# MASTERPLOTS II

## WORLD FICTION
## SERIES

# MASTERPLOTS II

## WORLD FICTION SERIES

## 1

A-Far

*Edited by*

## FRANK N. MAGILL

SALEM PRESS

Pasadena, California    Englewood Cliffs, New Jersey

**Library of Congress Cataloging-in-Publication Data**
Masterplots II: world fiction series.
  Bibliography: p.
  Includes index.
  Summary: Examines the themes, characters,
plots, style, and technique of 347 works by authors
from the non-English speaking countries of the
world, including Poland, France, Czechoslovakia,
Austria, Germany, and Russia.
  1. Fiction—19th century—Stories, plots, etc. 2.
Fiction—19th century—History and criticism. 3.
Fiction—20th century—Stories, plots, etc. 4. Fic-
tion—20th century—History and criticism. [1. Fic-
tion—Stories, plots, etc. 2. Fiction—History and
criticism] I. Magill, Frank Northen, 1907-    . II.
Title: Masterplots 2. III. Title: Masterplots two.
PN3326.M28   1988      809.3      87-33695
ISBN 0-89356-473-7 (set)
ISBN 0-89356-474-5 (volume 1)

# PUBLISHER'S NOTE

*Masterplots II*, World Fiction series, is the fourth set in the *Masterplots II* series, whose eighteen volumes to date—six covering short stories, four of American fiction (including titles from Latin America as well as the United States), four focusing on works from Great Britain and the Commonwealth nations, and the present four volumes, which survey fiction emanating from all corners of the non-Commonwealth Eastern Hemisphere—supplement and update the twelve volumes of original *Masterplots* (revised, 1976). Together, these thirty volumes document, both factually and analytically, nearly four thousand of the world's finest literary works.

The current four volumes account for 380 of those titles, covered in 347 articles. (Sequences of two or more novels are generally treated in a single article.) The need for such documentation arises from the proliferation of non-English-language titles that have appeared since the publication of the original *Masterplots* in 1949: Three-quarters of the titles covered in the following four volumes were published after 1945; nearly the same proportion were translated into English during that period—two-thirds, in fact, within the past twenty-five years.

The need for coverage of these new titles is clear when one recognizes that many of these recent works have achieved the status of modern classics and have been distributed worldwide: Yukio Mishima's tetralogy *The Sea of Fertility*, Aleksandr Solzhenitsyn's *One Day in the Life of Ivan Denisovich*, Camara Laye's *The Dark Child*, Peter Handke's *The Goalie's Anxiety at the Penalty Kick*, and the metafictions of Italo Calvino are among those titles covered here which have received both critical and popular acclaim within recent years. Similarily, the last quarter-century has seen the rise of several authors whose works were not represented in the original *Masterplots*, including eight Nobel Prize winners: Shmuel Yosef Agnon, Heinrich Böll, Elias Canetti, Yasunari Kawabata, Czesław Miłosz, Claude Simon, Isaac Bashevis Singer, and Aleksandr Solzhenitsyn.

By far the largest group of articles included here is concerned with the twentieth century productions of a broad range of nations, with emphasis on those whose authors have been widely disseminated internationally—France (with 77 articles), Germany (41), Russia/the Soviet Union (52), Italy (34), and Japan (32)—followed by Austria (20), Poland (20), Czechoslovakia (10), Israel (10), Sweden (10), and Spain (8). This scope is broadened by coverage of other Eastern and Western European works, as well as major works from regions whose literatures are beginning to enjoy long-deserved recognition, including the Far East (China as well as Japan), the Middle East (Saudi Arabia and Turkey), and the non-English literatures of Africa (including Cameroon, Guinea, and Senegal).

Of the 142 authors represented here, approximately a quarter of them gave birth to works covered in the 1976 edition of *Masterplots*. As the intervening years have witnessed the rise of new works by these authors, or in some cases the renewed critical esteem of works by them which previously were obscured, the current set contains articles on such masterpieces as Günter Grass's *The Flounder*, Hermann Hesse's *The Glass Bead Game*, Nikos Kazantzakis' *The Last Temptation of Christ*, and Franz Kafka's *Amerika*, in an attempt to complement their author's previous representation in *Masterplots*.

Similarly, a small number of articles are included here to cover major works of literature published before the twentieth century by non-English-language authors, works not included in the original *Masterplots* which merit inclusion in such a reference work: Hence, some previously excluded works by Honoré de Balzac, Fyodor Dostoevski, Saikaku Ihara, and Leo Tolstoy, among a few other recognized giants, are found here.

Finally, six articles have been reprinted from previous volumes in the *Masterplots II* series—two on works by Samuel Beckett and four on works by Isaac Bashevis Singer—to satisfy those who count these bi-national authors among the Continental Europeans.

Following the accessible format developed for previous sets in the *Masterplots II* series, this World Fiction set is arranged alphabetically by the title by which the work is best known in the United States. The individual essays are divided into six sections: 1) ready-reference top matter outlines publication information, type of work, and the principal characters; 2) "The Novel" discusses the action and plot; 3) "The Characters" analyzes the author's approach to characterization, using specific characters as examples; 4) "Themes and Meanings" brings into focus the primary themes (or issues) with which the author is concerned, as well as the devices and techniques which that author employs in their service; 5) "Critical Context" discusses the relevant environments in which the work was published, such as its place in the author's canon, significance in its generic, historical, and/or regional context, or general critical reception upon first publication; and 6) "Sources for Further Study" provides a listing of the best available secondary reference material that addresses both the specific work under discussion and its context.

At the end of volume 4 will be found an Author Index and a Title Index; the latter provides a complete list of titles with cross-references from all titles under which a work may have appeared in publication (including foreign-language titles). Also, a complete list of writers who contributed articles, along with their academic affiliations, is found in the front matter to volume 1.

# CONTRIBUTING REVIEWERS

Michael Adams
*Independent Scholar*

Patrick Adcock
*Henderson State University*

Andrew J. Angyal
*Elon College*

Norman Araujo
*Boston College*

Stanley Archer
*Texas A&M University*

Bryan Aubrey
*Maharishi International University*

Linnea Aycock
*California State University, Fresno*

Ehrhard Bahr
*University of California, Los Angeles*

Peter Baker
*Southern Connecticut State University*

Dan Barnett
*Butte College*

Thomas F. Barry
*University of Southern California*

Melissa E. Barth
*Appalachian State University*

Thomas Beebee
*Pennsylvania State University*

Elizabeth Berlings
*Saint John's University, New York*

Robert L. Berner
*University of Wisconsin-Oshkosh*

Terry D. Bilhartz
*Sam Houston State University*

Beatrice Christiana Birchak
*University of Houston-Downtown*

Carol Bishop
*Indiana University, Southeast*

Marion Boyle
*Bloomsburg University of Pennsylvania*

Harold Branam
*University of Pennsylvania*

Gerhard Brand
*California State University, Los Angeles*

J. R. Broadus
*Independent Scholar*

Robert R. Brock
*University of Montana*

Mollie A. Brodsky
*Rutgers, The State University of New Jersey*

Carl Brucker
*Arkansas Tech University*

Peter Buitenhuis
*Simon Fraser University, British Columbia*

William H. Burnside
*John Brown University*

Linnea Burwood
*State University of New York at Binghampton*

Edmund J. Campion
*University of Tennessee, Knoxville*

Rosemary M. Canfield-Reisman
*Troy State University*

Krista Ratkowski Carmona
*University of California, Los Angeles*

David A. Carpenter
*Eastern Illinois University*

Jocelyn Creigh Cass
*Fraser Valley College*

Deborah Charlie
*Antelope Valley College*

Dennis C. Chowenhill
*Chabot College*

Sandra Christenson
*California State University, Northridge*

C. L. Chua
*California State University, Fresno*

Ada Coe
*University of California, Davis*

John J. Conlon
*University of Massachusetts at Boston*

Frank Coppay
*Union College, New York*

Deborah Core
*Eastern Kentucky University*

Linda Seidel Costic
*Northeast Missouri State University*

Virginia Crane
*California State University, Los Angeles*

Frank Day
*Clemson University*

Charles Duncan
*Atlanta University*

Bruce L. Edwards
*Bowling Green State University*

Robert P. Ellis
*Worcester State College*

Thomas L. Erskine
*Salisbury State College*

Thomas H. Falk
*Michigan State University*

Donald M. Fiene
*University of Tennessee, Knoxville*

Edward Fiorelli
*Saint John's University, New York*

Robert J. Forman
*Saint John's University, New York*

Frank Gado
*Union College, New York*

Keith Garebian
*Independent Scholar*

Jill B. Gidmark
*University of Minnesota, Twin Cities*

Steven L. Hale
*Berry College*

Todd C. Hanlin
*University of Arkansas, Fayetteville*

Natalie Harper
*Simon's Rock of Bard College*

Sandra Hanby Harris
*Tidewater Community College, Virginia Beach*

Terry Heller
*Coe College*

Nina Hibbin
*Independent Scholar*

Hal Holladay
*Simon's Rock of Bard College*

Edelma Huntley
*Appalachian State University*

Archibald E. Irwin
*Indiana University, Southeast*

Philip K. Jason
*United States Naval Academy*

Shakuntala Jayaswal
*University of New Haven*

D. Barton Johnson
*University of California, Santa Barbara*

Ronald L. Johnson
*Northern Michigan University*

Jane Anderson Jones
*Manatee Junior College*

Alan Frank Keele
*Brigham Young University*

Steven G. Kellman
*University of Texas at San Antonio*

David W. Kent
*University of Louisville*

Karen Kildahl
*South Dakota State University*

Wm. Laird Kleine-Ahlbrandt
*Purdue University, West Lafayette*

Paula Kopacz
*Eastern Kentucky University*

Joseph E. Laggini
*Rutgers, The State University of New Jersey*

William LaHay
*Independent Scholar*

Frank S. Lambasa
*Hofstra University*

Harry Lawton
*University of California, Santa Barbara*

Leon Lewis
*Appalachian State University*

James Livingston
*Northern Michigan University*

Rita E. Loos
*Framingham State College*

# CONTRIBUTING REVIEWERS

Michael Loudon
*Eastern Illinois University*

Reinhart Lutz
*University of California, Santa Barbara*

Dennis McCormick
*University of Montana*

Lynn McDonie
*California State University, Northridge*

Hugh McLean
*University of California, Berkeley*

John L. McLean
*Northern Michigan University*

James B. McSwain
*Memphis State University*

Philip Maloney
*University of Montana*

Martha Manheim
*Siena Heights College*

Marsha Kass Marks
*Alabama A&M University*

Charles E. May
*California State University, Long Beach*

Laurence W. Mazzeno
*United States Naval Academy*

Jeffrey Meyers
*University of Colorado, Boulder*

Vasa D. Mihailovich
*University of North Carolina at Chapel Hill*

Jane Ann Miller
*Middlebury College*

Leslie Mittleman
*California State University, Long Beach*

Robert A. Morace
*Daemen College*

Katharine M. Morsberger
*Independent Scholar*

Robert E. Morsberger
*California State Polytechnic University,
  Pomona*

James Muhleman
*Hawaii Loa College*

Barbara Mujica
*Georgetown University*

D. Gosselin Nakeeb
*Pace University*

Greg Nehler
*Indiana University, Bloomington*

William Nelles
*Northern Illinois University*

Peter West Nutting
*Colby College*

George O'Brien
*Georgetown University*

Patrick O'Donnell
*University of Arizona*

Michael L. Otten
*Independent Scholar*

Robert M. Otten
*Assumption College*

David B. Parsell
*Furman University*

William E. Pemberton
*University of Wisconsin-La Crosse*

Robert C. Petersen
*Middle Tennessee State University*

Susan Piepke
*Elon College*

David Powell
*Western New Mexico University*

Norman Prinsky
*Augusta College*

Wade Provo
*Rockford College*

Charles Pullen
*Queen's University, Ontario, Canada*

Victor J. Ramraj
*University of Calgary*

John D. Raymer
*Independent Scholar*

Judith Ricker-Abderhalden
*University of Arkansas, Fayetteville*

Mac Linscott Ricketts
*Louisburg College*

J. Thomas Rimer
*University of Maryland at College Park*

Jerome J. Rinkus
*Pomona College*

David E. Robinson
*Winona State University*

Carl E. Rollyson, Jr.
*City University of New York, Bernard M. Baruch College*

Paul Rosefeldt
*Our Lady of Holy Cross College*

Joseph Rosenblum
*University of North Carolina at Greensboro*

Diane M. Ross
*Lake Forest College*

Robert Ross
*Southern Methodist University*

Victor Anthony Rudowski
*Clemson University*

Yvonne L. Sandstroem
*Southeastern Massachusetts University*

June H. Schlessinger
*North Texas State University*

James Schmitt
*Rockford College*

Lucy Schwartz
*University of North Dakota*

Francis Michael Sharp
*University of the Pacific*

John C. Sherwood
*University of Oregon*

Muhammad Siddiq
*University of Washington*

Armand E. Singer
*West Virginia University*

Gilbert Smith
*North Carolina State University*

Katherine Snipes
*Eastern Washington University*

Philip H. Solomon
*Southern Methodist University*

Leon Stein
*Roosevelt University*

David L. Sterling
*University of Cincinnati*

James Sullivan
*California State University, Los Angeles*

Roy Arthur Swanson
*University of Wisconsin-Milwaukee*

Patricia E. Sweeney
*Independent Scholar*

Daniel Taylor
*Bethel College, Minnesota*

Thomas J. Taylor
*Purdue University, West Lafayette*

Rita Terras
*Connecticut College*

Eric Thompson
*Université du Québec à Chicoutimi*

Lillian Vallee
*Merced College*

George W. Van Devender
*Hardin-Simmons University*

Dennis Vannatta
*University of Arkansas at Little Rock*

Michael Verdon
*Hollins College*

Nicholas Vontsolos
*Arizona State University*

John P. Welle
*University of Notre Dame*

James M. Welsh
*Salisbury State University*

Philip F. Williams
*Arizona State University*

Michael Witkoski
*South Carolina House of Representatives*

Karin A. Wurst
*University of Arkansas, Fayetteville*

# LIST OF TITLES IN VOLUME 1

# MASTERPLOTS II

# LIST OF TITLES IN VOLUME 1

# ABEL SÁNCHEZ

*Author:* Miguel de Unamuno y Jugo (1864-1936)
*Type of plot:* Psychological fable
*Time of plot:* Unspecified
*Locale:* Somewhere in Spain
*First published: Abel Sánchez: Una historia de pasión*, 1917 (English
    translation, 1947)

> *Principal characters:*
>     ABEL SÁNCHEZ, a famous painter
>     JOAQUÍN MONEGRO, a physician
>     HELENA, Abel's wife
>     ANTONIA, Joaquín's wife
>     ABELIN, Abel's son
>     JOAQUÍNA, Joaquín's daughter
>     JOAQUINÍTO, the son of Abelin and Joaquína

*The Novel*

Hatred resulting from envy is the consuming passion of which *Abel Sánchez* is the history. Indeed, because the novel is so dominated by Joaquín
Monegro's envy and hatred of his lifelong acquaintance, Abel, it has often
been suggested that hatred is the central character in the work. Moreover, although the novel focuses primarily on Joaquín, it is entitled *Abel Sánchez* because Joaquín's identity comes solely from his envy of Abel, thus making
Abel the work's focus.

The narrative is told primarily in the third person, but it is interspersed
with sections from Joaquín's memoirs (or *Confession*), which serve as his
own commentary on what Miguel de Unamuno y Jugo calls Joaquín's psychological disease or affliction. Since their infancy, Joaquín records, it was
always Abel who was the congenial one, while he himself was antipathetic;
thus, from the beginning, Joaquín envied him. The bare and understated
tone of the novel, as well as its simple and straightforward narrative line, suggests that Unamuno is working with the parable form here, in particular the
biblical story of Cain (Jo-Cain) and Abel; thus, because the biblical myth
demands it, the story moves relentlessly to an inevitably tragic conclusion.

The difference between the two boyhood friends is made clear when Abel
becomes an artist of some repute and Joaquín decides to become a physician
in order to rival him in fame. The rift between them becomes most pronounced when Abel marries Joaquín's cousin, Helena, the woman whom
Joaquín desires to wed. Joaquín records that on the night he realized that he
could not have Helena, he was born into his life's hell. From this point on, he

is nothing beyond his hatred for Abel. First, he decides to crush Abel's artistic fame with that of his own as a maker of scientific discoveries, a creator of works of scientific art. He also vows to find a woman of his own with whom he might take refuge from his hatred. Thus he marries Antonia not out of love but out of a need to find a motherly figure to succor him. Antonia marries him because she understands the nature of his obsession and hopes to cure him of it.

The crucial distinction between the two men is ironically emphasized by Abel's artistic ability, which most see as predominantly technical, even scientific in its approach, and Joaquín's scientific abilities, which Joaquín sees as basically intuitive, even poetic. Yet Joaquín becomes so involved in his daily medical practice that he neglects his aspirations to make great scientific discoveries. His hatred for Abel is increased when a woman for whom he has been caring dies and he discovers that Abel's painting of her allows her to live forever. The next stimulus to Joaquín's engulfing hatred is the birth of Abel and Helena's child, a boy whom the parents name Abelín, after the father. Joaquín vows that he will have an even more beautiful child.

When Abel proposes to paint the biblical story of the death of Abel at the hands of Cain, Joaquín is compelled to read Lord Byron's poetic version of the story, *Cain*, which he says penetrates him to the core. Joaquín realizes that his immortal hatred of Abel constitutes his very soul, and that he is doomed to live in this literal hell forever. When his daughter Joaquína is born, Joaquín vows that she will be his avenger against Abel.

In spite of his hatred, however, Joaquín is the chief eulogizer of Abel at a banquet given to honor the artist's painting of Cain's murder of his brother. The speech is so brilliant that those who hear it claim that it is greater than the painting, a work of art in itself, and that it is the speech that makes the painting. Unfortunately, because the speech is about Abel, the praise it receives only increases Joaquín's hatred.

While the son of Abel studies medicine, Joaquín lavishes all of his attention upon his daughter, who, like her mother before her, realizes that her father is more of a patient than a doctor. When Abelín's medical studies end, he become Joaquín's assistant; as Joaquín begins to try to use him to get revenge on Abel, his daughter decides to enter a convent as a way to save her father spiritually. Joaquín, however, convinces her to marry Abelín, for he says he will be redeemed if she will make Abelín his son.

After the marriage, Joaquín turns more and more of his practice over to Abelín, who begins to collect Joaquín's research notes in order to compile them into a book. At this same time, Joaquín begins to write his *Confession*, a diary which he addresses to his daughter. He also plans a literary fiction in which he says that he will portray the soul of Abel, whom he is convinced is dominated by the same intense envy from which he suffers. He takes solace in the hope that Abel will be remembered only as a creation of Joaquín;

ironically, Joaquín is unaware that he is only a creation of his hatred of Abel.

When Joaquiníto, the grandson of both Abel and Joaquín, is born, Joaquín tries to make Abel leave, for he believes that the child loves Abel most. When Abel tells Joaquín that the boy fears the contagion of Joaquín's bad blood, Joaquín grabs him by the throat and Abel suffers a fatal heart attack. For the next year, Joaquín lives in lonely melancholy, until he becomes ill; without Abel to hate, he no longer has an identity of his own. On his deathbed, he tells his family that his life has been like a nightmare, a living hell. His final recognition is that if he had loved Antonia, he might have been saved.

*The Characters*

The character of Joaquín dominates the book. All others, even Abel, who gives the work its title, exist only to serve as reflections of or counters to him. Nevertheless, Joaquín is less a realistic character than an embodiment of his own envy and hatred. His monomania, which transforms him into a flat, representative character, is what makes the book into the fable that it is. It is less true to say that Joaquín is mad than to say that he is a symbolic embodiment of the madness of hatred. Even on his deathbed, he asks what has made him so envious, but there is no way to account for what has made him that way, any more than there is to account for the envy and hatred of John Milton's Satan or William Shakespeare's Iago. It is the mystery of Original Sin that Unamuno wishes to personify in Joaquín. *Abel Sánchez* is not a psychological study of an understandable or curable psychic disease, but a symbolic fable about man's basic disease of hatred. Philosophy, not psychology, is necessary to understand the book.

Because the story is patterned after the biblical story of Cain and Abel, the characters are controlled by the role which they play in the narrative. Abel is the object of Joaquín's hatred and little else. His being an artist is meant to emphasize the gap between his intuitive self and Joaquín's coldly rational scientific self. No further psychological implications of these professional roles are explored in the novel. The children in the work, similarly, are merely ironic reflections of their respective fathers. Abel's son becomes drawn to Joaquín and his medical profession, while Joaquín's daughter becomes the sensitive and intuitive one concerned for her father's soul. The wives are also only slightly drawn. Helena is little more than a stimulus for Joaquín's envy, while Antonia merely plays the role of possible salvation for her husband.

Thesis, not character, is the center of interest in this work, for although he probes a psychological state, Unamuno is primarily interested in exploring a philosophical mystery—the mystery of hatred itself. Consequently, the novel is less realistic than it is allegorical; the characters represent unitary states rather than complex psychological personalities.

*Themes and Meanings*

The central mystery in *Abel Sánchez* is the mystery of the story of Cain and Abel in Genesis: why God looked with favor on the offerings of Abel and not with favor on the offerings of Cain. It is with this inexplicable distinction that hatred and murder are born into the world. Unamuno offers no answer to this basic enigma, except to suggest that with God's inexplicable choice, separation of one self from the other is emphasized as a result of the Fall. Cain, not Abel, is seen by Unamuno as the heroic and tragic figure in this archetypal tale, much as Milton presents Satan as his tragic figure, and much as Byron presents his version of Cain as the alienated and lonely outcast, the primal symbol of isolated man. Unamuno has said, in the preface to the second edition of his novel, that Joaquín is morally superior to Abel, for his passion is great compared to Abel's ordinariness.

In addition to this theological mystery, Unamuno is interested in the existential dilemma of the loss of selfhood. Instead of having an individual self, Joaquín is merely the sum of his hatred for Abel; thus, even though he hates Abel, he needs him to survive, for without his hatred, Joaquín is nothing. Throughout the novel, Joaquín moves back and forth between his hate and his desire to be freed of it, yet his need of his hatred is more powerful than his desire to be released. In fact, hatred in the novel is a pure existential state that Joaquín realizes to be immortal, existing as an essential part of the one who hates.

The most basic source of Joaquín's hatred is his lack of love for himself, a fact that he discovers when he realizes that he cannot obey the commandment to love his neighbor as himself because he does not love himself. At the time of his death, Joaquín has a final epiphany about the nature of his existence. Thus, when he dies, he is, if not redeemed, at least freed of the mysterious iniquity which has dominated his life. Too late, he realizes that he could have and should have loved Antonia, that to have done so would have been his salvation.

*Critical Context*

*Abel Sánchez* has been called Unamuno's first mature and fully realized novel. It is certainly his first starkly symbolic novel, for it is bare of any social or otherwise realistic context; the characters are allowed to stand alone on a stage of purely representative relationships. As such, the work falls into the tradition of the parable. Although the character of Joaquín seems to be thoroughly explored, he is the existential state of hatred brought mythically into the world by his namesake, the biblical Cain.

This short novel, like the other fictional works of Unamuno, is governed by the philosophical ideas which infuse it. The author, often called an early existentialist thinker, is here primarily interested in exploring, as he does in his other fictions, the implications of hatred as a basic human state which alienates the self and creates its own identity. Thus, *Abel Sánchez* is a thesis novel of some philosophical complexity, created in the period of time between the great poetic parables of the isolated man of the Romantic movement and the fictional depictions of the existential hero of the modern period.

*Sources for Further Study*
Barcia, José Rubia, and M. A. Zeitlin, eds. *Unamuno: Creator and Creation*, 1967.
Márias, Julián. *Miguel de Unamuno*, 1966.
Mora, José Ferrater. *Unamuno: A Philosophy of Tragedy*, 1962.
Valdés, Mario J. *Death in the Literature of Unamuno*, 1966.

*Charles E. May*

# THE ABYSS

*Author:* Marguerite Yourcenar (Marguerite de Crayencour, 1903-1987)
*Type of plot:* Period realism
*Time of plot:* 1510-1569
*Locale:* Reformation Europe
*First published:* L'Œuvre au noir, 1968 (English translation, 1976)

*Principal characters:*
ALBERICO DE' NUMI, a Florentine nobleman
ZENO, his bastard son, an alchemist, physician, and
    philosopher
HENRY JUSTUS LIGRE, Zeno's uncle, a powerful merchant
HENRY MAXIMILIAN LIGRE, his son, Zeno's cousin, a soldier of
    fortune
HILZONDA LIGRE, Zeno's mother, the sister of Henry Justus
JEAN-LOUIS DE BERLAIMONT, the prior of a monastery in
    Bruges and Zeno's protector
BARTHOLOMEW CAMPANUS, the brother-in-law of Henry
    Justus, canon and then bishop, Zeno's mentor at first and
    later his judge
SIMON ADRIANSEN, an Anabaptist merchant, Hilzonda's
    husband after Alberico's death
JAN MYERS, a barber-surgeon, Zeno's mentor in Bruges and
    later his host
PHILIBERT LIGRE, the son of Henry Justus and later head of
    the Bank of Ligre

*The Novel*

*The Abyss* is the story of one man's devotion to truth. As Zeno relentlessly searches for knowledge, vast historical forces—Catholicism and Protestantism, France and the Holy Roman Empire, agrarianism and commercialism—turn Reformation Europe into a bloodbath. Marguerite Yourcenar's careful documentation adds to this continent-sized clash between dissidence and dogma a great sense of period realism.

The story opens in 1530. Henry Maximilian Ligre runs into Zeno outside Dranoutre, Henry Justus Ligre's Belgian country estate, and the two discuss plans. At sixteen, Henry Maximilian is planning to serve with King Francis I. At twenty, Zeno is leaving to study alchemy in Spain. Both have abandoned the merchant House of Ligre. Henry Maximilian has chosen war, poetry, and women. Zeno has chosen a rendezvous with himself.

A flashback recalls Zeno's youth. His father, Alberico, was a friend of Michelangelo and prelate to Cesare Borgia. While staying with Henry Justus, his business agent in Bruges, he is smitten with Hilzonda. He later abandons her when she becomes pregnant with Zeno.

Alberico, a Roman cardinal by age thirty, is killed in an orgy. Simon Adriansen then courts Hilzonda. Zeno learns the classics from Canon Campanus and medicine from Jan Myers, and designs the mechanical looms used in the Ligre workshops. At the School of Theology in Louvain, Zeno comes to disdain dogma. His summer vacations are spent at Dranoutre, where his best moments are passed in alchemical speculations on the changing color of the leaves and the combustion of charcoal. He pities the numerous religious sects he sees forming and wishes to renounce his clerical vows.

One evening at Dranoutre, Henry Justus mounts a royal reception for Marguerite of Austria, who is there to ask for a loan. Henry Justus' weavers interrupt the festivities to request a raise and a pardon for their foreman, who has destroyed the looms. Henry Justus grants the loan, but no raise or pardon. Zeno, equally disgusted by the cynicism of the high life and the technophobia of the low life, departs in search of another critical mind. He will remain underground for the next twenty years.

Simon and Hilzonda are married and move to Münster, where they help found an Anabaptist City of God. A joint Catholic and Protestant army lays the city to siege. Inside, a mountebank proclaims himself God, executes the underzealous, and takes seventeen wives. The troops overrun the city and resume executions. Simon returns from a fund-raising expedition to find his wife beheaded. On his deathbed, he writes Salomé, his sister. She will rear Simon's surviving daughter, Martha.

Salomé is married to Martin Fugger of Cologne, whose money makes him more powerful than any prince of Europe. The elder Ligre has sent his son, Philibert, to learn banking under Martin. Martin betroths Philibert to his blood daughter, Benedicta. Benedicta, however, is stricken by the plague. Zeno, traveling incognito, visits and treats her. She dies, but Martin merely substitutes Martha's name on the wedding contract.

During the Council of Trent (1551-1552), Henry Maximilian again encounters Zeno at an inn in Innsbruck. Maximilian is employed by Marshall Piero Strozzi to spy on the Pope's messenger, Nuncio della Casa. Coincidentally, Zeno is Nuncio's physician and alchemist. The two cousins compare life histories. Zeno has performed dissections in Montpellier, invented liquid fire in Algeria, published a philosophical treatise, had an Arab male servant as his lover, and fought the plague of 1549. Henry Maximilian has served both France and Spain as a mercenary for twenty-five years. He sees Europe not only as a puppet show, with financiers pulling the strings, but also as a beauty pageant, with many a fair nymph for whom to compose verses. Henry Maximilian will die from a stray bullet at the Battle of Sienna in 1555.

Zeno escapes from Innsbruck a hair's breadth from the Inquisition. He is then successively an alchemist in Würzburg, a surgeon in Poland, and an astronomer in Uppsala. In Paris, the Queen Mother refuses her protection, and Zeno's *Protheories* are seized. He renounces his life as a fugitive and returns to Bruges under the guise of Dr. Sebastian Theus.

Jan Myers provides lodging for him. Zeno treats Jan's patients and discusses current events with Prior Jean-Louis de Berlaimont. Twice, the crude maidservant Catherine warms his bed. Catherine poisons Jan Myers, supposedly for Zeno. Outraged, Zeno inherits Myers' house but donates it to the monastery's hospice and retains only the duties of pharmacist.

Zeno can neither speak nor write freely. This deprivation triggers "the abyss," a deep descent within himself in search of pure concepts. Cleansed by this "black work" of mental alchemy (*l'œuvre au noir*), Zeno returns to everyday realities to find the prior terminally ill with an inoperable throat polyp. The atrocities of the Duke of Alba, a Spanish terrorist named Governor of the Low Countries in 1567, weigh heavily on the prior's conscience.

Zeno's innocent knowledge of a sex cult, "The Angels," imperils his life. The monastery's accountant, Pierre de Hamaere, and two monks, Cyprian and Florian, meet at night to "worship" the noble damsel Idelette de Loos. Zeno fears the consequences of a pregnancy. When the prior's death deprives him of a protector, he departs immediately. His plan is to cross the channel in a clandestine boat, but he is overcome by a feeling of "insupportable weariness" and returns to the hospice.

Idelette strangles her newborn child. Cyprian is arrested and falsely implicates Zeno. The physician is in turn brought to trial. The judge is Bartholomew Campanus, now a bishop. Pierre Le Cocq, the duke's representative, prosecutes. The indictment bears on every facet of Zeno's life. Zeno's coaccused are swiftly dispatched: Florian burns screaming, Idelette's head is hacked off; Pierre de Hamaere poisons himself. Catherine's ravings of intercourse with Zeno are particularly damaging.

Pierre Le Cocq is deeply indebted to the Ligre Bank, and the bishop writes to Philibert, asking him to sway the prosecutor toward clemency. With Martha's silent approval, Philibert does nothing.

Zeno is convicted of atheism and impiety. The bishop calls on Zeno to offer him a reprieve in return for a public retraction. Zeno refuses, having "lost his aptitude for lying." Choosing suicide over torture, he opens his veins. Zeno the wanderer finally keeps his appointment with himself.

*The Characters*

*The Abyss* has a cast of more than four hundred characters. There are men of money (the Ligres and the Fuggers), men of the cloth (Canon Campanus and Berlaimont), men of war (Marshalls Strozzi and Montluc), men of science (Zeno and François Rondelet), and "the lesser estate" (jailers, blacksmiths, and the like). Feminine characters consist primarily of self-interested royalty (Catherine of Médicis and Marguerite of Austria) and mystic martyrs (Hilzonda, Vivine, Benedicta, Idelette, and Martha). An exception is the Lady of Froso, a healer who was able to match Zeno's mind. Special sympathy goes to the aged: the prior, Jan Myers, and Bishop Campanus. The sheer numbers give an idea of the scale of Yourcenar's drama. Her characterization reveals what she values: intelligence, goodness, simplicity, and justice. Conversely, she detests brutality, violence, self-satisfaction, and connivance.

In an author's note, Marguerite Yourcenar reveals her numerous sources. Zeno resembles Erasmus (bastardy), Giordano Bruno (imprisonment), Tycho Brahe (astronomy), Paracelsus (alchemy), Tommaso Campanella (persecution), Étienne Dolet (violence), Leonardo da Vinci (inventions), and the latter four in his alleged sodomy. Michel de Montaigne inspired the prior, and the Fuggers were the true financiers of Charles V. Through his dissidence, Zeno also calls to mind Nicolaus Copernicus, Galileo Galilei, and Margaret Sanger. Alberico suggests both the Venetian painter Titian and Yourcenar's own father Michel Cleenewerke de Crayencour. Albrecht Dürer's engraving *Melancholia* inspired the first part of the novel, and the scenes of horror and disorder were influenced by Hieronymus Bosch and Pieter Brueghel the Elder.

Zeno dominates all other characters. Through his universal appetite for knowledge, he embodies the ideal of the Renaissance man. Successively theologian, alchemist, engineer, physician, astronomer, botanist, and philosopher, he is at the forefront of all these fields. His insistence on truth and his contempt for stupidity make him fearsome to others. In a hospitable world, there would have been no upper limit to his potential.

*Themes and Meanings*

During his trial, Zeno reflects that

> no lasting accord exists between those who seek, ponder, and dissect, and pride themselves on being capable of thinking tomorrow other than they do today, and those who accept the Faith, or declare that they do, and oblige their fellow men to do the same, on pain of death.

This reflection expresses the essential theme of the novel: polarization. Tension and hostility separate freethinkers, on the one hand, from hypocrites and fanatics, on the other. Four subthemes emerge as a consequence of this primary choice: danger, parallel worlds, self-transmutation, and paradox.

Any link involving Zeno is not only polarizing but also dangerous. Some associations form a clear and present danger: Zeno with Cyprian, or with Han, the injured Calvinist. Other associations, such as with Catherine, appear harmless but prove damning. Still others are directly or indirectly lethal: the Duke of Alba, whose murderous Council of Blood controls the prosecutor; Catherine of Médicis, who would not halt censorship; Philibert and Martha, whose inaction disowned and condemned a relative. These dangers give *The Abyss* some of the flavor of a spy novel.

Zeno's repeated exposure to the same persecution leads him to approve Democritus' hypothesis of an infinite series of parallel universes. Countless ironic juxtapositions demonstrate the theory. While Zeno awaits sentence in prison, Philibert sups with the Duke of Alba. As Henry Justus fetes Madame Marguerite, his weavers shiver from cold and hunger. While Zeno is plunged into the abyss, the prior passes through his own "dark night of the soul." The year 1491, carved on a beam of Zeno's monastery room, could as well have been 1941. Jan Myers is a comfortable Zeno. The Lady of Froso is Zeno as a woman. Zeno himself is that version of Galileo who refused to recant.

Merchants, who transmute labor into gold, and Inquisitors, who transmute flesh into ashes, are the true alchemists of the novel. In contrast, Zeno's aim is not gold, but knowledge, and he transforms his mind, as well as materials. The figure of Zeno thus unites the twentieth century goal of self-improvement with the medieval archetype of alchemy. The resulting "self-transmutation" is the process through which Zeno learns to recognize structural invariance in his Democritean universe of variation. The process has three recurring phases: black (analysis and synthesis), white (ascetic purification), and red (unity through passion).

Throughout the novel, the dichotomy between faith and truth remains intractable. This unresolved paradox is the abyss: the gaping absence of tolerance and reason, the void left by death and revolt, and the lack of causal dependency between compartmentalized worlds. Like his counterpart, Zeno of Elea, Zeno of Bruges also confronts the paradox of motion and immobility.

> It seemed to him now that he had almost insulted the infinite possibilities of existence by withdrawing for so long a time from the vast outer world. Assuredly, the mind's effort to penetrate the inner meaning of things leads to awesome depths, but it nullifies the very process which living is.

Zeno's skill with similarity transformations gave him mental mobility, but he had to give up life to pay for it.

### Critical Context

In the context of Yourcenar's personal canon, *The Abyss* points backward to her *Mémoires d'Hadrien* (1951; *Memoirs of Hadrian*, 1954) and forward to *Le Labyrinthe du monde*, an autobiographical project interrupted by the author's death. The first two works, monumental in scope and architecture, are credited with restoring the historical novel in France. The third is predicted by Zeno's phantasy vision in prison of a melancholy son by the Lady of

Froso. "If that phantom was his child, then he, philosopher though he was, was caught up in the game . . . ; he would not get out of this labyrinth until the end of time."

In the general current of French literary history, Yourcenar's treatment of difficult moral issues suggests comparison with André Gide. Her painful revisions recall the arduous polishing of Gustave Flaubert. Her classical erudition places her in the humanist tradition, but her focus on daily life more closely aligns her with the New Historians. Her taste for formula evokes the maxims of the seventeenth century moralists. Yourcenar's greatest stylistic achievements are her narrative voice, a kind of intimate third person, and her irony, a form of resigned disgust. In 1968, her forty years of work on *The Abyss* were recognized by the esteemed Prix Fémina, and in 1980, she became the first woman elected to the French Academy.

*Sources for Further Study*
Blot, Jean. "Le Romancier," in *Marguerite Yourcenar*, 1971.
Horn, Pierre L. "*L'Œuvre au noir*: A New Alchemy," in *Marguerite Yourcenar*, 1985.
Soos, Emese. "The Only Motion Is Returning: The Metaphor of Alchemy in Mallet-Joris and Yourcenar," in *French Forum*. IV (1979), pp. 3-16.
Spencer-Noël, Geneviève. *Zénon: Ou, Le Thème de l'alchimie dans "L'Œuvre au noir" de Marguerite Yourcenar*, 1982.

*Frank Coppay*

# THE ACCIDENT

*Author:* Elie Wiesel (1928-    )
*Type of plot:* Psychological realism
*Time of plot:* The late 1950's
*Locale:* New York City
*First published: Le Jour*, 1961 (English translation, 1962)

> *Principal characters:*
> ELIEZER, the narrator, a journalist
> KATHLEEN, his sweetheart
> HIS GRANDMOTHER, a victim of the Holocaust but still present in Eliezer's memory
> DR. PAUL RUSSEL, the young resident who cares for Eliezer in the hospital
> SARAH, a prostitute who as a twelve-year-old girl was sexually abused by the Nazis
> GYULA, a painter of Hungarian origin

*The Novel*

The Accident, a novella of little more than one hundred pages, is a psychological, philosophical, and spiritual journey. The narrator of the story, Eliezer, is a young journalist who has been spiritually immobilized by the Holocaust, in which he lost his family and of which he is a survivor. The narrative opens as Eliezer and Kathleen, his sweetheart, who loves him profoundly but to whom he is unable to make a commitment, are going to see the film version of *The Brothers Karamazov* in New York City. Hot, tired, bored, and lifeless, Eliezer lags behind Kathleen in crossing a street and is struck and dragged several yards by a taxicab. Suffering severe injuries, he is taken to a hospital and, after three days, is put into surgery. The young doctor who attends him, Paul Russel, takes a special interest in him, showing a curiosity which makes Eliezer suspect that the doctor knows something about him. The reader discovers that Eliezer was subconsciously a willing victim of his nearly fatal accident.

Dr. Russel's mention of Kathleen causes Eliezer to recall meeting her for the first time in Paris, some five or six years earlier. At that time, as now, he had come to the end of his hope and strength because of the oppressive memories of his experiences in the Holocaust. For years he has suffered from what is called "survivor guilt," just as, when a young boy, he felt guilty for being happier than a less fortunate orphan boy. Throughout the narrative, as it moves back and forth between present and past, Eliezer returns to thoughts of his grandmother and the rest of his family, all of whom were executed by the Nazis. He thinks of himself as being dead with them and the other six million people destroyed by the Holocaust. Kathleen attempts to alleviate his guilt and suffering by suffering herself; still, she is never able to penetrate the wall that Eliezer has put up around himself.

During his recovery from the accident, Eliezer wonders whether Kathleen knows the cause underlying it, and that he allowed himself to be hurt because he did not care enough to get out of the way. Dr. Russel, who has just felt the joy of saving a young boy's life, asks Eliezer one day why his patient does not care about living. Eliezer evades the doctor's angry questioning, but the reader is apprised of the answer. Those who have survived the Holocaust are no longer normal human beings; a spring has snapped inside them from the shock, and the results must appear sooner or later. Eliezer does not want the doctor to understand and thus lose his equilibrium. By abstractions and grandiloquence and evasions akin to lying, Eliezer persuades the doctor to believe that he does love life, proving it by his love for Kathleen.

Eliezer's relationship with Kathleen provides one of the main transitional devices in the narrative. For example, Kathleen asks him who Sarah is, since Eliezer, she says, had spoken her name during a coma. Sarah, he tells her, was his mother's name. It was also, however, as a flashback reveals, the name of a prostitute whom Eliezer had met in Paris long before he came to know Kathleen. That Sarah was twelve years old when she was sent to a special barracks for the pleasure of the Nazi officers at a concentration camp. Eliezer considers Sarah to be a saint, like his mother. Kathleen's slight resemblance to his mother turns Eliezer's thoughts back to the time of Kathleen's emotional struggle when they became lovers again after a separation of five years. The past—and all that it meant to Eliezer—stood between them; thus, Kathleen extracted a promise from him that he would allow her to help him in his fight against memories of the train station from which his mother and father and little sister were taken to their deaths.

The last chapter of the book introduces Gyula, a painter, originally from Hungary, who ignores Eliezer's attempts to explain his suffering and the reason behind the accident. Gyula pleads for him to forget the tragic past and make a commitment to life. He then paints a portrait of his friend in which the eyes are those of a man who had seen God commit the unforgivable crime of senseless killing. Enraged because Eliezer is intent on perpetuating the past rather than returning to the present, Gyula sets fire to the canvas and leaves, forgetting—as Eliezer says in ending his narrative—to take along the ashes.

## The Characters

Consonant with the story in which they appear, the characters in Elie Wiesel's novel are shadowy and disembodied, either alive in the midst of death or dead in the midst of life depending on their purpose in the narrative. The characters could be no other way, since the narrator sees life only with the eyes of death. His grandmother has long been dead, but she is more of a presence in the novel than the physically living Kathleen or any of the other characters.

Gyula and Dr. Russel are an evanescent opposition to the nihilism of Eliezer. They pass quickly through the novel without being fully developed. Wiesel wanted nothing more from them, artistically, than their appearance as voices in support of life and love. Kathleen is like them, ineffectual in spite of her love and energy. No character can counter the gloominess of Eliezer, while characters such as Sarah and his grandmother act as constant reminders of death.

Though Wiesel's characters are grounded in his own Holocaust experience, the story springs more from his imagination than from his life. There are many influences working on his imagination: culture, history, stories, myths, and the Bible. For example, from Jewish culture Wiesel draws the Hebrew name of God (El) in the naming of Eliezer; other characters— Sarah, Shmuel, and Sarah the prostitute—also have biblical origins.

*Themes and Meanings*

Self-annihilation by surrendering to death is a central theme of *The Accident*. Some years after surviving the death camps, in which he lost his family, Eliezer can no longer continue struggling to live. Even his love for Kathleen is insufficient to give meaning to his existence. It is easy, therefore, for the reader to accept that Eliezer passively intended to take his life when he stepped in front of the taxicab that seriously injured him. Suicide among survivors of the Holocaust is a phenomenon which Wiesel explicitly addresses in a preface written for the 1985 edition of *The Accident*. Referring to the hundreds of Jewish children in Poland who quietly surrendered to death after World War II, he suggests that they "were abruptly forced to realize to what extent they were depleted. And vanquished. And stigmatized. And alone." Eliezer's state of mind, affected by the same tragedy, is similar to that of those children.

The primary message of *The Accident* is that one who has experienced the Holocaust and survived it is almost certainly doomed to live it obsessively over and over again, to feel self-hatred as a consequence of survivor guilt, to resent those who are not outraged by the individuals responsible for the Holocaust, and to cry out against God for apparently acquiescing to the horror.

Life and love, the other central themes of the novel, are set in contrast to the themes of death and hatred and suffering. Eliezer is urged again and again to return to life, just as he is urged to put the past behind him and to accept love and give it. The effort to achieve forgetfulness is too much for him, however, and the last line of the novel ("He [Gyula] had forgotten to take along the ashes") reveals the finality with which Eliezer has chosen death over life. Neither love nor life can erase the ever-present memory of the Holocaust. The tragedies of the past make impossible any hopes for the present or the future for him.

## Critical Context

The Accident was Elie Wiesel's third book and should be read in sequence, following its predecessors. His first book, a memoir recounting his experience of the Holocaust, had a complex publishing history. Originally written in Yiddish, and running to some nine hundred pages in manuscript, it first appeared in its present form in French translation, radically condensed, as *La Nuit* (1958; *Night*, 1960). Wiesel himself has said that "*Night* is not a novel, it's an autobiography. It's a memoir. It's testimony." Nevertheless, it has frequently been classified as fiction. *Night* was followed by the novellas *L'Aube* (1960; *Dawn*, 1961) and *The Accident*. Unfortunately, the English title chosen for the latter obscures the thematic progression of the three books: *Le Jour*, the original French title of *The Accident*, means "day." Metaphorically, the French title suggests the survivor's full confrontation with the ongoing reality of life after the "night" of the Holocaust; the sequence of "night," "dawn," and "day" traces an ongoing struggle, not a neatly resolved movement from despair to hope.

As the winner of the Nobel Peace Prize in 1986, Wiesel has enhanced an already considerable worldwide literary reputation. He has long been recognized as one of the foremost interpreters of the Jewish experience and, inseparable from that experience, the Holocaust. Eliezer, the protagonist of *The Accident*, the victim, the survivor, may be seen as a living counterpart of any one of the six millions who did not survive the death camps. With other writers who cover the Holocaust—such as André Schwarz-Bart, Primo Levi, Nelly Sachs, Paul Celan, Ernst Weichert, Vladka Meed, Pierre Gascar, and Tadeusz Borowski—Wiesel has helped create a literature intended to assure that victims, living or dead, of any kind of inhumanity will never be forgotten.

## Sources for Further Study

Brown, Robert McAfee. *Elie Wiesel: Messenger to All Humanity*, 1983.

Fine, Ellen S. *Legacy of Night: The Literary Universe of Elie Wiesel*, 1982.

Knopp, Josephine. "Wiesel and the Absurd," in *Contemporary Literature*. XV (Spring, 1974), pp. 212-220.

Rosenfeld, Alvin H., and Irving Greenberg, eds. *Confronting the Holocaust: The Impact of Elie Wiesel*, 1979.

Wiesel, Elie. Interview in *The Paris Review*. XXVI (Spring, 1984), pp. 130-178.

*David Powell*

# ACQUAINTED WITH GRIEF

*Author:* Carlo Emilio Gadda (1893-1973)
*Type of plot:* Antistory
*Time of plot:* 1925-1933
*Locale:* The mythical city of Pastrufazio in Maradagàl, South America
*First published: La cognizione del dolore,* 1938-1941, serial; 1963, book; 1970, expanded (English translation, 1969, expanded)

> *Principal characters:*
> GONZALO PIROBUTIRRO DE ELTINO, the protagonist, an engineer and writer
> SEÑORA ELISABETTA FRANCOIS PIROBUTIRRO, his mother
> DOCTOR HIGUERÓA, their family physician

*The Novel*

Maradagàl is a South American country based upon Carlo Emilio Gadda's native Lombardy, specifically the Brianza region north of Milan. As *Acquainted with Grief* begins, Maradagàl has recently ended a war with neighboring Parapagàl, and both countries are experiencing modest economic recoveries. Gonzalo Pirobutirro de Eltino, a middle-aged engineer and writer, lives with his widowed seventy-three-year-old mother, Señora Pirobutirro, in their decaying villa outside the city of Pastrufazio. He has summoned the family doctor to the villa to have a checkup. Most of the first part of the novel is devoted to Doctor Higueróa's thoughts about Gonzalo's reputation in town as a stingy, temperamental misanthrope who is cruel to his ailing mother. This part also includes the physician's conversations with the servant, Battistina, and with Gonzalo himself.

Gonzalo is tormented by what he imagines is his mother's lack of affection for him; by her perpetual mourning for his brother, who was killed in the war with Parapagàl; and by his late father's having squandered most of the family's money on their elaborate villa. Gonzalo believes that he suffered as a child because of his father's excessive expenditures, and he continues to suffer by having to pay taxes on the estate. (All these elements of Gadda's story are autobiographical.) Gonzalo is also disgruntled by his mother's illusion that the family is still well-to-do and by her paternalistic attitude toward peasants. He suspects that she cares more for the servants than for him.

*Acquainted with Grief* was serialized in the Florentine literary review *Letteratura* between 1938 and 1941, but it was not published in book form until 1963 (with the inclusion of a fictitious dialogue between Gadda and his publisher about the "recovery" of the manuscript). The 1969 English translation and a 1970 Italian edition include two additional chapters. The first of these looks at Gonzalo's efforts to write a novel, and the second offers a strong plot element. Gonzalo has refused the services of the Nistitúo, a vigilante patrol hired by his neighbor, who fears thieves. On the night Gonzalo finally leaves home for good, the neighbor's security men hear strange noises coming from the villa. They find Señora Pirobutirro critically wounded, stabbed by an intruder; she says that her son was not involved in the attack. Like *Quer pasticciaccio brutto de via Merulana* (1957; *That Awful Mess on Via Merulana*, 1965), *Acquainted with Grief* is incomplete, ending without resolving the identity or motives of the attacker, though he may be an agent of the Nistitúo.

## The Characters

*Acquainted with Grief* is dominated by the lethargic sensibility of Gonzalo, caught in "the spreading shadows of neurosis." He recognizes and disdains his neuroticism, but he is also repulsed by what passes for normality in his society, represented for him by his mother's bourgeois values. Although Gonzalo is not the first-person narrator, the book is, in effect, his confession.

Gonzalo resents his parents for pursuing money, success, and prestige during his childhood while denying him attention and love. His neurosis centers on his ambivalent attitude toward his parents, and their country estate, for which he believes his life has been sacrificed. Gonzalo is tormented by not being first in his mother's affections and, at the same time, he is frustrated by his need for maternal love. Partly as an attempt to reject his family ties and partly because he sees everyone as a rival for his mother's attention, Gonzalo threatens and persecutes his mother. Since he both despises and desires his mother's jewels, it is appropriate that they are stolen in the attack on Señora Pirobutirro. It is also fitting that one of Gonzalo's last acts is to trample on a portrait of his father, an outburst against both the person and his property.

Gonzalo displays the jealousy and paranoia of a narcissist. As an aloof, ironic observer of the life around him, he becomes increasingly isolated. He is troubled by his view of a slovenly, incompetent world and by his repression of his anger at this world. His final tragedy is his awareness that love of no kind will ever touch him.

Like her son, Señora Pirobutirro is neurotic and narcissistic, though on a smaller scale. She claims to be self-sufficient, needing no one, including Gonzalo, but this attitude completely contradicts the reality around her. She fools herself into thinking that she possesses the economic and social status which she enjoyed when her husband was alive, for without such delusions, her life would be even emptier. Everything she does and stands for offends Gonzalo, especially her obsession with the memory of her dead son.

## Themes and Meanings

Gonzalo is closely based upon his creator. (Gadda was an engineer in Argentina from 1922 to 1924.) While the self-pitying protagonist is a target of satire to some degree, Gadda clearly shares some of his character's views.

*Acquainted with Grief* reflects Gadda's disillusionment with greed, vulgarity, hypocrisy, violence, and Fascism. He attempts nothing less than a subtle examination of the philosophical, psychological, and historical factors which transformed twentieth century Italy.

The novel's title is an ironic allusion to a biblical passage (Isaiah 53:3) often interpreted as a prophetic description of Christ: "He is despised and rejected of men; a man of sorrows and acquainted with grief. . . ." Through the experience of Gonzalo, a far from heroic "man of sorrows," Gadda depicts the process of learning about emotional pain. Gadda sees this process as the essence of life, as simultaneously pitiful and hilarious. He is concerned with the difficulty of knowing the truth about human behavior or of truly understanding any partial truth when confronted by it. Gonzalo considers himself all-knowing, but he is capable of very limited perception. One of his numerous deficiencies is the inability to communicate with others, his mother in particular. Gadda presents this barrier as an archetypal modern problem. Gonzalo tries to ignore the flaws in his character but cannot; as a result, he experiences unresolved guilt.

Much of Gonzalo's guilt and resentment are caused by sexual repression, and *Acquainted with Grief* is filled with Freudian overtones. Gonzalo resents his father and brother for having had the affection his mother has denied him, yet he also feels remorse for subconsciously wishing for their deaths. Gonzalo's psychological turmoil is an illness he thinks only he can understand. His malaise becomes a metaphor for modern man's isolation.

The emphasis on Freudian ideas is Gadda's response to Fascist Italy's rejection of Sigmund Freud as well as to the Fascist notion of Latin purity. Gadda's depiction of the chaos afflicting family and community life is his attack on the Fascist notion of an ordered society. Señora Pirobutirro's coercing others into feeling dependent on her is meant to resemble Benito Mussolini's paternalistic approach to political oppression. Gonzalo's ennui reflects the intellectual's feeling of impotence in the face of Fascism.

The main subject of *Acquainted with Grief*, however, is language or style, as is the case with all Gadda's writings. Gadda offers an unconventional, difficult narrative which challenges the reader to sift out the important ideas amid a multitude of extraneous details. Food is a prominent subject, as with this description of a local cheese: "This is a kind of Maradagàl Roquefort, but a bit fresher: fat, sharp, smelly enough to make an Aztec vomit, with rich mold of a dark green in the ignominy of its crevasses, very tasty to spread with the knife on the water-lily tongue and to chew over for quarter-hours in a foul mush." Drunk on words, Gadda revels in describing at length the seemingly irrelevant, his aesthetic and philosophical point being that the essential qualities of life are buried beneath tons of trivia.

Gadda's style, often called baroque, is his reaction to a chaotic, dehumanized world. He wants to liberate fiction from traditional rational structures. He celebrates the vitality and diversity of language, mixing regional dialects with standard Italian while tossing in slang, jargon, Latin, and Spanish. Gadda comments ironically on his critics when he has Gonzalo "furiously distilling from his memory one of those difficult words of his that nobody understood, with which he enjoyed decorating his prose (stiff, gluey, which nobody read)."

## Critical Context

*Acquainted with Grief* received the Fomentor International Literary Prize and is considered by many to be Gadda's masterpiece. As a portrait of suffering, it is a more human book than *That Awful Mess on Via Merulana*, and in it, Gadda takes even greater pleasure in linguistic gyrations. The novel has been called a major work of modernism, earning comparisons with the fiction of Henry James, Marcel Proust, James Joyce, Samuel Beckett, and William Faulkner, especially the latter's *The Sound and the Fury* (1929). Burdened with maintaining a myth of family respectability, Gonzalo resembles Faulkner's Jason Compson.

*Acquainted with Grief* encompasses two centuries of Italian literary traditions. Gadda's Maradagàl recalls not only his own Brianza but also that region as it is depicted in Alessandro Manzoni's *I promessi sposi* (1840-1842; *The Betrothed*, 1951). *Acquainted with Grief* was embraced by the Italian avant-garde writers of the 1960's as indicative of what they were attempting to achieve in their fiction, influencing the works of Nanni Balestrini, Angelo Guglielmi, Giorgio Manganelli, and Edoardo Sanguinetti. It inspired them through its use of language, its psychological insights, its fragmentation of reality, and its hostility toward contemporary society.

## Sources for Further Study

Adams, Robert Martin. "Carlo Emilio Gadda," in *After Joyce: Studies in Fiction After Ulysses*, 1977.

Biasin, Gian-Paolo. "The Pen, the Mother," in *Literary Diseases: Theme and Metaphor in the Italian Novel*, 1975.

Dombroski, Robert S. "Overcoming Oedipus: Self and Society in *La cognizione del dolore*," in *Modern Language Notes*. XCIX (January, 1984), pp. 125-143.

Lucente, Gregory L. "System, Time, Writing, and Reading in Gadda's *La cognizione del dolore*: The Impossibility of Saying 'I,'" in *Beautiful Fables: Self-consciousness in Italian Narrative from Manzoni to Calvino*, 1986.

Pacifici, Sergio. "Carlo Emilio Gadda: The Experimental Novel," in *The Modern Italian Novel: From Pea to Moravia*, 1979.

*Michael Adams*

# ACROSS

*Author:* Peter Handke (1942-    )
*Type of plot:* Philosophical novel
*Time of plot:* The early 1980's
*Locale:* A suburb of Salzburg, Austria
*First published: Der Chinese des Schmerzes*, 1983 (English translation, 1986)

> *Principal character:*
> ANDREAS LOSER, a teacher of ancient languages and an
> amateur archaeologist

## The Novel

*Across* is a first-person narrative with little plot action. It consists of three major sections and an epilogue. Andreas Loser is a teacher of ancient languages at a high school in a suburb outside Salzburg, Austria. He lives separated from his wife and two children. He considers himself to be an observer of, and not a participant in, life. One day, Loser deliberately knocks over a passerby while walking in Salzburg. He does not know why he does it, but only that he must act—that it is now or never. He is clearly undergoing some kind of inner crisis, and he believes that he needs time to assess himself and his existence. The day after this incident, he takes a leave of absence from his teaching post. Loser uses the free time to work on a treatise he is writing. His hobby is researching and excavating ancient doorsteps, or entryways (the German, *Schwelle*, also suggests a threshold or brink). During the rest of the first section of the novel, Loser remains an observer, describing his apartment and the suburb in which he lives. He longs to find those things that might still have meaning for him: landscapes and simple objects. He is very interested in the ancient Roman writer Vergil, especially his bucolic literature. Late at night, he hears a child wailing and reflects upon its distress.

In the second section, Loser becomes a participant in life, ironically through an act of willful destruction. He is on his way over the Mönch mountain to attend his monthly game of tarok cards with his friends. He describes the mountain and its landscape in great detail. He catches sight of an old man spray-painting swastikas on the trees and is seized by a tremendous feeling of melancholy and despair. Loser grabs a rock and runs toward the man, hurling the stone with all of his might and mortally wounding him. Undetected, Loser pushes the dying man over the cliff and then scratches out the signs the man had painted. He believes that he has acted decisively for once in his life. Continuing to his friend's house, he feels no regret or remorse. During the card game, he and his friends—a priest, a young politician, an artist, and a homeowner—discuss the meaning of the word "threshold." After the game, he and the artist walk through the city.

In the third section, which begins the next day, Loser remains in bed, thinking about his act of the night before, the theme of death, and his terrible isolation. Several days later, he emerges from his apartment and walks around the suburb. Days pass. His behavior becomes seemingly erratic. He takes a bus to the airport near the site of one of the excavations on which he is working. At the airport, he meets a woman with whom he spends the night. The next day, he visits his mother in a retirement home. He then flies to Milan, Italy, and on to Mantua to visit a landscape described by Vergil. He flies from Mantua to Sardinia and, finally, returns to his school in Salzburg to begin teaching again. (Later, he visits his family.) The epilogue consists of a description of a canal.

*The Characters*

Andreas Loser, the narrator of Peter Handke's *Across*, is typical of many of the author's characters. He is a solitary individual caught in an existential crisis in which the everyday meaning of his job and family has suddenly been lost. Loser desperately seeks to find significance for his existence. His violent act of murder is also seen in earlier Handke texts, notably in *Die Angst des Tormanns beim Elfmeter* (1970; *The Goalie's Anxiety at the Penalty Kick*, 1972), in which the protagonist randomly kills a cinema cashier. Other Handke characters have dreams or feelings of violence. This behavior is an aspect of the violent "break" with reality that plagues these figures and is indicative of their inner turmoil and rejection of society.

Loser's vocation as amateur archaeologist suggests his preoccupation with the past as a source of meaning for his life. This concern is also indicated by his job as a teacher of ancient languages. His interest in the doorsteps of ancient buildings represents the threshold or passageway that he has reached in his own existence. His restless wanderings during the course of the novel also point to his search for a new life.

*Themes and Meanings*

*Across* is a representative example of Handke's many novels. Loser is caught up in the midst of an existential crisis and must come to terms with the meaning of his life. He is a man on the "threshold" of a new existence. His quest is a search for authenticity. Like the crying infant he hears one night, he is in the process of being reborn to a new self. Nearly every Handke narrative begins on this existential note.

Loser's work with archaeology indicates his search for roots, his quest to return to an authentic beginning that will lend his life significance. That Loser teaches ancient languages (Greek and Latin) suggests his attempt to return to the foundations of Western culture, to the early myths through which man explained the events that shaped his life. In this sense, Loser is like Homer's Odysseus, a wanderer on a quest homeward, or like Sophocles'

Orestes, an outcast from society, plagued with guilt and longing to be relieved of his curse. It is an archaeology of the psyche that Loser ultimately practices. He longs for new "myths" that will give his existence meaning.

The work of the Latin poet Vergil is mentioned in the text, particularly his bucolic landscape verse (the *Georgics*). The Handke narrative itself is devoted to simple descriptions of the natural and village landscapes. Clearly influenced by the writings of the philosopher Martin Heidegger, Handke's character seeks authentic perception of being as it manifests itself in the simple objects and forms of nature around him. Loser looks to nature for "eternal laws" that will give his life meaning. Handke suggests here that it is society and its neuroses which produce the self-estrangement that tortures individuals such as Loser. Society promotes an inauthentic mode of existence among its members. This culminates in profound alienation. The transformation of nature and its forms into the transcendent forms of art is, as in Vergil, the goal of the character's quest.

The act of murder which Loser commits is disturbing. There is a sense that Loser's alienation is so great that a release of such violent proportions is the only mode of authentic behavior open to him. As mentioned earlier, acts of violence occur in several Handke texts. The novel *Die Stunde der wahren Empfindung* (1975; *A Moment of True Feeling*, 1977), for example, opens with the main character having had a disturbing dream that he has murdered a woman. In interviews, Handke has suggested that he attempts to include his own dreams in his works. The murdered woman may represent Handke's own mother, who committed suicide in 1971, and Handke may be addressing his own feelings of guilt over her act. The same is true of this text. Handke's real father was a German soldier during World War II, and the author has spoken of his firm rejection of this horrible war. Thus, the old man whom Loser finds spray-painting swastikas on the mountainside—a defilement of the purity of natural forms with the sordid forms of political and racial hatred—represents both Handke's father and the ideology of prejudice for which he fought. Loser's act is one of purification, an act that seeks to nullify or rectify the mistakes of Austria's past.

The figures at the card game that Loser attends represent various attitudes or perspectives on life. The priest suggests the traditional view of organized religion; the politician, the social and political world; the homeowner, the average bourgeois; and the artist, the aesthetic vision. For each, the definitions of life and the self are very different. Loser walks home with the artist, and it is to this perspective of art, and the transcendence it can bring, that he is ultimately committed.

*Critical Context*

Handke has been called a representative postmodernist author by a number of critics. Postmodernism is a literary and cultural movement that grew, in part, from the insights gleaned through the structuralist and deconstructionist movements of the 1960's and 1970's. Handke's earlier writings clearly show the influence of these trends of thought. "Reality," "truth," and other such absolute values are relative, a function of perception or one's perspective. This is the "deconstructionist" side to postmodernism. There is no absolute meaning to anything, only a point of view. Handke's texts repeatedly illustrate how "reality" is often a product or function of the language with which one describes it. The thrust of his first works was to demonstrate how what is taken to be "truth" is merely the linguistic sediment of words—fictions, as it were—that have become confused with a vision of reality. The construction of the "world" is, in essence, a creative act, a playing with fictions. This is what can be called the "constructionist" dimension of postmodernism. The fictional "truths" by which one lives can be trite and clichéd, or they can be challenging and liberating. Handke's postmodernist art seeks that latter, creative vision of reality.

It is clear why Handke places such value on the aesthetic mode of perception. Art and the imagination free one's static perspectives on existence and make it possible to envision other possible kinds of life. The creative act is the ultimate liberation and transcendence of being or nature. Loser is on a quest for "aesthetic myths" that will allow him to transcend the suffering he experiences. The original Greek word *mythos* means "plot" or "story." Art is the sole domain of mankind—only humans create works of art—and it is through creation that humanity gains its true meaning. In Heidegger's philosophy, genuine art attempts to capture the essence of what is, and art is equal in stature to philosophy. Handke's postmodernist quest is not for eternal truths per se, but for myths or fictions that can structure human existence.

*Sources for Further Study*

Enright, D. J. "Special Subjects," in *The New York Review of Books*. XXXIII (August 14, 1986), pp. 37-38.

Graver, Lawrence. "Personal Growth Through Murder," in *The New York Times Book Review*. XCI (July 27, 1986), p. 13.

Labanyi, Peter. "Thresholds," in *The Times Literary Supplement*. October 5, 1984, p. 1136.

Schlueter, June. *The Plays and Novels of Peter Handke*, 1981.

Sharp, Francis Michael. "*Der Chinese des Schmerzes*," in *World Literature Today*. LVIII (Summer, 1984), p. 405.

*Thomas F. Barry*

# AFTER THE BANQUET

*Author:* Yukio Mishima (Kimitake Hiraoka, 1925-1970)
*Type of plot:* Satire
*Time of plot:* The late 1950's
*Locale:* Tokyo, Japan
*First published: Utage no ato,* 1960 (English translation, 1963)

*Principal characters:*
KAZU FUKUZAWA, the proprietress of a famous Tokyo
    restaurant
YUKEN NOGUCHI, her husband, a retired foreign minister
SOICHI YAMAZAKI, Noguchi's campaign manager
GENKI NAGAYAMA, a politician of the conservative party

*The Novel*

*After the Banquet* is a political and social satire. Yuken Noguchi, the elderly politician in the novel, was based on an actual public figure, while the central character of interest in the narrative is Kazu Fukuzawa, the middle-aged proprietress of the Setsugoan restaurant, which was based on the famous Hannya-en restaurant in Tokyo. Although the work is written in the third person and the story is often told in a tongue-in-cheek style, the focus is on Kazu, who is treated more sympathetically than her elderly lover-statesman.

The novel begins with Kazu having arrived at a point in her life when her love affairs are past and when everything seems quite clear to her; she has divided human psychology into firmly defined compartments and is confident of her point of view and her position. Indeed, it is just this prideful confidence and certainty that the action of the novel serves to undermine. The narrative development of *After the Banquet* begins when Kazu finds herself attracted to the retired politician Yuken Noguchi.

Although many of Noguchi's gestures and comments make her think that he is an old man, Kazu is primarily fascinated by his dignified and stately manner. Furthermore, he seems to represent a world of the intellect, a realm of books and ideas and principles—all of which are alien to her rustic and intuitive nature. She develops an ideal image of the man, seeing him as one who has no self but the dignified, if somewhat stilted, aura that he presents to her. After their wedding ceremony Kazu believes that she has realized the goal of a lifetime: She has become the wife of a distinguished man.

Married life, however, is not without its difficulties—primarily resulting from the clash of Kazu's independence and masculine thinking with her husband's old-fashioned views on the propriety of woman's submissive role. Kazu, however, endures Noguchi's overbearing and misplaced sense of superiority and his formal aloofness, because she takes pride in now belonging to a noble family with a long lineage and dreams of being buried in the family temple; in this way, she believes that she has tricked eternity.

Noguchi's belief that the marriage is a refuge and a final home and Kazu's sense that she has found her rightful and secure tomb do not last. The pace of the novel shifts abruptly when Noguchi is asked to run for the governorship of Tokyo as a candidate for the radical party in Japan. Kazu's restaurant has been a favorite haunt for members of the conservative party; thus she has some ideas about the behind-the-scenes nature of politics. She feels quite confident in her political abilities, especially with the common people, and she is immediately obsessed with becoming directly involved in her husband's campaign.

Making Soichi Yamazaki, a master of campaign strategy, her coconspirator, Kazu begins her schemes to get her husband elected. She is possessed by a dream fantasy of using her knowledge of the ordinary Japanese people to sway their votes to the reserved and intellectual Noguchi. She meets secretly with Yamazaki to plan the campaign, throwing all of her resources and her time into the effort. At one point she has printed five million calendars with Noguchi's photograph on them. She even mortgages her restaurant to raise funds to pay for such campaign extravagances. Kazu believes that the election is her Heaven-appointed task. When Noguchi discovers what she has done and, out of pride and a sense of political decorum, beats her, his denunciations delight Kazu, because they embody the old moral virtues.

The election campaign, marred by Kazu's emotionalism and Noguchi's coldness, culminates with last-minute political tricks by the conservative party, including a scurrilous pamphlet about Kazu's past, promiscuous life, which guarantee Noguchi's defeat. Although Noguchi is reconciled to grow old peacefully after the frenzy of the campaign, Kazu discovers that she can never again tolerate emptiness and inactivity. She knows now that even if circumstances were to be tragic, she prefers a life of action to a void.

Torn between her comfortable image of being buried in the Noguchi family temple and the possibility of an animated life without resignation and abandoned hopes, Kazu is finally pulled toward the latter. When Noguchi, who cannot tolerate such aggressive behavior on the part of his wife, starts divorce proceedings against her, she returns to the Setsugoan and, with great joy, decides to reopen it.

*The Characters*

This is primarily a two-character novel based on the tension between the intuitive warmth and vitality of Kazu Fukuzawa and the cold and lofty ideals and principles of Yuken Noguchi. Secondary characters such as Soichi Yamazaki and Genki Nagayama are merely representatives of political positions of the Japanese radical and conservative parties respectively. Both are primarily defined in the novel by their relationships with Kazu, for she conspires with Yamazaki for Noguchi's election and consults with Nagayama, an old ally who ultimately betrays her. Both men understand her better than her husband does. Precisely because Kazu does not become sexually involved with either man, she can be comfortable with them. At the conclusion of the novel, there is some indication that Yamazaki will begin to play a more involved role in her life, with her divorce from Noguchi and the reopening of her restaurant.

Noguchi is representative of the old moral virtues; yet he is more European in his ideals than he is Japanese, filling his library with German books and his head with Western ideas. As a former ambassador and a member of a noble family, he condescends to Kazu and patronizes her, as he does the common people in general. He is driven mainly by logic and by principle and very little by human emotions. His old-fashioned view of the passive role of woman makes his marriage to Kazu an obvious mismatch which generates the basic conflict in the novel.

Kazu, on the other hand, is a romantic, filled with dreams and fantasies. Her plump, attractive figure is described by Yukio Mishima as bursting with energy and enthusiasm; her simplicity makes people with complex motives feel sheepish about their complexity. Combining a man's sense of resolution with a woman's reckless enthusiasm, she has powers that exceed those of most men. Although during her youth she has sold her favors to men, now as the owner of an influential restaurant where powerful politicians share confidences with her, she has reached a position in her life at which her confidence makes her see that all things have sharp outlines and are easy for her to understand; as Mishima says of her, it has been many years since she has been blind.

Her enthusiasm, energy, and considerable abilities make it difficult to understand why she is so in awe of the stodgy and safe Noguchi, who she allows to condescend to her and even to beat her. Kazu is a curious combination; she is the liberated woman proud of her freedom, but she still yearns for, or at least temporarily thinks she yearns for, the old moral codes and formalities that Noguchi represents. She thinks that she needs the static security that his dignity and his name promise. Although in some ways content to bask in the victories of her husband, at the same time she cannot simply hide in the shadows. Moreover, although she is extremely shrewd in her knowledge of the people with whom she comes in contact, there is also an element of naïveté about her that gives her a childlike quality.

Kazu's experience with the excitement of the election campaign is sufficient proof that she is not as content to slip quietly into death as she thought she was, in spite of the appeal of the nobility that Noguchi represents. The novel thus appropriately ends as it began, with Kazu once again bursting with energy, enthusiasm, and ambition, in her own way a much more able and wise politician than Yuken Noguchi ever was. Although she has seemingly come full circle, she has gained new knowledge and what Yamazaki calls a "peaceful uncertainty."

### Themes and Meanings

*After the Banquet* contains no complex philosophical or psychological themes, which readers have come to expect from many of Yukio Mishima's best-known works. Instead, Mishima has written more of a light entertainment than a fully developed novel. His primary aim seems to be that of satirizing Japanese politics, particularly the stiff Noguchi, and the social conventions of marriage, particularly the rigid relationships between men and women in Japan.

Beyond these obvious intentions, there is a dual theme that runs throughout the novel: First, there is the conflict between Kazu, the woman of warm blood and human vitality, and Noguchi, the man of lofty ideas and beautiful principles; second, there is the theme of Kazu's discovery that the true nature of politics is betrayal. In fact, what makes Kazu so adept at politics is her past experience with love, for she realizes that politics is like romance, indeed that politics and love affairs are identical.

The tone and style of the novel move between a kind of poetic lyricism and a subtle sarcasm. The combination is such that the reader is never quite sure when Mishima is being serious and when he is being satirical. Because the work is broadly critical of certain Japanese political and social customs, this uneasiness is even more pronounced for Western readers unfamiliar with the aesthetic conventions of Japanese fiction and the traditional social conventions of Japanese life.

Much of the novel's thematic complexity springs from the complexity of Kazu's motives. It would be untruthful to say that she works energetically for Noguchi's election simply to be the governor's wife, just as it would be inadequate to say that she does it for purely selfless motives. Both these motives are Western ideas that are alien to her. She is an ambitious woman. Her ambition, however, is not for herself but for her husband; thus she seems at once modern and old-fashioned. What she finally realizes about herself is that it is not any particular goal for which she strives, but rather the dynamic activity of life itself, in spite of the risks and dangers.

It is Yamazaki, Kazu's new friend and confidant, who has the final word in the novel, for he has understood the meaning of Kazu's experience with Noguchi. He tells her that although the election may have seemed a misfortune to her, it did well to expose her counterfeit happiness and reveal Noguchi's and her true natures to each other. Kazu returns to her vitality, determined to live, and Noguchi retreats back to his principles, content to die. As Yamazaki says, all is well.

*Critical Context*

One of the most striking features of Mishima's work is its variety; he adopted a style as if donning a mask. With its broad canvas and its political concerns, *After the Banquet* marked a new departure for Mishima; in this work, Donald Keene observes, "Mishima demonstrated that he was capable of writing a novel in the manner of nineteenth-century French fiction." On its publication, *After the Banquet* was both successful and controversial: As noted above, Mishima's plot was based in part on a scandal then very much in the news in Japan, involving prominent political figure Hachiro Arita, who sued Mishima and won a judgment against him. Despite the novel's political themes, there is no indication in *After the Banquet* of the commitment to a radical right-wing stance that was to lead to Mishima's suicide in 1970.

*Sources for Further Study*

Keene, Donald. *Dawn to the West: Japanese Literature in the Modern Era*. Vol. 1, *Fiction*, 1984.

Miyoshi, Masao. *Accomplices of Silence: The Modern Japanese Novel*, 1974.

Nathan, John. *Mishima: A Biography*, 1974.

Petersen, Gwenn Boardman. *The Moon in the Water: Understanding Tanizaki, Kawabata, and Mishima*, 1979.

Scott-Stokes, Henry. *The Life and Death of Yukio Mishima*, 1974.

*Charles E. May*

# THE AGE OF WONDERS

*Author:* Aharon Appelfeld (1932-    )
*Type of plot:* Social morality
*Time of plot:* 1938-1969
*Locale:* Provincial Austria
*First published: Tor-ha-pela'ot,* 1978 (English translation, 1981)

> *Principal characters:*
> THE SON (BRUNO), the book's central observer, who is twelve
>     years old in 1938
> THE MOTHER, who tries to keep the family together
> THE FATHER, a famous Austrian writer who abandons his wife
>     and son
> THERESA, a psychotic aunt who converts to Christianity
> STARK, a family friend who converts to a pious Judaism
> BRUM, a former family friend who renounces Judaism and
>     becomes an anti-Semite
> LOUISE, a family servant who becomes a prostitute

*The Novel*

Book 1, the longer of the novel's two parts, begins in 1938 on a train carrying a twelve-year-old boy, who serves as narrator and central consciousness, and his mother back to their hometown in provincial Austria. They had been vacationing in an unnamed retreat, quiet, little-known, beautifully located on a lovely riverbank. Mother and son were expelled from this apparent Eden. Aboard the train, the boy recalls, "the feeling that we were doomed seeped through me like a thick liquid."

Suddenly, the express train makes an unscheduled stop at a sawmill, far from any station. Politely yet ominously, "all foreign passengers and all Austrian passengers who were not Christians by birth" are requested to register with the "security forces." Why? The only official explanation is evasive: "Due to the special circumstances." Evidently, the Anschluss of March, 1938, has engulfed Austria within Adolf Hitler's Germany. Yet Aharon Appelfeld refrains here, as in his other fiction, from direct allusion to historic events. All the boy can be sure of is that "nothing would be the same again."

He finds his parents and their friends arguing obsessively about the nature and destiny of Jews and Judaism as anti-Semitic stresses, both upon and within them, increase. The boy's father is a famous Austrian writer, called, in Kafkaesque fashion, "A.," who is an intimate of such distinguished authors as Stefan Zweig and Arthur Schnitzler. The father's lofty reputation is venomously attacked in a sequence of journalistic articles calling his characters neither urban nor rural Austrians but, instead, "Jews who . . . were now useless, corrupt, perverted; parasites living off the healthy Austrian tradition." The critic himself turns out to be Jewish; unexpectedly, he dies soon.

The father thereupon adopts the same line of scurrilous anti-Semitism. He denounces the Jewish bourgeoisie as grossly materialistic; he claims that Jewish entrepreneurs should be wiped off the earth. He tries to become more Austrian than the Gentiles, flourishes his assimilationist views, and frantically curses the Jews who are "infesting Austria like rats, infesting the whole world, to tell the truth." The father drifts into madness as he writes pamphlets excoriating the Jewish petite bourgeoisie. Eventually he abandons his wife and son, fleeing to a Gentile, aristocratic mistress in Vienna. The son is expelled from school; later, mother and son are rounded up for a final journey on a "cattle train hurtling south."

Book 2 is subtitled, "Many Years Later When Everything Was Over." About thirty years have passed. The novel now shifts to the third person, with Bruno, the now-adult son, returning to his native town. His parents perished in the Holocaust. He has returned to his birthplace to confront its shame and affirm his identity. For several weeks he wanders in and out of the town's inns, streets, taverns, restaurants. He encounters several living relics from his boyhood. Some are partly Jewish, such as the singer Brunhilda. Louise, formerly a pretty maid who worked for Bruno's parents and was one of his uncle's mistresses, is now a worn-out, flabby, embittered old woman, who stereotypes Jews in a curiously positive fashion: "No Jew would take a pitchfork to a woman's thighs. Jews love women."

Most significant is Bruno's encounter with a former Jewish bachelor, Brum, who married his Gentile housekeeper, became a cattle farmer, wholly denied his Judaism, and survived the war. At first, the crippled, embittered Brum refuses Bruno's attempts at recognition. A short while later, he spews out hatred at Bruno. After several weeks, he tells him to leave town: "My hatred for Jews knows no bounds." Bruno hits him but finds that the blow does not reduce his despair. The next day he leaves, "empty of thought or feeling."

*The Characters*

Bruno as a boy and his parents and relatives are upper-class, cultivated Central European Jews who regard themselves as comfortably assimilated, with their Judaism only a marginal quirk in their characters. Traditional, religious Eastern Jews are exotic and barbaric specimens to them.

History soon smashes their illusions. Bruno, in the first book, is a sensitive, silent, but increasingly anguished observer of a society that degrades as well as disintegrates. In book 2, he is the age his father is in book 1 and has his own failed marriage—for unspecified reasons. He finds himself a stranger in his birthplace, revisiting a childhood traumatized by circumstances that cannot be expunged.

Bruno's mother is tender, weak, charitable, conventional, ineffectual. When the town's rabbi, following official orders, sends registered letters to all members of the Jewish community to come to his temple on a specified day, the mother asks, "What have I to do with them?" Once inside, she brandishes her umbrella at hostile neighbors and hisses, "Shopkeepers!"

The father is a prototype of the European artist as disdainful intellectual. Despising his fellow Jews, he regards himself as an Austrian luminary, with German his native tongue and Hebrew foreign to him. "Haven't I brought honor to Austria?" he asks jeering Gentile riders in a train compartment. When a distant relative in South America invites the family to resettle there, since Jews are not overtly hated in his land, the father feels insulted that he should be asked to go into business—no respect for the artistic life there, he rages, only for money, property, and survival above all! He tries to survive in his way by abandoning not only his family but also his heritage. His failure as husband, father, and Jew is accompanied by the growing acuity of Bruno's desolate awareness.

*Themes and Meanings*

*The Age of Wonders* is a chilling, plangent, remorselessly pessimistic study of Jewish self-denial, self-estrangement, self-hatred; of flawed human beings pushed into tight corners of base self-betrayal by motives and events whose enormity overwhelms description. Appelfeld's strategy, as a writer haunted by the Holocaust, is to dwell on its historical margins: either its prelude, as in this novel's book 1, or its aftermath, as in book 2. To deal directly with the twentieth century's most appalling horror would be, he told an interviewer from *The New York Times* in 1986, "like looking at the naked sun on a clear summer day. You couldn't stand the temperature. You can never understand the meaning of the Holocaust. You can just come to the edges of it. If you wrote about it directly, you'd end up trivializing it."

Everything in *The Age of Wonders* sooner or later finds its place in the context of anti-Semitism, with its resulting divisions and self-hatred among Jews. The first of several train scenes is paradigmatic of the overriding theme. As the coach comes to a halt in the middle of nowhere, with all "non-Austrian" passengers ordered to register their Jewishness, a varied lot of passengers descends into the night. A few comply forthrightly, particularly a loud, fat, cheerful, laughing woman who proclaims: "That means me! A Jewish born and bred!" A paralyzed boy is told by his nurse that the regulation applies only to healthy Jews—not to him; resolutely, he insists on registering. A diplomat's snobbish wife wants him to lodge a complaint against the procedure and assails the laughing woman for her "Jewish vulgarity." A refined baroness quietly registers. Bruno absorbs all of this with sorrowful fascination. What matters more than authorities identifying Jews is Jews identifying and either accepting or, mostly, rejecting one another.

Anti-Semitism spreads like a contagious disease, with Appelfeld often using train scenes to carry and publicize it. In the first of his novels to be translated into English, *Badenheim, 'ir nofesh* (1975; *Badenheim 1939*, 1980), the final paragraph abruptly moves previously comfortable resort guests to a freight train headed east, presumably to a Polish concentration camp. Not only do train journeys open and close *The Age of Wonders*, but also Bruno's mother makes weekly train trips to visit her schizophrenic younger sister, Theresa, temporarily settled in a sanatorium. On yet another train journey, Theresa, accompanying the family, drags them from their compartment in the middle of the night, searching the countryside for a church in which she, now a feverish Christian convert, can pray. When the family later hears of Theresa's death in a convent, the only available train to her funeral service is a local cattle run. As the family prepares to board it, a station guard calls out, "Austrian horses smell better than Jews."

The harshest dramatization of the gap between Jews also occurs in a railway station. The family notices a tightly huddled group of people dressed in black and striped garments, greedily gulping down sandwiches. The mother whispers, "Jews"; the father remarks, "Lately they've been appearing in droves"; for Bruno, this is his first sight of *Ostjuden*, Eastern European Jews. "They seemed chained to each other, even while eating. There was no glory in their nocturnal appearance." The image not only prefigures their actual enchainment-to-come but also highlights Central European Jews' haughty self-distancing from the alien and parochial manners of Polish or Russian Jews.

*Critical Context*

Aharon Appelfeld is himself a survivor of the Holocaust whose doom haunts his fiction. Born in Czernowitz, Bukovina (then Romanian, now within the Soviet Union), he was eight when the invading Germans sent him to a labor camp in 1940. His mother was killed; his father died in the camp; in 1941, the boy managed to escape into the inhospitable countryside, working as a shepherd and farm laborer for three years, hiding his identity from hunters of Jews, growing up without a proper adolescence. After the armistice, he made his way to Italy with a small tide of refugees, and from there emigrated to Palestine in 1946. Though he knew no Hebrew before the age of fourteen, he writes exclusively in his adopted language. His published works in Israel include six collections of stories, eight novels, and one book of essays.

Neither *The Age of Wonders* nor Appelfeld's other fiction directly alludes to the Holocaust's monstrous reality of deaths almost beyond reckoning. The horrors to come or just ended are a baleful flickering on the horizon of his muted, compressed, austerely understated perspective. His artistic strategy is to produce fiction whose structure, imagery, tone, and voice all meditate somberly on the precarious course of contemporary Judaism. He struggles unblinkingly with the culture of self-rejection to which all too many Jews succumbed in Central and Western Europe. In his flat, controlled, lucidly neutral prose, never thundering or moralizing, he presents scenes that pass a scorching judgment on the spiritual and psychological meanness of Jewish assimilation to and humiliation before a dominant Gentile society.

Like Gustave Flaubert, he flays his Bouvards and Pecuchets for their banal and narcotized acceptance of irrational hatreds. Like Marcel Proust, he depicts bizarre social snobbery and status-scoring, evasiveness, betrayal, and scapegoating. Like Franz Kafka, he ponders whether being Jewish is an incurable affliction. Appelfeld's art lacks the intensity, range, and imaginative power of these masters, but he shares with them the honesty of refusing to accept any easy solutions to basic problems of cultural separation and misunderstanding.

*The Age of Wonders* has its share of aesthetic flaws: The shift in point of view, from the first person in book 1 to the third person in book 2, is needlessly confusing; the number of minor characters is too profuse for a short novel; and the second part, amounting to an extended coda, is too long and dimly focused. Nevertheless, this novel is a noble achievement expressing eloquent grief at man's capacity for cruelty and victimization. Appelfeld bears tragic witness to a chapter in human history for which no explanations can adequately account.

*Sources for Further Study*
Agee, Joel. Review in *The New York Times Book Review*. LXXXVI (December 27, 1981), pp. 1, 20.
Alvarez, A. Review in *The New York Review of Books*. XXIX (February 4, 1982), pp. 33-34.
Lewis, Stephen. *Art out of Agony*, 1984.
Prescott, P. S. Review in *Newsweek*. CXCVIII (December 14, 1981), p. 108.

*Gerhard Brand*

# ALL OUR YESTERDAYS

*Author:* Natalia Ginzburg (1916-    )
*Type of plot:* Domestic realism
*Time of plot:* From the late 1930's through the end of World War II
*Locale:* An unnamed town in northern Italy and the village of San Costanzo in
southern Italy
*First published: Tutti i nostri ieri,* 1952 (English translation, *Dead Yesterdays,*
1956; better known as *All Our Yesterdays*)

> *Principal characters:*
> ANNA, a teenage girl as the narrative begins
> IPPOLITO and
> GIUSTINO, her brothers
> CONCETTINA, her sister
> GIUMA, the boy across the street and Anna's lover
> CENZO RENA, Anna's husband

## The Novel

*All Our Yesterdays* is divided chronologically and geographically. Part 1
describes the last school years and earliest adult experiences of the children
of a middle-class provincial family in the late 1930's. Part 2 takes Anna and
her husband away to the southern village of San Costanzo. From their perspective the reader observes the impact of World War II on the family and on
Italian society as a whole.

There is no single protagonist in the novel, which details the lives of the
children of two neighboring families. Anna's father, a widower, is an anti-
Fascist who spends the last years of his life writing his memoirs, which will
never be published. Anna's sister, Concettina, is preoccupied with her boyfriends and eventually marries Emilio, arousing the political disapproval of
several male members of the family. Anna meets Giuma, the youngest son of
the family across the street, on the day of her father's funeral. Giuma's
household consists of the old father who owns a local soap factory, his much
younger wife, Mammina, Giuma's elder brother, Emanuele, a rebellious sister, Amalia, and a mysterious German refugee, Franz, who is Mammina's
lover.

As Nazi Germany stands poised for the invasion of France, young Anna's
brother Ippolito, Emanuele, and their friend Danilo form a loose anti-Fascist
group, whose program consists largely of reading clandestine newspapers
behind closed doors. Ippolito becomes the first casualty of the war. Unable
to accept the collapse of France and Italy's collaboration with the Nazis, he
shoots himself one morning on a park bench in the center of the town. His
suicide coincides with Anna's realization that she has been made pregnant by

Giuma. She is sixteen years old. At this point an old family friend, Cenzo
Rena, reappears. Learning of Anna's crisis, he offers to marry her and takes
her back to his home in the South.

The second half of the novel is much more than the chronicle of Anna's
marriage. It is a careful portrait of a time and place. Cenzo Rena is the self-
appointed savior of the wretched village of San Costanzo, continuously
campaigning for the basic standards of civilized life, such as regular health
care for the women and children, and denouncing the doctor and school-
mistress for their ignorance, prejudice, and apathy. At first Anna, an outsider and still little more than a schoolgirl, feels completely alienated from
this foreign and largely male-dominated society. Gradually, however, her eyes
are opened to a new world which, while it offers her a spectacle of poverty
and misery, also bestows on her the warmth and generosity of its people. She
grows particularly close to La Maschiona, Cenzo Rena's faithful housekeeper.

The war comes to San Costanzo with the arrival of a handful of Jewish
refugees, a reminder of the special racial laws of 1938. Franz suddenly reappears, separated from his wife, Amalia, and rigid with the fear of captivity.
Local sons and fathers are shipped overseas to fight for what is an increasingly losing cause. The village is finally occupied by retreating German troops
in the summer of 1944. The occupation leads to inevitable tragedy when a
"friendly" German soldier discovers Franz and other fugitives in Cenzo
Rena's cellar. There are reprisals, and Rena sacrifices himself to save the
lives of innocent villagers.

Woven through these events is news of Anna's family, conveyed by letter
or visits. Her old governess, Signora Maria, is killed in an air raid on Turin.
Her younger brother, Giustino, and his friend Danilo join the resistance.
Emanuele edits a clandestine newspaper in Rome. Giuma turns up again,
married to an American student of psychology. The war over, Anna returns
with her daughter to the North to rejoin Giustino, Emanuele, and her family
to face the future together, uncertain of what lies ahead and how to deal with
the problems they will have to confront.

*The Characters*

This is a choral novel in which the collective experience of families and social groups is more important than that of separate individuals. One can
clearly distinguish the individual voices, but all are linked to the thematic and
historical chorus. Consequently, no one character stands out as the focus of
the book. By the end of Part 1, however, it is clear that the remainder of the
action will revolve around Anna and her middle-aged husband, Cenzo Rena.
Anna emerges only gradually from the shadows. As a schoolgirl, she thinks
of herself as unattractive and not very intelligent and is ashamed to have to
wear dresses made out of curtains. She accepts the courtship of Giuma out of

gratitude that someone is paying attention to her and in the full knowledge that he does not love her. Anna is completely passive in the acceptance of her pregnancy, Giuma's indifference, and her marriage. The reader must see this as a consequence of being born female in a patriarchal society and remember that Anna is still a child. In the circumstances, she is fortunate to find in Rena a protector who is wise and generous in spirit.

Natalia Ginzburg's characterization of Cenzo Rena is remarkable. Rena marries Anna out of loyalty and love for her father. He breaks in on the family's torpor at the most unexpected moments and attempts to breathe some vitality into their ennui and passivity. In sweeping Anna off to the South, he offers her a protection which reflects his social commitment to all the inhabitants of San Costanzo. He is sincerely committed to the future of his adopted daughter, to that of the villagers, and indeed to the whole of southern Italy. Cenzo Rena has plans for his village beyond the end of the war and the inevitable collapse of Fascism. He has even marked out a new mayor, the peasant Giovanni, whose function will be to put into practice all Rena can teach him about social welfare. Ultimately, Rena is a tragic figure obliged to offer his life to save others. The village, the South, and his young wife and child lose a man of action and moral energy.

The book's remaining characters are drawn with bold brush strokes, fully rounded in speech and gesture. The old governess, Signora Maria, is initially the glue that keeps the family together, with her punctilious observance of social convention. Concettina is busy with her boyfriends. Her vision grows even narrower after her marriage. Ippolito is silent; his mysterious smile cannot hide a growing, ungovernable despair. The generous Emanuele eventually learns the courage to break away from his family, and Anna's younger brother, Giustino, grows to political maturity through the war. Giuma, the spoiled boy, reverts to middle-class conformity at the end. Finally, there is the refugee Franz, who is numb with fear when he turns up at San Costanzo, carrying his tennis rackets to a mountain village in the midst of war.

## Themes and Meanings

In Natalia Ginzburg's fiction, the family and its relationships determine the parameters of the action. Domestic experience is the source of her inspiration, as it is the starting point of all human development. This novel, however, which draws on Ginzburg's own experience of the time she spent in the Abruzzi, where her husband was a political prisoner, has a historical dimension rare in her fiction. Her essential theme is the impact of history on private lives, the way public events have of intruding on personal existence and shattering the illusions of security and complacency. Every gesture seems politically determined, including the father's devotion to his anti-Fascist memoirs and the example he hands down to his son and friends, who establish their own anti-Fascist cell. Later, each member will offer a precise response to the war, beginning with Ippolito, whose suicide as a protest against the collapse of liberal Europe makes him the first war casualty. Anna's pregnancy coincides with Ippolito's death and the advance of Nazism. Her giving birth is, in context, an unconscious challenge to the atmosphere of violence and death and a vote of confidence in a future that will outlast the war. Her marriage to Cenzo Rena will open her eyes, and those of the reader, to the southern experience of which she was largely unaware, and ally her to a liberal reformer and the ideals of social engagement. Apolitical as she is, Anna cannot go unmarked by this experience and its tragedy.

The historical backdrop and the southern theme set *All Our Yesterdays* apart from the body of Ginzburg's fiction. Reading it, one is reminded of Carlo Levi's landmark work, *Cristo si è fermato a Eboli* (1945; *Christ Stopped at Eboli: The Story of a Year*, 1947), which set out to catalog all aspects of the problems of southern Italy in specifically sociological terms. Through the prism of personal observation, the reader sees a previously unknown world, one foreign to most Italian readers in 1952. The view includes now-familiar images of economic and human misery: the sick and semisavage children, and the perpetuation of the cycle of poverty, reflected in the unchanging round of the seasons. There is constant friction between the authorities and the peasants who visit Cenzo Rena's house. The reader is also made aware that forces are astir in the South which will dismantle the old feudal order that Fascism did nothing to dispel; these forces are represented by Cenzo Rena's careful instructions to the peasant Giovanni, whom he sees as the instrument of future local reform. The young men who join the resistance are fighting not only against an inhuman dictatorship but also for a complete revision of the country's priorities, beginning with the battle to turn the South into a civilized place. In Cenzo Rena the reader can discover a new Italian. Ginzburg portrays him with sympathetic humor as a flawed human being, but one who cheerfully shoulders his responsibilities. He is active rather than passive, hopeful rather than fatalistic, and is as capable of arousing people such as Anna and Giustino out of their torpor on the private level as he is of stirring a community out of its historical resignation.

## Critical Context

Natalia Ginzburg had already established an authorial voice in her earliest stories: "Un'assenza" (an absence), "Casa al mare" (house by the sea), and "La madre" (the mother). In *All Our Yesterdays* her style is even more firmly defined, as she outdistances her previous work in breadth and ambition.

The relationship of Ginzburg's voice to the post-nineteenth century tradition of the Italian novel is made clear in two respects in the novel. First, Ginzburg's polished control of indirect speech (which she prefers over direct dialogue) as the single means of narration places her in a direct line from the Sicilian novelist Giovanni Verga. Verga's cultivation of this device allowed the characters to speak for themselves, the author to absent himself from the novel, and for an appearance of objectivity. Ginzburg grants her characters autonomy by the same means, while staying closer to them in their sufferings and struggles. Second, she is more Manzonian than she might admit. Indeed, she has written a comprehensive biography of Alessandro Manzoni, chronicling the domestic life of the Milanese novelist. Since the publication of Manzoni's *I promessi sposi* (1827, revised 1840-1842; *The Betrothed*, 1828, revised 1951), Italian novelists have regularly explored the impact of history on individuals. Ginzburg's instinct is to limit herself to the vicissitudes of private life, but here, in what might be called her contribution to the resistance novel, she explicitly deals with the effects of Fascism and the war on those who find themselves unable to avoid the flood of history. In *All Our Yesterdays*, as in the works of Ignazio Silone and Alberto Moravia, history is a constant reminder of the individual's responsibility to his community—a challenge to which some are equal, while others are not. Seen in this light, history is the crucible of character, and thus the ally of the novelist.

*Sources for Further Study*

Bergin, T. G. Review in *The Saturday Review*. XL (January 5, 1957), p. 4.
Clementelli, Elena. *Invito alla lettura di Natalia Ginzburg*, 1972.
Piclardi, Rosetta D. "Forms and Figures in the Novels of Natalia Ginzburg," in *World Literature Today*. LIII (1979), pp. 585-589.
Quigley, Isabel. Review in *The Spectator*. August 24, 1956, p. 269.
Slonim, Marc. Review in *The New York Times Book Review*. LXII (January 5, 1957), p. 5.
*The Times Literary Supplement*. Review. September 14, 1956, p. 537.

*Harry Lawton*

# AMBIGUOUS ADVENTURE

*Author:* Cheikh Hamidou Kane (1928-      )
*Type of plot:* Philosophical realism
*Time of plot:* The early 1920's to the late 1930's
*Locale:* A Peul village and an unnamed town dominated by the French in Senegal, and Paris
*First published: L'Aventure ambiguë,* 1961 (English translation, 1963)

> *Principal characters:*
> SAMBA DIALLO, the protagonist, a young man of the aristocratic Diallobé family
> THIERNO, an aging, traditional teacher of Islam
> THE KNIGHT, Samba's father
> THE CHIEF OF THE DIALLOBÉ, Samba's cousin
> THE MOST ROYAL LADY, Samba's aunt and the chief's sister
> THE FOOL, Thierno's friend, a living symbol of the conflict between the West and Africa
> PAUL LACROIX, a French Catholic who discusses the values of the West with the Knight
> PAUL MARTIAL, a French Protestant in Paris who also discusses the spiritual values of the West with Samba
> LUCIENNE MARTIAL, Paul's daughter, a Marxist who debates materialism with Samba

*The Novel*

Written in the third person but from the protagonist's point of view, *Ambiguous Adventure* traces the education of Samba Diallo from the traditional Islamic practice of reciting the Koran in Senegal to advanced studies of philosophy in Paris. Difficult in French or English, the novel consists primarily of dialogue in which various characters espouse and debate distinctive philosophical values. Rather than merely recalling the chronology of an autobiographical journey into Western higher education, Cheikh Hamidou Kane immerses the reader in the complex dilemma of Senegalese aristocrats, who must decide how to reconcile their own Islamic faith with the materialism of modern Europe. As Samba pursues his adventure in ideas, he becomes increasingly alienated from the worldviews of both the West and French West Africa, thus raising problematic issues for French assimilationist policies in the wake of colonial conquest.

The early chapters of the novel center on debates among the nobility of the Peul people in Senegal. Samba is the spiritual and temporal heir to the traditions of the Diallobé family. By custom, he has been sent to a teacher, Thierno, who trains him in the lore and wisdom of the Koran at the Glowing Hearth, Thierno's household. As a result of the rigorous discipline which includes begging to sustain himself physically, Samba's intelligence and devotion prepare him to inherit Thierno's authority as teacher. Samba's spiritual revelations originate from his humility before God, allowing him to accept death as the salvation that transcends both the struggles of life and the fear of dying; yet his steadfast, youthful devotion is oblivious to the increasing material poverty that spreads among the people for whom he will eventually be responsible. Samba dreams only of becoming a teacher.

French administrators, however, are building schools in their effort to assimilate the conquered Diallobé. When Thierno refuses to advise the chief on whether to send his people to the new school, Samba's aunt, the Most Royal Lady, convinces the chief to enroll Samba, as a role model, in the belief that progressive French education will prepare the nobility to lead the Diallobé into material comfort. After formally concluding his studies of the Koran by reciting from the scripture throughout all of one night to honor his parents, Samba begins his adventure with Western values.

Samba does so well in his mastery of French, history, and other subjects that he becomes just as obsessed with understanding the values of the West as with nurturing his absolute faith in Islam. When the Knight, Samba's father, learns of the chief's decision to send Samba to the French school, he fears the loss of his son's quietistic perspective in the face "of this egotism which the West is scattering abroad." Although the Knight agrees with Paul Lacroix, a French Catholic, that "the era of separate destinies" for the West and for French West Africa has ended, he fears that Samba will be exiled spiritually while he pursues an understanding of the West's preoccupation with evidence, "a quality of the surface," thus undermining his son's identity as a Senegalese Muslim. Through dialogues between the Knight and Lacroix and between Samba and his father, a central question emerges: If Samba enters the thought of the West deeply enough to understand it, will he not then have lost his own worldview? As part 1 of the novel closes and part 2 opens, Kane shifts abruptly to Paris, where Samba is studying philosophy, seemingly confirming his father's worst fears.

Now mature but still a devout Muslim, Samba's academic success in comprehending Western thought from Protestantism to Marxism is accompanied by increasing despair over the uncertainty of his own beliefs. Intellectually, he rejects European materialism both in capitalism and socialism, but, emotionally, he feels his faith slipping away from him. When Samba expresses his spiritual anguish in a letter to his father, the Knight calls him back to the village in Senegal in order to protect him from atheism and materialism.

When Samba returns, he senses that he is no longer part of the community. In his absence, Thierno has died, and the new Koranic teacher has encouraged the people to attend the French schools. Trying to reaffirm his faith, Samba visits the grave of his former teacher with the fool, a man who went insane from his experience in Europe and who became dependent upon

Thierno for emotional stability. Because Samba refuses to pray at the dead teacher's grave, fearing that his uncertainty would be hypocritical, the fool stabs him, thinking that Samba has insulted Thierno. As Samba lies dying, he is mystically reunited with the earth and with the absolute nothingness that forms the core of his traditional belief. In his death, Samba affirms the values of Islam, but, dead, he offers little direction for the benefit of the Diallobé. Consequently, the novel ends in ambiguity over the possibility for reconciling the worldview of Islamic Africa with that of the West. Samba's individual intellectual and spiritual adventure has come full circle, but none of the complex, metaphysical questions developed throughout the novel has been resolved.

## The Characters

Schooled in the rich oral tradition of the Peul and firmly grounded in the Arabic scripture of the Koran, Kane draws clearly on his own experience, having pursued a French education in Paris. His affinities with his protagonist, however, resemble only the general movement out of Senegal. The name "Samba" was a title bestowed on the second son of the family, and Kane employs it to suggest a second generation of Peul-Muslim Senegalese who have to come to terms with their identity as French colonial subjects. Kane himself served both as the French regional Governor of Thiès and, after Senegal's independence, as cabinet director in the Ministry of Development and Planning of the new government. Remaining a devout Muslim but acknowledging his pragmatic perspective toward the French, Kane would say of "Europeanized Africans" that "we are cultural half-breeds. If we feel as Negroes, we express ourselves in French, because French is a language of universal vocation." That vocation, as writer and as political leader, however, serves only to arm Kane with diverse experience upon which he reflects in order to create the protagonist Samba and the other characters, all of whom are largely type characters who express distinct points of view through the complex discussions in the novel.

Of the West African characters, Thierno exercises the greatest determining influence on Samba, who serves as the conscience and identity upon whom all issues of the debates converge. Thierno is a stern, demanding master, shaping Samba's early consciousness. He demands perfect recitations and does not hesitate to draw blood in order to punish mistakes. From hour to hour, he sustains the principles of suffering and martyrdom in his training of Samba. Yet Thierno is also quietly compassionate, struggling not to show favoritism despite his pride in Samba's spiritual growth. When the fool returns to the village crazed by Europe's materialism, Thierno provides sanctuary for him. Thierno's world is entirely spiritual; he looks to God as "the totality of the world, the visible and the invisible, its past and its future." Consistent with this absolutism, Thierno disdains material achievements, disclaiming any responsibility for advising the chief on matters of French influence through the schools.

Like the chief, who recalls an aristocratic heritage that has succumbed to superior weaponry, the Most Royal Lady represents a type. The chief, paradoxically, must yield even more of his control if he is to preserve the society which he rules nominally. The Diallobé economic woes are such that the chief can see only further degradation if the Diallobé refuse French education. By encouraging his people to learn the colonial language and, inevitably, to assimilate aspects of French culture, the chief also realizes that the traditional Peul and Islamic basis for culture will be further diminished. For the Most Royal Lady, the choice is clear: assimilate or perish. While the chief contemplates the wisdom of permitting the Diallobé to perish as they were and are, thus maintaining cultural integrity and gaining martyrdom, the Most Royal Lady does not hesitate to champion the disappearance of traditions in favor of material survival. For her, authority and power are the only means to salvation. Rejecting the chief's contemplative understanding, she urges not the quietistic devotion to martyrdom, but a dedication to the "world of the living, in which the values of death will be scoffed at and bankrupt." From her perspective, assimilation is the ascent to power: "[W]e must go to learn from them the art of conquering without being in the right."

Of the European characters in the novel, Lucienne Martial poses the greatest challenge to Samba, for he harbors a romantic fascination with her. Yet her rigid Marxism, espousing atheism and scientific materialism, is a viewpoint which Samba cannot accept. When Lucienne argues the virtues of social and economic equality, Samba affirms his Diallobé faith in Islam: "As for me, I do not fight for liberty, but for God." More compatible with Samba's own spiritual devotion is Lucienne's father, Paul Martial. His colonialism, however, is spiritual; he mourns the loss of faith in the West and confesses that his zeal for missionary work was motivated by the hope that the example of Islamic faith would revive Christianity. Paul Lacroix, steadfast in his own belief, represents a worldview which holds that the emphasis on materialism, science, and progress is evidence of reason's "light." For him the spiritual light and the scientific light are nearly identical: Technological superiority confirms spiritual authority. Each of these characters represents an intellectual stance which Samba must at least partially accept in order to comprehend its force. In so doing, he moves further into a dual consciousness that seems to him only confusion and chaos.

*Themes and Meanings*

Characterization in *Ambiguous Adventure* is so pointedly typed that characters represent variations on the central philosophical tension in the novel: The values of the modern West force a movement from the values of traditional Islamic West Africa toward a universal destiny of oppositions united in nothingness. Science, progress, external evidence, materialism, and light oppose belief, stability, internal devotion, spirituality, and darkness. On the one hand, Islam, from the point of view in the West, is a "fascination of nothingness for those who have nothing. Their nothingness—they call it the absolute." On the other hand, the West, from the Islamic West African point of view, "is the triumph of evidence, a proliferation of the surface," which creates "masters of the external," exiling those masters to a superficial world. For Europeans, truth is revealed day by day. For West African Muslims, truth comes from the belief "in the end of the world" and "takes its place at the end of history." To the chief, Western values contract and constrain truth to increasingly relativistic, narrow, egoistic concerns. To Lacroix, the Diallobé pursue a cosmic drama that befits a defeated people who revel in absurd fears. Their common ground is only that both "shall have, strictly, the same future" of "the crucible in which the world is being fused."

That future is the torn conscience of Samba, in which the converging destinies of the West and Africa meet. Consequently, the novel's theme with respect to the individual turns on a double question: "[C]an one learn *this* without forgetting *that*, and is what one learns worth what one forgets?" For Samba, the price of his French education is despair, alienation, and death. Like the fool who kills him, Samba is of two minds. The fool wears a spotless white boubous; yet over it, he wears an old, dirty European frock coat. He has been destroyed by his experience in the West, yet he cannot shed that brittle, hardening experience. Ironically, the fool's murder of Samba is also Samba's freedom from his doubled-dressed, agonized consciousness. Kane, however, does not free the reader from the perplexing complications of the two ideologies that clash throughout the novel.

Although Samba finds salvation in a dubious martyrdom that results from his refusal to be hypocritical to the Word of the Koran and in his return to the visible natural world of an eternal, unseen creator, he also negates the very oppositions of the novel's tension. Death frees him just as Thierno taught him that it would. Dying confirms his devotion to the Word, vindicating his exile into a world of adventurous surfaces and precise evidence. The ideologies, however, remain; all the characters, all the variations of central opposing cultural viewpoints, survive Samba in the novel's closure of implied nothingness. What is left for the reader is an array of disparate ideas yet to be played out as long as humanity senses the movement of history—or awaits the apocalyptic end of it.

## Critical Context

*Ambiguous Adventure* is Kane's only novel, yet it represents a crucial step in the evolution of French West African literature. In its setting and theme the novel addresses a common dilemma of the intellectual elite in colonial Senegal and throughout Francophone Africa. One of the primary voices in the negritude movement, which espoused black cultural values and Africa as a source of inspiration, Kane rejects the position of earlier Senegalese novelists, such as Bakary Diallo, who sought to justify assimilation by demonstrating loyalty and by documenting the struggle to attain French citizenship. Indeed, Samba Diallo's last name suggests that Kane is quite conscious of his second-generation challenge to the assimilation supported by novelists from 1910 to the 1930's. The negritude writers, however, emphasized African heritage far more than they examined the implicit damage of colonialism. In this regard, Kane not only rejects the blind wish of earlier novelists to integrate culturally and politically with France but also anticipates postcolonial Senegalese novels, such as those by Ousmane Sembène, that are devoted to a political commitment in elevating those Senegalese who were not subjected to assimilationist policies.

Kane's novel is unique in that it represents the first direct challenge to the philosophy of assimilation. Moreover, Kane withheld publication of his novel for nearly ten years, waiting until independence to seek a publisher, perhaps to discern the political direction of Senegal and perhaps to hone the aesthetics of his craft to a sharpened if ambiguous clarity. In this respect, *Ambiguous Adventure* is also unique, for it offers a new language in African literature, setting a dialectical, discursive Western style against the repetitive lyricism of Koranic literary style. The linguistic synthesis reflects the duality of cultural perspectives within Kane himself, yet the novel—written in French—affirms the Islamic faith. The title of the novel identifies the aesthetic method, while, at the same time, it describes the strategies of an ideological battleground. Because *Ambiguous Adventure* is born of a particular period in Senegal's history, it remains a singular achievement. No other African novel is quite like it, and, given the waning of assimilation, another that belongs so much to its time and yet leaves so much ambiguously undetermined for the future is unlikely.

*Sources for Further Study*
Brench, A. C. *The Novelists' Inheritance in French Africa*, 1967.
Calin, William. "Between Two Worlds: The Quest for Death and Life in Cheikh Hamidou Kane's *L'Aventure ambiguë*," in *Kentucky Romance Quarterly*. XIX (1972), pp. 183-197.
Madubuike, Ihechukwu. "Aspects of Religion in the Senegalese Novel," in *Journal of Black Studies*. VI (1976), pp. 337-352.
_____. "The Politics of Assimilation and the Evolution of the Novel in Senegal," in *African Studies Review*. XVIII (1975), pp. 89-99.
Mbabuike, Michael. "Cheikh Hamidou Kane's *Ambiguous Adventure*: Dichotomy of Existence and the Sense of God," in *Journal of Ethnic Studies*. VIII (1981), pp. 114-120.

*Michael Loudon*

# AMERIKA

*Author:* Franz Kafka (1883-1924)
*Type of plot:* Magical realism
*Time of plot:* The early twentieth century
*Locale:* Chiefly New York City and unspecified environs
*First published:* 1927 (English translation, 1938)

### Principal characters:

KARL ROSSMANN, the novel's young hero from Prague,
    dispossessed by his family and adrift in America
THE STOKER, the first of Karl's ambiguous friends and guides
UNCLE JACOB, Karl's well-to-do uncle, owner of the Jacob
    Dispatch Agency
ROBINSON and DELAMARCHE, immigrants (one Irish, the other
    French) and unemployed mechanics whom Karl meets
    along his pilgrim's progress
GRETE MITZELBACH, formerly of Prague, like Karl, and now
    the manageress of the Hotel Occidental
THERESE BERCHTOLD, the manageress' secretary
BRUNELDA, an enormously fat singer

## The Novel

The plot of *Amerika* is deceptively simple, following a young immigrant's adventures from his arrival at New York Harbor to his "disappearance" on a journey to Oklahoma. The novel remains unfinished, yet it is paradoxically complete. Karl Rossmann's adventures—or rather his misadventures—begin even before he steps ashore. After seeing the Statue of Liberty (through Franz Kafka's surrealistic imagination, Liberty's torch is supplanted by a sword), Karl goes belowdecks to retrieve his umbrella. In typically Kafka-esque fashion, this simple act develops into a complex odyssey: He loses his way and, as a result, meets the Stoker, the first of many ambiguous guides and fellow sufferers. After listening to the Stoker's litany of wrongs suffered, Karl accompanies him to the ship's office, where the authorities' indifference prompts Karl to advocate the Stoker's case. That Karl should speak with such assurance about a man he hardly knows appears entirely natural given the dream logic of Kafka's seemingly realistic novel. In such a world, where sudden and comically absurd appearances are the norm rather than the exception, it is equally natural that his defense of the Stoker should lead Karl to his wealthy Uncle Jacob (or a man who believes Karl to be his nephew). In Kafka's fiction, everything is plausible and everything is in doubt.

The nearly penniless immigrant is thus saved—ironically and momentarily, for Uncle Jacob's protection is a mixed blessing. Even as he shields Karl from all the harshness of the immigrant experience, Uncle Jacob in effect imprisons his nephew in his house. He deprives Karl of any chance of freedom and demands total submission to his authority. When Karl chooses to accept an offer to spend the might with one of his uncle's business associates, Uncle Jacob banishes him from his house, his protection, and his sight. He watches Karl make his own choice and then suffer the consequences of his own decision, without first warning him of the effects. Driven from his uncle's house as he had been driven from his parents', Karl finds himself once again adrift and uncertain. In this state, he is easy prey for the two immigrant tramps, an Irishman called Robinson and a Frenchman called Delamarche. The tramps seem to befriend Karl, only to betray his trust repeatedly as they travel together to Butterford, the land of milk and honey and well-paying jobs that they never reach. Instead, Karl finds temporary refuge at the Hotel Occidental, where he comes under the patronage of Grete Mitzelbach, the hotel's manageress. Grete, like Karl (and Kafka), is a native of Prague. With her help, he becomes a lift boy, a position that gratifies Karl even as it makes him a virtual slave in the complex organization of the vast hotel.

Clearly, *Amerika* is not a Horatio Alger story of rags to riches and virtue rewarded. Dismissed for reasons that the head porter says are too serious to be specified, Karl once again takes up with Robinson and Delamarche, whose situations have visibly improved since their chance meeting with a wealthy and enormously fat singer, Brunelda. When he learns that he is destined to be one of Brunelda's servants, Karl balks. With no better prospects, however, he stays on until he chances upon a placard advertising positions with the Nature Theatre of Oklahoma. Karl goes to the Nature Theatre's temporary recruitment center, accepts a vaguely defined position as "technical worker," and continues on his way—this time toward Oklahoma, which is less a state of the union than a state of mind or, better, a state of Karl's and Kafka's absurdly hopeful imagination.

*Amerika* does, therefore, have an ending of sorts. Because the novel's plot is only apparently sequential, however, no conclusion is possible. In fact, the plot is recurrent and endless, the playing of the same basic situation over and over, a comic reenactment of Albert Camus' existential reading of the myth of Sisyphus. In Kafka's telling, the boy is banished from his home (and from the certainty and stability his home represents), goes in search of something more certain and more permanent, and, with the help of a benefactor (Uncle Jacob, for example, or the manageress), finds home, only to lose it as before. Traduced and yet again an outcast, Karl searches ahead for what he has lost behind him or perhaps never had—except as a dream or a delusion.

### The Characters

The novel's uncertainty, or doubleness, is implied in Karl's surname. As Rossmann, he is both horse (in German, *Ross*) and man (*Mann*), animal and human, flesh and spirit. Fifteen or sixteen years old (Kafka was inconsistent on this point), Karl is both a child and an adult. He is a sympathetic figure insofar as he seeks to be just and to be treated justly, yet he is comical as well in his naïveté and in his pompous, ill-founded certainties. Although banished from his home for having fathered a child by a maidservant, Karl is, in fact, more child than man and less the seducer than the one seduced. This is a pattern that repeats itself throughout the novel as the ever-hopeful, ever-trustful man-child succumbs to the charms not only of women but of all of his guides and benefactors as well. In a sense, Karl is doomed by his own will to believe, by a religious sensibility that makes him yearn for something more than he has, something finer and more final. Not entirely innocent, he is also not exactly guilty—whether the accusation is that of fathering an illegitimate child or shirking his duties as a lift boy. Ultimately, Karl is an undefinable being, the perfect hero for a novel of comic absurdity, a hero whose quest is less Odyssean than adolescent and whose nature is at once naïve and perverse, malleable yet intractable. As the half-maternal, half-sensual manageress tells him, "You're very obstinate, when people mean well by you and try to do you a good turn, you do your best to hinder them."

The reader may well agree, but—unlike the manageress—the reader will nevertheless have considerably greater difficulty in defining Karl. The entire novel, and the last two chapters in particular, make clear that Karl is searching not only for a home but for himself as well. He is looking for a role that will make him feel more secure, more at home in the vast and nameless void that Kafka has here chosen to call Amerika. Knowing this, the reader can better understand the appeal of the Nature Theatre of Oklahoma: not money (wages are never discussed or even mentioned) but, as the placard proclaims, "Employment for everyone, a place for everyone" (with the emphasis on *place*). The exact role Karl is meant to play in this Nature Theatre is left as vague as the nature of the Theatre itself, which combines aspects of the Christian afterlife, a vast carnival, a settlement company, a confidence game, a volunteer army of the unemployed, a relief agency, a quack religion, and an amateur theater on a national scale.

By the end of the novel, Karl has in a very real sense simply ceased to exist. Following the novel's relentless dream logic, Karl is too shy to give the recruiters his own name and provides them instead with "the nickname he had had in his last post: 'Negro.'" (This post and this name are the subjects of a chapter Kafka may have imagined but never actually wrote.) In this way, Karl, still hoping to fulfill "his old daydream" of becoming an engineer, is transformed into "Negro, technical worker," some hybrid of Mark Twain's Huck and Jim, of citizen and outcast, free man and slave. It is unclear whether this second issue of illegitimacy engendered by Karl marks the loss of his true self or instead constitutes a way of preserving it by keeping his essential self hidden under this pseudonym. What is less ambiguous is the fact that another of Karl's desires remains as strong as ever: "Besides, he kept on telling himself, it was not so much a matter of the kind of work as of establishing oneself permanently somewhere." Karl finds himself—or at least hopes to find himself—by losing himself in the vastness and variety of America itself. In this way, he proves to be just what Kafka called him in the novel's working title, *Der Verschollene*: the boy who disappeared. Easily distinguishable from all the novel's other characters, Karl is also quite like them with his immigrant status and all that it implies. Thus Karl, the only protagonist in a Kafka novel to have a complete name (the others are known simply as "K" and "Joseph K"), becomes an Everyman and, by virtue of his disappearance, a No-man as well—perhaps the only kind of Everyman still possible in these modern times.

### Themes and Meanings

Kafka seemed to intuit that being someone, or anyone, in the geographical vastness of America was not altogether different from the problem of being someone in the bureaucratic vastness of German-dominated Prague. Establishing an identity was, moreover, a problem compounded by the question of home, a question that was important both to the immigrant and to the Czech. "I want above all to get home," Karl points out early in the novel. By "home," he literally means the house of his Uncle Jacob but, figuratively, he is referring to that dream of a familiar place where he will feel secure, understood, accepted: the garden from which Karl, like Adam, has been banished. Because of his original sin, he has been condemned to wander the earth in search not only of a home, or refuge, but of justice and mercy as well. As he comes to realize, however momentarily, "It's impossible to defend oneself where there is no good will." What this sudden revelation suggests is that the absence of mercy, whether human or divine, makes justice impossible. Just as important, this situation renders all Karl's efforts not only existentially futile but—and this is Kafka's genius—comically absurd as well. The chance encounters that characterize the novel, the arbitrary exercise of authority by those who are in power (parents, uncles, head porters, and the like), the uncertain rules and regulations, and the various characters'—especially Karl's—precarious status constitute Kafka's fictional world.

This is a world that has as much in common with silent film comedies as with the philosophical essays, plays, and fictions of Albert Camus and Jean-Paul Sartre. Above all, it is a world that is blackly humorous. When Karl asks Robinson why he stays with Brunelda and Delamarche even though they treat him so badly, Robinson responds to Karl's "stupid question" with these words: "You'll stay here too, even if they treat you still worse. Besides they don't treat me so very badly." Robinson's words perfectly embody Kafka's point; they make ironically clear how desperately the individual (whether Robinson, Rossmann, or the readers) needs a place—any place, no matter what kind. These words also make clear, in Robinson's "Besides," how prepared the individual is to delude himself about what is intolerable and what is not, to confuse the ridiculous with the sublime.

Drawing on a host of sources—including Charles Dickens' *David Copperfield*, Benjamin Franklin's *Autobiography*, and the poetry of Walt Whitman—and calling to the reader's mind an even more formidable array of literary analogues—from William Shakespeare's one play set in the Americas, *The Tempest*, to Henry James's international novels and Horatio Alger's *Mark the Match Boy* guidebooks for country bumpkins dreaming of making their way in late nineteenth century urban America, Kafka conjures an America more fabulous than factual. Appropriately enough, in Kafka's America much of the action takes place in the deepest night, at the deepest levels of the subconscious and of the spirit.

*Critical Context*

*Amerika* (the title appended by his friend and biographer Max Brod) is Kafka's least overtly parabolic work and his most realistic fiction. It is, nevertheless, decidedly Kafkaesque in that it portrays a world both comically and tragically absurd, a reality at once solid and dreamlike through which the hero, or more properly the antihero, appears condemned to an endless and probably fruitless search for some stable identity, some final goal, some imperishable meaning that may or may not exist. Kafka's world is like his fiction: incomplete and labyrinthine, a world and a text in which certainty is what hero and reader desire and ambiguity is what they receive. Above all, *Amerika*, like all Kafka's stories and novels, is deeply autobiographical in its origins and implications. Still, the novel easily outstrips the limits of autobiographical and psychoanalytical interpretation. It is a text that does not so much describe and dramatize as evoke and unsettle, leaving the reader in endless confrontation with its enigma.

*Sources for Further Study*

Brod, Max. *Franz Kafka: A Biography*, 1960 (second edition).
Gray, Ronald D. *Franz Kafka*, 1973.
Hayman, Ronald. *Kafka: A Biography*, 1982.
Pawel, Ernst. *The Nightmare of Reason: A Life of Franz Kafka*, 1984.
Politzer, Heinz. *Franz Kafka: Parable and Paradox*, 1962.

*Robert A. Morace*

# AMONG WOMEN ONLY

*Author:* Cesare Pavese (1908-1950)
*Type of plot:* Symbolic realism
*Time of plot:* The late 1940's
*Locale:* Turin, Italy
*First published: Tra donne sole*, 1949 (English translation, 1953)

*Principal characters:*
CLELIA OITANA, the narrator
ROSETTA MOLA, a young girl who commits suicide
MOMINA, Rosetta's friend

*The Novel*

Clelia Oitana returns to Turin in the dim light of a snowy January day, a few years after the end of World War II. She registers at the best hotel, answers no telephone calls, and, in solitude, savors her return to her birthplace, a major industrial city in northwest Italy. The calm ends when she looks into the hallway to see medical attendants carrying away an unconscious young woman, who, while alone, took an overdose of Veronal. Clelia later discovers that the woman is Rosetta Mola, the daughter of an established Turin family.

Clelia, the narrator, is a successful couturiere in Rome, where she works in the establishment of "Madame," a major Italian designer. Madame has sent Clelia to Turin to prepare to open and then manage a new fashion house. The story takes place in late winter and early spring as Clelia works with an architect and construction contractors to prepare for the opening of the firm at a location on the Via Po.

Clelia, thirty-four years old, left Turin seventeen years earlier, determined to rise from her working-class background. On the first afternoon of the return, Clelia, alone, walks through her old neighborhood, which is smaller and dirtier than she remembers, and realizes that nothing remains there for her but memories. That evening she goes to a ball with Morelli, a friend who provides entrée into the fashionable world of Turin's salons, a world inhabited by the smart set that she wistfully envied as a working girl. She finds that if she does not fit into her old quarter, neither does this frivolous and unproductive leisure class attract her.

Yet the fashion business depends on high society. Interspersed with her work in getting the new business ready, Clelia attends fashionable parties, visits artists' studios, joins her new friends in slumming expeditions, and travels to nearby villas and casinos. The only members of the group with enough depth to interest her are Momina, a woman about her age, and Rosetta, twenty-three, who, recovering from the suicide attempt, returns to society.

Clelia moves back and forth between the construction work at the Via Po and the world of the salons, which are places of malicious gossip and restless searches for diversion. She senses that Rosetta is again irresistibly pulled toward suicide, unable to live with the pretension and hypocrisy surrounding her. Clelia knows that Rosetta is desperate but does not realize how near the crisis is. After a last-minute flurry of preparations before Madame arrives in Turin, Clelia learns that Rosetta has disappeared. Her body is found in a rented room, dead from poison. Clelia concludes that she could not have saved Rosetta: "You just can't love someone else more than yourself. If you can't save yourself, nobody can."

## The Characters

Cesare Pavese's beautifully depicted characters demonstrate his belief that while people cannot change fundamentally, they can become more knowledgeable about themselves. Clelia Oitana is strong and tough—streetwise and clever enough to escape the streets. She remembers the filth and stench of her neighborhood and the blighted lives of her childhood friends. She quickly corrects Rosetta, who romanticizes the lives of working girls. Clelia prides herself on her self-sufficiency. She remembers the frustration, even hatred, she felt as her father lay dying just before a pre-Lenten carnival season: "I thought that it was probably in that distant evening that I really learned for the first time that if I wanted to do anything, to get something out of life, I should tie myself to no one, depend upon no one, as I had been tied to that tiresome father." Her mother reinforced the lesson: Believe in nothing and nobody. Clelia broke away from the confining environment of her youth and won success and recognition in Rome. While she did not rise by ruthlessly stepping on others, she consistently shed lovers and friends as she moved onward through life.

Returning to Turin, she examines the meaning of her life and measures the cost of her achievement. Morelli tells her that she has one great vice: She is addicted to work. He asks her: Why not enjoy life along the way; why condemn people for their pleasures; why find people worthy only if they have suffered and struggled up out of a hole? Clelia understands and accepts his indictment. She also believes that Morelli has overlooked her biggest vice, her pleasure in solitude. Solitude and work have not brought her happiness, but they do, usually, bring her peace. In any case, they are an expression of an inner self that she cannot change, though they leave her isolated from other humans.

Momina is the daughter of nobles, well educated, economically and socially secure. Completely free to do what she likes, she is totally bored. Life is meaningless, nothing counts, she says. The world would be a beautiful place if people were not in it; life is zero. Ceaseless movement and an unending need for diversion characterize her life: "Seeing that nothing's worth anything, you've got to have everything." Unlike most of her frivolous companions, she realizes that something is wrong with their way of life, but she believes that she and others of her class cannot change.

Rosetta desperately seeks some purpose for her life. She considered entering a convent, and she believes that Clelia has found the secret in work, or perhaps the answer is in California, where, she has heard, people never die. Clelia respects Rosetta more than any other member of the Turin establishment. Rosetta is sincere and serious, and Clelia believes that she commits suicide to escape the empty life of her class. Contrasting the evil around her with her own need for order and decency, and unable to find acceptable compromises in the real world, Rosetta is vulnerable to the corrosive nihilism of Momina. In August, 1950, the month that he killed himself, Pavese wrote that when he was younger he had considered suicide but did not act: "Life seemed horrible to me, but I was still interested in myself. Now the opposite is true. I know that life is a tremendous thing, but that I cannot shape it to my own liking."

Clelia escapes the fates of Rosetta and Momina because she has absorbing work and healing solitude. If she is aware that work and solitude are vices, she also knows that they allow her to live. Nevertheless, she also is in a trap that may close in on her later in life. Her livelihood and success depend on the upper class, which she despises.

There is another way of life, that of Becuccio, the foreman in charge of renovating the Via Po shop. Becuccio is a Communist. If one cannot modify one's own character and individual destiny, one can find meaning in life by working to restructure the social conditions that will shape the characters and destinies of future generations. Clelia spends a night with Becuccio and experiences a feeling of authenticity and contentment that escapes her when she is with her fashionable friends. Yet she cannot understand his political message, for it would destroy the system within which she has achieved success. Nor can she escape her existential loneliness and submerge herself in a social movement. Becuccio and Clelia pursue their separate paths.

*Themes and Meanings*

Pavese's novels are thematically rich. Writing was a serious enterprise for him. He used fiction to explore the contradictions individuals confront in reconciling their needs with their social relations and responsibilities. *Among Women Only* scathingly indicts Italy's upper class. The shallow, futile nature of their lives has made them vulnerable to Fascism. They escaped the wartime devastation by retiring with their servants to mountain villas and seaside resorts, and Clelia joins them as they return to their urban haunts. Their empty lives are the product of a society without healthy core values, one incapable of providing its members with meaningful work or a productive social and political role.

Through Clelia, Pavese examines work and solitude, two of his own obsessions, finding them necessary and fulfilling but not fully adequate for a healthy life. Deprived of productive labor and frightened of solitude, Turin's fashionable set restlessly searches for diversion to combat boredom and avoid self-knowledge. People who do not work rot away, Pavese wrote in a letter to a friend. Momina and her friends go slumming for entertainment, viewing poor neighborhoods only as stage sets "got up" for their amusement. They regard art and music as important merely for the social occasion they provide. Even Rosetta's suicide attempt is important mainly because it provides a moment of drama and an endless opportunity for gossip. She arranges her death room like a stage set, a fitting end to a life of role-playing.

Pavese believed that Italy had to overcome its misogynistic traditions in order to achieve progress. He avoided stereotyping his female characters. Pavese did not regard women's lives as being emptier than those of men. He described class distress rather than a gender problem. If Clelia has not built an authentic, fulfilling life, it is not because she has abandoned the traditional role of wife and mother. Rather, it is because her society provides none of its members, men or women, with a productive role. Momina suggests that only by having children can women really become fully alive. Yet even this role does not provide fulfillment. Clelia's childhood friend, Gisella, remained in the old neighborhood to fulfill the traditional role of mother; rather than gaining life, however, she seems utterly drained, existing only through her daughters.

*Critical Context*

By the end of his life, Cesare Pavese had achieved critical and public recognition for his literary work. Shortly before his suicide on August 27, 1950, he received Italy's highest literary award, the Strega Prize. His life, work, and death made him into a cult figure, and admirers combed his novels for insight into the man. Pavese was as obsessed with work and solitude as Clelia and as compelled toward suicide as Rosetta. Like Becuccio, Pavese hoped through Communism to resolve the contradictions that warped individuals and society. Along with cult worship came world recognition of Pavese as a major literary figure, because he dealt seriously and directly with the central concerns of modern times. He may not have found solutions, but few have so clearly defined the problems. *Among Women Only* is a mature expression of his view of life and is considered one of his best books.

Pavese's writing style provided a firm foundation for his enduring popularity. It is lean and spare, with terse, elliptic dialogue. Each word helps to create atmosphere, character insight, and emotion. Pavese was a master of building suspense; without setting his characters in outwardly dramatic situations, he showed the agonizing and intertwined struggle of Clelia as she faces the turmoil that arises when she assesses her life after returning to the scenes of her childhood; of Momina as she wrestles with the void of nihilism; and of Rosetta, who is pulled toward suicide while frantically looking for life supports to prevent it.

Pavese's development of symbolic realism, his tight control of his material, and his fresh, terse style make him a writer to whom one can return confident of finding new levels of meaning. His ability to explore the major themes of human existence in the modern world maintains his popularity decades after his death.

*Sources for Further Study*

Biasin, Gian-Paolo. *The Smile of the Gods: A Thematic Study of Cesare Pavese's Works*, 1968.

Flint, R. W. Introduction to *The Selected Works of Cesare Pavese*, 1968.

Lajolo, Davide. *An Absurd Vice: A Biography of Cesare Pavese*, 1983.

Lucente, Gregory L. *The Narrative of Realism and Myth*, 1979.

Rimanelli, Giose, and K. J. Atchity, eds. *Italian Literature: Roots and Branches*, 1976.

Thompson, Doug. *Cesare Pavese: A Study of the Major Novels and Poems*, 1982.

*William E. Pemberton*

# ANNIVERSARIES
## From the Life of Gesine Cresspahl

*Author:* Uwe Johnson (1934-1984)
*Type of plot:* Historical realism
*Time of plot:* 1931-1968
*Locale:* New York City; Mecklenburg, East Germany; and Richmond, England
*First published: Jahrestage: Aus dem Leben von Gesine Cresspahl,* 1970-1983, 4 volumes (English translation, 1975; *Anniversaries II,* 1987)

> *Principal characters:*
> GESINE CRESSPAHL, a German émigré who has relocated to Manhattan
> MARIE CRESSPAHL, Gesine's daughter and confidante
> HEINRICH CRESSPAHL, Gesine's father, a German carpenter who resided in England for a time
> LISBETH CRESSPAHL, Gesine's mother, who was born into the Papenbrock clan
> PAPENBROCK, a self-made man, a prominent patriarch in the fictitious town of Jerichow, Mecklenburg
> DIETRICH ERICHSON, Gesine's present suitor, a professor and scientist working for NATO
> THE NEW YORK TIMES, the newspaper personified in Gesine's imagination as "Auntie *Times*"

*The Novel*

*Anniversaries: From the Life of Gesine Cresspahl* is a multileveled record of the ongoing lives of Gesine Cresspahl and her daughter Marie, counterpointed by Gesine's reconstruction of the past. The present encompasses the historically critical, highly eventful year of August 21, 1967, through August 20, 1968. Verbatim quotations from *The New York Times* provide a running chronicle that emerges as the nagging liberal voice of yet another character, "Auntie *Times*."

In volume 1 (volumes 1 and 2 of the German original), a heavy drama of the 1930's is framed by a relatively light, optimistic tale of newcomers to New York City (from August, 1967, through February, 1968). Day by day, as if making diary entries, the thirty-four-year-old Gesine Cresspahl, now a bank employee, notes both the immediate present and the events of the past, often occurring at the same time of year. Her attempts at reconstructing the past are increasingly aided by her gifted ten-year-old child, Marie, who responds, challenges, and evaluates, understanding more and more.

In the early 1930's, Heinrich Cresspahl, a German master carpenter comfortably settled in England, impulsively married a very pious, much younger

woman of a higher social status during a visit to Jerichow, a fictitious town in
Germany. Despite their real love, Cresspahl's wife, "our Lisbeth," could not
endure England and returned to the bosom of her patriarchal German family, the Papenbrocks, to give birth at home, in Jerichow. The only child of
this couple is Gesine. Cresspahl eventually joined his wife and was unable to
extricate himself or his family from increasingly Nazified Germany. While
Cresspahl pragmatically and phlegmatically made the best of things, however,
Lisbeth lost her sanity. Her last act was an illumination to others—including
the daughter and granddaughter, who subsequently reconstruct her life, helping each other.

Volume 2 (volumes 3 and 4 of the German original) covers the 1940's and
the early 1950's in Germany, and March through August of 1968 in New
York, with a whirling peripheral vision of the world outside. Now the reconstruction of the past, moving into the Soviet Occupation, the years under
Walter Ulbricht, and Gesine's conscious life, becomes more ironic while the
present, which had begun rather brightly, darkens.

In a sharp stroke of irony, the apolitical Cresspahl is made mayor of
Jerichow by the victorious British, only to be tortured and imprisoned by the
Russians who come to replace the British. Gesine's years of growing up, the
regime of a German secondary school (still very traditional despite the addition of political propaganda and Russian lessons), and the pairings and jealousies of adolescents are described with gentle irony. Before discovering
her latent love for Jakob Abs (Marie's father, who dies in an accident before
Marie's birth, without having married Gesine), Gesine had gone with the
touching, faintly ridiculous Pius Pagenkopf, son of a Communist Party official. Harsher satire is found in the story of Johnny Schlegel, who sets up
a wonderful agricultural commune in which everyone is supposed to be
happy—for which he is sentenced to fifteen years of hard labor.

Back in the present, the Vietnam War is escalating, Martin Luther King
and Robert Kennedy are assassinated, and demonstrations and riots are
everywhere. More intensely than before, Gesine begins reliving her mother's
obsession with guilt by association. Young Marie, though still loyal to her
new homeland, also feels disappointed and disillusioned (even with her erst-
while hero Mayor John Lindsay). Then Gesine suffers a personal tragedy
which she does not dare to tell her daughter: Dietrich Erichson, her longtime
suitor and almost a father to Marie, dies in a plane crash. Grasping for hope
around which to build a new life, Gesine commits herself to a dangerous job
with which she has been toying since the novel began: to become a discreet
representative for her employer, an international bank, in the recently awakening city of Prague. She would be authorized to offer millions of dollars in
credit (very quietly) to the Dubček government. Here, at last, is an upstand-
ing, guiltless, and idealistic regime that she could admire. Always ill at ease
with the West because of her Socialist-informed education and now uncom-

fortable with the spreading guilt of the Vietnam War and the many other troubles that she has long been imbibing through Auntie *Times*, Gesine uproots herself and Marie for a fresh start in a newly regenerated Czechoslovakia. Author Uwe Johnson leaves Gesine and Marie on the Baltic coast, in Denmark, poised for the last lap of their journey on August 20, 1968, the day before the Eastern Bloc's surprise invasion of Czechoslovakia and the crushing of the Dubček regime.

## The Characters

Gesine Cresspahl, the narrator and the central figure, remains the most elusive character, evidently because she herself wishes to be. Johnson even breaks in occasionally to complain to her about her self-willed behavior. She is driven by secret drives and obsessions with which she brooks no interference. The reader, however, is challenged to put all the pieces together and is allowed to examine all the evidence, including facts and thoughts to which even Gesine's daughter is not privy. Thus, there is something of the crime mystery and the spy thriller, brought to a high level of psychological sophistication, in Johnson's treatment of Gesine.

Gesine's extremely precocious daughter, charming in her process of Americanization, serves the literary device of confidante, drawing out her alter ego. Marie believes that "if a person comes to New York he must also come to his senses." She is more than a little reminiscent of the wise, doomed children found in the works of William Shakespeare. Yet Marie shows the psychological development of a real child in her growing trust of Erichson and in her relationships with other children, particularly a black classmate, Francine, who is also aware beyond her years.

Lisbeth Cresspahl is a mysterious figure. She has a mythical quality, partly because Gesine must strain to remember her, for all the scrupulous detail of her evocation: "When she removed the rings from the stove, she sometimes forgot she was still holding them with the hook, so lost was her gaze in the fire. . . . She was gone so suddenly; she was never mentioned. Seen no more."

Heinrich Cresspahl is the most solidly created figure, rooted in his occupation and cool, pragmatic approach to life. He can deal only with the external manifestations of his wife's behavior. When there is something on which he can get a grip, he acts swiftly and firmly, once saving his daughter's life and later coping with his wife's death.

The novel is lightened by a whole gallery of minor characters from New York City. Among them, *The New York Times* stands out as "she" develops over time from a prim, self-confident, didactic "Aunt" to "a shrewish, crafty old woman with a guilty conscience."

Johnson has long been known as a writer who makes his readers work. *Anniversaries* shows Johnson's bold ambition to create characters without reference to ready-made models. Johnson's characters are originals; each requires an entirely new (and at first glance, obscure) frame of reference to be understood. In *Anniversaries*, particular concessions to the reader's powers of imagination are made by enriching these new frames of reference with more detail than before. Thus, while new and unique, Johnson's characters acquire some of the solidity found in the more familiar world of Thomas Mann. By naming his local German clan (Lisbeth's family) the Papenbrocks, Johnson is beaming both a nod and a smile to the family depicted in Mann's novel *Buddenbrooks* (1900).

*Themes and Meanings*

The main theme of *Anniversaries* is recollection, the metaphor for which is "the cat of memory." How true is recollection, even when supported by physical evidence? How is this truth affected when challenged by a totally different viewpoint? Johnson affirms that, with much work, an approximation of the real truth is possible. The truth thus reached is satisfying on an intellectual, emotional, and aesthetic level. Johnson's quest recalls that of Marcel Proust or Jean Dutourd. Yet Johnson never relies on one viewpoint, and he requires documentary proof and physical evidence before he is satisfied.

Johnson's affirmation that truth exists and can be known is a counterbalance to the tragic content of the novel, centering on painful ethical issues. The most salient of these issues is collective guilt or guilt by association. Johnson accepts the thesis of collective guilt on principle but warns that it leads to madness. Suicide is raised as a moral and religious issue. The local pastor, when queried, is surprised to find that, in fact, there is no specific prohibition against suicide in the Bible, but "in place of the prohibition is the reminder of God's mercy that is put to the desperate person." He remembers, too late to help a suicidal but religious individual, that "suicide was not wicked in the eyes of men . . . suicide was a falling away from God."

Johnson's (or Gesine's) belief that "suicide was not wicked" in the fundamental moral sense has a bearing on many events in the novel. In addition to several outright suicides, there are the ambiguous accidental deaths of Jakob Abs—also the central figure of Johnson's first major work, *Mutmassungen über Jakob* (1959; *Speculations About Jakob*, 1963)—and Pius Pagenkopf, in neither of which is suicide to be completely ruled out. Since *Anniversaries* includes a seemingly disconnected news item about an American who has been found dead in the Vltava River in Prague, Gesine's final decision to go to Prague borders on self-destruction, despite her announced bright hopes.

*Anniversaries*, Johnson's last novel, ends literally on the brink: Gesine and Marie are left standing on the Baltic seashore, where Gesine's memories began. Readers will remain divided as to whether this equipoise, where Johnson deliberately stops (marking the novel as finished), means a new beginning or a most tragic end.

## Critical Context

The ambiguous deaths of several of his characters foreshadowed the end of Uwe Johnson's own life. He died in England at the age of forty-nine, not long after the publication of the final volume of *Anniversaries*. He had been dead for three or four weeks when his body was discovered, and the circumstances of his death remained unclear.

*Anniversaries* was Johnson's crowning achievement. Critics have noted that the completion of this book was necessary in order to make all of his preceding works understandable. Important characters from all of his earlier works, including Jakob, Karsch, from *Das dritte Buch über Achim* (1961; *The Third Book About Achim*, 1967), Cresspahl, and Gesine herself, are brought back to have some mysteries at least partly clarified and their portraits filled in or shaded. The consistency of Johnson's characters and the web of interplay among them over time recall the grand design of Honoré de Balzac's *The Human Comedy* (1829-1848) and, to a lesser extent, the work of William Faulkner.

Johnson borrows John Dos Passos' semidocumentary technique—but for a purpose other than to capture some kind of *Zeitgeist*. Johnson strives to reach the point of intersection of mind and reality. When he approaches such points, his language becomes poetry.

In *Anniversaries*, Johnson relaxes his devotion to a Spartan modernism just enough to accept some of the bourgeois sensuousness of Thomas Mann. He tips his hat to Mann both humorously, with his hapless "Papenbrocks" clan, and seriously, with the inclusion of a bona fide letter from Mann to Ulbricht (published for the first time). While Johnson was known during his lifetime for complicated political views and difficult techniques, his painfully verified characters, as if wrested from reality, overshadow technique and ideology as time passes.

## Sources for Further Study

Boulby, Mark. *Uwe Johnson*, 1974.

Hirsch, Marianne. *Beyond the Single Vision: Henry James, Michel Butor, Uwe Johnson*, 1981.

Howard, Richard. Review in *Saturday Review*. II (February 22, 1975), p. 38.

Pawel, Ernst. Review in *The New York Times Book Review*. LXXX (February 23, 1975), p. 4.

Thomas, R. Hinton, and Wilfried van der Will. *The German Novel and the Affluent Society*, 1968.

*D. Gosselin Nakeeb*

# ANOTHER LIFE

*Author:* Yury Trifonov (1925-1981)
*Type of plot:* Realism
*Time of plot:* The early 1970's
*Locale:* Moscow
*First published: Drugaya zhizn,* 1975 (English translation, 1983)

> *Principal characters:*
> OLGA VASILIEVNA, a research biologist, recently widowed
> SERGEI, her husband, a historian
> ALEXANDRA PROKOFIEVNA, Sergei's mother, a retired lawyer
> IRINA, Sergei and Olga's daughter

*The Novel*

*Another Life* chronicles a widow's progress in the months following her husband's untimely death at age forty-two. The narrative, presented entirely from Olga Vasilievna's point of view, switches from present to past and back again as she attempts to make sense of their life together and of her solitary existence now. She reviews their courtship, the course of their marriage, and the ups and downs of her husband's career.

Yury Trifonov eschews strict chronological order in favor of the workings of memory, at least in the first part of the novel. As *Another Life* opens, Olga is wide awake in the night, suffering from some undefined guilt. Others have blamed her for her husband's death, and she unwillingly seeks to discover the truth or falsehood of that charge. Her frustration with her own sleeplessness leads her to memories of her husband's restlessness and their late-night quarrels and conflicts. That in turn leads to worries about her current situation. She shares an apartment with her teenage daughter Irina and her dragonlike, vindictive mother-in-law, Alexandra Prokofievna. Scenes from the recent past float by without giving her any clue to a way out of her current dilemma: how to continue to live now that her husband is gone. She returns to one of her constant themes: her husband's previous lovers and what she supposes to be his real preference in women. At the same time, her practical side rebels against the futility of remembrance and dully looks ahead to the next few hours and her morning routine.

Olga and Sergei met through a mutual friend named Vlad, a kind, dull, pockmarked medical student Olga was seeing at the time. A biologist, shamefully unmarried at the age of twenty-four, Olga finds little joy either in the prospect of teaching at a local secondary school or in marrying faithful Vlad. He makes the fatal mistake of introducing Olga to Sergei, a quirky, brilliant young historian working "in some obscure institution in a job that was not in his field." Not until the following summer does Vlad begin to suspect his friends' mutual attraction, when the three of them plus a superfluous acquaintance named Rita scrape up enough money to spend a few weeks in Gagra, a fashionable resort town on the Black Sea.

These are Olga's glory days; young, slender, and athletic, she turns male heads and makes an enemy of poor Rita in the process. Nothing beyond her newfound happiness with Sergei seems to matter. Their return to Moscow, however, is not quite so idyllic; Sergei's mother takes perverse pleasure in unveiling the existence of a pregnant former girlfriend, who pathetically schemes to separate the new couple. The wedding reception, too, nudges Olga toward the realization that a marriage is not a question of two people alone but a "merger or a collision between two clans, two worlds," and that it will continue to be so even after the disappearance of one of the partners. Olga recalls her jealous accusations and confrontations in their old apartment, shared with her mother and stepfather, her unexpected pregnancy, and their move to Sergei's mother's apartment.

As Olga remembers, the narrative gradually assumes a more linear form, recounting Sergei's struggles at his institute. These struggles to write and publish a dissertation culminate in his resignation from the institute and eventually his death. Interwoven with Sergei's professional failure is the success of his former friend Gennadi Klimuk and the accidental death of his friend and patron Fedya. Fedya, as academic secretary of the institute where both Sergei and Klimuk work, has supported Sergei honestly in the midst of wavering and doubt. With Fedya's death, Klimuk begins to gain ascendancy, and Olga is faced not only with the triumph of a self-serving bureaucrat but also with the specter of Louisa, Fedya's hapless, distracted widow.

Although Olga, a successful research biologist who believes the world begins and ends with chemistry, cannot really understand her husband's seeming obsession with the workings of the czarist secret police, she never seriously questions his choice of topic and is truly distressed over his continuing difficulties. Yet her distress over his professional troubles takes second place to her dismay over their increasing separation and what she perceives as a change in his character. Tormented by his search for the threads that bind the present to the past, the individual to the common history, Sergei begins to seek those links in the occult. Increasingly distant and irritable, he both puzzles and disturbs the faithful and possessive Olga, who suspects that another woman is really the cause of it all.

Present and past merge in the penultimate scene of the novel, when Olga and Sergei are picking mushrooms in the forest, and she is finally able to ask him all the unanswered questions left after his death. It is all a dream, and she awakes to her customary seven o'clock alarm, but both she and the reader understand that some kind of reconciliation has taken place. Willingly or not, she has begun to make peace with this other, separate life.

The novel ends a year or so later, as Olga keeps a rendezvous with yet another troubled man and reflects on the turn of events that has led her to this new, unexpected life.

## The Characters

Trifonov usually draws his characters from the ranks of the Moscow intelligentsia, and *Another Life* is no exception to his general practice. He gives his Russian reader easily recognizable social types: the strong, motherly wife, the charming but undependable husband, the judgmental mother-in-law, the compromised artist.

Yet for all their familiarity, Trifonov's characters are not two-dimensional, predictable players in a Soviet soap opera. Olga, the main character and single voice, may be naggingly protective and jealous both of her husband and of her place in his life, but she is neither mercenary nor careerist. Her own career is a given, something which need not be discussed; it neither excites nor depresses her. Her entire emotional and spiritual life is "their life." Throughout the narrative she insists on the existence of their mutual life to such a degree that the reader realizes something must be radically wrong with this marriage. Sergei's intellectual skitterings, on the other hand, arouse more sympathy and interest in the reader, but stop short of making him a real seeker after truth. His torment is real, but so is his frivolity. There is no easy formula of assigning praise or blame to either one; there is only an effort to find an honorable way of living from day to day.

Though he spends less time developing them, Trifonov hints that his secondary characters, too, are not so easily reducible to cliché. Alexandra Prokofievna, Sergei's mother, is a typical "old Bolshevik," or at least typical of those who wish to be known as such. Loyal to a tradition of revolutionary asceticism and intolerant justice, she judges her daughter-in-law and granddaughter both, and finds them wanting. Her beloved son's death only makes their many faults more glaring and her isolation more bitter. Alexandra Prokofievna's close contemporary, Georgii Maximovich, is quite her opposite; an artist, once part of the avant-garde, purged, exiled, and rehabilitated, he is a kind and perceptive man. He has betrayed no one but himself, as he turns out safe, profitable, and mediocre landscapes for commissions.

There are no clearly heroic or even noble characters in *Another Life*. They are all achingly ordinary, and that is part of their appeal. Like Anton Chekhov, with whom he has been compared, and like Fyodor Dostoevski as well, Trifonov often endows his most unlikely characters with truths about human behavior and moral action. The fact that his characters inhabit a kind of gray zone should not be taken for neutrality, though, since that very ambiguous zone is full of moral choices and wrong turns, and often the turn becomes obvious only when it is miles or years past. Trifonov's characters often do not realize that they have made a choice until they are facing the consequences.

Olga, however, has another chance, a possible other life, whether she wants it in her grief or not. What is particularly interesting about Trifonov's characterizations in *Another Life* is his use of Olga as the narrative voice. Sometimes quoting her directly, sometimes moving into more neutral diction but still dependent on her view of things, he manages to portray her sympathetically but not at all uncritically. He allows her assumptions, her prejudices to work both for her and against her, so that the other characters emerge independently: They do not exist to prove Olga good or bad, right or wrong, but merely to be.

*Themes and Meanings*

Trifonov's title embraces a number of meanings. There is the underlying religious sense of life beyond the grave, a proposition which intrigues Sergei particularly in the last months of his life. His interest is genuine, but it is also fashionable in Moscow intellectual circles of the time: Without condemning Sergei, Trifonov casts a skeptical eye on the search for otherworldly peace of mind. There is the other life Sergei seeks while still on this earth, while still trapped in Soviet *byt* (routine, everyday life): his mental and spiritual existence, a life outside his family, which Olga finds so puzzling and threatening. There is Olga's unwanted new life as a widow and single mother of a teenager; there is Olga's new start at the end of the book. All these other lives, except for the last one, come together in Olga's remembrance without forming any coherent whole. Trifonov, in limiting her perception of events, examines the limits of any one person's perception in general, not as a literary exercise in the possibilities of point of view but as a moral and spiritual question. Just how is one to make sense of things?

In the course of their seventeen-year conversation, Sergei the historian asks Olga the biologist if she truly believes that "we disappear without a trace. . . ." She, the determined materialist, answers, "Do you really think we won't?" This difference in their habits of thinking and being goes beyond characterization to create much of the novel's sad irony. Seventeen years of genuine love—and genuine misunderstanding. Sergei has spent his short life in search of some elusive link between individual fate and national destiny— hence his confused explanation of his research, a jumble of family history and czarist police archives. Frustrated in these attempts by both his own uncertainty and the hostility of his colleagues, he turns to parapsychology and the occult as a way to connect past, present, and future, and to give him a vision of a life other than the thwarted one he now leads. Olga, however, stubbornly clings to a vision of "their life," which he has long since ceased to share.

Yet after Sergei's death it is Olga who finds herself the unwilling historian. She who has always regarded history as a collection of facts which simply need to be marshaled into coherent order now confronts troubling, unruly memories that refuse to be so easily organized. She may rationalize and explain, but she still cannot reduce such complex things as marriage and family and inner life to comforting clarity. Through Olga's effort to make sense of "their life" and her own, Trifonov works on two levels: the puzzle of human relations in general and the need to come to terms with both an individual and a collective past.

## Critical Context

Yury Trifonov emerged in the early 1970's as one of the leading writers of his generation and, suprisingly enough, as one of the most controversial (yet still publishable) of those writers. Lumped together with such writers as Vassily Aksyonov and Andrei Bitov as a practitioner of "urban prose" (as opposed to the "village prose" of Valentin Rasputin or Vasili Shukshin), he resembles them only in choice of milieu. Trifonov's densely packed, low-key treatment of the Moscow intelligentsia combines the impassivity of an uninvolved bystander and the rueful knowledge of an insider.

In Trifonov's world, as in Chekhov's, nothing happens—and everything happens: Marriages are made and destroyed; careers flourish or fail; men and women deceive themselves and others in search of security or even, sometimes, truth; people die. What has made Trifonov controversial is in part his lack of civic ardor; sober and detached observation paired with both moral and psychological intelligence does not equal an inspiring view of Soviet society.

He began his career as did many another young postwar Soviet writer, with competent and resolutely optimistic tales of his contemporaries. His novel *Studenty* (1950; *Students*, 1953) won a Stalin Prize in 1951, and was followed by *Utolenie zhazhdy* (1963; the quenching of thirst)—a novel about construction in Turkmenia—numerous short stories, and a film scenario. His tone changed with the publication of *Obmen* (1969; *The Exchange*, 1973), a novella chronicling the small but cumulative compromises that end in complete moral surrender for the main character. Shortly thereafter he came out with *Prevaritalnye itogi* (1970; *Taking Stock*, 1978) and *Dolgoe proshchanie* (1971; *The Long Goodbye*, 1978), both in the same uncomfortable vein. His preoccupation with assessing the past found overt form in *Neterpenie* (1973; *The Impatient Ones*, 1978), a historical novel about revolutionary Andrei Zhelyabov, while *Another Life* and *Dom na naberezhnoi* (1976; *The House on the Embankment*, 1983) explored the relationship of present to past in more intimate fashion. Trifonov's last published work in his lifetime, *Starik* (1978; *The Old Man*, 1984) and a posthumously published novella, *Vrema i mesto* (1981; time and place), continued to dig at questions of personal and historical responsibility.

*Sources for Further Study*

Hosking, Geoffrey. *Beyond Socialist Realism*, 1980.

*Kirkus Reviews*. Review. LI (September 15, 1983), p. 1019.

Pankin, B. "A Circle or a Spiral? On Iurii Trifonov's Novels," in *Soviet Studies in Literature*. XIV (Fall, 1978), pp. 65-100.

Proffer, Ellendea. Introduction to *The Long Goodbye*, 1978.

Updike, John. Introduction to *Another Life* and *The House on the Embankment*, 1986.

*Jane Ann Miller*

# AROUND THE WORLD IN EIGHTY DAYS

*Author:* Jules Verne (1828-1905)
*Type of plot:* Travel/romance
*Time of plot:* October 2 through December 21, 1872
*Locale:* London, India, Japan, America, and places between
*First published: Le Tour du monde en quatre-vingts jours*, 1873 (English
   translation, 1873)

> *Principal characters:*
> PHILEAS FOGG, a London gentleman who wagers on a trip
>    around the world
> JEAN PASSEPARTOUT, Fogg's French servant
> FIX, a private detective who follows Fogg
> AOUDA, an Indian widow of a rajah who is rescued by Fogg
>    and Passepartout and marries Fogg

*The Novel*

   *Around the World in Eighty Days* is, as the title suggests, the story of a
journey around the world. The focus throughout is on the remarkable journey by Phileas Fogg and his companions. The places visited, the people
encountered, the customs and cultures noted, the scenery observed—these
make up the fabric of this work.

   The situation at the beginning is twofold: For Fogg's newly hired valet, it is
an opportunity to work for a man who leads a steady, stable life. Passepartout believes that his new master never goes anywhere except to the Reform Club. Fogg does seem to have an extremely routine existence (even the
number of steps from his dwelling to the club is known). He frequents the
club, reading *The Times* and playing whisk with his acquaintances: "His daily
habits were quite open to observation; but whatever he did was so exactly the
same thing that he had always done before, that the wits of the curious were
fairly puzzled."

   This routine is altered drastically when a news item about a bank robber
leads Fogg to propose a wager that he can circle the earth in eighty days. He
establishes with his whist partners a wager of twenty thousand pounds, and
he announces that he will depart that very evening. Passepartout's expectations of tranquillity are shattered as he is set to work making preparations.
The only luggage is a large carpetbag, into which are placed a few articles of
clothing and toiletries, as well as a large sum of money in the form of nego-
tiable bank notes. The journey begins with the two boarding the Dover-to-
Calais train on Wednesday, October 2, 1872, at 8:45 P.M., exactly one and
three-quarters hours after making the bet.

   In addition to Fogg and Passepartout, the protagonists, there are two antagonists. Fix, an English private detective, jumps to the false conclusion that Fogg is the bank robber. In Suez, his expectations are twofold: the arrival of Fogg on board the steamer *Mongolia*, en route from Brindisi to Bombay, and receipt of a warrant for Fogg's arrest. When the latter does not come, he joins Fogg and Passepartout as a traveling companion. At Bombay, he takes note of Passepartout's offense against a temple.

The true antagonist, however, is time—or, more specifically, delay. The train ride across India ends abruptly when the track runs out; the long section through the interior, contrary to an earlier statement in *The Times*, has not yet been built. The ever-resourceful Fogg buys an elephant and hires its former owner as a guide. Together with Passepartout and a British military man met on the train, they begin the long, treacherous ride. En route they rescue a woman named Aouda from her husband's funeral pyre, and she joins them for the remainder of the trip. They arrive in Calcutta by train on time, only to be arrested (an arrangement made by Fix). Paying the bail, they sail to Hong Kong on the *Rangoon*, which Fix has secretly boarded. Delayed by weather, they nevertheless arrive in time to catch the *Carnatic*, which has also been delayed.

In Hong Kong, Fix contrives to delay Fogg by getting Passepartout intoxicated on drink and opium. Only the servant reaches the *Carnatic* before it sails for Yokohama. Fogg, in turn, charters the pilot boat *Tankadere* for Shanghai, which must ride out a typhoon before it reaches its destination. Meanwhile, Passepartout has arrived alone and penniless in Yokohama. Resourceful in his own way, he joins a troupe of actors as a clown and is reunited finally with the others after they have caught the *Rangoon* to Yokohama. Fix now has a warrant which he cannot use until he is again on British soil. All sail from Yokohama aboard the American steamer *General Grant*.

During the journey across America, the group is accosted by Colonel Stamp Proctor and diverted by a political rally in San Francisco; the train from Oakland is delayed for hours by a herd of buffalo; a Mormon diverts Passepartout; Fogg and Proctor begin a duel which is interrupted by an Indian raid; Passepartout again exercises his acrobatic skills by conveying himself from the rear car to the engine underneath the train, unhooking the engine and stopping the raid; and Fogg leads a body of cavalry to rescue Passepartout. In this novel of miraculous feats, even the train performs heroically, leaping over a weakened bridge at remarkable speed. All obstacles are overcome, but Fogg misses the *China*. Even the remarkable trip across the vast wasteland by sail-sledge has been in vain.

Not to be outdone, Fogg charters the *Henrietta*, commands her himself, buys her from the captain, and burns the wooden portions of the ship when there is no more fuel. Back in London, however, Fogg is in jail until Fix discovers that the real thief has already been caught. Ironically, Fogg has completed his journey around the world in eighty days but cannot collect on the bet. Back home, he and Aouda send Passepartout to find a minister for their wedding. The servant discovers that it is not Sunday but Saturday—the group has passed eastward over the international dateline without noting the loss of one day. Fogg arrives at the club with one second to spare to collect his twenty thousand pounds. Having spent nineteen thousand on the journey, he gives away one thousand and is left with exactly the forty thousand he had at the beginning. Except for finding Aouda, he has neither gained nor lost.

## The Characters

Phileas Fogg and Jean Passepartout are the most fully delineated characters in this work. Others are one- or two-dimensional, existing primarily to advance the plot.

Fogg is a combination of types. Larger then life, he is like Odysseus, a man who is never at a loss and never perturbed. When hardships or surprises delay his voyage, he remains calm and finds another way of accomplishing his purpose. Like Odysseus he deliberately delays long enough to rescue his traveling companions. Fogg is also, like Don Quixote, embarked on a perilous quest of questionable value, but he is an inverted Quixote; unlike Miguel de Cervantes' madman, he is completely rational, even machinelike, in his adherence to rote and in his total dependence on rational thought. He is a man of the Enlightenment, given over to reason, restraint, and decorum. Passepartout describes him as "repose in action" and "as exactly regulated as a Leroy chronometer," yet Fogg is also impulsive: He generously gives the elephant to his guide, the whist earnings to the poor, and profit from the wager to his companions, even to Fix, who has done everything possible to prevent the completion of the journey.

Passepartout is also larger than life, though contrasting with Fogg. In many ways, Passepartout (whose name means "goes everywhere") plays Sancho Panza to Fogg's Quixote. He is impetuous and vulnerable. He, too, is courageous, but in a more flamboyant manner: He climbs under moving trains, goes into a sacred shrine to rescue a woman, claims the right to a duel even though Proctor would surely kill him. Completely faithful to his master, he often uses poor judgment, thoughtlessly wearing shoes in a temple or confiding in his master's adversary. He is gullible, allowing Fix to get him intoxicated when his master's success depends on his delivering the news of the ship's early departure. Like Fogg, he is an overblown, stock character: here, the talkative servant and the acrobatic clown.

Fix, the villain in the melodrama, is yet another stock character. A man of singleness of purpose, he doggedly stays with his prey. Unintellectual and obstinate, he tenaciously holds on to his false belief. After becoming indebted to Fogg and learning to admire him, Fix nevertheless brings about his arrest. Of questionable intelligence and discernment, with a penchant for being wrong, he manages to be simultaneously dangerous and ludicrous.

Aouda is the least fully delineated of the cast of character-types, existing primarily to advance the plot, even though she is given a prominent place in its action. She is passive, a damsel in distress, admirable yet dependent. A familiar stock character, she provides the love element in the novel, though its presentation is subdued and limited in treatment.

All four are static rather than developing characters. At the end, Fogg and Aouda are largely unchanged. Passepartout may be wiser and humbler for his experiences, though the change is not emphasized. Only Fix seems to have undergone any change, having learned that he has hounded and arrested the wrong man. Still, there is no indication that his change is of any real significance.

## Themes and Meanings

In one sense, *Around the World in Eighty Days* is merely a superbly well-written romance of travel adventure. The form is what has been called traditional: chronological time and a single third-person narrator throughout. Though there is some dialogue, the focus throughout is on the action. Though some delineation of customs is evident, it is so limited that it hardly interrupts the rapid flow of the narrative. There are glimpses of religious customs in India and Utah, for example, and of American political procedures, but they are not developed.

The plot has affinities to two earlier works: It is a combination of an odyssey and a quixotic quest. The journey is arduous, with many hardships, many adversaries, many obstacles, overcome only by almost superhuman feats. The quixotic element is seen especially in the fact that the journey need not have been taken at all: It results from a whim and a wager. As Quixote at the end of book 1 is safe at home, so is Fogg, both having arrived under ignominious circumstances. Neither has actually profited from the original purpose of his journey: Fogg has not gained monetarily; Quixote has not bettered the people or society he has set out to serve; in several instances, both have brought hardship on not only on themselves but also those they have befriended. Quixote has his sanity back, but his further quests are suggested in the closing passage; Jules Verne's closing passage tells of Fogg's prize, his wife.

## Critical Context

This work marks a second turning point in Verne's career. The first came when he set aside the writing of plays and librettos for science-fiction romances, such as *Cinq Semaines en ballon* (1863; *Five Weeks in a Balloon*, 1876), *Voyage au centre de la terre* (1864; *Journey to the Centre of the Earth*, 1874), and *Vingt Mille Lieues sous les mers* (1870; *Twenty Thousand Leagues Under the Sea*, 1874). Although sometimes included with these and mistaken for the same genre, *Around the World in Eighty Days* is not science fiction: It employs the same journey motif and utilizes many of the same techniques (careful attention to technical detail, for example, and a detached, coldly scientific tone). Nevertheless, this work treats situations and incidents which though remarkable were not at the time of writing supernatural in any sense.

Pigeonholed as a writer of science fiction, Verne has been of most interest to readers and critics for works in this genre. His ultimate reputation as a literary author, however, would seem to hinge upon the critical reception of *Around the World in Eighty Days*. Critics regard this work as his most significant accomplishment, the one which enriched his fame and his financial status. It employs all the best techniques of the earlier science-fiction narratives, while allowing the journey its rightful place as the heart of the work, unhampered by the elements of the fantastic. It is regarded as pivotal in the Verne canon, in much the same way the best works of Verne mark the turn from nineteenth to twentieth century science fiction.

*Sources for Further Study*
Allott, Kenneth. *Jules Verne*, 1940.
Born, Franz. *Jules Verne: The Man Who Invented the Future*, 1964.
Boucher, Anthony. Preface to *Around the World in Eighty Days*, 1956.
Costello, Peter. *Jules Verne: Inventor of Science Fiction*, 1978.
Evans, I. O. *Jules Verne and His Work*, 1965.
Haining, Peter. *The Jules Verne Companion*, 1978.
Waltz, George H. *Jules Verne: The Biography of an Imagination*, 1943.

*George W. Van Devender*

# ARTURO'S ISLAND

*Author:* Elsa Morante (1918-1985)
*Type of plot:* Psychological realism
*Time of plot:* The late 1930's
*Locale:* The island of Procida, near Naples
*First published: L'isola di Arturo,* 1957 (English translation, 1959)

> *Principal characters:*
> ARTURO GERACE, a motherless boy in his early teens
> WILHELM GERACE, his father
> NUNZIATA, his teenage stepmother

*The Novel*

*Arturo's Island,* written in the first person, is the narration by Arturo Gerace, now an adult, of his memories of his childhood on the island of Procida. His memories are a clear, vivid, detailed, and sometimes agonizing account of his adolescent experiences and adventures. At the same time, they reveal the young boy's dreams and fantasies, his love for his father and for a mother he never knew, his absolute faith in his ability to live independently, and his difficult transition from adolescence to adulthood, from a fantasy world to the real world.

The novel begins with Arturo describing his life on the island. He makes it clear that he is proud that he has the absolute freedom to do as he pleases, and that he lives a carefree life that would be the envy of any boy. At the same time, however, he expresses his need for familial love, which he attempts to find in his father. The motherless Arturo adores his father, who, according to Arturo, constantly leaves the boy alone to go off on "fabulous adventures." Arturo lives for his father's return because he identifies with his father's lifestyle; thus, he augments his own fantasies of what adulthood will hold for him.

One day his perfect life is shattered by the arrival of a sixteen-year-old Neapolitan girl, Nunziata, who is Wilhelm Gerace's new bride and, therefore, Arturo's stepmother. Arturo's reaction is one of perplexity and defiance. It seems to him that this girl, barely two years older than he, has stolen his father's affection. His dislike of Nunziata is transformed slowly. First he feels something resembling a child's love for a mother: "Suddenly I saw in her a strange resemblance to my mother." That feeling changes into sexual love, although it takes a sexual encounter with the widow Assuntina to open his eyes to his desire for Nunziata. His entry into the real world by way of his encounter with Assuntina and his deepening love for Nunziata is beginning to destroy his perfect fantasy. The final blow, which completely shatters his dreams, is learning that his father is not the heroic man of his fantasies but rather a homosexual who loves a petty criminal and whose fabulous voyages are nothing more than visits to all the gay meeting places in Naples. Arturo has matured and decides to leave Procida forever, returning there only through his nostalgic memories.

## The Characters

The novel focuses on Arturo, for it is the inner being of the male adolescent that interests Elsa Morante. Arturo is not a typical teenager. He is, in many ways, an adult: He is alone much of the time; he is fiercely independent, without friends and without guidance; and he does not go to school. Nature and his own imagination are his teachers. Arturo looks at the other Procidians with disdain, because in his estimation they are inferior beings whose sole characteristic is "their everlasting dependence on the practical necessities of life." In his own "Code of Absolute Truth," the fourth law is that "No one living on the island of Procida is worthy of Wilhelm Gerace and of his son Arturo Gerace. For a Gerace to become friendly with a Procidian would be degrading." Women are even more unworthy of his attention; his father has already introduced him to misogyny. Thus, as he grows up, his solitude becomes more pronounced.

Despite his solitude, Arturo lives very happily in a magical world of his own creation, a world of pirates, knights, and conquerors. He is proud to have the name Arturo because it is the name of the great king who was lord of the knights of the Round Table. His second law states that "A man's true greatness consists of courage in action, scorn of danger, and valor in combat." For Arturo, his father is the embodiment of the true heroic figure, and when Wilhelm leaves the island for any period of time, Arturo imagines that his father is going forth on a glorious and heroic adventure. He imagines that sometimes his father is the scourge of pirates and bandits and that at other times he is a pirate or a bandit himself.

It seems that Arturo has everything, yet he lacks one essential ingredient for a happy life: affection. The affection for which he yearns is not to be found in his father. Wilhelm does not reciprocate Arturo's affection; he virtually ignores his son. Eventually, Arturo finds the affection that he seeks in Nunziata, an affection that soon turns into love and that ultimately thrusts him into the realization that he has grown up and must leave his perfect island to live in an imperfect outside world.

Nunziata at first seems to be a very simple, uncomplicated girl. She is awkward, clumsy, and childlike, although her body is that of a fully matured woman. She is from a poor Neapolitan family and does not want to marry Wilhelm but is forced to do so because of her family's economic problems. Nunziata is strongly religious and at the same time superstitious, but neither of these characteristics is all-consuming. Accustomed to living in a crowded and noisy house in Naples, and believing that human beings were created by

God to live together in harmony, peace, and love, she is uncomfortable and unhappy living in the oppressive solitude of the Gerace house. Even though she often is mistreated by both Wilhelm and Arturo, she treats them with respect and affection. Without Wilhelm's love, she falls in love with Arturo but refuses to be unfaithful to her husband. Arturo knows that he cannot live on the island with her and so must leave.

Morante has given Nunziata a simple quality, but at the same time she has endowed her with the traditional characteristics of Neapolitan women: an earthy sexuality, an inner warmth that exudes strength and firmness, and a natural coquettishness. Nunziata serves as the vehicle by which Arturo makes the transition from adolescence to manhood.

There is very little of a positive nature that can be said of Wilhelm. He is a restless soul who cannot stay in Procida for any length of time. He is bored with life on the island and with his new wife, whom he mistreats and insults constantly. He is ignorant of the needs of his son and treats him almost as if he were not alive. He is in love with a young man who is in jail and who makes Wilhelm wait on him like a slave. He certainly is not the heroic figure imagined by Arturo. In the end, Arturo's idolization of his father turns to compassion for him.

*Themes and Meanings*

Life is a mystery which unfolds through childhood via dreams, hopes, and aspirations, when all that is wanted is happiness. These dreams crumble when a person leaves the fantasy world of childhood and enters the adult world. Unfortunately, nothing becomes much clearer, for, as Arturo says at the end of the novel, "life remains a mystery, and to me the chief mystery of all is still myself." This is the main theme of *Arturo's Island*.

*Arturo's Island* explores the desire of human beings to create for themselves a biblical Garden of Eden, so perfect and so beautiful that one can believe that it is paradise on earth. Arturo's island, Procida, is such a place. The island is perfect because it has the unspoiled beauty of nature, the atmosphere of a primitive time when all was pure, and an isolation from the rest of the world. In such a Garden of Eden, one can sustain the illusion that there is no other kind of world. Just as the biblical Garden of Eden was destroyed by the original sin of Adam and Eve, however, so must all similar paradises be destroyed by the inexorable movement of time which propels human beings into adult knowledge.

Morante's novels often offer a nostalgic look at the happy innocence of childhood, and she enjoys exploring the workings of the minds of young people. Conversely, she presents a bitter view of reality. Her characters sometimes fail to make the transition from fantasy to reality and are destroyed in the process. This is especially true in her novel *Menzogna e sortilegio* (1948; *House of Liars*, 1951). Some, like Arturo, are fortunate enough to make the transition and also to relive their fantasy childhood through nostalgic memories.

*Critical Context*

*Arturo's Island* is considered to be Elsa Morante's most important novel. It was awarded the 1957 Strega Prize and received worldwide critical acclaim. The novel marks Morante's entrance into the small corps of Italian narrators who address the psychological problems associated with the adolescent child. While her theories on these problems are not new, they do represent a woman's sensibilities and sensitivities. More important, Morante has the ability to infuse her works with a lyrical, poetic quality which does not detract from, but rather enhances, the realism that is at the core of her novels. Her characters move within a world of reality surrounded by a mythological aura.

*Arturo's Island* is important for two reasons: First, it delves into the minds of young people to examine what their fantasy world is like and why they create such a world, and second, it is a strong and early example of a novelist easily and naturally dealing with the extremely difficult topics of incest and homosexuality.

*Sources for Further Study*

Caesar, Michael. "Elsa Morante," in *Writers and Society in Contemporary Italy: A Collection of Essays*, 1984. Edited by Michael Caesar and Peter Hainsworth.

Evans, Annette. "The Fiction of Family: Ideology and Narrative in Elsa Morante," in *Theory and Practice of Feminist Literary Criticism*, 1982. Edited by Gabriela Mora and Karen S. Van Hooft.

McCormick, E. A. "Utopia and Point of View," in *Symposium*. XV (1961), pp. 114-130.

Mitchell, Julian. "Absolute Beginner," in *Italian Quarterly*. III (1960), pp. 70-74.

*Joseph E. Laggini*

# AS A MAN GROWS OLDER

*Author:* Italo Svevo (Ettore Schmitz, 1861-1928)
*Type of plot:* Psychological realism
*Time of plot:* The 1890's
*Locale:* Trieste, Austria
*First published: Senilità,* 1898 (English translation, 1932)

> *Principal characters:*
> EMILIO BRENTANI, a clerk and novelist
> STEFANO BALLI, his friend, a sculptor
> AMALIA, his sister
> ANGIOLINA ZARRI, his mistress
> MARGHERITA, Balli's mistress
> ELENA CHIERICI, a widow

*The Novel*

Emilio Brentani is a man of thirty-five, a clerk in an insurance office, who lives in a drab apartment with his sister Amalia; he has literary pretensions and has published a novel which has had at least local success. He has fallen in love with a lower-class girl, Angiolina Zarri, who is remarkable for her blonde beauty and vibrant good health; she seems inclined to accept his attentions, though he is frank about his inability, or unwillingness, to marry. He begins to go for walks with her, during which she is affectionate enough, but already there are hints of trouble. From Sorniani, an older man with a bad reputation, Emilio hears that Angiolina was once engaged to a businessman named Merighi; the engagement was broken off, possibly because of Merighi's business losses, possibly because Angiolina was detected in an intrigue. Emilio's friend the sculptor Stefano Balli believes that there is danger in the affair.

Emilio visits Angiolina at her home and is well received by her mother, who seems a ruined version of Angiolina. The house is thoroughly shabby, except for Angiolina's bedroom, which is comfortably furnished but displays some photographs which Emilio recognizes as the portraits of some rather fast men about Trieste. He presses Angiolina for complete possession, and she would be willing if there were a third party on whom any results could be blamed.

Shortly thereafter, Angiolina announces her engagement to a tailor named Volpini, a man neither young nor handsome, though jolly and likable. She met him at the Deluigis', friends for whom she sometimes works. Though still trying to believe in Angiolina's respectability, Emilio realizes that he cannot "enjoy without suffering," cannot use Angiolina as a plaything without becoming emotionally involved. Balli refuses to give him any more advice but proposes that they should dine with him and his mistress, Margherita, a girl by no means as attractive as Angiolina, but meek and submissive. Balli treats both women rather coarsely, with the intention of discrediting Angiolina in Emilio's eyes, but Angiolina shows no resentment and Emilio is merely irritated with Balli.

Balli is in the habit of calling at the Brentanis', and this becomes the chief event in Amalia's gray life; she does not even resent her brother's affair, since it brings her in touch with romance. Balli has discovered that Margherita is unfaithful and in fact may be prostituting herself to support her family. Meanwhile, Volpini writes that he is unable to marry immediately but that if Angiolina will give him immediate enjoyment he will guarantee his good faith by a contract. Emilio still deludes himself about Angiolina and thinks of reeducating her.

It is now January, the time of the carnival, with all its tawdry gaiety, but also a time of wretched weather. Balli sees Angiolina in the company of a girl named Giulia and an umbrella maker, a man even less prepossessing than Volpini. Emilio confronts Angiolina and goes away, but his chief thought is that he could give her up more easily if he had once possessed her. Meanwhile, all is not well with Amalia, who has been talking in her sleep. Emilio discourages Balli's visits, saying, falsely, that a relative suspects an engagement. Then, when Amalia seems discouraged, he persuades Balli to return, but his coldness does more harm than good. A visit to the opera merely confirms Amalia's forlorn state.

Emilio begins a new novel, based on the reality of his affair with Angiolina, but finds it less vivid than the novel he wrote out of his fantasies. He believes that he can safely see her again, and a chance encounter is the beginning of an affair carried on in a sordid house of assignation. The affair is physically satisfying, but there are sour notes; she has given herself to Volpini, and she has taken a new lover whose personality Emilio can partially reconstruct: He is a student, apparently, for along with some indecent songs Angiolina has picked up a smattering of Latin. She maneuvers him into a confrontation with her father which only reveals the father's madness. Volpini sends a letter breaking off the engagement; Emilio helps Angiolina draft a reply full of injured innocence.

Emilio returns home to find Amalia half naked and delirious. As her state worsens, it becomes obvious that the content of the delirium is erotic and concerns Balli; she even imagines a rival, Vittoria. In the emergency, Emilio gets help from a neighbor, Elena Chierici, who loyally undertakes to nurse Amalia. Balli too is loyal and procures a doctor, who diagnoses inflammation of the lungs but startles Emilio by indicating that Amalia is an alcoholic. In fact, Emilio discovers by chance that she has been taking ether. Though Amalia is obviously dying, he leaves her to break off the relationship with Angiolina. Whatever his intentions, they quarrel for the last time. Emilio,

Balli, and Elena are present as Amalia dies. Emilio learns from Elena that the Deluigis are purely imaginary.

Some time later Emilio hears from Sorniani that Angiolina has run off with an embezzler. He calls on Signora Zarri, and Angiolina's younger sister flirts with him. Years later he looks back on the whole affair as one of the most luminous periods of his life, and in memory the figures of Angiolina and Amalia are somehow blended.

### The Characters

The key to Emilio is his *senilità*, his inertia. Like Hamlet, he combines a fundamental inertia with spurts of misdirected energy. It is significant that he has made no effort to pursue his promising literary career, or to better his financial situation, which prevents him from ever marrying without abandoning Amalia. Another area of his inertia is politics. He is a Socialist and free-thinker, and he dreams that under socialism he and Angiolina would have a better life; the only practical effect of his liberal ideas is that by banishing religion from his home he has deprived Amalia of its consolations.

The key to Emilio's affair with Angiolina is his inability to "possess without suffering"—to treat her as a plaything without being troubled by jealousy. He cannot or will not marry her, and yet he expects her to be faithful, even after he in effect cuckolds Volpini. Aside from the moral ambiguity of the affair, the notable element is Emilio's infinite capacity for self-deception with reference to Angiolina, or Ange (angel), as he calls her. The overwhelming evidence for Angiolina's real character—the gossip, the suspicions of Balli, the photographs in her bedroom, the mysterious visits to the imaginary Deluigis—is brushed aside until the crucial episode of the umbrella maker. Even after that, Emilio still believes that he can associate easily with Angiolina while knowing about her promiscuity.

Emilio's devotion to Amalia is creditable, and yet the clumsy and deceitful way in which he handles the affair with Balli in the end destroys her. The final irony is that the whole affair is not tragic for Emilio, who lives on with his pleasant, if distorted, memories.

Balli is offered as a foil for Emilio but should not be regarded as a simple opposite. As a sculptor he is not exactly a failure, and he certainly is no fraud, but he has never really been accepted by the official art world and his career is made possible by the capricious benevolence of an ignorant patron. As a lover, he seems a dashing success, at least in comparison with Emilio, but he settles for a mistress who is much less desirable than Angiolina and is himself cuckolded. Though he tries to demonstrate his power over Angiolina in order to disabuse Emilio, he himself falls under her power. He is, however, a devoted friend, and he expiates his careless treatment of Amalia by his vigil at her bedside.

Angiolina is a complex character who remains likable even after the exposure of her numerous deceptions. She is strikingly beautiful and notably healthy, and she manages to dress stylishly. It seems that she prostitutes herself to support her indigent family, but the evidence is inconclusive. From Emilio she gets little beyond sausages and cheese, and it must be assumed that much of her promiscuity arises from a compulsive need for admiration and approval. Her deceptions can be extremely ingenious but are sometimes so transparent that not even Emilio is fooled. Perhaps Emilio is right in regarding her as uncalculating; she might have used her beauty to make a good marriage, but instead she elopes with an embezzler.

*Themes and Meanings*

The Italian title *Senilità*, senility, cannot be meant literally, for Emilio is comparatively young; he is the age that Italo Svevo was when he married and embarked on a successful business career. The English title, which was approved by Svevo's friend James Joyce, suggests that the theme is not age but aging. It is possible to think of Emilio as one who is having a final fling before submitting to the aging process: At the end of the novel he is already living in his memories. Perhaps, however, senility in the novel is a spiritual state rather than a time of life, a state of inertia which would be excusable in a man actually old but which is inappropriate to a man in the prime of life.

Emilio's character belongs to the type of the antihero, which was popular at the end of the nineteenth century. There are Austrian examples in the works of Robert Musil and Arthur Schnitzler, and in English one thinks of characters in the works of Henry James and Joyce, of Leopold Bloom in particular. Emilio in a petty way does resemble the real tragic hero, for catastrophe does result from a mistaken action on his part, and Amalia could be compared to William Shakespeare's Ophelia or Cordelia.

The novel has been taken as an illustration of the ideas of Arthur Schopenhauer, in whom Svevo was interested, but it makes perfectly good sense without reference to any scheme of abstract philosophy. It has also been taken as a treatment of the theme of Jewishness, with Balli as Gentile contrasted to Brentani as Jew, but there are no references to Jewish beliefs or institutions, nor indeed any indication that Emilio is Jewish.

*Critical Context*

When *As a Man Grows Older* was published in 1898, it could have been regarded as part of an advance in fiction: a movement from naturalistic fiction, in which details are accumulated for their own sake, to modern fiction, in which, as in Joyce's works, details may be accumulated in a manner superficially naturalistic but in fact every detail is carefully selected for a total effect. Thus, for example, Svevo's descriptions of the furniture of Emilio's and Angiolina's apartments, of the house of assignation, and of Balli's studio are all significantly revealing. The novel, however, whether because it was privately printed in a city which was then part of Austria or because it was written in a kind of "business Italian," received almost no attention, and Svevo wrote nothing further until after World War I. Something significant happened in the interval, however; from 1907 on Svevo took English lessons from Joyce, who had come to Trieste to work in the Berlitz School. The two became friends and literary confidants; the character of Leopold Bloom owes something to Svevo, and his wife Livia, with her magnificent blonde hair, was one of the models for Anna Livia Plurabelle in *Finnegans Wake* (1939). They maintained only casual contact after Joyce left Trieste, but when Svevo published *La coscienza di Zeno* (1928; *Confessions of Zeno*, 1930), only to have it fall flat, he appealed to Joyce, and Joyce appealed to the French critics. The novel was translated and reprinted, and Svevo's fame spread back to Italy, where the younger novelists hailed him as "the aged great-uncle of our literature." It is pleasantly ironic that the author of *As a Man Grows Older* should have ended his life in a blaze of glory.

*Sources for Further Study*
Furbank, P. N. *Italo Svevo: The Man and the Writer*, 1966.
Joyce, Stanislaus. Introduction to *As a Man Grows Older*, 1932.
Lebowitz, Naomi. *Italo Svevo*, 1978.
Staley, Thomas F., ed. *Essays on Italo Svevo*, 1969.

*John C. Sherwood*

# ASHES AND DIAMONDS

*Author:* Jerzy Andrzejewski (1909-1983)
*Type of plot:* Political novel
*Time of plot:* May 5 through May 8, 1945
*Locale:* Ostrowiec, Poland
*First published: Popiół i diament*, 1948 (English translation, 1962)

> *Principal characters:*
> STEFAN SZCZUKA, the secretary of the Communist Party Area
>     Committee for the district of Ostrowiec
> MACIEK CHELMICKI, a twenty-four-year-old member of the
>     Home Army, the anti-German and anti-Soviet under-
>     ground organization
> KRYSTYNA ROZBICKA, an impoverished member of the gentry
>     who is currently employed as a barmaid at the Hotel
>     Metropol
> ANTONI KOSSECKI, a former jurist, now in his early fifties,
>     who has recently been released from a concentration camp
> ANDRZEJ KOSSECKI, a twenty-one-year-old member of the
>     Home Army and Mr. Kossecki's eldest son
> ALEK KOSSECKI, Andrzej's younger brother
> JULIUSZ SZRETTER, the charismatic leader of the conspira-
>     torial gang of which Alek is a member
> KATJA STANIEWICZ, Szczuka's politically conservative sister-
>     in-law
> FRANCISZEK PODGORSKI, Szczuka's loyal deputy

*The Novel*

The events which make up the plot of Jerzy Andrzejewski's *Ashes and Diamonds* occur over a period of four days in an industrial city of modest size called Ostrowiec. Situated approximately ninety miles due south of Warsaw, the city of Ostrowiec had already been liberated by Soviet forces in January, 1945. The novel itself formally begins on Saturday, May 5. It is on this day that Stefan Szczuka, a Polish Communist in charge of administering the entire district, narrowly escapes assassination at the hands of some members of the outlawed underground organization known as the Home Army. An unfortunate consequence of the miscarried ambush is the inadvertent killing of two innocent workmen from a local cement factory. Maciek Chelmicki, one of the participants in the ambush, is ordered by his superiors to make a new attempt to eliminate the Communist functionary. Chelmicki therefore checks into the Hotel Metropol, where he succeeds in obtaining a room immediately adjacent to the one occupied by Szczuka. In the reception hall at this hotel an official banquet is to be held later on that same day in anticipation of the imminent surrender of Nazi Germany. There is also a less formal assembly of townspeople in the bar situated next to the reception hall of the hotel. By reporting on both of these gatherings in great detail, the author is able to acquaint his readers with a host of characters drawn from a wide spectrum of Polish society without unduly complicating the structure of the plot.

One of the problems confronting Szczuka pertains to the ultimate disposition of a case involving a former jurist named Antoni Kossecki, a man recently released from the German concentration camp of Grossrosen. Szczuka, for his part, has firsthand knowledge of Mr. Kossecki's collaboration with the enemy, for he had also spent a few months at Grossrosen after his own arrest by the Gestapo before being transferred to other camps in Germany. Most distressed over the affair is Szczuka's deputy, Franciszek Podgorski. He had known Mr. Kossecki before the war and had always found him to be a man of unblemished probity. Podgorski visits the Kossecki household, and, after a lengthy discussion with him, instructs the former jurist to report to Szczuka at six o'clock on Tuesday evening. Podgorski then departs to attend the victory banquet at the Hotel Metropol. The festivities at the hotel begin at nine o'clock in the evening and terminate at dawn on Sunday morning as the last guests march out onto the street performing a polonaise to the discordant beat of the music provided by the hired orchestra.

Szczuka and Podgorski spend Sunday and Monday in the country on Party business and are not scheduled to return to Ostrowiec until Tuesday, when they will attend the funeral of the two men from the cement factory. During this interval, the novel focuses on the moral dilemma now confronting Chelmicki. Shortly after having checked into the Metropol, Chelmicki met and fell in love with a young woman named Krystyna Rozbicka, who is employed as a barmaid at the hotel restaurant. Because of her, he now desires to make a clean break with his violent life in the Home Army and lays plans to enroll at a polytechnic institute. Most important among the Home Army members who finally persuade Chelmicki to carry out his commission is Andrzej, the eldest son of Mr. Kossecki.

On Tuesday morning, Chelmicki goes to the cemetery where Szczuka is scheduled to attend the burial service. Even though it proves to be a painful ordeal for Chelmicki to witness the burial, he remains firm in his resolve to kill Szczuka at the most opportune moment. Subsequently, he trails Szczuka to a house where the Party secretary hopes to obtain information about the manner in which his wife perished in the concentration camp at Ravensbrück from another former female inmate. Chelmicki bursts into the house and dispatches Szczuka with his revolver.

On his way back to the Hotel Metropol, the loudspeakers in the town square announce that the unconditional surrender of Germany has just been formally ratified by the German High Command in Berlin. Tomorrow will be the first day of peace in Europe. Immediately, Chelmicki checks out of the hotel and heads for the railroad station to catch the next train for Warsaw, where Krystyna has agreed to meet him. When he is challenged by a military patrol consisting of three Polish soldiers, however, Chelmicki suddenly panics and runs from them and is shot dead by one of the soldiers. Thus, the lives of both Szczuka and Chelmicki are terminated by equally senseless acts of violence. Still to be resolved is the case of Mr. Kossecki. Because of Szczuka's death, it is Podgorski who must now pass judgment on the distinguished jurist. Readers of *Ashes and Diamonds* are, accordingly, left to wrestle with this ethical dilemma for themselves.

*The Characters*

While it is true that both Szczuka and Chelmicki are portrayed sympathetically throughout the novel, there can be no doubt that Andrzejewski draws a vital distinction between them on the basis of the political realities of postwar Poland. Despite his age, Szczuka represents the future of his nation in its role as a political and military ally of the Soviet Union. Since neither Szczuka nor his deputy are ever depicted in the act of enforcing any of the decrees issued by the Soviet-controlled regime in Warsaw, it is relatively easy for the author to present them in an entirely positive light.

In contrast to Szczuka, Chelmicki embodies the patriotic and conspiratorial tradition developed during Poland's tragic historical experience as an enslaved nation. The destructive aspect of this mentality is underscored by an incident that occurs with a band of youths who attempt to imitate their elders by establishing a conspiratorial organization of its own. While Mr. Kossecki's younger son, Alek, is one of its members, the moving force behind the organization is a charismatic youth named Juliusz Szretter. To instill a rigid sense of discipline among his subordinates, Szretter actually kills one of them for failing to comply with one of his demands. This deed is even more senseless than Chelmicki's assassination of Szczuka.

The moral problem involving Mr. Kossecki is of an entirely different order. Like many other men, he proved to be incapable of withstanding the pressures of cruelty and degradation to which the inmates of concentration camps were routinely exposed. For the sake of personal survival, he allowed the Germans to make him a block warden, and he frequently inflicted severe corporal punishment on his fellow prisoners as part of his duties. In addition, many of his former victims charge that he carried out these shameful acts with great zeal. The former judge declares to Podgorski that the traditional moral principles of everyday life do not apply to the abnormal circumstances which prevailed during the German Occupation. As Podgorski takes leave of Mr. Kossecki, the assistant administrator is pleased to recall that Szczuka is the one who is obliged to make the decision as to whether this case is to be prosecuted. Ironically, because of Szczuka's subsequent assassination, Podgorski himself will be forced to pass judgment on Mr. Kossecki.

*Themes and Meanings*

For Polish readers at the time of the novel's publication, the most startling aspect of *Ashes and Diamonds* was to be found in its portrayal of members of the Home Army. Andrzejewski's novel was actually the first work to be published in Poland under official government sanction, and this underground organization received much sympathetic coverage in place of the mandatory condemnation. Because of the constraints of censorship, however, Andrzejewski was unable to set forth completely the reasons for the Home Army's hostility toward the Soviet Union and its Polish henchmen. Much of the bitterness harbored by Maciek Chelmicki and Andrzej Kossecki toward their adversaries must surely have arisen because both men participated in the revolt against the Germans in late 1944, as the Red Army approached the Polish capital.

The Home Army, which was controlled by the London-based government-in-exile, sought to take control of Warsaw before the Soviet forces arrived and launched an attack on the Germans stationed within the city. Not surprisingly, the Soviet response to the insurrection was to cease all military activity against the Germans near Warsaw, and the Home Army was thus left to its own resources in battling the vastly superior Nazi forces. The bitter struggle lasted more than two months and cost more than 200,000 Polish lives. After the surrender of the Home Army, the Germans forcibly evacuated the city and then destroyed what was left of it, block by block. No reference to this background is contained within the novel itself, but Polish readers were fully aware of the political circumstances surrounding the destruction of their capital.

Thus, Andrzejewski's appeal to his compatriots was for both sides to end their self-destructive enmity and to unite in the task of rebuilding their devastated homeland. The alternatives are sharply delineated in the title of the novel, which was inspired by a poem by Cyprian Norwid, one of the major figures of the Romantic era in Polish literature. Andrzejewski hoped to remind his readers of the question posed by Norwid in his poem, whether all that is destined to remain of one's life is ashes or whether it is possible to conduct one's life in such a way that a diamond will be found among the ashes.

*Critical Context*

*Ashes and Diamonds* is by far Andrzejewski's best-known work. Not only was it widely translated into many other languages, but it was also made into a film by the celebrated Polish director Andrzej Wajda in 1958. The screenplay, it is interesting to note, was a collaborative effort by Wajda and Andrzejewski. When subsequently released abroad, the film received much critical acclaim and won many major awards for excellence.

The finest critical assessment of the novel itself is contained in Czesław Miłosz's collection of essays entitled *Zniewolny umysł* (1953; *The Captive Mind*, 1953). Much of this book is devoted to the fate of four writers in Communist Poland, and it provides a moving account of their gradual descent into spiritual slavery under Stalinist oppression. Although Miłosz designates these men only by abstract labels—Alpha, the Moralist; Beta, the Disappointed Lover; Gamma, the Slave of History; and Delta, the Troubadour—the writers' identities are not hidden from anyone familiar with postwar Polish literature.

Those who have read *Ashes and Diamonds* will have no difficulty in recognizing that "Alpha" is Andrzejewski. Miłosz's essay states the fact that Andrzejewski formally became a Party member shortly after the publication of *Ashes and Diamonds* despite his serious reservations over the official policy that made the practice of Socialist Realism mandatory for all Polish writers. It is important to recognize, however, that Miłosz's account is necessarily incomplete, and that Andrzejewski's adherence to Communist ideology proved to be merely a temporary phase in his literary career. By the mid-1950's, Andrzejewski came to reject the Marxist axiom that the laws of historical materialism ensure the triumph of Communism. He went on to write several novels in which he attacked the rule of totalitarian regimes. Foremost among these works are *Ciemności kryją ziemię* (1957; *The Inquisitors*, 1960) and *Apelacja* (1968; *The Appeal*, 1971). These books are unlikely to achieve the popularity of *Ashes and Diamonds*, but they may still be of interest to those wishing to read novels that explore the moral dimensions of politics with keen understanding and intelligence.

*Sources for Further Study*

Kryński, Magnus J. "The Metamorphoses of Jerzy Andrzejewski: The Road from Belief to Skepticism," in *The Polish Review*. VI, no. 1 (1961), pp. 111-116.

Krzyżanowski, Jerzy R. "On the History of *Ashes and Diamonds*," in *Slavic and East European Journal*. XVI, no. 3 (1971), pp. 324-331.

Miłosz, Czesław. "Alpha, the Moralist," in *The Captive Mind*, 1953.

———————. *The History of Polish Literature*, 1983.

*Victor Anthony Rudowski*

# ASYA

*Author:* Ivan Turgenev (1818-1883)
*Type of plot:* Psychological realism
*Time of plot:* The mid-nineteenth century
*Locale:* Germany, a small town on the Rhine
*First published:* 1858 (English translation, 1877)

> *Principal characters:*
> N. N., the narrator, a middle-aged Russian gentleman, who
> relates certain events of his youth
> GAGIN, a Russian gentleman and dilettante artist, sojourning
> in Germany
> ASYA, Gagin's half sister

*The Novel*

N. N., a lonely bachelor in his forties, tells the story of the lost love of his youth, twenty years ago. This is his story. A Russian gentleman in his twenties with ample private means, he has been vacationing in a picturesque small town on the Rhine, where he meets by chance two fellow Russians, a young artist named Gagin and a girl of seventeen called Asya (a diminutive of Anna), whom Gagin introduces as his sister. N. N., recovering from an unsuccessful flirtation with a young widow, feels ready for a new relationship. Apparently the only Russians in town, the three soon become close friends.

N. N.'s curiosity is aroused by Asya. She has a mysterious, untamed, elfin quality, now skittish and shy, now embarrassingly forward. Her manners and class markings seem quite different from Gagin's. The narrator imagines himself to be falling in love with her, but at the same time he is frequently irritated by her unconventional behavior. He suspects that she is not really Gagin's sister at all, and the belief that he is being deceived irritates him all the more.

This early mystery is soon resolved, however, when Gagin, in a reminiscence, tells his and Asya's story. Asya is his illegitimate half sister, the result of a liaison between his father and a serf woman some years after the early death of Gagin's mother. When his father died, Gagin, a young man in his twenties, found himself responsible for this wild creature, to whom he was bound both by ties of blood and by the dying words of his father, who had "bequeathed" her to him, revealing her true identity for the first time. She had been brought up entirely in the country, first by her mother as a peasant, and then, after her mother's death, by her father as a gentlewoman. After his father's death, Gagin had placed her for some years in a finishing school in St. Petersburg, and they had only just come abroad together.

The romance between N. N. and Asya continues to develop, reaching a climax on a perfect day marked by a long walk by themselves in a vineyard, followed by an evening of dancing to Gagin's accompaniment on the piano. The next day, however, Asya is strangely pensive and withdrawn, and N. N. finds himself unable to fathom her feelings or to sort out his own. The following day, he receives a summons from Asya. Gagin, however, intercepts N. N. with the startling announcement that his half sister loves him. She had spent a sleepless night, ultimately confessing her plight to Gagin with much sobbing. She is convinced, however, that N. N. despises her, presumably for her illegitimacy and peasant blood, and she had begged Gagin to take her away at once. Instead, Gagin has decided to talk to N. N. first, for to disappear would be tragic, if it turned out that N. N. also loved her. N. N. is thus forced into a difficult position: He must either propose marriage immediately or break off the relationship. The situation has suddenly become far more serious than he had anticipated, and once again his response is vexation.

In the denouement, N. N. has a secret meeting with Asya, arranged by her. At first, he draws her to him, but then abruptly he pulls back, saying that it is wrong of them to meet without her brother's knowledge, and she runs away. Later that night, she returns, but not before N. N. and Gagin have worried about her, and the next day N. N. learns that Gagin and his sister have left town without leaving any forwarding address. Now N. N. is filled with remorse and regret that he did not declare his love for her when he had the opportunity, but it is too late. He tries to follow them, to London and beyond, but in vain. All trace of Asya and her brother is lost, and now, twenty years later, N. N. looks back philosophically on this poignant episode of his youth. He suspects that it was all for the best: He would probably not have been happy with Asya.

*The Characters*

The narrator, N. N., is a familiar figure in Ivan Turgenev's fiction, similar to the heroes of several other works, such as *Pervaya lyubov* (1860; *First Love*, 1884) or *Veshniye vody* (1872; *Spring Floods*, 1874; better known as *The Torrents of Spring*, 1897). The character has obvious autobiographical elements. His age, sex, social position, and "philosophy" are more or less identical with Turgenev's own, but like other quasi-autobiographical characters, he is not endowed with the author's literary talent and success. Private means, from estate (and serf) ownership, supply the resources so that these young men can devote themselves entirely to private life; concerns over money seldom obtrude themselves. Like *Asya*, several of Turgenev's other stories take place outside Russia, particularly at spas in Germany (where Turgenev himself also spent much of his time until 1870), thus setting them apart from the Russian social concerns Turgenev evoked in such novels as *Nakanune* (1860; *On the Eve*, 1871) and *Ottsy i deti* (1862; *Fathers and Sons*, 1867). Asya's ambiguous situation, suspended by illegitimacy between two classes, echoes the position of Turgenev's own illegitimate daughter, Polina, and also that of the illegitimate daughter of his uncle, who was actually called Asya.

N. N. is also typical of other Turgenev heroes. He exhibits a certain sexual fecklessness, an inability to move beyond the early stages of courtship. When the woman, contrary to conventional expectations, takes the initiative in the affair, the skittish male takes to his heels, often evoking some "moral" rationalization for his craven flight. With the episode safely in the past, he then can use it to infuse his life with an aura of nostalgic poetry.

Except for his artistic interests, Gagin is almost a carbon copy of N. N. The reader, however, has no view of Gagin's inner world. Turgenev stresses the softness and sweetness of the artist's nature, which he identifies as a national and class trait, and Gagin himself attributes his lack of progress as an artist to his "cursed Slavic lack of discipline." He does, however, take seriously his responsibilities to Asya.

Asya herself is intended to produce an enigmatic impression; the puzzle of her social origin, solved early in the story, only partly solves the riddle of her character. She is more direct and uninhibited than the ladies of her brother's social class, but the key to Asya lies in the clash between her naturally outgoing, passionate nature and her pride, which fears rejection and humiliation at the hands of those whose legitimacy and class status are beyond question.

*Themes and Meanings*

The reminiscent mode has many advantages for Turgenev. With the immediacy of first-person narration, he can evoke the nuances of feeling, the stirrings, the hesitations, the sudden shifts and gushes of feeling in the early stages of a romantic relationship. He prefers, however, to present these experiences as "recollected in tranquillity," seen with the perspective of wisdom gained later and imbued with an aura of nostalgia and regret. Turgenev's "first loves" almost invariably end in rupture, and he never depicts married love, or its usual consequences of family life.

Lyric regret for lost love is fused with general regret for lost youth, and *Asya* concludes with a "philosophical" reflection on the ravages of time and the ephemeral nature of human life. The narrator, twenty years later, still has, pressed in a book, the geranium Asya had once thrown to him from a window. The flower still exudes a faint aroma, and he morbidly imagines that the hand that threw it may already be moldering in the grave, while for him the hopes and ambitions of youth have faded into nothing. "Thus," he concludes, "does an airy emanation from an insignificant blade of grass outlive all the joys and sorrows of man—outlive man himself."

*Critical Context*

In general, Russian criticism of Turgenev's time, more oriented as it was toward social commentary than artistic analysis, paid far more attention to the series of topical novels Turgenev produced during this period in his career, such as *Rudin* (1856; *Dimitri Roudine*, 1873; better known as *Rudin*, 1947), *On the Eve*, and *Fathers and Sons* than to such novellas as *Asya* and *First Love*, which deal with purely private themes. (In contrast, with the exception of *Fathers and Sons*, late twentieth century readers often prefer these shorter works to the novels in which the topical material, much of it now outdated, is not always well integrated with the plot.) *Asya*, however, was something of an exception, for the leading radical critic and ideologue, Nikolai Chernyshevsky, used it as the text for a famous article entitled "The Russian at the Rendez-vous" in 1962. Chernyshevsky's conclusion is that the Russian gentry, typified by N. N. and Gagin, are too lazy, shiftless, and incompetent to provide leadership for the country, which is entering a new era of progress and social change. This article became one of the classic texts of the radical Left.

Though many admired the story's psychological subtlety and lyricism, other critics have found the book fundamentally flawed. The character of Asya herself strikes some readers as contrived and artificial. The story's greatest weakness, however, may be a consequence of the first-person narrative. To a modern reader, perhaps standing on Sigmund Freud's shoulders, it seems clear that N. N.'s romance with Asya did not succeed because the narrator did not want it to succeed. Throughout his account of his encounters with Asya, he repeatedly expresses annoyance, irritation, and vexation with her behavior. He does not want the responsibility of a deep, lasting relationship, and he wriggles free from Asya's (and Gagin's) snares. There is, therefore, something spurious about his affectation of anguish and despair at the loss of Asya, his pursuit to London, and the aura of nostalgia that he casts over the memory. What is not clear, however, is the extent to which Turgenev has penetrated his character's rationalizations. The emotions the narrator claims to have experienced seem somewhat false, an effort at self-deception, but since the author has no voice other than the narrator's, the reader finds it difficult to know whether Turgenev sees through his creature's illusions or actually shares them.

On reading *Asya*, Leo Tolstoy wrote in his diary, "*Asya* is rubbish." He did not explain this harsh judgment, which may have been motivated by the jealousies of his personal relationship with Turgenev, but the story *Semeynoye schastye* (1859; *Family Happiness*, 1888), which he wrote soon afterward, clearly in some sense replies to Turgenev. Though as much a bachelor as Turgenev at that time, Tolstoy resolved in *Family Happiness* to do two things Turgenev never dared to do. He would present a first-person, reminiscential narrative of a romance from the woman's point of view, and he would carry the romance to the altar and beyond, into the notably un-Turgenevian region of married life and babies.

*Sources for Further Study*

Annenkov, Pavel Vasilevich. "The Literary Type of the Weak Man: Apropos of Turgenev's Story 'Asja,' " in *Ulbandus Review*. I (Spring, 1978), pp. 90-104.

Chernyshevsky, Nikolai. "The Russian at the Rendez-vous," in *Belinsky, Chernyshevsky, and Dobrolyubov: Selected Criticism*, 1962. Edited by Ralph E. Matlaw.

Dessaix, Robert. *Turgenev: The Quest for Faith*, 1980.

Freeborn, Richard. *Turgenev: The Novelist's Novelist*, 1960.

Schapiro, Leonard. *Turgenev: His Life and Times*, 1979.

Yarmolinsky, Avrahm. *Turgenev: The Man, His Art, and His Age*, 1977.

*Hugh McLean*

# AUGUST 1914

*Author:* Aleksandr Solzhenitsyn (1918-    )

*Type of plot:* Historical fiction

*Time of plot:* August, 1914, the beginning of Russian participation in World War I

*Locale:* The Russian farmlands of the North Caucasus, the battlefields of Poland and East Prussia, the town of Rostov-on-Don, in the Ukraine, and Moscow

*First published: Avgust chetyrnadtsatogo,* 1971; revised, 1983 (English translation, 1972)

*Principal characters:*

GEORGII MIKHALYCH VOROTYNTSEV, a dedicated army career officer and a strategist on the General Staff

ARSENII (SENKA) BLAGODARYOV, a quick-witted young peasant recruit whom Vorotyntsev adopts as his orderly

ALEXANDER VASILICH SAMSONOV, the commander of the Second Army on the Polish-Russian-German front

SASHA LENARTOVICH, a young army ensign from a family of liberal agitators; a Socialist

ISAAKII (SANYA) LAZHENITSYN, an idealistic college student from a tiny village in the North Caucasus

ZAKHAR TOMCHAK, the wily patriarch of the Tomchak family, which is living in sparsely settled territory near the Caucasus Mountains

IRINA (ORYA) TOMCHAK, Zakhar's daughter-in-law

ROMAN TOMCHAK, Zakhar's disappointing son and Irina's tyrannical husband

XENYA TOMCHAK, Zakhar's bright, sweet-natured daughter

## The Novel

*August 1914* examines an extremely broad cross section of Russian society within the telescoped time frame of a few critical days at the beginning of World War I. A major battle (and with it, an entire army) will be lost, at a moment when "[i]t only needed two or three such defeats in succession for the backbone of the country to be put out of joint forever and for a thousand-year-old nation to be utterly destroyed." Aleksandr Solzhenitsyn's thesis is that Russia itself was destroyed when it was replaced by the Soviet Union. The strands of his novel come together to emphasize that the Soviet Union was born out of war—the original harsh experience that colors the country to this day.

The author opens the novel with protagonists from his own preexistence. The models include his grandparents, Zakhar and Evdokia; his father, Isaakii; his elegant aunt, Irina, and difficult uncle, Roman; and his mother Taissia ("Xenya" in the novel). The family subplot, which recedes into the background of historical events, is precipitated by Zakhar's disillusionment with his son Roman; resulting in an unprecedented effort at first to educate Xenya, then in an abrupt decision to pull her out of school so that she can marry and produce a grandson.

Very much in the foreground are events on the Russian-German battlefront. Colonel Georgii Vorotyntsev plays the key role of linking the scattered sites together, as he rushes on his horse from one to the next attempting to straighten out the colossal, irreparable mess that has developed. The confusion is overwhelming, and this latter-day Saint George, though intelligent and dedicated, is highly fallible. He lacks the intuition or instinct for making blind choices. His errors, and the sheer impossibility of his mission, gradually turn this George into a Don Quixote, with his peasant orderly, Arsenii Blagodaryov, serving as a dignified Sancho Panza. Blagodaryov has an instinct of uncanny infallibility. The two become bonded during a trench battle. Becoming aware that they have survived, they look up to see a windmill burning. Its arms slowly begin to turn, not from wind but from the heat— giving the reader a first, faintly ironic glimpse of the symbol that dominates Solzhenitsyn's vision of Russian history (*Krasnoe koleso*, *The Red Wheel*, the title of the series of which *August 1914* is the first volume).

While Vorotyntsev, other officers, and the wretched recruits do their best to save the situation, General Samsonov, the commanding officer of the Second Army, stands at the center of a quicksand pit: "His was the helplessness of high position." Samsonov sees clearly that the extruding "arm" of Prussian territory must be struck "under the armpit," sending troops southwest, whereas the General Staff is fatuously determined to strike "on the elbow," sending troops in the opposite direction. In the struggle between Samsonov and the General Staff, Russian troops march and countermarch in fruitless zigzags, slipping into a void in which they are inexorably exterminated. The situation is aggravated by the Russians' failure to encode the messages that they send over an unfamiliar new invention, the wireless radio. "Far outstripping every horseman, the strength of the Second Army was leaking away on those vulnerable, invisible radio waves in the impenetrable darkness of enemy territory."

Samsonov, who identifies with his army completely, goes mad when it collapses; he dies with a medieval grandeur, which Solzhenitsyn links with the grandeur of Old Russia. In sharp contrast to Samsonov is the young Socialist, Sasha Lenartovich, who observes the benign, dying giant with pitiless eyes and thinks: "Just wait—there's more coming to you yet!" Lenartovich, who joined the army to carry on propaganda (in which his platoon of peasants show not the slightest interest), is Solzhenitsyn's prime representative of the whole range of radical youth, whose deeds are always described with mordant irony. Lenartovich "was not malicious but a young man with the sincerity and conviction that were the mark of the best Russian students." He, too, is drawn into a circle of survivors led by Vorotyntsev and Blagodaryov, with whose help he escapes the final debacle.

A far more sympathetic youth, Sanya Lazhenitsyn, introduced early in the novel as a village lad with schooling, reappears late in the action. He and a friend are spending their last day in Moscow before innocently joining an army that is about to be cut to ribbons. They meet an eccentric intellectual, Varsonofiev, with whom they discuss fashionable theories of the day, such as Tolstoyanism and Hegelianism. One may surmise that the eccentric's voice is that of his creator. Varsonofiev tries to guide the youths toward something deeper and more ancient: "Haven't you noticed what delicate complexity of thought there is in a riddle?" Varsonofiev moves easily from the riddles of Russian folklore to an echo of Taoism (itself rooted in folklore): "There is a justice which existed before us, without us, and for its own sake." The young men nickname this sage "Stargazer," thus tying Varsonofiev in with the stars that rise over Solzhenitsyn's hushed, blood-soaked battlefields at nightfall; and linking him also to Vorotyntsev, who will reluctantly answer his lover (in the next volume in *The Red Wheel*, *Oktiabr shestnadtsatogo* (1984; October 1916) that the only Russian author he can appreciate is Mikhail Lermontov, the soldier-poet whose line every Russian knows by heart: "The desert hearkens to God; and star with star converses."

## The Characters

In *August 1914*, most of Solzhenitsyn's characters are bathed in irony. This ranges from the gentle irony imbuing the Tomchak family and Vorotyntsev, to the mordant irony reserved for pompous generals and righteous radicals. Solzhenitsyn's ironic character descriptions depend to a great extent upon his quoting of the character's own favorite phrases and thoughts. Thus Sasha Lenartovich's motives are described as he contemplates desertion: "Surrender was a sensible and practical step: [T]he important things—his life, his educated mind, and his political views—would be preserved." The pompous, egotistical Roman Tomchak, who eagerly reads all the newspapers (which Solzhenitsyn gleefully quotes as a tissue of lies), contemplates the options open to him: "He might even have considered going in for socialism, if it had not been so closely akin to sheer robbery."

Because the action is confined to three days, characters are drawn with broad strokes, and substantial psychological evolution is possible only for those who are put into a veritable pressure cooker, such as Samsonov. When the mad general is at his most ridiculous, Solzhenitsyn's compassion lends Samsonov his greatest dignity as all irony is put aside.

## Themes and Meanings

The main theme of *August 1914*, arching over the obvious theme of war, is history itself, of which the sage Varsonofiev remarks: "History grows like a living tree. And as far as that tree is concerned, reason is an ax: [y]ou'll never make it grow better by applying reason to it." Looking back to Leo Tolstoy, his great predecessor in the genre of historical fiction, the theory of history, and the theory of warfare, Solzhenitsyn confronts him and his views.

Frequently, Solzhenitsyn's characters are influenced in their conduct by the examples of literature. One of the most reprehensible generals in *August 1914* models his career on that of the widely admired antihero Kutuzov in Tolstoy's *War and Peace* (1865-1869; English translation, 1886). "His long military service had convinced the general of the correctness of Tolstoy's views; there was nothing worse than sticking one's neck out by using one's initiative." Solzhenitsyn's would-be Kutuzov (General Blagoveshchensky) has been protecting his corps of soldiers by assiduously avoiding engagements, occupying deserted towns, and sending out dispatches announcing victories. He contributes in a crucial way to the final debacle.

Closely tied to the theme of war is that of treachery. In the final analysis, Solzhenitsyn harshly views the key to the Socialists' success as having been their willingness to commit treachery. Bolstering the Socialists' success, and adumbrating future developments, is the Russian intelligentsia's already well-established herd instinct and penchant for bullying any dissidents. Despite their alleged aim to build a new society, Solzhenitsyn's young Socialists find themselves at loggerheads with the real builders of the twentieth century: the engineers.

Until his death in 1910, one of the most influential gurus of the Russian radicals was Tolstoy, whose name runs like a red thread (or a railroad car) through this first volume of *The Red Wheel*. In applying the elegant ax of literature to Russian socialism, Solzhenitsyn hacks particularly at this thickest, most revered of its roots.

## Critical Context

As a young man, and at that time still a convinced Communist, Aleksandr Solzhenitsyn outlined a vastly ambitious project: a multivolume novel centered on the Revolution of 1917. He never lost sight of that goal. By the time he actually began the project, in the 1960's, his historical perspective had changed radically, but the basic conception of the work had not. *The Red Wheel*, as it came to be called, would re-create the period from the beginning of World War I to the Revolution; "its main dramatis persona," Solzhenitsyn has said in an interview, "is Russia as a whole."

*August 1914*, the first "knot" of *The Red Wheel*, was initially published in 1971. Following his exile to the West in 1974, Solzhenitsyn enjoyed access to historical materials which had not been available to him in the Soviet Union.

As a result, he published a greatly expanded version of *August 1914* in 1983. The revised version introduces a new historical theme: the assassination, in 1911, of prime minister Pyotr Stolypin, whose views Solzhenitsyn much admires and whose death, he believes, significantly diminished Russia's hopes for peaceful development.

Solzhenitsyn's achievement in *August 1914* should be seen in the context of a well-established tradition in Russian literature, where the historical novel is a respected genre; among Solzhenitsyn's distinguished predecessors are Tolstoy and Boris Pasternak, whose book, *Doctor Zhivago* (1957; English translation, 1958), picks up the thread of Russian history in 1905 and coincides with the pre- and post-Revolutionary period with which Solzhenitsyn is also most concerned. In this tradition, historical fiction is not a light entertainment but a laboratory for analyzing and experimenting with the historical process itself. Influenced by the very Soviet ideology that he opposed, Solzhenitsyn carries the experiment a step further: He has no doubt that literature influences life and that his interpretation of history cannot but influence the decisions of his readers and his government. This lends an undisguised polemical aspect to his historical novels.

Solzhenitsyn's interest in the medieval, pre-Petrine roots of Russia had surfaced in his early story, "Zakhar kalita" ("Zakhar the Pouch"). That theme is also continued in *The Red Wheel*, most obviously in the character of the medievalist (the "professoress" Andozerskaya, who appears in a minor role in *August 1914* and in a major one in *Oktiabr shestnadtsatogo*); more subtly in the linking of the grandeur of old Moscow with the tragic dignity of Samsonov and in the quixotic questing of Vorotyntsev, the modern Saint George (the rescuer of the Slavs).

The Red Wheel expresses Solzhenitsyn's drive toward a comprehensive view of all Russian society, encompassing the entire range of social positions and a tremendous inventory of psychological types, dwarfing the already Dantean range found in his earlier novels, *V kruge pervom* (1968; *The First Circle*, 1968) and *Rakovy korpus* (1968; *Cancer Ward*, 1968). With the multisided tableau of *The Red Wheel*, Solzhenitsyn confirms his own credo: the total inadequacy of any ideology to do justice to human life.

*Sources for Further Study*
Burg, David, and George Feifer. *Solzhenitsyn*, 1972.
Ericson, Edward E., Jr. *Solzhenitsyn: The Moral Vision*, 1980.
Kodjack, Andrej. *Alexander Solzhenitsyn*, 1978.
Moody, Christopher. *Solzhenitsyn*, 1976 (second revised edition).
Scammell, Michael. *Solzhenitsyn: A Biography*, 1984.

*D. Gosselin Nakeeb*

# AUTO-DA-FÉ

*Author:* Elias Canetti (1905-    )
*Type of plot:* Parody
*Time of plot:* Probably the 1930's
*Locale:* Vienna and Paris
*First published: Die Blendung,* 1935 (English translation, 1946; also as *The Tower of Babel,* 1947)

*Principal characters:*
> PETER KIEN, a world-famous sinologist with a private library of twenty-five thousand books
> THERESE, his vulgar and greedy housekeeper, whom he marries
> FISCHERLE, a hunchbacked dwarf who befriends Kien in order to swindle him
> BENEDIKT PFAFF, a sadistic house porter who becomes Therese's lover
> GEORGE KIEN, Peter Kien's younger brother, a distinguished psychiatrist

## The Novel

Elias Canetti divides *Auto-da-Fé* into three sections: "A Head Without a World," "Headless World," and "The World in the Head." The "head" is Peter Kien, a reclusive, internationally renowned sinologist who lives in a top-floor apartment, engulfed by his twenty-five thousand books. He is a purely cerebral bachelor, divorced from any awareness of human beings or human values. He has no significant contact with the world beyond his scholarly reading. Therefore, he believes that "Knowledge and truth [are] . . . identical terms. You draw closer to truth by shutting yourself off from mankind."

Kien hires a housekeeper, Therese, who is noiseless and seemingly devoted to each of his tomes, handling them with gloves. Soon Kien has a nightmare in which he is the sacrificial victim of two Mexican priests who, disguised as jaguars, drive books through his body and then burn both him and the books on an altar. Awakening, Kien dissects the dream rationally, finding the origin of each element in his recent reading and dismissing the vision's subrational omens. He decides to marry Therese, regarding her as "the heaven-sent instrument for preserving my library. If there is a fire I can trust in her."

Kien and Therese are soon at odds in a bizarre maze of misapprehensions and cross-purposes. The vehemently materialistic Therese screams greedy demands at him and insists on obtaining his bankbook; she also wants him to make his will in her favor. (She has the mistaken idea that her husband is wealthy.) When he refuses, she bodily ejects him from their apartment. Kien then meets Fischerle, a hunchbacked, dwarfish pickpocket who dreams of becoming the world's chess champion. Kien's demented devotion to books drives him to "buy" copies of a vast number by taking inventories in the city's bookshops of all available volumes that correspond to his own library. He then mentally "unloads" them in his hotel room each night, lifting "packet" after "packet" out of his deluded head. Yet he never actually purchases any of them. Fischerle profits from Kien's madness by inventing a quartet of quasi-sellers who "sell" books to Kien, while the dwarf pockets the lion's share of the money Kien has withdrawn from his savings account to pay for them.

Kien also imagines that his harridan wife, driven by her avarice, has taken no time to buy food and has, therefore, had to cannibalize herself, eating portions of her own body until she has consumed herself. Convinced that Therese is dead, Kien strenuously denies her weighty presence when she insists on having him arrested for the "theft" of their savings. In a grotesque address to the mentally retarded police officers, Kien asks them, in the terrifying presence of his wife, to "Liberate me from this hallucination!... Prove to me that she is dead!"

After Fischerle has been barbarously murdered and mutilated by one of his whorish wife's lovers, Kien returns to his home. Fearing Therese, however, he hides in the brutal caretaker Benedikt Pfaff's cellar apartment, subject to his cuffs and kicks. There, he is discovered by the novel's only sane and stable personality, Kien's younger brother George, director of a mental asylum in Paris. George is able to rid Peter of both Therese and Pfaff, and restore him to his library. Once George has returned to his patients, however, Peter breaks down completely. He imagines his beloved books revolting against their owner, with letters detaching themselves from their pages to assault his ears, footnotes kicking him, and the whole library becoming a "damnable mob." Fantasizing that even his brother is plotting to rob him of his books and that the police are outside the apartment door about to arrest him for having murdered Therese, Kien sets his books ablaze, climbs to the top rung of his ladder, and there awaits a Wagnerian self-immolation while laughing the loudest laughs of his life.

### The Characters

In an illuminating essay he wrote in 1973, Canetti summarized *Auto-da-Fé*'s composition and initial reception. In 1929 and 1930, he originally planned a Balzacian eight-volume cycle of novels that would constitute "a human comedy of lunatics... each focusing on a figure on the verge of madness, and each of these figures was different from all [the] others down to his language, down to his most secret thoughts." Kien was to be that "pure bookman." His name was initially Brand, German for "fire" or "burning"; it was eventually changed to Kien, which means "pinewood" in German, suggesting his combustibility.

Peter Kien is a forty-year-old hermit dwelling in the crabshell of his library, acknowledging no reality beyond the Chinese brushstrokes and pictures inscribed in his books. They are his mandarin masters of silence, insulating him from meaningful relationships with other human beings. Moreover, even his books are not entirely indispensable, for Kien has a superb memory and carries "in his head a library as well-provided and reliable as his actual library. . . ." In his schizoid self-deception, he regards his books as encompassing the whole world. Elias Canetti draws Kien as a bizarrely perverted Platonist, capable of denying or distorting phenomenal experiences while overloading his mind with abstract schemata. Like Don Quixote, Kien subjects empirical reality to confirmation or rejection by his preconceived ideas. Thus, he hears on one of his walks the cooing of pigeons. Having read that pigeons make such a sound, Kien agrees to receive it as a valid sensation: " 'Quite so!' he said softly, and nodded as he always did when he found reality bearing out the printed original."

Canetti's treatment of Kien and the novel's other characters is a fusion of comedy with horror, precision with fantasy, that can best be described as grotesque. Each of the characters elevates his or her fantasies to obsessionally held truths, unable or unwilling to check them against the perceptions of other people. Each is, therefore, driven by one or more monomanias. In addition to Kien's pathological bookishness, Therese is led by avarice and sexual frustration, Fischerle longs to dominate through chess triumphs, and Pfaff delights in brutal exploitation of physical weaklings. These characters are all demented subjectivists, ruled by an absolute inner world. Paranoia infects them all. Their eccentricities are extreme enough to render them psychotic.

Therese's characterization may be the most memorable and repulsive of this foursome. She is a misogynist's delight: vicious, greedy, gross, ugly, selfish, shrewish, and merciless. Her conversation consists largely of monotonous daily tags, such as "up already," "I ask you," or "I make so bold." Her torrents of platitudes and clichés become unbearably repetitive to Kien: "Several dozen times every day, she said the same thing." Her values are vulgarly materialistic, compounded by spiteful self-righteousness. Her ludicrous carnal cravings—never fulfilled by the asexual Kien—cause her to mistake the flattery of a furniture salesman ("the superior young man") for romantic interest. She imagines a liaison with him, laced with assignation lunches and nightly embraces. Her *idée fixe* leads her to public embarrassment: She literally confronts the salesman in the furniture showroom, undoes her skirt, and presses him to her fat body in a viselike embrace before a large, laughing crowd.

## Themes and Meanings

Canetti had originally titled his novel "*Kant Catches Fire*"; in 1935, when it was finally published after a four-year period of rejection, he renamed it *Die Blendung*—meaning the blinding, dazzlement, or deception. The second title is far more appropriate, since the protagonist is deceived by his reliance on pure intellection. The novel is a classic study of the violence subtly but incessantly present in abstract thought, the pathological undercurrent in rigidly schematized scholarship.

Insanity is the book's central metaphor. Even the only sane character, George Kien, is touched by madness in his position as director of an insane asylum in a Parisian suburb. The patient who most interests George is a catatonic schizophrenic known as "the Gorilla," who lacks the ability to separate his ego from the external world. In contrast to the rigidly reclusive Kien, the Gorilla reacts with stormy emotions. Presumably representing Canetti's own beliefs, George prefers the synthetic, undifferentiated perspective of the Gorilla to the dissociated, analytic, abstracted madness of his brother. In trying to stabilize and reassure Peter, George tells him, "If you [the man of facts] and I [the man of feelings] could be molded together into a single being, the result would be a spiritually complete man."

Such a harmonious synthesis is never realized in *Auto-da-Fé*. Instead, the novel dramatizes a world of confusion, fragmentation, and torment, amounting to an absurdist allegory of the disintegration of culture and degradation of man. For Canetti, the serenity of the ivory tower is a delusion; the rarefied discipline of philological scholarship is a thin patina over the lunatic violence of man's instinctual, brutish demons. Peter Kien's solipsism and sterility result in a conflagration whose flames herald the European Holocaust.

## Critical Context

Elias Canetti is a Bulgarian-born Jew of Sephardic ancestry who was brought up largely in Vienna, although he also lived in England and Germany. In the second of his autobiographical volumes, *Die Fackel im Ohr* (1980; *The Torch in My Ear*, 1982), as well as in the essay cited above, he tells how an episode that occurred on July 15, 1927, influenced him to write not only *Auto-da-Fé* but also his most important sociological treatise, *Masse und Macht* (1960; *Crowds and Power*, 1962). On that day, the Viennese newspapers headlined a verdict that Vienna's radicals regarded as a flagrant miscarriage of justice. Workers had been killed in the Austrian province of Burgenland, but their killers had been acquitted, and the acquittal was termed "a just verdict" by the government's party. Enraged, thousands of Viennese workers marched on the Palace of Justice and set it on fire. In retaliation, the police killed ninety of the demonstrators. That day, Canetti recalls, "I became a part of the crowd. I dissolved into it fully. I did not feel the least resistance to what it did."

One consequence of this profound experience was the writing of *Crowds and Power*, an impressively original study of the nature and structure of crowds. The other resulting work, *Auto-da-Fé*, was additionally prompted by Canetti's sighting a man in a side street moaning over the destruction of his files inside the burning Palace of Justice. "Better than people!" retorted Canetti. Peter Kien's characterization was born that day.

*Auto-da-Fé* is a forbidding novel with an uncompromising narrative style which reflects the claustrophobic inwardness of the characters' unbalanced minds. The novel has failed to gain widespread popularity, possibly because of the disagreeableness of almost all of its characters. Even George Kien, while empathetically humane to his patients, is an egotist, pleased to be the subject of their awe and adoration.

Nevertheless, the novel is a masterpiece. With it, Canetti joins such modernist authors as Franz Kafka, Hermann Broch, Robert Musil, Heimito von Doderer, James Joyce, Samuel Beckett, Günter Grass, and Nathanael West. Canetti recalls reading Kafka's *The Metamorphosis* (1915) while he was laboring on his novel: "Nothing more fortunate could have happened to me at this point. . . . [T]here was the rigor that I yearned for. . . . I bowed to this purest of all models. . . ." Kafka's example encouraged him to write a severely disciplined work, representing the abnormal and aberrant in a ruthlessly calm and factual manner. Beckett's fiction, particularly *Watt* (1953) and the *Unnamable* (1953), parallels Canetti's concentration on his characters' ludicrous delusions and elaborate speculations. The deformed physical and mental attributes of such people as Fischerle and Pfaff are akin to West's *Miss Lonelyhearts* (1933) or Grass's *The Tin Drum* (1959) or *The Flounder* (1977); indeed, *Auto-da-Fé* surpasses these satiric-absurdist texts in the intensity of its uncompromising focus on the grotesque. In stressing the divorce of abstract knowledge from vital experience and in suggesting madness as the sadly underlying agenda of the contemporary world, Canetti's work bonds with that of other noted Central European novels: Doderer's *The Demons* (1956), Musil's *The Man Without Qualities* (1930), and Broch's *The Sleepwalkers* (1931-1932). In addition, Joyce's stream-of-consciousness technique provides the narrative framework for the novel.

The saddest yet most instructive context for *Auto-da-Fé* is the twentieth century's history of totalitarianism. Power games may be confined to books, chess, money, and sex in this novel, but world events have unleashed its violence on a genocidal scale. The Reichstag fire, the Nazis' burning of humanistic books, concentration camp ovens, and the bombing of cities testify to the savage truth of Canetti's vision of the world as a self-destructive inferno.

*Sources for Further Study*
Canetti, Elias. "The First Book: *Auto-da-Fé*," in *The Conscience of Words*, 1979.

Enright, D. J. "*Auto-da-Fé*," in *Encounter*. XVIII (June, 1962), pp. 65-68.

Hulse, Michael. *Essays in Honor of Elias Canetti*, 1987.

Sokel, Walter H. "The Ambiguity of Madness," in *Views and Reviews of Modern German Literature*, 1974.

Thomson, Edward A. "Elias Canetti's *Die Blendung* and the Changing Image of Madness," in *German Life and Letters*. XXVI (1972), pp. 38-47.

*Gerhard Brand*

# BADENHEIM 1939

*Author:* Aharon Appelfeld (1932-     )
*Type of plot:* Historical fiction
*Time of plot:* 1939
*Locale:* Badenheim, an Austrian resort town
*First published: Badenheim, 'ir nofesh*, 1975 (English translation, 1980)

> *Principal characters:*
> THE HOLOCAUST, an unnamed ubiquitous presence
> symbolized by an orange shadow and generalized fear
> among Badenheimers
> THE SANITATION DEPARTMENT, both the symbolic and the
> literal agent of the Holocaust
> DR. PAPPENHEIM, the "impresario" and director of the
> summer festival in Badenheim
> TRUDE, the wife of the pharmacist Martin, considered
> "disturbed" because of her visions of the impending
> Holocaust
> SAMITZKY, a Polish musician and reflector of attitudes of and
> reactions toward Eastern Europeans relative to the
> impending Holocaust

*The Novel*

*Badenheim 1939* displays a sequence of both realistic and symbolic events beginning in early spring of 1939 in the resort town of Badenheim and ending with the deportation of the Jews in late fall of the same year. A third-person narrator, in detached and understated style, reports the steps taken by the Sanitation Department to gain control of the town and abridge the freedoms of its inhabitants, while revealing how specific people react to each succeeding deprivation.

In 1939, amid swirls of unidentified rumors, the novel opens as a foreboding, uneasy spring returns to Badenheim with the sound of country church bells ringing, two Sanitation Department inspectors examining the flow of sewage, and Trude delirious with a haunting fear that is also beginning to infect her husband. Shortly after the arrival of Dr. Pappenheim, the director of the summer festival, the perennial vacationers arrive and the town is abuzz with activity as the city people, anxious to relieve themselves of worry and the memories of an unusually strange past winter, stream toward the forest.

With the arrival of the feisty musicians, the vacationers wildly vent their emotions upon liquor and pastries, and an inspector from the Sanitation Department appears at the pharmacy, asking peculiar details about the business and taking measurements with a yardstick. As time passes, Trude worries even more about her daughter, Helena, who married a non-Jewish military officer against her parents' wishes and, in Trude's visions, is being held captive on her husband's estate, where she is beaten every evening when he returns from the barracks. Concurrently, the Sanitation Department expands its power to conduct independent investigations as it spreads all over town, taking measurements, putting up fences, planting flags, unloading rolls of barbed wire, and preparing cement pillars. The large south gate to Badenheim is closed, and a small, unused gate is opened for pedestrians. The guests, interpreting these activities as attempts to make the summer festival the best one ever, pursue gluttonous merriment even though Dr. Pappenheim's "artists" are breaking their promises to appear at the Festival. With a memory of the past summer, when the musicians surprised even themselves and annoyed the regular guests by sliding into playing Jewish melodies, a new theme is introduced.

Badenheimers become estranged, suspicious, and mistrustful of one another as the Sanitation Department completes its investigations and in the middle of May posts a "modest" sign requiring all Jewish citizens to register with the Department. Who is and is not Jewish becomes a matter of heated debate, with some denying Jewishness because of either personal conviction or conversion and others readily proclaiming their Jewishness. Foremost for all is the belief that they are Austrian first and Jewish second, and that their national allegiance supersedes all others. Badenheimers are discomforted, and several begin remembering their past while some of them blame the Department's intrusion upon the *Ostjuden*, the Eastern European Polish Jews, many of whom have not abandoned their Jewish heritage to assimilate into the Austrian culture.

As brief glimpses into the background of some of the guests are revealed and alliances and schisms among people are developing, the Sanitation Department posts pictures and descriptions of Poland and invitations to leave Austria and go to Poland. Twin-brother readers foreshadow the future by performing their specialty, readings of the death poetry of Rainer Maria Rilke, and the Sanitation Department denies everyone except the milkman and fruit truck entrance to or exit from the town. More deprivations follow as forest walks, picnics, and excursions are terminated as well as swimming in the pool, because the water supply is closed. Meanwhile, the non-Jews are leaving Badenheim.

The lives of other guests and their feelings about being Jewish are revealed as people are forced into closer contact with one another and the "alien orange shadow" and "leaden sun" symbolize the town atmosphere. Vegetation grows unchecked as people learn that they are prisoners in the town with no postal service and that all Jews, even Jews who renounced Judaism or whose parents had converted to Christianity, will be forced to "transfer" to Poland. With only a few exceptions, people accept the edict and many try to find the positive in the transfer. Food supplies begin to dwindle as the town fills with strangers—people dragged in from all over Austria because they were born in Badenheim. Even the feeble town rabbi, long ago relegated to an isolated old-age home, is brought into town. Derangement and chaos erupt as people seeking drugs loot the pharmacy and the musicians steal the hotel's dinnerware in preparation for their forced "transfer" to Poland. Finally, Helena, Trude and Martin's daughter, comes home without her non-Jewish husband. ("A goy will always be a goy. And your goy too is a goy. I'm not sorry," says Trude.)

Even the four dogs, pets of the headwaiter, try to escape by jumping the fence; driven back, all but one is shot. Ultimately, blame is placed upon Dr. Pappenheim as "the arch *Ostjude* and source of all our troubles," because he invented the Festival and "filled the town with morbid artists and decadent vacationers."

At last, the time for deportation arrives: "How easy the transition was—they hardly felt it." In fact, the policeman who escorts the Badenheimers to the train station has a very easy task because people, glad to be free of their confinement, are in fine spirits as they discuss the advantages of Poland. As if he were responsible for the "transition" as part of the happy festival arrangements, Dr. Pappenheim is overcome with tears of joy. As they are "all sucked in as easily as grains of wheat poured into a funnel" into the four filthy freight cars that come to take them away, the narrative ends with the impresario's observation: "If the coaches are so dirty it must mean that we have not far to go."

## The Characters

Rather than being rounded, the characters of *Badenheim 1939* are archetypes of people and conflicts repeated throughout the Holocaust. Unnamed and defying rational explanation, the Holocaust is the most powerful force in this novel. Revealed as a symbolic orange shadow enveloping Badenheim and gnawing at the geraniums, as a leaden sky blotting out the sun of the once-beautiful resort town, and as a general, undirected fear, its reality is confirmed only by its effects. Like William Blake, who cannot comprehend "The Tyger" although he sees it, the Badenheimers neither comprehend the actions of the Sanitation Department nor foresee the consequences of those actions. The power of evil is clearly felt, however, as it directs an increasingly and overwhelmingly destructive course.

The Sanitation Department, efficiency and thoroughness personified, is the agent of the Holocaust. As the orange shadow symbolizes the Holocaust, the Sanitation Department is both literally and symbolically the organizer and collaborator of the Holocaust—the Nazis and others who, in not defying them, become their agents. The Badenheimers never rise up against the Sanitation Department, a faceless, large, well-equipped omnipotent agency, because they cannot even imagine the Department's ultimate purpose. Instead of directing their anger about the increasing deprivations and humiliations toward the Sanitation Department, the Badenheimers make the grave error of assuming an unseen rationality and instead look to themselves for the cause of their problems.

Except for Trude, whose initial visionary perceptions of the truth and resultant fears are considered hallucinations and signs of disease, the characters remain blind to their mortal danger. Trude, like the other characters, however, is a loosely drawn type—one who sees the Holocaust coming but who is considered mad even to fear its portents. Still, when their daughter Helena returns home as Trude has predicted all along, "Martin knew that everything that Trude said was true."

Dr. Pappenheim, the impresario who has arranged for the town's summer entertainment for thirty years, was considered the most important person in Badenheim because summer was devoted solely to the pursuit of pleasure. With the confinement of Jews to the town and their imminent deportation, however, people blame the impresario and begin to treat him with hostility, which he does not recognize in his futile and continuing efforts to make the summer festival a success. Dr. Pappenheim's greatest pleasures appear to be making people happy and seeing the regulars return to Badenheim each summer. Ignoring each succeeding Sanitation Department imposition and perpetually rationalizing his way to optimism, Dr. Pappenheim tries to dispell the mounting anxiety about the Sanitation Department's increasing restrictions. He succeeds so well that a holiday atmosphere prevails as the Jews board the deportation trains to the sound of his optimistic prediction about the train ride.

Among other residents of Badenheim in 1939 is the musician Samitzky, who is the prototypical *Ostjude* whom the others hold responsible for their rejection by the Austrian world. Unpretentious, simple, and open, he is proud of his Polish roots, loves the Yiddish language, and becomes the lover of Frau Zauberblit, another prototype and an escapee from a nearby tuberculosis sanatorium whose non-Jewish husband has divorced her and whose daughter had brought her papers to sign renouncing all claims of motherhood. Thoroughly depressed and seeing no escape, Samitzsky chooses to spend each day in a drunken stupor.

*Themes and Meanings*

The Jews' perceptions of and reactions to specific government actions leading to the Holocaust are the focus of this novel. Badenheim and its inhabitants symbolize the Jews' tenure in Austria—outsiders enjoying a deceptively gay vacation in a death row which masquerades as a festival. The Sanitation Department, the organization and its agents who want to cleanse the city of its "waste" in the most expeditious manner, prepares for the Jews' deportation to the "Poland" of death. As the Jews' freedoms are increasingly abridged until they are prisoners, the naïve victims accept what the Department does with minor grumblings, some despair, and in some cases, great anger at one another for causing the problems. Excepting only a few people who consider themselves non-Jews but whom the Department nevertheless considers Jews, no one confronts the Department or even tries to leave, despite the ominous warnings. Situational irony, confirmed by an analysis of the historical period, highlights these opposites. Because the Jews were condemned as targets for the Sanitation Department, the deportation was tolerated by many rational "non-Jews." Yet the Jews' willingness to cooperate fully and be model citizens in a country they loved but which did not love them enabled the Department to deport them without encountering fierce attempts to ensure self-preservation. Similarly ironic, Trude, the only Badenheimer able to sense the impending catastrophe, is considered insane because of her fears; those who accept the unfolding plot by ignoring what they see or through frenzied drinking and gluttony are considered sane.

Dramatic irony, painful because the events are historical while also highly symbolic, pervades almost every line of the deceptively simple prose. Instead of perceiving the deportation to Poland as the next step toward death, the guests and Jewish townspeople, despite the forced return of all former Badenheimers to the town and many deaths among them, greet the filthy trains of death with joyful anticipation, seeing them as the vehicles of escape from their imprisonment.

Euphemistic symbolism names events and interprets actions with simultaneously figurative and literal images. The orange shadow that "gnaws at the geraniums" ominously predicts illness, death, and crematorium fires. As the vacationers compliment the thoroughness and efficiency of the Sanitation Department, they reflect both a historically documented pride in "their" country and the dramatically ironic efficiency of the technology and psychology used to exterminate them.

Because Badenheim is representative of Europe, each event symbolizes its larger European counterpart. Included are the initial acceptance of deprivations, the internal conflicts among Jews which hindered their leaving earlier, the carefree holiday illusions of security which clouded a clear image of reality, and finally, the misplaced optimism of a possible new "Golden Age," in which Jews would be fully enfranchised citizens, an idea which lulled them into believing that the evil would disappear with the orange shadow, leaden sky, and the cutting of the "creeping vines" which sealed the doors.

Other images which enhance the action include the forest, symbolizing freedom; the new blue fish placed into the tank, which are deceptively fun-loving during the day but which strew the tank with corpses at night; and finally the cliché reversal—instead of people being treated like dogs, dogs are treated like people and are killed.

Matching the simple naïveté of the unsuspecting but fearful Badenheimers is the deceptively simple writing style. Short, simple sentences predominate, but the reader must attend to every word, lest important ideas be lost. Subtleties shade and enhance nuances of meaning and reveal symbolic imagery requiring thought, and each subsequent reading opens new avenues for consideration.

*Critical Context*

*Badenheim 1939*, Aharon Appelfeld's first work published in English translation, introduced his writing to American readers. Although he had produced, in Hebrew, volumes of poetry, more than three hundred stories, and more than twenty volumes of fiction and essays, and although he emerged as a major Israeli author in the 1960's, he was largely unknown outside Israel until the publication of *Badenheim 1939* in English translation. Almost immediately, the novel was recognized as a new form of Holocaust literature, and each succeeding novel has enhanced the author's reputation.

The novel also established a set of images and techniques which Appelfeld has used in each of his subsequent novels, the most unusual being his treatment of the Holocaust, whereby he evokes its atrocities without direct allusion to the historical events that led to them, taking his readers "through the chill of enveloping horror without ever wallowing in the horror itself," as Stephen Lewis has put it.

Also introduced in *Badenheim 1939* are images found throughout Appelfeld's work—travel, trains, forests, abandoned children, lost mothers, ugly fathers, intermarriage, and the negative prewar Jewish image. All are woven into an allegorical but realistic world that intensifies the reader's vision of the inception of the Holocaust, and that have established Appelfeld as one of the most powerful voices of the Holocaust.

*Sources for Further Study*

Coffin, Edna Amir. "Appelfeld's Exceptional Universe: Harmony out of Chaos," in *Hebrew Studies*. XXIV (1983), pp. 85-98.
Lewis, Stephen. *Art out of Agony*, 1984.
Yudkin, Leon. "Appelfeld's Vision of the Past," in *Escape into Siege*, 1974.

*June H. Schlessinger*

# BAGA

*Author:* Robert Pinget (1919-     )
*Type of plot:* Fantasy
*Time of plot:* Unspecified
*Locale:* The fictional world of Fantoine and Agapa
*First published:* 1958 (English translation, 1967)

> *Principal characters:*
> ARCHITRUC, the king and narrator
> BAGA, his prime minister
> PISTON, one of the king's two musicians
> VIEILLE, the other royal musician
> CORNIFLET, the king's barber
> CONEGRUND, the queen of Doualia

## The Novel

So that his nephews, who will inherit his throne, will understand his life, King Architruc is writing his memoirs. Although his narrative is fragmented and even contradictory, one can piece together much of Architruc's life from the story that he tells. At twenty, he became king after his father was assassinated. On the day of his coronation, he named Baga to be his prime minister, because Baga gave him an antacid to soothe his churning stomach. At first, Architruc traveled around the country dispensing justice, but later he tired of all activity. He now believes that "what one has to find in life is a formula," and he has adopted one that suits him. He gets up at noon, does some simple exercises—which he hates because they require exertion—and examines his collections of pebbles, shells, leaves, and eyeglasses. Corniflet, the royal barber, arrives; after the daily shave, Architruc waters his pet plant, Ducky, dresses—always in white—and goes to the hall for his meal, which invariably consists of beef, followed by an omelet and a serving of cheese.

Anything that upsets this tedious existence threatens him, so when ambassadors from Novocardia arrive, he does not want to receive them. Not only will their visit disturb his routine, but also he suspects that they plan to cause trouble. Architruc's suspicions prove correct, for the Novocardians intend to occupy the valley of Chancheze, where Baga has been breeding rats. The rodents have been straying across the border and damaging Novocardian crops; despite repeated petitions to Architruc, nothing has been done to stop the depredations (probably because Baga has kept all these petitions from the king), and now Novocardia has determined to resolve the matter itself.

With the aid of the rats, Architruc defeats the invaders, but the ensuing war of attrition proves costly. Architruc's kingdom is almost depopulated, and he himself flees to the forest to live as a hermit. After a century, he tires of his loneliness; he then returns to his palace, pausing only to visit his two old musicians.

Soon, another intruder upsets the king's daily round of inactivity, though Conegrund, the queen of Doualia, is less bellicose than the Novocardians. Still, the royal treasury is hard-pressed to provide the pageantry and food she requires, and her voluptuousness even threatens to involve Architruc in love-making, until a black dishwasher satisfies her lust temporarily. The queen finds the dishwasher so satisfactory that she buys him for a thousand rupees, thus somewhat replenishing the king's coffers.

With this money, Architruc resolves to build a castle in the valley of Rouget. One day, while supervising the construction, he wanders off and finds Sister Louise. He joins her convent and even converts to being a woman, taking the name of Sister Angela. Together with Louise, he persuades a local girl, Mary, to join their religious order of Saint Fiduce. Mary and Sister Angela sleep together until the king regains his masculinity. Mary then loses interest in him, so Architruc once more returns to the palace to resume his former routine.

### The Characters

In the opening lines of the book, long before the narrator reveals his name, he asserts, "I am a king. Yes, a king of myself. Of my stagnation." These are the same words used by the nameless speaker in *Quelqu'un* (1965; *Someone*, 1984). Is he then the same person? Even after he begins to call himself Architruc, the reader can hardly be said to be enlightened, for Monsieur Truc is the French equivalent of Mr. What's-his-name, so that Architruc is simply King What's-his-name. Nor does his appellation inspire confidence, when one realizes that "truc" also means trick, making Architruc a master trickster, the archdeceiver.

One cannot even be certain whether Architruc is deceiving the reader or himself. He claims to be writing his memoirs so that his nephews will understand his life and presumably benefit from the account. Yet he adopts Rara, a dishwasher—the same one Conegrund buys?—as his heir, thereby subverting the purpose of his memoirs. He claims that he made Baga his prime minister out of gratitude, and in the course of the book he confers other honors upon him also: He presents Baga with the ribbon of the Order of St. Honoré, makes him his cousin, and proclaims him Count of Fidelity. Yet he also seems to distrust this man, stating that he named Baga his prime minister to lure him away from the Queen Mother, with whom Baga was having an affair.

Even more shadowy and enigmatic than Architruc is this prime minister. Is he merely the instrument of the king, the loyal umbrella carrier, or is he the power behind the throne? He knows more about the state of the country's military preparedness than the king, and he seems to have sought war with Novocardia. When Baga claims that only sixty people died in the war, should one trust his version of events or Architruc's? If Baga is such a schemer, why does he not take advantage of the king's lengthy absences to stage a coup? Or did he already engineer the one that put Architruc on the throne?

The identities of the other characters also pose challenges. The king cannot distinguish between his two musicians. In both name and character, Queen Conegrund closely resembles Voltaire's Cunegonde in *Candide: Ou, L'Optimisme* (1759; *Candide: Or, All for the Best*, 1759). Architruc's nameless father seems to be the king's double, not only in lack of name but also in behavior. The old king was killed because his subjects tire of his self-indulgent sloth. Significantly, in Pinget's play based on this novel, *Architruc* (1961), the title character is killed. Is one therefore reading a dead man's tale prepared for disinherited heirs?

## Themes and Meanings

All this confusion reflects the central concern of the book. Architruc's real audience is himself; he writes to learn exactly who he is. More accurately, he is trying to decide what role he wants to play. Baga tells him, "There's no 'life.' There's you. Your life. It's what you do, what you have done." Since reality is subjective, Architruc can shape his existence as he wishes. He can be hermit or nun, reigning monarch or deposed ruler. To write is to create a world; by changing the text, one can re-create existence.

Motivation is no clearer than identity in Robert Pinget's world. Just as Architruc tries to decide who he is, so, too, he seeks to understand why he behaves as he does. Is his choice of Baga as prime minister foolish impulse or shrewd policy? Does he want to live in a gaudy castle that dominates its surroundings or in a hut beside a spring? Does he want Mary to join the convent to rescue her from sensuality or to sleep with her?

At the center of the book, in the sixth chapter of eleven, Pinget casts even greater doubt on Architruc's ability to understand why he behaves as he does, and, by extension, on anyone else's capacity for self-knowledge. Here King Gnar converses with his adviser, a serpent, who says he made Architruc decide to leave the forest. Since Architruc is now bored, Gnar and the serpent agree to provide him with an occupation. Gnar therefore pulls a sock from the snake's bag and tosses it in the direction of the palace. The next morning Architruc tells Baga, "We're going to establish a sock store." Does some mysterious power control Architruc? Does Baga? Is Architruc king of himself, as he claims? *Baga* is a book of questions, fascinating because they have so many answers, or maybe none at all.

## Critical Context

In a lecture in 1970, Pinget observed that his characters and setting "exist not as defined but as in the process of definition"; he uses what he calls "continual metamorphosis" to mirror the uncertainty and instability of the late twentieth century. Architruc assumes numerous avatars in the course of the novel, as does his domain of Fantoine and Agapa. The valley of Chancheze in Pinget's previous work, *Graal flibuste* (1956), had contained a temple; now that building has yielded to a factory for manufacturing rat pelts.

While these constant alterations serve a serious thematic purpose, they also parody conventional genres. *Graal flibuste* rewrites the novel of quest as a journey to nowhere. Similarly, *Baga* assaults autobiographical fiction by presenting a narrator so unreliable that nothing is certain—not his age, not his sex, not even his actions or the reasons for them. *Baga* also shares the surrealism of Pinget's earlier books, in which a steeple (clocher) may be a coachman (coacher) and a cucumber may choose to get a suntan.

At the same time, this book's search for reality anticipates *Clope au dossier* (1961) and subsequent novels by Pinget in which various characters try to piece together reality from clues that refuse to yield their secrets. *Baga* thus occupies an important place in Pinget's canon, both epitomizing his earlier work and foreshadowing even the 1971 play *Identité, suivi de Abel et Bela*, which, as its name suggests, once more explores the problem of self-knowledge.

*Sources for Further Study*
Bann, Stephen. "Robert Pinget," in *The London Magazine*. IV (October 7, 1964), pp. 22-35.
Cismarie, Alfred. "Robert Pinget: An Introduction," in *American Benedictine Reivew*. XIX (June, 1968), pp. 203-210.
Henkels, Robert M., Jr. *Robert Pinget: The Novel as Quest*, 1979.
Knapp, Bettina, ed. *French Novelists Speak Out*, 1976.
Mercier, Vivian. *The New Novel from Queneau to Pinget*, 1971.
Oppenheim, Lois, ed. *Three Decades of the French New Novel*, 1986.

*Joseph Rosenblum*

# THE BARK TREE

*Author:* Raymond Queneau (1903-1976)
*Type of plot:* Antistory
*Time of plot:* The early twentieth century
*Locale:* The outskirts of Paris
*First published: Le Chiendent*, 1933 (English translation, 1968)

> *Principal characters:*
> MME CLOCHE, a lecherous, meddling matron who gives poor
>     advice on many subjects
> BÉBÉ TOUTOUT, a malicious and violent dwarf dedicated to
>     evil
> OLD TAUPE, a miser who lives in a hut beside a suburban
>     chemical factory and sells junk
> ERNESTINE, a young waitress who marries Old Taupe and
>     hopes that he has hidden a fortune somewhere
> ETIENNE MARCEL, an officeworker who is nearly run over one
>     day while en route to his place of employment, the Audit
>     Bank
> THÉO, a badly behaved child with a depraved interest in
>     women
> PIERRE LE GRAND, a cab driver and amateur philosopher
> NARCENSE, an unemployed saxophone player and would-be
>     writer
> SATURNIN BELHÔTEL, the keeper of a cheap hotel

## The Novel

Raymond Queneau's *The Bark Tree* is among the first antinovels and, as such, neither attempts to tell a carefully plotted story with beginning, middle, and end, nor strives to be coherent. In addition, it does not include well-developed characters or offer readers any moral or philosophical conclusion about life. *The Bark Tree* should be considered as an energetic, vibrant assault on convention, in which people are either things or real human beings. In many ways, the novel is a sustained joke about the random, precarious lives people lead and the ever-present threat of chaos and destruction with which they learn to live. Queneau, like James Joyce, uses language of his own invention and street slang to make more vivid what he has to say. By avoiding refined speech, he lets the characters be themselves: ordinary workers living in an ordinary suburb of a modern city.

Instead of providing a well-constructed plot, Queneau gives the reader a number of actions which may not be related. Etienne Marcel's narrow escape from death is observed by Pierre Le Grand, who informs Saturnin Belhôtel, who tells others. Meanwhile, Mme Cloche sees a rope with a noose tied at its end in a garden and wonders who left it there. Mme Pigeonnier flirts with the boy, Théo, while Etienne has a nightmare in which his mother wears a beard to serve boiled eggs. Yet Etienne does think about the rope (which he also saw) and wonders whether someone has tried to hang little Théo or a dog.

Throughout the novel, seemingly unrelated events somehow become connected, if only tenuously, by the links the characters forge between those events in their minds. Though their lives become accidently intertwined, the characters take an interest in what happens to one another, even though that interest is neither keen nor lasting. Queneau's people like to conjecture about others and to reconstruct events happening to others in order to pass the time and avoid ennui.

In their search to quell boredom the characters thrive on sensation. For example, when Ernestine, a poor waitress, marries Old Taupe, an equally penniless junk dealer of repulsive habits, the event causes much amusement and gossip for Mme Cloche and her fellows. They hope that, after marrying Old Taupe, Ernestine will find that he has stuffed thousands of franc notes under his mattress or in a tin can. Yet when no money has been uncovered, Ernestine's "friends" quickly lose interest in her. Only on her deathbed does Ernestine regain their attention, but after she dies, they go out in search of new gossip. Old Taupe's death is a nonevent and is completely ignored because it offers no surprises; he was only useful as a foil to Ernestine, and after her death, he becomes a bore. In the end, his hut is unceremoniously dismantled and burned, just as his body is tossed into a pauper's grave and forgotten.

Ultimately, the barren lives of Queneau's characters, their search for thrills, their love of novelties, and their selfishness lead them to indulge in the biggest thrill of all: war. At the end of the novel, an absurd war breaks out between the French and a group called the Etruscans. A motley collection of frenzied, yet purposeless, assaults and counterassaults, the war lurches on, until it degenerates into total farce as the eight remaining French soldiers surrender to a demoralized thirty surviving Etruscans. This war—which began because Queen Orlini of the Etruscans became angry with Anatole, King of the French, over a game of bezique—ends because that seems to be the thing to do. After all the bloodshed, the battlefield nightmare, the diseases of the trenches, and the massive trauma occasioned by the killing, it is apparent to the survivors that the conflict meant nothing. In fact, the French hold a banquet to celebrate the war's end, and the participants drunkenly banter with Mme Cloche about the weather and her love life.

At the end of *The Bark Tree*, Etienne and Mme Cloche separate after an argument about needing to relive life near a town, much like the one mentioned at the beginning of the novel, where flattened people go through only the motions of living. Thus, Queneau, while writing a novel seemingly devoid of structure, creates a plot in which the beginning and end flow into each other. In this merciless universe, Queneau appears to say, madness and violence will build until another absurd conflict arises. This slaughter will lead to a cessation of hostilities, which in turn will lead to truce, peace, and building resentment, which will lead again to war, *ad nauseam*.

## The Characters

Etienne is the most frequently mentioned character in *The Bark Tree*. His near brush with death helps him turn from puppet into person; he provides valuable commentary on the predicaments of the other characters; and he survives until the end of the book, when most of the others have vanished. Like the others, he is a common sort of person who does not cause events but to whom things happen. He attempts to make sense out of the meaningless events that form his life yet never manages to do so. Friends such as the innkeeper, Saturnin, and Mme Cloche simply confuse him further with their eccentric explanations of circumstances. As one of society's "little people," he finds himself at the mercy of others, especially the King of France, who involves the French in the absurd war. One of the sole survivors of the war, Etienne has no idea why he was spared, nor does he understand why the war ended: It has happened, he has survived, and now he will leave for home.

Pierre is another important character, but he is far more aware of the discontinuity of life around him. Instead of dwelling upon such inconsequential items as potato peelers and ducks (the stuff of Etienne's musings), Pierre thinks about the nature of reality and decides that it is irrational. In fact, Pierre is the one who notices that the little banker, Etienne, undergoes a transformation from nonentity to person after the near accident which left another person dead. Pierre's artistic power of observation allows Etienne to become a true, rounded character. As he watches Etienne in the train car, the cab driver imagines the banker changing from a flat cutout to a moving, breathing creation—his own. By doing so, Pierre takes the place of Queneau, his own creator.

Bébé Toutout, unlike Etienne and Pierre, is repulsive. A wizened dwarf, he tries to make others unhappy and thrives on their confusion and fear. Among other things, he is a child molester, swindler, braggart, liar, pornographer, and thug. As an agent of evil, he makes an already unstable world even more unpredictable.

Mme Cloche, the gossipmonger, is another negative character, one whose life is given over to lewd thoughts and bawdy jokes. She pushes young Ernestine into marriage with Old Taupe, hoping somehow to benefit from the fortune she is sure Ernestine will find in Old Taupe's mattress. When Ernestine marries the ugly miser and discovers that there is no hidden treasure, Mme Cloche maliciously nags the girl about her "folly," As the girl lies dying, Mme Cloche gives her only ten minutes in which to tell her life story.

Like Mme Cloche and Bébé, young Théo is an agent of destruction. A boy whom Saturnin would like to hang, Théo is a constant irritant to most of the novel's characters, as he lusts after older women, tortures animals, and steals. This young menace stirs up the others with his antics, if nothing else providing them with an incentive to forget temporarily their boredom.

Ernestine is a foil to Bébé, Théo, Mme Cloche, and the other, minor negative characters in *The Bark Tree*, for she is innocent, caring, and sensitive. She alone elicits compassion from the other characters, when she dies at such an early age. Her soliloquy, in which she talks about the random things which made up her life and about how disposable she is, resonates throughout *The Bark Tree*. Her anguish and sensitivity, as well as her acute self-awareness, make her a kind of modern martyr who suffers a meaningless death after living a pathetically brief and absurd life. The memory of her death stays with the friends present at the time.

*Themes and Meanings*

In *The Bark Tree*, the disconnected, violent lives of modern men create disconnected, violent times, which in turn create even more violent, disconnected lives. As the boredom and frustration build inside the characters, they find no outlet for these feelings, until at last they turn to war. A disregard for their own flattened lives leads Queneau's characters to devalue the worth of their fellows, so much that they wish to humiliate or destroy them. Ernestine's death can easily be forgotten, and the death of Potice, a man killed in a street accident, can be made into a source of entertainment. Nothing remains of those who have died to mark their passage through this world.

The lack of connection between characters creates sufficient inner turmoil to start the ridiculous war between the French and the Etruscans, when thousands are killed for absolutely no reason. The war, like every other event in the novel, is a diversion, although longer lasting, that passes the time.

A second theme is that of the deadly sameness of modern life. At the beginning of *The Bark Tree*, unnamed characters go through the motions of life like so many marionettes. They follow certain motions, until death ceases the charade. Only original thinking or the gift of some unexpected event such as Etienne's near death can propel these people into true life, which has a few major diversions or adventures, if not much meaning. As Ernestine dies, she recalls her life, telling the others gathered around her of the inconsequential events of her earthly existence. Her only adventure—the only thing that gave her life some flair—was her ill-advised marriage to the lecherous Old Taupe, but at least she had an adventure. Her death, Queneau hints, is similar to the later, meaningless deaths of the other characters.

*Critical Context*

*The Bark Tree* was Queneau's first and most influential novel. It has become well-known as the forerunner of the modern avant-garde novel and as one of the first works to use random events, minimal structure, and experimental language. His other works include *Un Rude Hiver* (1939; *A Hard Winter*, 1948), *Pierrot mon ami* (1942; *Pierrot*, 1950), *Le Dimanche de la vie* (1952; *The Sunday of Life*, 1976), and *Zazie dans le métro* (1959; *Zazie in the Metro*, 1960). Queneau also wrote a parody of traditional literary forms entitled *Exercices de style* (1947; *Excercises in Style*, 1958).

The wild humor of *The Bark Tree* is found in all Queneau's work. He delighted in manipulating language, reforming it to create new words or reshaping words to take on new forms, and *The Bark Tree* was his first attempt at achieving a break with literary convention and the French novelistic tradition.

Queneau also carefully hid any structure so as to give the reader, at first glance, a sense that *The Bark Tree* is formless, a collage of often unrelated elements. In so doing, he imitated the patterns and rhythms of life. Thus, all of his later works bear the stamp of seeming aimlessness found in *The Bark Tree* because Queneau believed that no one can reduce reality to a formula. Yet there is structure in Queneau's novels, hidden though it is: Events are connected to other events, however tenuously, and people's lives impinge upon the lives of others.

Queneau's characters helped change the twentieth century novel. They are at once both cardboard cutouts and memorable personages, aimless and strangely meaningful. The figures are not realistic, for they are not developed as fully as were the characters of Charles Dickens or Fyodor Dostoevski. More type than individual, the Queneau character nevertheless is a vibrant creation, full of life and enthusiasm.

*Sources for Further Study*
Guicharnaud, Jacques. *Raymond Queneau*, 1965.
Mercier, Vivian. *The New Novel from Queneau to Pinget*, 1971.
Shorley, Christopher. *Queneau's Fiction*, 1985.
Thiher, Allen. *Raymond Queneau*, 1985.

*John D. Raymer*

# BÀRNABO OF THE MOUNTAINS

*Author:* Dino Buzzati (Dino Buzzati Traverso, 1906-1972)
*Type of plot:* Psychological parable
*Time of plot:* The early twentieth century
*Locale:* The mountains around the village of San Nicola in northern Italy and a
farm in the valley
*First published: Bàrnabo delle montagne,* 1933 (English translation, 1984)

>    *Principal characters:*
>    Bàrnabo, a young forest-guard
>    Bertòn, also a forest-guard, friendly with Bàrnabo
>    Other forest-guards

*The Novel*
*Bàrnabo of the Mountains* follows the experience of one man, in his relationship with the forbidding but fascinating mountains, through a crisis of
honor and cowardice in the course of carrying out his duties as a forest-
guard, and his subsequent deeply felt need to prove and redeem himself.
Dino Buzzati openly acknowledged the influence of other writers, among
them Joseph Conrad, especially Conrad's *Lord Jim* (1900). This influence is
particularly strong in *Bàrnabo of the Mountains,* in the theme of redemption
and in the relationship of the characters with the elements and with their
environment.

Buzzati's novella opens with a fantasy map of the area and a precise
description of the setting in which the forest-guards live. They are moving
their headquarters into the "New House," built because their previous base,
the "Old Mardens' House," is falling into disrepair. One of their duties is to
guard the "Polveriera," or "Powder-Magazine," a hut nestled in the rocks. It
was built during a road-building project through the mountains as a place to
store explosives. The project abandoned, the explosives remained, and more
ammunition was added as the authorities recognized its safe location conveniently close to the border. In the course of the move to the New House, the
head forest-guard, an old man full of stories about the inaccessibility and
threat of the mountains and the people who died in them, is killed by mountain bandits. Thus, from the beginning, human temporality is emphasized in
opposition to the timelessness of the mountains. Del Colle, the old forest-
guard, is buried in the mountains, and his grave, with his plumed cap nailed
to the rock, remains as a symbol of man's affinity with this environment.

Buzzati places the reader in a world that combines myth and reality. The
towering mountain peaks of the map owe more to Grimm's fairy tales than to
any map of northern Italy, although the setting described is recognizable as
the mountains of the Alpine region around Belluno, where Buzzati was

born. The "bandits" belong as much to the world of opera as to that of reality. The forest-guards (*guardiaboschi*, a semimilitary organization responsible for the maintenance of order in the mountains and forest regions) reflect a code of honor as reminiscent of the Old French *chansons de geste* as of twentieth century militarism.

A hunt for the bandits fails to unearth any trace of them, but the foresters' interest does not abate. One day Bertòn, on guard duty, sees a column of smoke. He tells Bàrnabo and the two reconnoiter on their own. They do not find the bandits, but Bàrnabo rescues a wounded crow. On their return, Bàrnabo and Bertòn become separated. Back at the base, the bandits are discovered raiding the Polveriera. Bàrnabo, instinctively about to join his colleagues, is halted by another bandit armed with a rifle and stops. He is afraid. Bertòn, coming from another direction, joins in the fight and is wounded in one leg. The bandits escape safely, taking powder and ammunition. Bàrnabo, ashamed of his cowardice, wanders back into the woods, then returns, hours later, feigning ignorance at what has happened.

He is not shamed publicly for cowardice, but he is dismissed for abandoning his post. Bertòn covers for him by insisting that he was not there at all, but there is a certain ambiguity as to whether Bertòn knows or guesses what really happened and whether the Inspector knows. It may be only Bàrnabo's guilty conscience which makes him wonder, and the feeling of guilt which oppresses him.

Followed by the crow he rescued, Bàrnabo leaves the mountains and settles on his cousin's farm in the distant plains. Time passes. The crow becomes ill. Weakened, it flies off into the clouds toward the invisible mountains. Bàrnabo is ashamed at the sense of desolation he feels at its loss: the breaking of the final, tenuous link with the rocks, woods, and peaks he left behind in a past which he cannot recapture.

As the result of an unexpected visit from Bertòn, who has left the service of his own choice, Bàrnabo, five years after being dismissed, returns to San Nicola. Misunderstanding Bertòn's casual invitation, Bàrnabo takes out his forest-guard's uniform, now dusty, worn, and covered with moth holes, which he carefully mends before anyone has the chance to see them.

Things have changed in San Nicola. Following more raids by the bandits, the explosives and ammunition have been removed from the Polveriera to the nearest military post, thus relieving the forest-guards of this duty. The New House has been abandoned, the forest-guards billeted in the village and incorporated into the *guardiani communali*. Bàrnabo, by devious hints, elicits the offer of the position of a sort of caretaker of the empty New House. The other forest-guards emphasize the loneliness of the post, while promising frequent visits to him, and especially one visit on a specific date on which the brigands had defiantly promised to return.

In the New House, Bàrnabo finds things the same and yet different. He is painfully conscious of not being a forest-guard as before but one of their employees. He finds a certain tranquillity in the familiar woods but remains continually haunted by the idea of redeeming himself, of canceling out his past cowardice.

On the promised date, Bàrnabo makes extensive preparations for the expected forest-guards, who do not appear. He understands then that they have fooled him, that they never intended to visit him. Unlike Bàrnabo, they seem to be able to break away from the mountains casually and completely. On the following day, Bàrnabo goes to the Polveriera, and beyond it. Four bandits keep their appointment, and at first Bàrnabo is delighted at the victory within his grasp. He can shoot them and absolve himself of his earlier cowardice. When he observes them more closely, however, he sees that they are old men, thin, worn, and he does nothing—not out of fear or cowardice this time but because the need to kill them belongs to the past, like so many other events. To the present belongs a sense of joy and tranquillity, here in the mountains bathed in sunlight. Those men, he is certain, will never return: This is their last visit.

He returns to the deserted New House, empties his rifle, throws open the windows. Time, he knows, will flow evenly over him as over the mountains. While the night passes slowly, he stands in the doorway with his rifle, thinking he can hear, as in the past, the sentinel pacing near the Polveriera. Yet he knows the mountains are still and silent.

### The Characters

Buzzati's characters are invariably closer to being types or symbols than real people with individual characteristics or psychological depth. Unlike the other forest-guards, Bàrnabo is not given a last name in the novel; in the roll call of the forest-guards, he is the last: "they call him only by his name and he will later become Bàrnabo of the mountains." This lack of a family name emphasizes his isolation, the gap existing between Bàrnabo and the other forest-guards, the villagers of San Nicola, and later, the nebulous figures of his cousin and the other farm workers. His overwhelming characteristic is his close affinity with nature, with the mountains, which can be interpreted as the symbol of spiritual ascent toward an ideal. The initial punishment for dishonor is expulsion and exile. Once this exile has run its course, Bàrnabo can overcome and expiate his fault only by returning to the mountains.

The other forest-guards are equally undefined, lacking psychological delineation. They are figures that surround the central character. Bertòn, his closest friend, plays the role of Oliver to Bàrnabo's Roland: a companion and foil in the qualities he exhibits. Molo, a very minor character, serves to highlight Bàrnabo's heroic sensitivity and generosity when the latter fails to win a fight so as not to humiliate Molo. Montani is the forest-guard who encounters a brigand in the dark, in the deserted Mardens' House—an encounter narrated to Bàrnabo by Bertòn. Although the forest-guards have individual names, ultimately most of them are not much more clearly defined than the anonymous brigands who oppose them. Much more distinctive is the setting: the mountains in their beauty, in their variety of moods, whether friendly or menacing, and in their timelessness.

### Themes and Meanings

The theme of death and decay dominates this novella, from the first chapter with the anecdotes of people who have been lost and have died in the mountains to Bàrnabo's last sighting of the famed bandits as thin old men. Del Colle's grave, with his plumed hat nailed above it, is referred to at different stages in the story as a recurring thought haunting Bàrnabo. The Polveriera, constant reminder of the road that was never built, is a concrete symbol of the vanity of human aspiration and endeavor.

The novel juxtaposes two notions of time. On the one hand, there is the time which is measured by human standards: the shape on the wall betraying how long it has been since the rifles were last taken down, substantiated by the rust in the barrels; or the moth holes in Bàrnabo's uniform. On the other hand, there is the timelessness of the mountains and of nature, which dwarfs human experience.

The present is gauged as a failure against the aspirations of the past, but there is also a third dimension of time: the future. "It is today that time passes," thinks Del Colle, "tomorrow it has not yet passed." The future exists either within the limits of human aspirations, invariably to be disappointed, or in the endless permanence of nature. It is in this latter dimension that Bàrnabo, having realized the futility of any human gesture, finds peace and fulfillment.

### Critical Context

*Bàrnabo of the Mountains* was Buzzati's first published novel. In 1933, the Italian literary scene was already heavily influenced by Fascism, which encouraged a combination of rural peasant values and classical, mythical heroism. Buzzati, however, exploring his own internal world, was unaffected by the political developments and in no way reflected his historical situation. Neither *Bàrnabo of the Mountains* nor the novella which followed, *Il segreto del Bosco Vecchio* (1935; the secret of the old wood), attracted much attention from the critics. In its surrealistic quality of moral fable, *Bàrnabo of the Mountains* was too far removed from the specific reality required of literature at that time. On the other hand, it remained totally inoffensive to the regime and therefore aroused no opposition.

Buzzati is not totally divorced from reality. The setting of the novel is realistic, as are the characters. The surreality, or absurd element, derives from the atmosphere of anxiety and mystery. The brigands, for example, while on

one level real robbers or possibly smugglers, are invested with an almost supernatural aura.

*Bàrnabo of the Mountains* appears in English in a collection of Buzzati's
writings translated by Lawrence Venuti, *The Siren* (1984). This first novel
clearly announces the elements of existential angst intermingled with fantasy
parable which will continue through Buzzati's later work, especially in *Il
deserto dei Tartari* (1940; *The Tartar Steppe*, 1952), considered by many to be
Buzzati's major work.

*Sources for Further Study*
Gianfranceschi, Fausto. *Dino Buzzati*, 1967.
Laganà Gion, Antonella. *Dino Buzzati: Un autore da rileggere*, 1983.
*The New York Times Book Review*. Review. LXXXIX (October 28, 1984),
    p. 32.
Panafieu, Yves. "Aspetti storici, morali e politici del discorso sull'impo-
    tenza," in *Dino Buzzati*, 1982. Edited by Alvise Fontanella.
*Publishers Weekly*. Review. CCXXVI (August, 1984), pp. 75-76.
Spera, Francesco. "Modelli narrativi del primo Buzzati," in *Dino Buzzati*,
    1982. Edited by Alvise Fontanella.
Veronese-Arslan, Antonia. *Invito alla lettura di Buzzati*, 1974.

                                                                    *Ada Coe*

# THE BARON IN THE TREES

*Author:* Italo Calvino (1923-1985)
*Type of plot:* Fantasy
*Time of plot:* The late eighteenth century
*Locale:* Ombrosa, a fictional estate in northern Italy
*First published: Il barone rampante*, 1957 (English translation, 1959)

> *Principal characters:*
> COSIMO PIOVASCO DI RONDÒ, the protagonist, heir to the
> estate of Ombrosa
> BIAGGIO PIOVASCO DI RONDÒ, the narrator, Cosimo's younger
> brother
> ARMINIO PIOVASCO DI RONDÒ, the Baron of Ombrosa, father
> of Cosimo and Biaggio
> CORRADINA DI RONDÒ, the Baroness of Ombrosa, nicknamed
> "THE GENERALESSA"
> BATTISTA DI RONDÒ, their eccentric daughter, sister of Cosimo
> and Biaggio

*The Novel*

Set in the peaceful valley of Ombrosa during the period of intellectual and social ferment which characterized the Age of Reason, Italo Calvino's *The Baron in the Trees* relates the story of Cosimo Piovasco di Rondò, heir to the immense estate of the Piovasci. Cosimo rebels against the rule-burdened atmosphere in which he is reared by climbing into the trees on his family's estate at the age of twelve and remaining there for the rest of his life. His refusal to eat the snail soup and main course of snails prepared by his sister Battista is the issue which sends him into the trees, but he soon decides to make them his permanent home.

Cosimo's family makes a few perfunctory attempts to get him down. His mother, nicknamed "the Generalessa" because of her Austrian military ancestry, worries at first about Cosimo's falling. (His brother Biaggio, who becomes both observer of and commentator on Cosimo's unusual way of life, finds this concern ironic, noting that it would not have bothered their mother in the least to see her sons under cannon fire.) Eventually, she rather enjoys catching sight of Cosimo in one tree or another through her telescope, and she sends him messages with her military signal flags.

Cosimo's varied adventures in the trees make for enjoyable reading. At first these are boyish pranks, such as throwing a piece of bark at the boys' pompous tutor, the Abbé Fauchelfleur, or hair-raising encounters with the "fruit thieves," neighborhood boys who steal from the lush orchards in the area. One experience, however, has a lasting effect on Cosimo: meeting Violante (Viola) Ondariva. Their families have not spoken for years, but within minutes they are fast friends, and Viola is taken with Cosimo's unusual way of life. She even helps him escape from the fruit thieves in the guise of "Sinforosa."

Though Cosimo is a solitary figure, he does not avoid people. Indeed, as he matures, he provides useful services such as delivering messages. His agility allows him to pass easily from one tree to another, and, since he is bound by neither walls nor fences, he can travel great distances quickly. When huntsmen lose their quarry, he directs them to the fox. His perspective allows him to see which streams are best for fishing, and he often dangles his line from a convenient low-hanging branch. He finds it difficult but does, at least at first, attend High Mass by kneeling on a limb which is at the same height as a large church window.

Cosimo becomes close friends with his father's illegitimate brother, Cavilier Enea Silvio Carrega, who is also the family lawyer. Carrega is a secret beekeeper with beehives scattered throughout the valley. Cosimo helps him to gather bees and to devise a grandiose but unrealized scheme for irrigating the neighboring farmland. It does not bother Cosimo that the irrigation project never comes to pass. He realizes that tending the hollowed-out tree trunks that would carry the water would eventually prove a burden, binding him more closely to the earth. Escaping the burdens of everyday life was, after all, one of Cosimo's primary reasons for living in the trees.

Carrega has lived a life of secret resentment for many years. The Piovasco estate, where he lived as permanent houseguest, is the grandest in the valley, but no share of this wealth could ever be his since he is illegitimate. His smuggling activities, eventually revealed by Cosimo in a way that does not tarnish Carrega's reputation, represent a desperate attempt at revenge. Cosimo, by contrast, feels none of these burdens. Though heir to the Piovasco estate and fortune, and though reconciled at last with his father, he assigns all of his rights to his mother and brother. In return he receives a stipend adequate for his own maintenance, regular consignments of books by the authors he most enjoys, and the affection of many who live in the region.

In many respects Cosimo enjoys a surprisingly normal life in the trees. Though alone, he is rarely lonely. He meets a kindred spirit in Ursula, daughter of a noble exile from Charles III's Spain, Federico Alonso Sánchez y Tobasco. Federico's court has been granted permission to pass through northern Italy but only on the condition that they do not set foot on the earth. The entire entourage thus becomes tree-dwellers, though, unlike Cosimo, not by choice. Ursula desires to remain with Cosimo in the trees even after her family receives permission to return to Spain. She obediently, though reluctantly, accompanies them at last. Cosimo accepts this philosophically, as he does all human relationships, recognizing that all things end and pass away, even what one most treasures.

Cosimo lives in the trees well beyond the age of sixty-five and does not come down though he becomes old and infirm. His death, as unusual as his life, presumably occurs when he grabs hold of an anchor fastened to a passing hot-air balloon. Thus Cosimo's body, though of the earth, never returns to it again.

## The Characters

All of the characters in Calvino's novel are eccentric. The plainest and most conventional of them is Biaggio, the narrator. Biaggio profits handsomely from his brother Cosimo's life in the trees, for he becomes heir to the estate; nevertheless, Biaggio clearly regrets his own comparatively plain life, though he recognizes that he never would have been able to make a similar choice. Biaggio is, like many, successful by the world's standards but conscious of what might have been.

The boys' father, Arminio, the elder baron, has as his great ambition the regaining of his lapsed title, Duke of Ombrosa. His obsession with "genealogies and successions and family rivalries and alliances" contrasts markedly with Cosimo's nonchalance. Cavilier Carrega, Arminio's illegitimate brother, is only too well aware that though he lives amid Ombrosa's luxury none of its wealth will ever belong to him. He relies upon deceit (going so far as to steal food from the family table) and smuggling as revenge against his fate.

Arminio supports the Austrian monarchy, and this makes him conservative to the point of being politically reactionary. His wife, Corradina di Rondò, whose father, Konrad von Kurtewitz, commanded the troops which occupied the Genoese Republic, is a strange combination of the maternal and the military. Battista di Rondò, Cosimo's sister, inherits her mother's flair for the dramatic. She is given to spiteful scenes and retaliations. Cosimo's refusal to eat the snail soup she has prepared causes him to be sent from the table and provokes his escape to the trees. It is not Battista's snails but his family's aristocratic shallowness which Cosimo actually rejects.

## Themes and Meanings

Trees are archetypal symbols of knowledge and of life, as noted by the Swiss psychologist Carl Gustav Jung. Climbing the great variety of trees to be found in the vicinity of Ombrosa, trees which stretch, as Biaggio notes, as far as the border of Spain, is a means of perceiving the varied world at a comfortable distance. In other words, Cosimo remains in his world without being of it. Like the boy in Robert Frost's poem "Birches," Cosimo is "worldweary" and the trees provide a new perspective on familiar things.

Cosimo rightly senses the intellectual and political ferment of his times, and he realizes the essential stagnation of his family's way of life. They are anchored to a huge and isolated estate, and pursue, even though with eccentric élan, wealth, titles, and mundane comforts. It is at first Cosimo's natural rebelliousness, a reflection of the Age of Reason in which he lives, which causes him to vow never to descend from the trees. As he grows older, however, and begins to read avidly the authors of the exciting period in which he lives, especially Voltaire and Denis Diderot, he sees that life in the trees represents a symbolic as well as a literal escape from the everyday concerns which encumber the potentially rich business of simply living. Cosimo makes it a point of honor never to descend to the earth, to become entangled again with the sordid pursuits of those who live there.

Biaggio notes at the beginning of his narrative that he often played in the trees with his brother, though he was never as comfortable there as Cosimo. Biaggio is also aware, in later life, that his existence has never been as rich as that of Cosimo, primarily because he was unable to take the risk of living above the world's concerns. Though he becomes Baron of Ombrosa because Cosimo resigns claim to the title, Biaggio sees his life as less successful in the truest sense.

*Critical Context*

All of Calvino's works reflect an interest in fantasy and the fantastic. The unusual feature of *The Baron in the Trees* is that it reflects the supposedly contemporary idea of escape from an oppressive world against the intellectual and political ferment of the late eighteenth century. This was the period of the French philosophes, Deism, which claimed that God created the world but takes no active part in running it, and the American and French Revolutions.

In his later writings, Calvino played variations on fantastic themes drawn from semiology, the study of signs. *Le cosmicomiche* (1965; *Cosmicomics*, 1968) considers the relationship of picture and meaning. *Le città invisibili* (1972; *Invisible Cities*, 1974) reimagines Marco Polo—who, in Calvino's rendering, uses evocative language in the most precise way possible to describe cities which only he has seen to Kubla Khan, the Mongol emperor of China. *Il castello dei destini incrociati* (1969, 1973; *The Castle of Crossed Destinies*, 1977) employs speechless tellers of tales who use tarot cards to tell the stories of their lives, and *Se una notte d'inverno un viaggiatore* (1979; *If on a Winter's Night a Traveler*, 1981) presents numerous variations on a single event, a novel read with pages of another work mistakenly bound within it. Calvino's creative works are often read alongside his countryman Umberto Eco's essays on semiotics. Eco is himself the author of the semiotic mystery *Il nome della rosa* (1980; *The Name of the Rose*, 1983).

*Sources for Further Study*

Calvino, Italo. *The Uses of Literature*, 1986.
Carter, Albert Howard. *Italo Calvino: Metamorphoses of Fantasy*, 1987.
Eco, Umberto. *Travels in Hyper Reality: Essays*, 1986. Edited by Helen Wolff and Kurt Wolff.

Olken, I. T. *With Pleated Eye and Garnet Wing: Symmetries of Italo Calvino*, 1984.

Perosa, Sergio. "The Heirs of Calvino and the Eco Effect," in *The New York Times Book Review*. XCII (August 16, 1987), p. 1.

*Robert J. Forman*

# THE BASS SAXOPHONE

*Author:* Josef Škvorecký (1924-      )
*Type of plot:* Satire
*Time of plot:* A late summer and early autumn during the Nazi occupation of Czechoslovakia
*Locale:* A *fin de siècle* hotel in Kostelec, a Czech town in the Protectorate of Bohemia and Moravia
*First published: Bassaxofon*, 1967 (English translation, 1977)

> *Principal characters:*
>> THE NARRATOR, an eighteen-year-old jazz enthusiast who seeks political and artistic freedom
>> LOTHAR KINZE, the leader of a small German orchestra that roams through towns and villages along the war's sidelines entertaining the German communities throughout occupied Europe
>> THE GIRL FROM MOABIT, (SNOW WHITE), the vocal soloist in Kinze's orchestra, a beautiful girl with a Swedish face and blonde hair falling to her shoulders like broken swan's wings
>> HORST HERMANN KÜHL, the omnipotent Nazi authority
>> THE BASS SAXOPHONE PLAYER, a mysterious sleeping figure in a hotel room, who reclaims his place in the orchestra

## The Novel

This novella has an autobiographical significance, for when he was sixteen or seventeen, Josef Škvorecký played a tenor saxophone rather badly for a band called Red Music—modeled after a Prague group called Blue Music. He and his companions, living in the Nazi Protectorate of Bohemia and Moravia, did not know that in jazz, blue was not a color. Although the name itself had no political connotations, their music did, for jazz was condemned by the Nazis for being a creation of American black musicians and Jews. Jazz had to go underground, becoming, in effect, a protest against the Nazi's restrictions on creativity.

In *The Bass Saxophone*, Škvorecký tells the powerful, apocalyptic story of a jazz-obsessed lad, the narrator, whose passion for this "forbidden music" carries him into the center of an almost hallucinatory experience. Written in the first person, the novella shifts between the present and the past, mixing personal reminiscence with social and political history, fact with symbol, in a stream-of-consciousness dynamic.

As the story begins, at twilight, the young narrator is near a hotel in Kostelec, a town occupied by the Germans. A frail old man struggles off a gray bus with a big black case, and when the clasps fall open, the narrator sees a monstrous bass saxophone. He is urged to help the old man carry the instrument to a hotel room, where a man sleeps with his mouth open. Suddenly, the boy finds himself locked in the room, with nothing for company except the sleeping figure and a solitary fly which is about to die in the bell of the bass saxophone. The boy hears shouts from an adjacent room and recognizes the voice of Horst Hermann Kühl, the Nazi chief of Kostelec—the very man who had tyrannically confiscated one of the narrator's American jazz records some time earlier. Unable to contain his curiosity, the narrator plays the bass saxophone, frightening himself with its powerful, primitive, melancholy sound. The voice of Kühl is silenced, but the sleeping man does not awake.

The narrator is then surprised by a haggard little fat man and a procession of circuslike freaks. These characters turn out to be Lothar Kinze and his traveling orchestra. They offer to allow the lad a practice session with the fascinating saxophone. The narrator accompanies the orchestra to an auditorium, where he discovers in playing with the group that they lack imagination and genius. He is startled when Kinze and the blonde girl, the girl from Moabit, who is the band's vocalist, plead with him to play in the concert that evening, despite the evident threat this poses to both the narrator and the orchestra should the boy's real identity become known to the Nazis. Kinze disguises the narrator in the orchestra's garish green and purple uniform with white shirt and orange bow tie. After the practice, the narrator shares a meal with the orchestra, whose members launch into personal anecdotes which have a strange reality to counterpoint the dreamlike state of their collective appearance as a Spike Jones comic band.

At the concert, packed with Nazi dignitaries, the narrator ruminates about his own presence in this world of absurdity, danger, and disguise. Suddenly, he feels a hand on his shoulder and a loud, hoarse voice ordering him backstage. He recognizes the man as the sleeping figure from the hotel room. This stranger is the real bass saxophonist, come to reclaim his position in the orchestra. The boy listens as the bass saxophonist plays and is transported into a jazz hallucination, from which he is awakened by the abrupt arrival of Kühl. The boy is recognized by Kühl, who orders him to leave.

Upon arriving at the hotel room, the narrator experiences another mysterious vision. Left without a key to this puzzle, he walks the dark streets, acknowledging the reality of his own experiences and reaffirming his spiritual alliance with Kinze's orchestra as it moves across war-torn Europe. Dream, truth, and incomprehensibility are his mementos.

### The Characters

Taken in the context of Škvorecký's foreword, the anonymous male narrator is evidently a projection of the author. He is a youth with a romantic imagination for whom jazz is both a form of radical protest against political and artistic censorship and an expression of his youthful vitality and liberation from fear and self-pity. He knows the perils of indulging himself with the music, but he cultivates this indulgence with the same sort of deliberate air that he adopts for his foppish dress.

Škvorecký creates the myth of youth. When the narrator remembers his sister Anna, he remembers, too, the young Nazi soldier who would write her poems in a blue notebook as he sat on a riverbank. When the narrator thinks of his love of jazz, he recalls his jeopardy at the hands of tyrannical Kühl and all those European jazz-players who were swept underground by the laws against this "impure" music. The narrator is alert to the rurality of his home, which robs youth of its softness. There is also a strong note of fatalism in him, for his outlook on life is a bleak reconciliation to the idea of butchery. The specters of Auschwitz, Treblinka, and Majdanek hover over Europe, and nothing in life appears to be certain, except oppression. Nevertheless, there is jazz—a euphoric release from the gathering storm clouds over Europe.

The other characters reinforce an apocalyptic vision of the evil consequences of dictatorship. Kinze and his fellow musicians are "types" of grotesque dehumanization. Kühl is a monstrous personification of tyranny. The bass saxophone player is simply one more sad musician on the periphery of a disturbed world.

Because of its palpable, surreal effect on the story, the huge bass saxophone becomes one of the most vital characters. It is both fact and symbol, forcing others to struggle with its primitive power while leaving behind abstract waves of testimony to man's proud spirit of survival and creativity. The instrument is monstrous, yet seductive; grotesque, yet hauntingly beautiful. It is marked by physical decay, yet is a sort of polyrhythmic phoenix— ominous, tragic, incapable of extinction. It grows in the imagination while generating memories of the troubled history of man.

*Themes and Meanings*

The black comedy and the sadness of life under the Nazis are evoked by Škvorecký's quasi-surreal satire. Although there is a sense of dream that surrounds and permeates the novella, at its center there is an all-too-human destiny of restless flight. It is no small irony that the young narrator is on the "lee-shore of a land-locked lea in Europe," while feeling, at heart, forever one with American jazz-musicians, or wandering, in his mind and soul, with Kinze's orchestra across the war-torn countryside.

Jazz is forbidden music to Aryans, but this very stigma makes it especially attractive to all who resist state controls over life and art. Its wild jungle rhythms and sounds put it squarely outside the regulated, regimented way of life promoted by the Nazis, and so it becomes particularly seductive to the young narrator, who wants never to renounce his right to dream in music. The absurd Spike Jones look of Kinze's orchestra is a grotesque reminder of the hell of oppression. The assorted physical handicaps of its members are emblems of the cruel sufferings created by war. The anxiety and fear at the center of many of the players' lives reveal the resulting collapse of optimism.

Yet, although the novella is occasionally like a vision in one of Brueghel's disturbing paintings, it resounds with the idea of fidelity to real art. There is a schizophrenia in the narrator—especially as he disguises himself as a German to play a forbidden music that has come from another continent—but the moral of the tale is that the music joins him to a time and place and ideal from which he is separated by the vagaries of history. So long as he can play this jazz, he can communicate to the world a deep, sad, but ultimately triumphant, song of life.

*Critical Context*

An Editor's Choice of *The New York Times Book Review* and Book of the Year of *The Guardian, The Bass Saxophone* was Josef Škvorecký's first North American success in translation. Its satire is acute, its sense of atmosphere vividly compelling. Surreal images proliferate as the story grows before fading like music.

In a broad sense, Škvorecký can be placed in the category of émigré writers, for he is a writer in exile from his native land, who uses a foreign language by which to express his preoccupations. Although *The Bass Saxophone* is set in a Czech town, it does catch the feeling of social and political displacement—a theme that is enlarged in *Zbabělci* (1958; *The Cowards*, 1970) and *Příběh inženýra lidskych duší* (1977; *The Engineer of Human Souls*, 1984), for in these two novels, Škvorecký describes conditions in a small town in northeast Bohemia during periods of German Fascism and Soviet Communism. Other connections exist as well: The narrator and protagonist of *The Cowards* is Danny, a twenty-year-old zoot-suited, idealistic but innocent tenor saxophonist; the same character, now a middle-aged academic living in Canada, narrates *The Engineer of Human Souls*.

In all of his fiction, Škvorecký proves to be a realist—though not the type of social realist normally associated with East European writing, because he refuses to create an apocalyptic hero who sets a prescription for moral or political action. Škvorecký is against dogmatic ideas, and although he can sometimes be smug about his own vision, he does not believe in programs for human action or nature.

The grotesque elements of *The Bass Saxophone* bear affinities with the black comedy in *The Engineer of Human Souls* and are derived from a European tradition that encompasses Franz Kafka, Jaroslav Hašek, and Günter Grass. In the novella, the grotesque takes the form of characters, situations, and props that are both pleasantly ridiculous, as well as bizarre, frightening, and monstrous. The grotesque elements constitute a structure of estrangement for the narrator, who is strongly affected by a world that ceases to be reliable and which instills in him a fear of life rather than of death. The surreal moments fuse the fantastic and the satiric aspects of the grotesque, so that, while the narrator experiences moments of provocative vitality, he is also pushed along the borders of terror and loss.

*Sources for Further Study*

Balliett, Whitney. Review in *The New Yorker*. LV (October 22, 1979), p. 193.

Davies, Russell. "Dreams of Dixieland," in *The Times Literary Supplement*. No. 3977 (June 23, 1978), p. 694.

Maloff, Saul. "Music and Politics," in *The New York Times Book Review*. LXXXIV (January 14, 1979), p. 7.

Prescott, P. S. Review in *Newsweek*. XCIII (January 22, 1979), p. 76.

Škvorecký, Josef. "Some Problems of the Ethnic Writer in Canada," in *Canadian Literature*. Supp. 1 (May, 1987), pp. 82-91.

Windsor, Philip. "Jazz as Truth," in *The Listener*. C (August 17, 1978), pp. 220-221.

*Keith Garebian*

# THE BATTLE OF PHARSALUS

*Author:* Claude Simon (1913-      )
*Type of plot:* Antistory
*Time of plot:* The present, the recent past, and the ancient past
*Locale:* A sidewalk café in Paris, a train traveling through Europe, and a small Greek village
*First published: La Bataille de Pharsale*, 1969 (English translation, 1971)

>  *Principal characters:*
>  O., the narrator, who is an observer of life
>  UNCLE CHARLES, O.'s uncle, now deceased
>  ODETTE, an artist's model whom Charles had loved
>  O.'S LOVER, a woman who is unfaithful to O., causing him to suffer

## The Novel

*The Battle of Pharsalus* is not an easy novel to read. It has no linear plot, but rather presents a set of images or basic scenes that constantly recur. In these repetitions sometimes the elements are the same, but more often they shift, reassemble themselves, or have additional material in them. In these ways, Claude Simon forces the reader to participate actively in the reading of this novel.

Although the book is divided into three basic sections, it is not until the second section that Simon clarifies the elemental scenes reiterated throughout the work. The first section introduces these elements to the reader without making them fully intelligible. These basic scenes include several interesting pieces (as in a puzzle) that reflect various layers of time. These time layers represent the ancient Roman battle at Pharsalus, the narrator's boyhood struggle to translate the Latin account of that battle, his experiences in World War II, his recent train journey through Europe, his recent trip to Greece to find the site of the battle of Pharsalus, and the present time, represented by the narrator sitting in an outdoor café in Paris.

Scattered among these time levels are the various motifs of the novel. These motifs include O.'s memories of translating Latin with Uncle Charles, O. struggling to survive when he is unhorsed in a battle in Flanders, the story of a redheaded soldier who goes berserk in O.'s barracks one night, O. trying to break down his lover's door while she makes love to another man in her room, Uncle Charles watching his artist friend paint Odette nude, O. and a friend Nikos seeking directions on their trip in Greece, a soccer match on the fields near Pharsalus, the wreckage of an abandoned McCormick harvester-reaper on a field in Greece, O.'s train trip through Europe, the views O. sees from his outdoor seat at the Paris café, and the students in a political demonstration on a Paris street.

Most of these motif pieces merge frequently with one another, so the reader finds a battle scene from World War II blended into the ancient battle of Pharsalus. Such scenes are not merely juxtaposed to one another; they are literally woven together so that only a very close reading can discern where one ends and the other begins. Simon's point in doing this is to show that time is really continuous and that the past is always with his characters, even in the present. This disregard for a normal time continuum can confuse an unprepared reader.

Scattered throughout the three sections of *The Battle of Pharsalus* are moments in which the action freezes or stills itself. At such points, Simon reverts to descriptions of relevant paintings or works of sculpture. Most often these artworks he describes are of battle scenes depicting famous warriors. In this manner, Simon reiterates the timelessness of man's existence. All battles and sexual struggles become one; the experience is always the same. Even the young men playing a friendly game of soccer on a summer day in Greece are in fierce contention and conflict with one another.

When the novel closes, Simon has led the reader full circle. The narrator is sitting at a desk with a blank sheet of paper in front of him; on this sheet he inscribes the first lines with which Simon had begun part 1 of *The Battle of Pharsalus*.

## The Characters

As is the case with Simon's shifting of scenes in this novel, so his characters vary and merge somewhat from time to time. The two most clearly defined characters are Uncle Charles and O., the narrator (his nephew). Uncle Charles is now deceased; when he was alive he had a job in banking or accounting, for O. recalls his large desk full of money. Uncle Charles is intelligent and kind; he helps the young O. with his homework. In particular, Charles assists his nephew in translating Latin passages about Caesar's battle with Pompey at Pharsalus in Greece. After Charles's death, O. remembers these childhood lessons and sets out to see the actual battlefield at Pharsalus. Charles's life, unfortunately, had its unhappy aspects. He fell in love with the artist's model, Odette, who is unfaithful to him. Charles is not alone in his anguish over Odette, for the painter, Van Velden, also loves this beautiful young woman.

The narrator, who rather late in the novel refers to himself as O. for the first time, is a complex character. He most often represents Charles's nephew, but he sometimes becomes a female persona as well. For example, when O. attempts to break into his lover's apartment, he feels that he is both O. and the woman lover inside making love to another man. Similarly, at a few points in the book, O. seems to become Charles, as the distressed, jealous lover of Odette. Such character mergings in this novel can confuse the reader, yet they indicate the similarities of experiences between O. and Charles. When O. becomes a female, Simon seems to use this occurrence to emphasize the androgynous nature of all human experience.

There are only a few minor characters who appear in *The Battle of Pharsalus* who have discernible roles. One of the most fascinating of these is the redheaded soldier who goes crazy in a barracks, threatening imaginary opponents with his saber. Standing naked, drunk, and cursing on a cold winter's night, this soldier is described as an ancient gladiator by Simon. Despite his disheveled and wild appearance, this demented man takes on a heroic aura. When he is arrested and led away by an officer, the situation seems almost tragic—a great man has been subdued and diminished.

Simon's other minor characters in this novel serve merely as backdrops in various situations. There are the people who emerge from the subway in Paris and walk pass the café where O. sits. These pedestrians represent humanity in several of its aspects—they are carefree, worried, rich, poor, young, and old, all together; even Christ appears on this Paris street. These subway passengers resemble the people riding the train through Europe with O. They have a few distinguishing features but are basically an anonymous group that forms a backdrop and stimulates O.'s reflections.

Similarly, the soldiers in battle represent merely an aggregation of struggling human beings—in the armies of Pompey and of Caesar at Pharsalus, and in Flanders with O. in World War II. It is not important to distinguish fully between these two basic groups of warriors, for their function in the novel is the same—they represent frightened yet courageous men in battle. These sets of soldiers also blend in with the soccer players striving on the field in modern Greece, for their game is similar to a battle.

## Themes and Meanings

The most obvious distinguishing feature of Simon's novels is his radical break with traditional forms of fiction. His avant-garde style is inextricably interwoven with his themes. The narrator of *The Battle of Pharsalus* describes things and people as he observes them; he also intermixes sense memories and fantasies with his descriptions. This mixture of thought processes and sensations produces a style that goes a step beyond the stream-of-consciousness technique. By this method of narration, Simon is reinforcing his idea that all human experience is one. The past and the present are not distinct time periods for him, but a blend of experiences that cannot be neatly divided.

Another theme in *The Battle of Pharsalus* is the sadness of the human condition. O. continually repeats that he suffers. He suffers mainly from jealousy, his inability to trust his lover, as Uncle Charles suffered over Odette. This theme of jealousy, unfaithfulness, and their hurt is also developed in a scene in which Charles goes to Van Velden's studio to find Odette. There, Charles is confronted by Van Velden's jealous wife, who seems certain that her husband is also having an affair with Odette. Rather than talk directly about her suspicion, Mrs. Van Velden nervously chatters to Charles about her plans to visit Morocco with her husband.

Almost as pervasive as the theme of jealousy in *The Battle of Pharsalus* is the theme of aggression and hostility. The most obvious examples of aggressive behavior occur in the various battle scenes; yet even lovemaking, in Simon's depiction of it, takes on aggressive overtones. The soccer players sometimes display extreme aggression, as do the student demonstrators in the Paris streets. The aggression of the crazed, saber-wielding soldier is given a rather mythic stature; the invisible enemies against whom he rants seem real and threatening to him. Taken as a whole, Simon's view of aggressive behavior is mixed. While he condemns the horrors of war (often by graphic detailing of men's wounds), he also sees that human struggle can have an ennobling aspect. In Simon's view, man is doomed to a harsh existence, and anyone who can fight against his oppressors or tormentors has admirable traits.

Simon is at heart a pessimist: He believes that man's striving to overcome his ultimate fate (death) is valiant, but futile. The author sees death as all-pervasive, present even in the act of lovemaking. The best man can do as he moves toward his annihilation in death is to create powerful works of art. Simon's use of detailed analyses of famous paintings demonstrates his deep appreciation of and respect for the visual arts. He himself studied painting as a young man but chose a career in writing instead. *The Battle of Pharsalus* is inundated not only with descriptions of art but also with Simon's own painter's use of color and precision. Color especially plays a vital role for Simon and many vivid colors reappear throughout the various scenes; he relies, however, most heavily on yellow and its appearance in sunlight to convey moods. Yellow, for Simon, is both a funereal color and the color of jealousy, as well as of sunlight and gold coins. These basic images fuse with one another throughout the novel. Simon's use of these images results at times in a lyrical, almost poetic, quality in his prose. Some of his most vivid descriptions of nature remind the reader of those of William Faulkner, whom Simon has acknowledged as an influence in his career.

## Critical Context

Simon was awarded the Nobel Prize for Literature in 1985. His work as an avant-garde novelist and an individualistic writer made him worthy of such an honor. Simon, in such novels as *The Battle of Pharsalus*, has stretched far beyond the limits of the traditional European novel. The sets of images he creates and re-creates are perhaps the most accurate representations of the workings of a human mind ever accomplished in prose.

*The Battle of Pharsalus* is a work that stands midway between the author's earlier, less fully experimental novels, and his later works. Elements in *The Battle of Pharsalus*, such as the narrator's wartime experiences, reflect Simon's own life, as do elements in his previous books, such as *La Route des Flandres* (1960; *The Flanders Road*, 1961). In Simon's novels subsequent to *The Battle of Pharsalus*, personal experience is even more deeply submerged in complex linguistic structures.

*Sources for Further Study*
Gould, Karen. *Claude Simon's Mythic Muse*, 1979.
Jiménez-Fajardo, Salvador. *Claude Simon*, 1975.
Loubère, J. A. E. *The Novels of Claude Simon*, 1975.
Roudiez, Leon S. *French Fiction Today: A New Direction*, 1972.
Sturrock, John. *The French New Novel: Claude Simon, Michel Butor, Alain Robbe-Grillet*, 1969.

*Patricia E. Sweeney*

# BEAUTY AND SADNESS

*Author:* Yasunari Kawabata (1899-1972)
*Type of plot:* Psychological realism
*Time of plot:* 1961
*Locale:* The cities of Kyoto and Kamakura, Japan
*First published: Utsukushisa to kanashimi to*, 1961-1963, serial; 1965, book
  (English translation, 1975)

> *Principal characters:*
> TOSHIO OKI, a fifty-four-year-old novelist living in Kamakura
> FUMIKO, Oki's wife
> TAICHIRO, his son, a university professor specializing in
>     traditional Japanese literature
> OTOKO UENO, a traditional Japanese painter living in Kyoto,
>     who at the age of fifteen was Oki's mistress
> KEIKO SAKAMI, Otoko's student, companion, and lover

*The Novel*

    The action of Yasunari Kawabata's *Beauty and Sadness* develops out of an affair that Toshio Oki had twenty-four years earlier with a fifteen-year-old girl named Otoko Ueno. The book begins with Oki's decision to travel from his home in Kamakura, outside Tokyo, to Kyoto in order to surprise his former mistress, now a distinguished painter, with a request. Oki invites Otoko to listen to the tolling of Kyoto's temple bells at midnight on New Year's Eve. On the surface, Oki's motives are superficial and sentimental. He finds himself intrigued by a glimpse of Otoko in photographs in a magazine article about her work; he wants to see if she has retained the innocent beauty of the fifteen-year-old whom he seduced and made pregnant. At the end of their affair, Otoko stayed in a mental hospital, after the death of her baby. Yet Otoko's was not the only tragic loss resulting from the relationship. At the time, Oki was a married man with a young son; his wife, Fumiko, lost the baby she was carrying when the facts about her husband's relationship with Otoko were revealed to her in the manuscript of the novel that Oki wrote about his young mistress.

    Otoko finds this novel, which Oki has entitled *A Girl of Sixteen*, a curious document. While she recognizes his portrait of herself in the book, she does not find in it the mental anguish that she recalls as the most important characteristic of the affair. The novelist has softened and sentimentalized his account of their relationship; nevertheless, *A Girl of Sixteen* is his best, and most famous, book. When Oki telephones her from his hotel in Kyoto twenty-four years after their separation, Otoko decides to meet him to hear the temple bells, but she brings along her student, companion, and female lover, Keiko Sakami, to keep Oki from broaching the subject of the past. Keiko is only nineteen, but she knows of Otoko's affair with Oki, both from his version of it in *A Girl of Sixteen* and from Otoko's own account. Keiko is obsessed with understanding the bond between Oki and Otoko, and perhaps it is resentment and jealousy of the novelist's continued ability to affect Otoko's feelings that lead Keiko to mount a calculated assault upon the Oki family to extract what she calls revenge for Otoko's suffering.

After Oki returns home to Kamakura, Keiko delivers to him two of her own paintings, pieces more abstract and expressionistic than the work of her teacher. Fumiko, sensing the threat that Keiko poses, is tempted to destroy these pictures. Oki himself, however, does not see any danger, and he even takes the risk of going to bed with Keiko. She refuses him her right breast, suggesting that it is deformed or unresponsive to stimulation, and at a crucial moment in their lovemaking, she calls out Otoko's name and prevents Oki from achieving an orgasm.

Later, Keiko initiates a relationship with Oki's son Taichiro, granting him her right breast but not her left; she maneuvers Oki's son until she can telephone Fumiko with the claim that Taichiro has asked her to marry him. This telephone call comes from a hotel on the shore of Lake Biwa, just outside Kyoto, where Keiko has brought the young man so that they can take a moterboat out on the lake. There is a boating accident, perhaps planned by Keiko, and Taichiro is drowned. Otoko, Oki, and Fumiko meet in Keiko's room at the hotel, confronting in the tragedy of Taichiro's death the consequences of their own complex interrelationship. The beauty and sadness of Otoko's memories take on, in the light of Keiko's savage expression of resentment, a somberness not unlike the reaction of Fumiko, who accuses Otoko of engineering her son's death as revenge for the death of the artist's own baby daughter.

## The Characters

The central figures of Kawabata's *Beauty and Sadness* are Fumiko, Otoko, and Keiko, three women who suffer and cause one another to suffer because of their involvement with Oki and his son Taichiro. In marked contrast to the masculine perspective articulated in Kawabata's treatment of love in other novels, there is something surprisingly like a feminist viewpoint at work in this book. Of the three women, the most conventional is Fumiko. Devoted to family and home, she is the stereotypical middle-class housewife, and she struggles to control her feelings about her husband's infidelity by committing herself even more to her role of wife and mother. As her husband's typist, Fumiko sees it as a duty to prepare a neatly typed copy of *A Girl of Sixteen* for Oki's publisher, even though the book makes it clear to her that her husband continues to love Otoko. At the end of *Beauty and Sadness*, Fumiko must live with her awareness that Oki's passion for Otoko is as strong as ever.

For her, the incursion of Keiko into the lives of her husband and son merely confirms the emotional pain she feels.

By contrast, Otoko manages to find a degree of emotional tranquillity because circumstances allow her to develop an insight into her own feelings and a degree of control, denied to Fumiko, over her own behavior. The significant difference between the two women is that subsequent to her hospitalization Otoko becomes an artist and finds that she is able to channel her emotions into her painting. Largely unconscious of what she is doing, until Keiko joins her as a student, Otoko then develops the ability to recognize the self-deception in her work. She sees that even a portrait of her own mother is largely an idealized picture of herself as victim, and as her relationship with Keiko becomes overtly sexual, Otoko recognizes that in her treatment of Keiko she is repeating Oki's unconscious manipulation of her younger self. As she plans to paint Keiko in the guise of a Buddhist saint, a design stressing the girl's androgyny, Otoko uses her art to seek moral insight.

Kawabata leaves unresolved the question of whether Keiko is more than a projection of Otoko's subconscious desire for revenge on Oki. Keiko's volatile emotions are clear enough, even before Oki and his son come back into Otoko's life; so is her devotion to her teacher. There is a level on which she represents the elemental passions which Otoko and Fumiko control and fail to acknowledge, and it is tempting to see the three as the Freudian id, superego, and ego. Such a reading, however, would obscure the specific Buddhist context in which Kawabata places all three women, with the implication that Keiko is a tortured soul striving to achieve spiritual transcendence. She tells Taichiro, having brought him to the hotel at Lake Biwa and gone to bed with him for the first (and only) time, that she feels reborn. Kawabata deliberately leaves unclear whether Keiko's words refer to her emotions after intercourse or to her satisfaction in bringing Taichiro to the point of sacrifice.

*Themes and Meanings*

Far from resolving the thematic ambiguity of his treatment of Keiko, Kawabata reinforces the complexity of her characterization. At a significant point in the book, Taichiro discusses with his parents an article in a magazine on the excavation of the grave of Princess Kazunomiya (the wife of the shogun Iemochi Tokugawa), who died in 1877. The team of archaeologists finds, in the arms of the Princess' skeleton, a photograph on glass of a young nobleman in court robes. Exposed to light and air after so long a time, the image on the glass plate fades, and the archaeologists are therefore unable to determine if the picture was of the Princess' husband or of her reputed lover, Prince Arigusawa. Oki, Fumiko, and Taichiro discuss the article at length, and Kawabata intends that this conversation be applied to the other art objects in the novel. Oki's own *A Girl of Sixteen* is as much a picture of love's fragility as is the photograph in the grave of the Princess. Both are the images of a love lost, and both memorialize an absent lover.

Kawabata uses Otoko's and Keiko's own paintings to reveal their different personalities. Working in a traditional Japanese style, Otoko initially subsumes her emotions in her art and paints to project an idealized conception of herself and her dead daughter. She has tried over the years to paint a picture of this child, whom she never really saw, in the style of either Western paintings of the Christ child or Buddhist paintings of Saint Kobo. When Keiko asks to have her portrait painted, Otoko turns to the sketches for this abortive project. "Perhaps she could portray Keiko in the manner of the paintings of the boy saint. It would be a purely classical *Portrait of a Holy Virgin*. Though works of religious art, some of the saint's portraits had an indescribably seductive charm."

On the surface, this idea is ironic, for Keiko is not a virgin; Otoko's thoughts suggest Kawabata's purpose in his treatment of her. The idea of painting Keiko as a saint ascending toward the heavens suggests that in resolving this problem of representation, Otoko will achieve emotional and spiritual insight. "Why not paint a nude of Keiko, then? She could still follow the design of the boy saint's portrait, and there were even Buddhist figures that gave the hint of a woman's breasts." Only by rejecting an approach to painting that turns even a portrait of her mother into a picture of herself will Otoko be able to accept the loss of her child, reconcile herself to the pain caused by her affair with Oki, and break free of an obsession with the past. Her sexual feelings for Keiko, repeating the manipulation of her own feelings by her former lover, are a sign of her deeply troubled mind.

In a sense, Keiko is less a real girl than the projection of those emotions that Otoko has blocked out and sublimated in her painting. Keiko's pictures express the emotional turbulence that Otoko has excluded from her work, and they are not traditional in style. One of the paintings Keiko takes to Oki's house in Kamakura depicts a single large plum blossom against a background of mountains covered with snow. "But no real mountains narrowed at the base or were so jagged—that was the abstract element in her style. The background might be an image of Keiko's own feeling." The plum blossom itself is as large as the head of a child, and the petals are both red and white. Oki recognizes after a moment that Keiko has painted a plum tree in his own garden, whose unusual combination of red and white blossoms is something he had talked about with Otoko when she was his mistress. The painting reveals the depth of Keiko's knowledge about that affair. When she tells Otoko that she has gone to Oki's house and left this painting, she is scolded for meddling in something that does not concern her. Keiko reveals the extent to which she identifies with Otoko when she replies, "As long as I have you I'm not afraid. How do you suppose I'd paint if I lost you? Maybe I'd give up my painting—and my life."

Significantly, Kawabata shows that the emotional bond between Keiko and Otoko is the strongest one in the novel. The affair that Otoko had with Oki was equally passionate, but in that relationship, the partners were never equally committed. Oki always knew that the affair would end; there was no question in his mind of leaving his wife. His masculine ego was flattered by Otoko's youth, innocence, and depth of feeling, but he did not reciprocate her emotion; there was never any question of sacrificing himself to his passion. *Beauty and Sadness* suggests that this is something only a woman can do.

*Critical Context*

*Beauty and Sadness* focuses on the thoughts and feelings of female characters, not those of males as in Kawabata's *Yukiguni* ( 1947; *Snow Country*, 1956), *Sembazuru* (1952; *Thousand Cranes*, 1958), or *Nemureru bijo* (1961; *The House of the Sleeping Beauties*, 1969). Both the novelist Oki and his son Taichiro are peripheral to Kawabata's focus on the effects of creative, self-sufficient women's passion. Nevertheless, Oki and his son are typical of the men at the centers of other of his novels. They are attracted to women, drawn most strongly by the prospect of sexual innocence, but are incapable of relating to women on a level beyond the sexual.

It is Kawabata's characterization of Fumiko, Otoko, and Keiko that makes *Beauty and Sadness* unique among his novels. Because he portrays them from the inside and not through the eyes of a male protagonist as he does in other books, these three characters have a vitality and an integrity that his women often do not. In addition, Otoko and Keiko are shown as artists engaged in the kind of creativity often assumed to be a male prerogative. They are not the musicians, dancers, and practitioners of the tea ceremony found in Kawabata's other novels, women devoted to arts that are merely re-creative of the primary activity of composer, dance teacher, or tea master. Keiko and Otoko grapple with the primary materials of their art; they embody in their paintings a way of seeing the world, as Oki does in his novels. Based on the evidence of *A Girl of Sixteen* and the paintings done by the two women, it is clear that Oki is inferior as an artist to Otoko and Keiko.

*Sources for Further Study*

Keene, Donald. *Dawn to the West: Japanese Literature in the Modern Era*, 1984.

Lippit, Noriko Mizuta. *Reality and Fiction in Modern Japanese Literature*, 1980.

Petersen, Gwenn Boardman. *The Moon in the Water: Understanding Tanizaki, Kawabata, and Mishima*, 1979.

Ueda, Makoto. *Modern Japanese Writers and the Nature of Literature*, 1976.

Yamanouchi, Hisaaki. *The Search for Authenticity in Modern Japanese Literature*, 1978.

*Robert C. Petersen*

# A BEGGAR IN JERUSALEM

*Author:* Elie Wiesel (1928-    )
*Type of plot:* Impressionistic realism
*Time of plot:* 1967
*Locale:* Jerusalem
*First published: Le Mendiant de Jérusalem*, 1968 (English translation, 1970)

*Principal characters:*
DAVID, the narrator
KATRIEL, an Israeli soldier, David's close friend
MALKA, Katriel's wife
GAD, a lieutenant colonel in the Israeli army
DAN, the princely beggar
EZRA BEN ABRAHAM, an old Moroccan Jew
MENASHE, the matchmaker beggar
MOSHE, a mad beggar
SHLOMO, a blind Hasidic beggar
VELVEL, the joking beggar
YAKOV, the timid beggar, a schoolteacher
ZADOK, a Yemenite Jew

*The Novel*

Shortly after the Six Day War in June, 1967, a group of Jews gathers near the Wailing Wall in Jerusalem as the sun sets. Each night they assemble to recount the stories of their lives and to boast of their roles in the recent spectacular victory. Dan, for example, tells of his kingdom beyond the mythical river Sambatyon, which throws up stones six days a week and rests only on the Sabbath. Moshe speaks of participating in a theological dispute with Christian priests sometime in the Middle Ages. Zalmen recalls a visit from his regimental commander just before the outbreak of hostilities; the commander is Judas Maccabaeus. Shlomo tells of meeting Jesus on the day He was crucified. Velvel boasts of securing the capture of Jerusalem by rejoicing: "Had I stopped, had I shed a single tear, we'd have lost the war. . . ." His listeners dismiss this claim because each knows that he alone achieved the victory, Zadok by his prayers, Moshe by his singing.

David, who listens to all these stories, has two of his own to tell. One concerns his life, the other Katriel's. David was born in Transylvania; when World War II breaks out, he becomes a refugee. After the war he returns to his native town, where once a large Jewish community flourished. Now only three Jews remain, and all are insane. Two imagine that they still see the old world; the third tells David that he knows he is possessed because he cannot see it: "Imagine my seeing this town without its Jews. It sounds inconceivable, I know. And yet that is how I see it. . . . Still, I am not so mad as to suppose that my vision reflects any reality but my own."

Eventually David makes his way to Israel. As war threatens in 1967, he visits the headquarters of Gad, a former schoolmate in Europe and now a lieutenant colonel in the Israeli army. Reluctantly, Gad allows David to join his regiment, and there David meets Katriel.

Katriel is a sabra, born in Safed to a rabbi. Katriel joins the Israeli army in 1948 at the urging of his father. He marries Malka, and they have a son, Sasha, whose death places a barrier between them. Still, Malka loves her husband, and after the war she asks David to tell of her husband's final days.

David replies that in camp, before the fighting, he and Katriel make a pact; each agrees to bear witness for the other should one of them die. David expects to be the one who perishes. Instead, after the Israeli army captures Jerusalem, Katriel vanishes. He is listed as missing in action, so both Malka and David believe that he will return. As dawn breaks, Malka invites David to come home with her, but David declines. "Do you want me to go away?" she asks. "Yes," David replies. "Do you want me to come back?" Again the answer is yes. She will continue to listen, and David will continue to tell his story among the other beggars telling theirs.

*The Characters*

To an extent, David represents the author. They have a common birthplace, and both experienced the horrors of the Holocaust. Both are refugees; both are storytellers. David also resembles Samuel Taylor Coleridge's ancient mariner, a man obliged to tell his harrowing tale to anyone passing by, a man transformed by his experiences into a kind of specter. "Do his eyes disturb you?" Elie Wiesel asks. "They are not his, and he doesn't know it." They are not his because they belong to everyone. David has seen the Crusades, the Cossacks. "He who says 'I,' has said everything," David comments. "Just as every man contains all men, this word contains all words."

Most of all, David is Katriel. When people ask, "Still no trace of Katriel?" he replies, "His trace? I am his trace." Having agreed with Katriel to bear witness for him, to remember and record his experiences, he guarantees Katriel's immortality by becoming Katriel as well as David. Although in one sense Katriel's blind father in Safed could never have met David, certainly never fathered him, as Katriel speaks of his childhood David wonders whether they have met; he even considers that Katriel's parents may be his also. Later, Malka recognizes her husband in David and would take him home as her spouse. Finally, David cannot distinguish between the other man and himself: "What if I am dead and he is the survivor?" he wonders.

Reflecting this concept of the double is a story that Katriel tells shortly before the Six Day War. A man leaves his village to seek a magical city. At night, before he goes to sleep in the forest, he takes off his shoes and points them in the direction he is going, lest he become confused. While he sleeps, a practical joker happens by and turns the shoes to face the traveler's hometown. The next day, when the pilgrim resumes his walk, he actually returns home. To him, though, everything is new as well as familiar. He finds a family that reminds him of his own, whose husband and father has embarked on a quest for a magical city. At the urging of the wife and children, he remains, never seeking to return to his native village. The wanderer remains himself but has now assumed a second identity, too, and when Death seeks him, the wanderer cannot be found.

Just as David is himself, Katriel, and the Jews murdered in the Crusades and pogroms, so the other beggars have many lives. Zalmen lives in twentieth century Jerusalem, but he also fought against the Syrians more than two thousand years ago and joined Bar Kokhba's revolt against Rome in A. D. 135. "The Babylonians, the Greeks, the Romans, the Crusaders, the Moslems, all those wars they teach you about at school, remember that we took part in all of them," he says. An air force pilot who listens to these improbable tales thinks that the beggars are all mad, and so in a way they are. Yet Wiesel would agree with Emily Dickinson that such "madness is divinest sense."

## Themes and Meanings

Wiesel has written many novels, many stories, but they all concern one story, the dominant story of the twentieth century: the Holocaust. A survivor of Auschwitz and Buchenwald, Wiesel has dedicated himself to being a witness, saying, "I knew that anyone who remained alive had to become a storyteller, a messenger, had to speak up." Some of the most powerful scenes in the book deal directly with the Nazis' extermination of the Jews of Europe: the machine-gunning of a small Jewish community; David's narrow escape from a French mob that then turns its fury on the gentile woman who has saved his life.

Even the saga of David and Katriel, set in 1967, is in fact about the Holocaust. The pact that David and Katriel make is the same Wiesel made with his mother and sister, who were gassed at Auschwitz, with his father, whom he watched die at Buchenwald, and with six million of his coreligionists who perished. It is the promise to remember and remind the world of the existence of those who no longer can speak for themselves. "The way to fight death is to create life," Katriel's father says. One does so by overcoming silence, by speaking out. If Katriel were dead, David believes that he could revive him by telling his story.

Just before he disappears, Katriel stands with David in front of the Wailing Wall on the Temple Mount. Katriel tells David to follow the ancient custom of writing a wish on a piece of paper and then inserting it among the stones. In this way the writer actually becomes a partner in the construction and reconstruction of the Temple, a builder of the Jewish dream.

All the beggars are ancient mariners, telling their stories so that they, their ancestors, and their descendants can live. The madman in David's hometown is right when he says that he knows that the Jewish community destroyed by the Nazis still exists. Though no longer physically present, it endures in the minds and stories of people such as David.

David's teacher had told him that "the Romans and the enemies of the Romans, the Christians and the enemies of the Christians, the Moslems and the mortal enemies of Islam" shared the desire to silence the Jew because "the Jews are God's memory and the heart of mankind." Those who persecute the Jew would erase that memory and impose silence and sterility. To oppose them, David and the other beggars rely on the all-creating word that made the world and which alone guarantees its survival.

*Critical Context*

Wiesel's is a Jewish story, but it is not only a Jewish story. As Wiesel has noted, "The Jewish and human condition become one—a concentric circle, one within the other, not one against the other or one replacing the other." The Holocaust is a universal, not an ethnic tragedy, in the same way that Othello's tragedy is also Iago's, that Agamemnon's is also Orestes'. As Chaim Grade has said, in the Holocaust one-third of every person died. This disaster makes manifest the substitution of ideology for compassion, of technology for humanity, that has come to characterize the twentieth century. Biafra, Cambodia, Bangladesh; Auschwitz, Treblinka, Babi Yar; Dresden, Hiroshima, Nagasaki—the killing fields take many names, many forms, but all warn of the Final Solution through nuclear war.

Signs of the book's universal appeal include the reception of the prestigious Medicis Prize (1969) and sales of more than 100,000 copies in French alone. Readers and writers alike have acknowledged Wiesel's power, for they recognize the Jewish experience as at once common and unique. Jean-Paul Sartre wrote that modern man's greatest need is to bear witness to his time and to himself. In his Nobel Prize address, William Faulkner expressed an idea similar to Wiesel's when he concluded with the statement: "The poet's voice need not merely be the record of man, it can be one of the props, the pillars to help him endure and prevail." Each person must become a witness by telling another's story, for then, as Albert Camus has noted, "the tree is justified, love is born." To remain silent is no longer to be an innocent bystander; it is to become a conspirator with the forces of evil, and ultimately it is also to commit suicide.

*Sources for Further Study*

Abrahamson, Irving, ed. *Against Silence: The Voice and Vision of Elie Wiesel*, 1985 (three volumes).

Berenbaum, Michael. *The Vision of the Void: Theological Reflections on the Works of Elie Wiesel*, 1979.

Brown, Robert McAfee. *Elie Wiesel: Messenger to All Humanity*, 1983.

Cargas, Harry James. *Harry James Cargas in Conversation with Elie Wiesel*, 1976.

Estess, Ted. *Elie Wiesel*, 1980.

Ezrahi, Sidra DeKoven. *By Words Alone: The Holocaust in Literature*, 1980.

Fine, Ellen S. *Legacy of Night: The Literary Universe of Elie Wiesel*, 1982.

Green, Mary Jean. "Witness to the Absurd: Elie Wiesel and the French Existentialists," in *Renascence*. XXIX (1977), pp. 170-184.

Rosenfeld, Alvin H., and Irving Greenberg, eds. *Confronting the Holocaust: The Impact of Elie Wiesel*, 1979.

Roth, John K. *A Consuming Fire: Encounters with Elie Wiesel and the Holocaust*, 1979.

*Joseph Rosenblum*

# BERLIN ALEXANDERPLATZ
## The Story of Franz Biberkopf

*Author:* Alfred Döblin (1878-1957)
*Type of plot:* Expressionistic realism
*Time of plot:* The autumn of 1927 to the spring of 1929
*Locale:* Berlin and its environs
*First published: Berlin Alexanderplatz: Die Geschichte vom Franz Biberkopf,*
  1929 (*Alexanderplatz, Berlin,* 1931; best known as *Berlin Alexanderplatz*)

*Principal characters:*
  FRANZ BIBERKOPF, a heavy-set proletarian, about thirty years
    old, who has been a cement worker, furniture mover, and
    convict and who after his release from prison becomes in
    turn a tie-pin hawker, newspaper vendor, notions
    salesman, burglar, fence, pimp, and assistant doorkeeper
  HERBERT WISCHOW, a pimp and con man, a friend of
    Biberkopf before and after Biberkopf's imprisonment
  EVA (real name, EMILIE), Wischow's mistress, who is in love
    with Biberkopf before and after his imprisonment
  GOTTLIEB MECK, a friend of Biberkopf
  LINA PRZYBALLA (POLISH LINA), Biberkopf's first mistress
    after his release from prison
  CILLY, Biberkopf's second mistress after his release from
    prison
  MIEZE (MIEZEKEN, real name, EMILIE PARSUNKE, also called
    SONIA), Biberkopf's third mistress after his release from
    prison
  OTTO LÜDERS, Lina's uncle, a friend and the first betrayer of
    Biberkopf
  HERR VON UND ZU PUMS, the leader of a gang of burglars
  REINHOLD, a member of Pums's gang and a friend who
    betrays Biberkopf twice
  KARL MATTER, a tinsmith and member of Pums's gang

*The Novel*

*Berlin Alexanderplatz* covers some eighteen months in the life of Franz
Biberkopf, beginning with his release from Tegel Prison and ending with his
release from the Buch Insane Asylum. Within this period Biberkopf, a slow-
witted but vigorous man, suffers three shattering blows which mark his passage from naïve and hubristic individualism to a mature mutualism.

Biberkopf has served a four-year term for manslaughter: He had, in a
jealous rage, attacked his mistress Ida with a cream-whipper. Ida, whose

chest had been pierced by the wire coil of the implement, died after five weeks of hospitalization. Biberkopf, the ex-convict, is determined now to lead a decent life and to achieve an orderly existence. His determination is bolstered by his sense of self-sufficiency but will be frustrated by failings in his own character.

His reluctance to part from the gates of Tegel at the gateman's urging indicates that the order he desires is actually behind him, in the security of the prison. His release from prison is equivalent to expulsion from Eden. After a streetcar ride into Berlin, his insecurity becomes disorientation and terror before the chaos of freedom. He has hallucinations of roofs leaving their houses. He is taken in by two Jews, who befriend him and restore him to calm. Leaving them, he gets back into the stream of freedom by enjoying prostitutes and visiting Ida's married sister Minna, who shows affection for him but will not consort with him.

Aided by loans from a landlady and his friend Gottlieb Meck, Biberkopf begins to earn money, first as a street vendor, selling necktie clips and, eventually, newspapers, including the Nazi Party's *Völkischer Beobachter*, and later as a door-to-door salesman of shoelaces. He gains stability and secures Polish Lina as his mistress.

Then he suffers the first of the three blows. Lina's uncle, Otto Lüders, listens to Biberkopf's boasting about his conquest of a widow, who, grateful for his attentions, had purchased his entire sample of shoelaces. Lüders takes advantage of the information and forces himself upon the widow, taking back Biberkopf's sample and compelling the widow to give him money and valuables. When Biberkopf attempts to revisit the widow, he is repulsed and learns of his having been betrayed by Lüders. Crushed by Lüders' deceit, Biberkopf disappears for a time.

Recovering from his discomposure, Biberkopf makes a new start and falls in with a thief and womanizer named Reinhold. His attachment to Reinhold becomes quite strong, and he helps his new friend by systematically relieving Reinhold of each woman of whom his friend quickly tires. The first of these women is Fränze, the second Cilly. Cilly becomes Biberkopf's mistress after Reinhold is freed of her. She and Biberkopf then conspire to frustrate Reinhold in his desire to get rid of his latest woman, Trude. They persuade Trude not to let go; Reinhold, whose womanizing is a form of *Mädchenhandel* (white slavery), is stuck with her well beyond his usual four weeks of tolerance.

Reinhold is a member of Herr von und zu Pums's gang of burglars and persuades Biberkopf to join a job with the gang by fooling him into believing that the undertaking is simply a fruit pickup. Biberkopf does not realize that he has been duped into serving as a lookout until the gang begins to make its getaway. In the getaway car Reinhold clubs Biberkopf and pushes him out onto the street, where a pursuing car runs over his right arm. The arm is subsequently amputated at the shoulder, and Biberkopf has suffered his second blow.

Under the care of Herbert Wischow and Eva, he recovers and again achieves well-being, this time as a fence and a pimp. His new mistress, a pretty twenty-year-old for whom he pimps, becomes his true beloved. Her name is Emilie, but Biberkopf gives her the name "Mieze"; Eva, whose real name is also Emilie, had also been renamed by Biberkopf. Both Mieze and Eva love Biberkopf; Eva, sincerely encouraged by the barren Mieze, even becomes pregnant by him. The resilient but obtuse Biberkopf renews his friendship with Reinhold and, to the disappointment of Herbert and Eva, becomes a member of Pums's gang.

Then the third blow, the "hammer blow," is struck. Biberkopf boasts to Reinhold about Mieze's devotion and arranges for Reinhold to observe him and Mieze in the act of love. With Reinhold in concealment, Biberkopf, about to make love to Mieze, learns of her infatuation with another man and beats her severely but not, as he had beaten Ida, fatally. Later, they enjoy a sweet reconciliation. Some days afterward, Reinhold, bent on alienating Mieze's affections from Biberkopf, takes her to a rural area where, angered by her resistance to his advances, he strangles her and then enlists Karl Matter to help him bury the corpse. Karl will ultimately expose Reinhold, and Reinhold will be apprehended and sent to prison. (Alfred Döblin's chronology here is, whether deliberately or otherwise, confused. He has Reinhold murder Mieze on "Saturday, September 1st," which is two days before he meets Mieze "for the first time" on "Thursday, September 3rd." At the beginning of book 8, the narrator stipulates that the third of September was a Monday, as in fact it was in 1928, the year of the narrated action and the very year during which Döblin was at work on this novel. In a number of places in book 7, Döblin appears to have confused August with September; logically, Reinhold would have to meet Mieze for the first time not only before September 3 but also well before September 1.)

The murder of his beloved Mieze is the hammer blow that crushes Biberkopf. Lapsing into a catatonic state of acute melancholia, he is committed to an insane asylum. Here the would-be individualistic Biberkopf dies and the new mature Biberkopf is born. In his catatonic state Biberkopf, addressed by Death as Job had been addressed by God, had been berated for never blaming himself for his own actions. The new Biberkopf decides to listen to others the better to learn who he is and what his limitations and capabilities are, and he concludes that one cannot live without other people. He has passed from irresponsible individualism to authentic mutualism, among the principles of which are self-guilt, responsibility for self, and responsibility to others. Biberkopf, initially reluctant to heed the gateman at Tegel Prison, now becomes something of a gateman himself: At the novel's end he is employed as an assistant doorman at a factory.

## The Characters

Döblin has, with few exceptions, drawn all of his characters in *Berlin Alexanderplatz* from the lower classes and the underworld of 1920's Berlin. Minor exceptions include members of the constabulary and members of the psychiatric profession; both groups are subjected to the author's satire, particularly the latter, to which in real life Döblin, himself a neurologist and psychiatrist, belonged. The major exception is the unnamed narrator, whose speech patterns, varying from gutter slang to sophisticated High German, provide a cultural cross section of Berlin society. The reader's inclination to identify the narrator as Fate or as a type of Greek tragic chorus is checked by the narrator's overt opposition to the Greek concept of Fate and to classical concepts in general. The narrator insists that there are, not Erinyes and Fate, but people and Death; after presenting the lower stratum of Berlin's populace and commenting in voices from all strata of Berlin society, that is, after presenting real people, the narrator indirectly discloses himself as Death.

Biberkopf and Reinhold, the two people with whom the narrator is chiefly concerned, are complementary characters. Biberkopf is fat, naïve, extroverted, warmly amicable, and manic-depressive. Reinhold is thin, shrewd, introverted, coldly calculating, and consistent in temperament (inwardly sensitive but insensitive to others). As alter egos, each is a criminal, each is guilty of a woman's death and is accordingly given a prison sentence, and each is both attracted to and repelled by the other. Biberkopf is the more humane, but he does not attain to human fullness until he takes on the Reinholdian characteristics of shrewdness, calculation, and reserve. Both men learn dependence upon others, Reinhold because he will need his cohorts after his ten years in prison and Biberkopf because he can fulfill himself only through others.

Döblin's focus upon proletarian and underworld characters is a reminder that the values of any society are encapsulated in its dregs, wherein they can be known for what they are, undisguised by any bouquet of classical Greek concepts: When one character, a gray-haired former schoolteacher, says, "I am an opponent of Fate. I'm no Greek, I'm a Berliner," he is speaking for both the narrator and the author.

## Themes and Meanings

In *Berlin Alexanderplatz*, the major themes of authentic individualism (the self as subjectively inseparable from the other) and apolitical socialism (a mutualism among citizens of state that is not held in lockstep to party principles) are underscored by images of suffering, sacrifice, and conversion. The major image of suffering is the Old Testament figure of Job. Biberkopf is Job as a Berliner. He is restored, not to his fortunes after three pairs of confrontations with friends and one audience with God, but to himself after three exponentially severe blows and one audience with Death. There are two images of sacrifice: animals killed (by hammer blows) in a slaughterhouse symbolize victims ignorant of their being sacrificed, while the Old Testament's Isaac symbolizes the willing and knowing sacrificial victim. Biberkopf passes from ignorant victim to willing victim of society. Döblin's victim of society must adapt to life, as Döblin would have society itself adapt to reality, through learning that Death is the ruler.

This learning is an act or process of conversion, a dying and a rebirth, a transformation of the former Franz Biberkopf into the new Franz Karl Biberkopf. The prime image of conversion, recurrent like the images of suffering and sacrifice, is death. The image is carried by a poetic refrain: "There is a reaper whose name is Death, empowered by almighty God. Today he is his sickle's whetter, and indeed it cuts much better; soon he will cut with it and we must put up with it." The refrain is oddly reminiscent of Henry Wadsworth Longfellow's "The Reaper and the Flowers" (1839), which begins "There is a Reaper, whose name is Death" and which is optimistic in its presentation of Death as a beneficent power and a promise of life. The refrain anticipates the song that Death sings to the catatonic Biberkopf, a song optimistic in its assertion that Death is "life and truest power," without which life "can have no worth."

*Critical Context*

*Berlin Alexanderplatz* is Döblin's greatest novel and the one with which his name is immediately and, outside Germany, almost exclusively associated. He had won national renown before its publication: He was, with Herwarth Walden, a founder of the expressionist periodical *Der Sturm* in 1910; he furthered German avant-garde literature with works such as *Die drei Sprünge des Wang-lun* (1915; the three leaps of Wang-lun), *Wallenstein* (1920), *Berge, Meere und Giganten* (1924; mountains, seas, and giants), and his epic poem *Manas: Epische Dichtung* (1927); he had won the Kleist Prize in 1922 and was elected to the Writers' Society of the Prussian Academy of Arts in 1928. It was with *Berlin Alexanderplatz*, however, that he established himself as a major figure of world literature. This novel, written during 1928 and 1929, overshadows all that Döblin wrote both before and after it.

This novel is the culmination of Döblin's literary expressionism. It is marked by bold and broad exposition; kaleidoscopic shifts of narrative; catalogs of facts and data; collages of topographical, meteorological, medical, psychological, and mathematical details; montages of scenes and episodes; flashbacks and flashforwards; anticlassicism; antiheroism; and antibourgeoisism. Where it appropriates traditional forms, such as triadic structure or Menippean satire (the combination of prose and verse), it does so in a context of impudence. It is comparable to James Joyce's *Ulysses* (1922). Yet while Döblin expressed admiration for Joyce's novel, he denied its having served him as a model and insisted that both he and Joyce derived their methods from the expressionists, Dadaists, and similar schools.

*Berlin Alexanderplatz* was adapted by the author, in collaboration with Max Bing and Hugo Döblin, as a radio play in 1930, as revised by Wolfgang Weyrauch, in 1959. Döblin and Hans Wilhelm wrote the screenplay for its first adaptation to film in 1931. The novel was adapted to television in 1983 by Rainer Maria Fassbinder and was subsequently released as a theatrical film.

*Sources for Further Study*

Komar, Kathleen. "Technique and Structure in Döblin's *Berlin Alexander-platz*," in *The German Quarterly*. LIV (May, 1981), pp. 318-334.

Kort, Wolfgang. *Alfred Döblin*, 1974.

Prangel, Matthias. *Materialen zu Alfred Döblin "Berlin Alexanderplatz,"* 1975.

Schoonover, Henrietta S. *The Humorous and Grotesque Elements in Döblin's "Berlin Alexanderplatz,"* 1977.

Ziolkowski, Theodore. *Dimensions of the Modern Novel: German Texts and European Contexts*, 1969.

*Roy Arthur Swanson*

# BILLIARDS AT HALF-PAST NINE

*Author:* Heinrich Böll (1917-1985)
*Type of plot:* Social criticism
*Time of plot:* September 6, 1958
*Locale:* West Germany, presumably Cologne
*First published: Billard um halbzehn*, 1959 (English translation, 1961)

> *Principal characters:*
> ROBERT FAEHMEL, a forty-three-year-old architect and
>   demolitions expert
> HEINRICH FAEHMEL, an eighty-year-old architect and Robert's
>   father
> JOHANNA FAEHMEL, Heinrich's wife, a patient in a mental
>   hospital
> ALFRED SCHRELLA, a childhood friend of Robert
> JOSEPH FAEHMEL, Robert's twenty-seven-year-old son, an
>   apprentice architect
> HUGO, a seventeen-year-old bellboy in the Prince Heinrich
>   Hotel

*The Novel*

In this, one of Heinrich Böll's most structurally complicated works, the history of the Faehmel family over a fifty-year period is narrated by several family members. Through monologue, memory, and flashbacks, historical and personal events since the turn of the century are recounted, mirroring political and social developments in Germany itself. The eightieth birthday of the grandfather, Heinrich—September 6, 1958—marks a turning point for four members of the Faehmel family. Each of them has withdrawn from an active public life, preferring instead the protection of private routine. On this day, however, they will come to terms with the past that haunts them and forge a new identity as a united family. The time span of the novel measures approximately ten hours on this single day.

The first three chapters of the novel gradually clarify the mysterious behavior of the architect Robert Faehmel. Faehmel spends little time in his office, leaving punctually every day for an unknown destination. Faehmel's own secretary does not know where he goes, or why; she has only his explicit instructions that he is not to be disturbed. In addition, his two partners in the firm never visit the office, and all contact between them is carried out by mail. The reader soon discovers that Faehmel spends his mornings playing billiards in the Prince Heinrich Hotel, speaking only to a young bellboy, Hugo, who is there to guarantee Faehmel's privacy.

While standing at the billiard table, Faehmel reminisces aloud to Hugo

about the events in his life. During the advent of National Socialism, Faehmel was drawn instinctively to a group of dissenters and pacifists whom, in
retrospect, he characterizes as "lambs"; their amateurishly attempted assassination of a Nazi leader failed, and they were forced to flee the country to
escape punishment at the hands of the brutal Nazi conformists or "buffaloes." Faehmel later returned to Germany, was inducted into the army, and
spent the waning days of the war demolishing buildings for a demented officer who insisted on creating a "field of fire," a clear zone which was to provide an unrestricted firing line to the enemy. During his last mission, Faehmel convinced the officer to blow up St. Anthony's Abbey—built by his own
father, Heinrich Faehmel—though it was of no military or strategic value
whatsoever. Eventually, Faehmel reveals that this destruction was not an act
of hatred, perpetrated against his father, but rather an attempt to destroy institutions which had collaborated with the "buffaloes'" reign of terror.
Faehmel's comrades in this military venture have since become his two enigmatic partners in the architectural firm.

In an abrupt narrative change, the fourth chapter is devoted to Heinrich
Faehmel's reminiscences. He recalls the day, fifty years before, when he first
arrived in town. He was young and confident of his plans and thus of his future: Within a year, he would win the architectural competition to design St.
Anthony's Abbey, permanently establishing his professional reputation; he
would create an image or persona of himself, at once dependable and
unique; and he would marry a beautiful young woman from the higher social
circles. Recalling his fulfillment of those ambitions from the perspective of
his eightieth birthday, he is convinced that he can continue to live out his
days untouched by the chaos of historical events.

Chapter 5 presents the memories of Johanna Faehmel through an extended interior monologue. In 1942, alarmed at the insanity of a world which
was beyond her control, Johanna had herself committed to a mental hospital;
she has remained there voluntarily in "inner emigration" for the past sixteen
years. She now mirrors Heinrich's recollections, but from her own point of
view. She compares her two sons: Robert the "lamb," who is persecuted and
flees Nazi brutality, and Otto the "buffalo," who died in combat near Kiev at
the age of twenty-five, an unquestioning Fascist and conformist. In her disjointed ramblings, Johanna mourns her personal losses and pledges to sacrifice for the future good. On her husband's eightieth birthday, Johanna leaves
the mental hospital with plans to assassinate a former Nazi who has been
able to maintain a position in the present government. Later in the day, she
fires a pistol into the passing parade, but she only wounds her target. It is
clear that she will be returned to the mental hospital for the remainder of her
life.

From this point forward, the novel concentrates on the events of September 6, 1958, beginning with the return of the exile Alfred Schrella. He had

been tortured and persecuted by the Nazis because he was a "lamb"; his flight into Holland saved his life, as it did that of his friend Robert. Upon his return, however, Schrella feels that he cannot remain in present-day Germany—not simply because the "buffaloes" are still in power, but because he cannot find any "lambs." Schrella is not an activist and lacks political engagement, preferring to embarrass the police chief socially, rather than prosecute him for past criminal activities.

The youngest Faehmel, the grandson Joseph, is currently helping in the restoration of St. Anthony's Abbey. On this day, he discovers that his father was responsible for the wartime demolition of the abbey, his grandfather's most significant construction. Joseph does not know whether to continue with constructive architecture, move into demolitions, or abandon the profession entirely.

With Johanna's assassination attempt, the family's birthday celebration at the hotel is interrupted. Instead, they meet at Heinrich's old architecture office, the site of the family's original success. Sitting atop piles of old construction designs, the intimate circle eats a cake—designed as a replica of St. Anthony's Abbey—to celebrate their reconciliation.

During the course of September 6, 1958, each of the four Faehmels finds his or her way back into the family and, thus, back into the present. Johanna must attempt an act of political assassination to halt the spread of evil into the next generation. Heinrich supports his wife's decision to shoot a political opportunist and fight, however unsuccessfully, the continued dominance of the "buffaloes"; indeed, he accepts Schrella, the "lamb," as a son. Robert is reconciled with his father and, in turn, adopts the orphan Hugo as a representative of the next generation of "lambs." Joseph must still sort out the confusing events of the day, but it is clear that he will remain in the family and carry on either the father's or the grandfather's legacy.

## The Characters

At the novel's outset, each of the major characters is living a timeless existence, protected from contemporary reality. Heinrich Faehmel, patriarch of the clan, is a product of his own timeless myth, sure of the future because the present was always the fulfillment of the past. He came to town at the turn of the century with definite plans to attain his professional and personal goals. Heinrich succeeded precisely according to plan and on his own schedule, living to this day seemingly untouched by economic depressions, four governments, and two wars.

Heinrich Faehmel remains above everyday developments with an ironic stance. Unlike her husband, Johanna Faehmel openly condemns political criminals and acts to correct injustices. She is especially sensitive to blind nationalism and public respectability; this behavior is symbolized by her condemnation of Hindenburg, the German general and politician whose career spanned several generations, from the "blood and iron" years of the German Empire to Adolf Hitler's National Socialism in 1933, to which he capitulated. Johanna's lingering refrain, which summarizes those brutal years for the entire family, is the question, "whywhywhy."

Unable to cope with the increasing violence of the Nazi regime (which affected her own son Otto and caused the death of her daughter-in-law, Edith Schrella), Johanna has sought refuge in a mental hospital. There, in her "bewitched castle," she has been insulated from time. Despite her lengthy self-isolation, she is lucid and prepared to leave the sanatorium for one day, to avenge the past and save the future through an extreme act of political activism. Although she fails, she epitomizes the family's conscience. She has never capitulated to public weakness or opportunism, seeking instead a way to combat evil and promote goodness.

Living with unresolved memories of passive resistance to the inhumanity of the Nazi years, Robert has developed his own routine of self-protection. At his billiard table in the hotel, he, too, attempts to escape time. As a soldier, he had the unique opportunity to destroy some monuments of Nazi Germany (including his father's abbey) and thereby gain some sense of justice. Today, however, in his civilian occupation, Robert can neither ignore present injustices nor attempt to demolish them as he had been permitted to do earlier. By adopting Hugo as his son, Robert is finally able to make a constructive contribution to social betterment, as opposed to the destructive act attempted by his mother.

*Themes and Meanings*

The motifs, symbols, and plot strands are drawn together through the various and isolated memories of several narrators. This montage of dialogue, monologue, and interior monologue is structurally complicated and often confusing for the reader; only gradually, as in the construction of a mosaic, do the disparate pieces provide a unified picture of the past fifty years. The focus here is on the individual response to opportunism and barbarism. Many succumbed to this evil as corrupt "buffaloes"; a few resisted and attempted to maintain their humanity as innocent "lambs."

The title emphasizes two major elements of the novel: the game of billiards, which represents an artificial order, and the concept of time. The clean geometric patterns traced by the moving billiard balls reflect the architects' concern with a well-ordered life. Since no such order exists in the modern world—as exemplified by unexpected deaths and the political development of the "buffaloes" during the Nazi years—Robert hides behind a regimented schedule and the artificial beauty of the billiard table. All the while, he tries to fathom the moral events and challenges of the past. Time, however, effects change, as evidenced in the novel's structure. The preoccupation with the past gradually leads to a confrontation in and with the present; members of three generations must learn to make their peace, however tentative, with life.

Much of the novel's action transpires between the Prince Heinrich Hotel and St. Severin's Cathedral, between representative buildings of the secular (political and military) and religious power. Still, the predominant symbol for the family's fate remains St. Anthony's Abbey. The original creation of the elder Faehmel, it is leveled at the war's end by his son, Robert. The demolition is a symbolic act, and the ruins stand both as a memorial to all those innocents who perished (including Robert's wife, Edith) and as a protest against the Church's involvement with the corrupt political structure of the Nazis. Robert and his men also wanted to destroy St. Severin's Cathedral, the revered institution of all those responsible and respectable people who had been capable of so much hatred and murder.

The Abbey's symbolism is problematic. As a monument to the family's private success and to traditional German decency, it flourishes. During the war, however, Robert perceives the edifice as a reminder of the Church's capitulation to immorality and inhumanity, and he consequently levels it. With such a decisive end to this symbolic structure, Robert could hope for new beginnings, both politically and (for the Church itself) spiritually. Even before the novel begins, however, the decision has been made to rebuild the Abbey—on the original site according to the original plans, and with help from the youngest generation of Faehmels. Such circumstances imply a restoration of the past and do not bode well for fresh, thoughtful beginnings. At the novel's conclusion, the family cuts the cake (in the shape of the Abbey) and shares in the Abbey's "digestion," emphasizing a resolution to the family's differences. Nevertheless, this private act will in no way hinder the actual reconstruction of the public structure and will therefore not change the continued corruption of this representative institution of the Church and thus of society.

*Critical Context*

With its appearance in 1959, *Billiards at Half-Past Nine* was immediately perceived to be one of Böll's most significant works, and this opinion has not changed over the years. While his later novels and essays are concerned with contemporary German problems, this volume is the culmination of a series of works dealing with Germany's recent past, specifically the Nazi era.

It has been noted that this novel continues where Thomas Mann's *Buddenbrooks* (1900; English translation, 1924) concluded: While Mann's Buddenbrooks are nearing extinction at the turn of the century, Böll's Faehmels are just beginning their dynastic ascent. Because of its scope and ambition, this novel has created much controversy. Though recognizing its obvious strengths, critics have questioned the validity of its conclusion. How can one family represent the complex course of German history over the past five decades? Is this presentation not an oversimplification of those years, an attempt to portray world history as only good and evil, and thus to categorize Germans as either "lambs" or "buffaloes"? Also, how does the Faehmels' final, collective gesture—a political stance somewhere between resignation and companionship in isolation—offer constructive advice for social change? Still others have chided Böll for the seemingly happy ending, where the members of the family are reconciled with one another and with the past, while the young Hugo is unexpectedly elevated to the status of a Faehmel.

Heinrich Böll was one of the few contemporary German writers who consistently served as a conscience of the nation; in large part as a tribute to this moral engagement, he received the Nobel Prize for Literature in 1972. He actively championed frequently unpopular political causes, simply because he considered them to be correct. *Billiards at Half-Past Nine* is Böll's provocative reminder that the past cannot be ignored and that the future must be shaped by thoughtful action in the present.

*Sources for Further Study*
Bernhard, Hans Joachim. *Die Romane Heinrich Bölls*, 1970.
Conard, Robert C. "Novels of Conquering the Past," in *Heinrich Böll*, 1981.
Reid, James Henderson. "The Family Novels of the 1950's," in *Heinrich Böll*, 1973.
Ryan, Judith. "The Bewitched Castle: Heinrich Böll's *Billiards at Half-Past Nine*," in *The Uncompleted Past*, 1983.
Vogt, Jochen. ". . . nach fünfundvierzig der Aufbau nach den alten Plänen," in *Heinrich Böll*, 1978.

*Todd C. Hanlin*

# BLUE BOY

*Author:* Jean Giono (1895-1970)
*Type of plot:* Bildungsroman
*Time of plot:* c. 1900-1914
*Locale:* Provence
*First published: Jean le bleu,* 1932 (English translation, 1946)

> *Principal characters:*
> JEAN (THE BLUE BOY), whose development from earliest
>   childhood until his departure for World War I is the focus
>   of the novel
> PÈRE JEAN, the Blue Boy's father, a cobbler, a mystic, and a
>   healer; the true hero of the book

*The Novel*

*Blue Boy* is a fictionalized autobiography of Jean Giono's boyhood. Although much of the story is seen through the eyes of the young Jean, the novel is written in the lyrical style and language and with the voluptuousness and mystical insight which characterize Giono's greatest works. Sensuousness, the benign figure of Jean's father, Père Jean, and an intensely tender and loving regard for human suffering and for the beauties of the world provide a unity of tone and subject matter.

The first five chapters are dominated by three powerful influences on the young boy: his father, the life in a courtyard where "the night stayed from morning till evening," and music. *Blue Boy* is both the moving story of a father's subtle cultivation, enfranchisement, and liberation of a beloved son, and a son's loving tribute to his father.

Jean's earliest memories are of his father with his blue cobbler's apron sitting in his workroom with "a shoe in one hand and the awl in the other" talking with men who have come to him not for new boots but for help, who have come to be healed. By his example and later by his words, Père Jean encourages his son to become a healer, to use his gift with words to minister to human suffering and loneliness: "I tell you that you must put out the wounds. If, when you get to be a man, you know these two things, poetry and the science of extinguishing wounds, then you *will* be a man."

That the world is full of suffering and loneliness Jean's father does not have to tell him; the youth is preternaturally sensitive to the existence of grief and struggle around him. Jean spends many solitary hours looking down from the windows of his apartment at the dark well of a sheep court and into the windows and doors of other apartments which open onto that courtyard. For the dreaming, imaginative child, the guardian of this pitiful court is a lady whose face "dampness had traced on the walls," whose eyes are the green of mildew, a lady who, like the living inhabitants of the court, is "humanly beautiful and sad." The child does not know what to make of his perceptions, for he does not truly understand pain or suffering, and he spends much of his time being "borne away into the wide world" of his imagination. Nevertheless, when he hears the songs of the Passion according to Saint John by Johann Sebastian Bach, Jean imagines that "all the inhabitants of our poor sheep court were wailing."

Jean responds to the songs of his father's nightingale and to other music with such rapt attention that his father arranges for him to hear classical concerts played by two poor neighbors, Décidément and Madame-la-Reine, upon a violin and a flute. The child succumbs completely to "the intoxication of listening," demonstrating not only an intense sensuousness but also an innate capacity for transforming the language of music into words. He knows that the music of Mozart and Bach comes from the "very center of grief," but he also knows that there is celebration in the music—joy and pride and liberty.

The beginning of chapter 6 records the "sounds, the colors, the odors" which accompany the onset of a serious illness and Jean's descent into the "interior passages" of time. When he recovers, Jean is sent to live with a shepherd and his wife, Père and Madame Massot, in Corbières, a small mountain village, in order to regain his health, to learn "to see things as a whole. And to get some muscle." In the lush olive groves, vineyards, wheat fields, and pastures, the delicate, pampered child of dark tenements and city streets grows to the verge of manhood among shepherds, farmers, simple village folk, and animals. The turbulence, the vitality, the beauty, the tragedy of life flow forth all around and within him.

When the dark man of the sheep court, a former priest, comes to Corbières to serve as his tutor, Jean, the intellectual, the artist, the sensualist, thrives. Under the dark man's tutelage, Jean learns to respect the separateness and integrity of "the forms and life all about." Jean's pastoral vision of the harmony of life has its roots in the dark man's conviction that one has only to stoop and drink from the fountain of life to "have accomplished his work." Furthermore, the priest brings the world of the *Iliad*, of literature, alive for the boy. The vital, joyous, tragic world of Provence becomes inextricably linked for Jean with the heroic world of the Greeks, of men worthy of joy and sorrow and struggle. The boy also comes to see that the study of literature can, and should, lead to self-knowledge, to a richer understanding of and commitment to life.

Jean's sexual awakening also takes place at Corbières: "For the first time, . . . the odor of women reached me. . . . Then the song of the earth and waters changed its register." Jean is exhilarated, intoxicated, and saddened by his discovery. He is slightly more aware of his essential isolation after this moment, and he understands that "there is in sensuousness a kind of cosmic joy"; he also understands, however, "that the gestures that were so natural and simple for me were ugly, hypocritical, weighted with a sort of black slime for others."

By the time his father comes to take Jean back home, the boy has, as his father suspects, matured enough to be able to "see"; he is no longer a dreamy imaginative child. Père Jean is concerned that when his son actually "sees" the poverty and misery of his working-class tenement, Jean will despair. Père Jean warns the youth not to put his trust solely in what he "sees and hears, . . . in reason," for it is with reason "that a man puts the rope around his neck." Père Jean asserts that hope and the human heart are far stronger than suffering, than poverty, than reason. In spite of his father's words, Jean is deeply troubled by the pain and suffering he perceives all around him when he returns home. The sheep court and all the neighborhood "smelled of defeat and slavery. In this camp of the vanquished nothing remained but submission and death."

The final chapter develops the image of the dark courtyard as a well of consciousness, self-awareness, and self-knowledge into which Jean plunges deeper and deeper. An aging Italian aristocrat, Franchesc Odripano, comes to live in a room long closed, a room in which "the darkness had hardened." From this man, as from his father, Jean learns that it is possible to live with dignity and beauty and love amid the wounds of human life, to "belong to the sheep court" and yet to be clean and pure and undefeated. Franchesc Odripano is dedicated to life, to calling out loudly and bravely "the sound that comes from the heart," in spite of the fact that he knows that he can "no longer be heard" in this base world.

The novel concludes with "bitter and exalted" visions of Père Jean's and Franchesc Odripano's descents into death, of the glory of the natural world, and of the horrid, inevitable triumph of sterility and reason. The novel, Jean's childhood, and the vital, medieval world of Père Jean and his neighbors and friends in the village of Manosque end with the onset of World War I, the bloody child of man's senseless union with "things without thighs" and the grotesque father of the horrible mediocrity of the twentieth century. Jean, to his endless regret, sets out for the war "without any great feeling of emotion, simply because . . . [he] was young, and over all young men they were blowing a wind that sang of pirates and the ocean sail."

*The Characters*

Jean and his father are the central figures of the novel; both Giono's self-portrait and the loving study of his father are unforgettable. *Blue Boy* is, in fact, filled with finely rendered, striking characters. Two aspects of the characters and characterization are particularly interesting: Giono's ability to bring even a minor character vividly to life with a deft, individualizing stroke, and the fact that *Blue Boy* is replete with characters who reappear in Giono's later novels.

Giono was exceptionally sensitive to the "form, the color, the sound, the sensation" of the world and the people around him. The girls who work in his mother's laundry, the men who come to his father for help, the denizens of the sheep court, the men and women of Corbières are all brought convincingly to life; the unique humanity of each is seen so sharply and sketched so precisely that virtually all are indelibly imprinted in the reader's memory. For example, the fascinating gallery of women includes Sister Clémentine, who has the "nobility of a column" and whose body when she walks undulates like "waves, the neck of a swan, a moan"; Madame Massot, "an agreeable country lady; with so much goodness in her blind eye, so much goodness in her good eye, . . . in her sagging cheeks" that she seems to have been "cooked in the oven of goodness like a brick"; Aurélie, the baker's wife, with "hair so black that it made a hole in the sky"; and Anne with lips that "burned like live coals, . . . the cold, silent little girl, the sleeper with open eyes, perched in the trees like a fruit."

*Blue Boy* is a treasure house of stories; the famous tale of *La Femme de boulanger* (1942; the baker's wife), which Marcel Pagnol made into a celebrated film in 1938, is only one of many. Also, many characters from the novel reappear in Giono's later fiction; Madame Massot prefigures Pauline of *Mort d'un personnage* (1949) and the other good-hearted, self-sacrificing women in Giono's novels. Blanche Lambelle, who hangs herself, foreshadows many other unhappy, frustrated women for whom Giono cared so deeply. The tragedies and comedies of the people in and around Corbières are the source not only of the famous baker's wife but also of people and incidents in *Noé* (1947, 1961) and *Un Roi sans divertissement* (1947). The stories of the ball, of Costes, Costelet, Hortense, and Julie recur in *Le Moulin de Pologne* (1952; *The Malediction*, 1955). Clara and Gonzalès, whose marriage brings great pain and drama to Manosque, reappear transformed and transposed in *Le Chant du monde* (1934; *The Song of the World*, 1937).

*Themes and Meanings*

The principal concerns of the novel are nicely emblematized by Giono's division of himself into two parts near the end of the novel: "Come here," who works in a bank, understands "dignified politeness and beautiful penmanship" and earns "thirty francs a month"; and "Blue Boy," "the greater part, . . . [whom] the face on the wall, Décidément and Madame-la-Reine, Anne and the girl perfumed with musk" help to "escape to fair pastures." In this juxtaposition between the bank clerk and the poet, between the blue of his bourgeois suit and that of the "great blue cyclone of liberty," Giono establishes the major oppositions and motifs of the novel: the sterility, mediocrity, and vulgar sensuality of modern civilization against the fertility, vitality, and sensuousness of the natural, pastoral world; business, science, and technology against hope, love, and art; the prison of reason against the freedom of imagination.

Clearly, Jean Giono took the lessons of his father, Décidément, Madame-la-Reine, the dark man, and Franchesc Odripano to heart; his art and his life became a crusade against suffering, sterility, and death. He strove valiantly to transform the "stench" of the human condition into "the pure and somber beloved" as Bach had done; to prevent men from killing their hearts because it had become "too difficult to live with them"; to provide men with hope by giving them a vision of a living, vital pastoral world where the great forces of nature and of human passion and striving made life grand, heroic, worthy of love and struggle.

When young Jean Giono returned to Manosque after his glorious time in the countryside, he was almost overwhelmed by despair; he had an apocalyptic vision of civilization laying waste to the teeming medieval world of his childhood, of natural man dispossessed: "[T]here was my father with the others, seeing his city destroyed, his fields burned, and himself forced to set out alone on the highways like the rest." Yet Jean Giono did not despair; nor did he despair after seeing the slaughter of both world wars and the pollution of his native Provence. On the contrary, he found the courage and the strength to struggle to save and redeem men, to help them to know what was worthy of love, to enable them to see that "the whole happiness of man is in the little valleys." He did not, as it might seem, refuse to face the realities of the modern world or create a beautiful, imaginary world to which he might escape; rather, his vision pierced deep into the core of life, and he became one of the few men of the twentieth century whose life and work justified his father's vision of men of "hope":

> Men who arrive empty-handed. People scarcely notice that their open hands illumine the darkness like night-lamps. When they do notice them at all. And behold, the mountains arise and follow them.

### Critical Context

Jean Giono was the author of twenty-six major works of fiction, ten essays or collections of essays, and four plays, as well as syndicated columns. He is also well-known as a great prose poet of nature, an unrepentant social critic, a champion of the poor, a theologian, a mythographer, a scholar, a revolutionary, and a humanist. Throughout his career as a writer, he offered to his readers as an alternative to modern, urban, industrial civilization a harmonious, pastoral universe in the classical manner of Greek mythology. Giono was one of the most original and innovative of modern novelists.

*Blue Boy* is an early work which not only embodies the primary themes which Giono was to use all of his life but also reveals the sources and development of those themes. *Blue Boy*, along with his early pastoral trilogy—*Colline* (1929; *Hill of Destiny*, 1929), *Un de Baumugnes* (1929; *Lovers Are Never Losers*, 1931), and *Regain* (1930; *Harvest*, 1939)—is one of his most popular works. In addition, he is greatly admired for his later novels, including *Le Hussard sur le toit* (1951; *The Horseman on the Roof*, 1953) and *Le Bonheur Fou* (1957; *The Straw Man*, 1959), and for his last polemic, *Provence perdue* (1968; Provence lost), a scathing indictment of modern civilization for its pollution of Provence.

*Sources for Further Study*
Girard, Marguerite Mathilde. *Jean Giono: Mediterranean*, 1974.
Goodrich, Norma L. *Giono: Master of Fictional Modes*, 1973.
Peyre, Henri. "Jean Giono," in *French Novelists of Today*, 1967.
Redfern, W. D. *The Private World of Jean Giono*, 1967.
Smith, Maxwell A. *Jean Giono*, 1966.

*Hal Holladay*

# THE BLUE ROOM

*Author:* Georges Simenon (1903-       )
*Type of plot:* Mystery
*Time of plot:* The mid-twentieth century
*Locale:* Poitiers and a nearby small town and village in France
*First published: La Chambre bleue*, 1964 (English translation, 1964)

> *Principal characters:*
> ANTONIO (TONY) FALCONE, a seller of agricultural machinery
>     who is having an affair with Andrée Despierre
> GISÈLE FALCONE, his wife
> ANDRÉE DESPIERRE, the mistress of Tony Falcone
> NICHOLAS DESPIERRE, her husband, the owner of the store at
>     Saint Justin-du-Loup
> MADAME DESPIERRE, his mother

*The Novel*

The book opens with a conversation in the blue room between Tony Falcone and Andrée Despierre, who have just made love. Andrée asks Tony if he loves her: "Could you spend the rest of your life with me?" Tony answers Andrée lazily, mechanically, "Of course"; then he sees Nicholas, Andrée's husband, crossing the square toward the hotel. Terrified of discovery, Tony escapes through a skylight, leaving his mistress to pacify her husband. The reader quickly discovers that this scene, from which the plot springs, is not taking place in the present; Tony is re-creating the memory in response to interrogation. Flashbacks from his past are interspersed with the comments and questions of his interrogators. On that particular August 2, Tony returned to his home in Saint Justin-du-Loup and arranged to take his wife, Gisèle, and his six-year-old daughter, Marianne, to the seaside for a three-week holiday.

In the next section of the book, Judge Diem, who also has a wife and a baby—but who cannot understand Tony, though they are much of an age—gets him to re-create the events prior to August 2. Tony and his brother, Vincente Falcone, the owner of the Hôtel des Voyageurs, are sons of an immigrant Italian bricklayer. They went to school with Nicholas Despierre (then a fat, pasty, epileptic child, the only son of the richest family in the village) and Andrée Formier, "the great, tall girl from the Château." Andrée's father, the doctor, had died heroically in a concentration camp; the Château was dilapidated and Andrée and her mother were poor and hungry. By the time that Tony returns to the area with his wife to set up a business in the village, Andrée has married Nicholas and successfully banished her mother-in-law, Madame Despierre, from the shop to her bungalow at the bottom of the garden. The liaison with Tony begins when he stops to help start the Despierres' Citröen, which has had a flat tire on the way to Triant. Andrée seduces him—not a difficult task as he is a handsome man and a casually unfaithful husband. Andrée announces that she has always longed for Tony, and they meet once a month in the blue room at Vincente's hotel. Vincente and his wife, Lucia, are disapproving but loyal and silent, and the assignations continue until the Thursday afternoon when Andrée's husband appears, the August 2 which was re-created in the first part of the book.

After his narrow escape from discovery, Tony avoids the village store, ignores Andrée, and hopes that nothing will disrupt the routine of family and work which give meaning to his life. Nevertheless, he feels threatened. Then one day, the Postmaster hands him local, anonymous letters: "I haven't forgotten. I love you." "Soon. I love you."

The letters are only the beginning. Nicholas dies suddenly, and an anonymous letter spurs the police into exhuming the body. They discover that he was poisoned with strychnine.

In December, Tony receives another letter: "Happy Our Year." Little Marianne Falcone comes home from school one day to find her mother dying in agony. Strychnine is discovered in the half-eaten pot of plum jelly. For Judge Diem, Tony re-creates that day, though he persists in denying the existence of the letters: Before going to work Tony took Marianne to school, then joined the customers at the village shop. He was served first, and Andrée gave to him a pot of jam which she said that Gisèle had ordered. Tony left it in the kitchen for his wife and returned that evening to find her dead.

After a long imprisonment, several court appearances, and the elaborate reconstruction which largely forms the novel, the lovers are tried. Tony discovers that the village has always known about his affair with Andrée and sympathized with Gisèle. Piece by piece, the evidence that they give places him in jeopardy. There was strychnine in his shed but also there was some in the Despierres' storeroom; the Postmaster remembers giving Tony the letters, and Andrée has admitted to writing them. Madame Despierre's evidence is crucial; to ensure that both lovers pay for her son's death, she lies. When Andrée took over the store on the morning of Gisèle's death, according to Madame Despierre, customers were already waiting and the new consignment of jam was still in its package. Thus Tony took home an untouched jar of jam; Andrée, if one accepts her mother-in-law's evidence, would have had to open the package and add strychnine to the jelly while customers waited in the shop. Andrée is therefore found guilty only of her husband's death; Tony is found guilty of murdering Gisèle. Both are sentenced to life imprisonment. The novel ends, as it began, with Andrée speaking: "You see, Tony, we'll never be parted now!"

*The Characters*

In itself, calling Andrée and Tony lovers begs one of the major questions raised by *The Blue Room*. Tony finds Andrée sexually exciting, but he does not love her; she is obsessed by him. Georges Simenon carefully and unobtrusively puts in the details which help the reader to comprehend Andrée: the poverty; the gangling adolescent who watches the handsome boy choose other partners; the prudent marriage to the rich, sickly Nicholas; the possessive mother-in-law and her festering resentment. All the pieces are there. The reader, like Simenon's most famous creation, Inspector Maigret, can understand the growth of a personality capable of these crimes.

Tony is a picture of incomprehension. The interrogations clarify events for him as well as for the reader. He is largely incapable of analysis and his self-awareness is neither intellectual nor verbal. "Were there really people whose lives were devoted to self-examination, to gazing at themselves in a mirror, as it were?" he asks himself. What Tony actually says, therefore, is not as meaningful as what is left unsaid. "The words were without substance." Andrée, who hears what he says at the hotel, but only interprets it according to what she wants to hear, acts upon his words and destroys everything he values. "You know very well you said yourself. . . ." she argues.

Tony's wife, Gisèle, is a silent, pathetic figure, afraid to complain of her husband's philandering, terrified of losing him, isolated in the village to which she does not belong. Her husband no longer finds her attractive, but he loves his home and his daughter, and therefore also his wife. He loves the routine which Gisèle, a true housewife, carefully maintains. Yet Tony and Gisèle can only guess—wrongly—at each others' thoughts and feelings because the relationship has no words. Both afraid, each endures alone.

Because Tony is himself so limited, Simenon is able to surprise the reader with the importance of minor characters who lie outside Tony's awareness. Madame Despierre, for example, is the author of the letter which produces the police investigation. Her perjury convicts an innocent man.

The fact that Tony is himself finding out the truth as his questioners ask him things that he has never asked himself makes for both interest and limitation: interest in the discovery, limitation because he is passive and cannot offer information for which he has not been asked. Much of the technical interest of the book lies in Simenon's ability to draw a picture in words of a man who cannot verbalize his thoughts, who can, in fact, hardly think.

*Themes and Meanings*

The gap between law and justice, the difficulty of establishing guilt beyond doubt, even the nature of guilt itself, are all questions raised by *The Blue Room*. Tony is not guilty of the murder of his wife—but he is not innocent either and does not feel himself to be so. "It was, after all, because of me that she died," he says.

Simenon has said that he is not interested in men's social selves but in man when he is totally naked. This novel contains a totally naked man who sees himself for the first time in the mirror held up to him by his captors. Yet the shape of the book also produces the feeling of inevitability. Tony is the victim of a woman who is herself a victim. The conversation at the beginning of the novel is the trigger for all the other events which follow. Or is it? Does this trigger occur earlier? The events were "determined from the first day. And that was not the day of Nicholas' death nor the day of Gisèle's agony." Simenon does not tell the reader which day began the inexorable march of the events which are chronicled in *The Blue Room*. The title suggests that the events of August 2 were crucial, but reflection indicates that this may be too simple an answer.

*Critical Context*

*The Blue Room* appeared in the last decade of Simenon's career as a fiction writer. Between 1922, when he published his first novel, and 1972, when he announced that he would write no more fiction, Simenon authored more than 280 books. *The Blue Room* belongs in the category which he describes as "tragedy-novels." Usually these novels begin in a crisis, unravel its causes through a psychological investigation of the people involved, and proceed to a conclusion which is a logical but not necessary consequence of the events which have gone before. In his mature novels of this kind, Simenon uses a double plot: The truth unravels slowly, the suspense builds, because the knowledge may not be available in time to prevent a tragedy.

Like his famous inspector, often regarded as an incarnation of the author's creative process, Simenon thinks himself into the skins of ordinary, limited people who happen to commit criminal, violent, or irrational acts. When Georges Simenon, or Inspector Maigret, has finished, the event is seen to be not merely an accident but more the product of character, past events, environment, and opportunity, all fatefully conjoined. Like the Greeks, Simenon does not believe in free will. Also like them, he presents the harsh doctrine of necessity in many guises, using a short space of time, a limited cast, and a stark outline.

Nevertheless, Simenon's plate-glass style gives the reader a window on the world of mean urban streets, stuffy bourgeois interiors, small villages, and petty towns. His people are unprepossessing, ordinary, lonely, often incompetent, leading lives of routine desperation. The moment of action breaks the pattern, but the result is never fortunate.

Though the tragic pattern creates similarities of structure, each novel is particularized: The main characters and their settings are carefully dovetailed. *The Blue Room* is an excellent example of Simenon's technical brilliance and of his tragedy-novels.

*Sources for Further Study*

Becker, Lucille F. *Georges Simenon*, 1977.
Bresler, Fenton S. *The Mystery of Georges Simenon: A Biography*, 1983.
Mauriac, Claude. "Georges Simenon," in *The New Literature*, 1959.
Narcejac, Thomas. *The Art of Simenon*, 1952.
Raymond, John. *Simenon in Court*, 1968.

*Jocelyn Creigh Cass*

# BLUEBEARD

*Author:* Max Frisch (1911-    )
*Type of plot:* Psychological mystery
*Time of plot:* The late twentieth century
*Locale:* The environs of Zurich, Switzerland
*First published: Blaubart*, 1982 (English translation, 1983)

> *Principal characters:*
> FELIX THEODOR SCHAAD, a Zurich physician who had seven
>     wives and was accused of murdering the sixth one
> ROSALINDE ZOGG, Schaad's sixth wife and the victim in a
>     brutal strangling
> THE PROSECUTING ATTORNEY, the unidentified tormentor
>     within Schaad's mind

*The Novel*

This short, tantalizing novel is an adaptation of the tale of Bluebeard, a villainous knight who had seven wives and killed six of them. The hero in this modern rendition is Felix Schaad, a fifty-four-year-old Zurich physician accused of strangling Rosalinde Zogg, a call girl and his sixth wife.

Unlike typical murder mysteries, the suspense in this masterpiece does not lie with the jury's verdict, for the novel begins with the doctor having been acquitted on grounds of insufficient evidence. Instead, the drama revolves around a second, private trial within the courtroom of Schaad's own conscience. Confused and distraught by the jury's inconclusive verdict, Schaad relives the painful ordeal of his trial in an attempt to ascertain his own guilt. The narrative consists largely in remembered excerpts from the testimonies of Schaad's accusers, interspersed with comments and embellishments from the accused.

Although Schaad is legally acquitted, his attempts to return to the routine of his former life prove unsuccessful. With his once-thriving medical practice in ruins, Schaad finds himself alone in his office—a physician with few patients but with an abundance of time to think about his tragic past. Tormented, yet unable to silence the voices in his mind, Schaad seeks relief in drink, travel, and billiards. Such diversions, however, offer only momentary escape. Inevitably, Schaad's thoughts return to the testimonies of his accusers.

One by one, Schaad recalls the witnesses who brought testimony against him: his former wives, a cleaning lady, an antique dealer, a nurse, a custodian of the cemetery, and a janitor. While their testimony is contradictory and unsubstantiated, few come to his defense and an abundance of circumstantial evidence points toward his guilt. After all, he alone was known to have a key to the apartment of the victim; the crime was committed with his necktie; he was the last individual known to be present with the deceased; and it was he who sent the five lilies found lying across the breast of the lifeless body. Moreover, each of his three alibis—that he was walking in the woods, working on tax matters in his office, and viewing a Czech film—were successively disputed by other testimony. Indeed, Schaad could not recall where he was at the time of the murder.

Months pass, yet the cross-examination in his beleaguered mind continues. He is forced to sell his medical practice. His seventh wife returns from a business trip in Kenya with a new lover and announces her desire for a divorce. Meanwhile, details of Schaad's whereabouts and activities on the day of the murder seem to become more focused in his confused mind. With his professional and personal life in shambles, Schaad falls prey to hallucinations and suicidal urgings. Ultimately, he concludes that he is guilty, drives to Ratzwil—his birthplace, a town nowhere near the scene of the crime—and confesses to the murder.

In a surprising turn of events, however, the police reject his confession and inform Schaad that the true murderer has been apprehended and is in custody. Schaad is not the Bluebeard he has admitted to being. Yet this truth makes little difference. While driving back to Zurich, Schaad crashes his car into a tree in an attempted suicide. The story ends with Schaad's speechless body—if not lifeless corpse—lying in a hospital ward, and an anonymous female voice saying, "Why did you make the confession? . . . You are in pain."

### The Characters

A master of understatement and suspense, Max Frisch tantalizes the reader by systematically withholding information about his cast of characters, providing glimpses into the working of their minds but never the evidence necessary to answer the central questions of the reader's imagination. Using few transitions or introductions, Frisch has witnesses appear, respond, or refuse to respond to the questions of the unnamed prosecuting attorney and then dematerialize. From the testimonies of these witnesses, many details can be surmised about the hero and his many wives. Yet, consistently the most pressing questions cannot be answered from the sketchy and often irrelevant information presented. For example, while the testimony reveals the names and occupations of Schaad's ex-wives, and it suggests that each of his successive marriages was shorter and more chaotic than the last, the reader never learns why his marriages failed, why he married so many times, why he left his wives, or why they left him.

The fundamental questions of the work—Did Schaad commit the crime? If so, what was his motive? If not, who was the true murderer?—also are not answered in the interrogative scenes. Several of his ex-wives testify that Schaad was pathologically jealous. Evidence gathered from the doctor's private notebooks also suggest that Schaad was insanely protective of his wives. "I watch her peeling asparagus," Schaad confides, "We talk about nothing in particular, then suddenly I find myself counting the stiff peeled stalks of asparagus on the kitchen table, twenty-four; I say nothing, of course, but I think to myself: There's one missing." Other evidence, however, shows the doctor as an extraordinarily complacent husband who responds calmly and rationally to discoveries of his wife's extramarital relations.

Was Schaad capable of murder? His mother, coming to the witness stand from beyond the grave, admits that, as a boy, Schaad cut open his pet rabbit with a razor. In another flashback to childhood, the reader sees Schaad with several of his school chums binding the feet of a boy and leaving him exposed to the elements. As a witness himself, even Schaad admits: "Not since I was fourteen have I had the feeling of being innocent. . . ." Yet, others testify that the doctor was meek, harmless, and a man of great charity.

As to the victim and her relationship with Schaad, the evidence suggests that Rosalinde never enjoyed sex (though she had numerous lovers) and chose to become a call girl only after her divorce from Schaad. She had many friends of high social standing, gave parties for them, and retained, until the day of her death, a close friendship with her ex-husband. On one occasion, in an attempt to expose the irrationality of her former husband's jealousy, Rosalinde demanded that Schaad view a videotape of her coupling with her customers—an experience that, according to Schaad, cured him of his jealous tendencies.

The sum of the testimony brings the reader toward the same verdict as the original jury: There is suspicion but no proof; the evidence is inconclusive: Uncertainty prevails. Thus, whether Schaad is an innocent victim driven to madness by a cruel form of judicial torture or a "Bluebeard," a sadistic wife strangler, is a question never answered until the final page of the book. Even when the full truth is revealed, questions remain unanswered. The killer is a once-mentioned character, Nikos Grammaticos—a Greek student, bald with black beard, who speaks no German. Still, the revelation is unsatisfying. The novel ends without hint as to how or why the villain accomplished his grisly deed.

### Themes and Meanings

*Bluebeard* is a sparsely yet elegantly written tale about guilt and innocence in an age of bureaucracy. Schaad (the name itself means "damaged" in German) is a true self-tormentor who has worried himself into a state of suicidal guilt. Although wrongly accused of a serious crime, Schaad self-destructs when placed under intense public scrutiny and ultimately becomes the man others think him to be. With the headline "Bluebeard in Court" the press not only destroy his reputation but also succeed in convincing him of his own guilt. He is a tragic victim living within a highly civilized, technological age—

an age in which individuality is becoming increasingly irrelevant.

Yet, while not guilty of the specific crime, Schaad is far from innocent. Upon self-examination, he finds himself to be a blatantly egotistical creature who destroyed the loves of all the women who once adored him. A failure in seven marriages, he cannot even comprehend, much less learn from, his experiences. Schaad's refusal to respond to the prosecutor's disturbing question, "Is it correct to say. . . that the moment things go contrary to your masculine wishes, you very quickly lose your temper?" does not hide his sense of guilt. Indeed, Schaad was not the murderer, but he could have been, and perhaps, might have been had not another nonpersonality completed the deed for him. To Schaad, as to other characters in Frisch's works, memory brings not happiness but remorse; memory, by confronting individuals with their personal failures, merely reminds them of their inevitable jealousies, betrayals, and broken relationships. Schaad, like human nature itself, is morally corrupt—not because of a specific human act but because of the general condition of his soul.

Finally, Max Frisch uses the tale of Bluebeard to remind the reader that there is no simple prescription for truthful living. On numerous occasions, the unrelenting prosecutor instructs his witnesses to "Tell the Truth, the Whole Truth, and Nothing But the Truth" or face the penalty for perjury. Yet, as the story unfolds, it becomes increasingly apparent that there is a fine line between truth and fiction and that moral truth is not easily pinned down or established beyond doubt. Life must be lived in the face of ambiguity, for, to Doctor Schaad as well as to the author, the more important aspects of human experience are largely unknowable.

*Critical Context*

*Bluebeard* is a logical next step, perhaps the final step, in the intellectual and literary development of the Swiss author Max Frisch. A variant of this tale first appeared in Frisch's novel *Mein Name sei Gantenbein* (1964; *A Wilderness of Mirrors*, 1965). In this story, as in *Bluebeard*, a cultured man is accused of the murder of his former lover, a prostitute, and despite a lack of substantial evidence is unable to persuade the public of his innocence. Moreover, the themes and the plot of *Bluebeard* are reverberations of previous works. For example, in expressing his ideas about the deteriorating human condition, the relativity and unknowability of moral truth, the manner in which guilt erodes true identity, and the near impossibility of living truthfully, Frisch returns to themes about which he wrote with great inventiveness in his first grand masterpiece, *Stiller* (1954; *I'm Not Stiller*, 1958).

While Frisch's works reveal an underlying consistency, in more recent years he has developed a decidedly different narrative technique. Unlike his earlier novels, which were filled with eloquence and abundance, *Montauk* (1975; English translation, 1976) and *Der Mensch erscheint im Holozän*

(1979; *Man in the Holocene*, 1980) underplay his storytelling genius. In these works, he deliberately strips away all decorative speech until nothing is left but the pure, functional form. With *Bluebeard*, Frisch continues this stylistic shift toward literary silence. Blunt and more objective, the mature Frisch limits his expressiveness, often combining short introductory phrases with laconic sentence fragments. Such narrative techniques leave more space for interpretation and masterfully serve to remind his readers how little one truly knows.

Perhaps the last sentence of *Bluebeard*, "You are in pain," is in part an autobiographical statement of a chillingly frank artist who understands well the ontological suffering that accompanies moral uncertainty. At any rate, *Bluebeard* preserves Frisch's much-deserved reputation as a creator of cerebral labyrinths in the tradition of Franz Kafka and Jorge Luis Borges. This novel is another fitting encore to a brilliant career.

*Sources for Further Study*
Butler, Michael. *The Novels of Max Frisch*, 1976.
*The New Republic*. Review. CLXXXIX, July 11, 1983, p. 32.
*The New York Times Book Review*. Review. LXXXVIII (July 10, 1983), p. 9.
*Newsweek*. Review. CII (July 18, 1983), p. 69.
Probst, Gerhard F. and Jay F. Bodine, eds. *Perspectives on Max Frisch*, 1982.
*World Literature Today*. LX (Autumn, 1986). Special Frisch issue.

*Terry D. Bilhartz*

# THE BOOK OF LAUGHTER AND FORGETTING

*Author:* Milan Kundera (1929-      )
*Type of plot:* Novel of ideas
*Time of plot:* From 1968 to the late 1970's
*Locale:* Prague and a small town in Czechoslovakia, the Riviera, a provincial
    town in Western Europe, and a mythical isle of children
*First published: Le Livre du rire et de l'oubli*, 1979 (English translation, 1980)

> *Principal characters:*
> THE NARRATOR, an intrusive voice
> TAMINA, a widowed Czech exile in a small, provincial Western
>     European town

## The Novel

In part 6 of *The Book of Laughter and Forgetting*, Milan Kundera states
that the "entire book is a novel in the form of variations." He also declares
that "it is a novel about Tamina, and whenever Tamina is absent, it is a novel
for Tamina. She is its main character and main audience, and all the other
stories are variations on her story and come together in her life as in a mirror." In this authorial digression can be seen the nexus of the book. With
historical anecdotes, philosophical reflections, artistic criticism, and personal
revelations, Kundera weaves his own voice and experience in and out of the
stories he presents. Tamina epitomizes, perhaps, the soul in exile, besieged
by forgetfulness yet unable to forge a new life in an alien environment.
Kundera, on the other hand, is the successful exile, allowed to leave Czechoslovakia in 1975 for a university post in Rennes. Having settled in Paris in
1978, he survives in exile by evoking the life and spirit of his native Prague.

*The Book of Laughter and Forgetting* is divided into seven parts, a structure based on musical polyphony. In an interview with Philip Roth, Kundera
explains his theory of novelistic unity: "The synthetic power of the novel is
capable of combining everything into a unified whole like the voices of poly-
phonic music. The unity of a book need not stem from the plot, but can be
provided by the theme. In my latest book, there are two such themes: laughter and forgetting." Each of the seven divisions of the book is a different tale;
in only two, part 4 and part 6, does Tamina appear. The other five parts are
separate stories held together by the thematic variations, echoing incidents,
and the omnipresent narrator.

Part 1, "Lost Letters," opens with the narrator describing a famous Czech
photograph of Communist leader Klement Gottwald addressing the Czech
citizenry from a Prague balcony in February, 1948. In the original picture,
Gottwald was flanked by his comrade, Clementis, who, moments before,
had set his own hat on Gottwald's head to protect him from the snow. Four
years later, Clementis, having been accused of treason and hanged, was

airbrushed out of the photograph by the propaganda section of the government. Subsequently, Gottwald has stood on the balcony alone, but Clementis' hat remains upon his head.

This primary incident of "forgetting" in the book is accompanied by the sardonic humor implicit in Clementis' hat. The story of part 1 concerns Mirek, a former Party member, who was active in the Prague Spring reform movement and lost his position after the Russian invasion of 1968. At the time of the story, in 1971, he is working as a laborer. Having broken his arm, he has a few weeks free from work and is determined to retrieve old love letters from his former mistress, Zdena, who has remained a loyal Party member and who has continued to love him despite their political and personal disaffiliation. Mirek wants his letters back because he is ashamed of having loved a woman as ugly as Zdena; he wants to airbrush her out of his life just as the propaganda department has removed Clementis from Czech history. Zdena refuses to return the letters. In obsessively following this mission, Mirek has neglected to destroy papers which incriminate himself and his friends. The secret police, who entered his apartment soon after he left to see Zdena, greet him on his return. Mirek, his son, and several of their friends are sentenced to prison.

In part 2, "Mother," a married couple, Marketa and Karel, have invited Karel's mother to visit them for a week. Mother persists in staying an extra day, the Sunday on which Eva, Marketa's friend and Karel's lover, is due. Although Eva has come to participate in a "homespun orgy" with Marketa and Karel, the couple decide that Mother will go to bed early and not bother them. Marketa introduces Eva as her cousin, and Mother shows familial interest in Eva, who reminds her of an old friend, Nora.

When Karel sees the resemblance, his sexual lethargy, which had beset him early in the evening, dissipates, and he initiates a frenzied lovemaking session, inspired by his memory of Nora. As a four-year-old, he once caught a glimpse of Nora naked; the image and its accompanying dizzying sensation have remained imprinted in his memory. He transfers the image onto Eva and becomes a four-year-old satyr. Marketa, who has secretly been invited to join Eva and her husband for a similar weekend, manages to make love wantonly to her husband by imaginatively severing his head from his body.

In the morning, Marketa drives Eva to the train station and reaffirms their assignation with Eva's husband. Karel, still full of his excitement from the previous night, later drives Mother to the station and invites her to come and live with him and Marketa. Although she is grateful, Mother declines the invitation. Karel arranges a first-class coach for her and presses some money into her hand. She accepts it matter-of-factly, as a child accepts a gift of money from an adult. Karel stands on the platform waving until the train is out of sight.

Part 3, entitled "The Angels" (as is part 6), is a fable about two American girls, Gabrielle and Michelle, who are attending a summer-school course for foreigners in a small town on the Riviera. Mme Raphael, their teacher, assigns them to present a report on Eugène Ionesco's play *Rhinoceros* (1959). Enthralled by the recognition that Ionesco meant to create a comic effect with the symbol of the rhinoceros, the girls decide to present their report wearing horns on their noses. Mme Raphael is enchanted. The class reacts at first with sympathetic embarrassment, but when one student who dislikes the two girls recognizes a golden opportunity for revenge and neatly kicks each of them in the behind, the class breaks out in laughter. Mme Raphael, thinking the incident a prearranged part of the report joins in unrestrainedly. She misunderstands Gabrielle's and Michelle's embarrassed writhings as a dance and joins hands with them. The three dance in a circle around the room, until they begin to rise heavenward in their angelic circle of laughter, leaving the stupefied students below.

In relating this tale, Kundera interjects philosophical speculation on the nature of laughter, dividing it into two types: that of the Devil and that of the Angels. The first points up the meaninglessness of things; the second celebrates the rational order of the good and sensible conception of the earth. Taken to extremes, the former leads to despair, the latter to idyllic totalitarianism.

Kundera also relates his personal history of involvement with the Czech Communist Party. As a student in 1948, he danced in the circle that brought the Communists to power. Later, having been expelled from the Party and shut out of the circle for a political misstep, he witnessed the poet Paul Éluard's betrayal of his friend, Zavis Kalandra, who was executed as a traitor. When the Russians invaded Czechoslovakia, Kundera was not allowed to work. A young friend who edited a youth magazine hired him to write an astrology column under a pseudonym. While he was doing so, her boss, a high Party official, commissioned a personal horoscope which Kundera willingly, if ironically, provided for a high fee. The pseudonym ruse was discovered by the authorities, and Kundera's friend lost her position. At this point, Kundera realized that he would have to emigrate in order to avoid harming his friends. He believes that he continues to fall further and further away from the ecstatic circle dance of his youth.

Like part 1, part 4 is entitled "Lost Letters." Tamina's story begins here. She is a thirty-three-year-old native of Prague, now in exile in a small provincial Western European town where she earns a subsistence living as a waitress in a small café. She emigrated from Czechoslovakia with her husband, Mirek, leaving behind, in her mother-in-law's desk, her letters and journals which recounted their life together. When her husband died shortly after their emigration, Tamina, full of tranquilizers, attempted to commit suicide by swimming out into the sea; she did not fall asleep, however, and swam back to shore.

Now Tamina has begun to forget details of her life with her husband. When her friend Bibi plans a vacation in Prague, she consents to bring back the package of notebooks. With much difficulty, Tamina arranges for her brother to retrieve the notebooks from her mother-in-law and bring them to her father, who will give them to Bibi. Unfortunately, Bibi and her husband change their plans and cannot get the journals. Tamina confides her desire to retrieve her notebooks to Hugo, a writer and café regular, who is infatuated with her. He offers to go to Prague to pick up what he thinks are political papers. In gratitude and resignation, Tamina breaks her vow of faithfulness to her dead husband and sleeps with Hugo, but during the lovemaking she distracts herself by mentally enumerating the vacations she spent with her husband. Hugo feels let down after his sexual conquest because he cannot begin to penetrate Tamina's reserve, and finally he realizes that she is only with him because he has offered to go to Prague. When she asks him when he is going, he tells her that he cannot go, because an article he has written, analyzing the Czech power structure, would put him in danger with the authorities. She reacts with revulsion and nausea, and she never again contacts anyone in Czechoslovakia.

"Litost" is both the subject and the title of part 5. *Litost* is a Czech word which has no direct equivalent in any other language. Kundera defines it as "a feeling as infinite as an open accordion, a feeling that is the synthesis of many others: grief, sympathy, remorse, and an indefinable longing." More narrowly, however, it becomes "a state of torment caused by a sudden insight into one's own miserable self." Characteristic of immaturity, it "works like a two-stroke motor. First comes a feeling of torment, then the desire for revenge. The goal of revenge is to make one's partner look as miserable as oneself."

The sufferer of *litost* in this section is a student who has fallen in love with Krystyna, a small-town butcher's wife, whom he met during summer vacation. Failing to consummate his passion for her during his vacation, he invites her to visit him in Prague. Unfortunately, on the very day she is to arrive, he is invited to a gathering of the country's great poets at the Writers' Club; he declines the invitation because of Krystyna's arrival. Both are disappointed on their first meeting—he in her provincial appearance, she in the restaurant he has chosen for the rendezvous. On finding a more suitable dining situation, the student tells her of the invitation to join the poets; impressed, she insists that he go and requests that he bring her back an autographed book from the great poet whose poems she memorized in school. Gladly agreeing, he joins the gathering of poets and is treated warmly.

The student returns to Krystyna long after he said he would, but he placates her with the book in which the great poet has written a long dedication to her. Krystyna treats the student to exquisite sexual caresses, yet she will not allow him to penetrate her, despite his professions of intense and eternal love for her; she says that the act would kill her. Instead, she worshipfully holds his weapon in her hand as a precious object to be preserved and adored.

In the clear light of the next day, she tells him that her doctor has warned her that getting pregnant could cause her death. The student is dumb-founded that she would think him inexperienced enough to cause a preg-nancy, and he falls into despair because a sensible sentence from him would have gained for him his desire. Suffering from *litost*, but without an object for his revenge, since Krystyna has already boarded the return train, the stu-dent seeks consolation at the Writers' Club. There he descends into obses-sive *litost* by abandoning and being abandoned by the one poet who might have understood him.

"The Angels" reappear in part 6, which is the conclusion of Tamina's story. This section also encompasses Kundera's account of his father's dying. It begins with a repetition of the account of Clementis giving Gottwald his hat. In addition, Kundera tells the reader that the building on whose balcony Gottwald and Clementis stand once housed the ground-floor shop of Franz Kafka's father. The officials do not know about Kafka, nor would Kafka be surprised at their lack of knowledge, for Prague in his novels is a city without a memory, without even a name. Kundera reiterates this memory loss by tracing the name changes of the street on which Tamina was born. Five of them have occurred from the time when her father moved there until the day when she married her husband, each a memory loss induced by a change of government.

During the last ten years of his life, Kundera's father gradually lost his ability to speak. Ideas and objects were no longer associated with words. The author connects his father's growing silence with the silence imposed by the Russians, who dismissed 145 historians from their positions and forbade them to publish, and with the silence that gradually engulfs Tamina.

One day, a young man wearing blue jeans comes into the café and begins to talk to her, to question her. He offers to take her away from her sadness and despair at forgetting to a place where things "weigh nothing at all." Tamina walks out of the café with the young man to his red sports car; his name is Raphael. He takes her to a riverbank where a laughing boy in a row-boat transports her to an island of children. She is at first repelled and then seduced by the children. (Kundera's father died on the day that Gustav Husák, the Russian-appointed Czech leader, received the red handkerchief of the Pioneers; the air was full of the sound of children singing.) The chil-dren treat her to a purely physical sexuality, into which she escapes with angelic simplicity until one of them deliberately hurts her.

When Tamina shows the first sign of adult awareness, the children begin to torment her. She escapes, but when she is recaptured by the children she consciously plays by their rules. Then one day the boat boy returns with rock music which sets the children dancing. Nauseated, Tamina runs to the river and swims away from the island. After swimming all night, she tries to see the other shore by daylight. All that is visible, however, is the shore she had left, which is a few hundred feet away. Curious, a contingent of children come out in the boat and eagerly watch as Tamina drowns.

"The Border," part 7, which takes place somewhere in Western Europe, is full of scenes of empty sex, of sex that seems to have taken upon itself a ridiculous aspect. In the opening passage, Jan, a forty-five-year-old womanizer, reflects that what he finds most interesting about intercourse is a woman's face, but that of his present mistress, Edwige, remains a blank screen which torments him with questions. It is the question posed to sexuality, which he calls "the deepest region of life," that Kundera perceives to be the "deepest question." It is in questions, not answers, that Kundera finds wisdom. Questions keep the border between deathly meaninglessness and deadly certainty visible.

Part 7 is filled with sardonic echoes of the previous sections and with demoniac laughter at visions of soulless sex, which are sometimes twisted into ironic affirmations of life. There is the egocentric flirtation of Jeanne, an actress, with Passer, who is emasculated and dying of prostate cancer. Their dalliance disgusts Jan, but it leaves Passer with a final romantic vision. Then there is the sex party which is so precisely orchestrated by the hostess that Jan and a friend end up in peals of laughter at the ridiculous situation.

At the center of the story is Passer's funeral. In the midst of the funeral oration, a gust of wind blows a mourner's hat from his head and into the grave and atop the coffin. Despite their sorrow, the mourners are suffused with silent waves of laughter.

The novel ends with Jan and Edwige taking a final holiday at a nudist beach before he leaves for the United States. Jan dreams of pure arousal innocent of physicality, while Edwige invokes a return to pagan sensuality; they assent to each other's visions in mutual misunderstanding. In a discussion with a group of naked people, the end of Western civilization is brought up with enthusiasm by a paunchy man. "The others listened with interest, their naked genitals staring dully, sadly, listlessly at the yellow sand."

*The Characters*

At one point in *The Book of Laughter and Forgetting*, Kundera envisions himself atop a high rise in France looking toward Prague. It is from this vantage that the reader also views his characters. The men—Karel, Mirek, Hugo, the student, and Jan—are Don Juans who not very successfully seek in sexual encounters a kind of liberation, but as their sexual encounters tend to be empty of meaning, so also are their experiences empty of freedom. The women for whom the men lust—Marketa, Eva, Krystyna, Edwige—find sex most satisfying when it is soulless or unconsummated.

Each of these men and women is individually drawn and sympathetically, if amusedly, portrayed, but Kundera clearly points out their collective lack of self-awareness as they become unable to hold contact with the truth contained in memory and history. The characters revert to the angelic simplicity of infantile or childlike certainties. Only Tamina is fully aware of her growing amnesia and struggles to retain and re-create those memories which define her being. Nevertheless, even she falls prey to the temptations of the weightless forgetfulness on the isle of children. It is Tamina's total amnesia and the fragmented amnesiac qualities mirrored in the other characters which create the metaphor for the cultural and historical destruction of Czechoslovakia by totalitarian ideology.

*Themes and Meanings*

Just as James Joyce made Dublin a microcosm of modern European consciousness, so has Milan Kundera transformed Prague and the Czechoslovak experience into a microcosmic model of contemporary European destiny. He fears the loss of a European cultural heritage that he finds embodied in the Central European experience. Kundera chronicles the forced expulsion of culture and history from Central Europe by its Russian overlords and the dissipation of the same culture by the cacophony of the Western media. *The Book of Laughter and Forgetting* juxtaposes sexual farce, fairy tale, historical chronicle, political tract, literary criticism, autobiography, and musicology to offer multiple views of contemporary existence.

Just as Tamina is being led away to the children's island of "forgetting about forgetting," she regains a fragment of her memory. In a sudden moment of déjà vu, the clay slope of the riverbank brings back a visit she made to her husband at the construction site where he last worked in Czechoslovakia. She remembers the moment in all of its love and anguish and despair and suddenly realizes that her grief has content as well as form—a content for which she must continue to search. Yet it is too late for Tamina; the boat has arrived, and Raphael leads her to her Lethean journey across the river. His pleasant and infectious laughter, echoed by the boy who rows the boat, seduces Tamina with a promise of peace and joy. She steps into the boat, and her destiny is sealed.

Kundera implies that once an individual joins the laughing circle of certainties, the possibilities for questions and searching are forgotten. Defection from the assured circle allows one, again, to choose and question, but then one will forever suffer the grief of individuality and lonely knowledge. It is this self-awareness and individual consciousness that defines Western culture for Kundera. *The Book of Laughter and Forgetting* asks if the individual can survive in the contemporary world.

*Critical Context*

Although Kundera wrote *The Book of Laughter and Forgetting* in Czech, it was originally published in French, as were his earlier novels—*La Vie est ailleurs* (1973; *Life Is Elsewhere*, 1974) and *La Valse aux adieux* (1976; *The Farewell Party*, 1976)—and his subsequent novel, *L'Insoutenable légèreté de l'être* (1985; *The Unbearable Lightness of Being*, 1984). Only his first novel, *Zert* (1967; *The Joke*, 1969), and a collection of short stories, *Směšné lásky* (1969; partial translation as *Laughable Loves*, 1974) were published officially in Czechoslovakia by the Czechoslovak Writers' Union Publishers.

Kundera was honored in Czechoslovakia with the Klement Gottwald State Prize in 1963 and the Czechoslovak Writers' Union Prize in 1967. Nevertheless, because of his participation in the Prague Spring liberalization movement, Kundera lost his position teaching film studies at Prague's Academy of Music and Dramatic Arts. He emigrated to France in 1975 and since then has had his Czech manuscripts translated into French for original publication. After the publication of *The Book of Laughter and Forgetting*, Kundera was stripped of his Czech citizenship. The French have honored him with the Prix Médicis and the Prix Mondello; in 1981, François Mitterand conferred French citizenship upon him. Kundera was also awarded the Jerusalem Prize, for literature on the freedom of man in society, by the Israelis in 1985.

Although Kundera refuses the label of "dissident writer," his novels have always been enmeshed with the contemporary life of Prague. To read his novels purely as political statements, however, is to direct his vision into a much too narrow channel. All of his novels provide multiple perspectives that reflect the complexities of contemporary existence. Although *The Unbearable Lightness of Being* was greeted with near-universal acclaim, *The Book of Laughter and Forgetting* is considered by some critics to be Kundera's finest work and most sweeping commentary on the dangers of living under totalitarian rule.

*Sources for Further Study*

Di Pietro, Thomas. "Weighting for Kundera," in *Commonweal*. CXI (May 18, 1984), 297-300.

Eagle, Hubert. "Genre and Paradigm in Milan Kundera's *The Book of Laughter and Forgetting*," in *Language and Literary Theory*. Edited by Lubomir Doležel et al., 1984.

Kussi, Peter. "Milan Kundera: Dialogues with Fiction," in *World Literature Today*. LVII (Spring, 1983), pp. 206-209.

Lodge, David. "Milan Kundera, and the Idea of the Author in Modern Criticism," in *Critical Quarterly*. XXVI (Spring/Summer, 1984), pp. 105-121.

Roth, Philip. "Afterword: A Talk with the Author," in *The Book of Laughter and Forgetting*, 1981.

*Jane Anderson Jones*

# BOSNIAN CHRONICLE

*Author:* Ivo Andrić (1892-1975)
*Type of plot:* Historical chronicle
*Time of plot:* 1806-1814
*Locale:* Travnik, Bosnia
*First published: Travnička hronika*, 1945 (*Bosnian Story*, 1958; better known
  as *Bosnian Chronicle*)

> *Principal characters:*
> JEAN BAPTISTE-ETIENNE DAVILLE, a French consul in Travnik
> JOSEF VON MITTERER, an Austrian consul
> MEHMED-PASHA,
> IBRAHIM-PASHA, and
> ALI-PASHA, Turkish viziers

*The Novel*

*Bosnian Chronicle* is a chronicle of life in Travnik, a provincial Turkish
capital in Bosnia during the first two decades of the nineteenth century. Since
then, Travnik has lost all significance and is now merely a small town, but in
those days, it was an administrative seat at the westernmost border of the
Ottoman Empire and the residence of a vizier. Because the French occupied
nearby Dalmatia and the Turks were forced to retreat from Hungary, Travnik
became important beyond its true political and strategic value. It was so
important that in 1806 the French found it necessary to send a consul, Jean
Baptiste-Etienne Daville, to keep an eye on the Turks. This appointment, in
turn, prompted the Austrians to send their own consul, Josef von Mitterer.

Both consuls find themselves under the constant vigil of the distrustful
Turks. Non-Turkish inhabitants welcome them, each group in its own way:
Catholic Croats are friendly toward von Mitterer while shunning Daville; the
small Jewish community supports Daville; and the Orthodox Serbs distrust
both, pinning their hopes on Russia, which is expected to send its consul
also. Yet they are all powerless under the Turkish domination.

Daville, a middle-aged diplomat who writes classical poetry and tries to
keep the semblance of civilization in a town whose life-style resembles that of
the Middle Ages, finds it difficult to function, yet he endures for the sake of
his idol Napoleon Bonaparte and for the glory of France. Von Mitterer has it
somewhat easier, for Bosnia is in Austria's backyard and the non-Turkish
population is more sympathetic to him. Both of them, however, must deal
primarily with Turkish viziers, who wield all power and can thwart all of their
efforts by various means at their disposal. The work of the two Western consuls is further complicated by the necessity to play against each other. The
entire novel chronicles the lives and endeavors of these participants in world

politics in a most unlikely place—a sleepy provincial town in the Bosnian backwaters.

During the time of the novel, from 1806 to 1814, there are three Turkish viziers confronting Daville and von Mitterer. The first, Mehmed-Pasha, a Georgian by birth and a loyal servant of the empire, is a reasonable and good-hearted man. Daville has a relatively easy time dealing with him, and an aura of mutual respect and even trust develops between them. If he cannot succeed in every effort, Daville at least enjoys working with Mehmed-Pasha. After falling victim to internal Ottoman intrigues and struggles for power, Mehmed-Pasha is replaced by Ibrahim-Pasha, his exact opposite. Morose and taciturn, eaten internally by illness, Ibrahim-Pasha is extremely difficult, allowing the two consuls little room for success. His retinue of assistants and servants whom he brings from Turkey—the local people call them a "museum of monsters"—makes working with Ibrahim-Pasha even more difficult. Under this unpleasant veneer, Daville discovers a very unhappy man who is not as unpleasant and difficult as he seems, and with whom he develops a modicum of cooperation. The third vizier, Ali-Pasha, is the worst of the three. Frightfully efficient and merciless, he determines to execute immediately all thieves, gamblers, idlers, and even some political prisoners whom he finds in the prison. Having established his rule of terror and fear, he proceeds to be polite and even friendly with Daville and von Mitterer, as much as his position allows.

Even though the two consuls and their families eventually adjust to the unusual life in Travnik, both have difficulties leading a normal life, especially Daville's gentle wife, who during their stay loses a child and gives birth to two. Yet she is more practical and more religious than her husband and is therefore better equipped to cope with the life in a foreign land. When, finally, Napoleon's fortunes turn sour and Daville's mission is terminated, both he and his wife are glad to leave, as are von Mitterer and his family. The chronicle of the attempts of the Western powers to intrude on the life of this strange, though fascinating, country comes to an end, and Travnik again recedes into the darkness of a life outside history, leaving its people to remember for a long time "the times of the consuls."

## The Characters

Many characters parade through the novel, as befits a chronicle of turbulent, even if peripheral, events in history, the Napoleonic wars. Many of the characters, though masterfully sketched, remain sketches nevertheless, serving only to highlight the protagonists. Among the main characters are the two consuls and the three viziers.

Daville is a typical representative of the French power and culture of the times. Well educated, thoroughly civilized, and professionally trained, he does his job well, within the limitations imposed by circumstances. He also serves as a striking foil to the world in which he finds himself. Amid illiteracy and backwardness, he writes an epic poem about Alexander the Great, thus retaining a civilized decorum even when it seems out of place. He also keeps a polite demeanor even when most people around him either lose theirs or never had it. Not exceptionally clever or gifted, he nevertheless reaches the level of competence without losing the human touch that is often lacking among his cohabitants. At the same time, he is often unable to cope with the strange world, because he lacks temperament and strong individuality. He is therefore lonely, melancholy, and constantly worried. It is his faith in human values exemplified, in his opinion, by Napoleon, that enables him to survive even after the demise of his idol. In this sense, he is also a victim of his faith and ideals, yet he shows no regrets, resigning himself to his destiny. Lacking the religious fervor of his wife and the expediency and practicality of his younger assistant des Fosses, he seems to be ill-suited for the changes around him and certainly for the strange world into which he was thrust for a while. Yet he comes out of all these predicaments battered but not defeated, saddened but not bitter.

His counterpart, von Mitterer, is in many ways his opposite. Capable and meticulously efficient, purposeful, polite but unemotional, he does what he is supposed to do. He sees an enemy in Daville but not personally, realizing that he is only doing his duty and tacitly assuring Daville that their enmity is only on a professional basis. Confronted with the alien world and aware that Daville as a Westerner is still closer to him than the local populace, he nevertheless follows his sense of duty; he even seems to enjoy his skirmishes with his Western rival. Lacking the inner life and mental agility of his French counterparts and constrained by his military-diplomatic vocation, he is depicted much less favorably than Daville, mainly because he sacrifices his human qualities on the altar of duty and expediency.

The three Turkish viziers, though different in many ways, share the indelible stamp that their culture left on them. As representatives of an empire, they see it as their duty to uphold the laws and interests of the empire, yet they go a step further. Even when they are polite and friendly on the surface, they seldom show the concern for human values found among their Western counterparts. Ibrahim-Pasha, for example, flaunts a pile of cut-off noses and ears from the slain Serbian rebels. Whether it is the nature of their position that makes them inscrutable and efficacious or whether it is a conviction that an empire can survive only through rigorous means without sentimentality, they are all portrayed as ruthless and implacable servants of the state, embodiments of a way of life that is indeed different from that of the Western world.

Other characters are too minor to merit much attention. Daville's wife is depicted as the most humane of all the characters in the novel, a woman of simple yet true nobility. Daville's assistants and allies, des Fosses and d'Avenat, show a balance of virtues and vices. D'Avenat, an adventurer and a connoisseur of people, is especially colorful. Von Mitterer's replacement, von Paulich, is the exact pendant of des Fosses, young, energetic, practical, and unencumbered with superfluous concerns. They all serve to fill the rich tapestry of the life in Travnik and are indispensable even though they lack full portraiture.

## Themes and Meanings

There are several themes in *Bosnian Chronicle*, but the main one is the contrast between the West and the East. The comparatively enlightened world of the West, represented by the consuls of France and Austria, is counterposed by the backward, mysterious, dark world of the East as it exists in the Turkish Empire. Even though the opposing sides are not in an open conflict, the behavior of the players involved points to a tacit rivalry that is just as intense. The distrust with which the Westerners are met, not only by the Turkish officials but also by the people on the street, can only be explained by a deep-seated enmity. The antagonism goes beyond the political and national differences; it goes to the core of the way of life and the attitudes of the two worlds. Philosophical fatalism, resignation, deep mistrust of everything foreign, basic disregard for the rights of individuals—considered normal among the people of the East and the Turkish Empire—are pitted against the more open, compassionate, rational, and law-oriented ways of the West. Ivo Andrić presents this drama not so much by musings and discussions about history as through the interplay of people who are forced into situations beyond anything they have experienced before, thus adding a special dimension to the novel.

That this novel is not simply a historical chronicle but primarily a story of the people caught in the maelstrom of history is further demonstrated by the fine psychological studies Andrić invests in most of his characters, certainly the main ones. In all of his works, Andrić is at his best when he illuminates the deepest recesses of the minds and hearts of his protagonists no matter to what race, nationality, class, or creed they belong. This approach makes the novel more interesting than if it were strictly a historical chronicle. Thus Travnik, its historical significance at the time notwithstanding, becomes a backdrop for several human dramas that constitute the core of the novel. Even though almost all events and personalities can be traced to historical sources, which Andrić had researched diligently, the historical events—the Napoleonic Wars, the reforms of Selim the Third, and the first Serbian uprising—are never in the forefront. Instead, they cast their long shadows on the lives of Travnik's inhabitants. In the last analysis, the actions of the novel's characters are futile because everything is decided for them elsewhere; the actors are like puppets directed by remote control, achieving very little by themselves as far as history is concerned.

Another interesting theme is the role of women in the novel. Andrić sharply differentiates between his usual Oriental women, who are little more than objects of men's pleasure, and the emancipated Western women, who are, to some degree, like their male partners, with their own rights.

The universal meaning of the novel can be seen in the need for perseverance in a seemingly hopeless situation. This is symbolized by Daville's hope at the end of the novel, before leaving Travnik, that "the right road" will eventually be found despite his Bosnian experience.

## Critical Context

*Bosnian Chronicle* was the first of three novels—along with *Na Drini ćuprija* (1945; *The Bridge on the Drina*, 1959) and *Gospodjica* (1945; *The Woman from Sarajevo*, 1965)—Andrić wrote in Belgrade during the German Occupation of World War II. Together with the other two novels, it represents the culminating point in his career, winning for him the Nobel Prize in 1961. After years of writing short stories, he turned to novels, only to abandon this genre once again after the publication of these novels. Some critics consider *Prokleta avlija* (1954; *Devil's Yard*, 1962) a short novel, but it is actually a long story or a novella.

According to some critics, *Bosnian Chronicle* is a better novel than *The Bridge on the Drina*. It is certainly more of a true novel, preserving the unity of time, place, and plot. Yet the two novels should be considered organic pieces of a whole that, together with the unfinished novel *Omerpaša Latas* (1976; Omer Pasha Latas), constitute the true Bosnian trilogy.

Like many other works, this novel serves Andrić in part as a vehicle for his own thoughts and ideas about life and history. Furthermore, just as the bridge in *The Bridge on the Drina* is the symbol of bridging the differences between worlds, Travnik is a symbol of a *kasaba* (provincial little town) in the backwaters of an empire, where little is happening yet people continue to strive against all odds. Thus, even though the picture Andrić presents is often bleak and melancholy, life pulsates beneath the surface with full vigor. His skillful depiction of this multifaceted life made Andrić a leading figure in modern world literature. His mastery of the psychology of his characters against the backdrop of events over which they have little control reached its highest peak in *Bosnian Chronicle*.

## Sources for Further Study

Cooper, Henry R., Jr. "The Image of Bosnia in the Fiction of Ivo Andrić," in *Serbian Studies*. III (1984/1985), pp. 83-105.

Džadžić, Petar. *Ivo Andrić*, 1960.

Ferguson, Alan. "Public and Private Worlds in *Travnik Chronicle*," in *The Modern Language Review*. LXX (1975), pp. 830-838.

Goy, Edward D. "The Work of Ivo Andrić," in *Slavonic and East European*

*Review*. XLI (1963), pp. 301-326.

Kadic, Ante. "The French in *The Chronicle of Travnik*," in *California Slavic Studies*. I (1960), pp. 134-169.

*Vasa D. Mihailovich*

# BOTCHAN

*Author:* Sōseki Natsume (Kinnosuke Natsume, 1867-1916)
*Type of plot:* Comic satire
*Time of plot:* The 1890's
*Locale:* Tokyo, and a castle town on the island of Shikoku, Japan
*First published:* 1906 (English translation, 1918)

> *Principal characters:*
> BOTCHAN, the narrator and protagonist, a young Tokyo-born
>    teacher at a provincial Japanese school
> KIYO, an elderly maidservant of Botchan's family
> BADGER, the headmaster of Botchan's school
> REDSHIRT, the only university graduate teaching at the school
> YOSHIKAWA, nicknamed "CLOWN," the art master and
>    Redshirt's sycophant
> MADONNA, the object of Redshirt's marriage plans
> KOGA, a teacher and Madonna's fiancé
> HOTTA, nicknamed "PORCUPINE," the senior master at the
>    school

*The Novel*

Among the classics of modern Japanese literature, *Botchan* is probably the most frequently read novel and the most often anthologized work in Japan. Its action is set in the 1890's, during the Meiji Restoration, when Japan was making its cataclysmic metamorphosis from a cloistered feudal state to a major modern world power. The novel focuses on a few months in the experience of a neophyte teacher nicknamed Botchan (young master). Born and educated in Tokyo, he has accepted a job teaching mathematics at a middle school in provincial Shikoku. Botchan's personality, values, and Tokyo manners clash with those of his new environment, and out of this conflict Sōseki spins a comic tale that satirizes contemporary Japanese mores. The novel is narrated in the first person, and a substantial portion of its humor stems from Botchan's verbose and vigorous Tokyo dialect, which, by all accounts, Sōseki has brilliantly captured.

From his earliest childhood days, Botchan has been an impulsive and reckless scapegrace. He leaps from the upstairs window of his elementary school on a dare, fights with a neighbor boy in the middle of a vegetable garden, thus devastating it, and blocks up another neighbor's irrigation source out of sheer curiosity. Botchan's father dislikes him. Botchan's elder brother blames him for hastening their mother's death by his rowdiness. Through it all, Botchan grows into an unabashed and defiant individualist. Indeed, stubbornness, recklessness, and candor become marks of Botchan's character.

The only person with whom Botchan gets along is the family's elderly maidservant, Kiyo. Kiyo sees Botchan as a rough diamond. In contrast to everyone else, therefore, she plies him with delicacies, gifts, even money—including three yen notes which he accidentally drops into the latrine, and which Kiyo then fishes out, rinses, exchanges for coins, and returns to Botchan. In his rough-and-ready way, Botchan appreciates Kiyo's fondness for him, and their relationship borders on that between feudal serf and liege lord—in fact, it is she who has nicknamed him Botchan, and his acceptance of this sobriquet in turn acknowledges her authority to define his identity.

After their father's death, Botchan's brother sells their Tokyo home and departs for Kyushu, leaving Botchan only six hundred yen to defray his education for three years. Botchan manages to graduate (with neither distinction nor enthusiasm) from the Tokyo School of Physics and obtains his rather mediocre teaching post.

Botchan's Tokyo upbringing, individuality, and character clash with his new surroundings and acquaintances. He finds the provincial dress, manners, and (especially) dialect uncouth and disconcerting, and he is critical of his colleagues, whom he quickly dubs with satirical nicknames such as Badger or Redshirt. Badger, the headmaster, lectures Botchan during their first meeting and informs him that he should set a high moral example for his students away from school as well as in the classroom. Knowing his own foibles, Botchan resents this imposition and candidly offers to return his letter of appointment. Badger, who had expected Botchan to play his hypocritical game of keeping up appearances, is taken aback, then smiles away his pomposity by explaining that he has merely said what is usual for the occasion and that nobody expects anyone to live up to such ideals.

One of Botchan's new acquaintances is the senior teacher, Mr. Hotta, whom Botchan nicknames Porcupine for his closely cropped hair. Hotta is gruff and abrupt in manner but seems helpful. He finds lodgings for Botchan and treats him to a dish of fruit-flavored shaved ice; this act creates a bond of obligation (an important traditional Japanese concept termed *on*) between Botchan and Hotta.

Botchan is not a particularly dedicated teacher, nor do his students inspire him to become one. He finds them uncouth in manners and speech, and they disrespectfully make fun of his appetite for dumplings and noodles with tempura shrimp. When Botchan is assigned night duty at the dormitory, the students fill his bedding with grasshoppers. His ensuing fracas with the students, their cowardly lies, and an infestation of mosquitoes prevent Botchan from obtaining any sleep. He wants the students to be punished, but Badger decides to delay the decision until a staff meeting.

Meanwhile, Botchan goes fishing with Redshirt and Clown, two other teachers. The trip reveals to Botchan that Clown is a mindless toady of Redshirt and that they affect an entirely artificial Westernized sophistication.

For example, they catch a kind of fish that Sōseki calls *goruki*, and Redshirt and Clown parade their Westernized sophistication by pretending that they are hauling in the works of the Russian writer Maxim Gorky. Disgusted at this pretentious wit, Botchan refuses to fish any longer—especially when their boatman tells him that *goruki* are only fit for use as fertilizer. Botchan, however, overhears two whispered conversations between his companions, one mentioning a woman named Madonna and another insinuating that Hotta has incited the students to play their pranks on Botchan.

On the day of the staff meeting, Botchan so resents Hotta's alleged incitement of the students that he refunds one and a half sen to him for his shaved ice treat, thus removing his *on*. Hotta in turn tells Botchan that he must quit his lodgings, since the landlady is complaining to him of Botchan's rudeness—an example of the landlady's duplicity, for she wants Botchan to leave because he has not bought any of her husband's fake antiques. When the staff meeting begins, it is apparent that most of the teachers, swayed by Badger and Redshirt, are inclined to exculpate the students. In fact, Botchan is in disfavor with his colleagues because he has been observed openly going to the hotspring baths when he was on night duty (no one had told him that he should not). To Botchan's surprise, Hotta speaks against Redshirt and says that the students should be punished. He also says that Botchan was wrong in going to the hot springs, whereupon Botchan apologizes. Badger then launches into a homily that teachers are expected to cultivate spiritual pursuits such as fishing and haiku writing while shunning fleshly indulgences such as hot springs and noodles with tempura shrimp. Stung into retort, Botchan angrily asks whether seeing Madonna is a spiritual pursuit, a remark that oddly enough bows Redshirt's head and makes Koga (another teacher) blanch.

Unknowingly, Botchan has hit a sensitive nerve. Later, Hotta informs him that Koga was once engaged to Madonna, but Redshirt, noticing her charms, had broken up the engagement and set up a match between Madonna and himself instead. Now Redshirt has even obtained for Koga a transfer to a school in distant Kyushu, effectively banishing him from the town. Apprised of this, Botchan can hardly contain his indignation as he listens to Redshirt's outpourings of camaraderie during Koga's farewell party. Botchan is now certain that Redshirt had wanted him to overhear his mischievous remarks about Hotta's having egged the students on against him. Accordingly, Botchan takes back the one and a half sen he had earlier paid Hotta for the shaved ice, and the two men thus reestablish their friendship.

Redshirt's next move comes when a holiday is declared to celebrate Japan's victory over China. During the parade, a brawl develops between the students of a normal school and those of Botchan's school. Redshirt's younger brother, a student, appeals to Botchan and Hotta to quell the disturbance. When the two men try to do so, they are thoroughly beaten. To make matters worse, the next morning's newspaper reports the two men as having started the disturbance, and the two suspect that Redshirt drew them into the student fracas so that he could leak misinformation about it to the media.

Although both men are eventually exonerated, Hotta is asked to resign, and Botchan offers his resignation in sympathy. Since they cannot outintrigue Redshirt, Botchan and Hotta plan a more forthright vengeance. Botchan has suspected that Redshirt is the regular customer of a certain geisha. If this could be proved, then Redshirt's high intellectual and spiritual tone would be exposed as a façade. Botchan and Hotta rent a room across from a hotel of assignation and watch for their man. After more than a week, they finally see Redshirt and Clown enter the hotel at 9:00 P.M. and leave after 5:00 A.M. As Redshirt and Clown head back to school, Botchan and Hotta accost them, expose their unspiritual indulgences, and thoroughly pummel them, knowing that the hypocrites will not dare to press charges. Well satisfied, Botchan and Hotta then leave for Tokyo. In Tokyo, Botchan works happily as a mechanic. Kiyo comes to live with him, and when she dies, he honors her request to be buried in his ancestral temple grounds.

## The Characters

As their cartoonlike names and nicknames imply, the characters in *Botchan*, like those in many satires, tend to be types rather than fully rounded characters. Thus "Botchan" itself suggests certain character traits. Translating it as "young master" partly suggests the scion of a noble or feudal family, and Botchan does refer to the samurai past of his family, tracing his ancestry to the bodyguards of the shogun and to the Minamotos descended from the Emperor Seiwa. His relationship with the family retainer, Kiyo, also bears out this feudalistic trait of character, as does the nice pride with which he regards Hotta's treat of shaved ice. Samurai-like, too, is Botchan's forthright candor and dislike for intrigue, his physical courage and readiness to resort to fisticuffs. Yet if "Botchan" has these class connotations, it can also connote "greenhorn"—hence his inexperience at schoolteaching and ineptitude at intrigue.

Another important aspect of Botchan's character is his Tokyo background (or, as the Japanese commonly term it, "Edokko"—derived from Edo, the original name for Tokyo). Much of the Edokko flavor is conveyed in Botchan's language, and though some of its qualities are lost in translation, the tendency toward exaggeration and vituperation remains. The typical Edokko is also supposed to be a gourmand (for example, Botchan has an appetite for noodles), an anti-intellectual (he dislikes Redshirt's Western sophistication), and an honest, straightforward, helpful person.

The names or nicknames of the other figures are often indices to their characters. Hotta, the Porcupine, is irascible and bristles at the least slight; beneath his rough exterior, however, he is a caring and feeling person. Badger, the headmaster, has the Japanese folkloric attributes of the animal for which he is named: deceptiveness and empty authority. Clown (whose name could also be rendered as "Pimp") is clearly a toadying court jester who dances attendance on Redshirt. Redshirt, in turn, is probably an allusion to the then trendy pro-Western intellectual journal *Teikoku Bungaku*, which sported a red cover.

*Themes and Meanings*

Sōseki's satire couples his exposure of societal hypocrisy and pretentiousness with his endorsement of individual candor and personal loyalty. Redshirt, Clown, and Badger are obviously hypocritical and pretentious; insofar as their society rewards them with success and recognition, their society is at fault. Again, society is faulted when it fails to appreciate the qualities of individual candor and personal loyalty by which characters such as Botchan, Hotta, and Kiyo live and of which Sōseki obviously approves. Unlike their societally approved colleagues, Hotta loses his job, Botchan is too honest to fit with his so-called genteel profession, and Kiyo spends most of her life as a menial. In the historical context of the Westernization and modernization of Japan during the Meiji Restoration, it is significant that Sōseki makes the antipathetic Redshirt his main proponent of Western values and reforms (although it must be noted that Redshirt's understanding and practice of Westernization is of the shallowest kind) and that the sympathetic Botchan is portrayed as the chief exemplar of traditional Japanese values of the feudal Tokugawa shogunate (although Botchan's society-defying individualism is a deeply Western trait). Sōseki's satire is thus subtle as well as scathing.

*Critical Context*

*Botchan* belongs with *Wagahai wa Neko de aru* (1905-1906; *I Am a Cat*, two volumes, 1906, 1909) at the beginning of Sōseki's fiction-writing career, when he still treated human foibles humorously. Later works such as *Kokoro* (1914; English translation, 1941) and *Michigusa* (1915; *Grass on the Wayside*, 1969) present a darker and more tragic vision. Sōseki came to the forefront of the Japanese literary scene when Japanese writers were largely engaged in aping Western literary fashions, especially that of naturalism. Sōseki, however, who had studied English literature deeply, shunned mere imitation and developed his own voice and vision. Thus, though his works have been compared to those of Henry Fielding, Jane Austen, or George Meredith, they are distinctively his in execution and profoundly Japanese in sensibility. Indeed, Sōseki's total oeuvre establishes him as a master of the Meiji period and a pioneer of modern Japanese literature. Firmly in place within the Sōseki canon is *Botchan*, a book that has sold more copies than any other work of Japanese literature.

*Sources for Further Study*

Doi, Takeo. *The Psychological World of Natsume Sōseki*, 1976.

Jones, Sumie. "Natsume Sōseki's *Botchan*: The Outer World Through Edo Eyes," in *Approaches to the Modern Japanese Novel*, 1976. Edited by Kinya Tsuruta and Thomas Swann.

McClellan, Edwin. *Two Japanese Novelists: Sōseki and Tōson*, 1969.

Morita, Sohei. "On *Botchan*," in *Essays on Natsume Sōseki's Works*, 1972.

Yu, Beongcheon. *Natsume Sōseki*, 1969.

*C. L. Chua*

# THE BRIDAL CANOPY, IN THE HEART OF THE SEAS,
## and
# A GUEST FOR THE NIGHT

*Author:* Shmuel Yosef Agnon (Shmuel Yosef Czaczkes, 1888-1970)
*Type of plot:* Folk epic
*Time of plot:* The nineteenth and early twentieth centuries
*Locale:* Eastern Galicia and Palestine
*First published: Hakhnasat kala,* 1931 (*The Bridal Canopy,* 1937); *Bilvav yamim: Sippur agadah shel S. Y. Agnon,* 1934 (*In the Heart of the Seas: An Allegorical Tale of S. Y. Agnon,* 1947); *Oreach nata lalun,* 1939 (*A Guest for the Night,* 1968)

> *Principal characters:*
> REB YUDEL NATHANSON, a poor and pious Hasid seeking husbands and dowries for his three daughters
> NUTA, a drayman who provides him with transport and companionship
> REB HANANIA, a man who joins and aids a group of Hasids going to Palestine
> NILBAVIM, the enthusiasts traveling to Palestine
> THE NARRATOR, who is on a purportedly brief visit to his hometown of Shibush
> RACHEL ZUMMER, the hotelier's daughter
> YERUCHAM FREEMAN, a native of Shibush who has been expelled from Palestine

*The Novels*

*The Bridal Canopy* is set in the Jewish world of eastern Galicia in the early 1800's, in a culture still coherent and traditional, not yet fragmented by the impact of Haskalah (the Enlightenment) and emancipation. Most Jews lived either in a shtetl (small village) or in a larger town, such as Brody, the home of Reb Yudel. In dire poverty, without bed, table, or chair, Yudel spends his life "fashion[ing] a seat for the Divine Presence." A Hasid, he sees beneficent Providence in every occurrence and joyfully fulfills each of the 613 commandments of his religion. Unfortunately, one of these commandments is to bring the bride under the wedding canopy, and Yudel has three daughters, so he must disrupt his routine of prayer and study to go begging for three dowries and the first of three bridegrooms.

Yudel starts his journey on the wagon of Nuta the drayman. His travels to fulfill the commandment elicit hospitality and generosity, and he and his hosts entertain one another with stories. From time to time, the two horses tell each other stories as well. These stories have little connection with one another or with Yudel's quest; they are quarried from the rich veins of Jewish folklore and religious tradition, and are both didactic and steeped in the unquestioning acceptance of Providence and miracle.

When Yudel has collected two hundred gold pieces, he cannot continue to beg. He therefore installs himself in an inn and resumes his normal routine of prayer and study, with complete faith that God will provide. The townsfolk conclude that he must be rich, especially when they discover that his last name, Nathanson, is also that of a wealthy Brody merchant. Thus begins the series of coincidences and scenes of mistaken identity through which Yudel moves in pious serenity. He accepts a match for his daughter with the son of the town's wealthy merchant, pledging an enormous dowry despite his poverty.

After accepting the match, Yudel returns home and resumes his interrupted routine. He is untouched by the fact that his adventures have become legendary in the verses of the popular Brody singers. As the groom's family and the real Reb Yudel Nathanson finally discover the bride, Yudel's wife and daughters attempt to prepare a feast in their dank cellar room. They decide to cook the rooster who awakens Yudel for the morning prayers; it escapes, however, and as the women chase it, they stumble upon a fabulous treasure in a cave. Wealthy beyond measure, Yudel finds dowries and husbands for all three of his daughters. His family obligations fulfilled, he and his wife make *aliya*: They "go up" to the Holy Land and live out their days there.

*In the Heart of the Seas* begins, in a sense, at the point where *The Bridal Canopy* ends. A group of Hasidim from Buczacz, in Galicia, are preparing to make *aliya* when they are joined by Reb Hanania. Even more pious than his new companions, he has endured much travail to reach them. He occupies himself with both organizing their journey and repairing various ritual and secular objects. As the travelers move toward the sea, the Jews along the way provide them with aid and encouragement. Unfortunately, when their ship leaves Istanbul, they discover that Hanania is missing. A violent storm blows them back; repeating the voyage, they finally reach Jaffa, kiss the soil of Palestine, and soon discover that Hanania has already arrived. He had missed the ship when he delayed in order to give the religious authorities evidence of the death of a certain man, thus ending the dead man's wife's status as an *agunah*, a woman neither divorced nor widowed, in limbo because her husband's fate is unknown.

As the delayed Hanania had watched the ship leave Istanbul, God had suggested to him that he spread out his kerchief and sail upon it to the Holy Land. The Hasidim on shipboard had several times glimpsed this figure during their voyage and speculated upon it. While many of the Hasidim later encountered difficulties after settling in Palestine, Hanania grew stronger each year, dying at the age of one hundred; he was buried with his kerchief covering his eyes.

*A Guest for the Night* is narrated by an unnamed native of Shibush, in Galicia, who had been the first in the town to make *aliya*. When the 1929 Arab riots in Jerusalem destroyed his home, his wife and children went to stay with her parents in Germany, and he returned to visit his birthplace, arriving on the eve of Yom Kippur, the Day of Atonement. He hopes to draw strength from the sources of his childhood but finds only decay and despair. As recipient of the key of the *beit midrash* (house of study), he becomes provider of light and warmth in the central place of the religious tradition. Although the overwhelming desolation is attributed to World War I, it soon becomes obvious that the narrator cannot rejuvenate the fragmented and moribund traditional community. Instead, he aids the aged Reb Shlomo to join his dead son's comrades in Palestine. When the hotel keeper's daughter, Rachel, marries Yerucham Freeman, a disillusioned Zionist expelled from Palestine, the narrator presents their newborn son with the new key to the *beit midrash*.

Rejoining his family after a year and returning to Jerusalem, the narrator finds the old key in his luggage and recalls the tradition that in the messianic age all the synagogues and *beit midrash* of the Diaspora will be reestablished in the Land of Israel. The new child, the first to be born in Shibush for many years, named for the narrator, will thus be able to continue the tradition in the Land of Israel.

*The Characters*

The major, and most of the minor, characters in the novels are Hasidim, pious Jewish men rooted in the rabbinic tradition who spend their days and nights in prayer and study. Their purpose in life is to fulfill the commandments, which involves them in the life of the community but which also often means that they detach themselves from much of secular reality, instead relying completely upon the Divine Presence and accepting whatever occurs.

There is little or no character development. For example, Yudel remains essentially untouched by his experiences. While the many minor characters tend to personify the "types" of traditional shtetl Jews, they also provide much of the rich texture of the first two novels. The presence of the narrator is a constant reminder of the author, the real creator of these fictive worlds, whose pervasive if gentle irony undermines the characters' certainties. The spare plot line, essentially episodic, is developed by the interaction of the characters. While the narrator remains unseen, in *In the Heart of the Seas*, one of the nilbavim is clearly Shmuel Yosef Agnon himself, although no more developed or vital to the plot than is any other minor character.

In *A Guest for the Night*, however, the protagonist is a first-person narrator whose life apparently follows that of Agnon, including his two traumatic losses of house and library, his separation from wife and children, and his location in Buczacz and Jerusalem. Agnon grew up in Buczacz, in what was then known as Austria-Hungary, which appears as itself in the first two novels and is only thinly disguised as Shibush in the third. To leave either Buczacz or Jerusalem produces a sense of betrayal, either of one's roots or of one's heritage and destiny. It is clear, however, that the narrator is not even a fictionalized Agnon but Agnon's literary creation. For the novel, the complex personality of the narrator is crucial. His introspection, his deep feelings of guilt and futility, and his sense of alienation provide both the plot structure and the interaction with the novel's characters. These characters, essentially sketched through the narrator's eyes, manifest various aspects of twentieth century humanity. They remain static in their attitudes; the narrator changes, accepting the loss of his nostalgic ideal and the permanence of his future, his home, in Jerusalem.

## Themes and Meanings

Agnon's novels focus on the problems of faith, identity, and home. When Shmuel Yosef Czaczkes published his first story in Israel in 1908, he adopted the pen name (later his legal name) Agnon; that story's title, "Agunot" ("Deserted Wives"), refers to those in limbo, evoking a sense of loss and yearning. This thread runs throughout Agnon's works, intensifying in the later ones. Institutions and values crumble, but the redemptive power of a life of Torah, in the Land of Israel, remains. After World War II, Agnon's work, such as the 1945 novel *T'mol shilshom* (only yesterday), questioned even this assumption. The tension between Galicia—the Diaspora, exile— and Palestine is usually seen in the theme of *aliya*, "ascending" to the Holy Land, building and being built by it. Agnon's locales include both the traditional Jewish life in Eastern Europe and the tumultuous Palestine of the Second Aliya: He deals with both the rhythms of the early nineteenth century and the agonizing problems of the twentieth. Yet the Holy Land cannot invigorate the traditional religious community of the Diaspora, and even in Palestine, the community has neither coherence nor stability.

Agnon's skilled narrative technique produces an illusion of realism, so that the reader willingly accepts the plot developments, despite their mythic nature and the author's frequent and deliberately naïve commentary. Even his realistic detail is symbolic.

The Hebrew title of *The Bridal Canopy* resonates to the entire complex of traditional Jewish life which focuses on the family, the dominant metaphor for the basic sanctity and meaningfulness of life. *The Bridal Canopy* is a comic novel, its gentle parody of the Hasidic folktale reflecting the charm of its subjects (Yudel and the Jews of Galicia), yet finally it is corrosive. This ambiguity is structured by the author: His irony, filtered through the naïve narrator, rejects the basic values and assumptions of the characters. The providential world of Yudel, his epic of begging, and the miraculous happy ending, all had been subjects of bitter satire in previous Hebraic writing; Agnon draws them as fantasy in the detached style of midrashic prose, his amused sympathy keeping the reader aware that the skilled writer, and not a benevolent deity, is structuring the plot and deciding its outcome. The language agrees with the book's milieu: The late rabbinic Hebrew style, popular from the seventeenth to the nineteenth century, is fused with the Yiddish vernacular. This style of writing is calm and laconic but rich in biblical and Talmudic allusions immediately familiar to the educated reader.

*The Bridal Canopy* is structured around two cycles of departure from and return to Brody, with Yudel's home symbolizing tradition and continuity; at the very end, however, this symbol is replaced by the greater theme of *aliya*. Nightmare elements (death, the Devil), lust, and mistaken identity abound. Framed anecdotes, tales, parables, folk poetry, and rhymed prose maintain the tone of comic irony.

Just as *The Bridal Canopy* is less naturalism than fantasy, so *In the Heart of the Seas* is a playful treatment of the pious tale, in contrast to the serious and secular approach to such material that characterized Hebrew writing of the early 1930's. The sophisticated structure is evident here also: the picaresque episodes, the symbolic kerchief, and the motifs of temptation, *tikun* (repair, completion), exile and the Land of Israel. The novella follows *The Bridal Canopy* in its focus on the act of *aliya*.

*A Guest for the Night* is a further development, in both time and attitudes, of the milieu of *The Bridal Canopy*. It is Agnon's second major novel, midway between *The Bridal Canopy* and *T'mol shilshom*; despite the overwhelming atmosphere of decay and desolation, it is the most optimistic novel of the three, ending on a note of hope and affirmation. The wholeness and sanctity of the narrator's childhood have crumbled: The Hebrew root of *Shibush* implies error and corruption. The narrator is also an actor; he is both a wayfarer, and therefore a stranger, and a native. His nostalgic remembrance of and identification with Shibush turn inexorably into the nightmare of the recognition of the impossibility of its redemption and his own condition as an outsider. The painful transition to acceptance of his new home, Jerusalem, also means continuity; the child of Rachel and Yerucham, named (against convention) for him, represents the narrator's rebirth and the hope for the tradition in the Land of Israel.

### Critical Context

Agnon was recognized as a major literary talent with the arrival of his first Hebrew short story in 1908. He acquired fame, status as a classic writer, and numerous literary prizes in Israel (in 1966, Jerusalem put up a sign on his street: QUIET—AGNON IS WRITING). The scarcity of English translations of his works, however, limited his reputation among English-speaking readers, at least until he received the Nobel Prize for Literature in 1966.

Agnon belongs among the late nineteenth century neo-Romantic writers such as Micah Joseph Berdichevsky and Isaac Leib Peretz. Not influenced by Franz Kafka (also a product of that movement), Agnon's work nevertheless has often been compared to Kafka's, as Reb Yudel has inevitably been compared to Don Quixote. Critical opinion of Agnon is so varied that he has been labeled as both a traditionalist and a modernist. One of the causes for the confusion is that Agnon developed as a writer over a long literary life, frequently revising his works for later publication. In addition, he donned many public and private masks. These personas fed into critical analysis, especially since much of the raw material for his fiction was drawn from his personal experience and was then extensively reworked, and in fact distorted, by his artistic imagination. In reality, none of his work is in any real sense autobiographical.

Agnon was an individualistic and sophisticated literary craftsman. He was the master of the short story; his few novels are episodic. The quiet, yet lyric and flexible, Midrashic Hebrew style that he adopted is archaic but familiar to modern Hebrew readers and has influenced the development of modern Hebrew. Yet its simplicity in translation may seem lifeless and lose much of its charm, as well as its rich biblical and rabbinic allusions and wordplay.

Several themes recur in Agnon's works, and critics have debated their meaning. Agnon himself refused to provide any clues, declaring that a writer said all that he had to say in his writings. On one occasion, he went so far as to tell an editor, "I write things simply as they are." His fantasy intuitively recast reality. To recapture an ideal world is impossible, and turns nostalgia into nightmare; Agnon bridged the ideal and the real worlds through fantasy and his mastery of literary form.

*Sources for Further Study*

Alter, Robert. "Shmuel Yosef Agnon: 'The Alphabet of Holiness' and 'The Israeli Novel,'" in *After the Tradition*, 1969.

Band, Arnold J. *Nostalgia and Nightmare: A Study in the Fiction of S. Y. Agnon*, 1968.

Hochman, Baruch. *The Fiction of S. Y. Agnon*, 1970.

Ribalow, Menachem. "Samuel Joseph Agnon: Major Novelist of Yesterday and Today," in *The Flowering of Modern Hebrew Literature*, 1959.

Scholem, Gershom. "Reflections on Shmuel Yosef Agnon," in *Commentary*. XLIV (December, 1967), pp. 59-66.

*Marsha Kass Marks*

# THE BURN

*Author:* Vassily Aksyonov (1932-      )
*Type of plot:* Phantasmagoric modernism
*Time of plot:* 1970-1973, with flashbacks
*Locale:* Moscow and elsewhere
*First published: Ozhog*, 1980 (English translation, 1984)

> *Principal characters:*
> PANTALEI APOLLINARIEVICH PANTALEI, a writer
> ARISTARKH APOLLINARIEVICH KUNITSER, a physicist and space
>    scientist
> SAMSON APOLLINARIEVICH SABLER, a jazz saxophonist
> RADIUS APOLLINARIEVICH KHVASTISHCHEV, a sculptor
> GENNADY APOLLINARIEVICH MALKOLMOV, a physician
> TOLYA VON STEINBOCK, all of the above as a teenager in
>    Magadan, Siberia, during Joseph Stalin's last years
> ALISA, a young Magadan camp inmate who becomes an
>    amoral Moscow beauty of the 1960's and 1970's
> SANYA GURCHENKO, a Catholic camp inmate who escapes to
>    the West
> PATRICK THUNDERJET, an Anglo-American professor and
>    longtime friend of the heroes
> CHEPTSOV, a retired Stalinist KGB officer who arrested
>    Tolya's mother and Sanya Gurchenko twenty years earlier

*The Novel*

   *The Burn* tells the story of the Soviet generation that came of age in the years just after the death of Joseph Stalin. There are five more or less interchangeable heroes—or rather antiheroes—all members of Vassily Aksyonov's generation, all liberals, all superstars in their professions: Kunitser the physicist, Sabler the musician, Malkolmov the physician, Khvastishchev the sculptor, and Pantalei the writer. The disillusioned heroes have retreated from the successes of the socially concerned, optimistic 1960's into alcohol, sex, and work. Although the men do not know one another and lead independent lives, they have certain virtually identical and seemingly concurrent parallel experiences. Among them are encounters with an almost-recognized figure from the past who triggers flashbacks to a time when the five protagonists were one person, the teenage Tolya von Steinbock. Moreover, the identity of each of the heroes continuously revolves into that of another at the end of each episode.

   On the evening of the novel's first day, the collective protagonist encounters his old friend Patrick Thunderjet. Their drinking expands into a binge that takes the hero and Thunderjet through a set of riotous experiences ending in a police drunk tank in the Crimea. Too valuable to Soviet society to be written off, the collective hero is sent to a detox hospital, cured, and discharged.

Three years pass. The sobered heroes continue their lives engaged in major creative projects, including a secret satellite project; a miraculous serum, Lymph D; a gigantic marble sculpture of a dinosaur "Humility"; a jazz-rock fusion breakthrough; and the writing of a play, or perhaps *The Burn* itself. Each of these men has a professional colleague, a close friend from the early 1960's, when a radiant new future seemed imminent. The old friends have compromised with the renewed conservative government and risen to positions of power and influence. Judas-like, these former friends betray the heroes, who, at the moment of crisis, return to alcohol.

In the shattering finale the collective protagonist, now merged into a single nameless "I" (apparently the adult Tolya von Steinbock), descends into alcoholic madness. Attempts to save him fail because the hero can trust no one. In the last of a series of drunken hallucinations he leaps to his death, believing that he is an astronaut flying to the moon.

There is also a story-behind-the-story told in a series of flashbacks to events twenty years before. Tolya von Steinbock joins his mother in Siberia when she is released from a ten-year sentence toward the end of Stalin's government. He wants nothing more than to be a model Soviet youth and is vaguely ashamed of his ex-prisoner mother and stepfather, a doctor and Catholic lay priest of German origin. Among a group of new women prisoners being marched through the streets he sees a young Polish-English girl, Alisa, whom he dreams of rescuing. As he daydreams, an ex-prisoner named Sanya Gurchenko offers modest aid to the girl. Tolya becomes friends with Gurchenko, who knows his stepfather. The courage and idealism of the two older men greatly impress him. Tolya's mother is soon rearrested, as is Sanya. They are interrogated, Sanya brutally, by two political police agents, Cheptsov, and his superior. Sanya later escapes to the West, where he becomes a Catholic theologian.

These events lie deeply buried in the minds of the successful heroes. They do not wish to remember the past with its implications for the future, but it is very much with them. Wherever they go they encounter two old men, cloakroom attendants, drunk-tank aides, and so on, who are faintly familiar. They also yearn for a promiscuous beauty, who moves in Moscow intellectual circles and seems to be the Polish-English Alisa. The heroes are forced to confront both their impotent past and compromised present: a confrontation they cannot face. Unlike Sanya Gurchenko, who actively resisted, they compromised with the system. They fail to rescue Alisa, who has also been corrupted and who, like their friends, betrays them.

It is Gurchenko who offers the solution. On a trip to Rome the collective hero has an encounter with Gurchenko, now a Jesuit priest, who articulates his philosophy of "the third model." The basic postulate is that all men, atheist and believer alike, seek God. There are always two models before man: an idea and its comparison. What one must seek is a third model—one which is qualitatively different—through which one may strive to see the face of God. Man approaches it only in moments of intuitive, suprarational creative inspiration. Although many human emotions, such as fear, anger, courage, can be rationally understood, others, the higher emotions such as compassion for one's neighbor, charity, the urge for justice, are rationally inexplicable. Creativity is similarly transrational. Christianity, precisely because it is concerned with unaccountable human phenomena, offers a basis for moral action. The hero's final leap is, however, not an act of revelation, but one of despair. The weight of the past is too heavy and his moral complicity too great.

*The Characters*

*The Burn*'s five-in-one hero manifests different aspects of Aksyonov himself and his close friends, all members of the new young cultural and scientific elite in the 1960's. Most central of the generational spokesmen and closest to author Aksyonov is the writer Pantalei, who is caught up in the quest for the once-pure camp victim Alisa, now the beautiful vixen of the Moscow jet set and possible KGB informant. Malkolmov, like Aksyonov, is a doctor. Jazz saxophonist Sabler reflects Aksyonov's love of American jazz and popular music. Tolya von Steinbock's background closely parallels that of Aksyonov's youth. The heroes, although distinct in most respects, are not "real," individuated protagonists. They are, rather, richly drawn types chosen to convey different aspects of the experiences of a single generation. Their kinship is marked by their shared middle name, "Apollinarievich"; they are the figurative sons of Apollo, the Greek god of the creative arts.

Other characters are also treated as "sets." Each of the heroes is paired with a villain, a Judas figure. Aksyonov signals their nature by assigning them names that mean "silver" in various languages: Silvester, the jazz man; Zilberansky, the doctor; Argentov, a scientist; Serebro, a sculptor; and Serebryanikov, a writer. The "silver" refers to the thirty pieces of silver Judas received for betraying Christ.

*The Burn* offers a third, less sharply defined group of characters. These are the Stalinists headed by Lieutenant Colonel Cheptsov. Cheptsov and his henchmen appear throughout the novel in various guises and transformations: as cloakroom or drunk-tank attendants; as roving marauders who plunder Europe in earlier centuries; as a mercenary unit that attacks a United Nations hospital in Katanga; and as the Soviet tank crews that subjugate Prague in 1968. Cheptsov is often identifiable only by his "eyes like small, hot black cherries."

Perhaps the only characters who are truly individuals as opposed to representatives are the ex-prisoners Sanya Gurchenko and Tolya's stepfather, who,
supported by their religious beliefs, have actively resisted evil. Moral compromise and betrayal are unknown in their world.

## Themes and Meanings

*The Burn* is Aksyonov's chronicle of his generation in the nightmarish
context of twentieth century Russian history. How did the bright hopes of the
early post-Stalin years fade into the repressive mediocrity of the Brezhnev
era? Aksyonov holds that the Russian intelligentsia itself, past and present, is
responsible. It failed to provide moral leadership against tyrannical perver-
sions of its philosophical and political ideals. Not only has the intelligentsia
betrayed the people but it has also betrayed itself. Betrayal is a central theme
of *The Burn*. Not only is each of the heroes betrayed by an old friend, but
also each of them betrays himself by withdrawing into hedonism rather than
actively resisting evil. Aksyonov's answer to the moral debacle of his generation is found in the words of Sanya Gurchenko. "Christianity is like a breakthrough into space, that most courageous and far-reaching spurt toward the
third model." Aksyonov's collective hero perhaps pervertedly echoes this
thought when in a state of drunken paranoia he leaps to his death thinking
that he is a truth-seeking astronaut. The intelligentsia has again failed to confront evil, leaving it to Gurchenko who, whatever his origins, is not a member of that group. Nor is the materialistic Western intelligentsia a suitable
moral model for the Soviet Union. Patrick Thunderjet, the Western equivalent of the Soviet collective hero, is also spiritually bankrupt. It is perhaps
not too farfetched to see the belief systems Aksyonov associates with East
and West respectively as being the first and second models: Neither is satisfactory. Answers must be sought in the third model.

Aksyonov's long, complex, and seemingly chaotic novel falls into three
"books," which might be respectively characterized as drunken spree ("The
Men's Club"), sobriety and flashbacks ("Five in Solitary"), and alcoholic
hallucinations and death ("The Victim's Last Adventure"). The first book
covers a few days circa 1970; the second and third a short period circa 1973.
The form of the narrative is complex. Much of it is narrated from a perspective of drunkenness and even alcoholic dementia. The chaotic time line is
further fractured by both momentary and extended flashbacks. The text is
spangled with sections of surreal poetry mimicking jazz improvisations.
Numerous allusions to Russian history and literature and bits of Soviet realia
make *The Burn* a difficult but rewarding work for many readers. The novel's
seeming chaos is in fact cogently ordered by the religious mythology that
underlies its events.

*Critical Context*

The major theme of Aksyonov's oeuvre is the nature and fate of Russia, a country geographically and politically located between East and West. In the imagination of Aksyonov's generation, the East is associated with collectivism and despotism; the West with individualism and democracy. Stalin's tyranny turned Russia into a vast, culturally barren GULag. His perversion of Communist ideology had imposed a stultifying hyperrationalism on the country: Socialist Realism in the arts, atheism in religion, and materialism in philosophy. The Revolution had betrayed its idealistic perpetrators. With the death of Stalin in 1953, the debate over Russia's destiny was reopened by Aksyonov's contemporaries. The 1950's and early 1960's were a time of exhilarating ferment for young Russian intellectuals. Censorship eased. The official ideal of rigid rationalism was challenged by that of spontaneous creativity and Socialist Realism, by more exciting artistic forms. Some of the young rejected materialist philosophical views for religious belief and idealism. Western popular culture began to penetrate Soviet society. There was strong official resistance to these winds of change. By the mid-1960's, conservative forces had gained the upper hand. Trials took place; Czechoslovakia and then Afghanistan were invaded. Many disillusioned liberals withdrew into their private worlds, their dream of a new Russia dead. Some, like Aksyonov, emigrated—often with official encouragement. Aksyonov's works chronicle this period, first from the optimistic perspectives of a generation on the rise confident that a new day had dawned, then growing doubts, and finally compromises and retreat. These events, stages, and themes are mirrored in Aksyonov's fiction, the saga of a generation.

*Sources for Further Study*

Lowe, David. "E. Ginzburg's *Krutoj maršrut* and V. Aksenov's *Ožog*: The Magadan Connection," in *Slavic and East European Journal*. XXVII (1983), pp. 200-210.

Meyer, Priscilla. "Aksenov and Stalinism: Political, Moral, and Literary Power," in *Slavic and East European Journal*. XXX (1986), pp. 509-525.

Mozejko, Edward, Boris Briker, and Per Dalgard, eds. *Vasiliy Pavlovich Aksenov: A Writer in Quest of Himself*, 1986.

Proffer, Ellendea. "The Prague Winter: Two Novels by Aksyonov," in *The Third Wave: Russian Literature in Emigration*, 1984.

*D. Barton Johnson*

# CANCER WARD

*Author:* Aleksandr Solzhenitsyn (1918-    )
*Type of plot:* Domestic realism
*Time of plot:* 1955-1956
*Locale:* An unnamed city based on Tashkent in the Soviet Union
*First published: Rakovy korpus*, 1968 (English translation, 1968)

> *Principal characters:*
>
> KOSTOGLOTOV, a former labor camp inmate and now a
>   political exile suffering from stomach cancer
> RUSANOV, a loyal Party member suffering from a large tumor
>   on his neck
> DR. GANGART, a radiotherapist who takes a special interest in
>   Kostoglotov
> DR. DONTSOVA, the head of the radiotherapy department,
>   who dreads the discovery of her own cancer
> ZOYA, a young nurse attracted to Kostoglotov
> DYOMKA, a young cancer patient
> SIBGATOV, a patient slowly dying from cancer of the sacrum
> SHULUBIN, an old cancer patient and Kostoglotov's ally
> VADIM, a scholarly patient who fluctuates between accepting
>   his fate and fighting against it

*The Novel*

*Cancer Ward* is what its title suggests: an exploration of an institution
devoted to the care of cancer patients. In this public institution, people from
all levels of society find themselves in the same predicament, struck down by
a disease that terrorizes and enervates them. The doctors in the ward do
their best to keep their patients' hopes alive, and in some cases treatment
seems to be remarkably effective. Overall, however, there is a sense of gloom
and dread as patients worry over their "secondaries"—the tumors in other
parts of the body which reveal that their disease is spreading.

By beginning the novel with the arrival of Rusanov, a government official,
Aleksandr Solzhenitsyn quickly suggests the highly structured nature of Soviet society. Rusanov is upset that he is not being treated in Moscow. He dis-
trusts the doctors in this provincial city, and he finds his fellow patients
considerably beneath him. He is a stuffy, orthodox Communist who knows
very little about his own countrymen. He is quickly offended by Kostoglotov,
a hardened veteran of the labor camps and of political exile. Kostoglotov
finds Rusanov's political maxims hard to take, for he knows that Rusanov has
never confronted the realities of Soviet society.

Chapter by chapter each cancer patient's personality and background are revealed. Solzhenitsyn is careful never to supply the reader with too much information. Slowly, the story of Kostoglotov's arrival at the ward is explained. He is a man who considered himself near death, and the doctors have managed to save him through radiation treatments and drugs. Although his physical condition has improved, Kostoglotov tempers his admiration for the doctors with considerable skepticism. He believes that they take their therapeutic methods too seriously and actually overtreat their patients.

Kostoglotov's objections to the treatment are as much political as they are medical. He sees the doctors forming their own dictatorial society that cannot acknowledge the patients' right to know the exact nature of their disease. On the other hand, the doctors are shown to be extremely dedicated to their work, to making the correct diagnoses, and to protecting their patients from the dire consequences of their cancers.

The plot of the novel, then, centers on the dialogue between Kostoglotov and his doctors, who are alternately persuaded and repelled by his argument for releasing him before his full course of treatment has been completed. There is no question that Kostoglotov has a profound impact on the doctors, but, when he finally leaves the ward, he finds his sudden freedom to be an awesome and frightening responsibility.

*The Characters*

The main character and protagonist is Kostoglotov. He is the only one in the novel to challenge societal norms. He argues with everyone, even the female doctors whom he finds attractive. Having endured the cruelty of Soviet labor camps and the isolation of exile, he has toughened himself to the worst aspects of his native land, aspects his fellow patients and doctors scarcely recognize. An exception is Shulubin, another patient, who toward the end of the novel confesses that he has allowed himself to be cowed by the tyranny of the state. More than once he comes to Kostoglotov's aid in arguments with the smug Rusanov, who thinks nothing of informing on colleagues who have not, in his view, measured up to the high ideals of the Soviet state.

Dr. Gangart is enormously attracted by Kostoglotov's iconoclasm, even as she is puzzled by his seeming intractability. She comes to realize, however, that Kostoglotov is trying to remain his own man and to think and act and feel for himself. That is why he is horrified when he learns that the injections prescribed for him will take away his sexual drive. He does not want hormone treatments that will deprive him of the very desires that make him a man. Zoya, a sensitive and highly competent nurse, is won over by Kostoglotov and decides not to give him the injections. Kostoglotov is not, however, without his faults or without a certain foolishness, as when he believes that he can cure his cancer with a mandrake root.

Other characters are deeply moving. Vadim thinks that he has become reconciled to the fact that he has only eight months to live. He spends his time reading and studying, hoping to make a significant contribution to science. As his days dwindle, however, he cannot fight back the hope that some cure will be found for his disease. Similarly, Sibgatov's sacrum is slowly wasting away, but he patiently and uncomplainingly submits to treatment that can only prolong his agony. The young Dyomka must lose his leg and is painfully shy when a young girl, also a patient, counsels him not to consent to the amputation. One of the most moving scenes in the book occurs later, when she comes to him in the knowledge that one of her breasts has to be removed. She asks him to fondle it in memory of what she is about to lose.

Each of these characters is brought to life fully through vivid dialogue and description. There is, for example, the weary Dr. Dontsova, who has spent so many years in radiology that she apparently has become a victim of the very X-ray apparatus used to cure her patients. She lets months go by before she submits to an examination, for she dreads that her worst fears will be confirmed.

### Themes and Meanings

Although there are many discussions of politics and of cancer in *Cancer Ward*, the novel's themes and meanings are conveyed primarily through the characters themselves. They are all measured by the degree to which they have a consciousness of society. Rusanov, for example, is found wanting because of his lack of imagination. This is most evident when his son Yuri tries to show him that the state cannot govern its people as surely as Rusanov supposes. In his government job, Yuri notices that certain stamps are missing from government documents. He comes to suspect that one of two women in the office has been using the stamps to add to her income. He dates both women, thinking that he will find in one of their homes fine furniture or other evidence of earnings in excess of a government salary. He finds instead that neither woman lives in luxury. In fact, he learns that both of them have been stealing the stamps just to have enough money to live. Rusanov is disappointed when Yuri tells him that he has not turned in the two women to the authorities. He does not understand that his son has tried to tell him that life is much more complicated than his simple Party maxims about loyalty to the state.

The pervasive theme of *Cancer Ward* is the human inability to confront the truth—whether that truth be the onset of a fatal disease, the corruption of the state, or a character's blindness to his or his own limitations. Indeed, the novel ends with Kostoglotov, the bravest character in *Cancer Ward*, realizing that he too is afraid of real freedom, the freedom that finds people alone with the truth about themselves. Disease in this novel is the physical equivalent of the evil in human character. Just as there is something arbitrary about the cancer that can strike healthy human beings in their prime, so is there something arbitrary in the human character itself. *Cancer Ward* ends with Kostoglotov's visit to a zoo. He sees a sign that explains that "the little monkey that used to live here was blinded because of the senseless cruelty of one of the visitors. An evil man threw tobacco into the Macaque Rhesus' eyes." It is the senselessness of the destructive act that profoundly disturbs Kostoglotov; there is no rational explanation for it. In itself, the sign is remarkable because it does not contain the usual jargon of Soviet public language that attributes foul deeds to antihumanists and agents of American imperialism. The simplicity of the word "evil" arrests Kostoglotov's attention, for it is precisely the concept of evil that Soviet society no longer recognizes.

### Critical Context

Solzhenitsyn's *Cancer Ward* was a ground-breaking novel. A Soviet literary journal agreed to publish it in 1967 and then submitted the question of publication to the Board of the Union of Soviet Writers. The debate of that organization is included in the Farrar, Straus and Giroux edition of the novel, and it is indispensable to understanding that Solzhenitsyn was lifting the veil that had obscured the discussion of many subjects in the Soviet Union since the time of Joseph Stalin's rule. In the Board of the Union of Soviet Writers meeting, Solzhenitsyn was attacked for denigrating his society and for providing ammunition for the Soviet Union's foreign critics.

Solzhenitsyn defended himself by suggesting that he had forthrightly described what it was like to live in a cancer ward. He did not say so, but much of the novel was based on his personal experience. *Cancer Ward* is not a political parable; that is, it does not use the subject of cancer as a way of exploring politics. Instead, it suggests that the way people feel about their disease and the political positions they adopt are inseparable. Rusanov, for example, understands neither the nature of his disease nor the nature of Communism. He cannot fathom his own evil or the evil of those around him.

It had been the practice in the Soviet Union not only to suppress the crimes of Stalin's rule but also to make sure that literature conveyed only the positive aspects of life. Thus Solzhenitsyn's novel was viewed as subversive not only because of its political discussions but because it dared to raise the subject of cancer and of people's fears about it. Yet *Cancer Ward* is an impressively objective novel; it never forsakes characters for political arguments; rather, political considerations arise naturally out of human relationships in the novel.

Understanding the political and literary context of *Cancer Ward* undoubtedly adds another level of interest to Solzhenitsyn's work, but his novel should be read above all as an enduring human document. In *Cancer Ward* he explores the deepest questions about the value and meaning of life itself. In 1955 and 1956, the time of the novel, the Soviet Union was beginning to reconsider Stalin's legacy. In the novel, Kostoglotov learns that his political exile may end because of an impending period of liberalization. Ten years later, when *Cancer Ward* was considered for publication, a new era of intolerance was beginning. That *Cancer Ward* was even considered for publication in the Soviet Union suggests how powerful Solzhenitsyn's words are in challenging people who do not wish to acknowledge human suffering and who cannot admit that a society afraid of judging itself is already dead.

*Sources for Further Study*

Dunlop, John B., Richard S. Haugh, and Michael Nicholson, eds. *Solzhenitsyn in Exile: Critical Essays and Documentary Materials*, 1985.
Feuer, Kathryn, ed. *Solzhenitsyn: A Collection of Critical Essays*, 1976.
Kodjak, Andrej. *Alexander Solzhenitsyn*, 1978.
Rothberg, Abraham. *Aleksandr Solzhenitsyn: The Major Novels*, 1971.
Scammell, Michael. *Solzhenitsyn: A Biography*, 1984.

*Carl E. Rollyson, Jr.*

# CASSANDRA
## A Novel and Four Essays

*Author:* Christa Wolf (1929-     )
*Type of plot:* Psychological realism
*Time of plot:* c. 1200 B.C. in the novel
*Locale:* Mycenae and Troy in the novel; Athens, Crete, and Mycenae in the essays
*First published: Voraussetzungen einer Erzählung: "Kassandra"* and *Kassandra*, 1983, 2 volumes (English translation, 1984)

> *Principal characters:*
> CASSANDRA, the narrator, a Trojan princess and the priestess of Apollo
> PRIAM and HECUBA, Cassandra's parents, the King and Queen of Troy
> AENEAS, Cassandra's friend and lover, who is destined to escape from Troy
> ANCHISES, Aeneas' father, a benevolent old man who comforts Cassandra and other women of Troy
> PANTHOUS, a priest of Apollo, Cassandra's superior in the religious hierarchy
> AGAMEMNON, the leader of the Greeks
> HELENUS,
> TROILUS,
> PARIS, and
> HECTOR, Cassandra's brothers
> POLYXENA, Cassandra's sister, who is sacrificed on the grave of Achilles
> ACHILLES (THE BRUTE), a violent, lustful Greek warrior
> CLYTEMNESTRA, Agamemnon's wife, who kills both her husband and Cassandra

## The Novel

The captive Cassandra stands in Agamemnon's chariot outside the lion gate of Mycenae, awaiting her death at the hands of Clytemnestra. She knows that Clytemnestra is now killing Agamemnon in the palace. She says as much to the Greek elders who cluster around the chariot, but they, like her own people, do not believe or cannot understand her dire prophecies. She casts aside, as a bitter mockery, the insignia of her rank as a seeress and a priestess of Apollo. What time she has left she spends recalling her past, from the time she enjoyed the status of favorite daughter to Priam, her beloved father and King of Troy, until the time when Priam imprisoned her in the dungeon. She was punished because she would not cooperate in a plan to use her sister, Polyxena, as erotic bait to trap Achilles in the temple of Apollo. Achilles had demanded Polyxena as the price of giving back the body of Hector. According to the plan, while Achilles was making love to Polyxena, Paris would wound him in his vulnerable heel.

Cassandra's adamant refusal to cooperate with this plan was not motivated by any love for Achilles, whom she abhorred, nor was it a statement against the profanation of the temple, which had been declared neutral territory in the contest between Trojans and Greeks. To Cassandra, her refusal was a protest against a long process by which women had been deprived of all autonomy in this irrational war. This supposedly gallant contest over a woman was a lie from the very beginning. There was no Helen in Troy; the king of Egypt had taken her from Paris after Paris had abducted her from Menelaus' palace. The original kidnapping had been justified, presumably, by the fact that Priam's sister had been kidnapped by the Greeks in the past. Kidnapping was, after all, a rather common practice among the Greeks.

Cassandra, who began as a merry and thoughtless girl enjoying her privileges, realized that women were simply pawns in men's military and commercial rivalries. The Greeks did not want to acknowledge Trojan control of the commercial sea route between East and West. Besides, warfare was a way of life for the Greek soldiers, and it had become so for many of the Trojan men as well. Even the imperial Hecuba, Priam's wife, who had shared actively in government, was denied access to the inner councils, and old Priam was controlled by a military junta that cared little about family honor.

Cassandra had her first lesson in the necessity of submission to men at the time of her first menstrual period. Like all other women of that time, she had to sit before the temple of the love goddess until a man threw a coin in her lap; she then had to follow that man—whoever he was—into the sanctuary, where he would deflower her. (Herodotus describes this custom and notes that ugly women were forced to return again and again until they were chosen.) Cassandra was spared humiliation, however, because Aeneas hastened to claim her. Instead of violating the frightened girl, Aeneas simply reported to Hecuba that the deed was done. Cassandra fell in love with Aeneas because of his kindness on this occasion. She fantasized about him when the chief priest, Panthous, came to her bed at night.

Only much later did Aeneas actually become her lover. Perhaps the least plausible detail of this story (which is made more believable in many ways than the original epic) is Cassandra's refusal to leave Troy as it burns, when Aeneas asks her to flee with him. She says that he is going to be a hero and that she could not love a hero. "We have no chance against a time that needs heroes," she says.

*The Characters*

Cassandra, the narrator, is a much more complex character in Christa

Wolf's novel than the mythical prophetess, loved by Apollo, who gave her the power of prophecy and cursed her when she resisted his advances. According to the myth, Apollo asked for a goodbye kiss but spat in her mouth. After that, no one believed her. Here, Cassandra has a dream of Apollo, a nightmare in which he forces his attentions on her in the form of a wolf. This has some mythical justification, since the god of light was sometimes called Apollo Lykeios, a rather obscure god of wolves and mice. The mythic variant works well in this context, since it suggests that ideal masculinity has a dark and malicious side which is little recognized. Cassandra's experiences with her father, with the high priest of Apollo, and with some of her brothers (as well as Achilles and Agamemnon) contribute to her disillusionment with dominating males. By the end of the story, she withdraws from Aeneas, the hero-to-be, perhaps simply because she recognizes that power corrupts and heroes are prone to change.

She is complex in other ways, aside from her insight into male bravado. Much of her perfected wisdom is self-knowledge. She recognizes that she herself was part of the problem of a deteriorating Troy. She does not present herself as heroic or tragic, or even much concerned about others. She disdains marriage, wanting only to be a priestess—the sole "profession" open to a woman of her class. She resents the fact that her twin brother, Helenus, is made a priest first simply because he is a man, when she has a greater gift for the role. Her envy of her brother, however, does not make her any more compassionate toward her sister, Polyxena, who craves the attention that their father lavishes on Cassandra. As she grows older, Cassandra realizes that her sister's development into a coquette, who would even flirt with the unattractive Achilles, can be traced to her loveless childhood and low self-image. Thus, Cassandra's vehement refusal to cooperate with the plan to use Polyxena as live bait is prompted partly by feelings of guilt for having neglected her sister's welfare.

Cassandra's character becomes more compassionate with time. She begins to understand and empathize with other women through her friendship with her personal slave. Her slave introduces Cassandra to a group of women, both Trojan and Greek, who meet in a secret place in the mountains outside Troy. The only man who is often with these people is Anchises, Aeneas' father. He seems to be a kind of spiritual father to those in misery. He carves figures of animals out of wood and gives them to his friends. The figures become a secret signal of friendship, designating where one may find shelter in need.

Agamemnon is a weak man, sexually impotent but dangerous. Such men must act in a belligerent fashion to bolster their masculinity. He is burdened by guilt for having sacrificed his daughter, Iphigenia, to get favorable winds for the voyage to Troy. He is vaguely drawn to Cassandra, not out of lust, but because she reminds him of his daughter.

## Themes and Meanings

Wolf's realistic reinterpretation of the prophetess who told the truth but was never believed speaks as much to the present as to the past. An outline of the story was presented in 1982, when Wolf was awarded a guest lectureship at the University of Frankfurt. She delivered a series of five lectures relating to her Greek travels and studies, entitled "Lectures on Poetics." The four introductory lectures are published with the novel, which was expanded from a draft of the fifth lecture. She calls these essays "Conditions of a Narrative"; they throw considerable light on the genesis of the main character and the philosophic and psychological implications of the novel.

How does the past determine the present and the future and, conversely, how does the present determine the story one tells about the past? Though it includes no actual reference to modern times, the novel suggests not only the blindness of the Trojans and the Greeks to their own fates, but also the blindness of Germans to the consequences of the rise of Adolf Hitler and World War II. The novel also suggests an equal or worse failure of the contemporary world in foreseeing and forestalling the possibility of nuclear war. Men of every age seem to pursue death with blind abandon.

The first and second essays are travel reports about a trip to Greece that Wolf and her husband took in 1980. A chance mix-up about planes caused a day's delay—a day the author spent reading Aeschylus' *Oresteia*, the trilogy that begins with the murder of Agamemnon and Cassandra by Clytemnestra. The play illustrates one of Wolf's observations: that history and art are probably both reinterpretations of the past, distorted in one way or another by the storyteller. The *Oresteia* is a classical Greek's reinterpretation of a more ancient legend of blood revenge; the story is designed to glorify the Greek system of government of Aeschylus' time.

The second essay describes a journey to Mycenae and Crete, the center of the ancient female cults. There, Wolf makes a brief traveling acquaintanceship with two American feminists, who are eager for any evidence of the ancient preeminence of women in Minoan Crete. This hunger for vanished glory strikes Wolf as sad and ironic:

> What is proved by the fact, authenticated though it seems, that women led the early clans who lived by agriculture; that the children they brought into the world belonged to them; that they continued to determine the inherited succession even in later, highly organized kingdoms; that they were the originators of all cults, of taboo and fetish, dance, song, and many early crafts? Doesn't this harking back to an irretrievable ancient past reveal more clearly than anything else the desperate plight in which women see themselves today?

The author's suspicion that the feminists' veneration for the ancient cult of the mother goddess may reveal more about the present suggests that interpretation of the past often reflects the unconscious desires of the interpreter. She illustrates this tendency by pointing to nineteenth century attitudes toward ancient Crete as a peculiarly peaceful, therefore idyllic, culture brought down not by human error but by natural disasters such as catastrophic earthquakes. The novel suggests that people destroy cultures and that victims (that is, the Trojans) may contribute to their own destruction.

In another sense, the past exists in the present but is reinterpreted by the storyteller. Wolf illustrates this with the Greek Easter celebrations she witnessed, which center on the sacrificial lamb. She notes the similarity of the ritual to ancient fertility cults of Demeter and Dionysus. She points out that the ritual may have originally involved a human sacrifice, a young man representing the god's son, Dionysus; then, the lamb, as scapegoat, was substituted for the human being, and only with Christianity did the victim again become a man. Mythic patterns may govern history as well as literature—or perhaps only one's interpretation of history.

The third lecture is a work diary, much of it devoted to historical dilemmas, old and new, and the self-destructive course of history in the modern world. Here, Wolf suggests that male technological genius is coupled with an unrecognized irrationality and blindness about outcomes. She discusses the writings of Thomas Mann, Karl Kerényi, Lewis Mumford, and Stefan Zweig. The latter, living in a complaisant England when Hitler was invading France, wrote, "The old Cassandra feelings have come alive again."

While this diary may seem disorganized, even chaotic, its sheer range of thought does, in fact, suggest the "Conditions of a Narrative." All these observations on current events, political and moral realities, the history and subjugation of women, and men's pretensions to rationality and persistent pursuit of war relate to the dilemma of the truth sayer in a disintegrating society.

*Critical Context*

Christa Wolf is an East German writer who grew up in Hitler's Germany. This accounts for much of her distrust of heroes. Both the insecurity and the sense of guilt of Wolf and her parent's generation have left their marks on her writings. The early naïveté and uncritical acceptance of the young Cassandra which changed, in time, to disillusionment and horror may reflect the slowly developing perception of the author when she was a member of the Hitler Youth. Her autobiographical novel, *Kindheitsmuster* (1976; *A Model Childhood*, 1980; reissued as *Patterns of Childhood*, 1984), is filled with observations about how her contemporaries selectively forget or distort the recent past, unwilling or unable to face the reality of its cruelties. In that convoluted account, the child's mother is likened to Cassandra; she was punished by the Gestapo for saying that even a blind man could see that Germany would lose this war.

*Sources for Further Study*

Abel, Elizabeth. "(E)Merging Identities: The Dynamics of Female Friendship in Contemporary Fiction by Women," in *Signs*. LI, no. 3 (1981), pp.
413-432.

Keith-Smith, Brian. *Essays on Contemporary German Literature*, 1966.

Sauer, Klaus, ed. *Christa Wolf Materialienbuch*, 1979.

Stephan, Alexander. *Christa Wolf*, 1976.

_____. *Christa Wolf: Forschungsbericht*, 1979.

*Katherine Snipes*

# THE CASTLE OF CROSSED DESTINIES

*Author:* Italo Calvino (1923-1985)
*Type of plot:* Semiotic fantasy
*Time of plot:* The mythic past
*Locale:* A castle and a tavern
*First published: Il castello dei destini incrociati*, 1969; revised, 1973 (English translation, 1977)

> *Principal characters:*
> THE FIRST NARRATOR, an unnamed knight who has apparently faced many trials and difficulties
> THE CASTLE GUESTS, each of whom tells a tale of his or her own life by using tarot cards
> THE SECOND NARRATOR, also unnamed, who also has a tale to tell
> THE PATRONS OF THE TAVERN, also with tales told with the help of the tarot

*The Novel*

Italo Calvino's book, a series of short fantastic tales, falls into two major parts: "The Castle of Crossed Destinies" and "The Tavern of Crossed Destinies." In two isolated and mysterious settings, guests and patrons relate the stories of their lives. Since these experiences are extremely harrowing or traumatic, each storyteller, including the narrator-observer, has lost the power of speech. The method of narration, therefore, becomes the pictures on the cards of the tarot deck, which each guest arranges in the order that most closely corresponds to the story of his or her life. No one refrains from telling a tale; indeed, as the series of tales progresses, they fight for possession of cards crucial to individual stories. The tales validate the lives of these people and relating them justifies their experiences. Since pictures do not have the same precision of meaning as words, however, the reader has the option, at each phase of the story, of accepting the principal interpretation of the narrator-observer, one or another of the variants he offers as possible but less likely, or, because the cards themselves appear in the margin of the text, of fashioning his own interpretation of what was signified as each card was placed. Calvino thus allows the reader to become an active participant in the narrative process.

This unusual narrative method strips the tarot of its use for prophecy and makes it exclusively a tool of the archetypal past. One individual's story told in reverse (by transposing the order of the series of cards) becomes the tale of a second. As the cards lie face up, with each series revealing a story, every intersection of a series becomes the starting point for a new tale and the

experience of another narrator. Each narrator, therefore, becomes an archetype whose story transcends that individual's experience.

For example, the Popess, a card illustrated with a crowned, nunlike figure,
which accuses the Ingrate Knight of having offended the goddess Cybele by
deserting a woman who has befriended him, juxtaposed to the Ace of Cups,
becomes an inspiration for the Alchemist. The Emperor, the card which the
Alchemist selects next, suggests the prophecy of the forest witch that the Alchemist will become the most powerful man in the world, while the Juggler,
the next card in the Alchemist's series, coupled with the Seven of Coins and
the Two of Coins, indicates a barter of the Alchemist's soul for the secret of
gold.

Because the same cards have different meanings in the context of each
storyteller's experience, the quadrangle of Death, Pope, Eight of Coins, and
Two of Clubs, which had been elements in the story of the Doomed Bride
who chose to wed herself to the Devil rather than to God (a tale resembling
the abduction of Persephone by Pluto), becomes the the inspiration for the
Grave Robber. The narrator observes from the young man's dress that he
must have robbed only the graves of the illustrious or wealthy (popes, for
example), and that he used two clubs as levers. The Grave Robber's tale is a
classic one of choice. He climbs a huge tree (Life), reaches a suspended city
(the World), and is offered riches (Coins), power (Swords), or wisdom
(Cups). He characteristically chooses riches, but the archangel who offered
him the choice instead gives him damnation (Clubs).

Roland is also among the castle guests, and, as one might expect, uses the
cards to tell a story of chivalric romance. Despite warnings that he should not
enter the forest of love (Ten of Clubs), he does so to pursue Angelica, the
enchantress from Cathay who intends to ruin the French armies (Queen of
Swords). Roland finds her with the youth, Medoro (Page of Clubs), and pays
for his choice of love over war with the loss of his sanity. Force triumphs, and
Durendal, Roland's invincible sword, hangs forgotten on a tree, while lunacy
(Moon) reigns over Roland's earth. Justice is the penultimate card in Roland's series, followed by the Hanged Man. These last two cards may imply
that Roland's knights will save him from his fury, or only that Roland prefers
his madness.

The tales of the tavern patrons, also told with cards, similarly interlock,
though they use a different tarot deck, one consisting of seventy-eight cards,
for their intersecting tales. The major difference is that while the castle tales
appear in clearly defined vertical or horizontal rows, the tavern stories form
blocks with more irregular outlines; also, they are superimposed in a central
area, where the cards appearing in nearly all the stories are concentrated.
This new pattern allows the possibility of a different narrative method from
that used in the castle section. The Waverer, for example, is a young man
incapable of making choices, and the block arrangement underscores the

alternatives he faces as he vacillates, wrings his hands, and repeatedly changes the order of the cards. The Eight of Cups, the Ten of Clubs, and the Lovers indicate to the narrator-observer that the young man has deserted his bride on the day of his wedding feast. The second woman in The Lovers card implies a rival. Unable to decide which bride to choose, the Waverer chooses neither, and makes a forest journey but cannot decide which path to take. Since the coin he throws (the Page of Coins) remains erect in a bush at the foot of an oak, he climbs the tree to discover the best path, only to be blinded by the Sun. Identical twins confusedly gesture to a suspended city, perhaps the "City of All" where all choices are balanced. The Waverer can have the city, but after his long climb, he can think only of his thirst. He decides he cannot choose between two wells but instead wants the source of all water, the sea. A thunderbolt then smashes both tree and city, and Moon reigns. In the end, the Waverer confronts his double, the man prohibited from making a choice when the Waverer had refused to choose his bride.

The tavern section also contains literary montages which combine elements of the stories of Hamlet, Macbeth, and King Lear, as well as of Faust, Parsifal, and Oedipus. When the narrator tries to tell his tale, what emerges is Calvino's literary self-portrait: the King of Clubs, whose scepter resembles a cheap pen, and the Two of Coins (because the coins on the card form an *S* which the narrator reads as the essential of language, "signification"). The writer encounters unsavory reality (the Devil) and balances the elements with which he deals (the Juggler). Because his is a solitary occupation (the Hermit), the writer must ensure that he does not lose contact with the world about which he writes (the Knight of Swords). The narrator notes, as an afterthought, that paintings could describe his life as easily as does the tarot: Saint Jerome in place of the Hermit, Saint George for the Knight of Swords, Saint Augustine to represent the writer's restlessness.

*The Characters*

The narrators, who in reality are one person, are clearly the most important individuals in Calvino's collection of tales. They are the interpreters of the cards and therefore control the stories as they are told. This control is limited, however, since each person provides variant readings of the cards and even supplies narrative when gaps exist within the stories. Because the cards also appear in the margin as they are mentioned, the reader can also function as narrator by rejecting variants or by supplying personal interpretations, particularly of the evocative picture cards.

The other characters fall into three broad categories, themselves tangential: folkloric, mythic, and literary. Each has some hamartia or flaw which has led to a ruinous miscalculation in life. The Ingrate, for example, rejects the love of the woman who rescues him and pays for his ingratitude with his damnation in the forest of self-loss, the very place in which all Calvino's storytellers find themselves. Astolpho, the English knight and companion of Roland, ascends to the moon in an attempt to retrieve Roland's lost reason but discovers that every human undertaking begins and ends in the realm of madness. In the end, one always returns to the center of an empty horizon. The Waverer, like the Ingrate, also rejects love, though doing so because of indecision rather than selfishness. His near possession of the "City of All," the place where all alternatives are reconciled, is withheld when he insists on possessing the sea to satisfy his thirst. He, too, finds himself in the forest of self-loss and confronts his other self, the man prohibited from choice by his double's refusal to choose.

## Themes and Meanings

Doubt, loss, and missed opportunities haunt all lives, and the storytellers in this collection are no exception. Their crossed fates are doubly underscored, since they use the same cards to tell their tales and the intersecting cards of one are used for the story of another. In addition, they find themselves in an archetypal forest of doubt, but unlike Dante's forest (in the prologue to *Inferno*), here there is no hope of a resolution in Paradise. The raconteurs produce their stories with the same desperate necessity as Dante's sinners but without the same precision of language.

The tarot deck becomes a metaphor for the lives of these individuals, but a metaphor devoid of the literal weakens precision, even as it evokes a response. The cards, therefore, impose a similarity on ostensibly disparate experiences. They emphasize the similarity of all lives, from the most glamorous (the castle guests) to the most humble (the tavern patrons). That the narrator ultimately emerges as the author, who sees himself in the hermetic but sordid business of juggling the fates of others, reassures and at the same time terrifies the reader. Not even the master storyteller has an answer to what T. S. Eliot called "the overwhelming question" of life's meaning.

Despite the mythic past in which Calvino's tales are set, his narrators are, then, twentieth century personalities. Unlike Dante's Pilgrim, they cannot, because of weakness, ignorance, or inability to believe, make the journey which ultimately rectifies the false starts and missteps of earlier adventures.

## Critical Context

Like his other works, Calvino's *The Castle of Crossed Destinies* is considered fantasy because it describes the imaginative, the odd, and the visionary. It is, however, semiotic fantasy, since it uses tarot pictures as signs with which to construct the narrative. Its characters are even denied the use of words, which are merely the most conventional signs. Accompanying gestures are the only means, aside from the series of cards, that Calvino's characters have for telling stories which must be told.

Nonverbal signs interested Calvino throughout his life, and the challenge of constructing this book from two decks of tarot cards, a fifteenth century set by Bonifacio Bembo (for the castle narratives) and a larger, complete eighteenth century set printed in Marseilles, France (for the tavern stories), consumed many frustrating hours. In part, Calvino wanted to prove that such a work could be written; he did so when the castle section was first published in *Tarocchi: Il mazzo visconteo di Bergamo e New York* (1969; *Tarots: The Visconti Pack in Bergamo and New York*, 1975). Calvino explored related semiotic ideas in *Le cosmicomiche* (1965; *Cosmicomics*, 1968), *Le città invisibili* (1972; *Invisible Cities*, 1974), and *Se una notte d'inverno un viaggiatore* (1979; *If on a Winter's Night a Traveler*, 1981). Umberto Eco, his countryman, has brought semiotics to the mystery novel in *Il nome della rosa* (1980; *The Name of the Rose*, 1983). The French semiologist Roland Barthes noted that "everything signifies," that the smallest gesture and the most profound words carry meaning far deeper than surface appearance or literal content, and Calvino's semiotic fantasy hyperbolizes or exaggerates the communication process upon which every living thing relies. The imprecision of the process merely reflects the doubt and insecurity of those who use it.

*Sources for Further Study*

Calvino, Italo. *The Uses of Literature*, 1986.
Carter, Albert Howard. *Italo Calvino: Metamorphoses of Fantasy*, 1987.
Eco, Umberto. *Travels in Hyper Reality: Essays*, 1986. Edited by Helen Wolff and Kurt Wolff.
Olken, I. T. *With Pleated Eye and Garnet Wing: Symmetries of Italo Calvino*, 1984.
Perosa, Sergio. "The Heirs of Calvino and the Eco Effect," in *The New York Times Book Review*. XCII (August 16, 1987), p. 1.

*Robert J. Forman*

# CASTLE TO CASTLE, NORTH, and RIGADOON

*Author:* Louis-Ferdinand Céline (Louis-Ferdinand Destouches, 1894-1961)
*Type of plot:* Psychological realism
*Time of plot:* November, 1944, to March, 1945
*Locale:* Various German cities
*First published: D'un château l'autre,* 1957 (*Castle to Castle,* 1968); *Nord,* 1960
  (*North,* 1972); *Rigodon,* 1969 (*Rigadoon,* 1974)

> *Principal characters:*
> FERDINAND, the protagonist and subsequent narrator-author
>   of the novel, a doctor, who is fleeing Paris after having
>   been denounced as a pro-Nazi collaborator for his anti-
>   Semitic writings; the fictional persona of Céline
> LILI, his wife, a professional dancer
> LE VIGAN, a well-known actor in the French cinema,
>   condemned for radio broadcasts supporting the Nazis

*The Novels*

This trilogy of novels, *Castle to Castle, North,* and *Rigadoon,* informally
known as the wartime trilogy, traces the journey of the protagonist, Ferdinand, from Paris to Copenhagen in the wake of the collapse of the German
war effort. Denounced as a collaborator for his anti-Semitic writings and
consequently threatened with death by the Resistance, Ferdinand flees his
Montmartre apartment to seek the relative political safety of Denmark. Earlier, he hid money from royalties there to provide for such an occurrence.
Each volume of the trilogy begins with a preface by the narrator-author, an
older and more cynical Ferdinand, who informs the reader of his present
situation. He has settled in the Parisian suburb of Meudon and resumed his
medical practice after several years of detention in Denmark. Throughout
the trilogy, he asserts that he was made a scapegoat by the French government and never aided the Nazi occupiers of his country.

In the prefaces to the first and third volumes of the trilogy, *Castle to Castle*
and *Rigadoon* respectively, the narrator's return to his past, a narrative
metalepsis, is effected by means of a hallucinatory experience. In the first
example, he "sees" a boat moored nearby, and among its mysterious, hooded
passengers he recognizes several acquaintances from the war years, some of
them long since dead. In the second case, Ferdinand is caught in a rainstorm
while attempting to fend off interviewers who are intent upon verifying that
he is as loathsome in person as his public image would have him be. His subsequent illness is aggravated by a recurrence of the malaria he had contracted
in Africa. The resultant delirium and hallucinations dredge up materials from
his past. Hence the trilogy opens and closes with a signal to the reader that
what will be—and has already been—related is to be read as a fiction, a

creative delirium, no matter what autobiographical elements from Louis-Ferdinand Céline's notorious past may have served as its point of departure.

The three novels do not adhere in their internal order or that of their publication to the chronology of Ferdinand's journey: *North* should have been the first novel of the trilogy and *Castle to Castle* the second. Critics have remarked that this inversion was a result of Céline's perception that a novel that dealt with the officials of the collaborationist Vichy government, as does *Castle to Castle*, would sell better and thus more quickly reestablish his reputation, which had suffered after his return to France following his long exile in Denmark. The narrator gives a different explanation, stating that his violation of chronology is a sign of artistic freedom as well as a reflection of the disorder of the period he is describing.

Ferdinand, in the company of his wife Lili and the actor Le Vigan, begins the narration of his journey (according to the chronology of the events) after the trio has crossed the German frontier and arrives in Baden-Baden. Untouched as yet by the fighting, this resort city with its luxury hotels and famous casino is an oasis of tranquillity for the rich and powerful. The war finally comes to Baden-Baden, in the form of mass arrests following the unsuccessful officers' plot to kill Adolf Hitler in 1944, and Ferdinand and his companions are forced to leave the resort for war-ravaged Berlin.

Ferdinand discovers that he too has been marked by the ravages of the war. He begins to limp when he arrives in Berlin and notices that he has aged to the point that his face no longer matches the photograph in his identity papers. An acquaintance, Dr. Harras, a medical officer in the SS, invites the trio to share his well-furnished underground bunker. The presence of these French refugees arouses suspicions, however, and Harras is obliged to move them to Kränzlin—called Zornhof (anger estate) in the text—a vast property some one hundred kilometers north of Berlin. In the nearby town of Moorsburg, there is a refuge for diseased prostitutes. One can hear in the distance the muffled sound of bombs falling on Berlin.

In addition to the members of the von Leiden family, which owns the estate, Zornhof houses Polish serving girls, employees of the Health Ministry, French forced laborers, and conscientious objectors. Consonant with its name, Zornhof is a place of hatred, spite, and intrigue, notably on the part of the Baron von Leiden and his wife Isis. The Baron is a misanthropic cripple. His wife (ironically named after the Egyptian goddess of medicine and marriage) is obsessed with killing her husband and attempts to lure Ferdinand into becoming her accomplice. The Baron's father is a senile octogenarian who, one morning, dressed in his World War I uniform, rides off toward the front, only to be seized and severely beaten by a band of deranged prostitutes who have escaped from Moorsburg. Isis procures a hallucinogen which she gives to the Russian prisoner of war who carries the Baron from place to place. Disoriented by the drug, he drowns his master in a manure pond.

Ferdinand and his companions make every effort to avoid becoming involved in the antagonisms that imprison the von Leidens. When Le Vigan confesses to the murder of the Baron, Harras is called upon to restore order. Ferdinand and Lili receive permission to visit, as tourists, the northern coastal town of Wärnemünde, where they hope to find a boat that will take them to Denmark. Obliged to return to Zornhof after their mission proves fruitless, they discover that Ferdinand has been assigned to administer to the health needs of the colony of Vichy government officials that the Germans have transferred to Sigmaringen.

The population of Sigmaringen has been swollen beyond capacity by large numbers of pro-Nazi refugees seeking protection from the advancing Allied armies and the Resistance forces. The highest officials of the Vichy government, including Philippe Pétain and Pierre Laval, live in the luxury of the immense Hohenzollern château that dominates the town. Others, like Ferdinand and his wife, must find shelter in one of the town's inns and fend for themselves. Many of Sigmaringen's inhabitants, particularly those living in the castle, continue to delude themselves with visions of a final German victory that would draw upon hidden armies and secret weapons. Ferdinand sardonically mocks their fantasies and endeavors to deal with the realities of the situation into which he has been placed. Although the inhabitants of the castle lack for nothing, the numerous French refugees that he attempts to treat are not so fortunate, given the scarcity of medical supplies, poor nourishment, and overcrowded and unsanitary living conditions.

The death of a French official provides the opportunity for Ferdinand, as a member of the delegation attending the funeral, to travel to the town of Hohenlychen, twelve hundred kilometers north of Sigmaringen. His real purpose in going there is to obtain permission to practice medicine in Germany, as a means of enhancing his security and facilitating his eventual escape to Denmark. The German officer who is supposed to provide the requisite papers does not appear, and Ferdinand must return to Sigmaringen empty-handed and still very uncertain about his future.

The concluding volume of the trilogy deals with the passage from Sigmaringen to Copenhagen. Having made one more fruitless trip to the German coast to look for a boat that will take them to Denmark, Ferdinand and Lili stop briefly at Sigmaringen—Ferdinand has been relieved of his medical duties—before heading north again. Le Vigan will not accompany them, having decided to travel to Rome. The couple is placed in a locked boxcar along with members of a pro-Vichy commando unit. Their first stop is Oddort (Oddplace), a locale that is nothing more than a railroad station; those refugees unfortunate enough to stop there are executed. Warned in advance of the deception, the commando team kills the commander of the station and his guard. Ferdinand and Lili flee to nearby Hanover, a city in flames from Allied bombing. When they board their next train, they find themselves in a car filled with retarded children. The Frenchwoman supervising the children becomes too ill to care for them and places Ferdinand and Lili in charge of the group. A delay in their departure permits adults and children to wander among the ruins of Hanover, exploring buried sections of the city through fissures left by the bombs. Having resumed their journey north, Ferdinand and Lili are able to convince the officials at the Danish border that they are the children's escorts and are thus allowed to make their way to Copenhagen. The apparently peaceful streets of the Danish capital, however, do not reassure Ferdinand. He compares the city to the decor of a play, a decor that will collapse all around them, he indicates, with catastrophic results.

*The Characters*

Describing himself as a "lucid super-seer," the narrator implies by this term that the artist as visionary can provide a deeper insight into reality through the vehicle of fiction than would be possible in a merely historical account. Although he too has been condemned as a traitor and faces a possible death sentence should he be caught, Ferdinand, as protagonist and narrator of Céline's novels, maintains a degree of lucidity that sets him apart from those around him who entertain fantasies about their return to power and privilege. The vacationers at Baden-Baden and, particularly, the occupants of the château in Sigmaringen exemplify this attitude of self-delusion (to which Céline usually applies the term "delirium") in their persistent belief that somehow Germany will win the war. There is a price to be paid for refusing such facile escapism—the suffering concomitant with confronting the harsh realities of a world turned upside down by the war's devastation and the danger inherent in differing with those in positions of authority. It is ironic that a group of retarded children will provide the cover that will permit the super-seer to succeed in finally reaching Denmark.

Given his powerlessness and ambiguous status, Ferdinand is usually less an active participant in events than an observer of what takes place around him. One conspicuous exception to this attitude is the selflessness of his medical activities in Sigmaringen. Despite his past failures to sustain a viable medical practice, largely because of a deeply pessimistic view of society—a view sustained by humankind's penchant for war and self-destruction—and a disinclination to demand payment for his services, Ferdinand demonstrates a surprising devotion to his patients in Sigmaringen. He even goes so far as to purchase medicines for them out of his own limited funds. Ferdinand also excels, despite his mordant humor and trenchant language, at avoiding confrontations that might compromise his limited security.

Hanover furnishes Ferdinand with a different order of experience. Having known the city before the war as a rather sad, dull place, he perceives that it is becoming a more vital, more cheery city, as it is transformed by the vivid colors and changing rhythms of the flames that are devouring it. Such perceptions remind the reader of the metamorphosis of experience, however horrible or repulsive, that is effected by the mind of the artist and the work of art. Ferdinand's penetration into the subterranean galleries of Hanover reinforces his status as an underground man: an alleged traitor fleeing his country but also a person fascinated by the underside of life, instinctively drawn to the seamier, more revealing, aspects of existence. As Ferdinand penetrates into the underground vaults that conceal large sections of Hanover, he thinks of his medical practice. The doctor as author dissects society—with a pen instead of a scalpel—exposing its diseased organs, but, in his novels at least, offers no cure for its manifold ills.

Le Vigan functions as a double for Ferdinand with respect to the question of lucidity. The actor has specialized in playing the roles of alienated, mystical characters. As the journey progresses, and particularly during his stay at Zornhof, life increasingly imitates art as his mental state deteriorates. Housed in a vermin-infested room, he develops an unrealistic, almost paranoid, fear of being devoured by rats—a reflection, no doubt, of his terror of being captured by the Resistance and summarily executed. He attempts to block out reality by spending hours on his bed in a kind of trance, muttering to himself. His confession to the murder of Baron von Leiden has no basis in fact but arises from mingled feelings of guilt and fright. Putting himself under the protection of the law would give some coherence to his existence and end his flight from French justice. At the same time, by confessing to this other crime, he would exorcize his guilt for having been a collaborator and not have to confront the specificity of his crimes. By the time he decides to accompany Ferdinand and Lili no longer, he is close to insanity. He now has delusions of martyrdom, going so far as to imitate the position and expression of Christ on the Cross, as if he were assuming the world's guilt. His solitary voyage to Rome, the center of Catholicism, can be interpreted as a pilgrimage of sorts, one that will permit him to worship at the altar of his protective delirium.

Lili, Ferdinand's wife, is a professional dancer who has chosen to share her husband's fate. Never developed as a character, she is the embodiment of the gracious, uncomplaining survivor. She may also serve, in her efforts to maintain her dancing skills, as a reminder of the persistence of art, even under the most trying conditions. Ferdinand must survive so that he can transmute his experiences into the work of art that is the trilogy.

## Themes and Meanings

*Rigadoon* begins with a renewal of the narrative impulse that initiated the trilogy. The narrator's illness constitutes another variation on the head wound that appears so frequently in Céline's novels. The myth that Céline himself was trepanned (an opening made in the skull to relieve pressure on the brain) as treatment for a head wound suffered in World War I reinforces

the image of the narration as an outpouring from that wound, as an obligatory creative delirium that exposes the chaos lurking beneath the surface of
everyday reality. During the course of his voyage, Ferdinand is struck twice
on the head—a reminder of the novel's opening signals and an obvious link
between the protagonist and the narrator as suffering, creative selves.

Whereas the narrator's delirium is creative, resulting in a heightened
perception of reality, other forms of delirium serve to mask reality. Céline
uses the term delirium to refer to any obsession or mania which permits one
to escape from the disorder of contingent reality or, indeed, from the madness of the world in general. Insanity is the extreme form of delirium, an ultimate refuge, for the insane individual imprisoned within an aberrant psyche
is shielded from external reality and abdicates all responsibility. In this context, Le Vigan's descent into madness can be positively valorized and serve as
a temptation against which the protagonist must struggle.

It is the theme of the voyage north that links the three volumes of the
trilogy, and that particular direction is emphasized by the title of the second
volume. Copenhagen does indeed lie to the north, but the direction has
connotations in Céline's previous works that transcend geographical referen-
tiality and are relevant to the reading of the trilogy. Céline liked to think of
himself as a Breton, that is to say, a Northerner, physically and mentally superior to the ordinary Frenchman. In his anti-Semitic "pamphlets"—they
are, in fact, book-length volumes—North is opposed to South, to the Mediterranean Basin. As the homeland of the Jews, the latter becomes a source
of contagion infecting Europe. In Céline's first novel, *Voyage au bout de la
nuit* (1932; *Journey to the End of the Night*, 1934), northern climates are
deemed healthier, less likely to encourage the emergence of the conjoined
physical and moral decay to which humankind is heir. In the trilogy, the
France from which Ferdinand is fleeing is, analogously, an unhealthy climate,
a locus of contagion, of a vengeful justice bent on persecuting a writer who,
although he espoused the anti-Semitic rhetoric of the Nazis, claimed that he
was directing his vituperations against only those Jews who were forcing
France into yet another disastrous war with Germany.

Two of the trilogy's most salient images can be found in *Castle to Castle*.
One of these is the immense Hohenzollern castle in which the high officials
of the Vichy government are housed and which, topographically, dominates
the town. With its numerous portraits of previous occupants and the gradual
erosion of its foundations by the waters of the Danube, the castle conveys a
sense of the flux of human history, the impermanence of human structures of
all kinds, not the least of which is the Third Reich. The interior architecture
of the castle is consonant with the mental state of most of its inhabitants. The
castle is divided into a multiplicity of separate apartments, linked to one
another by a labyrinthine structure of corridors and staircases. That Ferdinand and Lili should be the only ones able to find their way through this

maze reflects the artist's ability to penetrate reality and link its otherwise disparate elements. The compartmentalization of the Vichy officials, separated from the outside world and from one another, encourages their delusions about a final German victory. If the castle is the "head" (however vacuous) of Sigmaringen, then its hotels, such as the Löwen, in which Ferdinand and Lili are housed, are its bowels. The continuously clogged and overflowing toilets in Ferdinand's hotel symbolize the disease, malnutrition, and overcrowding that constitute the reality of existence for Sigmaringen's refugees. In a more general sense, this divorce between "head" and "body," between the schemes of those in authority and the suffering that the powerless must endure in implementing those schemes, represents, for Céline, the folly of war: Governments plan wars and use their ordinary citizens as cannon fodder. The second image in question is that of the railway station, with its hordes of soldiers and civilians desperately seeking shelter from the conflict and exchanging food, information, and sexual favors. Ferdinand perceives a certain beauty in this anarchy, of which he and Lili will be a part, in the exoticism of voyagers arriving from or departing to the various countries of Europe. He admires as well the tenacity and vitality they manifest in their struggle for survival, qualities that he and Lili will share as they fitfully make their way to Denmark.

The trilogy constitutes a kind of rigadoon, a dance in which a couple moves one step backward for every step forward. Hence, there is motion without progress. The reader need not be acquainted with Céline's biography to know that Copenhagen will not provide Ferdinand with a haven. The narrator makes it clear that the initial tranquillity of Copenhagen will be quickly shattered and that years of detention in Denmark await him before he can be extradited to France and his case can be judged.

*Critical Context*

The publication of the trilogy—which appeared in three separate volumes over a period of several years—was greeted with largely negative commentary by critics, though it did succeed, as earlier postwar publications had not, in reestablishing the presence of Céline on the French literary scene. Céline's notoriety as a Nazi supporter and anti-Semite certainly played a part in the reception (and sales) of the trilogy. Some critics discerned a decline in the author's creative powers, condemning the work as rambling; they decried its lack of sustained plot development and overall interpretive framework that would convey an analysis of the historical situation in which Ferdinand finds himself as he attempts to seize History by means of Story. The emergence of the New Novel in France during the 1950's and 1960's, with its linguistic experimentation and ostensible rejection of traditional novelistic structures, no doubt obscured the more innovative aspects of Céline's writing, which, in some ways, were not so far removed from the conceptions of such New Novelists as Alain Robbe-Grillet, Nathalie Sarraute, and Claude Simon.

The passage of time has favored Céline, although he and, perforce, his writings remain subjects of controversy. As the events and the pervading attitudes of the World War II era have receded further into the past, there has been less concern with the author's politics and, concomitantly, a more detached perspective on his later works, such as the trilogy. Such a view fails to take into account Céline's attempt in the trilogy to exculpate himself by having Ferdinand proclaim his innocence and play the part of the scapegoat-victim. Can one read of and perhaps sympathize with Ferdinand's plight without recalling the many millions who rode the trains to such destinations as Treblinka and Auschwitz?

The relative discontinuity of the trilogy represents a departure, though not a radical one, from Céline's more traditionally structured earlier works, and can be interpreted as both a reflection of the chaotic period that is being described and an attendant calling into question of the nature of novelistic discourse. The trilogy's interest and originality reside in the conjoining of several elements: a particular vision of the general human condition, placed in sharper relief by the war; a rewriting of history that attempts to justify an individual destiny—Céline-Ferdinand's—by making it the paradigm of a collective tragedy; a deconstruction of the novel; and a language appropriate to these aforementioned concerns. As for that language, the three novels of the trilogy share those underground, subversive stylistic traits that characterize Céline's writing: the rejection of traditional literary discourse in favor of a popular, spoken level of language and the use of ellipses that set into sharper relief the essential elements of the phrase while bombarding the reader with rhythmic pulsations of verbal energy. Although giving the appearance of a crude first draft, an unrefinement that would be consonant with the nature of the events decribed and the outlook of the author, Céline's style is carefully concerted and his manuscripts are diligently edited so as to maintain a brilliantly orchestrated tension between the disorder of life and the order of art.

*Sources for Further Study*
Knapp, Bettina. *Céline: Man of Hate*, 1974.
Lottman, Herbert. *The Left Bank: Writers, Artists, and Politics from the Popular Front to the Cold War*, 1982.
McCarthy, Patrick. *Céline: A Critical Biography*, 1975.
Matthews, J. H. *The Inner Dream: Céline as Novelist*, 1974.
Noble, Ian. *Language and Narration in Céline's Writings*, 1987.

*Philip H. Solomon*

# THE CAT

*Author:* Colette (Sidonie-Gabrielle Colette, 1873-1954)
*Type of plot:* Psychological realism
*Time of plot:* The early 1930's
*Locale:* Neuilly and central Paris
*First published: La Chatte*, 1933 (English translation, 1936)

> *Principal characters:*
> ALAIN AMPARAT, the son of a wealthy manufacturing family
> CAMILLE MALMERT, the woman who marries him
> SAHA, his Russian Blue cat

*The Novel*

*The Cat* is a short novel about the rapid decline of a marriage. Both the young people involved, Alain Amparat and Camille Malmert, come from prosperous manufacturing families. The novel opens a week before the wedding at Alain's spacious but run-down old house at Neuilly, where he lives with his widowed mother and some ancient servants. Part of the house is being converted and modernized for the young couple. Until it is ready, however, they plan to live in a small studio at the top of a new nine-story apartment block. The apartment, lent to them by a friend, conforms to Camille's taste for everything up-to-date, but it offends Alain's fastidious and conservative nature.

It soon becomes evident that although Alain and Camille are physically attracted to each other, their engagement has more to do with family expectations than with a meeting of minds. Alain watches Camille nervously and is privately critical of her uninhibited manners and loud voice. He finds solace in the company of his beloved cat, Saha, a magnificent Russian Blue.

On the morning after the wedding, Alain, waking up in the ultramodern studio bedroom, is embarrassed to see Camille flitting about in the nude. He is nonplussed when she counters that he, too, is nude above the waist. This small incident is an early portent of the gap which is to widen between them. Later that day, Alain returns to Neuilly under the pretext of checking the building's progress. Camille teasingly accuses him of going to visit her rival, the cat. Taking her seriously, Alain protests that Saha cannot be her rival because there is nothing "impure" about his relationship with it.

During the hot summer months, they make love frequently, always at Camille's initiative. Alain becomes revolted by her open sensuality and longs for the sheltered security of his childhood home and for his cat, which is pining for him at Neuilly. Camille is annoyed when he brings the cat to live at the cramped top-floor apartment. Alain, however, lavishes all of his attention on the cat.

One day, Alain overhears Camille grumbling about that "filthy swine of an animal," which sparks a quarrel. At a restaurant that evening, Alain notices that Camille has put on weight and wonders with alarm if she is pregnant. Camille tells him that the owner of the studio will soon be coming back. She dreams aloud about the family they will rear when they return to Neuilly and she proposes redecorating his old room for the child.

Alain is aghast. His revulsion for her becomes crystallized into a single determination: On no account must she be allowed to share his childhood home. He tries to persuade his mother of this, but she prefers not to listen. Camille is deeply hurt when Alain takes to leaving their bed in the small hours and stretching out on a bench in a corridor, the cat lying on his chest. She makes it a point of honor not to complain, but instead tries to woo him back with her body—which only makes the situation worse.

Matters come to a head when Camille, waiting for Alain, plays a silent and menacing game with the cat. She forces it to jump from one part of the parapet to another. Suddenly, on impulse, she pushes it off the parapet. Camille expects Alain to accepts its death as an accident. The cat, however, is not dead. Its fall was broken; it is shocked but unhurt. Alain brings it upstairs in his arms, ministers to it lovingly, and asks Camille to feel its head for bumps. As soon as she stretches out her hand to it, it lets out a savage snarl and leaps away from her. Alain draws his own conclusions.

In the ensuing quarrel, Camille accuses him of loving the cat instead of her. He again insists that Saha is not her rival, but she continues the accusation: "I have seen you lying cheek to cheek. . . ." Alain forces her to admit that she tried to kill Saha. Then he installs the cat in a basket and tells Camille that he is—"we are"—leaving. Camille conceals her despair and, with a few sarcastic parting words, lets him go.

The following day, Camille arrives at the house in Neuilly with a suitcase of Alain's clothes. She finds him in the garden, disheveled, in torn pyjamas and in a state of near delirium. She tries obliquely to draw from him a hope for the future, but he is relentless. He calls her a monster for trying to kill a beautiful and defenseless animal. She replies that he is a monster to leave a woman for the sake of an animal. He does not deny it. Camille walks away and Alain is left—as he had contrived to be left—in the garden of his childhood, with his mother, his servants, and the cat.

### The Characters

To emphasize the incompatability of husband and wife, Colette created them in sharp contrast to each other. Both are outstandingly attractive: Alain is blond, delicate, and introspective while Camille is dark, easygoing, and uninhibited. Alain comes from a highly respected manufacturing family. Fatherless since childhood, he has been spoiled and mollycoddled by his mother and by the servants, who refer to him as "the young Master."

Camille is every inch a "modern girl" in the 1930's mode. She drives fast cars, dresses immaculately, smokes to excess, and uses coarse language. Alain is wholly conservative, locked in the habits and emotions of his childhood.

The biggest contrast between them concerns their attitudes to lovemaking. Marriage gives Camille the freedom of legitimized sex (denied to single women of the period), and she wants to take full advantage of it. Alain, who has had casual affairs in the past, is repulsed and perhaps frightened by Camille's open sensuality; he retreats from it into his relationship with the cat. The distance between the couple remains under the surface most of the time, emerging in the form of an occasional repartee.

Although Alain has the weaker personality, his self-absorption makes him more manipulative. He uses Camille's crude attempt to get rid of the cat as an opportunity, rather than as a reason, for leaving her. Camille has no inkling of the way she is being manipulated. She takes things at face value. Bold and outgoing, she is too proud to show any outward signs of disappointment. "I sometimes wish . . . ," she begins to say, but she cannot finish the sentence. Her only strategy for regaining Alain's affection is to tempt him physically, which she cannot resist trying even at their final parting: "She was going away, carefully avoiding holding out her hand to him. But under the arcade of clipped trees, she dared vainly to brush against him with her ripening breasts."

Colette's description of Saha's feline movements and behavior is so vivid that it gives the animal the force of a third character in an eternal triangle. Throughout the book the cat is referred to as "she," and there are incidents in which it does, indeed, appear to have its own free will. The cat is not only a "character" but also a symbol—to Camille, a symbol of an unfaithful husband and to Alain, of the privacy and serenity of a childhood which he hated leaving and to which he finally retreats.

The other characters are sketched impressionistically, with a few swift strokes. Madame Amparat emerges as an intelligent but preoccupied woman who would like to be relieved of the responsibility of an emotionally retarded son. The aging servants are obsequious to Alain and insolent to Camille. Émile, the butler, walks a fine line with double-talk which enables him to tear down Camille's character while apparently praising it.

## Themes and Meanings

*The Cat* is written with great stylistic economy; every sentence is redolent with meaning. Because, like most of Colette's works, it is a novel of the senses—with exquisite evocation of sound, taste, color, fragrance, and texture—it does not sustain a cohesive interior argument but is open to varied interpretations. Its central drive is an exploration of incompatability in marriage.

Although the gap between Alain's and Colette's expectations arises from the characters' very specific disparate attributes, there are some implied generalizations. As in *Le Blé en herbe* (1923; *The Ripening Corn*, 1931; also as *The Ripening Seed*, 1955), the author notes the sexual maturity of women compared to that of men of the same age. Colette also points to the difference between the social demands placed on men, who are expected to have sexual experience before marriage, and those placed on women, who are supposed to remain "pure."

On one of the rare occasions when the author uses her own voice, she hints at a more deep-seated and intractable gender difference. "Camille," she writes, "could not understand that a man's sensuality is brief and seasonal and that its unpredictable return is never a new beginning."

The conflict between modern and traditional attitudes to marriage is part of a social process which is observed throughout the novel. The stolid conventions of the old-style middle class are being replaced by the brasher life-styles of the newly rich. The big old Parisian estates are being split up into smaller units; tall buildings are mushrooming where villas once stood. The contrast between the rambling old house at Neuilly and the glass and chromium construction of the cramped studio is a key symbol of change. Nostalgia for an idyllic past that can never be recaptured is a recurring theme for Colette.

Alain's thoughts and feelings are given more prominence than Camille's, but the author distances herself from both with a degree of analytical coldness, reserving her warmth and enthusiasm for Saha the cat. Her description of Saha's movements and behavior is magnificent, a prime example of her ongoing exploration of the relationship between animals and human beings, which she once expressed in the proposition: "Our perfect companions never have fewer than four feet."

*Critical Context*

Colette's main characters are usually female, with the men in subordinate roles. Three remarkable exceptions are the eponymous hero of *Chéri* (1920; English translation, 1929) and *La Fin de Chéri* (1926; *The Last of Chéri*, 1932), Phil in *The Ripening Seed*, and Alain in *The Cat*. Although these male characters have very different personalities, they are all pampered, highly sensitive, and emotionally immature young men, exemplifying Colette's consistent rejection of gender stereotypes.

Colette's personal experiences and preoccupations are readily traceable in *The Cat*: her devotion to animals, her yearning for the trees and flowers of her childhood, her experience with the destructive force of jealousy, and her two broken marriages.

The novel was given a mixed reception when it was first published. "A fine talent demeaned by a ludicrous theme," wrote a reviewer in *La Gazette de*

*Paris.* Even in 1953, a review in *The Times Literary Supplement* of a then-new translation called it "a brilliant piece of writing, but a vile story." Edmond Jaloux, the distinguished Paris critic, however, recognized its qualities at once and called it "a masterpiece of art of classic perfection, told with the maximum of truth, of intelligence, and of poetry," an evaluation which has since become widely accepted.

*Sources for Further Study*
Cottrell, Robert D. *Colette*, 1974.
Crosland, Margaret. *Colette: The Difficulty of Loving*, 1973.
Goudeket, Maurice. *Close to Colette*, 1957.
Marks, Elaine. *Colette*, 1960.
Mitchell, Yvonne. *Colette: A Taste for Life*, 1975.
Richardson, Joanna. *Colette*, 1983.

*Nina Hibbin*

# THE CHAIN OF CHANCE

*Author:* Stanisław Lem (1921-     )
*Type of plot:* Science fiction
*Time of plot:* The late 1970's
*Locale:* Naples, Rome, and Paris
*First published: Katar*, 1976 (English translation, 1978)

> *Principal characters:*
> JOHN, the narrator, a former astronaut
> ANNABELLA, a girl whom John saves from death from a
>     terrorist's bomb
> DR. PHILIPPE BARTH, a computer scientist

*The Novel*

John, the narrator, a former astronaut, has been hired to investigate the death of a fellow American named Adams, who has died of unknown causes in Naples. This is only the most recent in a series of twelve strange deaths in which the victim first exhibited evidence of great excitement and aggressive behavior, followed by hallucinations and delusions of persecution, and, finally, total withdrawal, leading to death, in most cases by suicide. Though the twelve were unknown to one another, John believes that the pattern cannot be mere coincidence. Were they the victims of a great, mysterious conspiracy?

In an attempt to discover precisely what caused the death of Adams, John, monitored by two colleagues who follow at a distance, duplicates exactly the movements of Adams in Naples and Rome, hoping to tempt the presumed killer to attack him. He stays at the same hotel, drives the same highway from Naples to Rome, stops at the same service station, and registers at the same hotel in Rome. Although he is suspicious of some of the things that happen to him—a young woman in the service station, for example, approaches him and then faints—he learns nothing that can explain what happened to Adams.

He decides, therefore, to go to Paris to consult with Dr. Philippe Barth, a distinguished computer scientist who has been programming a computer to solve problems in which the amount of data exceeds the storage capacity of human memory. At the Rome airport, however, John is delayed when he saves a young girl from a terrorist's bomb which kills several people. At first he is arrested as the terrorist's accomplice; then, as a hero, he must endure a news conference, though he wishes to be anonymous. Eventually, he is able to deliver the girl, Annabella, to her father in Paris.

In Paris, he meets Barth, to whom he describes the twelve deaths and the problem inherent in the fact that they seem simultaneously related and unrelated. Barth is convinced that whoever is responsible for the deaths in Naples wants to create the impression that he does not exist; Barth believes that the only way to discover the motive and the perpetrator's method is to examine all the elements of the pattern. All the victims, for example, were bald, or balding, and all of them suffered from allergies, for which they were taking an antihistamine which contained the stimulant Ritalin.

When John leaves Barth's institute, his car is sideswiped, and he realizes that if he had been killed his death would have fit the Naples pattern. Later, at a party given by Barth, he meets a police inspector who tells him about the case of an optician who attempted to throw himself into the Seine and later died of heart failure. It was discovered that the optician had repaired the eyeglasses of a chemist who was doing research for the French government into depressants for chemical warfare. The glasses were contaminated by the drug. This story leads Barth and John to consider the possibility that the Naples victims were objects of an experiment by some secret agency that was testing some drug as part of a plot, perhaps to assassinate public officials in Italy.

To test this hypothesis, John prepares to return to Italy. Without realizing it, however, he commits a series of acts which finally explain the mystery. That night he eats some almonds, then sleeps in a bed in which Barth's superstitious mother, who has no confidence in his antihistamine, has sprinkled "flowers of sulfur" to cure his hay fever. The next day, at the airport, he gets a haircut, and the barber rubs a green jelly into his scalp. Unable to buy a plane ticket for Rome, he manages to get a room in the airport hotel without a reservation because he shows the clerk his picture in a newspaper article about his heroism in the Rome airport. That night he experiences a psychedelic nightmare and is prevented from leaping from a window to his death because he has managed during his "frenzy" to handcuff himself to a steam radiator.

John's bizarre experience leads to an explanation of the mystery of the Naples deaths—all of them the result of a coincidental combination of chemicals. One is present in the green jelly used in the treatment of baldness, and when it is combined with the Ritalin in the antihistamine it produces a mild form of the depressant which affected the French optician. When it is combined with cyanide and sulfur its toxicity is increased a million times. Almonds contain tiny traces of cyanide, and all the Naples victims ate almonds which had been contaminated with a disinfectant containing sulfur. John, therefore, experiences the suicidal hallucinations of the Naples victims because of the combined effect of the sulfur in his bed, the almonds, the barber's treatment of his scalp, and the Ritalin in his antihistamine.

*The Characters*

John—it is the only name given to the narrator—is the sole character in the novel who is developed at any length. John is a man of action, a World War II veteran who entered the astronaut program but was reduced to back-up status and finally dismissed from the Mars mission because of his allergies to grass and dust. Now, middle-aged, his only appropriate employment is as a private detective working for the executor of the Adams will.

His narration of the story is rather laconic and offhand, in the manner of the private detectives of the traditional American hard-boiled novel which, ironically, is Stanisław Lem's model. As a soldier, astronaut, and detective, John has learned to wait patiently for those moments when quick, decisive, unreflective action is required; in a sense, he is himself a kind of machine. (At one point he says that the only time he was excited during his simulation of Adams' experience in Naples and Rome was when he was frightened.) Furthermore, he does not undergo any transformation as a character. At the end of the story, he is the same person he was at the beginning, except that he now knows the answer to the puzzle.

Yet Lem's decision to employ such a character is appropriate, because he is dealing with a scientific puzzle which requires for its solution the kind of objectivity one expects from a technician, even in his account of the temporary psychedelic derangement which is the result of a remarkable chemical coincidence.

Barth, his colleagues, Annabella, and the optician are not characterized sufficiently to enable the reader to see them as fully rounded characters. That, however, must not be considered a flaw in the novel, because Lem's interest is less in the development of characters than in the explication of a scientific puzzle for the sake of its philosophical implications.

*Themes and Meanings*

The themes of *The Chain of Chance* have preoccupied Lem throughout his career. In 1968, he published a long treatise, "Filozofia przypadku" (the philosophy of chance), and in the autobiographical essay "Reflections on My Life"—in *Microworlds* (1984)—he indicated that this preoccupation origi-nated in the frightening coincidences and near-misses in his early life during the German occupation of Poland. In that essay, Lem poses a crucial ques-tion that echoes the title of the English translation of this novel (although not the original Polish title, which simply means "catarrh"): "Can all the factors that were responsible for my coming into the world and enabled me, al-though threatened by death many times, to survive unscathed... be re-garded only as the result of long chains of chance?" In his answer, Lem says that, while he does not believe in "predetermination," he suspects that the universe may often reveal "a preestablished disharmony, ending in chaos and madness."

This reference goes far to explain Lem's intentions in *The Chain of Chance*. Events in the universe that he describes are not predetermined (indeed, they would be more explicable and thus less frightening if they were). What Lem reveals in his novel is the way the universe, at least on occasion, reveals a tendency to produce a "disharmony" which is so extreme that it leads inevitably to "chaos and madness." The twelve victims in the novel are all driven into such chaos and madness by a "chain of chance" that the reader finds most appalling because it is clear that it actually could happen. The victims, who have nothing in common but their experience with hair restorative, antihistamines, and almonds, literally go mad in a chaos apparently inherent in the universe, in which, Lem believes, the only order, finally, is in coincidental structures of this kind.

Furthermore, it would appear that in Lem's view one must assume that such rips in the texture of the order of the universe are bound to increase, either as an inevitable consequence of entropy or as an accompaniment to the growth of the world's population. Saussure, a mathematician at Barth's institute, tells John that in physics everything is possible, because "the greater the set, the greater the chance of improbable events occurring within it." What causes the expansion of the "set" in human terms is population growth: "Mankind has multiplied to such an extent that it's now starting to be governed by atomic laws."

Saussure's example is of marksmen on a firing range shooting at a flyspeck on a postage stamp half a mile away. If a hundred marksmen continue to shoot week after week, a bullet will sooner or later hit the flyspeck. In a world in which population increases and science and technology produce an increasing number of increasingly complex substances, a series of events such as those that drove the Naples victims to madness and death is inevitable.

Ironically the mathematician who gives this lecture on probability is named Saussure, which is the name of the Swiss linguist Ferdinand de Saussure, whose early redefinition of the relation between language as words and language as structure is generally considered to be the first event in the development of structuralism. If structuralism asserts the importance of the role that the human mind plays in imposing order on reality, Lem's Saussure seems to be saying that the only order is that of the apparent disorder of the universe. Nothing is predetermined but chance, and sooner or later a bullet will hit the flyspeck and a dozen men will go mad and die in Naples.

This is a bleak view, and the narrator's references to terrorism and other elements in the social and political chaos of the modern world suggest that Lem intended his novel to serve as a commentary not only on the "chain of chance" that explains the universe as a whole but also on the increasing chaos that characterizes modern political, social, and economic life, a chaos for which the metaphor in the laws—and lawlessness—of physics is as good as any.

*Critical Context*

Lem apparently became disheartened with the writing of fiction in the 1960's, in part because of his disgust with the genre of science fiction itself. Particularly with *Solaris* (1961; English translation, 1970), he had established himself as a master in this field, even though he felt an increasing repugnance for it. With *The Chain of Chance*, however, he developed what, in a sense, is science fiction of a different kind—a fiction, that is, which deals with problems produced by scientific discovery in the contemporary world and which depends for its intellectual content on those problems and on their solution. *The Chain of Chance* begins as an apparently straightforward private-eye detective story, soon seems to become a story of international intrigue, and finally is found to be an account of the solution of a scientific mystery—all of this on behalf of Lem's explication of a profound statement about the nature of reality and the social state of the modern world. Because it is this kind of novel, it may disappoint readers who wish to place it within the narrow confines of the genres of detective, espionage, or science fiction. Those who read to challenge their intelligence, however, will be rewarded by Lem's brilliant handling of scientific data and ideas, and the development of their philosophical implications.

*Sources for Further Study*

Lem, Stanisław. *Microworlds: Writings on Science Fiction and Fantasy*, 1984.

Solataroff, Theodore. "A Master of Science Fiction—and More," in *The New York Times Book Review*. LXXXI (August 29, 1976), pp. 1, 14.

Steiner, T. R. "Stanisław Lem's Detective Stories: A Genre Extended," in *Modern Fiction Studies*. XXIX (Autumn, 1983), pp. 451-462.

Updike, John. "Lem and Pym," in *The New Yorker*. LV (February 26, 1979), pp. 115-121.

Ziegfeld, Richard E. *Stanisław Lem*, 1985.

*Robert L. Berner*

# A CHANGE OF HEART

*Author:* Michel Butor (1926-    )
*Type of plot:* Phenomenological and psychological realism
*Time of plot:* 1955 or 1956
*Locale:* The third-class compartment of a train traveling between Paris and
    Rome
*First published: La Modification*, 1957 (English translation, 1959)

>        *Principal characters:*
>            LÉON DELMONT, a middle-aged Parisian businessman
>            HENRIETTE DELMONT, his wife and the mother of their four
>            children
>            CÉCILE DARCELLA, his mistress, now working at an embassy
>            in Rome

*The Novel*

In *A Change of Heart*, Michel Butor describes the observations, recollections, thoughts, and fears of Léon Delmont during a twenty-two-hour train ride between Paris and Rome. For several years, Léon has traveled regularly in the first-class section in order to attend meetings at the Rome headquarters of Scabelli, the Italian typewriter company whose Paris office he directs. For the last two years, Léon and Cécile Darcella have been having an affair during his frequent trips to Rome. Léon has finally decided to separate from his wife, Henriette, and to live in Paris with Cécile, for whom he has found a position with a Parisian travel agency. Léon is paying his own fare for this trip to Rome and he plans to inform Cécile of his decisions.

During this lengthy and exhausting trip, Léon cannot fall asleep. He passes the time by imagining possible biographies for the other travelers in his compartment. His thoughts about his fellow passengers lead him to reflect on all of his previous trips between Paris and Rome, whether he was alone or accompanied by Henriette or Cécile. Perhaps unintentionally, Léon begins to consider the profound meaning of his relationships with these two women. Specific scenes observed through his train window remind him of significant but apparently now-forgotten conversations and experiences. *A Change of Heart* illustrates very effectively the influence of involuntary memory on the human thought processes. Léon comes to realize that his past has formed his present attitudes and feelings in ways that he had never even suspected. By the end of *A Change of Heart*, Léon has convinced himself that in the years to come he will be much happier with Henriette than he would be with Cécile. Shortly before his train reaches Rome, he reverses his earlier decision. Léon will not see Cécile during this visit to Rome; instead, he plans to end his affair and return to his wife and children in Paris.

*The Characters*

Readers of *A Change of Heart* receive the impression that the unidentified narrator has described the thoughts and opinions of the principal characters in a highly subjective manner, and they come to distrust the narrator. In addition, the basic narrative technique in this novel permits and even encourages widely different reactions to the three principal characters. *A Change of Heart* is a second-person narrative, but readers never know who is addressing whom. The narrator may be an omniscient novelist talking to Léon, Léon's conscience or subsconscious addressing him, or perhaps even Léon himself, who is writing the description of his trip for the reader.

Butor maintains an extraordinary degree of ambiguity throughout *A Change of Heart*. The opinions of Henriette and Cécile are always presented from the subjective viewpoint of either the narrator or Léon, and readers eventually conclude that neither woman is as self-centered as portrayed. The criticism directed against Henriette and Cécile tells readers nothing about the true feelings of these women but does reveal much about the frustration and sense of inadequacy felt by Léon.

Although Léon enjoys good health and a comfortable life-style, he is very unhappy. Neither his wife nor his mistress can determine how to satisfy his unpredictable emotional needs. Ironically, when Henriette and Cécile finally meet, they quickly become good friends and clearly prefer each other's company to that of Léon. Henriette is a considerate and patient wife who does not understand Léon's obvious indifference to their family life. Cécile tries to please Léon both sexually and emotionally. She, however, is confused and hurt by his insensitivity to her feelings. Cécile has rejected Catholicism, and for this reason she does not wish to visit the museum at the Vatican. Nevertheless, she does not object if Léon goes on his own. The result of this arrangement is that Léon complains repeatedly and irrationally that he cannot appreciate the art in the Vatican unless Cécile is at his side. Because of his selfishness, readers feel little sympathy for his emotional problems, which he has created for himself. Léon is also bored with his well-paying position as an office manager. He never wonders, however, whether Henriette and Cécile are satisfied with their jobs. Since Léon is so egotistical, readers do not truly care about the possible causes for his profound unhappiness. At the end of *A Change of Heart*, Léon affirms that he can love Cécile only in Rome. Were they to live together in Paris, their affair would soon end. Léon may well be sincere, but he is clearly superficial and self-centered. In Léon Delmont, Butor has created a marvelously ambiguous and unsympathetic character.

*Themes and Meanings*

*A Change of Heart* illustrates powerfully the close link between Léon's desperate search for meaning and his repeated efforts to interpret the world as he perceives it. During the first few hours of his ride to Rome, Léon imagines plausible histories for the others in his compartment. He convinces himself that two fellow travelers, a priest and a man whom he decides is a law professor, have found personal satisfaction in communicating abstract concepts of truth and justice to their listeners.

Léon, on the other hand, regrets that no ethical or spiritual code guides his existence. He feels alienated from society, and he has almost no self-confidence. When he sees an aged and bearded gentleman enter his third-class compartment, Léon associates this passenger with the Old Testament prophet Ezekiel, who, in Léon's opinion, has come to judge or condemn him for his sinful life. His extremely low self-esteem adversely affects both his perception of reality and his relationships with his family and mistress.

Surprisingly, this novel ends in a moderately optimistic manner. Léon finally accepts responsibility for his own actions when he decides to change his mind about separating from Henriette to live with Cécile. He comes to realize and accept the fact that people must find their own meaning in reality as they perceive it.

## Critical Context

Like such important contemporary French novelists as Claude Simon, Nathalie Sarraute, and Marguerite Yourcenar, Butor has explored the complex links between narrative techniques and the artistic representation of people's efforts to discover meaning for the different realities perceived at various times. Unlike most novels, *A Change of Heart* is written neither from an overtly subjective first-person perspective nor from the objective point of view of an omniscient narrator. The reader's reactions to this experimental second-person narrative are exceedingly complex. Although forced to view reality as Léon describes it, the reader frequently disagrees with his interpretation of past and present events, realizing that Léon's vanity causes him to interpret unjustly the innocent actions and comments of Henriette and Cécile. Although not able to identify with Léon's sentimental problems, the artistry of Butor enables the reader to experience the thought process which leads Léon to "modify" his original decision to separate from Henriette.

Butor wrote *A Change of Heart* near the beginning of his lengthy literary career, yet this early novel effectively illustrates a theme common to many of his writings. In his works of fiction and in his numerous essays on literary and philosophical topics, Butor has continued to explore techniques for communicating the meaning of perceived reality both to oneself and to others.

## Sources for Further Study

Albérès, R. *Michel Butor*, 1964.

McWilliams, Dean. *The Narratives of Michel Butor: The Writer as Janus*, 1978.

Mercier, Vivian. *The New Novel from Queneau to Pinget*, 1971.
Roudiez, Leon S. *Michel Butor*, 1965.
Spencer, Michael. *Michel Butor*, 1974.
Sturrock, John. *The French New Novel: Claude Simon, Michel Butor, Alain Robbe-Grillet*, 1969.

*Edmund J. Campion*

# CHÉRI and THE LAST OF CHÉRI

*Author:* Colette (Sidonie-Gabrielle Colette, 1873-1954)
*Type of plot:* Psychological romance
*Time of plot:* From 1913 to 1919
*Locale:* Paris and the French countryside
*First published: Chéri,* 1920 (English translation, 1929); *La Fin de Chéri,* 1926
   (English translation, 1932)

> *Principal characters:*
> CHÉRI (FRÉDÉRIC PELOUX), an immature but beautiful young
>    man
> LÉA DE LONVAL, who has been Chéri's mistress for six years
> CHARLOTTE PELOUX, Chéri's mother and, like Léa, a former
>    courtesan
> EDMÉE, the lovely daughter of another courtesan, who
>    becomes Chéri's wife at the age of eighteen
> DESMOND, Chéri's friend, a nightclub proprietor
> THE PAL, a friend of Charlotte Peloux in whom Chéri
>    confides

## The Novels

Even though *Chéri* and *The Last of Chéri* were published six years apart, they form one continuous love story. The two books relate the love affair between Léa, an aging courtesan, and extremely handsome but also extremely dependent Chéri; the two lovers' ages differ by twenty-four years. Together, the novels form a structurally perfect duet.

The liaison began in 1906, as Colette recounts in a flashback: Léa was forty-three to Chéri's nineteen when they found themselves alone, exchanged kisses out of boredom and curiosity, found their desires aroused, and became lovers. In the first novel's opening scene, set six years later, Léa is the gracefully protective mistress, Chéri the moody, petulant, narcissistic taker of her tenderness. Chéri will soon be married to Edmée, a beautiful, wealthy young woman; the young couple will then leave Paris for a six-month honeymoon journey.

Paying a social call on Madame Peloux during Chéri's absence, Léa is repulsed by the presence of an overdressed, wrinkled, ridiculous seventy-year-old woman with her seventeen-year-old Italian lover—a startling omen of what she and Chéri might become. Léa determines to heed the cautionary experience and to exit with dignity from Chéri's life before her beauty vanishes entirely. She leaves Paris for the winter.

Chéri returns from his honeymoon, tense and irritable; the marriage is going poorly. Léa is not yet back in Paris. He leaves Edmée, moves into a hotel with his friend Desmond, frequents an opium den, and awaits Léa's reappearance. When she comes back in late spring, he bursts into her bedroom and admits his love for her. Against her reasoned judgment, Léa yields to his beauty and need on that first evening.

With morning, however, the Dionysian ecstasy is replaced by Apollonian clarity. Chéri, pretending to sleep, stares at his middle-aged mother-mistress: "Not yet powdered, a meagre twist of hair at the back of her head, double chin, and raddled neck, she was exposing herself rashly to the unseen observer." Heroically, Léa takes the initiative in ending the relationship. She renounces her claim on Chéri, aware that he has discovered her to be an old, no-longer-desirable woman. She sends him back to his wife: "Quick, quick, child, run off after your youth!" She then sees him walking away from her apartment "like a man escaping from prison."

So ends the first novel. *The Last of Chéri* continues the action, in the summer and fall of 1919, against the background of a changing postwar Paris, where young people frantically dance, drink, fornicate, and speculate. Chéri, now thirty-two years old, is unable to cope with what he regards as the artificial, frenetic busyness of his wife and mother as administrators in a military hospital. He has survived a battle explosion in which a comrade's dead body saved him, but he was left "indignant and resentful," unable to take hold of life, apathetic, empty, idle. During a bitter talk with his mother, he tells her that people are "rotten" and that he is "nearly at the end of [his] tether." Madame Peloux thereupon phones Léa in Chéri's presence, clearly inviting her son to resume his former relationship.

Chéri returns to Léa, in the book's most significant scene. She is now fifty-six, and he finds her a corpulent, sexless, grey-haired woman, her mouth gold-filled, "with sagging cheeks and a double chin." Léa has put eroticism behind her, no longer bothers even to make up her face, and is enjoying a healthy, carefree late middle age, "jovial as an old gentleman." Desperately, Chéri seeks to rediscover the romance of her rose-colored bedroom, but Léa instead advises him to take better care of his kidneys and get his urine tested. She is impatient with his melancholy: "A certain kind of sickness of the soul, my child, of disillusion, is just a question of stomach." Chéri clings to his memory of Léa as his mother-mistress, refusing to accept the inevitability of natural changes. "This old woman is hiding her from me," he laments to himself.

The listless, disgusted Chéri now enters the antechamber of his disintegration and death, moving closer and closer to suicide. He runs into "the Pal," an old, opium-smoking friend of both Léa and his mother, with whom he can reminisce about the glorious years of his romance with Léa. Through her numerous anecdotes, the Pal feeds Chéri's hunger for his less demanding past. He gazes at the photos of Léa in her younger years that line the Pal's apartment walls. He suggests to Edmée that they have a child; she scornfully rejects Chéri's offer—having one child (her immature husband) is more than enough for her. Chéri thereupon spends most of his evenings in the Pal's apartment, cultivating his nostalgia for Léa. One day he picks up the Pal's revolver and fatally shoots himself in the temple.

## The Characters

Chéri begins and remains a pampered, inarticulate, spoiled, childish young man, self-absorbed, unstable, beautiful, wealthy, indolent, and lacking both intellectual depth and moral purpose. Léa is at once a degraded and exalted mother for him, a full-blooded woman with whom he can fuse the tender and sensual drives of his sexuality. Colette portrays Chéri as unloved and neglected by Madame Peloux, who has had him reared by indifferent servants and grim boarding schools. It is no wonder that he insults her, demands substantial amounts of money from his estate, and refuses to work.

Chéri never makes an adult, masculine adjustment to life, never finds a satisfactory career or other outlet for his energies. His tie to Léa is essentially incestuous: She loves him and is more charming, perceptive, stylish, attractive, and stable than is his true mother. Léa weaves around him a magic world of matriarchal understanding and indulgence, in the process encouraging him to remain the selfish, impatient Narcissus to her motherly, patient Demeter. He is her unruly, willful infant; she is his nurturing guide and unconditionally accepting lover. Their affair, while sexually grounded, primarily addresses complementary psychological needs.

Léa is one of Colette's strongest, most memorable female characters in a fictive world in which strong women invariably dominate weak men. She is ultrafeminine, yet sensible; worldly, yet vulnerable to sexual magnetism; humorous; solid; sadly renunciatory, yet ultimately adaptable to inevitable losses. She knows that Chéri's departure also means the departure of her alluring eroticism, but she accepts that fate with stoic wisdom, efficiency, and honorable grandeur. Colette invites the reader to consider Léa as archetypal Woman.

## Themes and Meanings

The opening pages of *Chéri* use sensory imagery with superb skill to illustrate the major theme of the novel: the reluctant but necessary dissolution of the liaison between a young man who will never grow up and a practical woman who learns how to grow old. In Léa's bedroom, the rose-colored curtains filter a pink light, the room has a rosy glow, the lampshades are pink and white, and even the servant is named Rose. Against this pastel background capers the goatish Chéri, described in the black-and-white colors of his demoniac and damned soul. He loves to play with Léa's necklace of forty-nine pearls, which he desires for his wedding trousseau. He taunts his mistress, "I dare you to say they don't look well on me!"

Léa no longer wears the pearls to bed at night, because she fears that Chéri, playing with them in the morning, will notice her aging, wrinkling neck. His conversation is filled with egotistic remarks, both petulant and insolent. Léa smiles at him with loving toleration: To her he is "rebellious only to become submissive, enchained lightly but powerless to free himself." The necklace will reappear throughout both novels as an emblem of their intimacy—every pearl necklace that Chéri sees will remind him of Léa and their love.

Léa and Chéri live their lives primarily through physical needs and comforts, stressing well-ordered food, wine, linens, jewelry, furnishings, and clothes. When decay eats into Chéri's fiber in *The Last of Chéri*, his taste and appetite also take an abrupt downward turn. He adopts the diet of a near-invalid, desultorily picking at his food. Léa's animalistic appetite, on the other hand, has become gourmandism in the second novel. She now relaxes in her old age, unconcerned over her appearance, gluttonous, and virtually hermaphroditic. In the concluding chapters, the Pal serves Chéri with only coffee, syrups, and ices—he cannot bear full meals. His reaction to aromas also becomes negative; Chéri enters a shadowy, comatose state in which he cannot distinguish among scents. He also has greater difficulty in breathing, with an increasingly oppressive atmosphere forming the harmonious complement to his *taedium vitae*. Colette specializes in rendering undercurrents of emotion through palpable imagery involving her characters' senses.

Colette also creates potently erotic scenes without explicit descriptions of intercourse, relying instead on oblique observations, sensuous suggestions, and an intricate network of the vital details and habits surrounding a relationship—all handed with impressive tact. Perhaps her happiest stroke is to start the Chéri-Léa involvement at a point close to its denouement, when the emphasis shifts from the affair's physical attraction to the actors' emotional torment, their psychological wounds. The reader is therefore ready to sympathize and empathize with them rather than to castigate them for offending against the natural process that separates generations.

*Critical Context*

The most important influence on both Colette's life and her writing was her mother, Sidonie, known as Sido. Sido had enormous energy, dignity, warmth, instinctual wisdom, and charm. What most fascinated her daughter was Sido's serene, pagan sensibility: She accepted whatever came her and her family's way of joy and sorrow as natural rather than supernatural, inevitable rather than miraculous. For her, as it later was for Colette, nothing in nature was evil, and all experiences merited attention, curiosity, and, if possible, love. Sido's sensitivity to the world's colors, odors, sights, sounds, and touches was passed on to her daughter. Both Léa's character and Chéri's urgent devotion to an ideal mother constitute tributes to Sido.

Unlike most French writers, Colette had few literary connections or philosophic-aesthetic interests. She did admire Marcel Proust's work and like him remained devoted to memories of childhood and youth. Nevertheless, she differed from André Gide and André Malraux, Albert Camus and Jean-Paul Sartre, in feeling no estrangement from the universe, no sense of anxiety or dread, forlornness or despair. Like these men, she accepted the world as godless but did not thereby feel forsaken or discarded. Rather, she delighted in natural objects and regarded life as the opportunity to explore and enjoy, endure and survive. Metaphysical angst was foreign to Colette's vocabulary.

*Chéri* and *The Last of Chéri* have evident flaws: Chéri's marriage is given scant attention, and Edmée is a cardboard figure. Chéri's shallow mother and her friends are grotesquely out of scale with Léa's sophisticated tastes, and Léa ages all too rapidly, with her looks in the second novel more appropriate to a dowager in her seventies than to a beautiful woman in her late fifties. Such weaknesses pale, however, beside Colette's achievement: These two novels constitute a diptych dramatizing unforgettably both the paradisiacal and infernal regions of love.

*Sources for Further Study*
Crosland, Margaret. *Colette: A Provincial in Paris*, 1954.
Goudeket, Maurice. *Close to Colette*, 1957.
Marks, Elaine. *Colette*, 1960.
Richardson, Joanna. *Colette*, 1983.
Wescott, Glenway. Introduction to *Short Novels of Colette*, 1951.

*Gerhard Brand*

# CHEROKEE

*Author:* Jean Echenoz (1949-　　)
*Type of plot:* Detective
*Time of plot:* The 1980's
*Locale:* Paris and the French Alps
*First published:* 1983 (English translation, 1987)

> *Principal characters:*
> GEORGE CHAVE, a private detective, the protagonist
> CROCONYAN, a criminal, George's friend
> FRED SHAPIRO, George's cousin, a trader and confidence man
> FERGUSON GIBBS, an English entrepreneur, Fred's employer
> JENNY WELTMAN, the girl whom George idealizes

*The Novel*

*Cherokee* is a detective story patterned after New Wave films. Unlike most detective stories, it presents characters and events to the reader without explanation and often without connection. Confusedly, George Chave wanders through these events, pursuing his ideal girl and haphazardly accomplishing his assignments while other characters pursue wealth, one another, and George. Only in the superb climactic scene of the novel, when one group of characters after another appears, do their relationships and the plot itself become clear. The ultimate detective, then, is the reader, who must watch the characters and the plot elements as Jean Echenoz masterfully juggles them, working toward a conclusion which the writer alone has in mind.

The novel begins with a chance encounter in a bar between aimless, unemployed George Chave and a large, mysterious man known only as Croconyan, whom George saves from a knife-flashing assailant. Thinking no more of the incident, George goes on his way, finally obtaining a job with a detective agency in order to be able to buy gifts for his new mistress. Unfortunately, the other two employees of the agency have been making no headway on the agency's three major assignments: to find a missing parrot, to locate a missing wife, and to ascertain who and where are the heirs to a fortune. Recognizing the husband's description of the wife's lover as Croconyan, George manages to locate and return the wife, who is released by her lover only because of his undying friendship with George. George's success in the parrot case is even more surprising, but the other two detectives employed by the agency can only assume that their status is threatened by a genius, and they begin to plot George's downfall, preferably before he can solve the inheritance case by finding the lost heirs.

Meanwhile, Ferguson Gibbs and his employee, the unscrupulous Fred Shapiro, are involved in two plots. By somehow impersonating the heirs to the fortune (the Ferros), they hope to inherit that fortune, and by convincing the members of the Rayonist cult that either Shapiro or Gibbs is their natural leader, they intend to seize the cult money. Thinking that George can be of help to them, Gibbs and Shapiro have him drugged and kidnapped. Meanwhile, the jealous detectives have put the French police on George's trail. George escapes and hides for a time with Croconyan, then flees to the French Alps, where Croconyan, George's mistress, and her lover join him. After the mistress is kidnapped, George finds himself at the Ferro estate, where a cult meeting is being held with Fred Shapiro and Ferguson Gibbs presiding and with the elusive Jenny Weltman acting as the cult goddess. Here more characters gather, including the remaining members of the detective agency, as well as police officers. In a gun battle which is a typical detective story finale, one member of the detective agency, who has throughout the story been injury-prone, is killed. The final scene is once again like a film script: a funeral procession, a burial, a mysterious car toward which Jenny Weltman beckons George, and finally, framed in the rearview mirror, Fred's eyes.

## The Characters

Because the characters are observed objectively, seen as they would be by the viewer of a film, their appearance and their clothing are fully described, while their thoughts and their motivations are usually masked, unless they happen to confide in other characters. Occasionally Echenoz will stop the story for an authorial explanation of a character's history, as he does early in the novel to clarify Fred Shapiro's involvement with Ferguson Gibbs; for the most part, however, readers must draw their own conclusions.

George Chave's motivations are always clear. He wishes to please his mistress, to buy her a yellow dress and other gifts. Therefore, he gets a job, which happens to be with a detective agency. His mistress' coldness and unfaithfulness, however, predispose George to another great passion. After a brief encounter with Jenny Weltman, he has a single goal: to find her, wherever she is. It is his quest for this ideal woman which takes him from adventure to adventure, accidentally surviving dangers and succeeding in detection, while others suspect him of being a schemer like themselves, rather than the innocent, single-minded lover that he is.

The other single-minded character in the novel is the criminal Croconyan, who subordinates his own interests to those of George, once he has become George's faithful friend. Whenever George needs help, Croconyan appears; indeed, when he finds himself in the hands of the Rayonists, George is disappointed, almost surprised, that Croconyan has not rescued him.

While George is pursuing Jenny and Croconyan is protecting George, several entrepreneurs are quite willing to resort to crime in order to make money. The Ferro inheritance and the Rayonist fund both inspire elaborate deception. The pleasant, wealthy Ferguson Gibbs and the scheming, violent Fred Shapiro, who has always quarreled with his cousin George, share an obsession with money and a delight in intrigue. The actors and actresses, including Jenny, whom they hire to further their plans, are not particularly concerned about what they must do in order to earn their fees. The hireling detectives are quite willing to have George beaten or killed in order to protect their own interests.

Certainly the objective approach and the comic tone of the novel are partially responsible for the one-dimensional quality of Echenoz's characters. Yet it is significant that the characters who are most fully realized are the two who are motivated by ideals: George, the determined lover, and Croconyan, the dedicated friend. Because they wear no masks, even in an objective novel they can be known as the schemers cannot.

### Themes and Meanings

If *Cherokee* is an imitation of life, then life itself is ruled by chance, not by design. Individuals pursue their own happiness, whether it seems to lie in the acquisition of money or in the fulfillment of love. Inevitably, they use one another, deceive one another, and intentionally or unintentionally interfere with one another's plans. Farcically, they tumble in and out of one another's lives, and although it might seem that the reunion of George with Jenny at the end of the book is the conventional, providential happy ending, the fact that George's cousin and old enemy Fred is driving the car does not promise a serene future.

*Cherokee* is also, however, a spoof of the traditional detective novel, or perhaps, more accurately, a realistic rendering of real-life flight and capture. One of the most clever themes in the novel centers on the numerous cars which are inevitably present in a contemporary thriller. They are not equipped, however, like James Bond's cars; they do not even work. Periodically, George visits his car, which is terminally ill in the repair shop, and rents worse and worse models. As the tempo of the novel quickens, the cars worsen. George's rented Opel, which has an ear-deafening motor and bad brakes, barely makes it to his hideaway. His mistress' kidnappers have to push their Talbot to get it started. When he pursues them, George is betrayed by the Opel, which loses its oil, forcing him into a car with strangers, who turn out to be kidnapping him. If cars are as unreliable as people, life itself is symbolized by the travels of the French police, who spend most of their time in their car on the beltways around Paris, circling the city and missing their targets as certainly as they miss the truth, which, circling, they sometimes approach.

Finally, like the usual detective novel, *Cherokee* involves flight and pursuit. In the customary pattern, a detective pursues a criminal, whom he unmasks at the end of the story. This story is more like real life, since everyone seems to be both fleeing and pursuing—fleeing from those who threaten them, while pursuing money, love, or some other goal which may well be unobtainable or illusory. It is significant that at one point in the story George wonders why he instinctively runs away, even when he is not aware of being in danger. George does not have the answer; the reader, however, knows that George is always in danger.

Comically exaggerated though the novel may be in its insistence on life as a badly executed series of pursuits of the unworthy or unsatisfying and flights from the unavoidable or unthreatening, it seems to suggest that such is reality. The detective story genre from which *Cherokee* was derived may have been far more illusory, presenting life as a puzzle which a good and rational person must, from time to time, solve, in order to set things right.

*Critical Context*

*Cherokee*, the second of Jean Echenoz's published novels and the first to be translated into English, won the Médicis Prize in 1983. Critics have described it as a detective story, a thriller, and a comic masterpiece with serious elements. That the setting is specifically French, from Parisian streets and highways to the French Alps, is pointed out by critics. This is not a modern novel which could have taken place anywhere that people are confused and unhappy. Yet the title of the book suggests also a kinship with American jazz, whose brief, intense phrases are the musical equivalent of the brief, intense, even violent scenes which make up the novel.

It is the contemporary film, however, which is the major influence on this work. The book opens like a film: A man walks out of a hanger and into a bar; minutes pass and suspense builds as Echenoz pans the scene in description; finally, without any real conversation, the man walks out of the bar, and the reader, caught, moves with him. The book ends with another familiar film scene: the funeral procession, the movement to a car, and the final frame, eyes in a rearview mirror and a brief question. *Cherokee* is a significant book because it brings new themes and techniques to an earlier form and because it successfully employs film techniques and conventions in the novel genre.

*Sources for Further Study*

McCarthy, Patrick. "Playing with the Parrot," in *The Times Literary Supplement*. October 14, 1983, p. 1142.

McGee, Celia. "Nice Guy, Private Eye," in *The New York Times Book Review*. XCII (September 20, 1987), p. 31.

Thiher, Allen. Review in *World Literature Today*. LVIII (Spring, 1984), p. 232.

*Rosemary M. Canfield-Reisman*

# CHEVENGUR

*Author:* Andrei Platonov (Andrei Platonovich Klimentov, 1899-1951)
*Type of plot:* Satire/surrealism
*Time of plot:* Shortly before and during the Russian Revolution and Civil War
*Locale:* The central provinces of Russia, and Moscow
*First published:* 1972 (English translation, 1978)

> *Principal characters:*
> ALEXANDER (SASHA) DVANOV, an orphan and Red Army
>   soldier
> PROKOFY (PROSHKA) DVANOV, Sasha's foster brother
> ZAKHAR PAVLOVICH, Sasha's guardian, a railroad mechanic
> SONYA MANDROVA, Sasha's childhood friend
> STEPAN KOPENKIN, a dedicated revolutionary

*The Novel*

*Chevengur* is the story of a quest—the search for a place where time is telescoped and Communism has managed to triumph in a matter of weeks. Episodic and fragmented, the novel follows the path of several characters on their way to the village of Chevengur, the workers' paradise on earth.

When Alexander Dvanov (Sasha) is orphaned, then turned out to beg by his impoverished foster family, he is taken in by Zakhar Pavlovich, a railroad mechanic who "wanted the world really to be endless, so that wheels would always be necessary, ever preparing the way for general happiness." As Zakhar Pavlovich declines, losing interest in his beloved machines, World War I comes and goes, the Civil War begins, and Sasha reads and studies, finding comfort, if not understanding, in algebra.

At this point the narrative jumps to Sasha's travels as a soldier in the Red Army and his wanderings during the Civil War. He leaves his regiment and returns home either to die or to recover from typhus; recovering, he falls in love with a neighbor girl, Sonya Mandrova, but leaves again, telling her that they will see each other after the Revolution.

Sonya leaves the town to work as a village schoolteacher, while Sasha travels through various villages, is wounded and captured by anarchist bandits, and then is rescued by Stepan Kopenkin, a troop commander who is temporarily without troops. Kopenkin believes that "all matters and roads of his life [lead] inexorably to the grave of Rosa Luxemburg"; he carries a picture of her in his cap and uses "Rosa" instead of "giddy-up" to urge his horse, Proletarian Strength, to great endurance in the name of the Revolution. The two set off to investigate the state of affairs in the district and to clear the road to socialism.

During their adventures they encounter more bandits, a knight of the

Revolution (clad in homemade armor), and finally Comrade Chepurny, otherwise known as the Jap. The Jap claims to be living in a village where Communism has already been achieved—that is, in Chevengur. Soon after their arrival in Chevengur, Sasha leaves again, but in the meantime Chepurny and Kopenkin help the Party committee purge the area of bourgeoises— they simply execute the male bourgeois population. Klavdyusha, Chepurny's female companion (since there are no more wives), collects all of their "noncumbersome manual objects." It turns out that Prokofy (Proshka) Dvanov, Sasha's opportunistic foster brother, is a member of the village committee and the local authority on literacy and Karl Marx. He is interested in acquiring both Klavdyusha and the village itself.

The problem is that once Communism seems to be established in Chevengur, no one quite knows what to do with it or how they should all spend their time. They make useless objects such as wooden frying pans in order not to exploit one another, and let the crops go so as not to exploit the land. They uproot all the houses and relocate them, but in the process realize that there is no one to live in them. They decide to recruit the poor folk of the district to resettle Chevengur, and so Prokofy is dispatched first to collect the proletarians and the landless peasants, and then later to bring back women for them all. The Chevengurians light a beacon to guide the "miscellaneous" (those who are not peasants or proletarians, but not capitalists) to their new home.

At this point, the action switches abruptly to Moscow, where Simon Serbinov, an inspector of sorts, runs into a mysteriously attractive woman aboard a streetcar. Serbinov keeps a list of the people he knows; he "would have liked to accumulate people like money, as a means of existence." This woman, who turns out to be Sonya, proves elusive.

Serbinov goes to Chevengur in his official capacity as agricultural inspector, and, like the rest of the people in the town, stays on for no definable reason. Sasha has returned, and they discover that they both know Sonya. Prokofy arrives with his wagonload of women, none of whom seems particularly interested in either socialism or sex. Pitiful, starved creatures, they want only food and warmth.

The Chevengurians try to keep themselves busy but unexploited by making tools and monuments to one another. In the end they are roused out of their uncomfortable idyll by a Cossack attack. In the battle, Kopenkin dies a heroic death and is carried off into the steppe by Proletarian Strength. Sasha goes after them, and in the wake of the fighting Prokofy vows to bring Sasha back.

## The Characters

Andrei Platonov's characters are not psychological studies—they are bodies plus consciousness. Both the body and the consciousness have an air of the grotesque about them, and some would seem monstrous (Pashintsev in his armor, for example, which is his only clothing) if it were not for the pensiveness and reflectiveness that nearly all the characters share.

That reflectiveness is most often a puzzled, all-pervasive melancholy. Zakhar Pavlovich the mechanic is sad and uneasy because he "cannot feel infinity" and because he cannot bear the thought that man is descended from worms, "a terrifying pipe with nothing inside." Sasha, as a boy, feels anguished sympathy with any life at all, to the point of pitying the passerby who coughs in the yard at night. Throughout the novel, the one emotion the characters feel for one another is not so much love as pity. Even their lust is somehow regretful. This compassion is a generalized and impersonal one, though, extending to railroad locomotives and horses and grass. All are equally vulnerable. The stranger who cuddles up next to Sasha for the sake of warmth in the middle of the open steppe is one example; the monuments the Chevengurians build is another.

The other element of consciousness common to the characters is their singular language—a hodgepodge of misunderstood and misused ideological abstractions, current names, and jargon forcing their way into colloquial speech. "Lenin tooketh away and now Lenin giveth," says an old peasant woman. As mangled syntax and ideological terminology come to describe not only politics but also the life of the soul and body, the characters' language simply takes them over. Zakhar Pavlovich tells Sasha that he has to feel imperialism with his body. By the end of the novel, Sasha looks at his fellow citizens and sees "their pitiful naked bodies as the stuff of socialism." Platonov's characters witness the word made flesh with a vengeance.

*Themes and Meanings*

The possibility of Utopia fascinated Russian writers at the end of the nineteenth and the beginning of the twentieth century, and none was more intrigued than Fyodor Dostoevski. His rejection of Utopia in *Zapiski iz podpolya* (1864; *Notes from the Underground*, 1913), on the grounds that what is defined and finished is dead, points the way for Platonov's *Chevengur*, a bizarre, surrealistic treatment of the revolutionary quest and its ultimate goal.

A quest implies a higher purpose and direction—perfect for a treatment of Marxism's supposedly inexorable progress toward history's final end, the resolution of all contradictions. Yet in the midst of turmoil, violence, and civil war, Platonov's characters move about almost randomly, accidentally, as if by inertia rather than will. Ragged, isolated even when together, they have little sense of what they are doing—even though they have a vocabulary for it. Even Kopenkin—the Bolshevik Don Quixote in search of his Dulcinea, Rosa Luxemburg (who is, moreover, quite dead)—wanders from place to place in a kind of limbo, covering great distances on his horse Proletarian

Strength but never really going anywhere.

There is a dreamlike unreality to time in the novel, partly because Platonov both expands it and contracts it, but partly because Chevengur itself has supposedly overleaped several historical stages to arrive at the end of historical time itself—a state of perfect equilibrium. The sun rises and sets, the grass grows, characters come and go, issuing directives and resolutions— all of which are taken absolutely literally—but time seems to be at a standstill; it all occurs in a vacuum, or at a dead end. The Chevengurians wait for Communism to show itself much as Samuel Beckett's characters wait for Godot.

*Critical Context*

*Chevengur* is a curious work in many ways, not the least because of its publishing history; this, Platonov's most ambitious work, finished sometime around 1929, has never been published in full in the Soviet Union. Drastically edited sections have appeared as short stories, but not until 1972 was the novel published in Russian in full—and in France. Even so, there are some missing links, and any effort at synopsis makes the novel seem more coherent than it is. Coherence, though, may not have been Platonov's point.

His body of work not published fully in the Soviet Union is large, including this novel and another major work, *Kotlovan* (1973; *The Foundation Pit*, 1973). Platonov first began to gain fame in the 1920's. Stories that would eventually go into his first collection, *Epifanskie shlyuzny* (1927; epiphany), attracted attention with their startling stylistic ingenuity. Platonov's eccentric language plus his fascination with the relationship between humans and their machines (he himself was an engineer) placed him among the ranks of young writers who were questioning the effects of a new ideology and new technology on an old rural consciousness.

Yet neither Platonov's idiosyncratic language nor his bleak pictures of rural life proved palatable in the 1930's. He was often attacked for "monstrous and unclean" attitudes and anti-Soviet slander. While he had his defenders and was able to publish such powerful stories as "Usomnivshiysya Makar" ("Makar the Doubtful"), "Vprok" (for the future good), and "Fro," hostile criticism—and the arrest of his only son—effectively put an end to his real writing career by the end of the decade. He continued to write, surviving on journalistic reworkings of folktales, until his death in 1951. *Chevengur*, in whatever form, is a powerful example both of Platonov's idiosyncratic sense of language and of his technological and spiritual preoccupations. Its absurd vision of the workers' Paradise Found is Socialist surrealism at its purest.

*Sources for Further Study*

Bayley, John. Review of *Collected Works, "Chevengur,"* in *The New York Review of Books*. XXVI (May 3, 1979), p. 37.

Brodsky, Joseph. "Catastrophes in the Air," in *Less than One*, 1985.
_____. Preface to *The Foundation Pit*, 1973.
Jordan, Marion. *Andrei Platonov*, 1973.
Olcott, Anthony. Foreword to *Chevengur*, 1978.

*Jane Ann Miller*

# CHRIST STOPPED AT EBOLI
## The Story of a Year

*Author:* Carlo Levi (1902-1975)
*Type of plot:* Social realism
*Time of plot:* 1935-1936
*Locale:* Gagliano, a small town in the southern Italian district of Lucania
*First published: Cristo si è fermato a Eboli*, 1945 (English translation, 1947)

> Principal characters:
>> CARLO, a political prisoner, a physician by training, an artist
>> by inclination
>> LUIGI MAGALONE, the mayor of Gagliano
>> DR. MILILLO, the mayor's uncle, an aged physician
>> CATERINA MAGALONE CUSCIANNA, the mayor's sister, the local
>> leader of the Fascist Party
>> GIULIA VENERE, Carlo's housekeeper
>> DON GIUSEPPE TRAJELLA, the parish priest

*The Novel*

*Christ Stopped at Eboli* is the story of a year in the life of a young man whose opposition to Fascism has resulted in his internment in a remote mountain village in southern Italy. The title refers to a saying of the local inhabitants. Nominally, Christianity exists in this poor, rugged, malarial region, but no real message of salvation has ever reached the people. No one comes to the area except for enemies, conquerors, and visitors without understanding. Carlo, a well-educated northerner, belongs to the last category, but during his enforced stay in Gagliano, he grows in knowledge of and sympathy for the villagers.

Carlo has been brought under guard from a larger town which boasts a few shops and amenities, but Gagliano, where the road ends and few vehicles ever come, is much more primitive. He sees a single treeless street flanked by the scattered one-room houses of peasants and a small number of more substantial dwellings of the local gentry. Nearby stands the barracks of the *carabinieri*, the policemen who loosely supervise the activities of the dozen political prisoners exiled to the town. Gagliano quickly discovers that the newcomer is a physician, although a nonpracticing one, and since the town's only doctors are the semiretired uncle of the mayor and another man who is both inept and insensitive to the people's needs, the inhabitants flock to Carlo. Although he lacks instruments, medicines, and practical experience, and would rather spend his time painting, Carlo provides what assistance he can to the peasants, whose ways and outlook on life draw his interest.

Inevitably, conflicts arise. Carlo is patronized by the mayor, Don Magalone, and his family, but Dr. Gibilisco, whose family and the Magalones have carried on a long-running feud, resents the newcomer's popularity with the townspeople. Carlo tries to keep clear of these rivalries, which seem to be the gentry's main occupation. Carlo may not leave the town and his activities are monitored and his mail censored (an indignity partly thwarted by the kindly postmaster), but he has the run of the town and can arrange for his own accommodations. With some difficulty, he secures a habitable house, and Donna Caterina, the mayor's strong-willed sister, finds for him a capable housekeeper named Giulia.

Carlo discovers that the insularity of the community extends even to those who have lived in the United States, for the returnees exhibit few traces of their experience abroad. It is a community oppressed by nature, exhausted by past generations, and neglected—save for taxation—by the central government. The people are passive, cheerless, superstitious, cynical of "the fellows in Rome," and indifferent to politics, but they are also patient, brotherly, and capable of great endurance and devotion. They identify more readily with the nineteenth century brigands—the memory of these men's violent but resourceful opposition to governmental authority has not been erased by the passage of nearly seventy years—than with the aspirations of Benito Mussolini. The brigands live on in romanticized legends as supporters of the peasantry against government; in 1935, government is concentrating on raising money and men for an aggressive war in Ethiopia.

Eventually, Carlo is threatened with full imprisonment if he continues to practice medicine, but he has attained the reputation of a miracle man among the peasants, and they continue to come to him under cover of darkness. Gradually, the young doctor comes to love and respect these people, ignorant of the world as they are, yet intelligent enough to understand and resent the indignity of their status. Because the authorities consider the peasants to be less than human, no one particularly bothers to investigate these violations of the governmental decree, and as long as Carlo does not practice medicine on the gentry, he is able to continue ministering to the sick and injured. A cycle of seasons passes. Suddenly Mussolini, encouraged by his army's successes in Ethiopia, grants amnesty to the political prisoners. Carlo, virtually absorbed into the rhythm of life in Gagliano, sadly prepares to depart, and, with promises to return, leaves the admiring townspeople and "the motionless time and dark civilization" of Lucania.

*Christ Stopped at Eboli* lacks a plot in the usual sense. Instead of a climactic narrative, the author conveys the sense of a year spent in a place and among a people unattractive in any conventional sense but strangely beautiful and cumulatively compelling. The structure of the book is thus true to life in Gagliano, which cannot reach any fulfillment or conclusion beyond that which Carlo has experienced during his confinement in the town.

*The Characters*

Carlo Levi makes no attempt to disguise the autobiographical nature of his main character. In all the important particulars, Carlo corresponds to the author of *Christ Stopped at Eboli*, and it is unlikely that Levi needed to invent many of the other characters. His mode of presentation might be described as good reporting, except that reporters seldom spend so much time with their subjects, interact with them so extensively, or reflect on them so profoundly.

The gentry are largely of the sort who would be inconsequential anywhere but in their own town. They are idle, petty, and pretentious. The mayor is quick to assure Carlo that he, too, is a cultivated man, and his sister assumes the responsibility for finding Carlo a wife from among the small number of local worthies, an honor which he carefully evades. She is the leader of the Fascist Party, despite her indifference to politics, because she knows that power and prestige accrue to the position. Old Dr. Milillo at once establishes his class's perspective on the peasantry: "Good people, but primitive." Thus deftly Levi conveys the dubious superiority exuded by the minimally functioning upper class of the town.

The peasants interest Carlo far more. Individually, they play minor roles, with only Giulia, the earthy housekeeper, present daily in Carlo's routine; collectively, however, they constitute the discovery that makes his year in Gagliano memorable. To this educated man from prosperous, cosmopolitan Turin, the rural south is another world. To them, Fascism—the evil Carlo has been sent here for resisting—is merely the latest version of an age-old repression. Resentful but resigned, they look kindly upon Carlo and the other prisoners (whom they call "exiles") as fellow sufferers. It is in a group effort that they best express their only seemingly extinguished spirit. When they hear of the decree against Carlo's medical practice, they sublimate their fury into the creation of an apparently impromptu play, in which a competent physician in white (they have borrowed Carlo's white jacket for the purpose) is opposed by another doctor in black. As the former, defending his patient, is about to triumph in the dispute between them, an emissary arrives from Rome and chases the good doctor away. Left in charge, the man in black proceeds to murder the patient by sticking a large needle into his heart—an effect simulated by the puncturing of a pig's bladder. The play ends in a dirge sung by the victim's mother and a chorus. Carlo cannot decide whether the play is truly spontaneous or a "reminiscence of an ancient art," but several performances of the play in various locations accessible to the local authorities show clearly that while the peasants know that they cannot rebel effectively, they can affirm their humanity in the face of officialdom's refusal to acknowledge it. Carlo's horizons widen during a year of encounters with people who are able to teach him more than he has previously suspected about the pervasiveness of brotherhood.

*Themes and Meanings*

At first, Carlo wishes to withdraw into his own quiet pursuits, to seek isolation in this essentially foreign environment. He forms the habit of lying in a
ditch in the cemetery which has been dug in anticipation of the next dead
body. In this open grave, he is close to the earth, and he achieves a feeling of
freedom and solitude: incidentally, he also escapes the oppressive summer
sun. He has little fondness for Gagliano's upper class, and he does not wish
to be appropriated by them. The mayor, also the town's schoolteacher, is
slow-witted and narrow-minded. Don Trajella, the priest, once an instructor
in a seminary, has gone to seed during his long and unsuccessful pastorate. It
is flattering to their egos to converse with this artist-doctor, and the fact that
he is a prisoner of a regime they tacitly support does not disqualify him in
their eyes, for they feel little enthusiasm for Fascism.

It is while lying in his open grave that Carlo meets the grave digger, a man
almost ninety years old, who exemplifies the timelessness, the primitive wisdom, and the collective memory of Gagliano. "The village is built of the
bones of the dead," the old man tells Carlo while carrying out the continuing
work of the living. Carlo's retreat has brought him into contact not only with
the earth but also with the people of the earth. For their part, the villagers
find it possible to respond to him more warmly after his sister pays him a
short visit. When they see that this stranger, whom they have regarded as a
sort of magician, is a person with blood ties and thus is potentially available
for the symbolic kinship known as *comparaggio*, the bond becomes more
powerful. Carlo discovers the ways in which the peasants are able to endure
their almost unvarying existence of poverty, toil, and disease.

In some ways, these people typify the Italian lower class, particularly in
the South, but Gagliano is an extreme case of a community afflicted by climate, topography, and official neglect. To be chosen as a prison site is in itself a token of official scorn. Malaria is endemic, and the required supplies of
quinine are not delivered. The land is so barren that the peasants must
trudge for miles to and from the fields in which they labor. Gagliano, the
south of Italy at its most pitiable, epitomizes for Levi the more unfortunate
of the two Italies, which are two civilizations that he sees as post-Christian
and pre-Christian. In the North, Christianity is exhausted; in the South, it is
not yet apprehended. Around Gagliano, the land is pathetically deforested,
the mountain streams have run dry, and the buildings of the town itself are
beginning to sink into the ravines below. Still, no industry has been established to compensate for the decline of crops and livestock. With emigration
restricted, taxation increased, and the Roman bureaucracy increasingly out
of touch with local problems, the lesser of the two Italies continues to
deteriorate. A recent decree exemplifies the general situation. On the theory
that goats destroy crops, the peasants have been ordered to slaughter their
goats, but in Gagliano, with no crops worth mentioning, to kill goats is to

eliminate the only dairy products that compensate for the foodstuffs which the villagers lack in the first place. Carlo concludes that only an "organic federation" of largely autonomous communities can solve the plight of a nation politically unified but in most other respects diverse and better able to deal with problems on a regional basis.

## Critical Context

*Christ Stopped at Eboli* stands as one of the more memorable works of a generation of writers who were born early in the twentieth century, lived under Mussolini's authoritarian rule during their formative years, and dedicated much of their imaginative energy to opposing his regime. The movement, which became known as the Italian Resistance during World War II, had already spawned such novels as Ignazio Silone's *Brot und Wein* (1936; *Bread and Wine*, 1936) and Elio Vittorini's *Conversazione in Sicilia* (1937, serial; 1941, book; *In Sicily*, 1948) before the war; others by Vittorini, Italo Calvino, and Cesare Pavese appeared shortly thereafter. These men set forth views that were usually egalitarian and, in some instances, communistic. Levi himself became a Communist member of the Italian Senate in 1963. Twentieth century Italian intellectuals tend to fear Communism less than a resurgence of the conservative and reactionary forces upon which Mussolini drew.

Political as it was, Levi's book caught and continues to hold the attention of readers because of its unforgettable verbal picture of a region rarely visited by tourists and little known even to many Italians. In this respect, *Christ Stopped at Eboli* belongs to an older tradition of fiction which presents the life of the Italian peasantry, a mode established by Giovanni Verga, especially in his masterpiece *I Malavoglia* (1881; *The House by the Medlar Tree*, partial translation, 1890, 1953; complete translation, 1964). As Verga revealed life in Sicily, so Levi unfolds life in Lucania. Although Levi is not primarily a novelist as Verga is, and although this book resists any neat classification, *Christ Stopped at Eboli* continues to transcend its specific concerns with the events of the 1930's and with the intensification of the totalitarian threat during World War II. The book evokes brilliantly the harsh beauty of a forbidding landscape and the timeless struggle of those who call it home.

## Sources for Further Study

Catani, R. D."Structure and Style as Fundamental Expression: The Works of Carlo Levi and Their Poetic Ideology," in *Italica*. LVI (1979), pp. 213-229.

Pacifici, Sergio. "Carlo Levi: The Essayist as a Novelist," in *The Modern Italian Novel: From Pea to Moravia*, 1979.

_____. "The New Writers," in *A Guide to Contemporary Italian Literature*, 1962.

Segrete, Carte. *Carlo Levi*, 1970.

*Robert P. Ellis*

# THE CITY AND THE HOUSE

*Author:* Natalia Ginzburg (1916-    )
*Type of plot:* Domestic realism
*Time of plot:* The late 1970's or 1980's
*Locale:* Rome; the countryside near Perugia, Italy; and Princeton, New Jersey
*First published: La città e la casa,* 1984 (English translation, 1987)

> *Principal characters:*
> GIUSEPPE GUARALDI, a middle-aged journalist who leaves his job in Rome to live with his brother in Princeton, New Jersey
> LUCREZIA, the mother of five children, wife of Piero, and former lover of Giuseppe
> ALBERICO GUARALDI, Giuseppe's son, a filmmaker and homosexual who dies a violent death at the age of twenty-eight
> ANNE MARIE GUARALDI, a scientist, the widow of Giuseppe's brother and later the wife of Giuseppe

*The Novel*

An epistolary novel consisting of more than ninety letters written during a three-year period, *The City and the House* brings together a colorful group of friends whose failed marriages, unhappy love affairs, and strained family relationships present a dismal view of contemporary domestic life. The breakup of the close-knit Italian family, the adoption of different sexual mores, and the rejection of traditional gender roles bring about new configurations in social relationships. Seeking their way as best they can, Natalia Ginzburg's wounded characters take refuge in human solidarity; enduring bonds of friendship ease the pain of problematic family ties.

As the novel begins, Giuseppe Guaraldi, the middle-aged protagonist, writes a letter to Lucrezia, his former lover, informing her of his intention to move to Princeton, New Jersey, to live with his brother, Ferruccio, a scientist who has been living in the United States for many years. In numerous letters written between this announcement and his departure, Giuseppe sorts out his emotions and reflects on his life. He recounts the failure of his first marriage and the effect it had on his son, Alberico. In writing to Lucrezia, he presents the problems that brought their love affair to an end. Lucrezia, in turn, argues that Giuseppe has never wanted to accept as his own Graziano, a child born from their relationship. Lucrezia accuses Giuseppe of being unable to play the role of the father.

Lucrezia and her husband, Piero, live with their five children in a large house called "Le Margherite" in the country near Perugia. This house is the scene of numerous happy gatherings as the friends meet there to spend holidays and weekends together. Lucrezia and Piero have an open marriage, and Lucrezia is prone to falling in love with other men.

Giuseppe settles into his new life in the United States. He begins to teach a course on Italian literature, to write a novel, and to play the role of house-husband. Barely two months after Giuseppe's arrival, his brother dies of a cerebral hemorrhage. In the wake of this unexpected death, Anne Marie and Giuseppe are brought together by their mutual loss. They develop a relationship based on their respect and love for Ferruccio. Eventually, they marry.

While Giuseppe is establishing a new life in the United States, his son is beginning to make his way as a filmmaker. Alberico has moved to Rome, where he is living with his friends Salvatore, a homosexual, and Nadia, a young Sicilian woman who gives birth to a child fathered by a Viennese journalist. Nadia has broken off her relationship with the child's father, who refuses to admit his paternity. Given his sexual orientation, Alberico will never be a biological father. He is happy, therefore, to claim Nadia's child as his own. Giuseppe, writing to one of his friends, describes the situation this way: "The baby is called Giorgia, just like my mother. Her last name is Guaraldi, just like mine. In some way I have become a grandfather."

While this unlikely family of two men, a woman, and a new baby is admired by their friends and neighbors for their ability to nurture one another, other family bonds are coming apart. Anne Marie's daughter Chantal gives birth to a child, Maggie. Soon after the birth, her marriage ends. Chantal and Maggie move in with Anne Marie and Giuseppe, who becomes attached to both the child and her mother. An ensuing brief affair between Chantal and Giuseppe casts a pall over this domestic arrangement and Chantal moves out, leaving Giuseppe to care for the baby.

A simultaneous domestic crisis occurs at Le Margherite. When Lucrezia falls in love with Ignazio Fegiz, an art restorer, her marriage suffers a shock from which it will not recover. Although she has had previous affairs, this act of infidelity moves Piero to leave her for a younger woman.

Alberico's experience of domestic tranquillity is also shattered. Attempting to protect Salvatore from a group of drug dealers who are angry with him, Nadia dies in a street fight. Her father arrives from Sicily and takes the baby back to the island. Alberico recognizes that Giorgia will be better off with her grandparents, and his experiment with fatherhood comes to a bitter end. In the wake of this tragic experience, Alberico, now a wealthy man as a result of the success of his film, decides to buy the house his father sold when he left Rome. He makes a down payment and writes to Giuseppe, inviting him to return. Before he can complete the final arrangements, however, Alberico, together with Salvatore, is murdered by the same group that killed Nadia.

Giuseppe returns to Rome for the funeral but must hurry back to Princeton because Anne Marie has been stricken with leukemia. She dies shortly after his return. The novel closes with a letter from Lucrezia to Giuseppe informing him that other friends have bought his house in Rome.

## The Characters

Ginzburg's characters are an odd group of lonely, suffering individuals who take comfort in friendship. The letters that they exchange allow the reader to see them from a number of vantage points. Their changing relationships, which form the heart of the novel, come through clearly in the epistolary format.

At the center of this group of prolific letter-writing friends, Giuseppe Guaraldi is a quirky and confused Italian male in the throes of a mid-life crisis. Unlike most Italians, who might be motivated to take up residence in the United States in a spirit of adventure, Giuseppe comes to America seeking shelter from life's difficulties. He relies on his older brother for both financial protection and guidance.

In their characterization of Giuseppe, his friends portray a man with a great capacity for friendship who lacks the backbone to be a strong husband and father. Giuseppe is somewhat afraid of life and describes himself as a weak person, a man always destined to lose. Because he is unable to play the role of the father, his relationship with his son, Alberico, is not a happy one. Giuseppe would have preferred a different life-style for his son. At the same time, he realizes that his son would have profited from a more capable and interested father.

The chief female character, Lucrezia, is a classical figure in the Ginzburgian repertoire. Her personal problems demand much attention. Her father died when she was very young and her relationship with her mother was overly dependent. Her lack of a father leads her to seek a surrogate father in the men with whom she comes into contact. Lucrezia's devotion to childbearing is not matched by a commensurate devotion to motherhood. She is fond of being pregnant but is not capable of providing a stable home life for her many children. She divorces Piero and leaves Le Margherite for a crowded and inhospitable apartment in Rome. Like many of Ginzburg's female protagonists, Lucrezia is lured by the attractions of life in the city. Her ensuing disillusionment forces her to realize that she is partly to blame for her unhappiness.

## Themes and Meanings

Human solidarity—friendship as the last refuge in a world where the family has disintegrated—is a central theme in *The City and the House*. Unsatisfactory family relationships—fathers and sons who barely communicate, mothers and daughters who cannot keep from inflicting pain, husbands and wives whose infidelity is endemic—create a dismal world in which the bonds of friendship become more enduring than family ties.

The narrative is divided among three locales—Rome, the Italian country-side near Perugia, and Princeton. As the title indicates, each of these three locations, or "cities" in a general sense, presents a particular house whose story intermingles with that of its inhabitants. The changing interpersonal relationships of the characters lead to changes in household arrangements. Giuseppe's house in Rome remains a recurring point of reference in the novel, as do the other two houses: Piero and Lucrezia's country house, Le Margherite, and Ferruccio's house in Princeton.

When Alberico expresses his intention to buy Giuseppe's house in Rome, the reader begins to expect a happy resolution to the novel. Giuseppe's homecoming seems to be a likely possibility. This happy ending is not to be, however, and the house passes into someone else's hands. In similar fashion, Le Margherite is sold when Piero and Lucrezia are divorced. This important dwelling, the scene of much happiness and frequent group celebrations, is transformed into a hotel and becomes unrecognizable after its renovation. Finally, Giuseppe's brother's house in Princeton provides a fitting setting for the novel's conclusion: Giuseppe has lost his brother, his wife, and his son and now finds himself alone in a house in which he has never felt comfort-able. Ginzburg's three households represent the widespread failure of the family as a social institution. Suffering from the effects of this social crisis, the individual remains isolated in a hostile environment.

*Critical Context*

*The City and the House* continues Ginzburg's fascination with the institu-tion of the family. Her depiction of the disintegration of the patriarchal fam-ily, as well as her insights into the family life of Italy's greatest novelist of the nineteenth century, Alessandro Manzoni, can be seen in her other works of the 1970's and 1980's: *Caro Michele* (1973; *No Way*, 1974; also as *Dear Michael*, 1975), *Famiglia* (1977; family), and *La famiglia Manzoni* (1983; the Manzoni family). Her early novels such as *La strada che va in città* (1942; *The Road to the City*, 1949) and *È stato così* (1947; *The Dry Heart*, 1949) present first-person female narrators whose destructive social conditioning con-stitutes an explicit condemnation of the traditional family. In her mature fic-tion, however, she moves beyond these perspectives to develop a pessimistic vision of modern society which suffers from a lack of parental authority. Her later works express a profound nostalgia for the stability that the traditional family once provided. Like Giuseppe and Lucrezia in *The City and the House*, the characters of her narrative works of the 1970's and 1980's are eternal adolescents engaged in a continual search for surrogate fathers.

More successful than her previous epistolary novel, *No Way*, *The City and the House* exploits the letter as a stylistic device well suited to Ginzburg's sparse, unadorned style, which is intended to reproduce the rhythms of speech. Divided between Italy and the United States, the cosmopolitan setting of the novel reflects the evolving interrelationship of social patterns throughout the West. One of the most important novelists of the second half of the twentieth century, Natalia Ginzburg provides an Italian perspective on an issue of great moment. *The City and the House*, her bleak depiction of domestic failures, is a fitting companion to her earlier highly acclaimed works.

*Sources for Further Study*
Bowe, Clotilde S. "The Narrative Strategy of Natalia Ginzburg," in *Modern Language Review*. LXVIII (1973), pp. 788-795.
Heiney, Donald. "Natalia Ginzburg: The Fabric of Voices," in *The Iowa Review*. I (Fall, 1970), pp. 87-93.
O'Healy, Anne Marie. "Natalia Ginzburg and the Family," in *Canadian Journal of Italian Studies*. IX (1986), pp. 21-36.
Piclardi, Rosetta D. "Forms and Figures in the Novels of Natalia Ginzburg," in *World Literature Today*. LIII (1979), pp. 585-589.

*John P. Welle*

# THE CITY BUILDER

*Author:* George Konrád (1933-      )
*Type of plot:* Psychological realism
*Time of plot:* The 1970's
*Locale:* An unnamed provincial city in Hungary
*First published: A városalapító,* 1977 (English translation, 1977)

> *Principal characters:*
> THE NARRATOR, a city planner
> HIS DEAD WIFE
> HIS SON, who may be dead

## The Novel

The City Builder is a stream-of-consciousness novel, narrated in the present tense, which explores the mind of a Hungarian city planner who has become disillusioned with his stagnant, bureaucratic, and repressive society. Each of the ten chapters has a central preoccupation and is further unified by the settings, characters, and symbolic patterns which are emphasized.

As the novel begins, the narrator is an airline passenger, resolving to withdraw into himself in order to avoid disturbing the fragile peace in the city where he will land. Yet his apartment, which should have been a haven, reminds him of the failures of his life: the ideal city, which was never realized because of bureaucratic corruption; the ideal marriage, which perished when his beloved wife was killed in a senseless car accident; the ideal son, whose own soul and body were damaged when he was thrown into prison and who at the end of the book may well have died in the earthquake which has destroyed the town.

In the second chapter, the airplane setting changes to a train, and the narrator thinks back to the waves of conquest which have swept across Eastern Europe from time to time as the train now moves across the land. The Romans, the Tartars, the Austrians, the Nazis have come and gone, leaving generation after generation of Hungarians to bury their dead, to rebuild the cities, and to begin living again.

Even times which seemed secure have been subject to sudden change. The house of the narrator's grandfather, on the family estate, appeared secure, and the hierarchical way of life, of which the narrator believes he must disapprove, offered a kind of solidity. Yet time brought industrialization and pollution in the form of a power plant built by the narrator's own father.

Recalling the birth of his son, the narrator mourns for another lost dream. Idealistic, philosophical, intense, the son fell afoul of the state. After three months in prison, he emerged broken in health and will. Meanwhile, the narrator's wife had been killed in an automobile accident, leaving only the bittersweet memories of their relationship, with which he must live. Among his memories, too, are those of his own parents when they were young: the lovely mother who had become an old woman when the narrator returned after being a prisoner of war, and the strong father, himself a private builder, defeated by death.

As he searches for something stable in life, the narrator questions God, in a segment reminiscent of Job, except that God does not answer his questions, even with the biblical insistence on his own existence.

At the end of the novel, the city planner is once again in motion, moving first on a ship through an idyllic holiday landscape, then shockingly through a city devastated by an earthquake, into which the military move, this time to rescue, not to subdue. Finally, it is a frozen winter night, New Year's Eve. The narrator is once again alone. God, he says, has been invited to join them, but has not appeared. Cut off from faith, he wishes to lose his loneliness at least in kinship to the people of his city. Remembering the bloody cruelty of his people, the whimsical condemnations of "enemies" whose only crime was to be different or irritating, the narrator tries, nevertheless, at the beginning of the New Year, to embrace them. The city is celebrating. Everyone seems free. Yet the narrator realizes that this brief respite from hate and oppression will end with the next dawn. The saving revolution has been an illusion.

## The Characters

Since the characters of *The City Builder* are seen through the eyes of the narrator, they reveal as much about him as about themselves. His grandfather, his mother, and his father, for example, all belong to a childhood of prosperity and security, of pleasure and joy. After he describes the autocratic grandfather, the important father, the passionate and beautiful mother, the narrator adds that he did not like their kind of life because it was founded on pride. Yet his description of that life indicates that his own memories are happy. The narrator's father, for example, is a lusty, gossipy, hot-tempered man, given to snatching at the maid, shouting at his son, and conversing with God as his equal. Certainly the bloated capitalist of propaganda, in the narrator's reminiscences he is infinitely preferable to the slavish officeholders of the new society, who are so busy protecting themselves that they accomplish nothing. Thus the narrator's own assessments of such capitalists, of whom he does not approve, are belied by the tone of his descriptions.

The narrator's most-admired women, like his father, are lusty and free-spirited. Acknowledging the peccadilloes of her husband, the narrator's mother obviously was delighted by him. The narrator details her sexual joy in her husband, a joy much like that of his own dead wife, whose sensuality, forever lost to him, is a constant torment. Both of them share the glitter of the long-dead lady who is described in the third chapter, jumping her stallion, dancing through life decorated with diamonds and furs, attended by colonels. Such individualists are not heroines of the collective.

Nor is the narrator's son at home in the society which he describes. From his childhood a questioner, he accuses his father of having too much faith in technocracy, too little interest in human individuality. Perhaps, thinks the narrator, he took pleasure in his son's inevitable fall. A dreamer, a theatrical promoter, a man who spoke his mind, the son was imprisoned because he refused to mouth the clichés of his state. To repression, he reacted with violence. Now hospitalized, he has returned to childhood, to begin again at twenty-two. The narrator examines his own feelings as he tells the story. Did he wish for his own argumentative son's downfall? Was the boy too much of a threat to his own hard-won assumptions? Or did he try to protect him too much? An intellectual, a natural skeptic, the son was honest with himself, and such honesty, broods the father, must end either in destruction or in a willingness to lie, to live the kind of life which the narrator has been willing to live.

Through the narrator's reactions to his own characters, through his sympathy with those who demand so much of life and of society, George Konrád suggests that the story of this novel is the narrator's examination of his own beliefs. His apartment, he says, is strewn with his own failures. In the light of those other lives, vibrant though doomed to disaster or death, the narrator is obviously having second thoughts about his own.

## Themes and Meanings

Konrád's major theme, the human need for freedom, is specifically spelled out in the sixth chapter, when the city builder, who once envisioned perfect cities in which human beings were efficient machines, expresses his new realization, that ideal cities must contain struggling, arguing, changing human beings, who are free to pursue perfection. After the Revolution has come a new stagnation. Born of independent thinking, the Revolution forced its own free spirits into fearful acquiescence. The new society punishes free thought of the kind which created it.

In Konrád's spoiled society, human beings learn to obey rather than risk dissent, to suppress original ideas rather than be suspected of treason, to praise the present rather than pursue a better future, to seek conformity in order to succeed, to live in fear. Communism, which moved to elevate the masses, has reduced those very people who would be the hope of its future to the level of its most dishonest, its least idealistic. Moreover, the prosperity which was its promise is not in sight, primarily because prosperity does not come from people who fear innovation. Therefore, Konrád points out, even the basic necessities are beyond the reach of most people, and thus private life cannot provide a pleasant refuge from the repression of the public world. Because the economy fails, deprived of the stimulus of ideas, salaries are low, and workers must struggle for food; because state-provided housing is insufficient, again because of the suppression of ideas as well as the overwhelming corruption, several generations are stuffed into tiny flats, where they quarrel, making home life as miserable as factory work.

The city builder hungers for a society not controlled by bureaucrats and spies, for a society in which differences of opinion are reflected in public meetings, in school discussions, in newspaper articles, in free elections, in real universities, in sidewalk performances, and even in graffiti. Clearly, those in power have betrayed the Revolution for which so many died. In an earlier time, the city builder's son would have been a leader in the struggle for freedom. In the society which pretended to bring freedom to the oppressed, he has been destroyed; sadly, the destruction of its natural leaders by this society frightened of ideas is leading the society, and the city which represents it, to its own stagnation and decline.

*Critical Context*

The justice of George Konrád's indictment of his Communist Hungary is evidenced by the fact that only his first book, *A látogató* (1969; *The Case Worker*, 1974), was printed in Hungary and that despite his growing international reputation only that work is mentioned in contemporary Hungarian literary histories. Budapest bookstores do not stock any of Konrád's works. Obviously they must be circulated privately, for intellectuals who will not discuss them are clearly familiar with them.

*The Case Worker* evidently did not offend the authorities because it did not seem to criticize the system, but instead expressed the frustration of a juvenile welfare worker whose acceptance of the realities of slum life is challenged by his feelings of responsibility for a five-year-old retarded child, whose parents have committed suicide. Even though *The Case Worker* denies the easy official optimism of Communism and points out the fact that society has no real answers for such problems, it does not focus on the shortcomings of the system, as do Konrád's later works.

While *The City Builder* lacks the unity which was provided by the earlier novel's focus on the relationship between two individuals and on one immediate problem, substituting the relationships between the narrator and his city, his parents and grandparents, his wife and his son, for a single, clearer line of development, it is a memorable book, primarily for moving scenes, such as those of the flood and of the earthquake, and for clearly realized characters, such as the father, the wife, and the son. In the book which followed *The City Builder*, *A cinkos* (1980; *The Loser*, 1982), Konrád moves from the essaylike technique, which can lose the reader, to more careful plotting and therefore to a stunning effect. As he has developed, it is clear that Konrád is one of the most important voices from contemporary Eastern Europe.

*Sources for Further Study*

Kessler, Jascha. Review in *The New York Times Book Review.* LXXXIII (January 22, 1978), pp. 13, 21.

Lardner, Susan. Review in *The New Yorker*. LIV (April 10, 1978), pp. 141-143.

Sanders, Ivan. "Freedom's Captives: Notes on George Konrád's Novels," in *World Literature Today*. LVII (Spring, 1983), pp. 210-214.

_____. "Human Dialogues Are Born," in *The Nation*. CCIV (April 23, 1977), pp. 504-506.

Solataroff, Ted. "The Weight of History," in *The New Republic*. CLXXXVIII (February 14, 1983), pp. 28-33.

*Rosemary M. Canfield-Reisman*

# CLOSELY WATCHED TRAINS

*Author:* Bohumil Hrabal (1914-    )
*Type of plot:* Impressionistic realism
*Time of plot:* During World War II
*Locale:* A provincial railroad station in German-occupied Czechoslovakia
*First published: Ostře sledované vlaky*, 1965 (English translation, 1968)

>   *Principal characters:*
>       MILOŠ HRMA, the narrator, a young train dispatcher
>       LADISLAV HUBIČKA, an older dispatcher, who is experienced
>           with women
>       LÁNSKÝ, the stationmaster
>       VIRGINIA SVATÁ, the station telegraphist
>       MARSHA, a young conductor, Miloš' girlfriend
>       VIKTORIA FREIE, a member of the anti-Nazi underground,
>           Miloš' first lover

*The Novel*

*Closely Watched Trains* tells the story of a young man's coming of age in Nazi-occupied Czechoslovakia. The novella, written in the first person, presents a wry account of the protagonist's comic struggles to achieve manhood. The plot unfolds in a series of disconnected episodes, using flashbacks, plot compression, and surrealistic imagery to unify the narration. The dreamlike tone is enhanced by the portraits of ordinary people surviving extraordinary events.

Miloš Hrma, the protagonist, is an apprentice railroad dispatcher working in a small station in a provincial Czech town. The time is the winter of 1945, during the final months of World War II, when the Nazis are fighting desperately to maintain their eastern front against advancing Soviet troops. The Nazis have already lost the air war over Czechoslovakia, and Allied dive-bombers are continually disrupting German rail transportation to the front. The countryside is littered with debris from aerial dogfights. Miloš has just returned to his dispatcher's post after being away on sick leave for three months, having cut his wrists in a hotel bathroom after finding himself unable to make love with his girlfriend. Though he is twenty-two, he has never been with a woman, and he lacks self-confidence. His fear of impotence led to his attempted suicide, though the townspeople think he did it simply to avoid work.

Miloš comes from an eccentric family. His great-grandfather, a retired army pensioner, was beaten to death by a group of unemployed quarry workers. His grandfather, a circus hypnotist, was crushed when he tried to prevent

German tanks from entering Prague. His father, a retired railroad engineer, collects scrap metal.

Miloš' troubles began when he took his girlfriend Masha to spend a weekend at her uncle's photography studio in Prague. Miloš was sleeping in the studio, under a backdrop of a large airplane, in front of which people had themselves photographed as pilots and observers. During the night, Masha came in and pressed herself against him. They embraced and were about to make love when Miloš wilted. Disappointed, Masha crept back to her aunt's room, leaving Miloš embarrassed and humiliated. The absurd scene climaxes when a bomb from an Allied raid blows the wall of the studio away and exposes a sign among the scattered debris: FINISHED IN FIVE MINUTES.

On Miloš' first day at work after recuperating from his suicide attempt, he learns that dispatcher Ladislav Hubička, who prides himself on being a ladies' man, has got himself into trouble for printing station stamps on the backside of the lady telegraphist, Virginia Svatá. The girl's mother has threatened to complain to the Gestapo.

Miloš contrasts his suicide attempt with his behavior during a real test of his courage when he is taken hostage aboard a German close-surveillance military transport train. The train has been delayed by the Czech dispatchers in his district, even though it was ordered to be cleared—an act that could be considered sabotage. He is taken aboard the locomotive by the German SS commander and two young guards, who hold automatic pistols to his side. Miloš is certain that he will be killed, but the commander notices the scars on his wrists and decides to release him. Miloš' colleagues at the station welcome him back, just as Slušný, the traffic chief, arrives to hold the inquiry about Hubička's behavior.

Disciplinary action is soon recommended against Hubička. Undeterred, Hubička proposes that he and Miloš try to sabotage a German ammunition train. The two men arrange a caution signal to slow the German transport long enough for Miloš to drop a bomb into one of the middle cars. Miloš must stand on the signal tower above the track, with the explosives, waiting for the train to approach. The bomb is smuggled into the station by Viktoria Freie, a Resistance fighter, who initiates Miloš into the mysteries of love on the stationmaster's couch. Once Miloš has thus proved his manhood, he is ready for his final challenge—blowing up the German ammunition train. He also feels confident enough now to agree to visit Masha again on her next free day.

Later that snowy evening, as the German train approaches the station, it whistles for an all-clear signal. As Miloš climbs the signal tower with the bomb under his arm, the signal turns green and the train approaches. Miloš waits until the fourteenth car passes and drops the bomb exactly in the middle of the train. As the last car departs, Miloš is spotted by the guard and the two men fire at each other. Both are wounded, and Miloš falls from the

signal tower as the guard drops from the rear of the train. The men embrace
in a macabre dance of death, one shot in the lungs and the other in the stomach. The German's legs move in a frenzy of pain, and Miloš shoots him in the
head before he himself weakens from his own wound. He holds the dead
German's hands as the ammunition train blows up in the distance. As he
loses consciousness, Miloš repeats into the ears of the dead German soldier,
"You should have stayed at home."

### The Characters

Miloš, the narrator-protagonist of *Closely Watched Trains*, is an ordinary
young man trying to grow up in a world distorted by forces beyond his control; Miloš has the misfortune to come of age during the Nazi occupation of
Czechoslovakia. Not only must he cope with the usual adjustments of gender
and identity, but he must also decide whether to join the Czech Resistance.
In his poetic account of Miloš' coming of age, Bohumil Hrabal stresses his
ordinary, even antiheroic qualities: his innocence and immaturity, his lack of
family distinction, his timidity and inexperience with women, and his over-
reaction to his problem with his girlfriend. The rich humor and pathos of this
novel arise from Miloš' fumbling attempts to come to terms with his absurd
situation. At times, he seems to be something of a Chaplinesque character,
asserting his humanity in a world largely hostile and indifferent to his needs.
Miloš wants to do his duty and prove himself as a man, though his first efforts are inadequate. The emotional complexity of his responses to his dilemma create the poignant comic tone of Hrabal's novella.

The two poles of Miloš' world are love and war. In each, he must prove his
ability in order to gain self-respect and overcome his postadolescent dif-
fidence. In a series of comic episodes, Miloš fails or succeeds not so much
through his own efforts as through chance. He has been in love with the
young conductor, Masha, ever since they kissed through a fence while painting at the railway yards. Masha, in turn, shows affection for Miloš, but
before they can consummate their love, Miloš must be initiated by an older
and more experienced woman, Viktoria Freie. Hrabal shows wisdom and humor in dealing with the problems of sex. Miloš' failure to make love to
Masha and his subsequent embarrassment are humanizing touches that make
his later heroism all the more impressive.

The other characters in *Closely Watched Trains* are comic caricatures who
sustain the tone of wry, earthy humor. Stationmaster Lánský is ambitious but
inept, a middle-aged, portly, balding prig who abuses his wife (and is in turn
abused by her), keeps pigeons, and shouts his frustrations into the heating
vent in his station. Mrs. Lánská is a heavyset housewife, beyond her middle
years, who is both shocked and sympathetic when Miloš comes to her for
advice about women. The train dispatcher, Hubička, is a flyspecked Lothario
whose nonchalance is somehow irresistible to women. His prowess evokes

jealousy in the stationmaster and awe in young Miloš, who envies his ease with women.

The women in this novel seem underdeveloped and serve primarily as foils for the protagonist. Miloš' mother and Mrs. Lánská merge as nondescript maternal figures—sources of comfort and consolation for the protagonist rather than self-motivated characters. Masha is young and sweet, with shiny cheeks, strong arms, and healthy instincts. The equestrian, Countess Kinská, is merely the object of Hubička's erotic daydreams, and even the well-endowed Viktoria Freie seems little more than a projection of male fantasies.

The other minor figures are stock characters. Miloš' father, grandfather, and great-grandfather are all allergic to work, content to "stroll their way through life." They serve perhaps as humorous allusions to the Czech willingness to enjoy life without strenuous exertion. Traffic chief Slušný and Councillor Zednicek are recognizable as Nazi collaborators, and the Nazis themselves are uniformly villains, though Hrabal does show some sympathy for the bald train guard whom Miloš shoots at the end of the story.

## Themes and Meanings

Despite its wry comedy, Hrabal's novella conveys a deep sense of the tragedy and futility of war, especially in its impact on ordinary people. There are no heroes in this book—only small people trying to cope with the disruptions and chaos of war. Hrabal's lack of ideological conformity typifies the experimental literature that emerged during the Prague Spring, the brief period of liberalization before the Soviet invasion in 1968. The setting may be World War II, but, as with so much of the contemporary literature of Central and Eastern Europe, there is a subtext that points to the misfortunes of history and geography that have denied small nations the right to self-determination. There is an intimation, in Miloš' fate, of the tragicomedy of individuals and nations pitted against events beyond their control.

## Critical Context

Though Hrabal's short-story collection, *Automat svět* (1966; *The Death of Mr. Baltisberger*, 1975), has also been translated into English, he is still little known to English readers, and *Closely Watched Trains* may be his best-known work. Hrabal collaborated with director Jiří Menzel in writing the screenplay for the brilliant film version of *Closely Watched Trains*, which won an Academy Award in 1967 as the best foreign film of the year. Hrabal's forte is clearly the light, ironic tale, or bagatelle, in the manner of the *fin de siècle* Viennese authors, who wrote complex and sophisticated tales of ordinary people forced to cope with circumstances beyond their control. In their struggles, even if they fail, they reveal their human and appealing qualities. Hrabal's works are much more impressive than the dull grist of Socialist

Realism that constitutes so much of postwar Czech literature. Hrabal's whimsical point of view in his work perhaps reflects the difficult circumstances of his own career. He studied law but was unable to practice during the Nazi occupation, during which time he worked at a variety of odd jobs. Hrabal did not begin his career as a writer until he was forty-eight, and though his output has been slight, his graceful, lyrical style and humane wisdom make him an appealing writer. Unfortunately, the Czech authorities suppressed his work after the 1968 Soviet invasion. All of his books were destroyed, and he was not rehabilitated until 1976. Along with fellow writer Milan Kundera, Hrabal stands as an important representative of postmodernist innovation in late twentieth century Czech literature.

*Sources for Further Study*

Hrabal, Bohumil. "Too Loud a Solitude," in *Cross Currents*. V (1986), pp. 279-332.

Škvorecký, Josef. "American Motifs in the Work of Bohumil Hrabal," in *Cross Currents*. I (1982), pp. 207-218.

_____. *Jiří Menzel and the History of the "Closely Watched Trains,"* 1982.

Souckova, Milada. *A Literary Satellite*, 1970.

*Andrew J. Angyal*

# THE CLOVEN VISCOUNT

*Author:* Italo Calvino (1923-1985)
*Type of plot:* Fable
*Time of plot:* The late eighteenth century
*Locale:* Terralba, a small state on the Italian coast
*First published: Il visconte dimezzato*, 1952 (English translation, 1962)

> *Principal characters:*
> VISCOUNT MEDARDO OF TERRALBA, a young Italian nobleman
> THE NARRATOR, a young boy of seven or eight, Medardo's
> nephew
> DR. TRELAWNEY, a shipwrecked English physician living in
> Terralba
> PAMELA, a young peasant girl

## The Novel

Medardo, the young Viscount of Terralba, goes off to fight the Turks, and in his first battle is blown apart by a cannon shot. The right-hand side of his body is saved by doctors, and Medardo returns home, half a man. Soon it is evident that Medardo's bad nature controls his maimed body. He tears apart one of his aged father's pet birds, and the old viscount soon dies. He tries to poison his nephew with deadly mushrooms. Medardo roams through the countryside, destroying things by halves: Pears are lopped in two as they hang on the trees; frogs are slashed in two as they sit by ponds.

The narrator and Dr. Trelawney, a shipwrecked English doctor, watch the Viscount as his actions grow more depraved. Medardo burns part of his own castle, and when Sebastiana, his old nursemaid, is scarred from the flames, he uses this as an excuse to exile her to Pratofungo, the seaside village of lepers. There seem to be no depths to which Medardo's evil half will not sink.

During one of his destructive rides through the countryside, the Viscount sees the young and beautiful Pamela tending her goats and ducks, and he falls in love with her. Yet even this passion is distorted in him. His messages to her to arrange meetings are such grisly mementos as halved bats and split jellyfish.

The other portion of the cloven viscount now returns to Terralba. This half is all good and soon embarks on a round of virtuous deeds: saving the narrator from the bite of a deadly spider, mending the sparrows maimed by the Medardo, and generally amazing people with his acts of goodness. Inevitably, he meets and falls in love with Pamela.

"The Good 'Un" and "The Bad 'Un," as the two halves of the Viscount are known to the people of Terralba, have a series of clashes which culminate at the marriage ceremony of Pamela and the better half of Medardo. A duel is arranged and the Viscount battles himself to a bloody draw. Dr. Trelawney quickly binds the two parts together, and Viscount Medardo is once again a single man, a normal mixture of good and bad.

## The Characters

The characters in *The Cloven Viscount* seem, at times, to be strictly stock figures: the good and the bad Medardo, symbolizing man's divided nature; the artless but beautiful goat girl, Pamela; the naïve young narrator, painfully discovering maturity; and the shrewd old nursemaid, unlettered but wise in the ways of the world.

In part, Italo Calvino is deliberately playing with these figures, arranging them in their expected postures to play their required roles. This is not unusual in a novel largely concerned with symbols and their use. On one level, then, the characters are themselves symbols, not realistic individuals.

This is true most obviously of Viscount Medardo, who spends most of the novel split into two parts, one of them thoroughly evil, the other unbearably good. Neither half of the cloven viscount would actually be able to exist in real life. This unreality allows Calvino to impress upon the reader that neither unadulterated evil nor good is possible in human lives. While this might seem a truism hardly worth mention, let alone elaboration, history might argue otherwise.

Calvino underscores this point further by the description of two communities which exist on the fringe of Terralban life: the Huguenots who live on the heights of Col Gerbido, and the lepers who inhabit Pratofungo. Each of these societies is flawed. The Huguenots have been separated from the rest of the world and their comrades for so long that they have forgotten all the essentials of their religion and no longer mention their faith at all, for fear of heresy. They have reduced their lives to an endless round of cheerless work rather than risk even inadvertent sin. The lepers, on the other hand, do nothing but make music and love throughout the day and night, forgetting their condition through constant revelry. Just as Medardo is split in two, so these communities divide the human condition in an arbitrary and untenable fashion.

Apart from the Viscount, most of the characters in the novel retain their stereotypical nature. The two exceptions are the narrator and Dr. Trelawney. The narrator, Medardo's nephew, grows in maturity and understanding throughout the work. By the end of the novel, the narrator has become more whole and unified, a development which parallels that of his uncle. The difference is that the young boy's metamorphosis is both more gradual and more realistic. This is fitting, because the young observer-narrator provides a factual, even unromantic, viewpoint on the fantastic events of *The Cloven Viscount*.

Dr. Trelawney also changes during the novel. At first he is detached, indif-

ferent to the people around him, interested only in his abstract and imprac-
tical experiments. Significantly, his chief concern during much of the book is
capturing will-o'-the-wisps from graves. As events unfold, however, Dr.
Trelawney gradually returns to practicing medicine and involving himself
with the human condition. He, like all the other characters in the work,
moves from a fragmented, isolated existence to a more unified, coherent life.

## Themes and Meanings

The central theme of *The Cloven Viscount* is the dichotomy between the
real and the ideal, and Calvino explores and presents this topic through a
variety of means.

The two sides of Medardo are known as "The Good 'Un" and "The Bad
'Un" by the people of Terralba, and both halves are unsatisfactory. "The Bad
'Un" is obviously a menace, hacking and burning his way through the
countryside, but "The Good 'Un" is equally, if more subtly, inhuman. His
meeting with the Huguenots at Col Gerbido, for example, is conducted with
decorum and excessive goodwill on both sides, but there is no real contact
between them, and the final effect is, in the narrator's words, "a bit chilling
on the whole." It is "The Good 'Un" who visits Pratofungo, the city of the
lepers, and argues them out of their carefree, if somewhat loose, lives. Deprived of that solace, they must face their disease and shattered bodies.

To those persons forced to endure it, unreal good is as dismal as unreal
evil. "Thus the days went by at Terralba, and our sensibilities became
numbed, since we felt ourselves lost between an evil and a virtue equally
inhuman."

The theme of unreality versus reality is further compounded in a corollary
topic, life as a series of symbols. Throughout the book, the central characters
refuse to face experience directly, but mediate it through signs and symbols.
The evil Medardo, for example, leaves a trail of bizarre messages for Pamela:
parsnips cut in two, daisies half stripped from their stalks, and chopped bits
of bats, birds, and jellyfish.

In a similar fashion, the good Medardo leaves iconic messages for Dr.
Trelawney, alerting him to the ills of Terralba's residents. He ties feeding
chickens to a terrace railing, their droppings indicating a case of diarrhea
inside the house; at another place, a row of snails diagnoses heart disease
within, and instructs the doctor to enter quietly. Life becomes a series of
mystical symbols to be read and deciphered, rather than events to be
experienced.

Much the same is true of Dr. Trelawney, whose interests early in the novel
are abstract and purely scientific. The narrator remarks on Trelawney's un-
concern with the patients who might need his services. The doctor's growing
involvement with sick persons and their cure is an echo of the integration of
Medardo through the fusing of his good and bad halves, and it is revealing

that Dr. Trelawney is the one who binds the two halves of the Viscount together. Calvino seems to tell the reader that a truly human being cannot be purely good or purely evil, as with the Viscount, or purely intellectual, as with Dr. Trelawney. Paradoxically, for humans to be whole is to be something less than perfect.

*Critical Context*

*The Cloven Viscount* is similar to other works by Calvino, such as *Il barone rampante* (1957; *The Baron in the Trees*, 1959) and *Il cavaliere inesistente* (1959; *The Non-existent Knight*, 1962). Three characteristics unify these books: They are about a past based on reality, yet transformed by imagination; they present fantastic events in a straightforward style; and they are concerned with the opposition of artifice and reality, symbol and fact.

These are themes and techniques which also appear in other works by Calvino, along with a rich fund of understated humor based on shrewd observation of human life. Beneath the wit, beneath the dazzling artistry, beneath the double-edged symbolism, however, Calvino's works have a profound and deeply rooted concern with the passions and problems of human life. *The Cloven Viscount* is a work about a number of subjects, but at its core it is concerned with people, how they live, how they make contact with one another, and how they grow and accept life.

When the young narrator of *The Cloven Viscount* hears that Dr. Trelawney is leaving with the famous Captain Cook, he rushes to the harbor: "But already the ships were vanishing over the horizon and I was left behind, in this world of ours full of responsibilities and will-o'-the-wisps." This combination of hard fact and fantasy, of duties and dreams, is characteristic not only of *The Cloven Viscount* but also of all Calvino's works, and it is his witty yet essentially serious exploration of these themes that makes him an enjoyable and an important author.

*Sources for Further Study*

Andrews, Richard. "Italo Calvino," in *Writers and Society in Contemporary Italy: A Collection of Essays*, 1984. Edited by Michael Caesar and Peter Hainsworth.
Calvino, Italo. *The Uses of Literature*, 1986.
Carter, Albert Howard. *Italo Calvino: Metamorphoses of Fantasy*, 1987.
Olken, I. T. *With Pleated Eye and Garnet Wing: Symmetries of Italo Calvino*, 1984.

*Michael Witkoski*

# THE CLOWN

*Author:* Heinrich Böll (1917-1985)
*Type of plot:* Social criticism
*Time of plot:* c. 1962, during the Economic Miracle
*Locale:* Bonn, West Germany
*First published: Ansichten eines Clowns*, 1963 (English translation, 1965)

> *Principal characters:*
> HANS SCHNIER, a professional clown
> MARIE DERKUM, Hans's beloved
> ALFONS SCHNIER, Hans's father, director of a coal-mining firm
> LEO, Hans's brother, a student at a Catholic seminary
> PRELATES SOMMERWILD, KINKEL, and ZÜPFNER, Catholic
> functionaries in Bonn

*The Novel*

*The Clown* is a first-person narrative which exposes the accommodations of postwar West German society to the success of the Economic Miracle, that astounding industrial recovery after the destruction of World War II. Members of the highest circles of society, with representatives from church and state as well as the military and industry, have conveniently forgotten the recent past in order to further their personal or institutional successes. They are conformists who no longer recognize their hypocritical existences—until reminded by a renegade clown. For his continued impudence, the clown must suffer without recourse. He lacks the unscrupulous behavior (often disguised as piety, generosity, and human concern) with which the others can so easily dispatch him.

Three months after his girlfriend, Marie Derkum, has left him, Hans Schnier falls during a drunken performance in Bochum and injures his knee. His career is faltering as he returns alone and destitute to his hometown of Bonn. From his apartment, he communicates with family, friends, and acquaintances by telephone, ostensibly to borrow money but also to rally support to reclaim "his" Marie. These calls are interspersed with his memories of past events. Thus, gradually, the chronology of the entire story unfolds. The novel's action spans no more than four hours on a March evening.

First, Hans telephones his mother, an "incredibly stupid, and stingy" woman. A German nationalist and racist during the war, when she sent her only daughter Henrietta to fight (and die) on the home front, she is now on the executive committee of the Societies for the Reconciliation of Racial Differences. Hans cannot bring himself to beg for money from this hypocrite, so he insults her with memories of her injustices during the Third Reich and hangs up.

During unsuccessful attempts to telephone his brother, Leo, in a seminary,

Hans recalls his seduction of Marie six years before, their affair or "marriage," her two miscarriages, and her leaving him in Hanover after meeting the Catholics Sommerwild and Züpfner. He is prompted to phone Fredebeul and then Kinkel, a liberal Catholic "thinker." He realizes that he may gain some degree of satisfaction from insulting these opportunists, but such behavior will not help him regain Marie.

Just before his bath, Hans's telephone rings. His agent, Zohnerer, advises him to forget his "childish" drinking, to train conscientiously for three months, and then to resume his career. Here, Hans repeats his dictum that, by age fifty, a clown has either made it to the palace or to the gutter; he must certainly realize that, at age twenty-seven, he is already not far from the gutter. Still, he cannot concentrate on his career. He weeps when thinking of Marie, Leo, Henrietta, and his father—people who have played significant roles in his past and are now effectively gone from his life.

In the pivotal thirteenth chapter (the structural and literal midpoint of the book), Prelate Sommerwild telephones Hans. Hans learns that Marie has married Züpfner and is now on her honeymoon, on the way to Rome, probably for an audience with the Pope. With Sommerwild's official confirmation of the marriage ceremony, despair sets in.

Hans's melancholy is interrupted by the doorbell. His father, Alfons Schnier, has come to hire an expert trainer and, thus, subsidize Hans's career, but Hans insists that he does not require an expert, only money. Despite their mutual respect, his father cannot give money to someone who will simply spend it and not invest it. Both father and son respect each other and yearn for the contact of a warm and loving relationship. Because of their differing attitudes, however, they can find no common ground, and the father leaves.

Finally Hans's brother, Leo, calls. Hans has pinned his greatest hopes on Leo, who has always been considerate and extremely generous with his limited funds. Unfortunately, Leo has little money and cannot come this evening. (He has a curfew in the seminary and will not break it.) In addition, Leo now seems to have joined the Catholic establishment that is trying to separate Hans from Marie. Disillusioned, Hans hangs up on his brother, thus forfeiting his last hope for outside help.

In desperation, Hans paints his face deathly white with cold cream; when dry, this mask begins to flake and crack, creating a deathly visage. He then takes his guitar and leaves for the train station, where he will sit on the steps, singing liturgical music and protest songs until Marie returns to the station from her Roman honeymoon. Her reaction, upon seeing Hans in misery, will determine his fate: She will either embrace him, and all will be well again; or she will ignore him, signaling his complete desolation. Since it is March and the middle of Mardi Gras, however, his garish appearance cannot be distinguished from those of the many costumed revelers. Is he to sit there throughout Lent as a sign of protest or penance? Will he be able to rise above his persecution as the religious season might imply, or will he commit suicide in recognition of his hopeless fate, as his death mask suggests?

## The Characters

Hans, as a clown, immediately evokes several cultural and historical associations. First, he is Pagliacci, the clown who is "laughing on the outside, crying on the inside" as a result of his separation from Marie. Despite his spontaneity and innocence, at the age of twenty-seven he is no longer a romantic youth but a mature adult who has not joined the establishment because of his nature and profession. He is not an acquisitive materialist; he enjoys simple pleasures such as playing Parcheesi, taking long baths, reading newspapers, singing liturgical music, and making love with Marie.

Second, Hans conforms to the archetype of the medieval fool, who, because of his fool's freedom, is allowed to speak openly; that is, he has official permission to make any statement, regardless of its veracity, as long as it is entertaining. Ironically, these pronouncements frequently represent truth or wisdom. As a clown, Hans shows audiences the comic nature of their everyday routine, the foolishness behind their overly serious drive to succeed and acquire. Hans's strength of character and single-minded purpose make him a sympathetic individual even though, in his private life, Hans cannot help but alienate those powerful figures whose lives he exposes.

Though Hans is an artist, and the reader learns much about his life-style and preferences, his experiences and convictions, this work is not primarily a *Künstlerroman*. Heinrich Böll uses the artist as an outsider, a knowledgeable but distanced observer of German society—most specifically, the influential circles of church and industry—with a strong personal interest in the outcome. Hans is innocent but not naïve; he observes and understands the power structure but without any desire to participate. Nevertheless, society cannot tolerate such an individual who, through his art, brings insight into the hypocrisy of everyday life.

Marie is a mysterious figure throughout the novel. She vacillates between her love and devotion to Hans and to the Church. She does not actually appear in the novel, other than through Hans's recollections and references from other characters. Why she ultimately left Hans to rejoin the Church and marry Züpfner is unclear. Feminist critics have emphasized Hans's ignorance of her individuality, but this argument is specious: Marie had made many choices of her own free will to reconcile with Hans after their inevitable lovers' quarrels, and he was the one who encouraged her wavering faith by waking her Sunday mornings to attend Mass. Regardless of her motivation, it is imperative for the novel's development that Marie, the one person in this outsider's life, be separated from him. He had hoped to live quietly with Marie on the fringe of society but soon learns that society will not allow him to do so. Now, completely alone, Hans is motivated to "fight for her," to voice his objections to the hypocrites and conformists who have stunted his development.

Though politicians and members of the military are criticized in passing, the industrial Schnier family and church hierarchy are the main targets of *The Clown*. The Schnier family itself represents a cross section of German society: the sister, Henrietta, is the innocent civilian killed in the futile war effort; the brother, Leo, is the uncertain youth who denies his heritage and converts to Catholicism, studying in the seminary and, thus, denying his worldly existence; the mother is the blind patriot, and materialist who adapts to prevailing social trends without hesitation; the father is the sensitive but responsible industrialist, brave in time of need but ultimately made impotent by his rigid standards of property and propriety. Of the entire family, Hans is the only one who will not, indeed cannot, forget the past.

There are several characters who represent different aspects of the Catholic establishment, including Sommerwild, Fredebeul, Kinkel, and Blothert, for example, though it is difficult to distinguish between them. They represent types more than distinct personalities, since their conformity tends to obliterate any distinguishing traits.

### Themes and Meanings

This work could be categorized as the first telephone novel in literary history. With the exception of his father's visit and a brief encounter in the hall with a neighbor's wife, Hans's contact with the outside world is maintained exclusively by means of this modern instrument. While Böll is able to create telephone dialogues as effective as traditional dramatic discourse, such conversations serve primarily as stimuli; they trigger Hans's memory, and the recollections, in turn, constitute the bulk of the novel. The various conversations also lend credibility to the predominantly subjective narrative stance from which Hans Schnier tells his own story; his monologues and memories could be seen as the mistaken ramblings of a paranoid young man were it not for corroborative statements made in these telephone conversations.

A recurring theme in Böll's works concerns the reactions of contemporary society to its guilt-ridden past of Fascism and war. Since society has repressed its historical past in favor of reconstruction and restoration, there is no one but this obscure clown to provide a social conscience. His commentary—indeed, his presence—is unwelcome, as it exposes hypocrisy in the highest circles. For Böll, the one institution which most dramatically exemplifies contemporary hypocrisy is the Catholic Church; since Böll has chosen Bonn as the site for this work, the Church there should be seen as representative of all West Germany. The primary aspect of the novel which calls the Church's hierarchy into question revolves around the timeless sanctity of marriage: Is marriage derived from a spiritual or a legal base? Is the Church's blessing vital to its existence? Finally, is marriage even possible in a corrupt society? These are questions that arise when Hans argues that his unlegitimized relationship with Marie was "moral," and that her present marriage (though legal in the eyes of the Church) is prostitution.

Böll intended such bold distinctions to provoke a thoughtful response to present practices within a church which has long prized its historical and theological mission of mercy and salvation. In Böll's works, the Church as an institution has aligned itself with the existing power structure to secure its own position within the status quo. Its representatives are no longer shepherds of the flock but personalities whose fashionable intellectual stance has perverted their mission. No church official of significance in the entire novel displays mercy, tolerance, or understanding of Hans's individual plight. In fact, they seem to be scheming either to incorporate him into the Church or to isolate him completely from society—in either case, to render him harmless. The ultimate antidote to this attitude is offered in the epigraph to the novel, a biblical quotation from Romans 15:21: "To whom he was not spoken of, they shall see; and they that have not heard shall understand."

*Critical Context*

*The Clown* was an immediate best-seller. (It was later produced as a play in 1970 and as a film in 1975, though without the success of the novel.) The novel represented a break from Böll's previous fiction, which had concentrated on experiences from the war. Beginning in the early 1960's, in fiction and in increasingly frequent essays, Böll critically examined postwar institutions as agents of restoration or corruption.

Böll originally began *The Clown* as a third-person narrative but soon allowed Hans to tell his own story. As one of Böll's few "active" heroes, however, Hans offered a solution which was neither practical in his own immediate situation nor a model for West German social protest in general. The novel was considered scandalous from the outset for its criticism of the Catholic Church. Böll repeatedly insisted that he was always faithful to that religion and, despite his withdrawal from the Church in his later life, must be considered a Catholic who attempted to improve an institution that he loved.

*Sources for Further Study*

Bernhard, Hans Joachim. *Die Romane Heinrich Bölls*, 1970.

Conard, Robert C. "Novels of Intensified Social Criticism and the Abandonment of Social Integration," in *Heinrich Böll*, 1981.

Hinck, Walter. " 'Ansichten eines Clowns'—heute," in *Böll: Untersuchungen zum Werk*, 1975.

Reid, James Henderson. "The Artist Novels," in *Heinrich Böll*, 1973.

Vogt, Jochen. "Der Clown als Stellvertreter," in *Heinrich Böll*, 1978.

*Todd C. Hanlin*

# A COIN IN NINE HANDS

*Author:* Marguerite Yourcenar (Marguerite de Crayencour, 1903-1987)
*Type of plot:* Social realism
*Time of plot:* 1933
*Locale:* Rome
*First published: Denier du rêve*, 1934; revised, 1959 (English translation, 1982)

>*Principal characters:*
>MARCELLA SARTE, a revolutionary who attempts to assassinate
>    Benito Mussolini
>MASSIMO, a double agent who is drawn to Marcella but is
>    disturbed at her ardor
>ROSALIA DI CREDO, a dislocated woman who longs for her
>    ancestral home in Sicily

## The Novel

*A Coin in Nine Hands* is a novel about a social group and about a period, the reign of Benito Mussolini in 1933. Marguerite Yourcenar uses the device of the circulating ten-lira coin to link her diverse characters, but they are also linked by the period and by the effect Mussolini had on each of them. The first three characters whom the reader encounters are all in search of some illusion that will enable them to survive. For example, Paolo Farina can still think of himself as a desirable man when the Roman prostitute, Lina Chiari, goes to bed with him. Lina can face the world with the help of cosmetics she purchases from Giulio. Giulio's difficulties are more complex—his wife is a shrew, his daughter's husband, Carlo, is in jail, and his daughter, Vanna, and her sick child live with Giulio—and his consoling illusion is the Catholic church. The relationships between these people are primarily commercial rather than human; they are selling and buying illusions.

Rosalia di Credo's story is somewhat different; her difficulty is her inability to recover or return to the family home, Gemera, in Sicily. Nevertheless, while Rosalia idealizes that home, its description and history suggest that it is merely another comforting illusion. Not only is Gemera decayed and decrepit, but its springs have dried up as well. In addition, Rosalia was driven from the decaying mansion by the enraged villagers, who think that her father is a demon. Rosalia comes to Rome with her mother to live out a meager existence. Rosalia's illusion of a return to Gemera is shattered when she receives a letter from her father announcing that Gemera is to be sold and torn down. Her response to the death of an illusion is to spend the ten-lira coin given to her by Giulio to buy hot coals, which she spreads upon her bed, making it her funeral pyre. When people rush into her apartment after seeing the smoke, they find a Rosalia who is "peaceful," who has "just reached the foot of a nocturnal, monstrous Gemera."

The next chapter, the central one in the book, brings together Vanna, Massimo, Dr. Sarte, and his wife, Marcella. Each wants something different. Vanna wishes to have her husband return, and she is "radiant" when she hears that Carlo has retracted his "errors." Marcella, the revolutionary, wants a dead martyr for her anti-Fascist cause rather than a living Carlo. Dr. Sarte, like Vanna, is worldly and opposed to the romantic idealism of Marcella. He and Marcella have separated because of a difference in political and social views. He informs Marcella that Carlo has died on the prison island of Lipari; this news, and the news that Massimo is a double agent, however, do not reduce her ardor for her revolutionary ideals. Instead, she is provoked to act; she tells her husband that she is going to assassinate Mussolini with the gun that she has taken from his desk. Dr. Sarte is not appalled by this proposed action; he is a student of human character and, although a Fascist, not committed to the cause of Mussolini. He even tells Marcella that he will be nearby to witness this intriguing event. Marcella passes the ten-lira coin to her husband as payment for his gun and as a symbol of her commitment. Marcella next tells Massimo of her plan, and a debate ensues; he argues that it would be a useless gesture, but she remains committed to the act—even if it is meaningless. She describes herself as doing "the dirty work no one else would do."

During the attempted assassination, Marcella thinks that she has been released from her flesh and become "pure strength." A moment later, she sees the act as absurd, yet at the crucial moment "she raised her arm, fired—and missed." She has put her illusions into action rather than rely on them to soothe her, as others have done, but the result is merely ridiculous.

The next chapter deals with Angiola Farina and is almost a commentary on the previous action of Marcella. Angiola is in a motion-picture theater watching her screen idol, Angiola Fides, whom she uses to supply the missing romance in her life. Dr. Sarte, whose wife has just played out a cinematic action, sees Angiola as an easy sexual conquest, and they enact a scene similar to that in the film they have just watched. They part, with Angiola in pursuit of a marriage to an Australian lord and Dr. Sarte in pursuit of some meaning in his life. Since Marcella has not met him as arranged, Dr. Sarte thinks that she also lacks courage, like everyone else in this society, but a bystander tells him that some madwoman attempted and failed to assassinate Mussolini and has been shot down. The chapter ends with a gruesome and realistic description of Marcella's body lying on a Roman street.

The rest of the novel is anticlimactic. Old Mother Dida is a miser who extracts work and profit from everyone with whom she comes in contact. Her old habits and thrift drive her, and she seems unable to change. At the end of the chapter, however, a slight transformation does occur. She is walking by a dark street in Rome, when she sees a poor man whom she distinguishes from the usual run of derelicts. She gives him the ten-lira coin that Dr. Sarte had given her earlier for flowers. Nevertheless, this realistic woman, who seems to have altered suddenly, falls prey to the same errors and illusions that the others do. The man to whom she has given the coin is not a poverty-stricken wretch but an artist suffering from angina.

The mistaken beggar, Clement Roux, and the enigmatic Massimo next encounter each other. Roux is an artist who mourns for the loss of the Rome he had known thirty years earlier. He meets Massimo, who is attempting to mourn for Marcella or find some expiation for his failure either to join or to prevent her attempt. Massimo has seen Roux's self-portrait in a museum and knows who he is, but they still talk at cross-purposes. Massimo continually refers to the attempted assassination, while Roux talks about either his art or his past. Roux, who is seventy, has had no experience with the realities of life; he was even too old for World War I, in which his brother died. In contrast, Massimo is twenty-two and seems to have experienced too much reality to be able to bear it. Roux's thoughts are of art and beauty, while Massimo's are of war, torture, and assassination. As they are about to part, Roux takes the ten-lira coin he received from Mother Dida and throws it into the recess of a rock, rather than into Massimo's hand. Roux is leaving Rome because of the climate and the changes brought about by the modern world. He leaves Massimo to the streets, as he returns to his comfortable home and the perceived safety it creates.

The last chapter of the book is a suitably fragmented survey of all the major characters in the novel. Paolo sleeps and is still unaware. Giulio is once more annoyed at the talk of his women and cannot sleep. Dr. Sarte is being interrogated by the authorities about his knowledge of his wife, Marcella, but remains in control of himself. Lina Chiari is lying on her bed thinking of Massimo—who is not thinking of her—and of her breast cancer. Angiola dreams of Angiola Fides, and Massimo collapses in weariness. Oreste Marinuzzi, a new character, appears and finds the coin, using it to get drunk and pass out—which makes him "as happy as a dead man."

*The Characters*

There is no one central character in *A Coin in Nine Hands*; instead, several characters have a tenuous relationship with one another and share a common need for illusion or obliteration. No one strives for meaningful action or consciousness; they simply act out predetermined roles or wear appropriate masks. Yourcenar's other novels are very different, especially *Mémoires d'Hadrien* (1951; *Memoirs of Hadrian*, 1954). One critic makes the differences clear: "In that early work, Yourcenar made modern characters of mythical ones. Here [*A Coin in Nine Hands*], she has reversed the process. Marcella, the assassin, is seen not as a modern woman, but as a doomed spirit of revenge." Yourcenar has also described her characterization as mythic; she suggests that "Massimo is of course Thanatos, the angel of death [and] Marinuzzi is Dionysus."

Two other characters deserve mention. Dr. Sarte is, in contrast to most of the others, objective and aloof. He is not the victim of illusion but sees the world as it is. He is, moreover, an opportunist who is using Fascism rather than being used by it. Nevertheless, he wants and needs to reestablish his relationship with Marcella, since without it, his life is empty. Another disinterested character is Massimo. He is the product of the modern world, not of Marcella's mythic one. He has been initiated by "hunger, war, escape, being arrested at the border." His only value is survival in a meaningless world.

### Themes and Meanings

The most important theme of *A Coin in Nine Hands* is the need for illusion in life. Without such illusions, most of the characters in the book would be unable to exist. The only two who live in reality, Dr. Sarte and Massimo, seem to be miserable. Clearly, the demand for supporting illusions is related to the political situation of 1933. Fascism seems to be an illusion in itself but not one that comforts the people; instead, it drives them deeper into other substitutes for life. Thus Mussolini is at the heart of the novel, even though his name is never mentioned and he is referred to only as "Caesar."

A related theme is the lack of love or even connection between man and woman. All the married couples are separated except for Giulio and his shrew of a wife. Potential relationships, such as those between Marcella and Massimo or Dr. Sarte and Angiola, are incomplete or distorted. One of the ideals of this Fascist state was family, but it seems to produce the opposite effect. Everyone, from the highest ranks—Dr. Sarte—to the lowest— Oreste—is alone. Yourcenar says that of one of the main purposes of the book is "to confront the hollow reality behind the bloated facade of Fascism," and it is nowhere more apparent than in these broken relationships.

### Critical Context

The reception of *A Coin in Nine Hands* has been mixed. Critics have usually praised the thematic content of the novel while damning the structure or technique. For example, one critic speaks of the novel as a "tragedy" which also depicts "the hope inherent in human lives." In contrast, another scathingly calls it a "disjointed and curiously artificial work, breathing a facile pathos." The fullest and most useful discussion of the novel is in *Marguerite Yourcenar in Counterpoint* (1983) by C. Frederick Farrell, Jr., and Edith R. Farrell; they place *A Coin in Nine Hands* into context with all Yourcenar's other works. Especially significant is the contrast with *Memoirs of Hadrian*; they point out that the characters in *Memoirs of Hadrian* are "introspective, and eminently capable of self analysis" while those in *A Coin in Nine Hands* are in need of "masks and mirrors."

Marguerite Yourcenar wrote eight novels, as well as plays, nonfiction, poems, and translations. Her best-known work is *Memoirs of Hadrian*. *A Coin in Nine Hands* is quite different from that famous novel on the Roman Empire, but it is also a novel that deals with a specific historical period. According to Yourcenar, in writing *A Coin in Nine Hands*, "Before me was a different set of models. For the first time in my life I felt aware of current events, of what was going on in that particular year of history, and I had to improvise my technique as the scene around me changed." Nevertheless, even though Yourcenar was dealing with the specific period of 1933, she gave the novel the mythic dimension that is present in all of her novels.

*Sources for Further Study*

Epstein, Joseph. "Read Marguerite Yourcenar!" in *Commentary*. LXXIV (August, 1982), pp. 60-65.

Farrell, C. Frederick, Jr., and Edith R. Farrell. *Marguerite Yourcenar in Counterpoint*, 1983.

Mellors, John. "A Coin in Nine Hands," in *Listener*. CIX (April 14, 1983), p. 32.

Weightman, John. "Adventures of a Ten-Lira Piece," in *The New York Times Book Review*. LXXXVIII (January 30, 1983), p. 10.

Yourcenar, Marguerite. *With Open Eyes: Conversations with Matthieu Galey*, 1984.

*James Sullivan*

# COMPANY

*Author:* Samuel Beckett (1906-    )
*Type of plot:* Internal narrative
*Time of plot:* The unspecified present
*Locale:* In the mind of the creator
*First published: Compagnie,* 1980 (English translation, 1980)

> *Principal characters:*
> A VOICE, which comes to one in the dark
> A LISTENER, who lies on his back in the dark
> ANOTHER, devising it all for company
> THE FATHER, who wanders the moors during his son's birth
> THE SON, who remembers his childhood and youth

## The Novel

"That then is the proposition. To one on his back in the dark a voice tells of the past." The action of *Company* is fundamentally the narration of stories by a voice to a listener lying in the typical Beckettian darkness. Some of the elements of the story are verifiable, some are conjecture, some are prediction. Like all Samuel Beckett's prose work, the narrative voice is that of the author, unable to cease telling stories, unable to express, yet obligated to express. Typical literary inquiries concerning the source of the voice, the identity of the supine figure on the ground, or the placement of the setting and time into a recognizable frame, cannot be satisfied in Beckettian novels; they are self-generating and self-referential, a trait of most postmodern fiction.

Uncharacteristic of Beckett's earlier prose, *Company* almost finds a way to discuss the undiscussable. It contains, embedded in the never-ending question of the reliability of the narrator, some poignant possible facts from a recognizable past, stories of childhood, and unforgettable moments in the memory of the listener. The narrative proceeds by a series of anecdotes told about the listener's childhood and youth. One story concerns the mother's reprimand at the child's innocent question about the nearness of the sky: "She shook off your little hand and made you a cutting retort you have never forgotten," the voice tells the listener. Another story describes the day of the listener's birth and his father's "tramp in the mountains" to avoid the noise and uneasiness of childbirth; suddenly, it is the listener himself who trudges along the narrow roads in the barren landscape. By means of stylistic techniques (perfected over a lifetime of writing in two languages), Beckett equates the listener with his father, whose "shade" accompanies him, "in his old tramping rags. Finally on side by side from nought anew."

Other stories keep the listener "company": an old woman who thought

she could fly, who tells the child "God save you little master"; the day the
child throws himself off the top of a great fir, the branches breaking his fall;
the hedgehog rescued by the child, only to die in its cage. As the stories
unfold, they are punctuated with further descriptions of the father/child
wandering in all weather through the moors outside his home. Interspersed
with the incessant self-examinations of the listener, the final story to be
pieced together is a love story involving an assignation in a log summerhouse,
a girl with long dark hair, and a quiet moment before the cycle of birth and
old age begins again.

Yet the most important "story" of *Company*, which encompasses all the
rest of the anecdotes, the wanderings in the landscape, and the attempts at
asserting epistemological truth, is the story of the need for "company." This
story is Beckett's way of expressing the mind's predilection for memories, for
"peopling" one's musings with recognizable characters and incidents from
one's real or imagined past. Thus the author, "devising it all for company,"
both invents and remembers, in order to avoid admitting the final existential
fact: There is no company; we are alone.

## The Characters

The term "character" does not apply comfortably to Beckett's novels, but
three figures form the main narrative in *Company*: a voice, disembodied,
neutral, without inflection, speaking in the second person ("You stand at the
tip of the high board. . . . You are alone in the garden"); a listener, on his
back in the dark, signified by the third person ("So with what reason remains
he reasons"); and "another" who hears the voice speaking to the listener and
ponders, "Is he not perhaps overhearing a communication not intended for
him?"

By exploiting the ambiguities inherent in pronouns with vague anteced-
ents, Beckett manages to blend the three "characters" into one unnamed
(because unnameable) first-person narrator who has "devised for company"
not only the normative characters residing in the stories (Mrs. Coote and Dr.
Hadden, for example) but also the speaking voice, the listener, and himself.
This "author" (a word Beckett does not use here) combines the traits of all
three: self-examining, suspicious by nature of the truth of all narration, obsessed with logic, overcareful of conclusions. It is, in fact, the singular creation which is found in all Beckett's prose work—the self-narrative presence,
Beckett's fictive equivalent of the self-defining existential man.

Two other characters deserve consideration as well. Through a technique
of gradual revelation, the father figure walking the moors becomes quite real
to the reader. He is dispassionate toward his son at birth, challenging of him
in youth ("He calls to you to jump. He calls, Be a brave boy"). The portrait
is one of reserve, of noncommunication, of isolation. The son as well becomes known to the reader: Sensitive to his parents' scorn, a loner, he tries

to capture the warm glow of their approval, but it dims quickly. After an unresolved love affair, he becomes old like his father, wandering the snowy pastures as he did, head bowed, listening to his own footsteps.

## Themes and Meanings

A succinct statement of Beckett's philosophy can be found in *Company*: He describes God as "Devised deviser devising it all for company." The traditional themes of isolation and doubt found in Beckett's work are joined here by a more poignant human emotional expression: loneliness. By reexamining the axioms of the Catechism, in which fundamental questions of God's motives in creating mankind are asked and answered, Beckett postulates that an immovable Prime Mover may have created the universe for "company," to alleviate a cosmic aloneness. Yet his thesis is by no means strictly metaphysical; the author himself may create characters for the same reason, as his sense of isolation overcomes him. Thus, the childhood memories that become stories from a voice to a listener are conjured up, partly remembered, partly reconstructed, partly made from whole cloth, to keep the author "company" in moments of unbearable loneliness. Beckett is submitting himself here to two kinds of personal exposure: the suggestion of autobiographical information regarding his relationship with his parents, and an undisguised admission of his own personal reasons for writing.

Any summary of Beckett's themes and meanings must necessarily reduce to banality what are, in fact, immensely complex metaphysical, aesthetic, and formalistic constructions. Taken together, his canon forms a sophisticated philosophical treatise on the implications and consequences of existential thought, at the same time vast in its comprehension and intensely personal in its expression. Like the great leap of the little boy into his father's arms, Beckett's *Company* is an act of bravery.

## Critical Context

The long novels of Beckett's earlier career, followed in the 1950's by dramatic work such as *En attendant Godot* (1952; *Waiting for Godot*, 1954) and *Fin de partie* (1957; *Endgame*, 1958), were in turn succeeded by shorter and shorter prose pieces, considered by some as mere exercises in anticipation of. yet another great prose work. It seemed that Beckett was following the patterns of his fictive counterparts, with longer and longer pauses between shorter and shorter "failures to not express." Minimalist pieces such as *Pour finir encore et autres foirades* (1976; *Fizzles*, 1976), a series of half-starts lasting only a page or two each, seemed to indicate that Beckett was simply emptying his notebooks of previous exercises or intentionally publishing fragments of what was to be a major final masterpiece. Surprisingly, *Company*, although fairly short, is a three-dimensional, fully articulated work. There is no sense that the piece is a part of something larger; on the contrary, it expresses with considerable economy the whole spectrum of Beckett's gifts, reflecting the storytelling qualities of *Murphy* (1938), the exasperating logic of *Watt* (1953), the ontological forlornness of *Waiting for Godot,* and the philosophical complexity of his trilogy: *Molloy* (1951; English translation, 1955), *Malone meurt* (1951; *Malone Dies,* 1956), and *L'Innommable* (1953; *The Unnamable,* 1958).

Beckett's prose work is often adapted to radio and the stage. *Company* was given a reading on the British Broadcasting Corporation by Patrick Magee (1980), and staged versions have been attempted at the National Theatre (London, 1980) and Mabou Mines (New York, 1983).

*Sources for Further Study*

Fehsenfeld, Martha. "Beckett's Late Works: An Appraisal," in *Modern Drama.* XXV (September, 1982), pp. 355-362.

Kalb, Jonathan. "Monologue of Solitude: Mabou Mines' *Company,*" in *Theatre.* XIV (Summer/Fall, 1983), p. 67.

Mitchell, Breon. "Beckett Bibliography: New Works, 1976-1982," in *Modern Fiction Studies.* XXIX (Spring, 1983), pp. 131-152.

Read, David. "Artistic Theory in the Work of Samuel Beckett," in *Journal of Beckett Studies.* No. 8 (Autumn, 1982), pp. 7-22.

*Thomas J. Taylor*

# THE COMPROMISE

*Author:* Sergei Dovlatov (1941-     )
*Type of plot:* Satirical realism
*Time of plot:* November, 1973, to October, 1976
*Locale:* Tallinn, the capital of the Estonian Socialist Republic
*First published: Kompromis*, 1981 (English translation, 1983)

>  *Principal characters:*
>  THE NARRATOR, a journalist for a major Russian-language
>       newspaper in the Estonian capital
>  MARINA, the narrator's mistress, a member of the secretarial
>       staff at the newspaper
>  MISHA (MIKHAIL BORISOVICH) SHABLINSKY, a reporter for the
>       "industry desk" at the newspaper and Marina's former
>       lover
>  HENRY FRANZOVICH TURONOK, the Estonian editor in chief of
>       the newspaper
>  ZHBANKOV, an alcoholic photographer for the newspaper

*The Novel*

    *The Compromise* only barely qualifies as a novel. It is highly autobiographical; the narrator retains the name and personality of the author and follows the exact path of the latter as a human interest reporter for the Tallinn newspaper *Soviet Estonia* from 1973 through 1976. The newspaper, however, is not named in the book; the name of the author's mistress (whom he in fact later married) is changed from Elena to Marina; and the tone of the narrative signals "fiction" rather than "nonfiction" to the reader.

    Other reasons that the work barely qualifies as a novel are its brevity (it is less than 150 pages long) and its division into eleven untitled sections (identified only as "The First Compromise," "The Second Compromise," and so on), which are more like separate short stories than chapters in a novel. Three or four chapters were published as stories in magazines before the book appeared. The "chapters" are presented according to a standard format: A brief, dated journalistic sketch is reprinted, one written by Sergei Dovlatov for the Estonian newspaper, followed by the "story behind the story," ranging in length from three to thirty-seven pages. These report the real personalities behind the bland facts and faces of the original text; or they tell how the reporter got into trouble with his boss, Turonok, for political "insensitivity"; or they describe incredible drinking bouts en route to, during, and after interviews of blue-ribbon milkmaids, crooked jockeys, and garrulous old war veterans. (One of the most humorous "compromises" concerns the discovery that the corpse of a Party official being eulogized at the grave site is the wrong body—but the burial proceeds as scheduled.)

The picaresque nature of Dovlatov's adventures, with their introduction of several dozen minor characters into the narrative, inhibits the classification of *The Compromise* as a novel. The narrator does remain a consistent personality throughout the book, however, and there is a certain development in his moral outlook, as he comes to realize the impossibility of continuing to work as a journalist who is never quite allowed to tell the truth. His first cousin, who had once been convicted of manslaughter, keeps telling him to take up some useful line of work. "Aren't you ashamed of what you do? . . . All I did was kill a man, . . . and try to burn his body. But you!"

If one adds to the above the frequent appearances of several of Dovlatov's colleagues, to provide a further sense of continuity, and of his mistress, Marina, who facilitates the portrayal of the private life of the narrator, one may be satisfied that this work is as much a novel as many another work so classified. The narrator's relationship with Marina never becomes a true element of the plot, but one senses a growing pressure toward marriage and character reform, as the young reporter drinks heavily in an effort to hold back the onset of middle-aged stability. He is behind in his alimony payments, wears nondescript clothes, is always hungover. Will he never change?

Dovlatov's journalistic work is the real subject of this book. Journalism, he says, resembles a peacefully flowing river—but one should not fail to notice the tin cans on the muddy bottom. He observes: "Journalism has its perpetually open markets, commissioned stores, and even flea markets. Which is to say, the selling-out is always going on, full blast." Because there is so much political stupidity in Dovlatov's anecdotes, it is tempting to assume that the main purpose of the novel is to attack the Soviet Union and its governmental system. A continually evident Gogolian humor, however, indicates that the real target of Dovlatov's criticism is himself—and humanity. Despite what ought to be bitterness toward his motherland, from which he was eventually forced to emigrate (in 1978), Dovlatov is surprisingly forgiving of it, and of humanity. It is journalism, newspaper reporting, that provides a window into the world of the modern Soviet Union, where, the author insists, "there are no angels or villains . . . no sinners or saints."

### The Characters

The narrator is identified once by the first name of the author and twice by the author's surname. Like the author, he is very tall. A pretty young Estonian girl named Evi, who falls in love with the journalist for a night, tells him that he looks like Omar Sharif. "Who?" he says. Yet the real Dovlatov, who is half Armenian and half Jewish, does indeed resemble Sharif. The narrator immodestly allows the reader to understand that he is an excellent journalist, except that the boss cannot trust him because of his perpetual drinking and his political irreverence—called "cynicism" by Turonok. A character emerges who is talented, intelligent, witty and handsome. Almost all the female characters in the novel either love him or have once loved him. He has a reputation for infidelity. Yet Dovlatov prefers to show the reader that his brief dalliance with the Estonian girl soon makes him feel guilty; he purposely drinks so much that he can no longer perform sexually with her. He thus does not quite appear to be a male chauvinist, as do almost all the other Soviet males in the book, but he is a type that women like, and he takes advantage of that. This causes him trouble and is a source for wry humor. Apropos of his relations with women, he declares that he is a "good man," adding that he can say that "without the slightest embarrassment, because it is nothing to be proud of." That is, "Women only love scoundrels, as everyone knows."

In short, Dovlatov has great potential as a human being, yet he is an alcoholic, a divorced person with a child, poor, morally weak in that he finally always writes what he is told to write, and a liar. He could almost qualify as a tragic figure if he did not behave so comically. He remains lovable because of his sins, not in spite of them. Through this major character the author shows how one may love a sinner who is not evil, but simply a person like oneself— and extend this tolerance to all humanity. What American readers especially must learn from this novel—and what the author intends for them to learn— is that nothing happening in the Soviet Union is worse than what happens every day in the United States (although that is bad enough and causes suffering).

About Dovlatov's mistress little is revealed beyond her age and occupation, and her despair of Dovlatov ever changing. The narrator notes that "something had been going on between us on the order of an intellectual intimacy. With shades of animosity and sex." Marina weeps despondently over her lover's unfaithfulness, irresponsibility, and lack of ambition. She is more a symbol for the universal suffering of women than a genuine character. Several minor female characters echo this role, so that it becomes a substantial motif in the novel.

Turonok, the editor, is a stereotyped "boss" and has one major task: to dictate the Party line as it applies to newspaper stories. Dovlatov carries this line to comic exaggeration, inducing one to see Communist inflexibility as perhaps more absurd than evil. This allows the novel to be viewed as satirical, though it may in fact be simply realistic.

The reporter Misha Shablinsky, who is exceedingly intelligent and ambitious, has a small role that depends on his having once been Marina's lover. When Dovlatov borrows a black suit from Shablinsky to cover the funeral of a Communist Party official, Marina, seeing Dovlatov in the suit, calls him "Misha" by mistake; the reader is obliged to consider what it might take to make this amiable drunk ambitious, and if that would be a good idea after all.

Most of the characters, whatever other roles they might play, lugubriously demonstrate the archetypal incompetence in everyday Soviet life.

*Themes and Meanings*

The personality of the narrator, together with his adventures as a reporter, is a source for several motifs. An obvious one is alcoholism—no doubt a true reflection of drinking life in the Soviet Union in the 1970's. (It is worth noting that as Mikhail Gorbachev took steps to curb Soviet alcoholism in the 1980's, Dovlatov the author managed to stop drinking upon emigrating to the United States.)

A more developed theme is that of Jewishness and anti-Semitism. These issues are not presented in a militant manner because the author, though half Jewish, was never religious and in general is not sympathetic to the religious cast of mind. Jews are not always presented as likable characters (for example, the alcoholic Zhbankov). All the same, the author is angry at Soviet anti-Semitism and the hypocritical denial of it by the government and the Party. When the narrator is told by Turonok to write a story on the four hundred thousandth baby born in Tallinn, he learns first that the baby must be a boy, second that it must not be half Ethiopian (this is also a reference to Aleksandr Pushkin), and third that it must not be the son of a famous Estonian poet who is also a Jew. Finally a newborn child is found whose father is Russian—an alcoholic shipyard worker who complains to Dovlatov that during intercourse his wife just lies there "like a codfish." Dovlatov finally chooses to fight Soviet anti-Jewish attitudes with humor, as when Evi declares to the narrator "the morning after" that when she marries again it will be with a Jew—because "Jews get circumcised."

The motif of sex occurs throughout the book, emphasizing the wantonness of youth, the insensitivity of males toward females, and the incredible ignorance and naïveté of both men and women in the Soviet Union concerning sex—a situation much like that in the United States of the late 1940's and early 1950's. (This may be construed as an attack on the puritanical character of the Party and its squeamish inability to provide complete and accurate information about sex.) Other themes include generational differences, the adoration of anything made in the West (except that Dovlatov has to make do with blue jeans made in Poland), and relations between Russians and Estonians, which are generally not very good.

*Critical Context*

Between 1979 and 1986, Dovlatov published ten books, most of them quite short and all of them written in the first person. None of his books appeared in the Soviet Union, nor could have. His laconic, witty, and humorous style appeals to both Russian and American readers. Certain Russian influences may be discerned in Dovlatov's writing, but more evident are the compressed style of Ernest Hemingway, the social alienation of J.D. Salinger, and the combined vulgarity and sensitivity of Kurt Vonnegut—writers all widely available in translation in the Soviet Union since the 1960's.

Dovlatov's works in English have received excellent reviews. His work has yet to receive more substantial critical attention (except in the Russian émigré press), but his success as a writer in the West was more than assured by the publication of seven stories in *The New Yorker* between 1980 and 1987—an unprecedented achievement for a Russian émigré writer. It is ironic that the perpetual "bad boy" has received so much attention from an essentially conservative literary magazine. Dovlatov's true role as a writer is thereby confirmed: to bridge the gap between the Russian and American cultures.

## Sources for Further Study

Bayley, John. "Kitsch and the Novel," in *The New York Review of Books.* XXXI (November 22, 1984), pp. 28-32.

Fiene, Donald M. "Sergei Dovlatov: *The Compromise*," in *Slavic and East European Journal.* XXVIII (Winter, 1984), pp. 552-553.

Karriker, Alexandra H. "Sergei Dovlatov: *The Compromise*," in *World Literature Today.* LVIII (Autumn, 1984), p. 622.

Rosenberg, Karen. "Of Compromise and Corruption," in *The Nation.* CCXXXVII (November 5, 1983), p. 437.

Serman, Ilia. "Teatr Sergeia Dovlatova," in *Grani.* L, no. 136 (1985), pp. 138-162.

Williams, Frank. "Bottle-Blight," in *The Times Literary Supplement.* December 16, 1983, p. 1413.

*Donald M. Fiene*

# CONCRETE

*Author:* Thomas Bernhard (1931-    )
*Type of plot:* Philosophical novel
*Time of plot:* The early 1980's
*Locale:* Peiskam, an estate in Austria, and Palma, Canary Islands, Spain
*First published: Beton,* 1982 (English translation, 1984)

> *Principal characters:*
> RUDOLPH, the narrator, a musicologist obsessed with writing
>     a monograph about Felix Mendelssohn
> HIS SISTER, a socialite
> ANNA HÄRDTL, a young woman the narrator meets in Palma

*The Novel*

Like many of Thomas Bernhard's novels, *Concrete* is written in the first person. It is a long, meandering monologue that has no paragraph breaks. The narrator, Rudolph, is an aging and sickly man who lives alone and is preoccupied with writing intellectual, scholarly treatises. He has tried to write essays on various musicians, philosophers, and writers such as Blaise Pascal, Johann Wolfgang von Goethe, Friedrich Nietzsche, and Alban Berg. His great torment is that he can never complete his work. He has been struggling for ten years with an essay on the Romantic composer Felix Mendelssohn but cannot put down the first sentence. Instead, he spends his time collecting materials and making notes. He is a gloomy and self-obsessed individual who harbors bad feelings against the society around him.

As the novel begins, he is railing against his sister, who, he claims, torments him and whose presence keeps him from writing. She comes to visit him and teases him about his presumed "work." At the same time, he is very much dependent on her. When she invites him to visit her in Vienna, he begins a diatribe against the boredom and sameness of the place, Austria's greatest city. He claims that the people, its culture, and "society" nauseate him. When he was a younger man, he had lived there and studied music. She continually taunts him about his failed writings. He ridicules her involvement in charity work, and he speaks vehemently against the Church. He also speaks against the Socialist government, which leads its people around by the nose. Then, he decides, with much hesitation, that he must travel to Palma, his favorite place to visit. He hopes that there he can begin work on his essay. His health is poor, and he is a resolute hypochondriac. Sitting in his favorite chair, he is devoted to morbid introspection and constantly berates himself while simultaneously blaming others.

He finally flies to Palma. There, he meets a young woman, Anna Härdtl, whose tragic story preoccupies him for the rest of the novel. She and her young husband were from a suburb of Munich, where they had opened an appliance store. The business had been plagued with numerous problems. They had taken a cheap vacation to Mallorca, where they had a nice room with a high balcony. She awoke early one morning to find a body on the ground below their balcony. Her husband was dead, and she was left alone with their child. The narrator does not finish his treatise, and when, several years later, he returns to Palma, he finds that the woman has committed suicide. He spends the next day in a state of heightened anxiety.

## The Characters

The narrator of *Concrete* is typical of the protagonists in Bernhard's novels. He is highly neurotic and unable to come to terms with himself and his existence; his alienation is suggested by the way in which, in the novel's opening sentence, he refers to himself as if he were another person: "From March to December, writes Rudolph, while I was having to take large quantities of prednisolone. . . ." His preoccupation with intellectual work suggests his entrapment within the confines of his own mind. His constant hesitation and his inability to complete any of his projects also indicate his estranged consciousness. Other Bernhard characters, such as Konrad in *Das Kalkwerk* (1970; *The Lime Works*, 1973), are obsessed with intellectual or scientific treatises, which they are unable to complete. They are, because of their acute intellects, indecisive human beings who cannot take a final and effectual step into the real world. Too much thought inhibits action. They fear and despise the hypocrisy and superficiality of everyday reality.

The narrator's mocking sister represents the society of individuals for whom taking action can be simple and unproblematic. A society woman, she is clearly the polar opposite of the intellectual narrator. Their relationship is a sick and sadistic one of mutual dependence. They hate each other, but one cannot do without the other.

Like the sister, the unfortunate woman, Anna Härdtl, is not a fully developed character but is seen only through the narrator's reflections. Her sad fate represents the despair and futility of life that the narrator sees all around him. Her story illustrates a deeply pessimistic view of existence.

## Themes and Meanings

*Concrete* is an existential novel that deals with the isolation of consciousness from the world and the endless suffering that this estrangement causes in the individual. In the existential philosophies of thinkers such as Jean-Paul Sartre and Martin Heidegger, the mind is fundamentally different from all being. Human beings are creatures who live not in the present, like animals, but in the future and are thus tormented by the awareness of eventual and unavoidable death. Life is viewed as a vale of tears in which one only suffers. Most people do all they can to avoid acknowledging such a truth. Nihilism and pessimism are attitudes that often accompany such gloomy, yet true, ideas. The intellectual and pessimistic narrator of the novel mentions Nietzsche, Arthur Schopenhauer, and Fyodor Dostoevski in his reflections and thereby clearly aligns himself with this tradition of existential thought.

The title of the novel suggests the impotence and paralysis of consciousness in reality. It is as if consciousness is stuck in "concrete," unable to move, fixed and unfree. The narrator's constant hesitation and his inability to take decisive action also indicate the image of the immobility and paralysis of consciousness. This inability to move and act as a result of a hyperintellectuality is a frequent theme in Bernhard's writings.

The narrator's failed efforts to write his treatise again point out his entrapment within his own mind. His project represents an attempt to assert the self within the world, to make an impact on it, to be "concrete." Like most of Bernhard's characters, he will not succeed, and the effort will drive him to the brink of insanity.

The narrator's sadomasochistic dealings with his sister suggest the author's dim view of interpersonal relationships. Bernhard, himself, lives alone and is of the opinion that suffering is the result of most contacts with others, especially those of the opposite sex. "Love" is an illusion and rests primarily on sick dependencies and mutual exploitation.

The story of Anna Härdtl, the death of her husband and her suicide, presents a totally bleak and pessimistic view of life. She represents an innocent and helpless creature who is crushed by the random and indifferent vicissitudes of existence. The news of her death deeply affects the narrator and leaves him in a state of high anxiety. All human life is weighted down by the "concrete" of existence, and the only escape is death.

*Critical Context*

The narrator of Bernhard's *Concrete* continues in the same vein established in his previous narrative monologues such as *Verstörung* (1967; *Gargoyles*, 1970), *The Lime Works*, and *Korrektur* (1975; *Correction*, 1979). Like the narrator, the characters of the latter two works are obsessed with writing treatises that they can never complete or even begin. They are preoccupied with composing the definitive text in their fields, with finding the ultimate truth. This vision of existence is a bleak one in which torment and suffering seem to be the norm. Bernhard's characters are all deranged by the horror of life. Yet these figures do not commit suicide; they all possess a spirit of resistance to the nihilism they see around them. The attempt to write a treatise or essay of some kind, to create meaning, is indicative of their efforts to resist the meaninglessness they perceive. This is a literary parallel to the spirit of Bernhard's own writing. His novels are documents of a profound pessimism, and their composition is the attempt to resist that despair by transforming it into art. Unlike the efforts of his characters, his works are completed. The characters' failed attempts are testimony to the author's own obsession and struggle with his writing.

*Concrete* is part of a tradition of monologue narratives which includes works such as Dostoevski's *Notes from the Underground* (1864) and Samuel Beckett's trilogy *Molloy* (1951), *Malone Dies* (1951), and *The Unnamable* (1953). Like the Underground Man of Dostoevski's novel, Bernhard's narrator is an obsessive, neurotic intellectual who exists on the fringes of society, unable to participate. He harbors vindictive feelings toward everyone and everything. Both are tormented and crippled by their heightened awareness of their existence. The protagonists of Beckett's novels are much the same: all caught within the confines of their minds and desperately seeking an exit where there is none. Dostoevski's, Beckett's, and Bernhard's characters are typical representatives of modern existential literature, which details the dilemma and paradox of human consciousness in a universe that resists all efforts to give itself meaning.

*Sources for Further Study*
Bartsch, K., et al., eds. *In Sachen Thomas Bernhard*, 1983.
Dierick, A. P. "Thomas Bernhard's Austria: Neurosis, Symbol, or Expedient?" in *Modern Austrian Literature*. XII (1979), pp. 75-93.
Fetz, Gerhard. "The Works of Thomas Bernhard: Austrian Literature?" in *Modern Austrian Literature*. XVII, nos. 3/4 (1984), pp. 171-192.
Meyerhofer, Nicholas. *Thomas Bernhard*, 1985.
Wolfschütz, Hans. "Thomas Bernhard: The Mask of Death," in *Modern Austrian Writing*, 1980. Edited by A. Best and H. Wolfschütz.

*Thomas F. Barry*

# THE CONFESSION OF A FOOL

*Author:* August Strindberg (1849-1912)
*Type of plot:* Psychological realism
*Time of plot:* The 1870's and the 1880's
*Locale:* Stockholm
*First published: Die Beichte eines Toren,* 1893; *Le Plaidoyer d'un fou,* 1895
   (English translation, 1912; also as *A Madman's Defense,* 1967, and *A
   Madman's Manifesto,* 1971)

Principal characters:
   AXEL, the narrator, a librarian at the Royal Stockholm
      Library and a writer
   MARIE, the Baroness
   GUSTAV, the Baron
   MATILDA, the Baroness' cousin

*The Novel*

   *The Confession of a Fool* is its first-person narrator's account of painful
and scandalous events during a thirteen-year period of his life. Axel, the
twenty-seven-year-old narrator and protagonist, is a librarian at the Royal
Stockholm Library and a writer. Seeking a patron for one of his plays, he
calls on the Baron, Gustav, and the Baroness, Marie. Axel is immediately
drawn to the Baroness. She is attractive, aristocratic, and passionately interested in the theater. He becomes a frequent visitor to Marie and Gustav's
home and is soon the couple's intimate and constant companion. Axel wor-
ships Marie as a Madonna, despite the fact that the Baron and Baroness
have been married for three years and have a daughter. He does not think of
Marie as a sexual being, but he becomes aware that Gustav is having an
affair with his wife's eighteen-year-old cousin, Matilda, and moreover, that
Marie knows of and consents to her husband's unfaithfulness. Axel believes
that Gustav's neglect of Marie is shameful and that Marie's lack of jealousy is
further proof of her sainthood. When Marie finally does mildly criticize her
husband's behavior to Axel, however, Axel's feelings of male solidarity with
Gustav cause him to insult her and to accuse her of being a disloyal wife.
Somewhat irrationally, Axel believes that she is trying to make a confidant of
him, that she has insulted the man in him, and that "she was taking the first
step toward breaking her marriage vows." Significantly, he.adds, "[A]t that
moment the hatred of her sex was born in me." His image of chaste perfection shattered, he can no longer sublimate his sexual feelings for her. She has
become a mere woman and, even worse, a woman he desires. Through pro-
fane revels with bohemian friends and visits to brothels, he desecrates his sacred image of her and vows never to see her again.

Axel finds it impossible to break off his close friendship with Gustav, however, and soon the three of them have resumed their old relationship. Finally, desperate to tear this tormenting love for Marie from his heart, he decides to leave Stockholm. Axel stages a tearful, dramatic farewell dinner in his artist's garret for Marie and Gustav and takes a ship to France. After only a few hours on board, he suffers a hysterical attack and is put ashore. He exhausts himself swimming in the sea and then sits naked for hours in the chill October winds, attempting to catch pneumonia. He then goes to a hotel ready to die—but only after telegraphing Gustav that he is ill. In a matter of hours, Gustav and Marie arrive. Axel is not physically ill, although he pretends to be so that Marie will be his nurse.

Back in Stockholm, Axel notes that Marie is increasingly bored and restless. She complains of having no purpose in life and talks of going onstage. (This seems impossible for her because of her husband's social position; in that era, actresses were regarded with contempt.) She ignites Axel's jealousy by flirting with young men at parties. Gustav's behavior with Matilda, their frequent houseguest, becomes ever more outrageous. Finally, the growing emotional pressure culminates in Marie and Axel's confessing their true feelings for each other. Theirs will be a love without passion: It is "beautiful, new, almost unique—to love, to tell one another of it. . . . Nothing else!" Yet their resolve to be as brother and sister soon collapses, and they become lovers.

Marie's frequent visits to Axel's garret occasion many rumors, so Gustav and Marie decide to divorce. Gustav is threatened with financial ruin because of a bank failure, and life becomes a dreary round of legal bickering. When Marie leaves to establish residence in Copenhagen for purposes of divorce and also to pursue a theatrical career, she demands that Axel accompany her. Despite his belief in free love, he refuses, fearing that all Stockholm would see it as an elopement. Professing concern for Marie's reputation, Axel also has an inordinate fear of scandal and a fierce need to maintain his honor. Marie's letters from Copenhagen distress him, because he fears she is flirting again and spending her time among second-rate people. When she returns, a divorced woman, he finds her coarsened. They do not marry because of Marie's disdain for marriage and motherhood and Axel's fears that the responsibilities of marriage would distract him from his writing career. All Axel's and Marie's friends drop them. This is a society that winks at adultery but severely censures divorce (especially divorce involving a woman who abandons her child). Ironically, Marie has not even legitimately gained her freedom. For propriety and out of financial necessity, she lives with her mother and an aunt, who closely oversee her every move; this makes Axel and Marie's illicit relationship even more difficult. Finally, through Axel's efforts, Marie launches a theatrical career in Stockholm. The course of their disastrous relationship is set.

Axel becomes jealous of Marie's newfound success and is emotionally wounded by her patronizing attitude toward him. Marie has maintained friendly relations with Gustav and now prefers his advice on theatrical matters to Axel's. In Marie, Axel sees a shallow, egotistical woman and a mediocre actress. Bitter fights ensue, and love grows cold. Loathing what Marie has become, he leaves for Paris, uncertain of when or if he will ever see her again.

When Axel receives Marie's letter telling him she is pregnant and asking him to save her from dishonor, he rushes joyously back to Stockholm. They marry, determined that theirs will be a model marriage: Expenses will be equally divided, cooking and housework will be done by a servant, and each of them will have autonomy, privacy, and freedom. Axel is once again in love with Marie. Throughout their marriage, he is happiest when she is pregnant, fulfilling what he regards as the highest ideal for a woman: motherhood. Marie gives birth to a premature baby who soon dies, a baby whom Axel later becomes convinced was fathered by Gustav. Their marriage begins to degenerate into a marital inferno. Axel becomes fiercely jealous of a pet dog which Marie acquires; he is also jealous of her friends, particularly a woman who Marie invites to stay in their country cottage. Increasingly, Axel is convinced that Marie is perverse and faithless, flirts with men and women, and has affairs with both sexes. With him, she is cold. Marie returns from a theatrical tour in Finland and is uncharacteristically passionate with him. Much later, he decides that she became pregnant in Iceland and wanted him to believe that the child was his. He begins to think that she hates him and would like to get rid of him.

Axel's satirical, eccentric writings and relentless denunciations of feminism give rise to attacks on him in the press. The rumor that he is insane eventually leads to a court trial for blasphemy. Feeling surrounded by enemies, he moves his family to Paris, where there are friends who can reassure him that he is not insane. Axel believes that Marie plans to have him committed to an insane asylum and that she would welcome his death. (He suspects her of putting cyanide in his tea.) In Paris, he believes that his wife's infidelity has become common knowledge, that Henrik Ibsen's play *The Wild Duck* is about him and his marriage. He opens Marie's mail and spies on her, obsessed with finding the truth. During the next years, he moves his family to Switzerland and Germany, but he becomes ever more isolated and suicidal, tortured by the questionable paternity of his children. When at last they return to Sweden, people treat him as if he were mad and treat Marie as a holy martyr. Axel decides it is time "to write the story of this woman, the true representative of the age of the unsexed."

In an epilogue to the novel, Axel reviews the charges which have been made against him: the selfish sacrifice of his wife's theatrical career for his own ambition and the squandering of his wife's fortune. He finds himself innocent on both counts. He rejects the idea that he was ever ill or insane. His only crimes are having allowed himself to be seduced by a married woman and having consented to a financial arrangement which allowed Marie continually to cheat him. In short, he is guilty of being a fool. He renounces revenge, instead vowing to discover the truth about his wife's constancy, his children's paternity, and his own sanity. He appeals to the reader's judgment for a verdict.

## The Characters

Axel is an undisguised August Strindberg; the Baroness is an equally undisguised portrait of Strindberg's first wife, Siri von Essen, the Baroness Wrangel at the time that he met her; and the Baron is Baron Carl Gustaf Wrangel. Even the Baron's mistress, Matilda, has a real-life counterpart in Sofia In de Betou, Siri's cousin.

The extent to which *The Confession of a Fool* may be read as a reliable account of Strindberg's relationship with Siri von Essen is a matter of continuing controversy. Some have argued that Strindberg, in writing, gives free rein to his imagination, his fancies, and his speculations; thus, the story is fiction or at least semifiction. One critic suggests that Strindberg the dramatist has created in Axel a fictional character who behaves not as Strindberg behaved, but as he would have behaved if he had been insane. What is beyond doubt, however, is the number of striking correspondences between the novel and the well-documented fourteen years of Strindberg's life from his first meeting with Siri von Essen in 1875 to the final separation in 1889.

Axel, like Strindberg, is an employee of the Royal Library, a contributor to newspapers and magazines, author of several published plays, and a member of a society to promote free love. Like Strindberg, he attributes his nervous excitability and oversensitivity to being born prematurely. Axel also relentlessly denounces feminism, proclaims male superiority, and alternates between misogyny and deification of women—all traits of Strindberg. Axel is always looking for a mother in the women he meets and believes that motherhood is a woman's highest achievement. He is easily made jealous, is aware of his susceptibilities to mental delusions, and is inclined to a defensive paranoia. Like Strindberg, the son of a servant, Axel is painfully conscious of class; he is as obsessed with orderliness and cleanliness and as convinced of his own inherent superiority as was his creator.

The degree to which Marie is an accurate portrait of Siri von Essen is more difficult to ascertain because of doubts about the reliability of the narrator. According to some, the book is wholly vindictive; it has been called published malice. Others believe that it gives a substantially truthful, if not complete, account of their marriage. Ironically, despite Axel's intention to present himself as a victim of his wife's "brutality, inconstancy, and dishonesty," the novel's first readers regarded Marie as a heroine—to

Strindberg's everlasting chagrin. Trying to account for this reaction, Strindberg argued that it was the depth of his love for her which allowed readers to sympathize with her, a love so great that it not only survived the brutality described in the novel but also effectively communicated itself to the reader. Like Axel in the epilogue, Strindberg continued to think of himself as an innocent victim, a Sampson whose vicious wife had shorn his lion's mane and, hence, his powers.

### Themes and Meanings

*The Confession of a Fool* gives powerful expression to many of Strindberg's obsessive themes: love as a struggle for power and dominance; sex as a cruel battle between blind desire and hatred; marriage as warfare; and women as Madonnas who are actually predators—"treacherous, faithless, with sharp claws." Fatherhood was important to Strindberg; he believed that a man's children are his immortality; thus, the matter of paternity is crucial. Like Axel, Strindberg was tortured by the thought that, once he no longer trusts his wife, a man is unable to know for certain that he is father of his child. This dilemma was the subject of one of Strindberg's best-known plays, *Fadren* (1887; *The Father*, 1899). What is only a possibility in *The Confession of a Fool* is there fully expressed: A cruel woman systematically drives her husband insane by raising doubts about the paternity of their daughter. Provoked into throwing a burning lamp at his wife, he is pronounced insane, and a motherly nurse tenderly helps him into a straitjacket. Strindberg, an astonishingly prolific writer (with fifty-eight plays; fifteen novels; more than one hundred short stories; and numerous poems, historical works, and essays to his name) returns again and again to the subject which obsessed him: warfare between the sexes.

Beyond its plot and characterization, *The Confession of a Fool* conveys a sinister image of woman through its language. Woman is a temptress, a vampire who sucks Axel's brain dry and consumes his heart, a sorceress, a despot, a witch, a she-devil, and a devouring spider. Strindberg could, however, occasionally even appall himself by the vehemence of his hatred. He once explained his misogyny as "only the reverse side of my fearful attraction towards the other sex." Like Axel, Strindberg needed to deify woman, to worship her as a Madonna, a pure woman who is paradoxically both virgin and mother. He desperately needed to fill the void left by his failed religious faith with her image. Not surprisingly, no woman could ever fill this role for him. He required a nurturing, motherly woman but was attracted to emancipated, career-minded women. At the same time, he was terrified by the feminine side of his own nature and insecure about his masculinity. Strindberg continued to swing between veneration and vilification, desire and disgust, idealism and cynicism, trust and paranoia, and love and hate. All these tortuous contradictions threaten to drive Axel insane and make *The Confes-*

*sion of a Fool* a painful book. The only respite from human anguish is found in nature. Axel's occasional solitary sojourns into the mountains and forests renew not only him but also the reader. Such scenes, minutely and lovingly described, bring a bit of light into a dark novel.

### Critical Context

*The Confession of a Fool* is the author's most notoriously autobiographical novel and the most sensational of his writings. The novel is responsible for the view that Strindberg was mentally unbalanced. Its publication in Germany caused him to be charged with indecency and immorality. Of this book, Strindberg himself wrote, "This is a terrible book. I fully admit it, for I regret that I ever wrote it. How did I write it? Because I felt under a powerful and justifiable compulsion to wash my corpse before it was laid in the coffin for ever." Thus, it was written when Strindberg believed himself ready to die (he lived another twenty-five years) and ostensibly for reasons of catharsis, to cleanse himself of filth. It appears, however, that his motives were mixed. Strindberg always needed money, and he feared that a friend would soon write this book if he did not. He also obviously intended the book as revenge on his wife and as vindication of himself. Strindberg consistently put his life to use in his writings, but he suffered guilt for doing so. Later, leaving literature and turning to science, he confessed his relief that he would no longer have "to use his own wife as a rabbit for his vivisections or to flay his friends and offer the skins for sale."

Aside from being notable for its virulent misogyny and for the lurid light which it casts on Strindberg's life, *The Confession of a Fool* is also notable for its minute psychological analysis. Writing before the vogue of psychoanalysis, Strindberg was intent on studying, analyzing, and describing a whole range of mental and emotional states. He struggled heroically to put his pain to some use, to gain some insight into paranoia, jealousy, guilt, hate, hysteria, and all the dark things which, like the poet William Blake's invisible worm that flies in the night, eat away at our greatest joys.

### Sources for Further Study

Johannesson, Eric O. *The Novels of August Strindberg*, 1968.
Johnson, Walter. *August Strindberg*, 1976.
Lagercrantz, Olof. *August Strindberg*, 1983.
Lamm, Martin. *August Strindberg*, 1971.
Reinert, Otto, ed. *Strindberg: A Collection of Critical Essays*, 1971.

*Karen Kildahl*

# CONFESSIONS OF A MASK

*Author:* Yukio Mishima (Kimitake Hiraoka, 1925-1970)
*Type of plot:* Psychological realism
*Time of plot:* The 1920's to the late 1940's
*Locale:* Tokyo and its environs
*First published: Kamen no kokuhaku,* 1949 (English translation, 1958)

> *Principal characters:*
> KOCHAN, the narrator, an upper-middle-class youth
> OMI, a schoolmate of the narrator
> SONOKO, the sister of another schoolmate

## The Novel

*Confessions of a Mask* is a first-person narrative about a Japanese youth growing up from infancy to young manhood in and around Tokyo, Japan, from 1925 to about 1947. The narrator-protagonist is psychologically burdened by a sexual inversion, making him a latent homosexual. The novel deals with the manifestations of this latent homosexuality, the protagonist's growing awareness of it, and his struggle to live with it in Japanese society. These elements are presented in four chapters of unequal length, and these chapters in turn informally comprise two halves, the first dealing chiefly with the narrator's epiphanic moments of self-discovery and encounters with males (especially school friends) and the other half describing his encounters with women (especially Sonoko, whom he almost marries).

The novel begins with the narrator-protagonist's precocious claim that he saw and remembered events at his own birth, especially his first bath. Born in 1925, into an upper-middle-class family that has seen better days, the narrator is reared by his sickly, strong-willed grandmother, who snatches him from his parents. At the age of one, the narrator, nicknamed Kochan, falls down a stairway and grievously injures his forehead. At the age of four, he suffers monthly attacks of autointoxication in which he undergoes the symptoms of death for some hours, then revives with a urination.

These precocious or anomalous incidents precede several moments of illumination. The first is a chance view of a night-soil collector who crosses Kochan's homeward path. Kochan is fascinated by the handsome physique, robust health, and thigh-hugging trousers of this menial, who balances buckets of excrement from a shoulder yoke. It is an epiphanic moment: For Kochan, the excremental and the beautiful have become inextricable. A second such moment occurs when he lovingly admires the picture of a knight in armor and then imagines an even more beautiful picture of the knight dead. He is strangely disappointed, however, when told that the knight is really a woman, Joan of Arc. Here Kochan discovers that he cannot find beauty in woman and that transvestism can mask sexual identity. Not surprisingly, when Kochan plays at dressing up, he likes to impersonate powerful women such as Tenkatsu (a female magician) and Cleopatra, roles of which his elders disapprove. In Kochan's games with his girl cousins, he senses that he is expected to play the role of male and warrior, and he tries his best to act out this societally imposed masquerade, though doing so runs counter to his nature. Chapter 1 closes on a symbolic scene depicting the conflict between order and chaos, outer mask and inner nature. During a summer festival, the orderly processional bearers of a portable shrine (which encloses or masks a pocket of inner darkness beneath the outer blaze of noonday sun) suddenly lose all restraint and create chaos in Kochan's garden by trampling its flowers. As Kochan watches the scene, he dimly realizes that, like the rioting bearers, there is in his character a lack of restraint that attracts him to males, to the lower classes, and to an obscene disorder which culminates in death, whereas his society dictates that he find beauty in females, in the aristocratic, and in a life-enhancing orderliness.

Chapter 2 deals with Kochan's early teen years. With the advent of puberty, Kochan's aesthetic sense becomes more physical and more sexual. Significantly, his first masturbatory ejaculation is inspired by a reproduction of Guido Reni's painting of Saint Sebastian, which depicts a handsome loincloth-clad Roman youth achieving Christian martyrdom by being shot with arrows. This chapter, however, is dominated by Kochan's infatuation with an older schoolmate, Omi. Omi is a delinquent lout, masculinely hirsute and reputedly sexually experienced. Several moments of intense feeling between Kochan and Omi occur. One snowy morning, Kochan follows Omi's footprints, which appear black through the masking white snow to where Omi has printed his name in giant characters in the snow. Figuratively, Kochan is following the exposed and unmasked marks of his nature to his inner identity. Then, as the boys talk, Omi rubs his leather gloves on Kochan's cheeks, and this touch of masculine abrasiveness makes Kochan realize that he is in love with Omi. Again, during gymnastics, Kochan admires Omi's well-developed body, especially his armpits, to which he becomes fetishistically attracted, so much so that later, on an oceanside outing, Kochan's own armpits become his onanistic objects. Never robust, Kochan develops anemia during this time, and he lapses into daydreams of a sadistic murder theater that includes his practicing anthropophagy on a delectable schoolmate. Through these psychological experiences and physical affinities, and recognizing that he misses the point of many standard male jokes and innuendos about women, Kochan has become aware that his psychological makeup is radically different from that of his male peers.

The second half of the book, chapters 3 and 4, shows the narrator floundering pathetically with his sadohomosexual nature. He evolves a complex attitude toward sexuality and death. One possible solution to his predicament is to feign sufficient heterosexuality to maintain a masquerade of normal family life. The other solution to his problem would be death—on the battlefield or in an air raid. Yet, although the narrator sees death as a possible final solution, he takes advantage of his medical history and also induces symptoms of illness in himself during his military health examination, which he flunks. He wants to live, and to do so, he desperately dons a mask of normative heterosexual behavior.

The most extensively elaborated of the narrator's attempts at a heterosexual self-rehabilitation or masquerade is the account of his relationship with the eighteen-year-old Sonoko, the sister of a school friend. By this time, the narrator is a twenty-year-old university student; it is 1945, when American B-29's are conducting air raids over Japan. He desperately hopes that he can learn to love a girl without being sexually attracted to her initially. He pins his hopes on Sonoko, of whose presence he first becomes aware through her piano playing—one is reminded that music is the most abstract and bodiless of the arts. When the narrator first sees Sonoko, he is very taken by her beauty. He determinedly begins a flirtation with her as he joins her family on an excursion to the barracks of their recently conscripted son. Sonoko proves receptive. The narrator now feels so attracted to her that he is confident of experiencing heterosexual desire once he manages to kiss her—this despite the fact that he has been entirely unruffled by other girls' kisses. On a carefully planned outing in an idyllic countryside, the narrator and Sonoko kiss. She responds warmly, but the narrator, who had high hopes of this moment for a sign of his sexual corrigibility, feels no sexual stirring. Instead he now has the task of extricating himself from the matrimonial expectations of Sonoko's family without betraying his shortcoming. He fends off marriage by pretending family obligations. Then, in a pathetic effort to evince some vestige of heterosexual response, he allows himself to be led to a brothel, and there he experiences an unequivocal fiasco. His last hope for a solution to his problem, therefore, becomes his death in a bombing raid. In this, too, however, he is disappointed. Peace is made, and he finds himself alive.

Meanwhile, Sonoko has quickly married another man. By accident, she and the narrator meet again and begin to see each other for almost a year. Mingling hope and self-deception, the narrator looks forward to these trysts as if they were again manifestations of his possible heterosexuality. The book ends on the description of their final rendezvous for lunch one summer day when Sonoko questions the point of their meetings, asking him outright whether he has ever slept with a woman. The episode is also subtly interwoven with images emblematic of emptiness and waste. During their talk, the narrator is once again aware of Sonoko's beauty. He is also aware of his inability to enter into a sexual relationship with her. Shaken, he upsets a water vase over their elegant restaurant's tablecloth. They leave the restaurant and go to a cheap dance hall. As they sip soft drinks at a table, the narrator sees a well-built young gangster with an unbuttoned shirt. As he looks, the narrator feels that he is becoming sexually aroused. At this point, he realizes that he can no longer attempt to hide behind a mask of heterosexuality by paying court to Sonoko. (He never seems to care much what Sonoko feels.) As he and Sonoko part, the narrator looks back at the young gangster's now-empty table on whose top a spilled beverage glistens menacingly.

## The Characters

*Confessions of a Mask* is tantalizingly autobiographical. The narrator-protagonist is born the some year as Yukio Mishima, into similar social and familial circumstances. Furthermore, the narrator is nicknamed Kochan, a common diminutive form of Kimitake, Mishima's real given name. Mishima's homosexuality and fascination with death are well documented, and one of the better-known photographs of Mishima depicts him as a loincloth-clad Saint Sebastian, complete with arrows protruding from his sides—and his left armpit. Mishima's fascination with death eventually led to his *seppuku* (ritual suicide), which was a media event in 1970. Yet however closely *Confessions of a Mask* may conform with the circumstances of Mishima's youth, it should still be read as a novel.

The narrator-protagonist is a psychological portrait of a sexually anomalous male growing up in modern Japan. He is a sexual invert, a homosexual, and one with an attraction to thanatos. When he becomes aware of his anomaly, he hopes either for death in war or else the ability to carry on a heterosexual masquerade. The dashing of his hopes fills him with anguish and emptiness, and he may be viewed as a societal and sexual misfit who is the victim of a genetic quirk.

The other characters of the novel, major and minor alike, are neither independent nor rounded out but exist strictly for their relationship to the narrator-protagonist. Omi, the narrator's school acquaintance, is a physically attractive male whose only role in the novel is as an obsessive object of the narrator's desire. Similarly, although presented throughout half of the book, the young woman Sonoko is portrayed mainly as a necessary catalyst for the narrator-protagonist's test of his heterosexuality in the laboratory of life.

## Themes and Meanings

*Confessions of a Mask* is the study of a psychologically and sexually anomalous person and his unsuccessful attempts to accommodate himself to the heterosexual norms of his highly structured society. Beyond being a psychodrama about conflicting aspects of the same self, the novel may be read as a variation on the theme of an individual in conflict with his society. The reader who finds the narrator-protagonist's anomalies unsympathetic or incomprehensible will read the book as a narrative in the ironic mode. Yet if one finds the narrator-protagonist's plight and his attempts to correct it to be sympathetic, then one will be struck by the tragic qualities of his situation, one not of the protagonist's choosing but rather determined by genetics or fate. It is probably in order to achieve this latter effect that Mishima keynotes his novel with an epigram drawn from Fyodor Dostoevski's *Bratya Karamazovy* (1879-1880; *The Brothers Karamazov*, 1912), where the sensuous and romantic Dmitri tells his saintly, ascetic brother Alyosha: "Beauty is a terrible thing! . . . A man of noble heart and lofty mind sets out with the ideal of the Madonna and ends with the ideal of Sodom. . . ."

Although the novel's narrative unfolds chronologically, Mishima's method is to focus intensely on certain master images or spots of time rather than to provide a smoothly connected sequence of events. Isolated people, incidents, and images tend to take on powerful symbolic suggestions—for example, the staining images of spilled drinks in the closing pages of the novel link with the water of the narrator's postpartum bath in the opening scene of the novel and with the description of his first onanistic ejaculation, which bespatters his desk and books.

*Critical Context*

Published when Mishima was twenty-four, *Confessions of a Mask* created a sensation and propelled its author to the forefront of the Japanese literary scene. The novel belongs to the widely practiced genre of the Japanese "I novel" (*shi shosetsu*), about whose authenticity, fictitiousness, and artistry there has been much debate in Japan. In this context, Mishima's very title for his book suggests an ironic deconstruction of its genre. Confessions are candid; masks are not. How honest, then, can be the confessions *of* a mask (not of the *man behind* the mask)? Futhermore, Yukio Mishima is the author's pseudonym, a name which masks the author. Yet Mishima's unflinching use of unsavory and unflattering details in this work would seem to challenge other I novelists to greater heights of authenticity. In the wider context of world literature, parallels to Oscar Wilde's *De Profundis* (1905) or André Gide's *L'Immoraliste* (1902; *The Immoralist*, 1930) come to mind, but it must be said that Mishima's novel suffers by comparison to Gide's, which casts its net more inclusively over larger social and ethical issues.

*Sources for Further Study*

McCarthy, Paul. "Mishima Yukio's *Confessions of a Mask*," in *Approaches to the Modern Japanese Novel*, 1976. Edited by K. Tsuruta and T. E. Swann.

Miyoshi, Masao. *Accomplices of Silence: The Modern Japanese Novel*, 1974.

Nathan, John. *Mishima: A Biography*, 1974.

Petersen, Gwenn Boardman. *The Moon in the Water: Understanding Tanizaki, Kawabata, and Mishima*, 1979.

Scott-Stokes, Henry. *The Life and Death of Yukio Mishima*, 1974.

*C. L. Chua*

# CONFESSIONS OF ZENO

*Author:* Italo Svevo (Ettore Schmitz, 1861-1928)
*Type of plot:* Psychological realism
*Time of plot:* From the 1880's to 1916
*Locale:* Trieste, Graz, and Lucinico, Austria
*First published: La coscienza di Zeno*, 1923 (English translation, 1930)

> *Principal characters:*
> ZENO COSINI, the protagonist, a businessman
> AUGUSTA MALFENTI COSINI, his wife
> GUIDO SPEIER, his business partner
> ADA MALFENTI SPEIER, his sister-in-law, Guido's wife
> CARLA, Zeno's mistress, an aspiring singer
> GIOVANNI MALFENTI, his father-in-law
> OLIVI, the administrator of Zeno's family business
> DR. S., Zeno's psychoanalyst

*The Novel*

In "The Last Cigarette," the first of the six major sections of *Confessions of Zeno*, Zeno Cosini chronicles his efforts to quit smoking and the amusement of others at his increasing indulgence in the habit. This account of his intended abstinence helps to establish his larger attempt to make some sense of his life: "[D]id I really love cigarettes so much because I was able to throw all the responsibility for my own incompetence on them?" Zeno goes on to outline the numerous defects in his character, including hypochondria and the desire to possess most of the women he meets.

*Confessions of Zeno* is presented as the protagonist's autobiography, written to further the work he is doing with his psychoanalyst, Dr. S. If the first section offers fairly superficial information for Dr. S., the second, "The Death of My Father," is more substantial. Zeno considers his father's death the most important event in his life because, with it, he lost faith in his own possibilities. He is bitter at his father for dying before he has had a chance to prove himself. The dying man is angry for reasons Zeno cannot fathom and strikes his son at the very moment that he dies. Zeno decides that the violence cannot have been intentional, but his father strikes an even greater blow after his death by leaving his business to Olivi, an employee, rather than to the ineffectual son whom he clearly does not trust.

In "The Story of My Marriage," the most comic chapter, Zeno makes Giovanni Malfenti his business mentor and father-substitute. He decides, even before meeting them, that he will marry one of Malfenti's four daughters. He chooses Ada, the most beautiful one, and pursues her like a clumsy schoolboy. His courtship of Ada is so awkward that she thinks he is interested in Augusta, her plain sister. After being refused by both Ada and Alberta, their pretty younger sister, he gives in and proposes to Augusta—all on the same day. Although he tells Augusta that he loves Ada, she marries him.

"Wife and Mistress" describes Zeno's marriage and his surprise at finding that he loves Augusta: "I discovered that far from being a blind beast driven by another's will, I was a very clever man." His affection for his wife, however, does not prevent him from taking the first opportunity to acquire a mistress. Zeno convinces himself that he needs and deserves Carla, an aspiring singer. He rationalizes his adultery with the argument that it strengthens his marriage by making him feel even more tender and passionate toward Augusta. He soon decides, however, that he despises Carla and wants to be rid of her. When she falls in love with the singing master he has hired for her, Zeno's ego forces him to try to keep her.

The section "A Business Partnership" focuses on Zeno's relationship with Guido Speier, who has married Ada. Perversely, Zeno would rather try to teach business practices to the impulsive Guido than learn them from Olivi at his own office. He sees his devotion to the irritating Guido as "either a real manifestation of disease or of great benevolence, both of which qualities are closely related to each other." Zeno indulges Guido despite his friend's unwise investments and an affair with Carmen, who works in their office, because he admires recklessness. Hoping to make Ada regard him more highly, Zeno promises to supply the money to save Guido's failing business. Ada has lost her beauty through ill health, and Zeno feels both desire and disgust for her. She refuses to allow him to bail out her spoiled husband. In an attempt to make Ada give him the money herself, Guido takes a poison he knows will not kill him if he receives prompt medical attention. Through a series of mishaps, a competent physician arrives too late to save Guido's life. Ironically, Zeno recovers most of the business losses on the day of Guido's funeral. Ada, however, continues to blame him for the tragedy.

In the final section, "Psycho-Analysis," Zeno attacks Dr. S.'s treatment for having made him "more unbalanced and in worse health than ever." He considers it ridiculous that the psychoanalyst has reduced all of his miseries to an Oedipus complex. Zeno determines that he no longer needs Dr. S. and within a year reports that he has cured himself through exercise, a renewed interest in business, and "self-persuasion."

*The Characters*

Italo Svevo succeeds in making the reader sympathetic to his characters by exposing their humanity and weaknesses. Despite his neuroses and lies, Zeno triumphs through his sense of humor and irony. He is a hypochondriac because he needs a disease to impose some order on his rather pointless life: He is in ecstasy when he thinks that he has diabetes. His imaginary illnesses are, in an ironic sense, more serious than the real diseases that plague his father and Ada. His sickness has no cure—regardless of his self-delusion at the end of the narrative. He also thinks that business is a source of form and discipline and resents Olivi for doing the work he could do himself, yet he finds little of the same order at Guido's office. His quick settling of Guido's affairs shows that he could force himself to be a good businessman. He is simply too self-indulgent.

Zeno's motivations are complex and contradictory. He is at first devoted to Guido as a public display of his indifference to losing Ada, but a true affection eventually develops, making Ada's harsh judgment of him after her husband's death more painful. While vacationing in Lucinico during the war, Zeno tells a peasant that the fighting will not spread to his village. He does not want the man to worry, but he is also being irresponsible. He has tricked himself into thinking that all of his lies are equally harmless.

Humor and irony come into play most strongly when he tries to explain himself: "Everything I have put down in my notebooks proves quite clearly that I have, and have always had, a strong impulse to become better; this is perhaps my greatest misfortune." Why, then, does he lie so much? He tells Carla that the then-beautiful Ada is his wife so that she will think twice about leaving him. He habitually exaggerates, claiming, for example, that his father's striking him "deprived me of all my courage and of all joy in life." This statement comes from a man who lives for comfort and pleasure. Zeno fluctuates inexplicably between melodramatic despair and what he calls "my usual incurable optimism."

The other characters in the novel are important only as satellites to this self-centered storyteller. Augusta is the most notable figure; only she recognizes the comic nature of her husband's life. She loves Zeno uncritically and is the true source of order in his life.

### Themes and Meanings

Although Zeno's attacks on Dr. S. can be seen as defensive, Svevo questions the adequacy of psychoanalysis for dealing effectively with humankind's more urgent problems. Zeno may indeed have an Oedipus complex, but he refuses to be defined by it. Dr. S. wants to reduce people to stereotypes, but every page of Zeno's confession shows the complexity of human emotions. Dr. S. proves the point himself in his preface by admitting that he is publishing his patient's autobiography as revenge for Zeno's abandoning his treatment. Psychiatry is also seen as incapable of recognizing simple truths when they do appear: Zeno says that Dr. S. "must be the only person in the world who, hearing that I wanted to go to bed with two lovely women, must rack his brain to try and find a reason for it!"

Svevo uses Freudianism and Darwinism to express his doubt that any orthodoxy can explain the complexities of life. It is a joke on Darwinism that Zeno, hardly the fittest of his friends and associates, is the only one to survive. *Confessions of Zeno* ends with an apocalyptic vision of something resembling nuclear war which results when all human theories have failed. Because no philosophy can come close to explaining all life, Zeno settles for a simpler view: "Life is neither good nor bad; it is original."

### Critical Context

*Confessions of Zeno* is considered to be the first novel to employ Freudian theory extensively. Svevo had read Sigmund Freud's works and discussed his ideas with a friend who was a psychoanalyst, as well as with James Joyce. (He sent a copy of the book to Freud, who did not acknowledge receiving it.) The influence of Svevo's friend Joyce may be seen more clearly in the novel's modernist characteristics. It has been called the first modern Italian novel for its representation of the totality of a person's social and psychological existence. It is also a notable example of modernism in its treatment of time, as Zeno rearranges the events of his life to support his rationalizations: "Time, for me, is not that unimaginable thing which never stops. For me, but only for me, it comes again." He also complains that time "is really very ill-ordered!" Zeno is the epitome of the modern person desperately seeking order in a period when chaos is on the rise.

Zeno is in the tradition of Sinclair Lewis' George Babbitt and Arthur Miller's Willy Loman: the businessman who, above all else, wants to be well liked. As a self-serving liar, he is one of the best examples of the unreliable narrator. In the Jewish literary tradition, he is also a classic schlemiel, a comic fool who wants his weaknesses to be seen as his strengths. *Confessions of Zeno* has been widely admired by post-World War II American novelists. Its protagonist resembles the schlemiels in the fiction of Saul Bellow, Bruce Jay Friedman, and Philip Roth. Though Svevo has influenced many Italian writers, including Alberto Moravia, *Confessions of Zeno*, his masterpiece, has been compared more often with the works of German writers, particularly Thomas Mann's *Der Zauberberg* (1924; *The Magic Mountain*, 1927). This connection is only fitting, given Ettore Schmitz's German ancestry and his pseudonym, which means "Italo-German."

### Sources for Further Study

Biasin, Gian-Paolo. "Zeno's Last Bomb," in *Literary Diseases: Theme and Metaphor in the Italian Novel*, 1975.

Furbank, P. N. *Italo Svevo: The Man and the Writer*, 1966.

Lebowitz, Naomi. *Italo Svevo*, 1978.

Lucente, Gregory L. "The Genre of Literary Confession and the Mode of Psychological Realism: The Self-consciousness of *Zeno*," in *Beautiful Fables: Self-consciousness in Italian Narrative from Manzoni to Calvino*, 1986.

Moloney, Brian. *Italo Svevo: A Critical Introduction*, 1974.

*Michael Adams*

# THE CONFORMIST

*Author:* Alberto Moravia (1907-    )
*Type of plot:* Social realism
*Time of plot:* 1920-1945
*Locale:* Rome and Paris
*First published: Il conformista*, 1951 (English translation, 1952)

> *Principal characters:*
> MARCELLO CLERICI, a bureaucrat in the Fascist secret police
> GIULIA, his wife
> LINO, a chauffeur
> PROFESSOR QUADRI, an anti-Fascist organizer, who is living in
>     Paris
> LINA, the professor's wife
> ORLANDO, a Fascist policeman and assassin

*The Novel*

   *The Conformist* is an attempt to trace the origins of the impulse toward Fascism in an individual mind. The novel portrays the life of Marcello Clerici from his childhood in the home of wealthy bourgeois Romans to his death in a random air raid at the end of World War II.

   Marcello's father, an ex-military man, ignores his son, and his mother alternately spoils and neglects him. He gets off to a bad start by deriving most of his childhood pleasures from destroying plant and animal life in the overgrown garden of his parents' villa. Because of his feminine appearance, he is abused and bullied by his schoolmates. He becomes obsessed with the idea of obtaining a revolver so that he can demonstrate his power to his tormentors. One day he is picked up by Lino, a chauffeur and an ex-priest. With the promise of providing Marcello with a revolver, Lino lures him to the home of his employer, who is out of the country. There Lino attempts to seduce the boy. Marcello fights him off and picks up the revolver. The guilt-stricken Lino implores the boy to shoot him. Hardly realizing what he is doing, Marcello pulls the trigger and escapes from the house through the bedroom window. Later he reads that the chauffeur has died in the hospital, believed to be a suicide.

   The next section of the novel takes up Marcello's career as a minor Fascist bureaucrat with the secret police. He proposes to his superiors in the ministry a plan to entrap and destroy Professor Quadri, who had been his supervisor at the university, and who has fled Rome to fight against Fascism from a base in Paris. By this scheme, Marcello hopes to demonstrate his loyalty to the state and his reliability as a ruthless Fascist. When asked how he can find an excuse to call on the professor, Marcello suggests that he visit Paris on his upcoming honeymoon.

Before the wedding, Marcello goes with his mother, now a pathetic, drug-dependent, and slovenly woman, to see his father, a megalomaniac confined to an insane asylum. Marcello has completely rejected his parents in order to marry into a conventional middle-class family and is seeking to conform to their sentimental style of life and behavior. He can feel no love for Giulia, his fiancée, only the low-keyed affection one might have for a household pet.

Shortly before the wedding, at the urging of Giulia, the agnostic Marcello visits a church to make his confession—the first in thirty years. Marcello has not told Giulia of the killing, but he confesses his crime to the priest. The priest absolves him, but this does little to diminish Marcello's continual and vague sense of guilt and fear. The honeymooning couple travels to Paris, and on the journey Marcello does what he can to assuage the sexual desires of his passionate bride.

In Paris, he seeks out Professor Quadri and takes Giulia to meet him. In the professor's apartment the couple also meets Lina, his young wife. For the first time, Marcello feels real sexual desire for a woman, and he takes the first opportunity to try to seduce her. Lina appears to respond, but she is really attracted to Giulia and only feigns interest in Marcello to get at his wife. Giulia, however, is indifferent to Lina's advances.

Quadri tells Marcello that he is planning to leave Paris the next day to travel to Savoy and asks Marcello and his wife to come with him. Marcello refuses. He later tells his henchman Orlando of Quadri's planned route so that his victim can be intercepted and killed. The two couples go out to dinner. This occasion has been planned in advance so that Marcello can point out Quadri to his assassin. Quadri tries to persuade Marcello to join the anti-Fascist movement, without success. The four go on to a lesbian night club, a favorite haunt of Lina. There Marcello tries to persuade Lina into an affair, and Lina tries to seduce Giulia, both without success. The frustrated Lina decides to leave with her husband to travel to Savoy for the summer instead of staying on in Paris as she had planned. Both are killed by the Fascist assassin.

After his return to Rome, Marcello is informed by Orlando that the order for the assassination had been countermanded so that relations between Italy and France would not be upset. The order had come too late to save Quadri and Lina. Marcello's treacherous act had been both unnecessary and counterproductive.

The last section of the novel takes place at the time of Italy's defeat at the hands of the Allies. Like other Fascist officials, Marcello is facing the loss of his job and his home, but he and Giulia go out in the streets to observe the celebrations. In the Borghese Gardens, Marcello encounters Lino, who did not die in the hospital as had been reported. Marcello discovers that the slaying that changed his life and caused him so much fear and guilt had never taken place at all.

The next morning Marcello and Giulia, accompanied by their little girl, leave Rome for the refuge of a country town. On the way, their car is machine-gunned by a plane. The whole family is killed.

## The Characters

The major emphasis of the novel is on Marcello, the man who is so aware of his criminal and violent nature that he wishes to conceal it by conforming totally to his social and political surroundings. His beliefs, his wife, and his style of life are all taken on in order to make him fade into his background. To do so, he rejects his mad father, his eccentric mother, his social class, and his freedom of will. Having, as he believes, already killed a man, he feels no compunction about destroying his former teacher.

The other characters, with the exception of Quadri, represent various sexual tendencies. In the cases of Lino and Lina—whose similar names represent to Marcello the fated nature of his life—these tendencies are perverted. In Giulia's case, the tendency appears to be natural. Even Giulia, however, has been sexually abused and blackmailed for years by an old family friend, and she has a greedy sexual appetite. Marcello's parents are the unhappy victims of a terrible mismatch. His father is much older than his mother, and is harsh and joyless. Marcello's mother pathetically seeks for pleasure and is frustrated at every turn by her husband.

Of all the major characters, Quadri appears to be the only one with any balance—and the only one who resists Fascist tyranny. He, too, is mismatched, with a lesbian wife. The mismatches and sexual dislocation with which the novel is filled seem to be a counterpart to, and partly an explanation for, the politics of Fascism.

## Themes and Meanings

The novel is a complex mixture of many themes: social, philosophical, and political. Alberto Moravia was a sworn opponent of Fascism, and yet he was fascinated by a political movement which could attract so many people and extract from them so much devotion. This devotion led to many of the horrors of the twentieth century: political assassinations, oppression, militarism, and a hatred of minorities that could lead to such monstrosities as the Nazi concentration camps.

In portraying Marcello, Moravia attempted to analyze the genesis of a particular mindset. Marcello was a neglected child, and his fantasy world was one of violence and revenge. When coupled with a servile deference to authority and convention, this violence develops into a political attitude. Marcello becomes a natural convert to Fascism. In volunteering to betray his former mentor, Professor Quadri, he reenacts Judas' betrayal of Christ. Even after recognizing the analogy, he goes through with the betrayal.

In addition to being an examination of the development of a Fascist type, the novel is also a portrayal of a figure familiar in European postwar fiction: the man without identity, a tool of his emotions and of the forces of society. Moreover, the novel delineates a man whose every important act seems fated to be mistaken or ineffectual. The novel is an examination of existential nihilism, and is chilling in its revelation of philosophical bankruptcy. Marcello lives a life without authenticity and without value.

*Critical Context*

*The Conformist* is one of a series of novels in which Moravia attacked the moral bankruptcy of the Italian bourgeoisie, beginning with *Gli indifferenti* (1929; *The Time of Indifference*, 1953). Much of his fiction of the 1930's was written as satire against the Fascist government of Italy. He was forced to flee Rome to find refuge in a remote mountain area of Italy to avoid prosecution and probable imprisonment. With his postwar novels, Moravia became one of the major European existentialist novelists—along with Nikos Kazantzakis in Greece and Jean-Paul Sartre and Albert Camus in France—who explored the consequences of the devastation of the war.

*The Conformist*, which was adapted for a film version by Bernardo Bertolucci in 1970, is an engrossing, simply told tale of a man who is both a victim of his age and a perpetrator of its crimes. No one has analyzed more tellingly than Moravia the psychological bases of Fascism and the consequences of nihilism.

*Sources for Further Study*

Lewis, R. W. B. "Alberto Moravia: Eros and Existence," in *The Picaresque Saint: Representative Figures in Contemporary Fiction*, 1959.

Pacifici, Sergio. *The Modern Italian Novel: From Pea to Moravia*, 1979.

Rebay, Luciano. *Alberto Moravia*, 1970.

Ross, Joan, and Donald Freed. *The Existentialism of Alberto Moravia*, 1972.

*Peter Buitenhuis*

# CORRECTION

*Author:* Thomas Bernhard (1931-    )
*Type of plot:* Philosophical novel
*Time of plot:* The early 1970's
*Locale:* Altensam, an estate in Austria
*First published: Korrektur,* 1975 (English translation, 1979)

>*Principal characters:*
>THE NARRATOR, a sickly individual who is obsessed with
>    reconstructing Roithammer's posthumous work
>ROITHAMMER, a brilliant man who is obsessed with con-
>    structing a round building and with writing a treatise on
>    his native village
>HÖLLER, a taxidermist from whom Roithammer rents a room

*The Novel*

*Correction* is a first-person narrative written, as is typical of many of Thomas Bernhard's works, in one sustained statement that has no paragraph divisions. The first of its two sections contains the ruminations of the unnamed narrator. The narrator, who is plagued with lung infections, meditates on the life and suicide of his friend, Roithammer, a brilliant and obsessed man. The narrator has moved into the attic apartment of his deceased friend; he tries to assemble the numerous notes that the latter had collected in his attempt to write a treatise on his life in Altensam, the Austrian estate where his brothers and sisters reside, and on his architectural plans to construct a round building in the woods for his deceased sister.

The second section represents the narrator's paraphrase of his friend's writings. Roithammer, once an outstanding student and tutor at the University of Cambridge, returned to the stifling and petty atmosphere of Altensam. For him, the community and its narrow attitudes became a kind of spiritual prison which eventually led to the taking of his own life in a clearing deep in the woods. He was an exceedingly intellectual individual whose interests included philosophy, mathematics, and modern music. He rented an attic apartment in the home of the taxidermist, Höller. Everyone considered the scholar somewhat of an eccentric. He planned, for example, to sell the family estate and to donate the proceeds to the inmates of the local prisons.

The second son of the family, Roithammer received his father's huge inheritance and proceeded with a fantastic plan to design and build a round structure for his beloved sister. He constructed the edifice and, immediately thereafter, the sister died. He went back to England but soon returned and began to write his treatise in several, ever more succinct, versions. Isolated and in a profound despair, he took his own life.

Living in Höller's attic room, the narrator becomes himself obsessed with the "correction" of his friend's manuscripts and confronts his own desperation and despair. He becomes almost an alter ego of Roithammer and, like Roithammer, verges on the brink of suicide.

## The Characters

The two main figures of *Correction*, the narrator and the deceased Roithammer, are again typical of many Bernhard characters, such as the obsessed Konrad of *Das Kalkwerk* (1970; *The Lime Works*, 1973) or the depressed narrator of *Beton* (1982; *Concrete*, 1984). All these individuals are highly intelligent, intellectual men driven by a desire to complete some great work. Roithammer and the others are fundamentally alienated from existence and look upon it with a certain detached horror. Roithammer's concern with mathematics expresses his wish to construct a world which is logically pure and free of contradictions. His treatise is, in part, an attempt to analyze his childhood and the origins of his personality. Bernhard's characters are acutely self-conscious individuals who constantly reflect upon the conditions of their existence. The death of Roithammer's sister, ironically upon the completion of the structure he built for her, seems to be the pivotal point in his life, and his alienation culminates in his eventual self-destruction.

Bernhard's method of characterization in *Correction*, as in many of his other novels, is somewhat indirect. Since the truth of any person's existence is, at best, an elusive property, the description of an individual's motivations and ideas must remain largely circumstantial. Truth is, in existential terms, not absolute or universally valid, but a function of the individual perspective of each person. Bernhard is also well aware that language, which is imprecise and misleading, often tends to obfuscate rather than clarify reality. Thus, he tends to characterize his figures obliquely, through the views of others. That places a greater burden on the reader to construct the character from the evidence presented, quite different from the more traditional techniques of characterization in novels that employ an omniscient narrator. In *The Lime Works*, for example, the story of Konrad and his wife is told through the views and opinions of neighbors and officials. In *Correction*, the reader learns of Roithammer's life and death mostly indirectly through the observations of the narrator and through the account of his last weeks by the landlord, Höller. These are clearly biased accounts. The narrator both admires and fears Roithammer, whose powerful intellect has dominated his friend's life. Höller admires and respects his tenant.

Conversely, what is known of the narrator is learned through his obsession with Roithammer. Even though the text is a monologue, the former's personality is revealed only as a result of his attempt to explain his friend's project and his suicide. Even in the last section, when the narrator comes to talk more of his own feelings, these thoughts are more a reflection of

Roithammer's personality, since the narrator himself seems at the brink of suicide. Living in the attic room where his friend spent his last days and obsessed with carrying out the latter's revisions of his work, the narrator becomes Roithammer.

## Themes and Meanings

*Correction*, as is the case with Bernhard's other writings, is a chronicle of existential despair. Its form, a sustained monologue, suggests the theme of isolation and estrangement; there is no dialogue with others, only the single voice speaking out into the silence of a universe that is essentially indifferent to mankind and its need to give suffering a meaning. As with the death of the sister after the building has been completed, life is a series of tragic ironies.

Intellectuals such as Roithammer and the narrator illustrate a fundamental theme in Bernhard's writing: the basic alienation of human consciousness from being. His characters evidence a profound pessimism concerning the meaning of existence. They are all plagued by an exaggerated sense of self-consciousness, an awareness of their otherness in the midst of life. As in the philosophy of the pessimistic thinker Arthur Schopenhauer, whose name appears in *Correction*, existence is regarded as a random and pointless exercise from which only pain and horror can result. These individuals suffer from this estrangement and their inability to "correct" life, to make it consonant with consciousness. The narrative is a meandering chronicle of their despair. The ultimate "correction" of life for Roithammer is suicide.

Roithammer's plans to construct a round building in the middle of the desolate woods serves as a symbol of his otherness and alienation. It is a fantastic project, unprecedented and extravagant, an unusual architectural feat. The plans are an attempt to defy society and the opinions of the community. They suggest Roithammer's exceptional and atypical character, his otherness within the world. The building itself is also an attempt to defy nature and gravity. A round building, a circle, is not a natural form; perfect, geometrical circles do not exist in nature. As such, the structure serves as an existential emblem of human self-consciousness which is fundamentally alien to, eternally other than being (nature). The circle has traditionally been a symbol of eternity (in the wedding ring, for example) and here again suggests the tragic and ironic existential fact that every human being must die. Roithammer's building is, at a basic level, an attempt to defy death. As the prefatory quotation indicates, a major architectural concern in constructing such an edifice would be the issue of providing stability in such a structure. That again becomes emblematic of Roithammer's own consciousness, his efforts to provide stability, meaning, and purpose in his own life. The building is a monument to his sister, and, tragically, she dies after its completion.

The characters' obsession with writing a great intellectual treatise is their final attempt to "correct" existence, to fashion a reality that is subject to the control of the individual. Roithammer's great treatise is, in one sense, an attempt to come to terms with his own childhood and his parents. It is, to a great degree, a positive gesture, a kind of affirmation—as well as a model of Bernhard's own writing: Art is a heroic effort, vain though it may be, to refashion life.

## Critical Context

*Correction*, and all Bernhard's writings, should be considered in the context of modern existential literature. The experience of the alienation of consciousness from being that pervades his texts is akin to the fundamental assumptions that inform the works of French existential writers and thinkers such as Jean-Paul Sartre and Albert Camus. The former's well-known novel, *La Nausée* (1938; *Nausea*, 1949), for example, highlights the same kind of experience that motivates Bernhard's figures. Roquentin, the narrator of Sartre's work, repeatedly confronts the brute otherness of existence and becomes, much like Roithammer and the narrator in *Correction*, a lone and solitary individual, estranged from society and from his own consciousness. Roquentin does not, however, commit suicide.

The issue of suicide also links Bernhard to Camus. In his famous essay "The Myth of Sisyphus," Camus suggests that, given the ultimate absurdity of human existence, the first question of any philosophy must be whether one commits suicide. If one rejects that alternative, then one turns to "revolt" against the meaninglessness of life. For Camus, the highest form of protest is art or "absurd creation," the temporary transcendence afforded the individual through the creative use of the imagination. Art allows humankind, if even for only a moment, to escape the suffering that existence inevitably entails. This is closest to Bernhard's project as author. He and his characters are engaged in the monumental effort to write, be it a novel or some great intellectual dissertation that stands as a revolt, a rejection of the despair that plagues them. Bernhard's texts also carry a distinct resemblance, both in themes and style, to the writings of Samuel Beckett. They both create extended monologues of isolated characters who reflect upon the horror and absurdity of existence. Bernhard can justifiably be called an "Austrian Beckett."

Within the tradition of modern German literature, Bernhard stands in close relation to earlier authors such as the pessimistic German poet Gottfried Benn and the unparalleled writer of existential alienation, his fellow Austrian Franz Kafka. Benn's early poetry and novellas are some of the most nihilistic visions of the pointless suffering and horror engendered by human self-awareness in its confrontation with the indifference of existence. Bernhard has sometimes been referred to as a latter-day Kafka. The former's themes—estrangement, despair, and acute self-awareness—are in the same vein as those of Kafka. Of contemporary German language writers, Bernhard also stands in close relation to the Austrian author Peter Handke, whose texts also deal with the themes of alienation and the search for transcendence through art.

*Sources for Further Study*

Botond, Anneliese, ed. *Über Thomas Bernhard*, 1970.

Dierick, A. P. "Thomas Bernhard's Austria: Neurosis, Symbol, or Expedient?" in *Modern Austrian Literature*. XII (1979), pp. 73-93.

Fetz, Gerhard. "The Works of Thomas Bernhard: Austrian Literature?" in *Modern Austrian Literature*. XVII, nos. 3/4 (1984), pp. 171-192.

Meyerhofer, Nicholas. *Thomas Bernhard*, 1985.

Rietra, Madeleine. "Zur Poetik von Thomas Bernhards Roman *Korrektur*," in *In Sachen Thomas Bernhard*, 1983. Edited by K. Bartsch, D. Goltschnigg, and G. Melzer.

Wolfschütz, Hans. "Thomas Bernhard: The Mask of Death," in *Modern Austrian Writing*, 1980. Edited by A. Best and H. Wolfschütz.

*Thomas F. Barry*

# COSMOS

*Author:* Witold Gombrowicz (1904-1969)
*Type of plot:* Philosophical realism
*Time of plot:* The 1960's
*Locale:* Poland
*First published: Kosmos,* 1965 (English translation, 1966)

> *Principal characters:*
> WITOLD, the narrator
> FUCHS, Witold's classmate
> KULKA WOJTYS, the housewife who rents a room to Witold
>    and Fuchs
> LEO WOJTYS, Kulka's husband
> LENA, Kulka's daughter
> LOUIS, Lena's husband
> KATASIA, Kulka's poor relative, who helps in the kitchen

*The Novel*

Two students, Witold and Fuchs, rent a room in the mountain resort of Zakopane in Poland in order to prepare for exams. Perhaps because they are students and therefore in the habit of studying things for their meaning, they begin to observe certain signs that they think are meant to be interpreted. During their first day in Zakopane, they come across a dead, hanging sparrow, and they wonder what message was intended by this sight. They discover a crack in the ceiling that seems to be an arrow. Where is it pointing? Witold is particularly bothered by the way people look. Katasia, who works in the kitchen, has a cut across her lip to which he attributes a sinister meaning. Lena, on the other hand, has a mouth that seems fresh and unspoiled, but for that very reason it haunts him. Witold wants to believe that somehow these two women are related to each other, and that "Katasia's dissolute perverseness, that indecent, gliding mouth movement" is connected with "Lena's fresh, virginal, half-open lips."

Witold and Fuchs search Katasia's room hoping that they will find evidence with which to interpret the mysterious signs. Witold is well aware that their suspicion of her may be no more than their wild imaginings, but he cannot resist pursuing even the remote possibility that Katasia's room might provide at least a "partial revelation." Nothing significant is found, yet Fuchs and Witold are later beset by a number of hanged objects. Witold becomes so upset that he hangs Lena's cat. By initiating an action, he temporarily feels in control. All along he has had the feeling that Lena wants to tell him something, yet almost no communication occurs between them.

Witold's satisfaction over hanging the cat turns to puzzlement as he realizes that he "acted out of sheer excess and superfluity." Reality had been giving him too many signs; he had had too much evidence to interpret and had wanted "to force reality to declare itself." Still, the killing of the cat is something of which Witold finally knows the full meaning, and he hopes that by his own intervention he has been able to build a bridge between his feelings about Katasia and Lena.

In fact, Witold learns very little from his act. What seems clear by the end of the novel is that each character has revealed his or her obsessions, and that these obsessions do not necessarily add up to some great whole. The most dramatic event, near the end of the novel, concerns Witold's discovery of Lena's husband, Louis, hanging from a tree. One interpretation of this scene suggests that Louis has had an obsession with hanging which has ended in his own suicide. Unfortunately, Witold takes Louis' hanging as a sign that he must now hang Lena, but Lena's illness prevents him from doing so. Instead, he returns to Warsaw and his parents' home to resume "warfare with my father" and his regular life. The novel ends with his mundane and anticlimactic statement: "Today we had chicken and rice for lunch."

## The Characters

Except for his hanging of the cat, Witold is a passive character. To say that he is in love with Lena is not quite accurate, since he never actively pursues her and is put off by even minor obstacles. He takes the path of least resistance and is somewhat upset when Fuchs assumes command of their interpretative quest. It is Fuchs who announces to their landlady's household that he and Witold have become intrigued by the signs evidently left for them. Witold suspects that Fuchs has attached himself to the Wojtyses for lack of anything better to do, because Fuchs has had trouble with his employer and now seems to be compensating by trying to master this new situation. This explanation might prove to be as accurate for Witold, whose family quarrels have driven him away from home.

Each character in the book brings to the world a very private, compulsive way of looking at things. Kulka, for example, is obsessed with her housecleaning. Her husband, Leo, is the epitome of the tendency to create a private reality that others cannot imagine. For years, he has cherished the memory of a brief episode of lovemaking with another woman. He even brings his boarders to the location where he had made love to this woman—although he does not tell them in so many words about what the site commemorates for him. Witold is the only one who realizes that Leo is lost entirely in a world of his own making. The only way to enter that world is through "berging," the term Leo has made up to express his divorce from the mundane reality of his marriage. When Witold says the word "berg," Leo realizes that he has met a kindred spirit, for what Witold finally discovers is not some overarching meaning to the signs that have troubled him but rather the human knack for creating signs. Berging, or sign making, is the acknowledgment that humans are free to interpret their existence as they choose. There is no one objective meaning to be grasped, as Fuchs and Witold had supposed.

## Themes and Meanings

That characters are inseparable from the themes and meanings that they create or have imposed upon them seems to be the point Witold Gombrowicz makes in calling his novel *Cosmos*. Witold's odd way of describing himself and others is perfectly natural to him, because he sees correspondences between himself and others that someone else would not necessarily acknowledge. When he says that "Katasia advanced from the sideboard to clear the table, and her deformed, gliding, darting mouth approached the mouth opposite me," Witold has arbitrarily chosen to associate Katasia's mouth with that of Lena, who sits across from him at meals. Another character might find some other feature to establish a different relationship which is just as arbitrary. Witold realizes this when he discovers a photograph of Katasia that shows her with a "perfectly normal mouth, a decent, honest, peasant mouth."

Like most of the characters in this novel, Witold finds things significant because he has made them so. He returns to the same subjects repeatedly, until he is convinced of their import. That his ideas are, in fact, unsupported by reality is revealed by the lameness of his language: "when something was repeated more often than it ought to be, well, we knew what it was like when something was repeated more than often than it ought to be."

*Cosmos* does not have a plot as such, because the very idea of a plot involves moving to a destination or a definitive ending, and this maneuver is not possible in Gombrowicz's mundane world. Despite all the pseudoprofundity of his speculations, Witold ends his narrative by mentioning what he had for lunch. This is a pathetic ending, but it is what the author intended. In the words of Czesław Miłosz, "Gombrowicz's destructive talent has always been directed toward depriving the reader of his certainties and his presumed values"; Miłosz adds that Gombrowicz has no respect for literature or philosophy and not the slightest interest in comforting his readers with great themes or ennobling thoughts. Thus his novel will not end with a grand summation; it will conclude, rather, with the narrator's current state of mind, which has no final revelation to offer.

Yet *Cosmos* is not a nihilistic or unfeeling novel. It reveals great compassion for adolescents who are often peculiarly concerned with being authentic, with finding models of behavior that can be safely and successfully imitated. If there is great arbitrariness in the inconsistency of adolescence, there is also great freedom to be creative. Perhaps this potential explains why Gombrowicz preferred the company of a generation younger than himself and took special delight in pointing out how adolescence survives into so-called adulthood.

*Critical Context*

*Cosmos*, the last novel that Gombrowicz wrote, is the culmination of his longer fiction, which he began in 1937 with *Ferdydurke* (1937; English translation, 1961) and continued with *Trans-Atlantyk* (1953) and *Pornografia* (1960; English translation, 1966). These works share many of the same themes and fictional structures. All three books concentrate on a narrator and his male companion. The narrator has doubts about his friend but does not have the mental resources to resist a stronger intelligence than his own and thus is drawn into situations that are of his friend's devising. In each case, the two males project a meaning onto circumstances and are fairly successful in getting others to accept and to act upon that meaning.

This, then, is a recurrent theme. Gombrowicz explores again and again the ways in which human beings are manipulated by form, whether that form be the shape of a person's face or the structure of an institution such as a school. In each instance, the individual becomes what Gombrowicz calls in his preface to *Pornografia*, "Ferdydurkean man[,] . . . a constant producer of form: he secretes form tirelessly, just as the bee secretes honey." Thus Witold in *Cosmos* gives the world its peculiar form of hanging objects and provocative mouths. Yet Gombrowicz notes that man "is also at odds with his own form," as Witold is when he confesses that he has trouble holding together his own narrative. Near the end of *Cosmos*, Witold notes that "I shall find it difficult to tell the rest of this story. Incidentally, I am not sure that it is one. Such a continual accumulation and disintegration of things can hardly be called a story."

What makes Gombrowicz such an intriguing and complex author is his talent for making stories out of the elements of "antistory." The events of *Cosmos*, it is true, do not lead anywhere. Nevertheless, because reality itself is shown to be composed of fictive elements, of the forms people impose on themselves and on others, it is fascinating to watch Gombrowicz's characters make and remake one another. This creative process must be something like the author's, and perhaps that is why he chose in his last two novels to give his narrator his own name.

*Sources for Further Study*

Fletcher, John. "Witold Gombrowicz," in *New Directions in Literature: Critical Approaches to a Contemporary Phenomenon*, 1968.

Freeman, G. Review in *New Statesman*. LXXIV (November 17, 1967), p. 685.

Miłosz, Czesław. *A History of Polish Literature*, 1983 (second edition).

Thompson, Ewa W. *Witold Gombrowicz*, 1979.

Veeder, William. " 'A Call to Order': *Cosmos*," in *Cross Currents*. IV (1985), pp. 125-144.

*Carl E. Rollyson, Jr.*

# COUP DE GRÂCE

*Author:* Marguerite Yourcenar (Marguerite de Crayencour, 1903-1987)
*Type of plot:* Existential realism
*Time of plot:* The years following World War I and the Russian Revolution
*Locale:* Kratovitsy, a fictive Baltic estate threatened by the Bolshevik army, and its vicinity
*First published: Le Coup de grâce,* 1939 (English translation, 1957)

> *Principal characters:*
> ERICK VON LHOMOND, the narrator and protagonist, an elegant, youthful soldier of French, Balt, and Prussian ancestry
> CONRAD DE REVAL, Erick's cousin, a boyhood friend and later comrade-in-arms against the Bolsheviks
> SOPHIE, Conrad's sister, who is hopelessly in love with Erick

*The Novel*

Marguerite Yourcenar wrote *Coup de Grâce* in the style of a classical French *récit*, a first-person narrative severely limited in time, place, and action. Erick von Lhomond, an elegant soldier of fortune approaching forty as the story begins, recalls an episode connected with his youth. Though the story begins at the Pisa, Italy, railroad station as Erick is waiting to return to Germany after having been wounded at Zaragoza (presumably in the Spanish Civil War), the entire focus of his tale remains on his experience in the Baltic regions of Livonia and Kurland as the Bolshevik army approaches Kratovitsy, the estate of his cousin and boyhood friend, Conrad de Reval. Erick briefly recounts his first visit to Kratovitsy. He is innocent in every sense of the word, little more than a boy, and the place seems an Edenic paradise. He and Conrad become strong friends. Sophie, who evidently cares for Erick even at this point, remains merely an unobtrusive distraction for him.

In the wake of the Russian Revolution, Erick returns to Kratovitsy as a Prussian-trained officer fighting in the White Russian army and determined to stop the advance of Bolshevik forces in the Baltic states. He serves with his boyhood friend Conrad and eventually arranges to be billeted at Kratovitsy. He discovers that war has brought a general neglect to the once excellently managed estate. He notices changes in his feelings for Sophie as well; her kiss makes him determined to view her as the sister he never had. It was general knowledge among those living in the house that Sophie had been raped by a drunken Lithuanian sergeant. Her brother Conrad never learns of the incident, but the fact that she has been "sullied" makes Erick feel a new affinity for her.

Erick does not love Sophie; rather, he views her as he sees himself, as a creature degraded by circumstances. Sophie does not understand the complex workings of Erick's mind, and he never is willing, perhaps is not even able, to describe his feelings for her. She is puzzled and embarrassed when Erick does not respond to her advances; even so, she realizes that he never rejects her, merely that he does not respond. She cannot understand why Erick misses no opportunity to belittle her and is puzzled by the oblique ways he chooses to do this, registering his disgust when she wears clothing he does not think appropriate, when she dances with officers stationed at Kratovitsy, when she drinks more than he considers proper, or does not pay sufficient attention to her appearance.

Such incidents become the norm during the winter lull between battles. Erick grows careless of Sophie's safety, sending her on dangerous but nonessential errands to the front. Sophie, for her part, becomes unconcerned about her own safety and that of the others residing at Kratovitsy. For example, she intentionally stands on a lighted balcony as the estate comes under aerial attack. She is shaken but feels no remorse when a bomb falls on the stables, causing the horses a painful death. When her dog Texas is killed by one of the soldiers, she retreats into drink but shows no outward sorrow. In short, she comes to accept the brutality and wickedness around her as the norm and becomes indifferent to the possibilities of life or death.

Erick, not Conrad, witnesses Sophie's sudden departure from Kratovitsy, alone and on foot. Erick hypothesizes to himself about what, if any, progress she is likely to make in winter weather, but the thought of her death does not especially bother him. He does not, predictably, tell Conrad that she has left. Routine search parties fail to discover any definite information about her whereabouts or, indeed, whether she managed to survive.

On patrol and under threat of the advancing Bolshevik army, Erick seizes the pretext of levying supplies to set out for Lilienkron, home of Gregory Loew, a Jewish bookstore clerk who had in past years been a friend of Sophie. Loew, an intellectual and, by this time, long gone from his home to fight with the Bolsheviks, had had long, pleasant discussions with Sophie about books in the years before and just after the start of the war. Erick, bitterly amused at the prospect, had always suspected that Loew loved Sophie. He realized that Sophie might have been attracted to Loew as well, though he characteristically had never even mentioned his feelings to Sophie.

When Erick recognizes Loew's mother wearing Sophie's coat, the one she had worn when she left Kratovitsy, he ruthlessly interrogates the old woman and searches the Loew home. He eventually learns that Sophie had indeed come to Mother Loew's home and had borrowed some of Loew's clothes in order to dress like a man.

Inevitably, the cause of the White army deteriorates under pressure from the Bolsheviks. Conrad dies a painful death, and Erick comes by chance upon the body of Loew. Shortly thereafter, he discovers Sophie, who had been hiding with several exhausted Bolshevik soldiers in the hayloft of a barn. No prisoners can be taken because of the hard-pressed circumstances of the White army, and a tall, blond soldier who had been Sophie's companion and protector is killed immediately. Erick knows that he can intervene to save Sophie's life. Yet, having told her of the deaths of Conrad and Loew, he orders the execution of all prisoners. He orders Michael, the former butcher at Kratovitsy, to do this, and one by one the prisoners are shot. Sophie is last, but just as Michael is about to pull the trigger she requests that Erick kill her. With the thought that he wishes finally to put an end to Conrad, Erick, turning his head away "like a frightened child setting off a torpedo on Christmas Eve," destroys Sophie's face with his first shot but does not kill her. It requires a second shot to end her life. Erick first believes that Sophie had intended this act as a final indication of her love. He interprets it ultimately, however, as her wish to take revenge and cause him to feel remorse. Though he admits that he occasionaly does feel remorse, his more overwhelming feeling is that he has been trapped, as, he believes, one always is in dealings with women.

### The Characters

All the characters in Yourcenar's *Coup de Grâce* are peripheral to the complex relationship among Erick, Conrad, and Sophie, and, true to the style of the French *récit*, even the reader's understanding of that relationship is carefully controlled by Erick's highly subjective recounting of it. It is he who views Sophie as first innocent, then morally loose, enamored of him, and ultimately vengeful. The approximately fifteen years which intervene between the events and Erick's recollection of them further serve to color his memories, and since all the principals are dead except himself, one has only Erick's testimony that there is a likeness between himself and Sophie and that he feels a haunting but forbidden attraction to Conrad, one which he seeks to obliterate through his clumsy execution of Conrad's sister.

Clearly the episode haunts Erick's life, and he feels a need to recount the compromising story to present comrades-in-arms, despite what it reveals about his own ruthlessness and not least about his inner psychic state and predisposition. His obvious self-hatred results from his latent homosexuality, though he is completely unaware of the latter and so remains totally oblivious of just how personally compromising his story is.

Erick remarks repeatedly that he wishes his narrative to be uncompromisingly honest. This attempt to be dispassionate, especially about a situation whose essence is passion, causes him to present himself in a consistently unfavorable light, though he never judges his own actions as either justifiable or wrong. The perceptive reader, similarly, has difficulty assessing blame since everything Erick does, especially his coldness and cruelty, stems from abysmal ignorance of his inner self.

Sophie is also ignorant, though in a different sense. She never realizes why Erick repeatedly denies her advances. Indeed, every relationship she has had with men has been one of use or convenience. It seems she expects no more than this from Erick, even if he were to respond. Erick cannot countenance this moral standard in a woman whom he has preferred to view as a sister and in whom he sees an aspect of himself. Though he never consciously realizes it, his brutal execution of Conrad's sister is a pathetic attempt to banish at once his feelings for Conrad and his inability to respond to Sophie.

Conrad is the most silent and enigmatic member of the trio. He withdraws from all action increasingly until he literally becomes inert in his rooms at Kratovitsy. He often witnesses Erick's cruelty to Sophie, yet he never intervenes. The reader, always governed by Erick's perceptions, never knows Conrad's feelings about his cousin. Conrad, until the moment of his death, remains the essential ingredient as well as the most unknowable unknown of this relationship.

## Themes and Meanings

*Coup de Grâce*, as are Yourcenar's novels generally, is set in a precarious historical period. Another era, in this case the Fascist, is about to begin, and the tragedy is that all the individuals of the novel have been so brutalized by preceding events that they no longer recognize evil for what it is. They have developed an existential amorality which accepts all things as normal.

This is obvious in all the characters. Erick can blame Sophie's desire that he inflict the *coup de grâce* (the death blow) on her as revenge. It is actually a perverse act of love which frees her from the pain of living with unrequited love. Conrad accepts his own *coup de grâce* fearfully but ultimately with as much dignity as he can muster. Lowe has received his own death blow on the battlefield, and his death compels Erick, however reluctantly, to accept the Bolshevik as a comrade-in-arms. It remains for someone else to administer Erick's *coup de grâce*. In the meantime, he tells his story to whomever may listen (presumably often to captive audiences such as that at the Pisa station) and is always on guard to make its retelling impartial.

Erick, it follows, controls the narrative, but he has an amazing lack of insight in its telling. He never understands what it is about himself or the overwhelming events through which he has lived that allows him neither to respond to love nor to rise above the amoral world about him. His *récit*, or recital of events as he sees them, marks him and the others in this story as yet more spiritually hungry souls of the twentieth century.

## Critical Context

Yourcenar's *Coup de Grâce* is one of her early works. It was written in the deceptively peaceful atmosphere of Sorrento, Italy, just before the beginning of World War II and just a year before she established her home in Maine with her American companion and translator Grace Frick. Yourcenar takes pride in her Belgian origins and would deny the strong existentialist tone of this and her other works, a predisposition of many writing in French during and after World War II. Nevertheless, her works share the theme of protagonists unable to rise above the moral chaos of their lives, usually because they cannot see the origins of the problem as eminating from themselves. Yourcenar saw *Coup de Grâce* as a commentary on the state of the world at the brink of what was then considered total war. It was based on an episode, supposedly true, which had been related to her, but it has the potential to be of any time or any place.

*Sources for Further Study*

Blot, Jean. *Marguerite Yourcenar*, 1971.
"Marguerite Yourcenar," in *Current Biography*, 1982. Edited by Charles Moritz.
"Marguerite Yourcenar Will Be Honored at National Arts Club," in *The New York Times*. CXXV (February 26, 1986), sec. III, pp. 22-25.
Yourcenar, Marguerite. *The Dark Brain of Piranesi and Other Essays*, 1984.
_____. *With Open Eyes: Conversations with Matthieu Galey*, 1984.

*Robert J. Forman*

# COUSIN BAZILIO

*Author:* José Maria de Eça de Queiróz (1845-1900)
*Type of plot:* Satiric realism
*Time of plot:* The 1870's
*Locale:* Lisbon
*First published: O primo Basílio*, 1878 (*Dragon's Teeth*, 1889; better known as
  *Cousin Bazilio*)

*Principal characters:*
    LUIZA, a beautiful, sensual, and shallow young wife
    JORGE, her husband, a decent, honest, and self-satisfied
        mining engineer
    BAZILIO DE BRITO, Luiza's handsome, arrogant cousin and
        lover, recently returned from Brazil
    JULIANA CONCEIRO TAVIRA, Luiza's ugly, ailing, and malignant
        maidservant
    JOANNA, Luiza's loyal and good-natured cook
    LEOPOLDINA, Luiza's unhappily married school friend
    FELICIDADE DE NORONHA,
    COUNCILOR ACCACIO,
    SEBASTIAN,
    JULIAO ZUZARTE, and
    ERNESTINHO, regular members of Jorge and Luiza's Sunday
        evening circle

## The Novel

Jorge and Luiza have a happy but unexciting marriage. Luiza, childless and bored, amuses herself with music, romantic novels, and visits to her dressmaker. Immediately after Jorge leaves on a mining expedition to the south of Portugal, Bazilio returns to Lisbon after a seven-year absence in Brazil and France. Luiza has fond memories of her tall, bronzed, and mustached cousin, with whom she had had a youthful romance. Bazilio's ruthless character, scorn for social conventions, and seduction and abandonment of Luiza provide a striking contrast to her husband's circle of bourgeois friends. Only Luiza's intimate friend Leopoldina, whom Jorge despises because of her immoral life, is sympathetic to Luiza's love affair.

Bazilio's seduction slowly progresses from provocative familiarities, tender kisses, and ardent embraces during rides in closed carriages, to its consummation in Luiza's drawing room. Bazilio then finds a squalid room, which the lovers ironically call their "Paradise," where they can secretly meet. He completely dominates her, teaching her new sexual sensations, to which she responds deliriously. Yet Luiza's disillusionment is foreshadowed by her comparison with a yachtsman on a romantic voyage who anchors on the mud banks of the Tagus River and must breathe the surrounding marshy stench. Bazilio soon loses interest in his prey: He abandons his pretense of affection for Luiza, treating her in a brutal manner; humiliates her by openly expressing his boredom; and refuses to run away with her as promised.

This degrading love affair, which echoes Leopoldina's coarse liaisons with numerous lovers, is contrasted not only with Luiza's affectionate marriage to Jorge but also with Felicidade's absurd attempt to arouse the amorous interest of Councilor Accacio—she even tries the magic of a fraudulent wisewoman—and with Joanna's frankly carnal connection with a carpenter. Only Juliana—embittered by poverty, hard work, and bad health—is completely without an emotional life. She consults an "arranger" about how to deal with Luiza (just as Felicidade consults a wisewoman) and vents her sexual frustration on her indolent and egoistic mistress.

The maid steals Luiza and Bazilio's love letters, using them to blackmail her mistress. While waiting for her money, Juliana seizes control of the household, changes places with Luiza, and degrades her mistress in a lingering martyrdom—as Bazilio did after his passion subsided. Juliana works less and less, goes out whenever she pleases, takes the best food and wine, brutally insults her mistress, and forces her to fire Joanna (who had struck the intolerable Juliana). Luiza meekly submits to her grasping maid and makes excuses for Juliana's bizarre behavior. Aware of her impending tragedy, and imagining the ruin of her marriage and the loss of her reputation, "she felt that, at the very centre of her being, something had been broken off and was bleeding painfully."

Faced with Juliana's blackmail, Bazilio follows the advice of his cynical friend Viscount Reynaldo and offers Luiza money, which she refuses, and then leaves Lisbon as suddenly as he had appeared. Jorge returns from his long trip and, though everything is now changed, on the surface everything is the same. Luiza resumes the role of devoted wife, but Jorge, increasingly suspicious of the maid's arrogance, finally insists that they dismiss Juliana.

In desperation, Luiza asks Leopoldina to arrange a meeting with old Castro, who has always lusted for Luiza, so that she can get money for Juliana from him. Yet she is repelled by his anticipated advances and, in a grotesquely comic scene, expresses her rage against Bazilio and Jorge by seizing a cane and slashing the flabby flesh of the astonished lecher. In a final attempt to save herself, Luiza confesses to Jorge's friend Sebastian, who is sympathetic and promises to help her. He brings a policeman to the house to frighten Juliana and provokes her fatal heart attack. Luiza falls into a fever from the shock of happiness but begins to recover.

Unfortunately, Jorge intercepts a letter from Bazilio that reveals the sordid story and becomes frantic. He loves Luiza more than ever, but with a carnal and perverse love. Mad with jealousy, he confronts his wife with Bazilio's letter. She faints, and he pardons her with a long kiss. Becoming delirious, Luiza moans lascivious words to Bazilio, falls into a coma, and dies. When Bazilio returns to Lisbon and learns of Luiza's death, he regrets only that he has not brought his French mistress to amuse him.

## The Characters

Like most nineteenth century novelists, José Maria de Eça de Queiróz makes moral judgments of his characters, but his tendency to moralize is complemented by his caustic vision of the pretensions and stupidity of mankind. The novel is called *Cousin Bazilio*, but the seducer is merely a catalyst. Luiza is the main character. Despite her intellectual and emotional limitations, Eça de Queiróz remains sympathetic to the beautiful young lady. As Sebastian observes, "There aren't any bad women, my dear Senhora, there are only bad men." The most interesting aspect of Luiza's character involves the violent conflict between propriety and desire. Her voluptuous response to the dangers of adultery and the rapture she experiences from openly breaking laws and conventions is described as "the soul [seeking] its own discomfiture with sensual appetites and tremblings of desire." Despite her humiliations and punishments, Luiza never fully abandons her passion for Bazilio.

Bazilio is a callous and predictable stage villain who triumphantly twirls his mustache after sexual conquests: "Adultery appeared in his talk as an aristocratic obligation. After hearing him one would have thought virtue was the defect of mediocre spirits." Jorge, though a decent man, suffers because of his complacency and his inability to sustain a lasting passion with Luiza. During a theoretical discussion at the beginning of the novel, Jorge exclaims that he would kill his wife if she were unfaithful, and he finally becomes the inadvertent cause of her death. Councilor Accacio is an effective comic caricature, and the scene in which he insists on accompanying Luiza, who is desperate to meet Bazilio at their Paradise, is brilliantly executed. The most interesting and most repulsive character is the sexually starved Juliana. She personifies pure hatred and forces Luiza to pay for her sin.

## Themes and Meanings

*Cousin Bazilio*—written while Eça de Queiróz was in Great Britain on consular duty, which gave him a more objective view of his own country—presents a vivid portrait of the inert and boring society of old-fashioned Lisbon, which nourishes ennui, dreams, and illusions. The novel also offers a bitter and cynical exposé of the then-current patriotic and religious cant, as well as a devastating condemnation of the romantic idea of passion. Luiza and Bazilio share a bond of blood and memories of a youthful attachment. In her eyes, he is exotic and exciting. Though he is her only surviving relative, he destroys her instead of protecting her. Both lovers are aroused by the hint of incest mingled with adultery. Like Gustave Flaubert's *Madame Bovary*

(1857) and Leo Tolstoy's *Anna Karenina* (1875-1877), *Cousin Bazilio* portrays the themes of seduction and adultery, sin and punishment.

## Critical Context

*Cousin Bazilio* has been criticized for imitating *Madame Bovary*, though Eça de Queiróz's defenders have demonstrated his original treatment of a similar story. In a savage essay, Eça de Queiróz's contemporary, the Brazilian novelist Joaquim Maria Machado de Assis, condemned *Cousin Bazilio's* unconvincing plot and sensational sexuality. The book's portrayal of sexuality and frank expression of a woman's desires are the best aspects of the novel, but the plot does have two radical weaknesses. Juliana's theft of the love letters and Jorge's interception of Bazilio's letter seem contrived, though people communicated more frequently by letter before the invention of the telephone. The other problem concerns the successive and convenient deaths of Juliana and Luiza. Juliana had been suffering from heart disease, but Luiza, who faints all too frequently during crucial moments of the novel, dies merely from emotional shock and not from any physical cause. Despite these relatively minor defects, *Cousin Bazilio* is a masterpiece of satiric realism, giving a lively picture of Portuguese society, passionate love, and a vengeful servant. It fully justifies Eça de Queiróz's reputation as one of the major novelists of the nineteenth century.

## Sources for Further Study

Coleman, Alexander. *Eça de Queiroz and European Realism*, 1980.

Fedorchek, Robert. "Luiza's Dream Worlds in *O primo Basílio*," in *Romance Notes*. XV (Spring, 1974), pp. 532-535.

Pritchett, V. S. "A Portuguese Diplomat: Eça de Queiroz," in *The Myth Makers*, 1979.

Rougle, W. P. "The Role of Food in Five Major Novels by Eça de Queiroz," in *Luso-Brazilian Review*. XIII (Winter, 1976), pp. 157-181.

Stevens, James. "Eça and Flaubert," in *Luso-Brazilian Review*. III (May, 1966), pp. 47-61.

*Jeffrey Meyers*

# THE COWARDS

*Author:* Josef Škvorecký (1924-    )
*Type of plot:* Social realism
*Time of plot:* 1945
*Locale:* Kostelec, a fictional town in Czechoslovakia
*First published: Zbabělci*, 1958 (English translation, 1970)

*Principal characters:*
DANNY SMIRICKI, an eighteen-year-old youth, a saxophone
    player in a jazz band, and a would-be revolutionary
IRENA, the girl with whom he is in love
ZDENEC, Irena's boyfriend
BENNO, another young member of the jazz band
PREMA, a revolutionary

*The Novel*

The action of the novel takes place during one week, between May 4 and May 11, 1945, the period between the defeat of the occupying Nazis in this area of Czechoslovakia and the takeover by the Soviets. The title refers to the fact that in spite of all the brave sentiments mouthed by the townspeople, few of them really want to be involved in the fight against the Nazi troops, until the issue is no longer in doubt.

The novel is narrated in the first person by Danny, a self-obsessed and self-conscious youth, who is often more worried about his unsuccessful courtship of Irena and his relationships with his peers in the jazz band than he is about the important events taking place around him. Danny is a member of the bourgeoisie and thus cannot really identify with the proletarians who are in favor of the approaching Russian troops. Nevertheless, he understands and fully exploits his privileged position. When he is arrested by the Germans during a demonstration early in the novel, he is saved from punishment, and possibly even execution, by the intervention of Dr. Sabata, a town official and a friend of Danny's father. Danny then joins a partisan group and is issued a submachine gun, but immediately afterward, most of the group tamely turns over these guns when ordered to do so by the town authorities. The only holdout is Prema, their leader, who refuses to give up his gun and is jailed as a result.

The hopes and fears of the townspeople rise and fall at the confused news from the nearby front. The town organizes a militia, supposedly to keep order and to guard against an uprising of the local Communists. The militia marches around in the streets in small bands, but without guns. Danny joins this force too, but he feels silly while engaged in this pointless exercise. The militia engages in a number of fights with Communist insurgents, but since the town's makeshift army remains unarmed, its efforts are futile. Eventually, Danny deserts.

The next development takes place when hundreds of prisoners of war, escaping from camps after German defeats, straggle into the town. Danny, who speaks English, becomes responsible for a group of English escapees and finds billets for them through his extensive contacts with bourgeois families. The next day, however, German troops on the retreat start moving through town, and Danny goes back to the militia, thinking that the time for real action has come at last. He finds another submachine gun and joins in the confused battle that soon erupts in and around the town between the advancing Russians and the retreating Germans. He loses his fear as he thinks of his love, Irena, and is caught up in the excitement of battle. Later, he meets Prema, his former revolutionary leader, who has escaped from jail. Together they set up a heavy machine-gun emplacement on the outskirts of town and destroy a German tank. Soon after, the battle ends, and Danny returns to the town, where he finds some townspeople taking a grisly revenge on a group of captured Germans. This sickens him. He seeks out Irena, who has been working for the Red Cross and discovers that her boyfriend, Zdenec, has not yet returned from the battle. Danny comforts her, all the while seeking to seduce her, but she resists his advances and he returns home in despair. The novel ends with his jazz band playing in the town square to celebrate the arrival of the Soviets and the end of the war. Irena is dancing with her boyfriend, who has returned, so Danny's saxophone sobs out a melody that elegizes the end of his youth and signals the beginning of a new era. This is an era, however, that is fraught with new menace.

### The Characters

Danny is a self-centered young man, given to fantasies. The novel is focused so strongly on him that the other characters do not emerge with any great clarity. He lives with his parents but returns home only to sleep and to eat; otherwise, he is constantly looking for action, seeking always for something to make himself glamorous in the eyes of Irena, who remains cool to him in spite of his best efforts. Danny, in fact, seems to be an arrested adolescent whose interior reality, in spite of all the momentous events occurring around him, is stronger than any reality in the exterior world. In a rare moment of self-recognition, Danny wonders how he could be so self-absorbed during the biggest war of all time, in which millions have been killed, millions wounded, and millions more destroyed in concentration camps.

The other characters become real only when they impinge on Danny's reality. Most vivid is Prema, the dedicated revolutionary, who has kept a heavy machine gun hidden in a cellar since 1938, when the Nazis marched into Czechoslovakia. His single-minded dedication is the mark against which the performance of all the other characters, including Danny, is measured. Prema's resolve inspires Danny when the time comes to act against the Germans.

Irena is of a lower social class than Danny. Her very unattainability, both, socially and physically, makes her the ideal fantasy figure for Danny; she is the necessary focus for all of his sexual and social confusion. The stolid and powerful Zdenec, her boyfriend, is an expert mountaineer, dependable and courageous; the reader can scarcely blame Irena for preferring him to Danny.

Benno is the trumpet player in the jazz band. Rich, fat, lazy, and cowardly, his one rule is self-preservation; he lies at the other end of the scale from Prema. Benno is dominated by his girlfriend and humiliated by his peers. Like Danny, he is conscripted into the militia, but when any danger threatens, he takes to his heels. He survives the war, while brave men perish in the battles of liberation.

### Themes and Meanings

One of the epigraphs to *The Cowards* is Ernest Hemingway's assertion, "A writer's job is to tell the truth." This is the supreme virtue of the novel. Its truths are seldom palatable, for they expose the devious and often nasty workings of the human heart. Danny is the character least spared by the author, even though he is closely modeled on Josef Škvorecký himself. In fact, Danny has been the protagonist of many of the novels that Škvorecký has written. In the author's preface to one translation, Škvorecký mentions that, at first, critics "charged that the novel was an offense against concepts sacred to the Czech and Slovak people and that it caricatures and insults the Red Army." Škvorecký claims that this criticism is beside the point. He believes that the book was absolutely realistic and portrayed his people and the Red Army as they were, warts and all. "Danny and his friends," he writes, "do not insult the revolution, but mock the way the bourgeoisie play at making one." After the failure of the uprising against the Soviets in 1968, the writer emigrated to Canada.

For Danny, jazz is another way of mocking the bourgeoisie and an attempt to express his spontaneous feelings, but Danny's problem is that he cannot escape his bourgeois rearing, which he is unwilling to forsake. His moods fluctuate between exultation and despair as he feels raised up by his hopes and dreams and then dashed by the realities and disappointments of life. This account of the life of a romantic youth is highlighted by the events swirling around him during the last days of World War II, when bombing raids, battles, and sudden death became part of everyday life. Ironically, a youth's egotism can overshadow even the cataclysm of a world war and a revolution.

### Critical Context

*The Cowards* was Škvorecký's first novel, and it contains themes and metaphors which have recurred often in his work. Jazz has remained an important metaphor of freedom and resistance to authority, and the individual's perception of reality, as opposed to the "official" versions of life, has become a central theme in his work. Clearly, Škvorecký is not a man who could remain content under an authoritarian regime, and all of his work has been a claim for the supremacy of the human imagination and freedom over the demands of the state.

Although he has been an exile from Czechoslovakia since the late 1960's and has taught for much of that time at the University of Toronto, Škvorecký has continued to write in Czech, which reflects his obsession with his own identity and his situation as an exile. He has tried to maintain relations with his homeland, having translated many books from English into Czech and helping to run a Czech-language publishing house started by his wife. He won the Governor-General's Award of Canada for his novel *Příběh inženýra lidskych duší* (1977; *The Engineer of Human Souls*, 1984) and is the best known of all the writers in exile from Central Europe living in Canada.

*Sources for Further Study*

Fulford, Robert. "Another Country," in *Saturday Night*. January, 1983, pp. 5-6.
Fyfe, Robert. "Bridge over the Credit," in *Brick*. Winter, 1986, pp. 29-33.
Hancock, Geoff. "Interview with Josef Škvorecký," in *Canadian Fiction Magazine*. Nos. 45/46 (1983), pp. 63-96.
Kundera, Milan. "1968, Prague, Paris, and Josef Škvorecký," in *Canadian Forum*. August, 1979, pp. 6-9.
*World Literature Today*. LIV (Autumn, 1980). Special Škvorecký issue.

*Peter Buitenhuis*

# THE DARK CHILD

*Author:* Camara Laye (1928-1980)
*Type of plot:* Autobiographical *Bildungsroman*
*Time of plot:* The mid-1930's to the mid-1940's
*Locale:* Kouroussa, a village in French Guinea, and Conakry, the capital of
 Guinea
*First published: L'Enfant noir*, 1953 (English translation, 1954)

> *Principal characters:*
> THE NARRATOR, a youth of the Malinke people, growing up in
>  Upper Guinea
> HIS FATHER, a skilled village goldsmith
> HIS MOTHER, a woman endowed with magical gifts

## The Novel

*The Dark Child* tells the story of the author's youth. Yet, the style, structure, and purpose of the book cause it to be classified as a novel as well as an autobiography; Camara Laye has molded his materials in such a way that it is not he, himself, who emerges from the book but rather a representative man. In this way, *The Dark Child* is similar to other "shaped" autobiographies such as Robert Graves's *Goodbye to All That* (1929), Maya Angelou's *I Know Why the Caged Bird Sings* (1970), and even D. H. Lawrence's *Sons and Lovers* (1913).

Laye's account is structured through a dozen chapters, each evoking a particularly meaningful and poignant memory. The first chapters show Laye as a small child, playing about his father's hut, where he observes his father caressing and talking to a small snake. His mother tells him that this snake is the guiding spirit of his father's people; it gives his father knowledge and the special skills which make him a highly praised, prosperous goldsmith. His father tries to share this same knowledge with the child, but both father and son sense that the transference will never occur, that the son's destiny lies elsewhere.

Another part of Laye's heritage is related in the next two chapters, as the child visits his maternal relatives in the village of Tindican. Here, he participates in the rice harvest. The narrator captures the many rituals associated with the harvest as thoroughly as he detailed the ritualistic aspects of his father's trade. Above all, he recalls the joy of the participants in these rituals. Laye's artistry works to create a sense of foreshadowing here, as, amid joy there are notes of sorrow or potential sorrow. Laye's village, Kouroussa, is much larger than Tindican. Thus, in Tindican, he is regarded as a "town boy." He is dressed differently and is not permitted to perform labor. Though everyone is kind and loving, he is different, set apart. This difference and his slight uneasiness about it foreshadow the greater alienation he is preparing to undergo as the book ends.

As the boy grows older, he attends schools, Muslim and then French. Although he values his religious and intellectual education, he details more fully the particularly African education he receives through undergoing rites of manhood, including circumcision. Through this ritual, he and his friends become reborn as men. Laye describes the many rituals surrounding this event and makes clear the powerful bonding that results. He views the experience not simply as a chance to show courage or gain the prerogatives of adulthood; rather, the experience is valued because it makes him truly at one with his people. For the expatriate, this aspect of the memory is most powerful.

To further his education, Laye now travels to Guinea's capital, the coastal city of Conakry, four hundred miles from home. Equipped with magic elixirs and talismans, he makes the journey successfully, settles in with relatives, and eventually falls into a childlike love affair with a girl named Marie. After a few false starts at school, he is graduated at the top of his class and is given an opportunity to study in France. He accepts, then faces the painful task of telling his parents. His father and finally his mother agree to his going, and the novel ends as he sits on the airplane with a map of Paris in his hand, grieving but looking forward.

*The Characters*

The central character is Laye, himself. He portrays himself as a happy child, fitting perfectly into a coherent and benevolent culture in which each individual has an identity and a role. As he grows into young manhood, though, he finds himself pained by his need to leave the village and travel farther away in order to fulfill himself intellectually. He seems to know early that this separation is his fate, so he experiences nostalgia for his home long before leaving it.

Other than this feeling of loss (or perhaps because of it), Laye portrays himself as happy and content. When he has problems with school, his father solves them. When he loses a friend to death, he is comforted by thoughts of religion. It is important to the central idea of the story that this character should be happy; he is the product of a culture which is being idealized.

Laye's father and mother represent two aspects of the African culture which Laye idealizes. The book begins with a poem of dedication to his mother, a prayer that she will know how much he loves and values her. It is she with whom he has an emotional relationship: She represents a more passionate, mystical side of life, and it is significant that her family are farmers, closely attuned to life through their rituals. Also, his mother is a healer with magical gifts. Laye, in his Westernized narrator's voice, seeks to explain the miracles she performs but cannot.

The family's respect for the mother is nearly absolute. Laye notes that people often believe mistakenly that the African woman's role is subordinate; such stereotypes, he says, are far from the truth. His mother runs the house and, partly through custom and partly through their great mutual affection, controls much of her son's life—chasing off friends she deems unsavory and checking his room to see that he is not sneaking in girls. Because of her strident nature, some critics have viewed her as a negative character. The narrator makes it clear, however, that her role is appropriate. It is she who links him to the part of the past for which he yearns, unconditional acceptance and love.

His mother has both magical power and the power of love over her son, yet she is doomed to fail when the issue that matters most emerges; despite her pleas, her son leaves for school in France. In recognition and love, his initial poem calls out to her and to that part of Africa which she represents:

> Black woman, woman of Africa, O my mother, let me
> thank you; thank you for all that you have done for
> me, your son, who, though so far away, is still close
> to you!

Laye's father represents a different side of experience. He seems to know early that his son will not follow his trade. He teaches and protects his son, guiding him closely in the ritualistic attainments of manhood. The attitudes learned in these rituals—courage, self-control, and respect for community— become the valued traits of the soon-to-be expatriate.

### Themes and Meanings

*The Dark Child* is, in one sense, a highly personal book. Laye wrote it when he was a very young man, living in Paris and homesick for his family and village, and he has said that in writing the book, he no longer felt alone or abandoned. Looking at the book in this light, one is not surprised to find that its vision of African life is largely Edenic.

Laye's account, however, was not written solely for himself. It is clearly written with an audience in mind. He shapes his experiences into twelve brief chapters, each one a step forward in his journey to maturity. In crafting the book, he had European influences, including Gustave Flaubert and Marcel Proust, whose writings on memory flavor both style and content in *The Dark Child*. Laye's experience and heritage are different from that of these Europeans, so he crafts his work not only to articulate his world but also to articulate it to an audience of non-Africans. Therefore, his realism can never be casual; it must be clear and credible to the uninitiated, the alien.

His realism in the early chapters involves a child's-eye view of things. Quickly, the reader sees the customs and community structure that shaped the adult narrator's life. Often, the narrator presents, side by side, the "real" and the magical, showing the essence of the African experience to the Westerner. Most sections end with a personal note, however, an exclamation of sadness for what has been lost. The narrator cannot return to the safe, blissful world of his childhood; no one can. Perhaps more significant, he implies that his very nature, which demands education and a broader life, prevents him from ever participating in the adult life of his village. He may go home, but he would have no place there, in a community where everyone must have a role. This implied loss is at the heart of *The Dark Child*'s nostalgia.

*Critical Context*

The popularity of *The Dark Child* established Camara Laye, among Westerners at least, as a notable African voice. His fellow African writers, however, were not always united in praise of the book. *The Dark Child* portrays a childhood lived under a colonial government. To many critics, his idealistic portrait of a childhood under colonialism was comparable to an American black writing, in 1865, of the joys of his childhood in slavery. *Négritude*, African consciousness, was the key theme of the day, and Laye did not conform to its attitudes. Laye has commented that there were few whites where he lived; he simply did not feel the oppressions of colonialism as others did. Therefore, conflict in *The Dark Child* is not between the French and the Guinean, but between two sides of the self. The side of Laye which was destined to leave Africa always seems to dominate. Nostalgia and loss then, not anger, inform his style (though anger was more fashionable).

When Guinea gained its independence in 1958, Laye returned to fill political roles. After seven years, however, he left Guinea for the political reasons detailed in his second autobiographical novel, *Dramouss* (1966; *A Dream of Africa*, 1968). His bitterness and lack of distance made this novel a failure as a work of art. His last work, *Le Maître de la parole* (1978; *The Guardian of the Word*, 1984), is more successful. In it, Laye again addresses African history—specifically, where the present Africans might find the seeds of redemption. It appears that Laye's great strength was his powerful recounting of the virtues of the past. With *The Dark Child*, he has left a wealth of knowledge and wisdom as well as a moving work of art.

*Sources for Further Study*

King, Adele. *The Writings of Camara Laye*, 1981.

Lee, Sonia. *Camara Laye*, 1984.

Moore, Gerald. "Camara Laye: Nostalgia and Idealism," in *Seven African Writers*, 1962.

Olney, James. "Ces pays lointains," in *Tell Me Africa: An Approach to African Literature*, 1973.

Palmer, Eustace. "Camara Laye," in *An Introduction to the African Novel*, 1972.

                                                                    *Deborah Core*

# THE DEATH OF A BEEKEEPER

*Author:* Lars Gustafsson (1936-    )
*Type of plot:* Fictional diary
*Time of plot:* The 1970's
*Locale:* The countryside in Västmanland, a Swedish province
*First published: En biodlares död,* 1978 (English translation, 1981)

*Principal character:*
LARS LENNART WESTIN, the narrator, a retired public-
school teacher

*The Novel*
   *The Death of a Beekeeper* opens with what Lars Gustafsson calls a "prelude" in which he says good-bye to the readers of this, the last part of his
five-volume novel sequence, *Sprickorna i muren* (1971-1978; the cracks in the
wall). He presents himself as merely the editor of notes left behind on Lars
Lennart Westin's death, telling the reader that the speaker to whom he now
hands over the narrative suffers from cancer of the spleen. As the narrative
proper begins, the reader knows more than the protagonist.
   The documents used for the narrative are a yellow notebook, the source
of most of the entries in the novel, a blue notebook which contains stories
(some of them science fiction) that Westin has written, and a torn notebook
in which the progress of Westin's illness is recorded. They cover a period
from 1970 to 1975 and have supposedly been found in Westin's home by his
literary executor, Lars Gustafsson.
   When the school where he was teaching was consolidated with a bigger
school, Westin opted for early retirement. He has decided to settle in the
country and keep bees. In an early entry, he worries about the well-being of
his bees—he has not winterized the hives properly because he has not been
feeling well all fall.
   Another early indication of Westin's illness is the fact that his dog does not
seem to recognize him any longer. Westin speculates that perhaps the old dog
is losing his sense of smell, or that Westin's own smell has changed radically.
In another entry, Westin relates his reactions on receiving a letter from the
hospital where he has gone for tests: He decides not to open the letter, rea-
soning that if his illness is not life-threatening, it will simply pass, and if the
news is about a fatal illness, he does not want to know it. He burns the letter
unread.
   The second part of Westin's narrative tells of his marriage, which was
based on a tacit agreement with his wife that they would not get too close
to each other, not invade the other person's private sphere. The spouses
acknowledge the emptiness of their marriage after Westin meets a woman

doctor, Ann, on a train. They have a brief affair but, more important, they keep in close touch by phone and by letter. Westin tells his wife about Ann and, to his surprise, she is delighted and tells him to ask Ann over for a visit. The two women become friends and, gradually, Westin is the one left alone.

Westin recalls his childhood and tells anecdotes of his relatives. He also has a visit from two twelve-year-old boys, Uffe and Jonny. The boys have a fascination with horror and adventure comics, and Westin begins writing a science-fiction story for them. A feature in the first story is an immense pipe organ which produces intolerable pain. The pain replicates the pain Westin himself feels—a pain which becomes more pronounced as the narrative continues. For a few weeks, however, there is a cessation of pain. Westin decides that the episode of terrible pain he endured meant he had passed some kidney stones and that now his illness is over; he defines paradise as the absence of pain.

Paradise is also defined by Westin as a place where there are no lies. In another science-fiction story, he describes a society in which it is impossible to tell lies since communication is by object and action rather than by words.

The fifth section of the novel consists of a more developed science-fiction story, entitled "When God Awoke." In this version, God is female. She has been asleep for millions of years, but now She wakes up and starts hearing, and answering, human prayers. When an archbishop prays for peace in the world, She responds by turning all fissionable matter and all weapons into gold. Eventually, since all wishes are immediately fulfilled, language disappears. Humanity, the reader is told, realizes that it has labored under a misapprehension in imagining a punishing paternal god: The truth is that there is a boundlessly indulgent maternal deity. The section ends: "IF GOD LIVES, EVERYTHING IS ALLOWED."

In the final section of the novel, Westin experiences a return of pain. He finally feels real, but also feels that this new reality is terrible. The novel ends with Westin waiting for an ambulance and hoping that it will not have an accident on the slippery roads.

*The Characters*

The only main character in the novel is Lars Lennart Westin; his wife, Margareth, and his onetime lover, Ann, are characters about whom he writes but who do not actually appear in the novel. Westin and his wife have had an agreement "not to see" each other. For both of them, Ann is a possibility of liberation from a sterile relationship. Margareth is as repressed as her husband; Ann is described as warm and maternal. She is someone who is able to "see" Westin, but when she forges a bond with his wife, he loses her and the possibility of her liberating influence, which he considers his last chance to understand and define himself.

The two boys who come visiting appear within the time frame of the novel, but they are minor characters, an occasion for Westin to write science-fiction fantasies. The book is Westin's, and the people in his life, past or present, are interesting to the reader only in their relationship to the narrator. Some visiting relatives are never even individualized by names; others, who are named and characterized, are people in Westin's stories. The narrator is someone who has avoided personal relationships as much as possible. He believes that his one chance, Ann, was taken away from him by Margareth. It is in character for him to keep his illness to himself, to retreat to the solitary existence of a beekeeper, to decide not to let society get hold of him in his weakened condition. Westin's remark that he has wanted too little all of his life, especially wanted too little from, and too little to do with, other people, shows his increasing self-awareness. Now, when the events of his last few months make him feel real, he cannot accept the change and considers it terrible.

## Themes and Meanings

The science-fiction story of a maternal deity mirrors Westin's comment on Margareth's and Ann's relationship. He had not realized that what Margareth needed was a mother; the science-fiction story implies that the need for an indulgent maternal figure is universal. This fable constitutes a literal apotheosis of the female principle, a development that started in his poem "*Kärleksförklaring till en sefardisk dam*" ("Declaration of Love to a Sephardic Lady") and continued with other female figures in the first two volumes of *Sprickorna i muren*. In *The Death of a Beekeeper*, Ann is an ineffectual liberator, but the god of the science-fiction story becomes the culmination of liberation—from war, from materialism, from pain, from language, and, eventually, from personality itself.

In the novel, it is the cessation of pain, rather than the absence of pain, which is paradise. If there had never been any pain, it would be impossible to become aware of its absence as something desirable. Without hell, in other words, there could be no paradise.

In spite of Westin's positive invention of a prayer-granting god, a comment in one of the last diary entries is more revealing of his metaphysical attitude. He says that perhaps a more interesting heresy than the denial that there is a god who has created humanity would be a heresy that says yes, there is a god who has created us, but there is no reason to be either impressed by or grateful for this fact. If there is a god, Westin states, our task is to say no. Westin has consistently said no to life. In burning the letter from the hospital, he attempts to say no to death as well.

## Critical Context

*The Death of a Beekeeper* is the last in a sequence of five novels with the overall title *Sprickorna i muren*. The structure is based on Dante's *Divine*

*Comedy*. The first three novels, *Herr Gustafsson själv* (1971; Mr. Gustafsson himself), *Yllet* (1973; wool), and *Familjefesten* (1975; the family party), describe the Inferno, while the fourth, *Sigismund* (1976; English translation, 1985), takes the reader through Purgatory.

The Death of a Beekeeper is the ironically conceived Paradise section. It is actually a story of death. In it, many characters and themes from the earlier novels recur. The science-fiction elements present in *The Death of a Beekeeper*, for example, have appeared in earlier novels, in particular *Yllet* and *Sigismund*. Also characteristic of Gustafsson is the way in which Westin's thoughts return to the idyllic landscape of his childhood—the section devoted to childhood memories is entitled "Memoirs of Paradise." The auto-biographical elements—so prominent in the first two parts of the novel sequence—are absent here, except for the "prelude." Many of the ideas presented in the earlier novels are made clear and brought to a conclusion in *The Death of a Beekeeper*. The five novels have a common theme: lies and hypocrisy in public and private life. In the last novel, Westin confronts the problem of lies in his science-fiction story about objects replacing language.

Gustafsson explores other ideas present in the earlier novels: the limits of the self, the relation of the individual to society (Westin retreats from society so completely that he elects to face death in solitude) and—more important in this last novel—to the uncontrollable forces of illness and death. Westin's contact with reality has been brought about not by love or by immersion in nature but by pain. *The Death of a Beekeeper*, as Gustafsson himself has said, paraphrases René Descartes in proclaiming, "I suffer. Therefore I am."

Critics consider *The Death of a Beekeeper* as Gustafsson's best novel before the equally acclaimed *Bernard Foys tredje rockad* (1986; Bernard Foy's third castling).

*Sources for Further Study*
*Antioch Review*. Review. XL (Summer, 1982), p. 374.
*Best Sellers*. Review. XLI (February, 1982), p. 409.
Mortensson, J. "Gustafsson's *The Bee Keeper*," in *Swedish Books*. II (1979), pp. 6-7.
Updike, John. "*The Death of a Beekeeper*," in *The New Yorker*. LVII (January 11, 1982), p. 92.

Yvonne L. Sandstroem

# DEATH ON THE INSTALLMENT PLAN

*Author:* Louis-Ferdinand Céline (Louis-Ferdinand Destouches, 1894-1961)
*Type of plot:* Social and psychological realism
*Time of plot:* Mainly the first decade of the twentieth century
*Locale:* Principally Paris
*First published: Mort à crédit*, 1936 (English translation, 1938)

> *Principal characters:*
> FERDINAND, a medical doctor who narrates the incidents of
>    his boyhood and adolescence
> CLÉMENCE, his mother
> AUGUSTE, his father
> ÉDOUARD, his maternal uncle
> CAROLINE, his maternal grandmother
> NORA MERRYWIN, the wife of the headmaster of Meanwell
>    College
> COURTIAL DES PEREIRES, an eccentric genius, editor, inventor,
>    and philosopher

*The Novel*

*Death on the Installment Plan* takes the form of a review by an adult Ferdinand of his boyhood and adolescence. Ferdinand's reminiscence reveals the harsh, cruel world in which he grew up and shows the germination of his present attitude and temperament. In the opening fifty pages, Louis-Ferdinand Céline introduces the narrator as a gloomy, disillusioned doctor who views medicine cynically and is irritated by his patients. Employed at the Linuty Foundation Clinic, he is surrounded by sickness and corruption. His cousin, a doctor at a venereal disease clinic, is dying of cirrhosis of the liver, and his typist wants to be an abortionist. Ferdinand is gravely ill when the novel begins. His mother comes to visit him, and it is a vicious quarrel with her, not warm maternal-filial feelings, which conjures up his childhood memories and initiates the flashback that constitutes the novel.

It is a grim childhood, as one after another of the numerous recalled incidents and episodes of his childhood evocatively indicate. He grew up in a filthy apartment in a glass-encased passage in Paris, to which the action turns: There is no warmth, no love in his home. Ferdinand is constantly beaten and abused by his father, Auguste, an insurance clerk who, a failure himself, belittles his son. His mother, Clémence, runs a clothing shop, and though she has aspirations for her son and is solicitous of his welfare, she provides little emotional or material comfort and constantly nags him. His grandmother, Caroline, is one of two family members who show him any affection or kindness, but she soon dies. She secretly buys for him a copy of

*Illustrated Adventure Stories*, of which his father disapproves. In it, he discovers the story of King Krogold, which inspires him to create his own King Krogold stories, set in a fictional world into which, as a child and later as an adult, he often escapes. Uncle Édouard, whose joviality and optimism contrast sharply with the gloom of this household, displays some interest in young Ferdinand. The other uncles and aunts, a grotesque bunch, care little for him. The neighbors, generally repulsive, are no warmer than Ferdinand's relatives, and their harsh treatment of him makes him more withdrawn. There are many instances in which his painful, negative experiences cause him to vomit, to defecate in his pants, and to masturbate. The only happy period of his childhood is a short vacation the family spends at Dieppe, but even this respite is marred by his brush with death by drowning.

A poor student, he manages to be graduated from elementary school and begins searching all over Paris for employment. When he does find work, his employers take advantage of him. He is fired from his first position as a stockboy and from his second as a clerk for a jeweler, whose wife introduces him to passionate, animal sexuality and later falsely and deliberately accuses him of theft. Unable to hold a job, he is abused and chastised by his parents. This is a period of great anguish for him. Hoping to make something of him, his parents accept a loan from Uncle Édouard which enables them to send him to learn English at Meanwell College in England.

At the college, where Ferdinand spends eight months, he refuses to speak in French or English, associating only with the retarded Jongkind. Nevertheless, life at the college is better than at home, and though Ferdinand isolates himself, he does not find his life to be unpleasant. The college, run by a strict headmaster, Merrywin, is close to financial collapse. The headmaster's wife, Nora, seduces Ferdinand, who is entranced by her beauty. A moral but sexually frustrated woman, she feels guilty about her infidelity with Ferdinand and commits suicide. Her suicide has a profound effect on Ferdinand and marks his passage from childhood into adolescence. The school fails soon after Nora's suicide and Merrywin goes insane. Ferdinand returns to Paris, leaving behind a world that, only slightly more pleasant than his home, is portrayed through disgusting images of filth and nausea, passion and rage, despondency and defeat.

Back in Paris, Ferdinand tries unsuccessfully to find work. Constantly abused by his father, he eventually strikes him, almost causing his death. Thrown out of the house, he is rescued by Uncle Édouard, who introduces him to Courtial des Pereires, an eccentric inventor, editor, and philosopher. For the last half of the novel, Ferdinand's life is dominated by Courtial. When they first meet, Courtial is editor of a popular magazine, *Genitron*, whose subscribers are themselves quixotic minor inventors. Courtial flees Paris when some of his subscriber-inventors who were cheated by him sack his office. He acquires a farm and, with his wife and Ferdinand at his side, tries his hand at novel agricultural and educational practices: He cultivates vegetables by passing electric shocks through the soil and runs a pension for underprivileged children who, exposed to both mental and manual activities, are expected to become model citizens. Both experiments fail: The vegetables rot away, the children are delinquents, and the neighboring farmers become antagonistic. With everything crumbling around him, Courtial commits suicide.

Ferdinand is once more left on his own. Distraught and discouraged, he once again is rescued by Uncle Édouard, who provides him with a home and tries to rally his spirit. He is grateful to his uncle, but he does not want to be a burden on him or on anyone else, including his parents, who have given up on him since his fight with his father. Now about seventeen, he decides to join the army, and the novel ends where Céline's first novel, *Voyage au bout de la nuit* (1932; *Journey to the End of the Night*, 1934) begins.

*The Characters*

Céline draws heavily on his own life in his portrait of Ferdinand. Despite the many similarities in their temperaments and experiences, however, it must be remembered that *Death on the Installment Plan* is a work of fiction; the distinction between author and protagonist must be maintained. As a doctor, the adult Ferdinand is cranky, disillusioned, and embittered. There is a mutual disgust between him and his patients and neighbors. He suffers from insomnia, paranoia, and frequent bouts of hallucinations and delirium, the consequence of a wartime wound, of malaria contracted in Africa, and of his traumatic, unhappy childhood. He is also a poet and storyteller, who is preparing a mock medieval romance, *The Legend of King Krogold*, a work that tells of violence and death but is romantic enough to offer him some measure of escape from his drab and dismal life. As a child, Ferdinand devises similar stories of King Krogold. King Krogold is a medieval warrior; he defeats his enemy, Gwendor the Magnificent, and indiscriminately wreaks havoc on Gwendor's subjects.

Young Ferdinand is tough, resilient, and filled with curiosity and a lust for life. These qualities help him survive the jungle in which he finds himself. He defends and protects himself with an ingrained hostility. As a boy, he beats his dog, treating it the way his father treats him. As an adolescent, he almost kills his father in a fight. He defecates in his pants to defy his parents and repel them. They perceive him as a total failure, stupid and obnoxious, when in fact he is lonely and in desperate need of comfort and encouragement. Though stubborn, violent, and filthy, he elicits sympathy in the reader, which is augmented by an awareness of his sensitivity and creative imagination. The adult Ferdinand's review of his life shows how, in many instances, the child is father of the man—though it is difficult to see how the slovenly, barely educated boy will evolve into a physician.

The other important and absorbing character in the novel—and the most important in young Ferdinand's life—is Courtial des Pereires, the eccentric self-styled genius. Céline depicts him comically and sympathetically as a lovable rogue. Courtial is an idealist who, forced to live in a practical world, is not above using chicanery. He is Ferdinand's mentor and Ferdinand is his willing disciple. Ferdinand recognizes that he is a clarlatan but is responsive to his infectious zest, ingenuity, and enthusiasm, his dislike of systems, and his striving after truth. While Ferdinand's parents and friends belittle him, Courtial teaches him to believe in himself and makes him recognize and accept that the price of living is death.

The novel has a full gallery of rich secondary and minor characters, some significant in Céline's scintillating portrayal of the protagonist's development, others in his brilliant evocation of the life and times. Ferdinand's parents are the most important figures in his early life. His father, ironically named Auguste, has little dignity. He wants to be a merchant navy officer but must settle for a post as an insurance clerk with no prospect of advancement. He perceives his son as a burden and is convinced that he will be a thief. Clémence, Ferdinand's mother, spends her time eking out a living in her shop. Hers is a miserable life. Though her robust husband constantly rebukes her, she admires him and allows him to abuse her puny, unpromising son. She comes to realize that she has inadvertently nurtured her son's hatred for his father. When Ferdinand leaves home because of the rift with his father, she blames herself. Guilty and depressed, she loses interest in life.

The two figures who exert a positive influence on Ferdinand are Grandmother Caroline and Uncle Édouard. Caroline is understanding, warm, and considerate. After her death, Uncle Édouard takes her place in Ferdinand's life as the only positive familial influence. He is an optimistic, understanding man, a foil to Ferdinand's father. Outside the family, Nora Merrywin is one of the more significant characters. She is a moral, affectionate woman. Ferdinand is enthralled by her beauty, perceiving her as a phantasmagoria. She represents a feminine warmth and beauty to which he never was and never again will be exposed.

### Themes and Meanings

In *Death on the Installment Plan*, Céline is obsessed with human suffering and death and with the individual's efforts to cope with those horrible realities. At the end of the novel, Ferdinand becomes aware that from the moment of birth the individual is being prepared for the grave. Initially, Ferdinand, exposed to so many instances of emotional, spiritual, and physical deaths, is overwhelmed by despair, but he comes to understand and accept the frightening truth that all are paying for death on the installment plan. This realization enables him to cope with his existence. He is able to pick up the pieces and survive.

The novel is an indictment of Céline's society, which he perceives as vicious and as the primary agent of death, whether emotional, spiritual, or literal. The conditions of modern life encourage distrust, betrayal, rancor, brutality, persecution, and selfishness. Céline believed that it was his duty to open his readers' eyes to the baseness and ugliness spawned by French society. He provides graphic, naturalistic details of dust, decay, stench, vomit, and excrement. He portrays the destruction of family life, the bankruptcy of business, the callousness of the health care system. He is unsparing in his evocation of the revolting and the nauseating.

Such a world forces Ferdinand to withdraw into himself and to develop a loathing both of it and of himself. Céline's vision of society, however, is not totally bleak: There are pockets of decency that occasionally counter the pervasive brutality and corruption. In Ferdinand's case, under the mitigating influence of the few considerate characters in the novel—Caroline, Uncle Édouard, Nora Merrywin, and Courtial des Pereires—he progresses from hatred (including self-hatred) to an awakening of warmer emotions and a recognition of his worth.

The novel is very much a book about the writer and writing. Céline discusses the importance of the imaginative and the cerebral, the hallucinatory and the conscious in the creative process. He also examines its consolatory and therapeutic effect: Both the adult and the young Ferdinand find temporary respite in imaginatively creating the romantic world of King Krogold.

The legend of King Krogold functions not only as a means of escape for the narrator-protagonist; it is significant to Céline's main theme as well. He uses it as a myth to explore a truth in human nature: In the story, Gwendor the Magnificent asks Death to spare his life until he finds and destroys his betrayer, thus ridding the world of evil. Death reprimands him for wanting to live in a dream world, telling him that pain and evil are a part of life, which cannot be only joyful and beautiful.

### Critical Context

*Journey to the End of the Night* and *Death on the Installment Plan*, Céline's first two novels, are considered his most significant works and two of the greatest novels in any language. Critics are divided on which of the two is the more impressive, but they all agree that both have had a significant impact on the modern novel. Alain Robbe-Grillet has called Céline the greatest writer of the period between the wars and a major influence on *le nouveau roman*, the New Novel. Céline was admired by Jean-Paul Sartre and Jean Genet as well. Several North American writers have been influenced by him, including William Burroughs, Joseph Heller, Jack Kerouac, Henry Miller, Mordecai Richler, and Kurt Vonnegut, Jr.

When *Death on the Installment Plan* was first published, its obscene images, vulgar diction, and bleak picture of lower-class life in Paris evoked a hostile response from many reviewers. There were, however, several who recognized Céline's novel as a work of genius. Céline was neglected after World War II because of his anti-Semitic, pro-Nazi stance during the war. Contemporary writers and critics, however, have come to see him as one of the few innovative writers of the twentieth century. In his first two novels, particularly *Death on the Installment Plan*, he forced readers to open their eyes to the darkest aspects of society. He gave currency to the telegraphic, elliptical style (*les trois points*) as a means of conveying his characters' urgency and intensity of feelings, their emotional agitation, and their disturbed thought processes. He emphasized the effectiveness of everyday speech and slang (in his case, Parisian argot) in evoking the common life powerfully and authentically. He made the obscene poetic. He probed the subconscious, using the hallucinatory, delirious point of view. And he sought to free the novel from the traditional, linear, cause-and-effect narrative pattern by employing a loose, unconstrained, digressive, and rambling structure.

*Sources for Further Study*
Flynn, James, ed. *Understanding Céline*, 1984.
Hanrez, Marc. *Céline*, 1961.
McCarthy, Patrick. *Céline: A Critical Biography*, 1975.
Nettlebeck, Colin W. "Journey to the End of Art: The Evolution of the Novels of Louis-Ferdinand Céline," in *PMLA*. LXXXVII (January, 1972), pp. 80-89.
O'Connell, David. *Louis-Ferdinand Céline*, 1976.
Solomon, Philip. "Céline's *Death on the Installment Plan*: The Intoxication of Delirium," in *Yale French Studies*. L (1974), pp. 191-203.
Thiher, Allen. *Céline: The Novel as Delirium*, 1972.
Woodcock, George. "Céline Revived," in *Tamarack Review*. XLIV (1967), pp. 94-99.

*Victor J. Ramraj*

# THE DEFENSE

*Author:* Vladimir Nabokov (1899-1977)
*Type of plot:* Philosophical realism
*Time of plot:* The 1910's and 1920's
*Locale:* Russia and Germany
*First published: Zashchita Luzhina,* 1929, serial; 1930, book (English
translation, 1964)

> *Principal characters:*
> ALEKSANDR IVANOVICH LUZHIN, a world-class chess player
> MRS. LUZHIN, his fiancée and, later, his wife
> MR. and MRS. LUZHIN, SR., Luzhin's parents
> LUZHIN'S AUNT, a vivacious, redheaded young woman and the
> mistress of Luzhin, Sr.
> VALENTINOV, a chess promoter and, later, a film producer
> TURATI, Luzhin's chess opponent

*The Novel*

*The Defense* is the story of Aleksandr Ivanovich Luzhin, a brilliant Russian chess master, who is locked in a losing chess game with madness and death. Having lost one match which ended in madness, he devises a special defense which proves ineffectual in his fatal rematch.

As the novel begins, Luzhin is a morose, solitary boy of ten, spending the last days of summer at the family's country house near St. Petersburg. His father has just given him the unpleasant news that he is to start school upon their return to town. The boy loathes school. The only person for whom he feels any affection is his pretty young aunt, who proves to be his father's mistress. She introduces little Luzhin to chess on the very day that his mother learns of the affair. The boy begins skipping school to visit his aunt's apartment, where he plays chess against one of her admirers. The following summer, Luzhin, Sr., learns of his secretive son's talent, and the prodigy makes his public debut. Dropping out of school, he devotes himself exclusively to chess until he falls ill. During his prolonged recuperation, he is taken to a German health resort where, by chance, a major international chess tournament is being held. Luzhin's career is launched.

Sixteen years elapse in the course of a paragraph, and Luzhin is still at the same health resort, talking to a young woman who will become his wife. Socially, Luzhin at thirty has progressed little beyond the morose, taciturn boy of his childhood. During the intervening years, his youthful career has been managed by a Svengali-like chess promoter, Valentinov, who long since dropped his aging prodigy. Luzhin now faces a major tournament and has come to the resort to prepare himself. His bride-to-be is not put off by his eccentric, boorish behavior. After a bizarre courtship, he sets off for his tournament in Berlin, which is also the home of his fiancée's dismayed parents.

Luzhin plays brilliantly, progressing toward a final match with an opponent named Turati, against whose novel opening move he has devised a new defense. (He has lost an earlier match to Turati.) In the evenings, Luzhin visits the kitschy home of his fiancée's philistine parents. As the days pass, Luzhin, whose grasp of reality is faint at best, becomes ever more absorbed in the patterns of chess, which he imposes on his surroundings. The final match with Turati begins, but without the opening move against which Luzhin had devised his special defense. Luzhin is now so deeply sunk into the world of chess that he cannot regain the world of reality. When the game adjourns for the night, he hears a voice say "Go home."

Luzhin awakes in a sanatorium attended by a black-bearded psychiatrist who, along with Luzhin's fiancée, assures him that he must forswear chess if he is to save his sanity. Through a window, Luzhin observes a scene reminiscent of the Russian countryside and thinks, "Evidently, I got home." Luzhin successfully suppresses his chess memories and re-creates his past starting from his prechess childhood. Soon released, he returns to Berlin, where he marries his fiancée. Luzhin's new life without chess proceeds smoothly until he attends a charity ball. There, he encounters a dimly remembered childhood acquaintance who reminisces about their school days. Unaccountably distressed, Luzhin lies awake, pondering the secret meaning of the encounter. He resolves mentally to "replay all the moves of his life from his illness until the ball" in order to discover an unfolding pattern. The attentions of Luzhin's wife are now distracted by the appearance of a guest, a childhood acquaintance who has arrived on a visit from Russia with her morose eight-year-old son, who is much like Luzhin. The woman knows the aunt who taught Luzhin to play chess. Shielded by his bride from all things that might remind him of chess, Luzhin chances to overhear the guest mention his aunt. He suddenly grasps the unfolding chess moves: "With vague admiration and vague horror he observed how awesomely, how elegantly and how flexibly, move by move, the images of his childhood had been repeated (country house . . . town . . . school . . . aunt), but still he did not quite understand why this combinational repetition inspired his soul with such dread." Each stage of his life since the breakdown has repeated, in variant form, a stage of his childhood leading up to his discovery of chess which ended in his madness. Many other details are part of the repeating pattern. While his wife is preoccupied with her guest, everything seems to conspire to bring Luzhin back into the fatal world of chess. Each defensive move he makes is thwarted by an unseen opponent. At length, Valentinov, his old chess promoter, locates him with a proposal to act in a film together with his old foe Turati. Luzhin now realizes that he has lost. He chooses to resign the hopeless game by committing suicide.

## The Characters

Vladimir Nabokov once referred to his characters as "galley slaves," thus denying them the human credibility that realistic literary figures supposedly display. On the surface, Luzhin would seem to be an exception. Nabokov himself describes his lumpish, overweight, inarticulate hero as "uncouth, un-washed, uncomely—but . . . [with] something in him that transcends both the coarseness of his gray flesh and the sterility of his recondite genius." This contrast between the master of the beautifully elegant, abstract world of chess and the inept, doomed human being stirs the reader's compassion. Nevertheless, Nabokov remains remote in the treatment of his protagonist. Luzhin acquires a first name and patronymic (the usual Russian form of address) only at the moment of his death. All the actions that give Luzhin's character the illusion of humanity prove to be part of a developing novelistic chess pattern, not life. They are "moves" orchestrated from above.

Luzhin's nameless wife, the novel's only other sympathetic character, is his only link with human reality. Her love for the strange chess master is rooted in compassion rather than passion, but it is, nevertheless, real. For Luzhin, sex is obscurely linked with chess, perhaps because of his aunt's sensuality and his wife's quiet acquiescence in their asexual marriage. His wife tries only to protect Luzhin from his past, by building a normal, "chess-free" existence for him. Her valiant attempt is at first marginally successful—until her vigilance is distracted by the Russian guest, leaving Luzhin to his fatal obsession with chess.

Luzhin's parents are little more than novelistic props to establish the stages in the boy's life that will later be fatally repeated: country, town, school, aunt, and chess. It is the revelation of the father-aunt affair, coinciding with the boy's introduction to chess, that underlies the sublimation of his sexuality (and entire existence) into chess. The parents are also a target of Naboko-vian social satire. Luzhin's father, a writer of saccharine children's books, and his hypochondriacal mother present a mordant picture of Russian bourgeois high culture. This is contrasted with Luzhin's true artistry as a chess player, which the father is completely unable to comprehend, as it does not fit the stereotypical image of the child prodigy. Strangely, it is the boy's free-spirited aunt who senses his hidden talent and cultivates it with appropriate presents. The hero's reluctant in-laws, a wealthy emigrant business family, are the chief objects of derision; their Berlin apartment is filled with nostalgic fake Russian gimcracks.

Valentinov, the entrepreneur who takes over the young Luzhin's career, is a typically Nabokovian character type. He is the unscrupulous minor artist figure. A gifted man of many talents and a shrewd organizer, he coldly manipulates the lives of all whom he meets. Having launched Luzhin's career as an international chess prodigy, he drops him. Valentinov returns only to deliver the *coup de grâce*, inveigling Luzhin back into the world of chess as a bit player in a film he is producing. It is in his studio office that Luzhin finds the film magazine photo that gives him the idea for his suicide leap.

## Themes and Meanings

Chess has often been used as a metaphor for life. Nabokov uses it as a metaphor for art and art's relationship to life. Inept in life, Luzhin is a near-genius in the supremely abstract, elegant world of chess, that is, art. He is so immersed in chess that he perceives life only in terms of chess patterns. Sensing a chesslike attack being mounted against him for the second time, he correctly recognizes the unfolding pattern but mistakes the very nature of the game. He prepares the wrong defense and dies. Luzhin ultimately understands chess (art) no better than life. It is not by chance that he fails to reach the pinnacle of the chess world. Luzhin falsely believes that he is a player in a chess game with death, a game he can win if he can find the correct defense. His misconception is that he is a player, a king in the game. In reality, he is merely a pawn in a chess problem conceived by his author. The game is "fixed" by the outside, controlling artist, its creator.

*The Defense* displays a strategy common to many Nabokov novels which take the relationship of art and life as their theme. The fictional characters think that their artificial world is real. There are, however, small signs that their universe is not real, but created and controlled from outside—that is, from the world of their author. In some Nabokov novels, the protagonist, often an artist figure, senses the presence of the author-creator and is "saved." Luzhin, the failed artist, does not and is destroyed.

In some ways, this tightly constructed chess novel resembles a mystery. Like Luzhin, the reader must be on the lookout for clues, the key repetitions that form the mounting attack on the hero's sanity. Almost every event in the second part of the book subtly echoes an aspect of Luzhin's life before he learned chess. Told in the third person by an omniscient narrator and almost entirely without dialogue, *The Defense* superficially mimics a traditional realistic work but proves to be simply an elaborate game.

## Critical Context

Nabokov was a gifted composer of chess problems as well as a brilliant writer. *The Defense* brings together the two passions, justifying his remark that both require "the same virtues that characterize all worthwhile art: originality, invention, conciseness, harmony, complexity, and splendid insincerity." *The Defense* was Nabokov's third novel and firmly established him as the most important of the younger generation of Russian émigré writers. He was controversial even then, however, for many considered his concern for formal elegance rather than social and spiritual truths to be counter to the tradition of Russian literature. This reaction became even more pronounced as Nabokov moved from the relative "realism" of *The Defense* to the highly sophisticated modernism of his later masterpieces, *Invitation to a Beheading* and *The Gift*. In 1940, the bilingual Nabokov started to write almost exclusively in English, with such works as *Lolita* (1955), *Pale Fire* (1962), and *Ada or Ardor: A Family Chronicle* (1969), which brought him international acclaim. Banned in his homeland during his lifetime, Nabokov's fiction at last took its place in Russian literature with the Soviet publication of *The Defense* in 1986.

*Sources for Further Study*

Cockburn, Alexander. "Paths of Exile: Nabokov's Grand Master," in *Idle Passion: Chess and the Dance of Death*, 1974.

Johnson, D. Barton. "Text and Pre-text in *The Defense*," in *Worlds in Regression: Some Novels of Vladimir Nabokov*, 1985.

Moody, Fred. "Nabokov's Gambit," in *Russian Literature Triquarterly*. XIV (1976), pp. 67-70.

Purdy, Strother B. "Solus Rex: Nabokov and the Chess Novel," in *Modern Fiction Studies*. XIV (Winter, 1968-1969), pp. 379-395.

Updike, John. "Grandmaster Nabokov," in *Assorted Prose*, 1965.

*D. Barton Johnson*

# DEMIAN

*Author:* Hermann Hesse (1877-1962)
*Type of plot:* Bildungsroman
*Time of plot:* 1905-1915
*Locale:* Germany
*First published:* 1919 (English translation, 1923)

> *Principal characters:*
> EMIL SINCLAIR, the protagonist and narrator, a young student
> MAX DEMIAN, a fellow student
> FRAU EVA, Demian's mother
> PISTORIUS, an organist and former theology student; Sinclair's mentor
> KNAUER, a younger schoolboy
> FRANZ KROMER, Sinclair's adversary, also a student

## The Novel

*Demian* narrates the life of its protagonist, Emil Sinclair, from the age of ten until past the age of eighteen from the viewpoint of an older Sinclair looking back upon his youth. Essentially a *Bildungsroman* with heavy emphasis on psychology, the novel focuses on persons and experiences that contribute to the protagonist's development and to his uniqueness as an individual. In his preface to the novel, Hermann Hesse emphasizes the significance of the individual human being, who "represents the unique, the very special and always significant and remarkable point at which the world's phenomena intersect, only once in this way and never again."

At age ten, Sinclair belongs to a comfortable, secure middle-class German family that includes his parents and two older sisters, yet he stands on the verge of troubling and sweeping changes in his life. One day at school, in an effort to impress other boys, he invents an account of stealing apples from a local orchard and swears to its truth. This false confession leads to distress when Franz Kromer, an older boy, informs him that the orchard owner has offered a reward for information about the theft and then blackmails Sinclair over a period of months.

During this time, a boy named Max Demian enrolls in the school and notices Sinclair. Sensing Sinclair's anguish, Demian learns its cause, and soon afterward Kromer's intimidation ceases, though Sinclair never learns how. Demian, who thinks for himself and seems to possess unusual psychic powers, interprets the story of Cain and Abel to Sinclair in such a way that Cain becomes the hero. Thereafter, Sinclair recognizes the mark of Cain on himself and others as a mark of distinction. Demian also assures him that although an individual does not have free will, he can achieve anything upon which he concentrates his entire will and effort.

Once freed from Kromer, Sinclair, like the prodigal son, returns to the secure and ordered family life that had been strained by his ordeal. After seeing little of Demian for several years, Sinclair encounters him again in confirmation class. The rapport between them is restored when the teacher alludes to the Cain and Abel story. Demian explains other biblical stories to Sinclair, offering interpretations different from those usually accepted. Just as he admires Cain, he also admires the steadfastness of the unrepentent thief on the cross. When the class ends, Sinclair leaves the city to enroll in a boarding school, and the tie with Demian is broken.

At boarding school, Sinclair finds himself lonely, homesick, and generally miserable. He wanders through the streets alone, drinks too much, and neglects his studies. When Alfons Beck, an older boy, boasts of sexual exploits with older women, Sinclair thinks that this bragging is degrading to the ideal of love. While walking alone, he sees an attractive girl and begins to build a fantasy based upon this brief meeting. Naming his idealized love Beatrice, he resolves to live nobly in accordance with the image he has created. He gives up his bad habits, applies himself in school, and begins to paint.

In an effort to reestablish contact with Demian, he paints a sparrow hawk escaping from an egg and leaves the painting at Demian's last known address. Later, he finds inside a book on his desk at school a note from Demian interpreting the painting. The note mentions the Gnostic deity Abraxas, a figure unknown to Sinclair, who combines within himself both the holy and the satanic. To Sinclair's surprise, his teacher discusses Abraxas in the daily lesson. As his ideal of Beatrice fades, Sinclair seeks self-understanding through dreams and symbols.

On one of his walks through the town, he encounters a church organist named Pistorius, a former theology student who knows about Abraxas. Pistorius becomes Sinclair's mentor, assisting him with the interpretation of dreams and symbols. Yet Sinclair finally parts from him because the organist's interest lies in the past, not the future. His knowledge helped Sinclair toward self-understanding, but as Sinclair recognizes, it did not help Pistorius find his own way. Sinclair has, however, learned enough about good and evil to help others. He saves a boy named Knauer, guilt-ridden over his sexual urges, from suicidal despair.

Seeking Demian once again, Sinclair finds at his former home a photograph of Demian's mother, Frau Eva, whom he has not met. She becomes a dream image for him, an ideal and an object of Platonic love. Obsessed with her image, he searches for her and Demian until he discovers them living in a university town. In their home, where he spends many happy hours, he learns that like Demian she possesses psychic powers and knows about Abraxas. Among their circle of acquaintances, which includes a variety of seekers, Sinclair discusses and debates questions concerning philosophy and religion.

The joy and tranquillity of this life are shattered by dreams portending the destruction of Europe. Demian, predicting war, believes that humanity will be destroyed and reestablished on a higher plane. When war comes, both Demian and Sinclair are called to military service. They meet once during the conflict, as casualties in a military hospital. Recognizing Sinclair, the dying Demian kisses him and promises to remain with him. Afterward, when Sinclair looks into a mirror, he recognizes features of Demian as part of himself.

*The Characters*

Sinclair, the narrator-hero of *Demian*, represents a largely autobiographical figure. Both the setting and the school experiences reflect Hesse's youth in Calw, his native town, located near Germany's Black Forest. The character of Pistorius is based upon the Swiss psychologist Dr. J. B. Lang, who treated Hesse and introduced him to Carl Gustav Jung's psychoanalytic theories.

Sinclair struggles to achieve his own individual identity, described metaphorically as a path or way to meaning in life. He feels compelled to break out of his conventional background and establish his independence, even though he realizes that the way or path never ends, that stasis can never be achieved. For his understanding of himself, he draws upon symbols, dreams, an evolutionary perspective, and insights provided by other characters. Sinclair is depicted as vulnerable, sensitive, and intelligent.

Other characters are less clearly drawn; indeed, they often seem to be shadowy abstractions existing primarily to contribute to the hero's growth and development. Among them, only Demian appears throughout most of the novel. Older and more mature than Sinclair, he becomes a kind of model and a source of encouragement; as Theodore Ziolkowski notes, he represents a Christ figure. Demian possesses a magnetic personality, strong independence, and insights beyond his years. Something of a mystery to others and usually aloof, he can interpret symbols and dreams.

Franz Kromer is portrayed as a clever and cunning opportunist willing to take advantage of weaker boys such as Sinclair. Pistorius, the theologian-organist, contributes to Sinclair's development by explaining symbols and dreams to him, yet because he is oriented toward the past, he is unable to find his own way.

Demian's mother, Frau Eva, clearly demonstrates the subordination of characters to the protagonist's development. A wealthy middle-aged widow, she treats her son more like a friend than a child. Endowed with warmth and dignity, she is cultured, profoundly learned, and intuitive. In her romantic outlook, she emphasizes the mutual attraction of human beings, yet Sinclair never approaches her too closely. In his dreams and fantasies, he transforms her into an earth goddess, a mother of mankind like Eve, and a Platonic love

ideal. As his earlier idealistic image of Beatrice had, his love for Frau Eva
contributes to his emotional development and powerfully influences his behavior. In his evolutionary view as applied to mankind, she becomes a symbol
of rebirth and renewal.

## Themes and Meanings

*Demian* has as its dominant theme the development of the individual from
dependency to independence, from innocence to understanding and acceptance. Hesse's views on human development encompass a wide range of earlier psychology and philosophy. The Romantic individualism of Jean-Jacques
Rousseau and Novalis, the primacy of will as envisioned by Arthur Schopenhauer and Friedrich Neitzsche, neo-Darwinism, and the psychological theories of Sigmund Freud and Jung are among many sources influencing the
novel's perspective.

In order to explain Sinclair's painting of the sparrow hawk, fully mature,
emerging from a sphere as if from an egg, Demian wrote the following: "The
bird fights its way out of the egg. The egg is the world. Who would be born
must first destroy a world. The bird flies to God. That God's name is
Abraxas." George Wallace Field has shown that the passage reflects Jung's
psychology of symbols, but it also represents a cryptic index to the novel's
main themes. The bird represents both the individual and mankind in general. The individual discovers his identity only by breaking ties to his past. In
doing so, he experiences sorrow and guilt, which can be dealt with successfully only through dreams, myths, and symbols such as the god Abraxas, who
combines or synthesizes good and evil and represents a symbol of Nietzsche's
conception of an existence beyond good and evil.

To project idealized dream visions upon persons, as Sinclair does with
Beatrice and Frau Eva, is to experience what Freud called the process of
sublimation. Sexual energy is thus channeled into something outside reality.
To go beyond this and endow the images with symbolic significance, treating
the symbols as universals, is to incorporate Jung's view that psychic energy
thus channeled leads a person to profound insights and contributes to psychic
integration and development.

When Sinclair joins Demian and his mother, he finds that those in their
circle study symbols in order to understand contemporary events. The novel
at this point conveys a decidedly antitechnology theme, technology being
viewed as destructive to individualism.

The theme of the isolated individual seeking identity through exertion of
the will has its origin in the philosophy of Schopenhauer and Nietzsche. The
idea that one survives as a seeker only if one achieves integration of personality through symbols with religious meanings derives primarily from Jung.
The novel clearly reflects Hesse's view that the unique individual represents
the highest value. The purpose of the individual in life is self-discovery and

development; these goals are achieved through suffering, through unconscious illumination, through interaction with others, and through an understanding of universal symbols.

*Critical Context*

Although Hesse had published five novels before *Demian* appeared, this novel was his first to be widely acclaimed in Europe, and it still ranks alongside *Siddhartha* (1922) and *Der Steppenwolf* (1927; *Steppenwolf*, 1929) as one of his most widely acclaimed works. All three of these novels are concerned primarily with the search for identity, and all are loosely autobiographical. *Demian* received high praise from Thomas Mann when it first appeared; in addition, it was published under the pseudonym Emil Sinclair and received the Fontane Prize of the City of West Berlin for the best first novel of its year. Hesse promptly returned the prize, since he was not qualified according to its terms, and the author's identity became generally known by 1920.

Although Hesse lived in Switzerland and became a Swiss citizen, his works were published in Germany and distributed by German publishers. Because his works were objectionable to authorities during the Nazi era, his popularity with readers declined. When he received the Nobel Prize for Literature in 1946, it was for his total contribution to literature and not for a particular work. Along with Hesse's other important novels, *Demian* was widely read in the United States during the 1960's, when the hippie movement made Hesse a kind of counterculture hero.

The novel's appeal diminished somewhat, as did that of Hesse's works in general, after 1970. It is sometimes regarded as an important example of the existential novel, although it can hardly be said to anticipate later existential philosophy. The idea that an individual develops primarily from within his own psyche, a view that largely ignores heredity and the external influences of education and culture, reflects a limited and extreme legacy of Romanticism. Except for Sinclair, few of the characters are memorable or well-rounded. With its prophecy of change, which envisioned a new Europe and a new European man, the novel proved excessively optimistic.

*Sources for Further Study*
Boulby, Mark. *Hermann Hesse: His Mind and Art*, 1967.
Field, George Wallis. *Hermann Hesse*, 1970.
Mileck, Joseph. *Hermann Hesse: Life and Art*, 1978.
Otten, Anna, ed. *Hesse Companion*, 1977.
Ziolkowski, Theodore. *The Novels of Hermann Hesse: A Story in Theme and Structure*, 1965.

*Stanley Archer*

# THE DEMONS

*Author:* Heimito von Doderer (1896-1966)
*Type of plot:* Historical chronicle
*Time of plot:* 1926-1927 and 1955
*Locale:* Vienna and its environs
*First published: Die Dämonen: Nach der Chronik des Sektionsrates*
  *Geyrenhoff*, 1956 (English translation, 1961)

### Principal characters:

GEORG VON GEYRENHOFF, the narrator, a retired civil servant
IMRE VON GYURKICZ, a newspaper cartoonist, a painter, and
  a friend of Charlotte von Schlaggenberg
MARY K., a widow who has lost a leg in a streetcar accident
LEONHARD KAKABSA, a young factory worker who educates
  himself
ANNA KAPSREITER, the widowed sister of Mathias Csmarits,
  a keeper of a dream-book
FINANCIAL COUNSELOR LEVIELLE, the villain
GÉZA VON ORKAY, a Hungarian diplomat, the cousin of
  Geyrenhoff
FRIEDERIKE RUTHMAYR, an immensely wealthy widow
CHARLOTTE VON SCHLAGGENBERG (QUAPP), an aspiring
  violinist
KAJETAN VON SCHLAGGENBERG, a novelist and Quapp's
  brother
GRETE SIEBENSCHEIN, René von Stangeler's girlfriend
RENÉ VON STANGELER, a brilliant young historian
RUODLIEB VON DER VLÄNTSCH, the author of a late medieval
  manuscript

## The Novel

A retired civil servant, Section Councillor Georg von Geyrenhoff keeps a chronicle for a group called "Our Crowd," which has come together in Vienna during the fall of 1926 and the spring of 1927. As narrator, Geyrenhoff commissions the novelist Kajetan von Schlaggenberg and the historian René von Stangeler to assist him in writing this diary, while numerous lesser characters become unwitting collaborators, spies, and reporters of unwitnessed events. The final report on the people and events is not issued until twenty-eight years later, in 1955.

There are 142 characters, of which more than thirty are main characters, while about three dozen play not insignificant roles in the development of the novel. Additionally, another two dozen or more appear as nameless and minor or auxiliary characters in this 1,330-page novel. It is not possible to speak of a plot of *The Demons* in the traditional sense; one simply observes the development of various characters, some events, and several documents as they are presented by the chroniclers.

With the benefit of hindsight, Geyrenhoff is "preparing to summarize and revise the whole story" now, in 1955:

> Terrible things took place in my native land and in this, my native city, at a time long after the grave and lighthearted stories I wish to relate here had come to an end. And one thing that lay curled amorphous and germinal within the events that I must recount, emerged dripping blood, took on a name, became visible to the eye which had been almost blinded by the vortex of events, shot forth, and was, even in its beginnings, recognizable—gruesomely inconspicuous and yet distinctly recognizable for what it was.

The historical events that Heimito von Doderer describes in great detail, although they are almost totally peripheral to the development of the main characters, are those which led to the burning of the Palace of Justice in Vienna on July 15, 1927. By the mid-1920's, there had been many confrontations in Austria between right-wing Fascist and left-wing Socialist paramilitary groups. Often these clashes occurred in the countryside adjoining the Hungarian border, in the Burgenland province. It was in the village of Schattendorf on January 30, 1927, that members of the Socialist Republican Protective Association staged a march. In the novel, they are met by supporters of the right-wing Veterans of the Front, who fatally wound a war veteran, Mathias Csmarits, and a young boy, Pepi Grössing. Although two men were charged with the murders, when they came to trial on July 14, 1927, they were acquitted. This was the fifth time that crimes of violence committed by right-wing organizations had gone unpunished. The Socialists saw this as another example of injustice to the proletariat and resolved to stage a peaceful strike and a workers' march in Vienna on the next day. The peaceful protest march turned to violence, and the marchers set fire to the Palace of Justice. Doderer notes that the destruction of this great symbol of justice "signified the Cannae of Austrian freedom. But no one knew that at the time," least of all the characters of the novel.

Historically, it can be seen that the open fights between the Republican Protective Association (the Socialists who comprised about 40 percent of the population) and the Austrian Fascist Party (the Home Defense Front, which was a very small political entity) led to the internal weakening of Austria at a time just shortly after the collapse of the six-hundred-year-old Habsburg monarchy. This internal crisis in the mid-1920's made it possible for Fascist Germany to annex Austria in 1938 and led to destruction and defeat in 1945. Doderer recognized this as an important moment in history, when his native land began the pursuit of an ideology—he calls it a "second reality"—that could only lead to destruction. The chronicler Geyrenhoff had to experience the totality of that "second reality" before he could tell the whole story from the perspective of twenty-eight years later.

Geyrenhoff does not write about each main character in diary fashion. If one can speak at all about a plot in *The Demons*, it would be the efforts of Financial Counselor Levielle to cheat Charlotte von Schlaggenberg out of her inheritance. From this situation emanate a multitude of subplots, many highly convoluted and fragmented, not necessarily following a common chronology and not always set in Vienna during that 1926-1927 period. Geyrenhoff advises the reader in the "Overture" to the novel: "[I]n fact you need only draw a single thread at any point you choose out of the fabric of life and the run will make a pathway across the whole, and down that wider pathway each of the other threads will become successively visible, one by one."

Charlotte von Schlaggenberg, usually called "Quapp," is an aspiring violinist. She is of the opinion that she should become a soloist and learns only in time, as well as through failure at an audition, that she has no real musical talent. In time she also learns that she is the illegitimate daughter of the late Captain Georg Ruthmayr, a wealthy landowner, and Baroness Claire von Neudegg. Her problems are solved when she inherits large sums of money from the estates of her natural parents.

The financier Levielle is the villain of the novel. As executor of Captain Ruthmayr's will and financial adviser to Ruthmayr's widow, Friederike Ruthmayr, Levielle stands to have access to great sums of money, especially if he does not reveal the facts of Quapp's parentage. Geyrenhoff and a group of boys retrieve the captain's will, locate Alois Gach, who witnessed the will when he served as a sergeant in Ruthmayr's regiment, and send Levielle packing for Paris.

Quapp's brother, Kajetan von Schlaggenberg, is a professional writer and Geyrenhoff's collaborator in writing this chronicle. He only agrees to help, however, if he can include his own "Chronique Scandaleuse," a manuscript that makes up the chapter entitled "Fat Females." Geyrenhoff agrees to use only a small "censored" portion of this document, which serves as an example of "Kajetan's Theory of the Necessity of Fat Females to the Sex Life of the Superior Man Today." In the introduction, Geyrenhoff suggests that "this minor insanity clearly exposes how utterly foolish so-called 'ideologies' in general are, by contrast with the life they would hope to improve." In spite of the perverse humor this chapter adds to the novel, it is an important example of Doderer's attempt to reveal how an ideology can be rendered a scientific theory through the employment of "pseudoscientific words" and an acceptable "methodology." Geyrenhoff writes, "In times to come, we would find similar words playing the same role in a different context: 'Provocateurs,' 'saboteurs.' . . . In times to come, we would find altogether different things being turned inside out—among them, for example, conscience."

Another manuscript included in the novel is usually identified by the name of its author, Ruodlieb von der Vläntsch, and entitled "Specyfyeth of how the sorceresses delt wyth atte Neudegck whan that they were taken Anno MCCCCLXIIIJ." The manuscript is written in the Bavarian dialect of Early New High German, and the translators have rendered the late medieval manuscript in the language of William Caxton, the first English printer (c. 1422-1491). In order to assist the modern reader, who may have difficulty in understanding the older language, René von Stangeler reads the manuscript and offers interlinear glosses.

The story which the manuscript relates is the trial in 1464 of two women charged with practicing sorcery. This trial examined an aspect of sorcery which had not been considered at that time, namely, the sexual power of magic. According to the manuscript, the master of the castle, Achaz Neudegg, tried to gain control over two women under the guise of a trial. Each evening, the women were brought before the judges to confess that they were witches, which they denied. The bailiffs, Heimo and Ruodl, then took them to a special torture chamber where they were undressed and struck with a light satin-covered rope. The only harm they suffered was the indignity of appearing nude in the presence of the bailiffs. Achaz Neudegg participated only as a voyeur, while the bailiffs became personally and sexually involved with the witches. Heimo thrived in this "Sodhom and Ghommorah," but Ruodl, "an innocent lamb," suffered great pangs of conscience. Each time Ruodl reflected on what he was doing, he realized that his lustful desires were the result of a divided personality over which he had no control. He observed, "[I]t was like a border goeth thurgh me, on one syde am I Ruodl and on tother am I al wode." Again, Doderer has created a character who experiences a "second reality," a personality alien to himself.

The castle in which the medieval manuscript is found has just been inherited by Jan Herzka, who enlists the aid of René von Stangeler to read and interpret the text. René also oversees the modernization of the castle and is given the publication rights for the manuscript. With this good fortune in his professional life, René now enjoys a marked improvement in his relationship with his fiancée, Grete Siebenschein, and is regarded as a favorable choice of husband by the Siebenschein family. The family has created a typical bourgeois concept of life and has imposed this "second reality" on their prospective son-in-law.

A third manuscript included in the novel is "Kaps's Night Book." It is a diary by Anna Kapsreiter, a relative of the victims of the January, 1927, Schattendorf killings. The two chapters of the novel devoted to this manuscript record only thirteen dreams. Although the dreams are related directly to Anna's waking life, they reveal a highly prophetic insight into the life and times of many characters and events treated in the novel. Whereas the other two manuscripts reveal a "second reality" from a contemporaneous and a historical perspective, "Kaps's Night Book" demonstrates a future "first reality": a valid apperception of events of which Geyrenhoff speaks when he talks of "terrible things [that] took place in my native land and in this, my native city" twenty-eight years after the personal and historic events that constitute the novel.

## The Characters

When Geyrenhoff sets out to write the diary of "Our Crowd," he is dealing for the most part with characters from similar social and economic backgrounds, that is, the upper-middle class in Vienna. The group is occasionally brought together by Captain von Eulenfeld for a night of drunken carousing, wild automobile chasing through the various districts in Vienna, and generally debauched disturbances of the peace. The membership of "Our Crowd" includes the narrator; Kajetan and Quapp von Schlaggenberg; René von Stangeler and Grete Siebenschein; the history student Dr. Neuberg and his fiancée, Angelika Trapp; the newspaper cartoonist Imre von Gyurkicz, who is a friend of Quapp; and the Hungarian diplomat Géza von Orkay. They seem to believe that they have to play the role of the younger generation, since they have experienced World War I and the subsequent change from the monarchy to the republic. In reality, however, they were no longer part of that generation; they were living in a "second reality."

Leonhard Kakabsa belongs to a very different part of Viennese society. He is a young factory worker who is satisfied with his position in life and seeks no change in his occupation. Quite by accident and out of curiosity, he begins to teach himself Latin one day. He works hard and diligently on this task, but without a particular goal or change in life-style in mind. In time, he realizes that he has acquired the ability of intellectual freedom, since he can now use language in any social setting in an appropriate and productive manner (Doderer refers to this as the "crossing of the dialect barrier"). Through his studies, Leonhard also learns of Pico della Mirandola's essay "On the Dignity of Man," which gives him a philosophical and theological basis for his life. Through his acquaintance with Mary K., a woman who has come to terms with her life after she lost a leg in a streetcar accident, Leonhard meets Prince Alfons Croix and finds a new vocation as his librarian. In his relationship with Mary K., he never takes an aggressively active role, and in time they enjoy a mature, loving, and sensitive life together.

Leonhard is the most fully developed character in the novel. Unlike the members of "Our Crowd," he is capable of always apperceiving his own level of development and consequently lives in a constant "first reality."

Other characters in the novel include representatives of all sections of the Viennese world of 1926 to 1927. They range from the elegant world of the now-immensely wealthy widow Friederike Ruthmayr to the underworld of the barmaid Anna Diwald, the prostitute Anny Gräven, and the murderer

Meisgeier. Doderer has painted a great panorama of Vienna in its "ecstasy, despair, boredom, or triumph."

## Themes and Meanings

In the penultimate chapter of _The Demons_, entitled "The Fire," Doderer not only brings the historical events of the novel to a conclusion but also brings the major characters to a critical conclusion in their lives. Leonhard's story is one of success, because he has not been encumbered by a "second reality." He is a free man who has become self-sufficient as a human being; he has not fallen prey to the ideologies, misperceptions, and demons that haunt most of the other characters.

On the day that the Palace of Justice burns, many members of "Our Crowd" experience some sort of shock which enables them to apperceive the world in which they live. Kajetan has given up his mania for fat females and will begin again as a novelist; René von Stangeler will marry because he is now established as a historian; Quapp realizes that she has no talent for playing the violin and—now that she is also rich—will marry Géza von Orkay, who will be an important diplomat for the Hungarian government in Basil. Geyrenhoff, now that he has exposed Levielle as an embezzler and sent him into exile, will marry the wealthy Friederike Ruthmayr.

Doderer sees the day of the fire not as the idyllic moment that the individual characters experience but as the "Cannae of Austrian freedom." The annexation of Austria by Nazi Germany and World War II became for him and his country a terrible time of living in a "second reality." It was only with the collapse of Nazism and the passing of the great conflagration of World War II that a "first reality" was regained. Doderer is by no means naïve enough, however, to think that totalitarian ideologies cannot return. It is only through a constant apperception of all aspects of one's world that the demons of the "second reality" can be exposed and that life in a "first reality" is possible.

## Critical Context

Heimito von Doderer devoted twenty-five years to writing _The Demons_. This major novel secured for Doderer a position as one of the major European novelists, along with Thomas Mann, Robert Musil, Hermann Broch, Marcel Proust, and James Joyce. He started writing the book in 1930 and finished the first part in 1936. In the years from 1951 to 1956, he completed the novel in its present form. In the intervening years, he also published, among numerous other works, the two other novels that belong to his cycle of Viennese novels: _Die erleuchteten Fenster: Oder, Die Menschwerdung des Amtsrates Julius Zihal_ (1950; the illuminated windows: or, the humanization of councillor Julius Zihal) and _Die Strudlhofstiege: Oder, Melzer und die Tiefe der Jahre_ (1951; the Strudlhof steps: or, Melzer and the depth of the years). *The Demons* is the most complex of that cycle, containing a complete exposition of Doderer's views on the basis and function of the novel and his role as a novelist. Furthermore, it offered Doderer a context in which to articulate his views on critical philosophical, psychological, and historical issues.

The response to *The Demons* has been slow in coming but for the most part positive. The size of the novel, as well as its structural and thematic complexity, has made it somewhat problematic for many readers. With the publication of Doderer's diaries *Tangenten: Tagebuch eines Schriftstellers 1940-1950* (1964; tangents, diary of a writer) and *Commentarii: Tagebücher aus d. Nachlass* (1976), along with other works of a novelistic and essayistic nature, there has been substantial and continuous scholarly work devoted to interpreting *The Demons*.

*Sources for Further Study*
Bachem, Michael. *Heimito von Doderer*, 1981.
*Books Abroad*. XLII, no. 3 (1968). Special Doderer issue.
Falk, Thomas H. *Heimito von Doderer's Concept of the Novel: Theory and Practice*, 1970.
Hamburger, Michael. *From Prophecy to Exorcism*, 1965.
Hesson, Elizabeth C. *Twentieth Century Odyssey: A Study of Heimito von Doderer's "Die Dämonen,"* 1983.
Politzer, Heinz. "Heimito von Doderer's *Demons* and the Modern Kakanian Novel," in *The Contemporary Novel in German*, 1967. Edited by Robert R. Heitner.
Weber, Dietrich. *Heimito von Doderer*, 1987.

*Thomas H. Falk*

# DEVOTION

*Author:* Botho Strauss (1944-     )
*Type of plot:* Psychological realism
*Time of plot:* Summer, 1976
*Locale:* West Berlin
*First published: Die Widmung,* 1977 (English translation, 1979)

>    *Principal characters:*
>        RICHARD SCHROUBEK, thirty-one years old, a former
>            bookseller
>        HANNAH BEYL, the girlfriend who has left him

*The Novel*

Devastated by the sudden and unexplained departure of his girlfriend, Hannah Beyl, from his Berlin apartment, Richard Schroubek quits his job in a bookstore and waits in vain for her return. After a few days of roaming around the divided city, Richard barricades himself in his apartment, closes the curtains, and begins writing a journal dedicated to her (hence the story's German title, *Die Widmung,* "the dedication"). His notes are at first short and aphoristic, but as the weeks go by he writes more and more and eventually spends seven or eight hours a day writing. Regarding the separation as only temporary, he writes in the hope that she will return one day and read "his conscientious and terrible protocol of her absence."

In order to pay off their accumulated bills, Richard sells an inherited etching by the German expressionist Max Beckmann, but very little money remains afterward. One morning, he is visited by a fat young man named Fritz, who claims that he has spent three days with Hannah. She has deserted him as well, and he comes hoping to find out why. Unnerved by someone who regards himself as Richard's "companion in misery," Richard locks himself in Hannah's room, where he has been keeping the manuscript for her. The telephone, which was disconnected because of overdue bills, rings in another room. It is Hannah, who has apparently paid the telephone bills. She wants to talk to Richard, but Fritz answers and excitedly agrees to meet her. By the time Richard unlocks Hannah's door, Fritz is gone, and there is only a dial tone on the telephone.

His money spent, Richard fires Frau N., the cleaning lady and his last living connection to the outside world. Having given up books for television, he watches intently the news accounts of the catastrophic heat wave that has enveloped Europe since the beginning of the summer. He begins to develop bad habits, such as not bothering to clean the apartment, wearing the same clothes every day, and not bathing. One day, he absentmindedly tips over the honey jar onto his papers. He notices the honey only when he gets stuck in it on the floor. In a panic, he pours a box of laundry detergent and a basin of water over it, then mops up the ensuing mess with old shirts. Another accident soon occurs. He pulls the chain on the toilet too hard and breaks the shut-off valve. In the process of repairing the toilet, he falls into the toilet bowl and breaks his glasses. After he has fixed the valve ("my last silent film," he says to himself with a bit of satisfaction), he mops up the considerable amount of water on the floor with the gray flannel suit that he wore to work.

Richard writes during the day and spends his evenings in front of the television. In his "TV delirium," he switches back and forth between channels but retains little of what he watches, besides the latest news about the heat and the payoff of a children's lottery in which a little girl won a thousand identical dolls. Having consumed the last of the TV dinners and yogurts in the refrigerator, he realizes that he will have to break his isolation soon. He begins to admit defeat: "I can see how my heroic and festive despair is shriveling into a miserable petty-bourgeois sadness," he writes in one of his last entries.

In his weakened condition, Richard can no longer write. The television is on constantly now, even after the broadcasts have stopped. Hannah calls and wants to meet him at a bar. Oblivious to his filthy appearance, he runs out of his apartment but falls in the corridor, where he remembers his writings, the "biography of his empty hours," which he gathers together into an old briefcase. On the way down the stairs, he hears his phone ring. He falls again on the way up, but the ringing has stopped by the time he reaches his door. When he meets Hannah outside the bar, she tells him that she called a second time to tell him not to come. She is drunk and disheveled and has ordered a taxi. Richard gives her the briefcase with the manuscript through the taxi window. She promises to read it.

Feeling released from "his stubborn neglect of himself," he resolves to start a normal life the next day. He finds a new job selling books, cleans the apartment, and restocks the refrigerator with delicacies for her return. When she has not called after a week and a half, he goes to the bar where he last saw her. The host has not seen her recently, but a package has been left for him. It is the briefcase with the manuscript. Hannah left it in the taxi. Richard returns to his apartment and turns on the television. An aging pop singer is performing on a request concert. The man, "dragged in out of the past," tries to synchronize with the scratchy recording of his own song but can no longer remember the lyrics.

### The Characters

When he wrote *Devotion*, Botho Strauss was, like his protagonist Richard Schroubek, thirty-one years old, a resident of West Berlin, and an apolitical recluse and introspective survivor of the German student movement of the late 1960's. Despite these similarities and Schroubek's Strauss-like observations on Berliners and contemporary West German cultural stagnation, Strauss distances himself from his character by making him comically grotesque. The deeper Richard works himself into his self-imposed isolation and verbal narcissism, the more ridiculous he becomes. As he tries to cover up with a bohemian existence the emotional and social emptiness of his life, his despair becomes a pose, his increasing slovenliness a façade. He is aware of his own comic posturing as "Richard-without-life" and adds that "the comedy is only a protective ether that keeps the pain fresh."

Richard's greatest fear is of his own normality, the fact that he might be just like every other jilted lover, "lethargic, dim-witted, constipated," as Fritz tells him. Although Richard misses the cleaning lady after her dismissal, she, twenty-five and happily married, epitomizes for him the kind of person he does not want to be, a self-satisfied, comfortable, unenlightened member of the consumer society. He, on the other hand, claims to long for poverty, solitude, shabby physical surroundings, and an erotic sensitivity to phenomena. Yet his growing addiction to television and his rapid return to normality after his brief encounter with Hannah unmask his own basic shallowness.

Lacking political and social energy, Richard has no creative outlet outside his writing. Yet his own attempts to intensify experience pale beside the great works of literature. When he reads Ivan Turgenev's *Fathers and Sons*, he finds that the novel's characters live "on a higher plateau of sensibility" that has no correspondence to the "low-calorie emotional diet" of contemporary daily life. Without a sympathetic and faithful listener or reader (such as his idealized Hannah), Richard's utterances threaten to deteriorate into inarticulate gurglings, like those of the Dante's *accidiosi*, the melancholy and apathetic slime dwellers of the Inferno. Nevertheless, compared to the "dull tumult of images" emerging from the television, writing, "the great intensifier, the *tracing*, . . . the lasting spoor of language," is the sole activity that makes him feel alive.

When Richard finally meets Hannah again, he hardly recognizes her. She is in some ways a mirror image of his own appearance: "[B]oth were dirty and had lost weight, were in rags, and unprepossessing to the point of being unrecognizable." The narrator dryly calls them two "social casualties of love." Although very little is revealed about Hannah, her love is likely not for Richard and perhaps not even for the unattractive school porter Fritz, who was with her at the bar. While *Devotion* invites comparison to Johann Wolfgang von Goethe's *Die Leiden des jungen Werthers* (1774; *The Sorrows of Young Werther*, 1779), Richard is at best an emaciated Werther, and Hannah, rather than being the subject of Richard's adoration and praise, as was Werther's beloved Charlotte, is the object of his self-indulgent fantasies. Richard's solipsistic world thus remains virtually intact once he returns to his apartment after retrieving his manuscript. Without the hope of ever reaching his lover through his writing, he seems condemned to a lifeless existence in front of his television set.

## Themes and Meanings

Hannah's departure forces Richard to realize more keenly that he lives in an empty present, a present devoid of memory, history, and personal biography. Although he ultimately—and comically—fails as a writer, his manuscript does leave a genuine trace of who he is and was. As such, it counteracts the "verbal free-for-all" and "nervous synchronism" that the narrator sees as characteristic of contemporary Germany. Strauss, through Richard, condemns those performing artists who create a false presence of a text by destroying its historical con-text, "its secret as a relic": "In the presence of such people, memory fails us; they wipe out the written, the diachronic desire." Writing, then, is the only means for combating the epoch's ahistoricity, memory loss, and obsession with an all-consuming present.

Writing, however, does not have as its primary function enlightenment, either in the form of greater self-understanding or critical cultural analysis. Rather, it offers a compensation for the shallowness of experience, a momentary withdrawal from the thin and smug public sphere. Richard's self-analysis similarly aims not to unmask the unconscious but to enrich it. He would want as his conversational partner not a disinterested psychoanalyst but a seductive tempter such as Mephisto, whose "moving concern" and "delighted interpretation" intensify Faust's desire instead of curing him of it in Goethe's *Faust*.

The seriousness of Richard's failures is contrasted by the ironic, and often comic, undertones of the narration. The introduction to Richard's manuscript and the epilogue, entitled "Berlin Without End," are reported by a sympathetic, but coolly objective narrator, who, in addition, interrupts Richard's monologue for four of the eleven chapters of the main body of the novel, "For H." This disrupted narration prevents the story from sinking to Richard's level of self-pity or to the meaningless gurglings of Dante's melancholics. Indeed, the novel's changing narrative perspectives, ironic tone, and feuilletonistic style give it a buoyancy that starkly contrasts with the grimness of the protagonist's decline.

## Critical Context

*Devotion* is Botho Strauss's most successful and accessible narrative. Together with his drama *Trilogie des Wiedersehens* (1976; trilogy of reunion), *Devotion* marks the turning point in his writing career. Strauss's earlier plays, *Die Hypochonder* (1971; the hypochondriacs) and *Bekannte Gesichter, gemischte Gefühle* (1974; familiar faces, mixed feelings), and the two stories published under the title *Marlenes Schwester* (1975; Marlene's sister) were too esoteric and complex to reach a wide audience. Strauss's later works, however, reflect the emotional reality of a politically quiescent Germany in the later 1970's and the 1980's with a precision unmatched by any other German writer. With the dramas *Gross und Klein* (1978; big and little), *Kalldewey, Farce* (1981), *Der Park* (1983; the park), and *Die Fremdenführerin* (1986; *The Tourist Guide*, 1987), Strauss has become the most performed contemporary dramatist on the German stage. The short prose collected in *Paare, Passanten* (1981; couples, passersby) further develops Strauss's acerbic observations of people groping to find love and meaning in a nervously satiated society. The first of his two longer novels, *Rumor* (1980), deals with the disintegration of a father involved in an incestuous relationship with his daughter. The second, *Der junge Mann* (1984; the young man), is a loose series of realistic, parodic, allegorical, and imaginary narratives centered on the fifteen-year career of a young theatrical director.

*Devotion* contains *in nuce* many of Strauss's main themes and motifs: melancholy self-observation, political resignation, impossibility of love, escape into literature, and longing for depth and meaning in one's life. Despite the thematic bleakness, Strauss's macabre humor, self-assured style, and meticulous attention to detail make this short novel one of the more interesting and appealing works of modern German literature.

*Sources for Further Study*
Adelson, Leslie. *Botho Strauss and West German Prose of the 1970's*, 1983.
_____. "Subjectivity Reconsidered: Botho Strauss and Contemporary West German Prose," in *New German Critique*. XXX (Fall, 1983), pp. 3-59.
Dickstein, Lore. Review in *Saturday Review*. VI (July 21, 1979), p. 50.
Judd, Inge. Review in *Library Journal*. CIV (July, 1979), p. 1487.
Shrimpton, Nicholas. Review in *New Statesman*. XCIX (February 29, 1980), p. 325.

*Peter West Nutting*

# DIARY OF A MAD OLD MAN

*Author:* Jun'ichirō Tanizaki (1886-1965)
*Type of plot:* Psychological realism
*Time of plot:* June 16, 1960, to mid-April, 1961
*Locale:* Tokyo and Kyoto
*First published: Fūten rōjin nikki*, 1961-1962, serial; 1962, book (English translation, 1965)

*Principal characters:*

TOKUSUKE UTSUGI, the affluent seventy-seven-year-old protagonist, rather corpulent, in ill health, and infatuated with his daughter-in-law

SATSUKO, Tokusuke's flirtatious and self-seeking daughter-in-law, a former chorus girl who, with her husband and son, lives in Tokusuke's house in Tokyo

JOKICHI, the only male of Tokusuke's three grown children, thirty-six years old and immersed in his own business and extramarital affairs

HARUHISA, Tokusuke's devious nephew, who embarks on an extramarital affair with Satsuko

NURSE SASAKI, Tokusuke's burdened live-in private nurse, one of several medical professionals attending him

## The Novel

Nine-tenths of *Diary of a Mad Old Man* is composed of entries from the protagonist's diary (from June 16 to November 18, 1960) up to the point at which a series of seizures incapacitate Tokusuke and bring an end to his written autobiographical introspection, in which he has engaged for many years. The work's remainder is composed of respective extracts from Nurse Sasaki's report (November 20), Dr. Katsumi's clinical record (from December 15, 1960, to February 7, 1961), and notes by the protagonist's widowed elder daughter, Itsuko Shiroyama, which bring the story up to Tokusuke's recuperation in mid-April, 1961.

Basically, the novel chronicles Tokusuke's increasing obsession with Satsuko while his health and his relationships with the rest of his household and family deteriorate. The sexually impotent Tokusuke constantly schemes to be alone with Satsuko, and then, with her encouragement, to obtain a caress or kiss; Satsuko exacts material rewards for these favors: an automobile, an expensive beige suede handbag, and finally a fifteen-carat cat's-eye ring costing three million yen (roughly $17,000), this last item perhaps symbolizing her feline predacity. Tokusuke's wife (never named in the diary, suggesting the protagonist's estrangement), younger daughter, Kugako, and elder daughter are increasingly chagrined by Tokusuke's preferment of Satsuko and the callousness, spitefulness, and niggardliness he shows to them.

When, three-quarters of the way through the novel, the hope for a quick cure, through spinal injection, to the now-excruciating neuralgia in Tokusuke's left hand is raised and then thwarted, the episode suggests that life's problems are not so easily solved, as well as the Tanizakian notion that a novel's plot cannot be resolved so quickly and neatly—as indeed it is not in this work. The rest of Tokusuke's diary recounts his trip to Kyoto to arrange for his burial, his surreptitious plan to incorporate Satsuko into his Buddhist monument, revealing the protagonist's deification of a femme fatale, a theme in many of Jun'ichirō Tanizaki's works. Tokusuke's quarrels about Satsuko with Itsuko—earlier the most retiring of his children—at the conclusion of the Kyoto trip and back in Tokyo precipitate Tokusuke's stroke and angina pectoris, the latter emblematic of the heartache the old man feels in his frustrated, impracticable sexual longing. In a shift from the subjectivity of Tokusuke's diary, the objective third-person accounts in the closing extracts document Tokusuke's decline and convalescence, from hospital to home, unwittingly pointing to the crucial connection between clinical facts and emotions, desire, and mind. Unbeknown to Itsuko, her concluding matter-of-fact report on the impracticality of the beginning of the excavation of the garden for a swimming pool (since Tokusuke will not be allowed outdoors in the sun) recalls the diary entries of August 12, September 13, and October 23, which all mention the swimming pool and intimate that Tokusuke's yearning to see Satsuko in her swimsuit is the spark that keeps him alive. The novel's ending leaves unresolved the questions of whether Tokusuke's convalescence is completed, whether he lives, whether the swimming pool is finished, and whether he ever sees Satsuko in the pool.

## The Characters

A crux, implied by the work's title, is whether—or to what extent—the protagonist is insane. Although Tokusuke uses or reports Satsuko's words, such as "crazy" and "lunatic," to refer to his infatuation no fewer than seven times, the overall clarity of his mind is confirmed by the astute analysis in his diary entries, his own anxieties about his mental health, and finally a psychiatrist's opinion (quoted in Nurse Sasaki's extract) that he is not mentally ill, though subject to abnormal sexual impulses. The power of sex to require an outlet, direct covertly much of human activity, and preserve or destroy life is recognized by both Tokusuke and Tanizaki. Blocked by impotence, Tokusuke is naturally attracted to the alluring former chorus girl who is constantly in his presence.

Abnormality arises in the hint of incest, analogous to that in Tanizaki's "Yume no ukihashi" ("The Bridge of Dreams") and emphasized by Satsuko's reiterated term "father," whenever addressing Tokusuke; foot fetishism (similar anatomical fetishes occur in many of Tanizaki's other works); and the typical Tanizakian masochism, which with the preceding abnormality is symbolically blended in Tokusuke's final choice of a burial monument having Satsuko's footprint (in the guise of Buddha's) placed over, as if stepping on, his remains. Also abnormal is Tokusuke's abetting of a triangle among Satsuko, Haruhisa, and Jokichi, which has analogues in *Tade kuu mushi* (1928-1929; *Some Prefer Nettles*, 1955), *Kagi* (1956; *The Key*, 1960), and "The Bridge of Dreams." Yet while Tokusuke claims that he would pursue the erotic even to death, it actually leads to the prolongation of his life, in contrast to its opposite result for the protagonist, the Professor, in *The Key*.

Also helping to create Tokusuke's complex character, like the others in the novel a mixture of good and bad, are Tanizaki's techniques, appropriate to the diary form, of juxtaposition of or consistency and inconsistency between entries. Both the silliness and the slyness of Tokusuke's attempt to wrest a kiss from Satsuko by exaggerating his neuralgia and tearfully feigning a child-like entreaty (October 9 and 13) are set off against the six-year-old Keisuke's genuine, innocent concern for his grandfather's pain, which furthermore evokes from Tokusuke admirably authentic feelings and tears (October 19). Tokusuke's machinations regarding Satsuko are satirized by the comical in-consistency of his plans for a trip to Kyoto, vehemently expressed in the entries of July 12 and November 10 ("There's no need to be in a hurry!" versus "This isn't the kind of thing you can afford to put off!"). His self-deceit and deceiving of the reader occur in the inconsistency between the entries of November 9 and 10, where in the former Tokusuke asserts that the time is ripe for the Kyoto trip because of the abeyance of his pain and the too-long protraction of delay, but in the latter that this is only another chance to flirt with Satsuko. Tokusuke does, however, show commendable steadiness in his resolve to face death, as suggested by the consistency in his accounts, in the entries of June 19 and October 22, of his feelings about his X rays appearing to yield a fatal prognosis.

Related to Tanizaki's novelistic credo of leaving some points obscure or "in shadows," Tokusuke's craftiness in plotting is suggested by the meaning-ful reticence in certain entries. Tokusuke never explains his statement in the June 17 entry, "I had something else in mind." The reader infers later that the "something" was his twenty-five-thousand-yen gift (or bribe) to Satsuko. The reader must infer from the July 29 entry that Tokusuke's postponement of a trip to the resort town of Karuizawa is to enable a tête-à-tête with Sat-suko; an obligatory inference from the August 19 entry is that Tokusuke's whole detailed house-remodeling scheme is intended to incarcerate his wife, allowing him greater freedom with Satsuko.

### Themes and Meanings

Two themes, beyond those already mentioned, are the pervasiveness of dualities in Japanese culture and life's ironic reversals. The first theme occurs in nearly all Tanizaki's fictional works from the 1920's onward that are set in the twentieth century, such as "Aoi hana" ("Aguri") and *Some Prefer Nettles*. Characters are aware of and often comment on the tensions resulting from these dualities. In *Diary of a Mad Old Man* they include regional dichotomies (Tokyo food and drama versus those of Osaka, and the inhumane chaos of Tokyo versus the quiet of Kyoto), hemispheric dichotomies (Western dress, food, and culture—particularly films—versus their Asian counterparts), the present versus the past (particularly concerning the change in Japanese women), ugliness versus beauty, old age versus youth, and disease or illness versus good health.

The second theme is embodied, literally, in Tokusuke's ailing physiology. For example, despite Tokusuke's prior heroic resolve about death, his deep anxieties, and all the superstitious precautions taken about good and bad days (according to the almanac of such matters), the instant cure (or calamity) promised from the spinal injection technique of Dr. Fukushima comes to nothing when the physician, previously infallible at the procedure, has two unsuccessful dry runs on Tokusuke and declines to attempt the operation. Further, though Tokusuke states with some satisfaction near the novel's beginning that his bowel movements are unimpaired, Dr. Katsumi's clinical record at the novel's close reveals that Tokusuke's attacks were associated with "straining at stool" and subsequent bowel movements.

## Critical Context

Among Tanizaki's twenty-five or so original novels, *Diary of a Mad Old Man* falls among those that are short—the majority, with the notable exception of *Sasame-yuki* (1943-1948; *The Makioka Sisters*, 1957), set in the twentieth century (the other novels being set in the past, anytime from the Fujiwara to Tokugawa periods) and written after Tanizaki's transforming experience of the great Tokyo-Yokohoma earthquake of 1923 and his subsequent resettlement in the Kyoto-Osaka region. The novels of this period are generally considered his best; indeed, up to his death, Tanizaki was regarded as a leading candidate for the first Nobel Prize for Literature to be awarded to a Japanese writer.

The continuity in Tanizaki's works is evidenced by his portrayal in the early ones of the femme fatale, as in "Shisei" ("The Tatooer") and of the elderly, as in Misako's father in *Some Prefer Nettles*. In the works *The Makioka Sisters*, *Shōshō Shigemoto no haha* (1950; *The Mother of Captain Shigemoto*, 1956), *The Key*, "The Bridge of Dreams," and *Diary of a Mad Old Man*, Tanizaki increasingly focuses on old age, aging, disease, illness, and death, very probably reflecting the concerns of an aging author, from his fifty-seventh to seventy-sixth year. Of these latter novels, *Diary of a Mad Old Man* has the closest affinity with *The Key*, which is also in the diary form (a professor's and his wife's respective diaries). While in *Diary of a Mad Old*

*Man* Tokusuke views his escalating contact with Satsuko in popular-culture terms, as an "erotic thriller," in *The Key* the Professor views his improved sexual relations in the more philosophical light of rationality surrendering to the animal. Moreover, Tokusuke repeatedly requests that Satsuko masticate some medication and administer it mouth to mouth to him, symbolizing the maternal life-giving force she is to him. In *The Key*, however, the Professor chews medication and transmits it mouth to mouth to his wife, symbolizing the life-draining force she is to him, which ultimately leads to his death (and cessation of his diary) toward the end of the novel.

*Sources for Further Study*

Keene, Donald. *Dawn to the West: Japanese Literature of the Modern Era.* Vol. 1, *Fiction*, 1984.

Kimball, Arthur G. *Crisis in Identity and Contemporary Japanese Novels*, 1973.

Lippit, Noriko Mizuta. *Reality and Fiction in Modern Japanese Literature*, 1980.

Petersen, Gwenn Boardman. *The Moon in the Water: Understanding Tanizaki, Kawabata, and Mishima*, 1979.

Ueda, Makoto. *Modern Japanese Writers and the Nature of Literature*, 1976.

*Norman Prinsky*

# DOG YEARS

*Author:* Günter Grass (1927-    )
*Type of plot:* Social realism
*Time of plot:* The mid-1920's to the late 1940's
*Locale:* Danzig and West Germany
*First published: Hundejahre,* 1963 (English translation, 1965)

> *Principal characters:*
> EDDI AMSEL, the narrator of book 1
> WALTER MATERN, Eddi's friend and the narrator of book 3
> HARRY LIEBENAU, the narrator of book 2
> TULLA POKRIEFKE, Harry's beloved cousin, to whom he addresses his narrative letters
> JENNY BRUNIES, a Gypsy child adopted by Herr Brunies

## The Novel

*Dog Years* has three narrators who, together, tell the story of Germany from the mid-1920's to the late 1940's. Eddi Amsel, the first narrator, is also the protagonist of book 1. He grows up in Danzig after World War I. The area is not yet a part of Germany, although it has a predominant German population, with conflicting ethnic and religious groups. The Mennonites and the Catholics, for example, distrust one another, and the Jews are discriminated against. Eddi's ancestry is somewhat clouded, but he is reputed to be half-Jewish. He is also an artist, a creator of amazingly lifelike scarecrows that disturb not only the birds but also his fellow Danzigers, who treat Eddi as an outcast.

Book 1 explores both the history of Danzig and the history of the families of Eddi and his friend Walter Matern. These are the "dog years," in the sense that, threaded through this dynastic saga, is the story of the Matern family's dogs. The dogs' pedigree finally makes one of their breed a fit choice for the führer, Adolf Hitler. The emphasis on dog breeding is an implicit comment on the growing German obsession with "Aryans." Eddi's friendship with Walter grows in spite of Eddi's tainted blood, yet Walter cannot seem to help himself; his prejudice shows when he calls Eddi a "sheeny." Eddi, himself, is not immune to racism and adopts the philosophy of a virulent anti-Semitic author who contends that Jews have no souls. In spite of his effort to assimilate the racial prejudices of his fellow Germans, Eddi is finally attacked by Walter and other Nazi zealots. He decides to leave Danzig and assume a new identity.

Book 2, narrated by Harry Liebenau, reflects this young man's obsession with his cousin, Tulla Pokriefke. Through his evocation of her character in a series of "love letters," the growing intolerance and violence of Nazi Germany are dramatized. Tulla hates Jenny Brunies, a Gypsy child adopted by

Herr Brunies. Like Eddi, Jenny is the artist as outcast. Her Gypsy origins are just as unacceptable as Eddi's Jewish background. Like Eddi, her art derives from her suffering. Just as he fashions scarecrows that are shocking revelations of his brutal community, so she becomes a slender, beautiful ballerina after having been assaulted by Tulla. Eddi and Jenny fail to realize that their art allows them to transcend the indignities heaped upon them by their community. Eventually, they combine forces. Eddi designs mechanical scarecrows for one of her ballets. These are precisely the beings without a soul that Eddi's favorite anti-Semitic author described in his book.

Book 3 is narrated by Walter, who finally recognizes the evils of Nazism and sets out to punish his comrades who made Hitler's demonic vision a reality. In nearly every case, however, Walter's revenge on these postwar survivors of Fascism is ineffective. His own complicity in evil is so great that he does not realize or even remember how he helped to persecute Eddi Amsel and other Jews, creating the conditions for their extermination in concentration camps. The people of postwar Germany do not come to terms with their guilt; instead, Walter is befuddled by the country's booming economy, which is based on forgetting the past and rationalizing evil.

### The Characters

The relationship between Eddi Amsel and Walter Matern is at the center of *Dog Years*. Eddi is a gentle, brilliant, and creative person. Whatever anger he might feel is expressed through the creation of his artful scarecrows. He never fights others; on the contrary, he tries to ignore all expressions of hostility toward him. Evidently, Walter is impressed by this quality in Eddi, for he defends his schoolmate from the other boys who have beaten Eddi on numerous occasions. Yet, Walter is a crude character, incapable of reflecting on the way society inflicts cruelty on anyone it deems inferior. Walter shifts from being a Communist, to a Nazi, to a Catholic, without ever reflecting on the root causes of his restlessness. Yet the two boys have sworn a blood brotherhood and, after their long separation during the war years, Eddi reminds Walter of their bond.

Tulla Pokriefke is the malevolent force in *Dog Years*. She seems to hate Jenny Brunies for no reason at all. Tulla is sadistic and, for the sheer fun of it, enjoys making Jenny abase herself. She holds her cousin, Harry Liebenau, in thrall precisely because of her self-sufficiency and her effortless ability to order people around. She is Harry's Hitler. If she has a redeeming quality, it is her candor. When she finds human bones near a concentration camp, she bluntly identifies them for what they are and does not try to ignore the obvious evil, as her fellow Germans do.

Jenny Brunies is the female counterpart of Eddi Amsel. Like Eddi, she grows up as a fat child, persecuted by the group. It seems improbable that she would become a ballerina, but some need to express herself is released as a result of Tulla's persecution. Tulla's behavior then changes when she sees that Jenny has found individuality. Tulla is no longer able to control Jenny.

Harry Liebenau is not a well-defined character—but that seems to be Günter Grass's point exactly. Harry is an observer, a follower who is obsessed with his Tulla as the Germans were with their führer. Harry seems incapable of thinking for himself. Instead, he writes "love letters" to Tulla, recalling all of her callous behavior and his inept efforts to please her and win her favor. He is pathetic.

*Themes and Meanings*

Günter Grass grew up in the region about which he writes in *Dog Years*. He was a young Nazi and served in the German army. Only after the war did he come to realize how evil the Nazis were. His novel sets out to show how a whole society collaborated in the creation of Fascism. Germans were proud of their führer. They wanted to dominate the weak, to expand the nation's power, and to create a master race. There were very few dissenters. Grass shows that even where Jews were completely assimilated into the community (as Eddi Amsel was), they were doomed. Eddi survives only by changing his identity and fleeing Danzig.

What makes Eddi's fate particularly dreadful is that he and Walter are, in a sense, parts of the same self. No less than Eddi, Walter is an outcast. He is expelled from group after group because he does not fit in. He takes up a career as an actor, plays many roles, but is accepted nowhere. Similarly, Eddi adopts many guises (Herr Brauxel, "Goldmouth," and others), but he never finds acceptance as himself.

Eddi's creation of scarecrows is a mockery of the German people who have acted as though they have no souls. When Eddi creates mechanical figures that are propelled by a mechanism in their bellies, Harry Liebenau recalls, "We felt our own bellies, looking for the mechanism inside us: Tulla had one." Tulla has one because she is the quintessential Nazi: obedient and actively evil. If Harry cannot feel his own mechanism, it is because he is so passive, a weak person who simply goes along with the evil, like so many of the other minor German characters in the novel.

By giving such a full history of Danzig at the beginning of *Dog Years*, Grass is at pains to show that Nazism is no aberration. It develops out of deep-seated prejudices, including religious intolerance that has split families and incited violence. Sooner or later, every human being is implicated in this insidious evil—especially since Grass's characters are largely unconscious of the cultural forces that have shaped their outlook. Human appetite overcomes human reason. For example, when Walter Matern tries to confront one of his Fascist enemies after the war, he is stymied; first, he is welcomed as an old buddy and then, he is offered his buddy's wife in bed.

What Walter, a fairly simple man, cannot see is also what Germany's thinkers have obliterated. *Dog Years* contains a vicious attack on the philosopher Martin Heidegger, who expressed initial enthusiasm for the Nazis and who never clearly repudiated them. In Grass's opinion, Heidegger helped to promote a simplistic view of human character and wrote in a turgid, obscure style that epitomized Germany's blindness to reality. One German army officer speaks in Heideggerian language when he calls underdone potatoes in their jackets, "spuds forgetful of Being." This abstract language, which has no grounding in actuality, repels Grass. Heidegger's philosophical vocabulary, Grass suggests, reveals a basic inhumanity, which he connects to the fact that Heidegger abandoned his mentor, the distinguished philosopher Edmund Husserl, who was Jewish.

*Critical Context*

*Dog Years* is part of Günter Grass's *Danziger Trilogie* (1980; Danzig trilogy). *Die Blechtrommel* (1959; *The Tin Drum*, 1961) and *Katz und Maus* (1961; *Cat and Mouse*, 1963), the two novels that precede *Dog Years*, share the same three-part structure. Twentieth century German history is divided into three periods: prewar, war, and postwar. In each novel, Grass takes a very careful historical approach which attempts to explain the seeds of Nazism. He demonstrates that many of the evils of Nazism have yet to be addressed because of the amnesia of the German people who refuse to shoulder the burden of the evil done in their name.

*Dog Years* is the most sophisticated novel in the trilogy because of its employment of three very different narrators: the inventive and oblique Eddi Amsel, the passive Harry Liebenau, and the aggressive but largely unconscious Walter Matern. Each narrator presents a distinct frame of reference through which many of the same historical events are viewed. Thus, Grass evokes the way history is actually experienced by different personalities.

*Dog Years* is also the most explicitly political novel in Grass's trilogy. Nazi ideology, German philosophy and history, and German political figures are treated more directly than in the other novels. *Dog Years* engages in a powerful attack on pernicious political ideas. If the novel seems heavy with Grass's diatribes against these ideas, his profound grasp of history and human character ultimately convinces the reader of the correctness of his vision.

*Sources for Further Study*
Cunliffe, W. Gordon. *Günter Grass*, 1969.
Hayman, Ronald. *Günter Grass*, 1985.
Leonard, Irène. *Günter Grass*, 1974.
Reddick, John. *The "Danzig Trilogy" of Günter Grass*, 1975.
Yates, Norris W. *Günter Grass: A Critical Essay*, 1967.

*Carl E. Rollyson, Jr.*

# THE DOUBLE

*Author:* Fyodor Dostoevski (1821-1881)
*Type of plot:* Fantasy
*Time of plot:* The 1840's
*Locale:* St. Petersburg
*First published: Dvoynik*, 1846; revised, 1866 (English translation, 1917)

> *Principal characters:*
> YAKOV PETROVICH GOLYADKIN, SR., a senior clerk in a
> government office
> YAKOV PETROVICH GOLYADKIN, JR., his double

## The Novel

*The Double* centers on the mental disintegration of Yakov Petrovich Golyadkin, Sr., the assistant to the chief clerk in a government office in St. Petersburg. The first four chapters lead up to his breakdown. In chapter 2, a visit to his German doctor, Krestyan Ivanovich Rutenspitz, reveals the protagonist's highly agitated state of mind. He has enemies, he says, who are trying to destroy him and he complains that a younger colleague of his, the nephew of his superior, Andrey Filippovich, has been awarded the promotion that he, Golyadkin, Sr., had been anticipating. His chances of a successful romance with the desirable Klara Olsufyevna have also been harmed. Soon the reader discovers that some ugly rumors have been spread about Golyadkin, Sr., to the effect that he has been involved with a disreputable German woman, Karolina Ivanovna, and that he has behaved dishonorably toward her.

Later that day, he is refused admission to Klara's birthday party. He slips in unnoticed but clumsily draws attention to himself, tries to dance with Klara, and is escorted out. This humiliation proves to be the crucial moment in the narrative.

Fleeing down the miserable, wet November streets, attempting to escape from what he thinks is persecution, he senses someone near him. A stranger passes by, yet somehow he seems familiar, and he is dressed exactly like Golyadkin, Sr. The stranger passes by again a few minutes later. Golyadkin, Sr., recognizes him; he knows him only too well. He follows the stranger to the entrance of his own apartment and finally into his own bedroom. Trembling with horror, his hair standing on end, the protagonist realizes that he has met his double, a man exactly like him in all respects.

The next day, the double turns up at the office and secures a job as a clerk. No one but Golyadkin, Sr., takes much notice, or remarks on the strange resemblance, but Golyadkin, Sr., is in a state of continual anguish, as if he is being roasted on a fire. In the evening, he finds himself inviting his double back to his apartment for dinner and literally and figuratively is beside himself with amazement. His guest is humble and deferential as he tells his story. The double was poor and without a job, driven from his previous position by his enemies, and had sought out Golyadkin, Sr., because of their remarkable resemblance. They talk amiably and appear to become friends.

Yet Golyadkin, Sr., awakes in the morning suspicious and resentful of what he now believes to be his double's cunning. He resolves to have nothing more to do with him. In the office the next day, Golyadkin, Jr., has changed his manner. Now aloof and self-important, he seems to have taken the real Golyadkin's place, fawning on his superiors, while they act disdainfully toward the original Golyadkin. An unpleasant confrontation follows, and Golyadkin, Sr., fails to retain his presence of mind. He is convinced that there is a conspiracy against him and believes that he is being treated "like a rag used for wiping dirty boots." A series of confrontations with his double always yields the same result. Golyadkin, Sr., is humiliated; his double seems to have taken over his life and outmaneuvers him when challenged.

That night, Golyadkin, Sr., dreams that he is in the midst of good company; he is witty and courteous, and everyone likes him. Then Golyadkin, Jr., appears and instantly blackens his character; the group believes the slander and turns against him, while Golyadkin, Jr., succeeds in making everyone like him. In the streets afterward, the desperate Golyadkin, Sr., finds another Golyadkin springing up at every step he takes. All the fake Golyadkins run after one another in a long chain, following the real Golyadkin so that there is no escape for him.

The next morning, he decides once more to confront his double. He plots and schemes, hoping to outwit the plans which he assumes his opposite is making, but he meets only with further insult. He complains to his superior, who confronts him with accusations about his conduct at the previous evening's party, his behavior toward the German woman, and his slander of Golyadkin, Jr. Eventually Golyadkin, Sr., loses his job, and his servant leaves him.

The story reaches a climax when the protagonist receives a letter from Klara Olsufyevna, begging him to elope with her. The letter probably exists only in his mind. He waits for two hours outside Klara's home, but his double discovers him and invites him inside. The center of attention, Golyadkin, Sr., is guided to Klara, who stands with her newly betrothed fiancé. Her father shakes the protagonist's hand and everyone looks at him with sympathy and curiosity. Then Krestyan Ivanovich, Golyadkin's doctor, suddenly and unexpectedly enters the room. With all eyes on him, Golyadkin, Sr., is escorted to a waiting carriage. He finds himself traveling down an unfamiliar road, and the doctor has taken on a demonic appearance, his eyes glittering like fire. He tells Golyadkin, Sr., "You will get quarters at public expense . . . firewood, light, and service, which you don't deserve." Golyadkin cries out; it is a fate which he has been expecting for some time.

*The Characters*

The main interest of the story lies in the character of the protagonist; the other characters are sketched only thinly. The only exception is the sullen and sarcastic servant, Petrushka, who knows his master well enough to ignore him most of the time. Fyodor Dostoevski clearly establishes his hero's character in the first few chapters, before the mental disintegration becomes fully manifest. Golyadkin, Sr., is first seen on a shopping spree, riding in a splendid rented carriage and wearing a new suit of clothes. He is obviously a man who has social ambitions, but he is too self-conscious to carry off the act successfully and suffers from acute embarrassment whenever he encounters any acquaintances. In spite of the great show he makes by flourishing his savings—he even goes so far as to change large notes for small, so that he appears to have more money—he buys almost nothing. He is an ineffective man, unable to assert himself in the way that he wishes. He puts on a show of bravado toward people he knows he can bully, such as his servant, but his timidity and awkwardness ensure that he is fatally divided against himself— he cannot become the person he wishes to be. The pettiness of his ambitions, his servile attitude toward his social and professional superiors, his suppressed feelings of guilt, and his self-righteous belief that he is an honorable man being destroyed by unscrupulous enemies do not encourage the reader to feel any sympathy toward him. (The consistently mocking tone of the narrator further alienates the reader.) In his rapid alternation between clumsy attempts at self-assertion and a bewildered state of paralysis, Golyadkin, Sr., is a victim of his own inability to be whole.

His double is a projection of the deeper, suppressed forces of his own psyche. These forces are both good and bad. Golyadkin, Jr., is immediately successful, in both his personal and professional relationships. His relations with his colleagues are easy and cordial. He acts with great charm (which Golyadkin, Sr., finds revolting and insincere) in company. The double's efficiency is noted by his superiors, and he is fully accepted in the home of Klara. All these things infuriate Golyadkin, Sr.

Yet in dealing with Golyadkin, Sr., the double adopts something of what is probably his counterpart's own disingenuousness. When pressed to explain himself, the double veers between an excessive formality, which renders Golyadkin, Sr., speechless with frustration, or an inappropriate informality which offends his interrogator's sense of decorum. This *Doppelgänger* also insults Golyadkin, Sr., in public and taunts him with his secret sense of guilt, calling him a Faublas (the name of an immoral lover in an eighteenth century Russian novel). These are things of which Golyadkin, Sr., does not want to be reminded. By now, the protagonist has lost rational control of himself, and his subconscious impulses confront him as if they were coming from the external environment, rather than from himself. He therefore regards his double not only as his deadly enemy but also as an impostor, not related to him at all. Only occasionally is his condemnation mixed with some measure of self-awareness, as when he exclaims, angered by his own inability to keep control of himself, "I'm my own enemy, I'm my own murderer!" The words carry a deeper meaning than he realizes.

## Themes and Meanings

Dostoevski prepares for the appearance of the double with careful foreshadowing. In the first chapter, after passing his office superior, while traveling in the hired carriage, Golyadkin, Sr., is overwhelmed by confusion. He wonders whether he should pretend not to be himself, "but somebody else strikingly like me.... Just ... not me, not me and that's all." After the humiliating experience at Klara's birthday party, the narrator comments that Golyadkin, Sr., "was killed entirely, in the full sense of the word." He wants not only "to run away from himself, but to be obliterated, to cease to be, to turn into dust as well."

The most notable aspect of Dostoevski's narrative technique is his ability to blend the realistic with the fantastic. In spite of the effectiveness of the foreshadowing, the status of the double is never made completely explicit. His first emergence, on a wet foggy night, could be seen as a hallucination, existing only in the protagonist's disordered mind. Dostoevski keeps this possibility in the foreground: After the double has spent the night at the house of Golyadkin, Sr., he appears to vanish without a trace in the morning, and the servant, Petrushka, acts as if nothing untoward has happened. Other characters are completely indifferent about the matter, apart from a casual remark or two about coincidence, and on two occasions Golyadkin, Sr., sees the double in a doorway, which he took to be a looking glass. Nevertheless, the fantastic elements are balanced by a carefully developed realism. The double has a personal history (which he explains to Golyadkin, Sr., on their first acquaintance), and an objective life which is independent of his counterpart's own mind. Others recognize and acknowledge his existence. The balance is maintained up to the last episode: The German doctor's transformation into a demon is purely fantastic, but his announcement of his patient's fate is grimly realistic.

## Critical Context

*The Double* was Dostoevski's second novel, appearing a year after *Bednye lyudi* (1846; *Poor Folk*, 1887). Following its publication, the leading Russian literary critic of the day, Vissarion Belinsky, mixed his praise of the book with censure for its fantastic elements, which, he said, have their place "only in madhouses, but not in literature." Dostoevski himself, commenting on the reception of his novel, said that "everybody... found Golyadkin so boring and dull and so long-winded that it was impossible to read it." This is a verdict with which the modern reader may agree, and Dostoevski admitted that "alongside brilliant pages there is trash and rubbish." In spite of his own criticisms, however, the author believed that *The Double* was a significant work. He later claimed that although the story did not succeed, the idea with which it dealt was more serious than anything else he had contributed to literature. He was sufficiently convinced of the novel's value to revise it in 1866, while he was finishing *Prestupleniye i nakazaniye* (1866; *Crime and Punishment*, 1886). The revised version, simpler and shorter than the original, is the form in which the novel is generally known.

In writing *The Double*, Dostoevski was influenced by the work of the German writer, E. T. A. Hoffmann, and by Russian imitators of Hoffmann, such as Nikolai Gogol, although the influence of the latter is less apparent in the revised version of *The Double*. There are also some autobiographical elements: Golyadkin's acute shyness, and his belief that he is being persecuted, have their origins in certain aspects of Dostoevski's own personality.

Dostoevski was frequently to return to the theme of the double; Golyadkin is the forerunner of the many split personalities which appear in Dostoevski's fiction, who are often confronted by their doubles or near doubles. Although there is much that the modern reader may find puzzling or repellent about *The Double*, the best portions of the novel present a subtle and horrifyingly compelling portrait of a man sinking into a dark psychic realm of his own creation. It serves as a prelude to the great novels of Dostoevski's maturity.

*Sources for Further Study*
Chizhevesky, Dmitri. "The Theme of the Double in Dostoevsky," in
     *Dostoevsky: A Collection of Critical Essays*, 1962. Edited by René Wellek.
Dostoevski, Fyodor. *The Unpublished Dostoevsky*, 1973-1976 (three volumes). Edited by Carl R. Proffer.
Frank, Joseph. *Dostoevsky: The Seeds of Revolt, 1821-1849*, 1976.
Hingley, Ronald. *Dostoevsky: His Life and Work*, 1978.
Terras, Victor. *The Young Dostoevsky, 1846-1849*, 1969.

*Bryan Aubrey*

# A DREAMBOOK FOR OUR TIME

*Author:* Tadeusz Konwicki (1926-    )
*Type of plot:* Impressionistic realism
*Time of plot:* The 1930's to the early 1960's
*Locale:* Poland
*First published: Sennik współczesny*, 1963 (English translation, 1969)

> *Principal characters:*
> PAUL, a disillusioned veteran of anti-Nazi and anti-
>     Communist conflicts
> JOSEPH CAR, the leader of a religious cult
> JUSTINE, Car's young wife
> REGINA, the operator of a grocery cooperative
> MALVINA KORSAK, Paul's landlady
> ILDEFONS KORSAK, Malvina's brother
> SZAFIR, the local Communist Party official
> DEBICKI, a railroad foreman
> JASIU KRUPA, a railroad worker and a former partisan
> COUNT PAC, another railroad worker
> SERGEANT GLOWKO, the local policeman

## The Novel

In a remote Polish village, Paul works as a laborer building an extension on the railroad. The other villagers, though friendly, are suspicious of the middle-aged stranger because he seems educated and says little about himself. Paul rents a room from Malvina Korsak, who is unmarried and lives with her elderly brother, Ildefons. The other characters in the novel include Regina, a lusty woman who runs the local grocery cooperative; Jasiu Krupa, a former partisan with only one hand; Count Pac, a railroad worker who, despite his name, insists upon his humble origins; Debicki, who oversees the work on the railroad; Sergeant Glowko, a policeman; Szafir, the local Party official; Joseph Car, a mysterious stranger who leads a religious cult to which most of the villagers belong; and Justine, Car's young wife.

The fragmented narrative jumps between Paul's experiences in the present and his past life, mostly his serving with the Home Army, which battled the Nazis during World War II, and with anti-Communist guerrillas who fought the Soviets after the German Occupation of Poland ended. Paul was expelled from the Home Army for killing German soldiers when ordered not to do so. Later, with the guerrillas, he grew sick of killing and attempted only to wound a man he had been ordered to assassinate. Paul is sure that Joseph Car is this man, and his mixed feelings of guilt and anger are intensified by his falling in love with Justine. She rejects his pleas to run away with him.

The villagers' despair at their seemingly meaningless lives increases when engineers arrive to dam the Sola River and create a reservoir, thereby flooding their community. Forces over which they have no control seem to be out to destroy their efforts to conduct a normal existence. They find some solace in Joseph Car's cult and seek scapegoats to blame for their troubles, beating Paul and Szafir, who dies soon afterward.

### The Characters

*A Dreambook for Our Time* opens with Paul's attempted suicide. He thinks that he can no longer live with his guilt and despair. He feels guilty for his mother's arrest by the Nazis and her subsequent death, for his accidental killing of a young comrade he mistook for a German, for surviving the war when so many of his friends and countrymen did not, for his failure and that of his society to live up to their potential. He has seen too much death, too many broken promises. Tormented by his memories, he sees his past in the often-accusing faces around him: "I look for meanings everywhere. Every face I see grows over with the thicket of memory. I shall never extricate myself from it." While the villagers can find some respite in religion, Paul cannot: "I don't need a faith from outside. I want to find peace in myself." Tadeusz Konwicki offers little hope of his character's ever finding it.

Paul is an idealist who has lost all of his ideals. Count Pac tells him, "You wanted to set the world right, make people happy. You swallowed any amount of these ideas, and they've eaten you up inside. Only have to touch you with one finger, and you all fall apart, like rot." Paul's decay is presented as that of Poland. He fought the Nazis and the Soviets to preserve his country's integrity. Then he joined the Communist Party, only to be disillusioned.

Paul thinks that if he confronts Joseph Car his torment might be somewhat alleviated. Yet this mystic only adds to his confusion by first admitting that he is the man Paul wounded during the war and then claiming that he is not. Paul wants to save himself by proving that he can care for another human being. "I'll make you a gift of the last remains of my feelings," he tells Justine. When she refuses to leave her husband, Paul's sense of hopelessness grows.

Joseph Car is Paul's psychological double, a reflection of Paul's past. "The same sin links us, the same memory," Paul tells him. Car says that Paul sees only his guilt, is motivated only by his desperation to reassemble some of the pieces of his broken life. Car does this himself by unifying the villagers in a cult through which he hopes to release them from the burden of their pasts.

Like Joseph Car, most of the characters are primarily symbols, representing different types of victims. Because she is an orphan who knows neither her true identity nor her nationality, Justine must be loyal to her husband, the only stability she has ever known. Accepting her fate, Malvina hides behind homilies and claims that she has chosen not to be happy. Her brother,

Ildefons, blames the world's troubles on humans trying to be wiser than God. He attempts to escape by writing stories about fantastic animals and plants, yet when his sister reads and criticizes them, he destroys years of work. The most complex of the characters, Regina, wants affection but fears intimacy. No longer able to bear her loneliness, she leaves the village only to return to marry the dull Debicki. She is the character most capable of sympathizing with Paul's pain.

## Themes and Meanings

Konwicki offers an existential view of postwar Poland in which no one knows how to contemplate happiness. Although Paul and his coworkers build railroad tracks leading away from the village, there is no escape. No trains even appear until the end of the novel. While *A Dreambook for Our Time* presents political criticism of Poland under Communism, the characters are imprisoned, as much as by anything else, by their weaknesses. They represent the despair of modernity, as well as of twentieth century Europe.

A sense of doom pervades the novel. The impending flood is but the latest uncontrollable event to uproot the characters. Something bad is always about to happen, and once it occurs, some other problem will follow. Every event in the characters' lives underscores the futility of finding lasting happiness, the impossibility of sharing one's life. Neither Christian nor romantic love seems to work. Nevertheless, Konwicki considers the search for meaning and understanding admirable; Paul admits that he does not understand how people live, but he persists in trying to find out despite his alienation from them.

The need for political, social, and personal order is emphasized throughout *A Dreambook for Our Time*. Paul says that their lives are "the result of our getting a handful of playing cards and then to the end we shuffle and rearrange them, seeking order and meaning." During the war, Paul crumples a piece of paper ordering him to carry out an assassination and tosses it into the snow: "I know it will drown in this fluff, the rain will wash away everything written on it before the grass breaks through and the trees turn green. I know that this white, soaked leaf will be carried away by some bird to make a nest of it."

Faith in the order of nature, however, is presented as somewhat naïve. Not only is the village about to be destroyed by man's control over nature, but also the forest the water will cover is a symbol of man's chaos, since centuries of wars have occurred there. Trees will be buried beneath the reservoir, but so will the graves, mostly unmarked, of thousands killed in war. Rains pour down throughout the last half of the novel, creating a natural flood in anticipation of the controlled one. Nature's excesses and unpredictability reflect those of the characters.

The water symbolism is appropriate for a novel whose events are nightmarish: The rain heightens the unreality of this chain of terrible events. At the end of the novel, Paul longs to awake from the "stifling dream" of his life and scramble "to an ordinary, commonplace day, with its usual troubles, its everyday toil, its so well-known, familiar drudgery." Willing to settle for uneventful lives, these characters are unable to escape from chaos.

*Critical Context*

Tadeusz Konwicki's early fiction was in the Socialist Realist vein dominant in postwar Poland, but with novels such as this one, he helped lead Polish literature into more ambitious spheres. The experimental qualities of *A Dreambook for Our Time* can be seen primarily in its fragmented structure. Paul's life in the present is interrupted by flashbacks to his past, but these earlier events do not occur in chronological order: Paul's period with the guerrillas, for example, comes before his expulsion from the Home Army. There are flashbacks within flashbacks, a method which helps to emphasize the chaos of war and the characters' turmoil. Since there is no pattern to the history of Poland, a seemingly random structure is fitting for a novel attempting to capture the essence of life in that country.

*A Dreambook for Our Time* is frequently described by critics as surrealistic and nihilistic. The former quality results from Konwicki's slight distortion of reality as the best means of depicting the everyday nightmares of life in the twentieth century. The charge of nihilism seems inaccurate, since Konwicki's characters rarely give up on life despite the diminishing possibilities they encounter.

*Sources for Further Study*

Kołakowski, Leszek. Introduction to *A Dreambook for Our Time*, 1976.
Krzyżanowski, Jerzy R. "The Haunted World of Tadeusz Konwicki," in *Books Abroad*. XLVIII (1974), pp. 485-490.
*The New York Times Book Review*. Review. LXXV (May 17, 1970), p. 5.
*Saturday Review*. Review. LIII (June 20, 1970), p. 43.
Wegner, J. *Konwicki*, 1973.
*World Literature Today*. Review. LI (Summer, 1977), p. 464.

*Michael Adams*

# THE DWARF

*Author:* Pär Lagerkvist (1891-1974)
*Type of plot:* Parable
*Time of plot:* The Renaissance
*Locale:* Unnamed Italian city-states
*First published: Dvärgen,* 1944 (English translation, 1945)

*Principal characters:*
THE DWARF (PICCOLINE), the narrator, a misshapen,
  misanthropic factotum of the Prince's court
THE PRINCE, the cultured ruler of an Italian city-state
BERNARDO, a brilliant scientist and artist
ANGELICA, the Prince's naïve young daughter
GIOVANNI, Angelica's lover and the son of the Prince's enemy,
  Lodovico
DON RICCARDO, the Prince's swaggering courtier
TEODORA, the Prince's wife and Don Riccardo's lover
BOCCAROSSA, a condottiere and leader of mercenary troops

*The Novel*

*The Dwarf* is the acrid journal of a court freak, a twenty-six-inch-tall misanthrope whose name, Piccoline, is mentioned only once, in passing, by another character. Thereafter called the Dwarf, he offers a distorted perspective on the fortunes of the Italian city-state whose prince he serves. Though generally slighted by them as an insignificant retainer, the Dwarf is able to observe important public figures and bear witness to actions that have dramatic consequences.

After strangling Jehosophat, the Dwarf has become the only dwarf at court and the reluctant pet of Angelica. The Dwarf is discomfited by the arrival in the city of the inquisitive genius Bernardo and gratified by that of the mercenary leader Boccarossa. With Bernardo's war machinery and Boccarossa's soldiers, the Prince attacks the enemy Montanzas led by Lodovico. Reveling in battle, the Dwarf reports his disappointment over delays caused by rain and over the retreat necessitated by insufficient funds to pay Boccarossa. He is nauseated when he witnesses the sexual adventures of the Prince and Don Riccardo with prostitutes. He regrets that Don Riccardo, whose illicit love letters he has been forced to convey to Teodora, has not been killed in battle.

During a truce, Lodovico and his followers are entertained at the Prince's court. The Dwarf follows what he assumes to be his master's orders and serves poisoned wine to the enemy, but he intentionally kills the vainglorious Don Riccardo as well. Lodovico's followers regroup and, with the support of

Boccarossa's mercenaries, lay siege to the Prince's city. When the Dwarf discovers that Giovanni, Lodovico's son, has been surreptitiously spending the night in the bed and arms of Angelica, the Prince's daughter, he informs on them. After the Prince beheads Giovanni, Angelica, lovelorn, drowns herself.

Meanwhile, an epidemic of plague devastates the city, ending the war but resulting in the deaths of many at the court. Before expiring in agony, Teodora comes under the diabolical domination of the Dwarf, whom she accepts as a scourge for her sinful past. When she dies, Bernardo paints a beatific portrait of her, and she becomes an object of veneration throughout the city. For his part in her painful death and in the suicide of Angelica and the poisoning of Lodovico, the Dwarf is imprisoned. While chained in the fastness of a somber dungeon, he writes his final lines, certain that they will be followed by others.

*The Characters*

Although his position permits him access to privileged information, the Dwarf is about as unreliable as a narrator can be. Stunted emotionally as well as physically, he imagines himself central to the life of the court, when in fact, if the Prince notices him at all, he considers the Dwarf a disposable lackey. "Reality is the only thing that matters," declares the Dwarf, who admits that he cannot perceive the stars or value dreams. He also concedes that he cannot understand love, yet love, whether that of Angelica for Giovanni or that of Teodora for God, is crucial to the events he narrates. The Dwarf's version of reality is so circumscribed as to be almost solipsistic, like Pär Lagerkvist's final image of him, chained in the darkness of a solitary cell. Some of the Dwarf's most confident assertions are immediately refuted by events, as when, seeing them during the military truce, he proclaims that Angelica and Giovanni, clandestine lovers, are obviously bored with each other. "It is difficult to understand those whom one does not hate," says the Dwarf, who succeeds in hating everyone but the Prince and understanding no one, including himself.

Bernardo, a brilliant scientist, artist, and inventor, is a fictional version of Leonardo da Vinci and, more generally, the archetypal Renaissance man. Animated by boundless curiosity, he might have adopted the Humanist motto "humani nihil a me alienum puto" (nothing that is human is alien to me). By contrast, the Dwarf, considering himself to be a member of an alien race, despises human beings. While the Dwarf has a pathological dread of the body and of being touched, Bernardo exemplifies another Renaissance ideal, the sound mind in the sound body, and he is intent on studying anatomy. Bernardo's moments of exuberance alternate with moments of severe depression when, aspiring to accomplish everything, he realizes the futility of attempting anything. Many of his projects remain incomplete.

Like a Borgia or a Medici, the Prince is an amoral leader motivated by vanity and personal pleasure. No one is a hero to his dwarf, and, though the narrator expresses admiration for the Prince, the endorsement comes for all the wrong reasons and from the wrong source.

Each of the characters in this short novel is a victim of the insufficiency of the human self. The only ones to suggest the possibility of transcending the inadequacies of the merely human are the two main female characters: Angelica with her doomed love for another human and Teodora with her confused gropings toward God.

### Themes and Meanings

Unreliability is not simply a flamboyant accessory of this first-person narrative; it is the very subject of the novel, set during a period when medieval pieties were being challenged and skepticism coexisted with immense worldly ambition. *The Dwarf* is brief, bare, and deliberately vague, the better to extrapolate its story into allegory, the universal drama of grappling with the essence of humanity.

In its contradictory energies, the Renaissance was an emphatically manic-depressive period, and, though the cynical, reductive Dwarf is as much at home in the era as was Niccolò Machiavelli, he is as puzzled as the reader is by the spirit of the age. "One minute it is a chorus of jubilation over the glory of being a human creature. The next minute it is nothing but hopelessness, complete futility, despair."

Though parabolic, the novel does not preach but, through its patently unreliable perspective, forces its readers to try to fathom the contradictions of human nature. Are men closer in character to the Dwarf, Bernardo, or the Prince? Or do the three constitute the id, superego, and ego of the complete personality? The Dwarf attributes his ability to frighten others to their recognition that he represents malevolent internal forces to which they would just as soon not admit: "They think it is I who scare them, but it is the dwarf within them, the ape-faced manlike being who sticks up its head from the depths of their souls."

Baptized as a joke and acting as a sadistic confessor to Teodora, the Dwarf provides a demoniac parody of traditional religion. *The Dwarf* provides its audience with a modern perspective on the heart of darkness lurking in each person, but it also suggests the limitations of the humanist perspective. Readers take the limited measure of the deluded Dwarf and become skeptical over the arrogant credo that man is the measure of all things. The Dwarf complains that Bernardo's "mind is so presumptuous that it would fain lord it like a prince over a world which it does not own." Yet Bernardo does not finish his paintings, and, though convinced that he will live to walk out of prison and continue his notes, the Dwarf does not finish his narrative.

*Critical Context*

Lagerkvist's first published novel, *The Dwarf* was both a commercial and a critical success. It remains, along with *Barabbas* (1950; English translation, 1951), published a year before he received the Nobel Prize for Literature, the best-known work of the best-known Swedish novelist. In its recognition of the power of evil, *The Dwarf* is as much a product of the continuing preoccupations of its author as it is of the somber *Zeitgeist* of World War II.

Lagerkvist has been discussed as an heir to Fyodor Dostoevski and Franz Kafka and within the context of European existentialism, though he remained aloof from organized Continental movements. His was a religious sensibility, not merely in novels such as *Barabbas*, *Sibyllan* (1956; *The Sybyl*, 1958), *Ahasverus död* (1960; *The Death of Ahasuerus*, 1962), and *Det heliga landet* (1964; *The Holy Land*, 1966) that recycle biblical texts. *The Dwarf* explores the frailties of individual consciousness in a world bereft of the consolations of the absolute. A powerful narrative of skeptical spirituality, *The Dwarf* is no small achievement.

*Sources for Further Study*

Ramsey, Roger. "Pär Lagerkvist: *The Dwarf* and Dogma," in *Mosaic*. V (1972), pp. 97-106.

*Scandinavica*. X, no. 1 (1971). Special Lagerkvist issue.

Spector, Robert Donald. *Pär Lagerkvist*, 1973.

Vowles, Richard P. "The Fiction of Pär Lagerkvist," in *Western Humanities Review*. VIII (Spring, 1954), pp. 111-119.

Weathers, Winston. *Pär Lagerkvist: A Critical Essay*, 1968.

                                                                                      *Steven G. Kellman*

# ELSEWHERE, PERHAPS

*Author:* Amos Oz (1939-　　)
*Type of plot:* Social realism
*Time of plot:* The early 1960's
*Locale:* Kibbutz Metsudat Ram, near the Israeli-Jordanian border
*First published: Ma'kom a'her*, 1966 (English translation, 1973)

> *Principal characters:*
> REUVEN HARISH (originally HARISMANN), a poet, teacher, and
>     tour guide at the kibbutz
> NOGA HARISH (nicknamed STELLA MARIS and TURQUOISE),
>     Reuven's daughter, age sixteen
> EZRA BERGER, a kibbutz member and truck driver
> BRONKA BERGER, Ezra's wife and Reuven's lover
> AVRAHAM ROMINOV (known as RAMI RIMON), Noga's
>     boyfriend, age eighteen

*The Novel*

　　*Elsewhere, Perhaps* is set in the Israeli kibbutz of Metsudat Ram, which is located within sight—and gunshot—of the disputed Israeli-Jordanian border. Through the course of the seasons the members of the kibbutz go about their affairs, traveling through passages of life and death, change and continuity that are particularly Israeli yet universally human. The unnamed narrator of the novel is obviously one of the settlers at Metsudat Ram, and the reader also comes to enjoy at least honorary membership in the commune.

　　The action in *Elsewhere, Perhaps* is deceptively slow-paced, with a rhythm that echoes natural cycles. As befits a novel about Jewish characters, many of whom are survivors of the Holocaust or who are descended from the original generation of Israelis, memory and past events play a large part in the book. Persons and their actions are scrutinized, puzzled over, teased into meaning. As a character remarks, "I'm not a wise man, but I do know how to think. If you think the same thought a hundred times, it ends up by being very refined."

　　Reuven Harish, the book's central character, has much about which to think. Years earlier his wife, Eva, ran away with a cousin who was visiting the kibbutz. Ironically, and symbolically, Reuven has now assumed the position of tour guide as well as teacher for the commune. When not teaching he writes poetry, for which he is well-known, and he struggles with rearing his children, Noga and Gai.

　　After his wife's departure, Reuven's friendship with Bronka Berger gradually ripened into a love affair. At the same time, Bronka and her husband, Ezra, silently drifted apart, neither daring to admit openly what both knew privately. Now Ezra takes on double duty as a driver to deliver the kibbutz's fruit to Tel Aviv; that way, he is seldom at home and can avoid confronting his wife or facing the situation.

Rami Rimon, Noga's boyfriend, struggles to convince himself and others of his manhood. Although sensitive and caring, he tries to disguise these qualities, believing them to indicate weakness on his part. When his feigned roughness and attempts at lovemaking are rejected and mocked by Noga, Rami enlists in the army, full of self-pity and thoughts of a hero's death.

In the meantime, Noga has begun to spend time with Ezra, and their originally innocent meetings develop into a love affair which parallels that of Bronka and Reuven. Ezra gives Noga the nickname, Turquoise, because she originally asked him to bring her back some thread of that color from one of his trips. By the time of the summer festival, Noga realizes that she is pregnant.

Zechariah Berger, Ezra's brother, arrives from Germany to sign up artists for European tours; in Munich he runs an entertainment business with Eva's second husband. When Zechariah learns of Noga's condition, he plots to have her return with him to live with her mother. Zechariah's plans are clever, and his arguments persuasive, but Noga and Reuven have already moved toward a silent, awkward understanding. At the same time members of the kibbutz unite to show Noga a flood of compassion, demonstrating a solidarity that is one of the enduring features of true communal life.

As the Hebrew calendar moves toward the end of the year, the kibbutz experiences changes in the lives of its members, some minor, others major. Committee memberships are reshuffled, preparations are made for the New Year's festival. A long-anticipated clash with Arabs over disputed territory takes place. There are only two casualties from the kibbutz: a farmer killed while plowing the fields and Reuven Harish, who dies in his room during the battle.

The new year brings renewal both in the land and in the people. Even before Reuven's death, Bronka and Ezra had gradually repaired their relationship. Noga and Rami are married, and on the day of the spring festival Noga gives birth to a daughter.

### The Characters

Although *Elsewhere, Perhaps* is set in an Israeli kibbutz and its characters are undeniably Jewish, the reader is most struck by their overwhelming humanity. With affectionate, careful strokes, Amos Oz has created a gallery of persons who are recognizable both in their individual ways and their common traits. Even the minor characters are well-rounded and believable because their traits and personalities are both distinctive yet universal.

In writing his novel, Oz has brought the reader into the circle of the kibbutz; it is a circle as close and intimate as a family, and in a sense, it is a family. The unnamed narrator, obviously a member of Metsudat Ram, presents not only direct descriptions of actions but also the commentary on those actions by the kibbutz members. In this fashion the same event will be examined from several different perspectives, and this gives additional resonance and vividness to even the most mundane activities. In this sense, as the narrator remarks, gossip is not mere talk, but "our collaborator in this story."

Reuven Harish is described by Oz as "a man of learning and at the same time a peasant, a man whose life has been enriched by suffering . . . one of our most remarkable men." About the age of fifty, Reuven is a dedicated teacher, writer, and father. He is basically direct and honest, and his illicit relationship with Bronka Berger stems primarily from loneliness and grief over the desertion of his own wife, rather than passion or lust. Yet Reuven is acutely aware that in securing solace for himself, he has wronged Ezra Berger, and his attempts to resolve this dilemma add complexity and realism to his character.

Reuven's relationship with his children changes through the course of the novel. Noga Harish experiences the changes, both painful and joyous, of developing womanhood and grows more distant from her father. Further, there is the dislocation and pain which followed when Eva Harish abandoned her husband and her children. This seemingly inexplicable act continues to puzzle and torment the family, especially Reuven, who believes that he may have precipitated the event, and Noga, who fears that she may repeat it.

On a wider scale, Noga and her brother Gai are of a newer, and different, generation of Israelis than Reuven, and this adds to their puzzled, yet essentially loving, misunderstandings within the family. To the normal complexities of adolescence is joined the constant threat of violence.

This violence, the sense of being surrounded by enemies, causes Rami Rimon to mistrust his own nature. Although sensitive and thoughtful, Rami attempts to project a tough, brusque image, which he hopes will make others see him as forceful and masculine. Noga, who perceives his pointless charade, laughs at him; in despair, he enlists in the army. Rami's only brother has been killed while in the service and is remembered as a hero; Rami has self-pitying daydreams that he will follow him.

Ironically, it is in military service that Rami comes to terms with his true nature. He learns that a real man need not reject sensitivity and compassion, that true strength is not merely brute force. As Rami changes in military service, so does Noga in pregnancy, gaining more maturity and greater understanding. By the end of the novel their personalities have been sufficiently tempered so that marriage is not only appropriate but, within the universe of Metsudat Ram, almost inevitable.

The seeming inevitability of marriage is also present with another couple, Ezra and Bronka. Although their union is apparently shattered by Bronka's affair with Reuven, the two continue to preserve the rudiments of married life. Even when they are estranged, Ezra and Bronka are clearly a couple, their characters complete only when together. At first glance a simple, slightly educated truck driver, Ezra is a complex character, difficult to comprehend because of his allusive nature. He answers questions with proverbs, biblical quotations, and uses these techniques to deflect others when they try to approach him. Yet these methods reveal that the burly, barrel-chested worker is deeply if not widely read, especially in the Bible, and a patient, methodical thinker. Bronka is a more profound, less explicable character. She seems haunted by some lingering and secret sorrow whose effect Oz captures but whose cause he does not reveal. Her gradual return to married life and modified happiness is sparked, in ironic but inevitable fashion, by Noga's pregnancy. They take different paths to their goal, but by the end of the novel, Ezra and Bronka have managed to reconnect and become once again a real couple.

## Themes and Meanings

There are two essential themes which run throughout *Elsewhere, Perhaps*. The first is of change and continuity in the world and people's lives; the second, how human beings can transcend their limitations through love and communion.

Throughout the novel Oz uses a variety of devices, both literal and symbolic, to underscore the theme of change and continuity. Events in the kibbutz proceed within the time frame of the Hebrew calendar; forthcoming festivals—for spring, summer, fall, the New Year—are important milestones in the lives of the residents of Metsudat Ram. The endless cycle of the year, which repeats itself both in nature and in the individual, is an integral part of an agricultural society such as the kibbutz. Yet in *Elsewhere, Perhaps* the ebb and flow of time becomes an important symbolic motif of the continuation of human life across the generations.

Change is seen most obviously in the manner in which characters alter their names or adopt new ones. Reuven Harish was once Harismann; Tomer and Oren, the sons of Ezra and Bronka, have changed their last name to Geva, to be more Israeli, and Rami Rimon's original name was Avraham Rominov. Tellingly, these persons have shifted their names to reveal, rather than hide, their identities. They aspire to return to a culture that is both traditionally Jewish and yet authentically new, a culture that embraces the best of the past and the future.

Such is not the case with Zechariah Berger, the Munich impresario. His revised name is Siegfried, which he wears as a taunt against the Germans among whom he lives. Zechariah/Siegfried takes delight in humbling and insulting his German neighbors, hiring former army officers and Nazi officials at pitiful wages and reveling in their groveling thanks. At least, that is his story for the residents of Kibbutz Metsudat Ram when he comes to visit them, but Oz allows a haze of mystery to remain over Zechariah and his activities. The man might be something of a poser, perhaps even a fraud. The reader is never quite certain.

The reader, however, is certain about the residents of the kibbutz. The changes which they experience are real and meaningful. Those which are ordinary and mundane form the backdrop for the more dramatic events and shifts in life: the affair between Ezra and Noga, a sudden and unexpected rainstorm which disrupts the May Day Festival, the climactic gun battle with the Arabs across the border. All these changes, whether slow and peaceful or abrupt and violent, are part of the life at Metsudat Ram.

Change is important because it happens to human beings, and the second pervasive theme in *Elsewhere, Perhaps* is the ability of those human beings to transcend their limitations, to become part of a larger whole, through accepting change. Throughout the novel, Oz repeatedly uses the image of the tongue or clapper of a bell; it appears as a chapter title and later reappears as the title for part 2 of the book. Noga's daughter is given the name of Inbal, which means the tongue of a bell.

The significance of this symbol is clear in *Elsewhere, Perhaps*. The community of the kibbutz—the people, united in their beliefs and their efforts— form the tongue of the bell. Without a clapper, a bell is a hollow, empty shell, incapable of sound, unable to fulfill its purpose. Thus, a land without people to care for it and work it would be hollow and useless.

Further, Oz seems to be saying that the individual pulled from society is hollow, unable to make those connections which give joy and meaning to life: "There is a moral in this: men are not condemned inevitably to an accursed, tedious life of sterility. With an effort of will a man can avert the curse and hew out a path of his own." That path may be his own but cannot be alone; *Elsewhere, Perhaps* is ultimately a novel about community.

*Critical Context*

*Elsewhere, Perhaps* explores territory, both fictional and literal, that Amos Oz knows well. Like Reuven Harish, Oz was a long-standing kibbutz member, dividing his time between teaching and writing. Unlike Reuven, on the other hand, Oz is closer to the "new generation" of Israelis, who seem more confident, more self-assured, more at home, in a sense, in the land they claim as ancestrally theirs.

This division between the "generation of 1948" and the one which followed it (the generation of Oz) marks the main dividing line in contemporary Israeli literature. The older generation of writers lived through the founding days of the new Israel, and their works reflect an intense moral and patriotic vision. The new wave of Israeli authors, such as Oz and A. B. Yehoshua, are different in their outlook, and *Elsewhere, Perhaps* is an excellent example of this.

Oz sees the endemic armed conflict in which Israel lives as an existential fact, rather than a special case. He uses modern politics, including terrorism, as means to probe the individual human being and to see how a particular character will react to the common human dilemmas.

In works such as his collection of short stories *Artsot ha-tan* (1965; *Where the Jackals Howl and Other Stories*, 1981) and the novel *La-ga'ath ba-mayim, la-ga'ath ba-ruah* (1973; *Touch the Water, Touch the Wind*, 1974), Oz continues and refines the techniques he first established in *Elsewhere, Perhaps*. From his first novel he has developed an outlook that is Israeli in setting and feeling but universal in scope and sympathy.

*Sources for Further Study*
Batzdorff, S. M. Review in *Library Journal*. XCVIII (September 1, 1973), p. 2464.
Sheppard, R. Z. "Independent States of Mind: In New York, International P.E.N. Generates Heat and Light," in *Time*. CXXVII (January 27, 1986), p. 75.
Wood, Michael. Review in *The New York Review of Books*. XXI (February 7, 1974), p. 12.

*Michael Witkoski*

# ENEMIES
## A Love Story

*Author:* Isaac Bashevis Singer (1904-        )
*Type of plot:* Domestic realism
*Time of plot:* The postwar 1940's
*Locale:* New York City
*First published: Sonim de Geshichte fun a Liebe,* 1966 (English translation, 1972)

> *Principal characters:*
> HERMAN BRODER, the protagonist, an irreligious Jewish
>     survivor of the Holocaust
> YADWIGA, his Polish wife
> MILTON LAMPERT, a sixty-four-year-old rabbi who is Herman's
>     employer
> TAMARA LURIA, Herman's first wife, presumed killed by the
>     Nazis
> MASHA TORTSHINER, Herman's mistress and later his third
>     wife
> SHIFRA PUAH BLOCH, Masha's mother

*The Novel*

The only child of Reb Shmuel Leib Broder of Tzivkev, Herman studies philosophy in Warsaw. There he meets the daughter of the rich Reb Shachnah Luria, Tamara, who is studying at the Wszchnica. Despite their parents' objections, the two marry, but they quickly begin quarreling and are separated, about to be divorced, when World War II breaks out.

During the war, Yadwiga, a Polish peasant who had worked as a maid for the Broders, hides Herman in a hayloft. At the war's end in 1945, he learns from eyewitnesses that Tamara and their two children have been killed by the Nazis. He marries Yadwiga, and together they move to Brooklyn, close to Coney Island.

To support himself, Herman becomes a ghostwriter for Rabbi Milton Lampert, but he tells Yadwiga that he earns his money as a traveling bookseller. This lie allows him to spend nights with his mistress, Masha. Suspicious, bitter, and fearful, Masha wants Herman to divorce Yadwiga and marry her; she intends to divorce her unfaithful husband, "Doctor" Leon Tortshiner. When Masha tells Herman that she is carrying Herman's child, he agrees to the marriage but not to the divorce.

To complicate Herman's life further, Tamara appears in New York, the reports of her death having been premature. She was shot by the Nazis and her children were murdered, but she, like Herman and Masha, has survived. Although she has the most legitimate claim on Herman, she alone makes no demands. On the contrary, she attempts to help him.

At a party given by Rabbi Lampert, the secret of Herman's three wives comes out. Masha leaves him, and he realizes that he can no longer work for the rabbi. Tamara finds him a job—as a bookseller. Her uncle, Reb Abraham Nissen Yaroslaver, wants to sell his bookstore and move to Israel, but no one will pay his price. Since he suspects that he may wish to return to America someday, he offers the bookstore to Tamara, who in turn offers Herman the chance to manage it.

Herman, however, cannot settle down. When Masha suddenly reenters his life, telling him that she is planning to leave for California the next day, he decides to join her. That very night, though, Masha's mother, Shifra Puah, dies. Herman wants to leave anyway, but Masha now insists on waiting until after the funeral. Herman leaves her and disappears from the world of the novel; Masha, having lost her only ties to life—her mother and Herman—commits suicide.

Yadwiga gives birth to Herman's child, whom she names Masha. Mother and daughter move in with Tamara, who is managing the bookstore. Rabbi Lampert, a frequent visitor, tells Tamara that as a deserted wife she is free to remarry, but Tamara replies that she will keep faith with the feckless Herman.

### The Characters

Herman is deeply affected by the Holocaust. Everywhere he goes in New York City he seeks potential hiding places from imaginary Nazis. When he vanishes at the end of the novel, Tamara speculates that he has found another hayloft. Yet he flees not so much from the Nazis as from himself, his own greatest enemy. As Isaac Bashevis Singer writes in the author's note to the novel, "the characters are not only Nazi victims but victims of their own personalities and fates."

Nazis do not compel Herman to become a polygamist. Tamara offers to divorce him, as does Yadwiga. Masha is willing, however reluctantly, to leave him. It is his desire for all three women that deters him from living with only one. Even before World War II, he was a womanizer, and he was first attracted to Masha when he and Yadwiga were still in Germany waiting to sail for America.

Herman is also a victim of his nihilistic philosophy. Representative of modern Jewry, he is "without belief in himself or in the human race, a fatalistic hedonist who lived in presuicidal gloom," as Singer describes him. He does not mourn his murdered children—whom he did not want in the first place—nor does he intend to become a father again. When Tamara asks what provisions he has made for Yadwiga's pregnancy, he replies that the neighbors have done everything. Tamara reminds him, "But it's your child, after all." He does not respond but thinks, "So what?" Attached to nothing and to no one, he is finally blown into oblivion by the whirlwind of passions.

Masha, too, is a modern Jew who has rejected a God who could permit the Holocaust. Like Herman, she is bitter and self-centered, caring only for her own pleasures. She has no qualms about tearing Herman away from his wife—or wives. Her one constant link to the world is her mother, whom she rescues from death at the end of the war; yet even with her mother, her relationship includes as much hate as love, as much selfishness as generosity.

Herman's other two wives are as selfless as Masha and Herman are selfish. Before the war Tamara had been self-centered, like her husband, more concerned with crusades than with people. The war, however, has chastened her. She sees much cruelty, noting that under stress most people sink beneath humanity. Some, however, transcend their human limitations to become saintlike, and she chooses to imitate these. Hence, she makes no demands on Herman; instead, she helps him as much as she can and cares for his wife and child after he abandons them.

Yadwiga, too, is saintlike. She risks her life to save Herman from the Nazis and later, in an effort to be closer to him, embraces his religion. When Tamara visits them for the first time, Yadwiga offers to return to Poland so that Herman can live with his first wife—both Tamara and Yadwiga are willing to relinquish their own claims in favor of each other's claim to Herman. When Herman hastily goes off with Masha in the midst of a snowstorm, Yadwiga throws his galoshes out the window after him.

Between these two poles of selfishness and generosity is Rabbi Lampert. Like Herman, he is a charlatan, building a scholarly reputation on ghost-written sermons, articles, and books. Like Herman, too, he is lustful, always trying to seduce women. Yet he is also capable of great compassion and tries to help Herman, Masha, and others. He pays for Shifra Puah's tombstone, and one senses that he joins with Tamara in providing for Yadwiga and her infant.

Completing this rich tapestry is Shifra Puah, another Holocaust survivor. Masha has been embittered by her experiences, and her faith has been shattered; Shifra Puah's faith has been strengthened by the Holocaust. Her husband had been a nonbeliever, but she had always adhered to Jewish traditions. In America, her devotion increases, and her faith gives pattern and meaning to her life.

## Themes and Meanings

*Enemies* indicts modern Judaism, which Singer regards as vulgar and materialistic without being real. Yadwiga, seeking to convert to Judaism, attempts to learn about the religion from her neighbors. From them she gets the impression that "the insurance policy and the dishwasher were both necessary aspects of Jewish observances." Implied is Singer's harsh condemnation of Jews who fail to perpetuate their heritage. Significantly, Masha thinks that she is pregnant but is merely suffering from nerves: She can produce only death, not life. Herman also dissociates himself from birth; he wants no children and does nothing to help Yadwiga through her pregnancy. It is she who says, "I want to have a Jewish child"—she who wants someone to say the memorial prayer for her.

Herman periodically attempts to reform. He puts on his skullcap and returns to the sacred books. During these intervals he is at peace with himself and the world; like Shifra Puah, he finds consolation in religion. Yet his belief is not as strong as hers—he cannot remain faithful to tradition and so is ultimately lost.

Though Singer sees Jews tormenting themselves, he also sees them saving themselves. If some are their own worst enemies, some also show love. For a selfish Herman there is a generous Tamara; for the sterile Masha there is the fecund Yadwiga. With the birth of a new Masha at the end of the novel, Singer extends hope for a new and better generation. Perhaps this new Masha, safe from the Nazis, reared in a world of loving care, will carry on the tradition that her namesake and her father rejected.

*Critical Context*

*Enemies*, Singer's fourth novel to be translated into English, was his first with a contemporary American setting. His America is a bleak, winter wasteland, a gray background of deserted beaches, steamy subways, and seedy cafeterias. Singer's New York City is a fitting place for the hollow men and women who inhabit it.

Despite its grim setting and tragic conclusion, *Enemies* is essentially comic. Herman speculates that Tamara may be a ghost but rejects this possibility when he notes that she is gaining weight. His juggling of wives is farcical, and his elaborate lies are themselves a tour de force. Where indeed but in comedy would the central lie—his occupation—become truth? Yadwiga's confusion over the ritualistic importance of an insurance policy and dishwasher, while symbolic, is at the same time amusing. Even the ending may be regarded as part of the fertility ritual that underlies comedy—the old Masha is slain so that a new Masha may be born in the late spring.

Like Singer's other novels, *Enemies* uses a simple narrative to raise complex metaphysical questions. Is there a God? Does He care about the world? Is He benign or malign? How can or should man relate to Him? In Singer's novels one senses an increasing dissatisfaction with easy answers. *Der Knekht* (1961; *The Slave*, 1962) concludes with the canonization of its hero and heroine, whose son is carrying on their beliefs. In *Enemies*, the ending is ambiguous. Herman vanishes, leaving behind a child whose life is yet to unfold. In *Neshome Ekspeditsyes* (1974; *Shosha*, 1978), Singer implies that no answers are possible; one is left literally as well as spiritually in the dark.

Although Singer lacks answers, he remains one of the few contemporary writers to pose ultimate questions. In this lies much of the lasting significance of his books.

*Sources for Further Study*
Alexander, Edward. *Isaac Bashevis Singer*, 1980.
Buchen, Irving. *Isaac Bashevis Singer and the Eternal Past*, 1968.
Kresh, Paul. *Isaac Bashevis Singer: The Magician of West 86th Street*, 1979.
Malin, Irving, ed. *Critical Views of Issac Bashevis Singer*, 1969.
Walden, Daniel, ed. *Isaac Bashevis Singer: A Reconsideration*, 1981.

*Joseph Rosenblum*

# THE ENGINEER OF HUMAN SOULS

*Author:* Josef Škvorecký (1924-    )
*Type of plot:* Psychological realism
*Time of plot:* Winter, 1976, to spring, 1977
*Locale:* Toronto, Canada
*First published: Příběh inženýra lidských duší,* 1977 (2 volumes; English
   translation, 1984)

Principal characters:

DANIEL SMIRICKY, a forty-eight-year-old Czech émigré, a
   writer and Edenvale College literature professor
IRENE SVENSSON, the affluent nineteen-year-old student at
   Edenvale who becomes Smiricky's lover
LARRY HAKIM, a student in Smiricky's sophomore literature
   class, an intense Socialist ideologue
VERONIKA PRST, a student at Edenvale, a Czech exile who
   chooses to return to her homeland
NADIA JIROUSKOVA, Smiricky's teenage love who died in
   Czechoslovakia on January 23, 1946, at age twenty-one
PREMA SKOCOPOLE, a friend of Smiricky and the teenage
   leader of the Kostelec underground during the German
   Occupation, who later emigrated to Australia
JAN PROUZA, Smiricky's friend, a poet who remained in
   Czechoslovakia, battling the constraints of Socialist
   Realism until he committed suicide in August, 1972
VACHOUSEK, Smiricky's foreman in the Messerschmitt factory
   during World War II, a lifelong resistance leader, captured
   and executed in the 1970's
MILENA CABRICAROVA, the Czech émigré known as DOTTY,
   Smiricky's dearest friend in Toronto, who marries a
   businessman and happily adjusts to Western life

*The Novel*

Daniel Smiricky, the narrator of *The Engineer of Human Souls,* writes by
force of circumstance. He fled his native Czechoslovakia at the time of the
Russian invasion, in 1968, and resettled in Toronto, Canada. Although he
feels "utterly and dangerously wonderful in this wilderness land," he is,
nevertheless, a man on the margins of two cultures, East European and
Western, belonging totally to neither. In 1976, he finds himself in the anomalous position of a Czech teaching American and English literature to blasé
Canadian and foreign students who are generally ignorant of world history
and politics and largely insensitive to any language. As a writer, he is without

a literary audience; as a teacher, he is without literary proselytes. Sadness pervades his life. Smiricky laments his disconnection from his past and dwells poignantly on the days of his ardent youth, days full of precious friends, loves, adventures, and delights. He mourns the plight of his homeland under German, then Russian, domination since World War II.

As Smiricky's mind continually scans his own life, past and present, East and West, his personal narration constructs a historical, literary, and political picture of the last thirty years of international events. *The Engineer of Human Souls'* unusual narrative structure consists of brief segments of experience, each only a few pages in length, each isolated like the separate frames of a film before it comes to life as a "moving picture." Punctuated by black dots at the center of the page, these discrete segments about different times, places, and people cumulatively build separate and distinct narratives, unified through Smiricky's consciousness. The present-tense frame narrative of the novel depicts Smiricky teaching his classes, meeting with his academic colleagues, participating in the Czech émigré community, attending holiday parties, and starting an affair with one of his students. Although unendingly interrupted by moments from the past, this frame narrative proceeds in discernible chronological order: from the dreary opening sophomore literature class on Edgar Allan Poe in the winter of 1976 to the novel's comic resolutions in the spring of 1977, when Smiricky's friend Dotty marries a prosperous businessman, and Smiricky goes on a romantic excursion to Paris with his new lover, Irene Svensson.

In the course of his day-to-day activities, Smiricky's mind returns to his youth in his hometown, Kostelec. This set of recollections creates, within the frame narrative, an emotionally intense memory narrative covering a brief time, from 1942 to 1944, thirty years in the past. Against a horrifying backdrop of world war, bombings of Europe, concentration camps, and random local instances of Nazi brutality, Smiricky's enthusiastic skirt chasing, raucous camaraderie, and amateur heroics shine in memory's spotlight. The ugly face of his uncertain future, the closure of Czech universities and his subsequent machining of parts for Messerschmitt fighter planes, pales in the rosy hues of the memories of his first love, Nadia Jirouskova. These Kostelec youths are unmindful of the ghastly historical moment they endure. As Smiricky ironically observes, "we were young and free in that awful dictatorship, and we had no respect for its glories."

Another memory narrative reveals Smiricky's more mature awareness of personal fears and political atrocities. Loosely linked experiences from the time of his postwar departure from Kostelec through the development of his writing career, his expatriation, and his first years in Toronto are unified by accounts of secret agents, informers, political persecution, censorship, and the ongoing resistance to Communist control within and beyond Czech borders.

A narrative of letters, individually fixed in time and space but appearing out of chronological order, provides biographical sketches of Smiricky's hometown friends since World War II. Since 1942, their lives have taken diverse courses. Jan Prouza, the poet, stayed in Czechoslovakia, futilely resisting censorship. Prema Skocopole escaped to Australia, where he was plagued by homesickness for the rest of his life. Nadia died of tuberculosis shortly after the war and Rebecca survived a concentration camp and emigrated to Israel, only to lose her family to a terrorist's bomb. In chapter 7, "Lovecraft," this epistolary narrative becomes a necrology, a record of the deaths of most of Smiricky's friends. The last letter shows Lojza, a Czech Babbitt, thriving in his homeland, benightedly singing the praises of socialism for peasants such as himself.

These four narratives alternate with irregular rhythms through the seven chapters of the novel. Each chapter is identified with a well-known literary figure: Edgar Allan Poe, Nathaniel Hawthorne, Mark Twain, F. Scott Fitzgerald, Stephen Crane, Joseph Conrad, and H.P. Lovecraft. These "heroes of the pen" provide literary rubrics for Smiricky's history, and classroom discussions of their works establish his preoccupations of mind and spirit: war and peace, oppression and freedom, horror and beauty, fear and hope, loss and love, death and life. Although Smiricky's forty-eight years have been more eventful than most lives, conventional plot and action are minimized by continuous narrative disjunctions and implied associative leaps. The drama of a man, "a living stream of consciousness," is constructed with bits of thinking, feeling, and remembering—in response to life, death, love, fear, and art. The motion of a life is not to be captured in a linear plot or a single crystal of meaning. Like the world, like this novel, Smiricky's life is a plethora of sensations, reflections, and experiences. His life eludes definition but is replete with significance. There is no one meaning in *The Engineer of Human Souls* for "something written well, as Ernest Hemingway once said, can have many meanings. . . ."

### The Characters

In many ways, the life of the narrator of *The Engineer of Human Souls* resembles that of his creator, Josef Škvorecký. Škvorecký also survived the German Reich protectorate, earned a Ph.D. after the war, and became a nationally renowned but officially banned writer. Relocated in Toronto after the Soviet invasion of August 21, 1968, Škvorecký became a literature professor at Erindale College, University of Toronto, and an active member of the Czech émigré community. His lifelong interests in swing music, cinema, mystery novels, and world literature are also shared by his protagonist. Smiricky's personality, however, seems to more closely resemble that of T.S. Eliot's Prufrock. Aging, no longer easily set on fire, self-absorbed, and plagued by vestigial fears, Smiricky is a man nearly drowning in his own memories. By his own estimation, he is prone to sentimentality, full of grief, and dependent on women. He is not above consciously exaggerating both the "heroic connotations" of his war experiences and the dangers of his writing activities to add allure to his image.

Several groups of characters from Smiricky's past and present are shown through his consciousness. Many of those with whom he grew up in Kostelec are now dead, irretrievably lost and painfully unforgotten, and they haunt him. A large part of Smiricky's story is written by and for these dead. Re-creating their shared moments of love, humor, friendship, bravery, and cowardice, Smiricky elegizes his friends: Nadia, the honest, simple girl from a lower social class; Benno, the musician; Jan, the poet; Prema, the saboteur; Vrata, the artist; and Vachousek, the factory foreman.

The spies, informers, and paranoid citizens of communist-controlled Czechoslovakia encountered by Smiricky during the 1950's, 1960's, and 1970's constitute a second set of characters. Most are shown in wonderfully farcical anecdotes, for "the alchemy of time transforms everything into comedy." The long arm of totalitarianism is demonstrated by the alleged and real defections of Dr. Toth and the trap sprung by Uher, the malicious Czech secret agent, to force Smiricky to inform on a Czech tourist during one of his literary tours. Critical commentary on Czech literary production and censorship is implicit is Smiricky's hilarious efforts to get the frightened Czech book smuggler, Novak, to turn over a contraband book to him in the Toronto airport toilet. On a university visit, a Czech poet, Vokurovski, arrives accompanied by a secret agent "translator" who speaks no English. Burlesque tales such as these disclose the inherent absurdities of the sophisticated terrors of modern totalitarianism.

At Edenvale, Smiricky deals with students guilty of "Blessed ignorance! That unforgiveable sin of transatlantic civilization!" Most see the world through television and glossy magazines and maintain their parochialism by resisting acquaintance with history, literature, and politics. Fellow émigrés, Dotty Cabricarova, Milan Fikejz, Mrs. Santner, Mr. Pohorsky, Bocar and Margitka, and Veronika Prst (among others) are torn between East and West. Many are sick with longing for their homeland yet appalled by its state. They are at once enchanted by the freedoms of the West and terrified of being "infected" by its political obliviousness and its commercialism. These groups of characters share Smiricky's experiences in different ways at different times over several decades. Together, they display a spectrum of ideologies, ethics, and emotions which counterpoints and amplifies Smiricky's perceptions.

*Themes and Meanings*

The subtitle of *The Engineer of Human Souls* sweepingly declares it "An Entertainment on the Old Themes of Life, Women, Fate, Dreams, the

Working Class, Secret Agents, Love, and Death." Central to all these concerns, however, is Škvorecký's ironic use of the phrase "the engineer of human souls." The author asserts that this was Joseph Stalin's definition of the writer: "As an engineer constructs a machine, so must the writer construct the mind of the New Man." Smiricky is a writer who is not writing at the moment. He is a writer without an audience, for his work is banned in his homeland and ignored in Canada—even by Czech exiles. His plight poses the most pressing questions of the novel. What is the writer's place in today's world? When all the themes in this world are "old," why write? When imperialisms, personal and political, persist and when Eastern writers are not free to write and Western readers are free not to read, then why write? Smiricky himself offers an answer in his discussion of F. Scott Fitzgerald: "perhaps because so much that is human is still alien to so many people." *The Engineer of Human Souls*, as a whole, exemplifies the poet Prouza's vision of the writer's special talent for "mimesis," his ability to represent the "individual *uniqueness* of man, who lives out what *everyone* lives out: his unique variation on the general theme." The writer must continue to resist suppression, fight audience indifference, and struggle to disclose the universal truths in particular experience.

Reader indifference is as threatening to the writer as his own despair and ennui. Such indifference is made real in Smiricky's classroom. Eating their lunches, painting their fingernails, and courting covertly, students from every walk of life and nations around the world listen passively with seldom a live thought, a sympathetic ear, or a feeling response. When active, they are generally mouthing the purloined words of the critics to whom they turn for facile analyses. However powerful the works they read, Smiricky's students seem to fail to recognize and value writing's "secret ability, inaccessible to the reason, to awaken in the reader the joy of recognition. . . ." *The Engineer of Human Souls* calls the writer to write, against all oppositions, all apathy. The novel also challenges the reader to read with all the powers of his mind and spirit. Škvorecký's complex, fragmented narrative with its constructions of multiple perspectives, evocations of times, re-creations of places, and interpretations of human experiences intentionally coerces readers into a more active role in the creation of meaningfulness. Succinctly, Smiricky sermonizes "unmarxistleninistically" on the need for this special kind of literary coercion: "The real religion of life, the true idolatry of literature, can never flourish in democracies, in those vague, boring kingdoms of the freedom not to read, not to suffer, not to desire, not to know, not to understand." With his fable of an individual consciousness, Škvorecký may move men to read, to suffer, to desire, to know, and to understand. When both writer and reader move beyond unenlightened self-interest, national allegiances, and political ideologies, they move closer to the universal truths which may make it possible to "construct the mind of the New Man." Such writing and such reading are imperatives, "because so much that is human is still alien to so many people."

## Critical Context

Josef Škvorecký won the Neustadt International Prize for Literature in 1980, and *The Engineer of Human Souls* was awarded the Canadian Governor General's Award for Literature in 1984. Since he emigrated to Canada, Škvorecký's reputation as a novelist has grown rapidly in the West. His warm, humorous, and melancholy treatments of life, love, and politics are frequently compared to the cool ironies of his countryman Milan Kundera, to the autobiographical narratives of Czesław Miłosz, or to the depictions of terror and totalitarianism in the works of Aleksandr Solzhenitsyn.

Daniel Smiricky is also the protagonist of several other Škvorecký novels: *Zbabělci* (1958; *The Cowards*, 1970) and *Prima sezóna* (1975; *The Swell Season: A Text on the Most Important Things in Life*, 1982) and two untranslated, *Tankový prapor* (1971; the tank corps) and *Mirakl* (1972). Škvorecký's first novel, *The Cowards*, though banned for depicting both Germans and Russians as less than heroic, established his reputation in Czechoslovakia. When he left in 1968, Škvorecký was one of the nation's most popular novelists and a prolific editor, translator, essayist, and screenwriter as well.

Both *The Cowards* and *The Swell Season* are set in the dramatic closing days of World War II, and both follow youthful Danny Smiricky, then an innocent amid chaos, chasing beautiful girls relentlessly and blowing his saxophone in rebellion. The narratives of both novels are limited to narrow parameters of time and space and provide more straightforward exposition of plot and more conventional treatment of characters than does *The Engineer of Human Souls*.

The protagonists of the two novellas in *Bassaxofon* (1967; *The Bass Saxophone*, 1977) and the young hero of *Lvíče* (1969; *Miss Silver's Past*, 1973) each bear a strong family resemblance to Smiricky with their respective enthusiasms for jazz, beautiful women, and literary freedom. The seemingly improvisational narrative flow of *The Bass Saxophone* anticipates the subtle emotional and intellectual fusions of *The Engineer of Human Souls*.

With its innovative narrative techniques and challenging visions of life, art, and politics, *The Engineer of Human Souls* has taken its place among outstanding postmodern novels. Like most major works of world literature, its art reaches beyond national borders, transcends cultures, soars over Iron Curtains, and defies ideological dogmatisms to address an international audience, all humanity.

## Sources for Further Study

Hames, Peter. *The Czechoslovak New Wave*, 1985.

Hancock, Geoffrey. "An Interview with Josef Škvorecký," in *The Canadian*

*Fiction Magazine.* Nos. 45/46 (1982/1983), pp. 63-96.

Škvorecký, Josef. "Why the Harlequin?" in *Cross Currents.* III (1984), pp. 259-264.

Solecki, Sam. "The Laughter and Pain of Remembering," in *The Canadian Forum.* XXXIX (1984), pp. 39-41.

*World Literature Today.* LIV (1980). Special Škvorecký issue.

*Virginia Crane*

# ENVY

*Author:* Yury Olesha (1899-1960)
*Type of plot:* Satire
*Time of plot:* The 1920's
*Locale:* Moscow
*First published: Zavist,* 1927 (English translation, 1936)

>     *Principal characters:*
>       NIKOLAI KAVALEROV, a homeless drunk, the narrator of the
>         first part of the novel
>       ANDREI BABICHEV, the Director of the Food Industry Trust
>       IVAN BABICHEV, the brother of Andrei, a semicrazed dreamer,
>         an opponent of the twentieth century
>       VOLODYA MAKAROV, a star athlete and engineering student,
>         the new Soviet man
>       VALYA, the daughter of Ivan, who is loved by both Volodya
>         and Kavalerov

*The Novel*

Andrei Babichev, the very efficient Director of the Food Industry Trust, brings home a drunk whom he has found in the gutter, Nikolai Kavalerov. Kavalerov, who is an individualist and completely out of sympathy with the new Soviet way of life, both likes and dislikes his new protector. Kavalerov discovers that Andrei also supports Volodya Makarov, a student from the provinces who is also a star athlete and a staunch believer in the Soviet system. Volodya is away for the summer holidays, so Andrei showers his attention upon Kavalerov. While the latter appreciates the concern, he grows in his hatred of Andrei's emphasis upon the collective and upon machinery in place of individuals. His rage grows such that he writes a letter to Andrei, criticizing the views of the official and stating that he, Kavalerov, as the representative of individuals, is superior to a system which caters only to the material needs of its constituents.

Kavalerov mistakenly believes that Volodya must also feel this way, for the latter is a talented youth who is forced to depend upon a mere bureaucrat with no pretensions to intellect. When Kavalerov finally meets Volodya, he realizes that Volodya is an avid disciple of Andrei; even worse, he discovers that both Andrei and Volodya view him with at best pity, at worst contempt. The enraged Kavalerov leaves the Babichev household, vowing to kill his former benefactor.

At this point Kavalerov meets Ivan Babichev, the brother of Andrei, who is completely opposed not only to the Soviet emphasis upon the collective and machinery but also to any form of technology. The two men collaborate in an attempt to restore the primacy of feelings and respect for the individual in the Soviet Union; they also wish to rescue Valya, Ivan's daughter, from the views of Andrei and Volodya, whom she greatly admires. Because they have no plan, but only vague theories and desires, Kavalerov and Ivan are unsuccessful; at the end of the novel Valya has rejected her mad father and his ally, and the reader realizes that the two men are also being rejected by the course of history, at least in the Soviet Union. Kavalerov and Ivan are content to move in with a fat widow, who is willing to support them in return for their attentions.

### The Characters

The characters in this novel represent two conflicting attitudes in the Soviet Union of the 1920's: the old order, expressed in respect for individual achievement and individual feelings, and the new order, expressed in mammoth construction projects and emphasis upon the group. Nikolai Kavalerov has grandiose dreams of becoming famous but cannot find a way to do so in the Soviet system; the only people who become famous are people such as Andrei Babichev, who invents the perfect sausage and dreams of large collective dining halls serving inexpensive meals, thus making the family kitchen and its accompanying drudgery unnecessary. Kavalerov's hatred of Andrei is based upon envy, thus the title of the novel; Andrei becomes famous and Kavalerov, his intellectual superior, becomes a useless alcoholic.

Ivan Babichev is a more extreme Kavalerov; he rejects the entire twentieth century, with its emphasis upon technology and efficiency. While Kavalerov is merely a romantic out of tune with the times, Ivan is mentally ill and a pathological liar, potentially very dangerous. The author may be pointing out that Kavalerov's path toward rejection of reality may lead to a much more serious condition than alcoholism and romantic nostalgia.

Volodya Makarov is a more extreme Andrei Babichev. While Andrei uses machines and has, by Kavalerov's standards, rather mundane goals, Volodya has no goals other than to become a human machine with no signs of inefficiency or feelings to hamper perfect production, whether it be in athletics or labor.

In the midst of these male characters is Valya, the daughter of Ivan and apparently the symbol of the typical 1920's Soviet girl. Valya seems to be the female equivalent of Volodya, but she values feelings. She also arouses feelings in the men of the novel, some romantic, some paternal or avuncular. In this sense Valya seems to represent the old order of feelings and cultivation of beauty, as well as the new order of physical fitness and social usefulness. In the end, she rejects her father and Kavalerov; she becomes a staunch member of the Andrei/Volodya camp, reflecting the actual course of history in the Soviet Union as well as pointing out the ineffectiveness of Ivan and Kavalerov.

*Themes and Meanings*

The central theme of the novel is embodied in the eternal struggle between the old and the new, certainly not a new theme in literature, but one particularly appropriate for the postrevolutionary transitional period of the 1920's in the Soviet Union. Authors such as Yury Olesha had been educated to the traditional ideals of culture, beauty, and individual achievement, while the new Soviet leaders cultivated the more prosaic ideals of industrialization, egalitarianism, and collective achievement. The conflict between these sets of ideals raged not only among political and social groupings but also within individuals. None of the characters is very attractive; each seems to be lacking something essential to an integrated human personality. The author may well be using this theme, demonstrated through these flawed characters, to demonstrate his own ambivalence toward the old and new orders; instead of showing readers the best of both worlds, he presents the worst of both as a warning of the dangers inherent in each view: excessive rigidity and lack of human feelings on one hand, and rejection of reality with actual improvements in the human condition on the other.

Although it is not explicit in the novel, Valya seems to represent a possible synthesis between the two orders, uniting feelings and beauty with the benefits of material progress. A possible reason for the nondevelopment of this theme may have been the inability of the author to envision how such a synthesis could come about.

This main theme is complicated by Kavalerov's attitude toward the new society. While he seems to be a proponent of the old order, his feelings of animosity are fueled by his inability to fit into the new order; in other words, an almost adolescent rejection of the adult world which will end if Kavalerov can fit into the new society. The rejection is based upon principle as much as upon personal experience, thus somewhat negating the theme of rejection of the new order. If Kavalerov can achieve some form of personal fame, his revolt will end.

A secondary theme is the opposition between Russia and the West, a perennial topic among Russian writers, both pre- and post-revolutionary. Kavalerov expresses the wish that he had been born in Western Europe, where the individual can become famous. At first glance, this statement might seem anti-Soviet, a criticism of the collectivized society; in fact, many nineteenth century Russian writers used that same theme to portray the lack of opportunity in the Soviet Union for the talented individual. Intellectuals of both the new order and the old have felt out of place in their country and looked to the West as a sort of Promised Land, although most did not wish to emigrate from their beloved Russia. The result is a love/hate relationship, often leading to an almost schizophrenic attitude toward Russia as the land of good and evil.

*Critical Context*

*Envy* is easily Olesha's most important work; it is the only one of his novels to achieve the status of a Soviet classic—although it is not reprinted in the Soviet Union—and it is the one work of the author which is known to most students of Soviet literature. His work was greeted favorably when it was published because most critics misunderstood what the author was trying to achieve in it. Orthodox Marxist critics viewed the novel as a vindication of the new Soviet system because Ivan and Kavalerov are completely ineffectual and end up sharing the attentions of the fat widow; in effect, kept men who are unable to cope with reality. Opponents of the Soviet system viewed the novel as a call for more individualism in a society which was rapidly becoming collectivized, more emphasis on feelings rather than utilitarian worth. In the end the latter group of critics prevailed, and *Envy* is a banned classic in the Soviet Union. The truth of the matter is probably in the middle: The author was repelled by aspects of both sides in the dispute.

The real attractiveness of the novel was the freshness which Olesha brought to the theme. Critics of all persuasions praised the author's style, which is a combination of symbolism, realism, and fantasy. The author deals with a very realistic problem of the times and enhances the main themes with a liberal dose of fantasy in order to emphasize the realistic nature of the situation. Such a method requires great virtuosity if it is to be successful, and most critics agree that Olesha was such a virtuoso. Using colorful images and a fast-paced narrative, the author managed to restate an old problem in a new form. Because of the Draconian restrictions placed upon Soviet literature soon after the publication of this work, its method was not repeated until the 1960's, when Olesha became an openly acknowledged master for a new generation of Soviet writers.

*Sources for Further Study*

Brown, Edward J. "Prophets of a Brave New World," in *Russian Literature Since the Revolution*, 1982.

Struve, Gleb. *Russian Literature Under Lenin and Stalin*, 1971.

Tucker, Janet. "Jurij Olesa's *Envy*: A Re-Examination," in *Slavic and East European Review*. XXVI (1982), pp. 56-62.

Wilson, Wayne. "The Objective of Jurij Olesa's *Envy*," in *Slavic and East European Review*. XVIII (1974), pp. 31-40.

*Philip Maloney*

# EQUAL DANGER

*Author:* Leonardo Sciascia (1921-    )
*Type of plot:* Parodic fable/murder mystery
*Time of plot:* The 1970's
*Locale:* Imaginary "Spanish" cities, probably analogues to those of Sicily
*First published: Il contesto: Una parodia,* 1971 (English translation, 1973)

> *Principal characters:*
> INSPECTOR ROGAS, the protagonist and the shrewdest
>     investigator on the police force
> CRES, the antagonist and the purported assassin, who is never
>     seen
> NOCIO,
> GALANO,
> THE MINISTERS, and
> PRESIDENT RICHES, the representatives of both private and
>     governmental morality
> CUSAN, a writer and friend of Rogas

*The Novel*

When the district attorney in charge of prosecuting an infamous murder case is himself assassinated one evening in May, the Minister of National Security assigns Inspector Rogas to the case. No sooner is he given charge than news arrives of the murder of another judge in a neighboring city. Besieged by questions of motive and character, Rogas begins to sift among possible explanations.

When yet a third official is gunned down, Rogas concludes that one man is responsible for all three murders. His conclusions lead him through a series of interrogations and interviews which form the heart of this short novel.

One suspect, the victim of wrongful imprisonment, is found sitting in the sun, reticent, stoic, seemingly indifferent to life. A second man, now a mechanic and also unjustly convicted, has become cynical and embittered, a helpless victim of "the system."

Rogas' investigations take a different direction when he is presented with an absurd tale about a pharmacist's wife who has accused her husband, Cres, of trying to kill her with poisoned rice and chocolate. Discovering evidence that suggests that Mrs. Cres framed her husband, tricking the court system into putting him in prison while she ran around with other men, Rogas pursues the idea that Cres, recently released after serving five years, may now be taking revenge on those who convicted him.

Meanwhile, Cres has become invisible. Though Rogas learns something about the subject's strange personality from one of the ex-pharmacist's friends, Cres himself has somehow acquired a new identity, eluding even Rogas' expert surveillance. Significantly, Rogas begins to develop a sympathy for his antagonist. Convinced of his guilt, he is determined to find him.

His determination is ironically thwarted, however, when a fourth murder convinces the Government that a left-wing revolutionary group is responsible for the murders. Rogas is pulled off the Cres case and given orders to work with his colleague in the political section, an assignment which he views as punishment for his zeal.

His first interview under this new line of investigation is to be with the editor of the notorious left-wing magazine *Permanent Revolution*. The editor, Galano, is the houseguest of a celebrated writer, Nocio, who has become disaffected with the sociopolitical establishment and has written a poem which underscores in seamy images the sterility and rankness of society.

Galano is evasive, but Rogas meets him finally at the house of a suspected neoanarchist. With them is a top Government Minister; the startled Minister orders Rogas to appear in his office the next morning. When Rogas stands before the Minister, he is told that what he saw the night before was simply a matter of political accommodation, and that he should continue to investigate the "real" enemy, the revolutionaries.

Convinced now that the next victim is to be President Riches, Rogas succeeds in warning the President. Certain that Cres is still his prime suspect, Rogas is shocked when he realizes that the man he has just passed in the elevator is Cres, who, with his new identity, has taken lodging in the same building as the President, the better to assassinate him.

Rogas determines to stop Cres, but he realizes now that someone—the Government, perhaps—is having him followed. He evades surveillance and goes to a café where he tells his friend, Cusan, a committed writer and an honest man, everything about the case. Cusan agrees to help.

The point of view now shifts from Rogas to Cusan. The writer learns through a news broadcast that Rogas has been killed at a museum, together with a member of a rival political party. At about the same time, President Riches is shot dead in his house. Fearing for his own life, Cusan goes to the headquarters of the Revolutionary Party for a final interview. There he learns that Rogas was killed by a Government agent as part of a chaotic plot to forestall an imminent revolution.

*The Characters*

The characters of *Equal Danger* are virtual abstractions. Except for Rogas, from whose point of view the story unfolds, the politicians and would-be reformers are mere parodies of corruption and ineptitude.

Inspector Rogas, whose surname derives from the Latin verb, *rogare*, "to ask," is an honest philosopher-cop who seeks the truth but whose interrogations lead only to more questions. He is well read, sensitive, and sympathetic. The reader is told, in fact, that Rogas is a man of principles in a country where no one else believes in them anymore.

His principles lead him to ask questions that the Government finds embarrassing. Though he follows orders, he does so only out of a professional sense of duty. Like all good philosophers, Rogas is not far from the truth even when he seems to be sidetracked. Despite impediments, his investigations take him inevitably closer to the real assassin, Cres.

Significantly, the character around whom the plot revolves is unseen—or only briefly, in disguise. This elusiveness, a virtual invisibility, is a crucial aspect of the meaning of the plot. The other characters doubt Cres's guilt. They are thus unable or unwilling to recognize or believe in the truth. Cres's name literally suggests "credibility." Though the real assassin, he is ultimately let alone, ignored, even patronized. He becomes the agent, a sort of angel of death, wreaking havoc on society.

The characters of *Equal Danger* are thus not flesh-and-blood human beings but representations, analogues of certain destructive attitudes toward justice. The two suspects whom Rogas interviews at the beginning of the novel, for example, depict what happens to ordinary men who come up against the injustice of the court system: They become cynical, despairing, frightened creatures who sit mindlessly in the sun.

Galano, Nocio, the ministers of state, even President Riches, are not shown as individuals but as stereotypes—the intellectuals, the bourgeoisie, the corrupt and inept government officials. Each has his views about the political structure of society, but none can act to save it without being corrupted by it.

*Themes and Meanings*

The narrative structure of *Equal Danger* is that of one variation of the classic detective novel, in which the criminal is known but his whereabouts are not. The method implicit in such a literary form allows for a density of meaning. On the simplest level, there is the implied parody of the form itself. Leonardo Sciascia uses the detective novel—with its trail of clues and dead ends and its laconic, unadorned style—to parody the detective novel.

On a deeper level, the story is a philosophical inquiry into the nature of a society whose system of justice has broken down. Sciascia has called his novel a "fable." The fable here is the symbolic interplay of the characters within a toxic social system. The flat literary tone reinforces the theme of helplessness within the system—a system without honor, faith, or justice. Rogas' murder and the consequent shift of the point of view to Cusan suggest a further complexity: The pursuit of truth will continue, despite failure and death, but such a pursuit must be conducted amid indifference, helplessness, and a sense of doom, as if the entire enterprise were meaningless.

The "equal danger" of the title points to a paradox. Society must be saved from the barbarians, but the saviors are equally barbaric, the injustice of the social system crying out that it is, in fact, not worth saving. The world represented by the fictionalized Spanish milieu thus hovers on the brink, awaiting the revolution that must come.

*Critical Context*

Sicilian-born Leonardo Sciascia has produced novels, short stories, and essays which focus on a recurring theme: the individual's search for justice in a society essentially bereft of it. The society is recognizably Sicilian, and the problem which emerges is Sicily's inability to defeat the evil represented by the Mafia, a criminal organization that controls all aspects of Sicilian political and social life. This corruption fostered by the Mafia has destroyed honor and decency; justice has become a sham and reason has fled.

The method characteristically used by Sciascia to express this theme is that of the detective novel. Four of his books deconstruct the "whodunit" formula, and *Equal Danger* is central among them. Like the hero of an earlier work, *Il giorno della civetta* (1961; *Mafia Vendetta*, 1963; also as *The Day of the Owl*, 1984), for example, Rogas is an enlightened policeman, the embodiment of a rational, philosophically balanced intellect, who seeks order amid chaos. Like the other novels of this kind, also, *Equal Danger* ends inconclusively, on the verge of despair, with the social fabric at the breaking point, and is compact, concise, and taut, stripped of all ornament except wit.

*Equal Danger* differs from its kin by maintaining an almost surrealistic tone. The setting is not explicitly Sicily, or Italy, but a vague Iberian region curiously nonpictorial. Of Sciascia's major novels, *Equal Danger* is the vaguest in terms of place and even characterization. There is an abstract feel to the work, as if Sciascia were trying to fictionalize a philosophical discussion of justice, to give narrative structure to an essay. Sciascia himself has admitted that the difference between his narrative and journalistic methods is often marginal.

Such an abstract quality has the effect of universalizing the problem. The corruption and near-anarchy is thus not a Sicilian or Italian predicament but a condition facing all humanity. The evil is not of Sicily but of the world, of civilization which has abandoned the principles of truth and honor. In this respect, *Equal Danger* presents a darker view than Sciascia's other novels in this genre, a view more despairing and less certain of the future.

*Sources for Further Study*

Cannon, JoAnn. "The Detective Fiction of Leonardo Sciascia," in *Modern Fiction Studies*. XXIX (Autumn, 1983), pp. 523-534.

Jones, Verina. "Leonardo Sciascia," in *Writers and Society in Contemporary Italy: A Collection of Essays*, 1984. Edited by Michael Caesar and Peter Hainsworth.

Prescott, P. S. Review in *Newsweek*. LXXXII (July 16, 1973), p. 88.
Vidal, Gore. "Sciascia's Italy," in *The Second American Revolution and Other Essays, 1976-1982*, 1982.

*Edward Fiorelli*

# THE ERASERS

*Author:* Alain Robbe-Grillet (1922-    )
*Type of plot:* Detective
*Time of plot:* Probably after World War II
*Locale:* An unnamed northern French city
*First published: Les Gommes*, 1953 (English translation, 1964)

> *Principal characters:*
> WALLAS, a detective
> LAURENT, a police commissioner
> DANIEL DUPONT, the victim
> EVELYNE DUPONT, his ex-wife
> GARINATI, an assassin
> DR. JUARD, a friend of Dupont

*The Novel*

*The Erasers*, Alain Robbe-Grillet's first published novel, is about a detective, named Wallas, who is sent from the capital to a northern city to investigate the latest in a series of political assassinations. The most recent victim, Daniel Dupont, was, however, only slightly wounded in the attempt. His friend, Dr. Juard, hides the fact that Dupont is still alive and also withholds his "body" from the police in order to protect him from a possible second assassination attempt.

Wallas is on his first solo mission for a governmental intelligence agency and is to take charge of the investigation. Parallel to Wallas' search for a murderer is his attempt to procure a certain type of eraser that he once saw, hence the title of the book. Although the reader does not see the hero of the novel, Wallas, in the first part of the prologue, it is eventually revealed that Wallas arrived late the night before and has taken a room in a café-hotel and that the owner is to call him at an early hour.

As the prologue begins, the café owner is preparing for the day's business and recalling bits and pieces of conversations from both the distant and recent past. The passages are written exactly in the way that one would think to oneself about such experiences, leading to sudden shifts of time or of locale and persons and giving the reader no sense of chronology or any explanation for the sudden changes. This method of writing, the suppression of linear time and space, seems to owe much to Marcel Proust; it is one of the hallmarks of the New Novel.

Included in the owner's thoughts is the fact that Dupont is not dead. Since Dupont's phone was out of order, his housekeeper had called the police from the café, telling them that Dupont was only slightly wounded in the arm. At the same time, Robbe-Grillet seems to warn the reader that there will be the classic red herrings of the detective novel in this book, since the café owner has seen a newspaper relating Dupont's death and thinks to himself that they can print anything they want but that they will never make him believe stories deliberately made up to fool people.

In the same manner, the reader is introduced to the murderer, Garinati, and his chief, Bona, who is giving his subordinate instructions on how to proceed with entering the house and killing Dupont. The reader makes a tour, through Garinati's eyes, of Dupont's house and witnesses the assassination attempt. The reader is also present at a meeting of Dupont and his friends while they discuss how to save him from the killers. Everything is presented to the reader in a series of flashbacks, without preamble or explanation. Finally, the prologue concludes with three words: "Wallas, Special Agent."

Wallas has risen early and walks through this unknown city of labyrinthine streets looking for the central police station. He asks directions of various people and, not wishing to make his identity known, lies to them, saying that he wants to go to the post office. This method leads to various complications, and he then gives, to himself, true answers as well as other false ones that lead to more complications.

Wallas finally meets with Commissioner Laurent, and they discuss the case. Laurent is rather annoyed at Wallas' being put in charge of the investigation but does his best to conceal it. Laurent is also bothered by the fact that he does not have a body to examine. The commissioner is not sure if Dupont was murdered, killed himself, or died accidentally.

Wallas goes to Dupont's house and interviews the old housekeeper. He also examines the study where Dupont was shot. Wallas takes to the streets again, and, quite by accident, enters the stationery store of Evelyne Dupont while looking for the elusive eraser. Wallas realizes that she must be the ex-wife when he sees a picture of Dupont's house. He interrogates her, and she assures Wallas that Dupont could not possibly have committed suicide. Meanwhile, Laurent has also been conducting his part of the investigation, weighing all the possibilities, interviewing witnesses, imagining what might have happened.

Wallas eventually returns to Dupont's house to reexamine the office where the attempt on Dupont's life occurred. He is in the study when Dupont arrives on the scene, looking for important papers that he needs to take with him in his temporary flight. At the same time, Laurent is in his office, scoffing at the report of a young and overzealous subordinate who, believing people who were obviously playing a joke on him, has cooked up a theory that Dupont had an illegitimate son about twenty years ago. It is then that Laurent concludes that if he cannot find a body, it is because Dupont is still alive. He calls Dupont's house to tell Wallas, but the call is too late: Wallas has just killed Dupont.

## The Characters

It is difficult, if not impossible, to talk about the characters in a normal sense, that is in the sense that Honoré de Balzac or Gustave Flaubert created characters. The central characters, Wallas, Laurent, and Garinati, have no first name and very little or no background. For example, all that the reader is told about their physical makeup is that Laurent is bald and that Garinati is small and has the face of a sad spider. The physical description of Wallas is limited to the fact that he is big and shaved his mustache for this assignment, and that his mentor and hero, Inspector Fabius, almost rejected him because his forehead measured only forty-nine square centimeters instead of the required fifty. Beyond that, the reader is told only that Wallas has a mother and that he had come to this particular city, as a child, to see his father, but that he did not meet him. It is also known that his previous assignment was keeping an eye on some Theosophical groups. There is strong evidence to suggest that these characters are to be seen not as individuals but as objects to be described as part of the art of writing. Such an indication comes in the interview with Evelyne Dupont, when she tells Wallas that Dupont was never alive, and when Robbe-Grillet adds, during Wallas' interrogation of Dupont's housekeeper, that Dupont's death is now an abstract event being discussed by mannequins.

## Themes and Meanings

The novel begins with a citation from Sophocles, "Time that sees all has found you out against your will." The book is then divided into five chapters and an epilogue, which suggests the form of a classical tragedy, such as *Oedipus Tyrannus*. Elements that indicate that the novel is a reworking of the Oedipus legend are to be found in such passages as those that show Garinati seeing debris floating in a canal, debris that forms, among other things, a sphinxlike monster. There is also a scene in which Wallas sees, in a curtain, the depiction of a child nursing a sheep. There is even a drunk who poses, along with two others, the sphinx's riddle: What animal walks on four legs in the morning, two at noon, and three at night? There is a statuette that shows a child leading a blind man. The child, however, is male, and Oedipus was led by his daughter, Antigone.

Nevertheless, the most important clue is taken to be the eraser that Wallas seeks. That eraser was so worn that there were only two letters left of the brand name: ——di——. For most critics, the name suggested would be *Oedipus*. Because of that and other clues that seem to point to the Oedipus legend, it is generally believed by critics that the book is a modern version of that myth, particularly so since Wallas accidentally kills Dupont at the end of the book. Yet such an interpretation would be rather simplistic and certainly not consistent with the claims made by critics that Robbe-Grillet is a great innovator in the novel. One should then look at Robbe-Grillet's critical writings, keeping in mind what he wrote about Wallas' hero and mentor, Inspector Fabius.

When faced with difficulties, such as having to lie about where he wishes to go, or having to fit in at a workingman's bar, Wallas often asks himself what Fabius would do in a similar situation, even to the point of becoming Fabius in his mind. Fabius, a name that suggests the French verb, *fabuler*, to make up fantastic stories, is, perhaps, another warning to the reader about Robbe-Grillet's intentions. Fabius, according to the novel, no longer accepts the most obvious evidence or believes that any solution is possible.

*Critical Context*

In his collection of essays *Pour un nouveau roman* (1963; *For a New Novel*, 1965), Robbe-Grillet states that the hero of the New Novel is not to be seen as a person in the traditional sense but as the "simple subject of the action expressed by the verb." Robbe-Grillet also derides the notion that the novel must contain psychological truths. According to him, the most ridiculous thing that critics say is that author so-and-so has something to say and says it well. Could one not maintain, asks Robbe-Grillet rhetorically, that the true artist has nothing to say, only a way of saying it? Robbe-Grillet also says that the true work of art does not contain anything, message or other, as a box might contain something foreign to itself. To the contrary, he states that writing is an art and must be sufficient unto itself and that it is time to stop fearing art for art's sake. In this vein, if there is a scene in *The Erasers* that is admired both by Robbe-Grillet's supporters and by his detractors, it is the one describing a slice of tomato. The description of the tomato has the absolute precision of an anatomical plate and has nothing to do in any way with the novel itself. Its very gratuitousness would seem to bear witness to Robbe-Grillet's seriousness about his theories on the art and goals of writing. (It should be mentioned that the passage is much more impressive in French than it is in English.) Critics dismiss Robbe-Grillet's critical writings as unimportant or as totally exaggerated. Regarding *The Erasers*, however, a case can be made for such an interpretation, that is, of art for art's sake.

First, Robbe-Grillet does not identify Wallas as being or not being the son of Dupont, and such an omission is contrary to the normal practice in a detective novel, in which there is a definite answer to every given problem. Second, Wallas is still young (*encore jeune*), that is, in his forties, and therefore much too old to be that son, since Dupont was fifty-two when he died. There are also the warnings about reading too much into the "evidence," and also Wallas' interview with a Mme Bax who, when he suggests what she might have seen or heard, tells him not to add too much detail for fear that he will make her think she "saw the whole thing," when she saw only a man who stopped in front of Dupont's gate.

The most important argument against an Oedipal interpretation, however, is the fact that most elements of any importance in *The Erasers*, other than the erasers themselves, and certainly including all the Oedipal clues, (and indeed, the very name Wallas), seem to have been taken bodily from *A Gun for Sale: An Entertainment* (1936; published in the United States as *This Gun for Hire: An Entertainment*) by Graham Greene, a book for which there is no possibility of giving an Oedipal interpretation. (Note also that, again besides the eraser, the major elements found in *The Erasers* serve as the basic elements in the construction of *Dans le labyrinthe* (1959; *In the Labyrinth*, 1960). Therefore, if Robbe-Grillet has been faithful to his theories, he has taken a number of elements from a novel by Greene and created another work from them, a work that stands on its own as a work of art and that contains nothing external to its own writing. Robbe-Grillet does note, however, that the individual reader is perfectly free to interpret any work according to his own interests or preoccupations but adds that such a reading will be only a reflection of that reader's mind and will have nothing to do with the novel as it stands.

*Sources for Further Study*

Brock, Robert R. "Robbe-Grillet's *Les Gommes* and Graham Greene's *This Gun for Hire*: Imitation or Initiation?" in *Modern Fiction Studies*. XXIX (Winter, 1983), pp. 688-694.

Gardies, A. *Alain Robbe-Grillet*, 1972.

Morrissette, Bruce. *The Novels of Robbe-Grillet*, 1975.

Rahv, Betty T. *From Sartre to the New Novel*, 1974.

Stoltzfus, B. F. *Alain Robbe-Grillet and the New French Novel*, 1964.

Sturrock, John. *The French New Novel: Claude Simon, Michel Butor, Alain Robbe-Grillet*, 1969.

*Robert R. Brock*

# FAMILY HAPPINESS

*Author:* Leo Tolstoy (1828-1910)
*Type of plot:* Psychological realism
*Time of plot:* The 1850's
*Locale:* A country estate, St. Petersburg, and a spa in Baden-Baden
*First published: Semeynoye schastye,* 1859 (English translation, 1888)

> *Principal characters:*
> MARYA "MASHA" ALEKSANDROVNA, the narrator, a young
>     Russian gentlewoman
> SERGEI MIKHAILYCH, her guardian and later her husband

*The Novel*

*Family Happiness* is divided into two parts. In the first, Masha, a girl of seventeen whose mother has just died, relates the story of her romance with her guardian, Sergei Mikhailych, a man of thirty-six and a former friend of her father (who has died some years earlier). The romance culminates in their engagement and marriage. The second part concerns Masha's married life. The couple's relationship temporarily deteriorates, as Masha is corrupted by the false values of high society in St. Petersburg but is eventually restored on a new, "realistic" plane of serenity (or perhaps merely resignation and habit).

The first part of the novel is lyrical and evocative, as it proceeds with acute psychological subtlety to depict the growth of an intense man-woman relationship. There are formidable obstacles to be overcome, since the problem here, unlike that in the conventional boy-girl encounter, is not the formation of an entirely new relationship but the transformation of an old one. Masha must cease to think of Sergei Mikhailych as a surrogate father and must substitute him for the youthful, melancholy, romantic hero of her fantasies; and Sergei correspondingly must learn to regard Masha as his equal and no longer as a child. Sergei must also abandon his mocking and suspicious attitude toward "romance" itself and take Masha seriously as a woman, at the same time as he learns to view himself as an acceptable suitor for her despite the gap in their ages. These adjustments take considerable time. The underlying sexual attraction is impeded, mainly by Sergei's strong sense of moral responsibility and by his belief that he is too old for Masha, but she too has to outgrow negative feelings, those engendered by her rebellion against his paternalism. There are many stops, starts, hesitations, and misunderstandings, all handled by Leo Tolstoy with great delicacy in a poetic, summer atmosphere learned from Ivan Turgenev, complete with gardens, nightingales, and music. Even after their mutual love has been acknowledged, Sergei continues to play the role of Masha's mentor, while she finds herself more and more his "creature," thinking his thoughts and sharing his emotions. At last, Masha, now thoroughly in love, breaks down Sergei's scruples; they become engaged and soon afterward are married. Their relationship is strongly marked by male dominance, but Masha seems to like marriage that way. "I felt," she says after the wedding, "that I was completely his, and that I was happy in his power over me."

The marriage is at first idyllically happy, though Masha feels some twinges of guilt that their happiness is too self-absorbed, too lacking in social usefulness. Since they are living in his mother's house, Masha has in fact no responsibilities and very little to do. She begins to grow bored, especially since Sergei refuses to allow her any share in his business affairs. They quarrel, and eventually he agrees to take her to St. Petersburg as a diversion. In the city, she displays a talent for social life and becomes caught up in it, enjoying the excitement and the attention she receives. Sergei is now bored in turn, but their return to the country is repeatedly postponed. Quarrels occur more and more frequently, and they sense a gulf opening between them.

Three years pass and a baby son is born. At first, Masha is absorbed by maternal feelings, but after she begins to go into society again, she loses all feeling for her child. Sergei and Masha go abroad to take the waters in Germany, where Masha flirts with a sexy Italian marquis but pulls back, frightened, from the brink of adultery. The couple return to their estate in the country (Sergei's mother has died), another child is born, and slowly they settle into a tranquil, contented life. This new serenity lacks the intense happiness of the honeymoon period but is seemingly destined to last.

### The Characters

For a male author to write a first-person narrative from the woman's point of view was something of a tour de force for Tolstoy, as it was a feat never attempted by his rival and model, Turgenev (nor, indeed, ever again by Tolstoy). The consensus is that he succeeds remarkably well, especially in the first part. The complex and often contradictory emotions experienced by a girl on the verge of womanhood; her lost and helpless feeling as the senior surviving member of her family, to some extent responsible for her younger sister yet at the same time filled with the exuberance of youth and the desire to have a fulfilled life of her own—all this Tolstoy renders with acute psychological insight. To be sure, the form presents some difficulties. Like most reminiscential narrators, Masha, recalling these events in later years, is credited with a mnemonic capacity that far exceeds the limits of plausibility. More important, her understanding is necessarily limited; the reader has only her inferences about the inner life of Sergei Mikhailych, rather than the full revelations Tolstoy was able to provide when he used the perspective of the omniscient author (as he did in his great novels).

Masha's development in the second part of the novel is, for the most part, handled convincingly. It is a process of maturation, as she outlives the romantic ecstasy of the honeymoon period, passes through what amounts to a "wild oats" phase, and finally settles down into a more realistic version of "happily ever after" (the title given the story in one English translation).

The chief weakness of *Family Happiness* is Tolstoy's rendition of the effect on Masha of motherhood. Here Tolstoy's intuition failed him. He had not yet had any experience of paternity, and his description of Masha's babies, and her feelings about them, remains quite unreal and seemingly introduced, at least in part, only to make Tolstoy's polemical point about the corrupting effects of high society even on such a basic biological response as maternal love.

On the other hand, the characterization of Sergei Mikhailych has vitality. He is a vigorous, well-balanced, good-natured man with a strong sense of moral responsibility. He is both scrupulous and intelligent: He will not allow himself to take advantage of his privileged position as Masha's guardian, and he also wonders, for both their sakes, whether it is wise for two persons so far apart in age and experience to marry. In the second part of the novel, Sergei is perhaps a bit improbably passive. Stating his view that people have to learn such things for themselves, he abandons entirely the mentor role he had earlier played and simply bides his time while Masha painfully discovers for herself the ultimate emptiness of high society and the danger of toying with sexuality. Not without reason, she reproaches him bitterly for thus casting her adrift.

### Themes and Meanings

There is an autobiographical context to *Family Happiness*. During 1856, Tolstoy had carried on a somewhat desultory and cerebral courtship of a young lady named Valeria Arseneva, who lived on an estate near his. Her situation was similar to Masha's: She was an orphan, living with her aunt, sisters, brother, and a governess. As the brother's guardian, Tolstoy had easy access to the family, and he initially assumed toward Valeria the informal role of tutor. He played this part far more crudely than did Sergei Mikhailych, writing Valeria a series of peremptory and often scolding letters, full of advice about even such things as the style of her hats. Tolstoy was especially displeased with her for being caught up in the excitement of festivities during the coronation of Alexander II. Later he "tested" himself and her by going to Moscow and St. Petersburg for several months to determine whether their attachment would survive the separation. It did not, and the relationship was broken off, leaving Tolstoy feeling guilty for having toyed with the girl's feelings. The story obviously reproduces these experiences in a much purified form, giving them the somewhat muted happy ending they did not have in life, punishing the girl for her immaturity, and making his alter ego, Sergei Mikhailych, rather wiser and more benevolent than Tolstoy was himself.

The story is also to some degree a response on Tolstoy's part to writings of the period on the "woman question," notably Jules Michelet's *L'Amour* (1858; *Love*, 1860) and Pierre-Joseph Proudhon's *De la justice dans la Révolution et dans l'église* (1858; *On Justice in the Revolution and the Church*, 1858), both of them strongly antifeminist, and, on the other side, the novels of George Sand. *Family Happiness* was perhaps intended as a statement in favor of male dominance, but in the actual story, Tolstoy's theoretical stance was considerably mitigated by his psychological intuition and his artistic sensitivity. The themes of courtship, marriage, parental responsibility, conjugal relations, and adultery were later explored, more deeply and penetratingly, in *Voyna i mir* (1865-1869; *War and Peace*, 1886) and *Anna Karenina*, (1875-1877; English translation, 1886).

*Critical Context*

*Family Happiness* is the last work in the series that might be called early Tolstoy, extending from *Detstvo* (1852; *Childhood*, 1862), his first published work, through *Otrochestvo* (1854; *Boyhood*, 1886) and *Yunost* (1857; *Youth*, 1886), and several short stories. He had dealt with a wide range of themes: the subjugation of the Caucasus, the Crimean War, agriculture, art and the artist, death. In *Family Happiness*, he took up the classic literary subject he had not yet treated, love. Of necessity, this change of subject put him in competition with Turgenev, whose specialty was "first love." Tolstoy, however, had no sympathy with Turgenev's minor-key poetry of lost loves, being skeptical in general of romantic exaggerations and idealizations and having a strong sense of biological imperatives. Nature cares nothing for lost loves, he insisted; nature wants fertilization, babies. He would therefore write a Turgenevesque idyllic love story, but unlike Turgenev, he would carry it past the altar into married life, shown with both its warts and its nightingales. Even in the courtship phase, despite the book's genuine lyricism, Tolstoy debunked some romantic clichés.

The aftermath of *Family Happiness* marked a crisis in Tolstoy's career. The enormous success of *Childhood* and the Sevastopol sketches had not been sustained, and his later stories attracted little attention. Tolstoy was becoming disgusted with the literary life in St. Petersburg, with its factions, it politics, and its vanities. *Family Happiness* itself was hardly noticed by the critics, who at that time were interested primarily in muckraking exposés of social evils. Tolstoy himself lost confidence in his capacities as a writer and in the validity of the literary profession. "*Family Happiness*," he wrote in his diary, "is a shameful abomination," and in a letter to a friend he stated, "I am buried as a writer and as a human being. . . . There is not a live word in the whole thing. The ugliness of language, which derives from the ugliness of thought, is inexpressible." He retreated to his estate at Yasnaya Polyana, resolving to have nothing more to do with literature, and for four years he did not publish another line of fiction.

*Sources for Further Study*

Bayley, John. *Tolstoy and the Novel*, 1966.

Christian, R.F. *Tolstoy: A Critical Introduction*, 1969.

Gustafson, Richard F. *Leo Tolstoy, Resident and Stranger: A Study in Fiction and Theology*, 1986.

Kisseleff, Natalia. "Idyll and Ideal: Aspects of Sentimentalism in Tolstoy's *Family Happiness*," in *Canadian Slavonic Papers*. XXI (1979), pp. 336-346.

Poggioli, Renato. "Tolstoy's *Domestic Happiness*: Beyond Pastoral Love," in *The Oaten Flute*, 1975.

*Hugh McLean*

# FAREWELL FROM NOWHERE

*Author:* Vladimir Maximov (Lev Samsonov, 1930-      )
*Type of plot:* Künstlerroman
*Time of plot:* The late 1930's through the early 1950's
*Locale:* The Soviet Union
*First published: Proshchanie iz niotkuda*, 1974 (English translation, 1978)

> *Principal characters:*
> VLADIMIR (VLAD) SAMSONOV, a Russian youth
> SAVIELY MIKHEYEV, his grandfather, a retired railroad worker
> ALEXEI SAMSONOV, his father
> FEDOSYA SAMSONOV, his mother
> BORIS ESSMAN, an artist who Vlad meets in Krasnodar

*The Novel*

   *Farewell from Nowhere* traces the physical, spiritual, and emotional journey of a young Russian boy, Vlad Samsonov, through his turbulent adolescence and tentative venture into early manhood. Written in four sections,
each comprising from seventeen to twenty-five brief chapters, the novel shifts
the chronology of events frequently, so that it is necessary to read through to
virtually the end of the work to understand the context or import of events
that were related much earlier.

   Vlad begins his role in the narrative as a boy of about seven or eight, the
son of a peasant woman and a politically outspoken father whose Trotskyist
leanings have led to his arrest and imprisonment. With his father absent,
Vlad often goes to stay with his grandfather, Saviely Mikheyev, and spends
the rest of his time reading and conversing with his neighbors in the Moscow
suburb of Sokolniki. Vlad fancies himself a poet and writes tributes to the
righteousness of the Soviet state. His neighbors, less enamored of Joseph
Stalin's government, are alienated and annoyed by Vlad's blind allegiance. To
Vlad, this loyalty is merely the mark of a good citizen, and he fulfills his
"civic duty" even to the extent of reporting a classmate who tells an anti-
Stalinist joke.

   Gradually, Vlad's experiences begin to change his attitude about political
dissidence. He spends a summer at a Pioneer camp, part of a government-
run youth-league program. At first, Vlad feels comfortable in the group atmosphere, but the troop leader's dislike of him eventually makes him reluctant to participate, and he is accused of an "alien spirit of individualism." To
compound his difficulties, Vlad is smitten with love for a girl who is indifferent to him. Misreading her intentions during a war games exercise, he is
caught off guard and forced to surrender. Dejected, Vlad deserts the mock
battlefield and seeks solitude in which to lick his emotional wounds. He

ducks inside the sewer pipe under an outdoor latrine, but even there he cannot escape his misfortune. His daydreams of victory are rudely interrupted
by the arrival of the troop leader, who has come to use the latrine. Terrified
of being found out, Vlad can only remain still and brace himself for the del-
uge. The event is both humorous and prophetic, for it turns out to be a portent of Vlad's future encounters with the state.

The narrative shifts next to Vlad's home life. His father, only recently released from prison, is drafted into the army and dies in his first week at the
front, where Russian troops are struggling to contain Adolf Hitler's invading
army. Vlad returns to his grandfather and travels with him transporting secret
documents as part of the war effort. When Saviely's village of Uzlovaya is
freed from German occupation, they return, but soon afterward Vlad is summoned home by his mother. At the train station, Vlad says good-bye to
Saviely and feels, accurately, in the light of the events that follow, that his
childhood is closing behind him. He returns to a gloomy Moscow and works
at a variety of odd jobs, but when these fail him, he resorts to stealing. Life
at home with his mother, his sister Katya, and his aunt Maria (Mikheyev) is
full of conflict and becomes even more bitter when Vlad learns that his
beloved grandfather has died. As he did when a young boy, Vlad seeks sanctuary in books and one day comes across Alexei Svirsky's *Istoriia moei zhizni*
(1935; the story of my life). The book is an account of Svirsky's solitary travels as a youth, and it inspires Vlad, now twelve, to run away from home.

This decision marks the beginning of a radically different life for Vlad. He
adopts the life-style of a transient: hopping trains, joining with other run-
aways in order to get money or food, and then leaving again to roam on his
own. The sheer struggle for existence pushes his resourcefulness to the limits. He works for a drug smuggler, indulges in petty thievery and drinking
binges, and changes his name frequently in order to get odd jobs on river expeditions or collective farms. Intermittently his luck runs out and he is sent
to a reformatory or prison, though his incarcerations are generally short-
lived. For a time, each release leads only to a new round of drinking and
debauchery, but eventually Vlad realizes he must sober up and stop ruining
his chances for a better life.

Through a series of serendipitous events, Vlad lands a job as a theater
director and life becomes more stable and settled. His tranquillity is disturbed, however, when a friend introduces him to a writer who has been
imprisoned and beaten because of his "subversive" work. Vlad reveals his
own ambitions to write, but the guest expresses reservations about Vlad's
sincerity and desire for truth, knowing that it will be his downfall. He reads
some of Vlad's poetry, which he disparages as being too ethereal and self-
consciously literary, but he recognizes the "genuine spark" of a writer and
says that fate will not allow Vlad to escape his vocational responsibility. Vlad
does not yet fully appreciate the writer's wisdom, but it has left its mark. He

returns to his theater job uninspired, and after antagonizing his boss he is fired.

Destitute, Vlad drifts awhile until he meets a Party official who, sympathetic to Vlad's plight, offers him a factory job near the prosperous city of Krasnodar. Vlad continues to write but has changed his intent, realizing that the squalor and difficulties of his everyday life are what he must transform into poetry. Encouraged by his coworkers, he travels to Krasnodar to have his work appraised. The editor of the Party newspaper reluctantly rejects the poems as immature and awkward, a pronouncement that sends Vlad spinning into despair. Before leaving the city, however, he tries his luck at a small publishing house, and there his work is well received. With the prospect of publication almost certain, Vlad returns elated to his job at the brick factory. Soon afterward he is summoned by three Party officials who have come to sponsor him at the regional writer's conference. He is given new clothes and offered the position of director of the district's House of Culture in Krasnodar. On the train to his new job assignment, Vlad meets a disgruntled former journalist who was fired, he claims, for telling the truth about government corruption. Blinded by his own good fortune, Vlad dismisses the man as a drunken malcontent, though the ignored warning turns out to be prophetic.

Once in Krasnodar, Vlad is hailed as the "peasant poet" and wallows in his newfound success. He meets Boris Essman, an established artist who warns him about the Party's motives and tells him a story titled "The Master Craftsman Who Knew," a parable about artistic integrity. Essman feels that he himself has become complacent and false, and he admonishes Vlad to avoid the local literati and focus on his work. Soon things take a turn for the worse; Vlad, already plagued by scandal because of an affair with a Cossack girl, loses his job and falls out of favor with both government and literary circles. He is publicly accused of anti-Soviet activity, and when his association with Essman threatens Boris' job, Vlad realizes he must leave for Moscow. He finally returns home to Sokolniki, knowing that his family has long since left to live in Jerusalem. Back in his birthplace, Vlad reflects on the experiences and other lives that have shaped him, and feels that he is an unwanted stepchild of Russia. He senses that he too will leave, but also that he will return so that his country will finally understand and accept him.

*The Characters*

As the protagonist of *Farewell from Nowhere*, Vlad is largely a portrait of Vladimir Maximov as a youth. The events in the story, although dramatized, correspond closely with the author's experience; Maximov has stated in interviews that the novel is autobiographical. Since the book is essentially a coming-of-age chronicle, it is not surprising that its focus is somewhat narrow and that Vlad emerges as the only fully rounded character, indeed the only figure who is present throughout the entire novel. Other names and faces meander in and out of the narrative, some making an entrance and exit within the space of a single page. As such, they serve mainly to illuminate Vlad's struggle toward maturity.

Vlad's quest is really threefold: He must discover and establish his own identity, he must come to understand other individuals and human nature in general, and he must posit himself in relation to his nation and culture. He accomplishes this through his interaction with the other characters. Vlad's experience of his father, though limited, is a source of both his outspoken political nature and his individualism. Counterbalancing Alexei is Vlad's mother, Fedosya, who bitterly views her husband's dissident activity as merely an invitation to trouble. Uncle Mitya, Fedosya's brother, echoes this sentiment, warning that books can lead one astray and that "Life's much easier if you keep going steady and don't stick your neck out." Mitya sees his country's problems, but considers silence prudent. Vlad ignores the conventional wisdom and learns the painful lesson at first hand.

Another, more personal facet of Vlad's development centers on a perennial ordeal of youth: learning the virtues of compassion and forgiveness. With the love and trust bestowed upon him by his grandfather as a touchstone, Vlad gradually comes to appreciate the healing power of mercy, especially when extended to those who have shown him none. When his grandfather's friends (a married couple and their children) are invited to share Saviely's private railroad car one night, Vlad is resentful and finds himself disliking the man's quarrelsome and irascible wife. When he awakens that night to hear her crying in fear and pain to her husband, he realizes that passing judgment on his fellow human beings without understanding them is sinful and ignorant.

The final and perhaps most important contribution that the other characters make to Vlad's life is the recognition, encouragement, and at times the safeguarding of his poetic gifts. Despite his rebellious and maverick temperament, Vlad receives support from such a diversity of people that he eventually learns to believe in his gifts himself. The return home after his long sojourn makes him realize that his past is an ineluctable part of who he is, and that this "discovered" self, the foundation for the self he must establish, has rendered his future vocation as a writer just as inescapable.

### Themes and Meanings

Several themes are woven throughout the fabric of *Farewell from Nowhere*, the most obvious one being the redemptive power of compassion as it is embodied in the lives of individuals and institutions. At one point, Vlad describes himself as a baton being passed in a relay race and acknowledges that his survival has often depended upon the kindness of others, some poorer than himself, without whose help he certainly would have perished. Equally conspicuous is the absence of any such benevolence in the workings of the Stalin regime, and here Maximov unleashes his fiercest contempt. Throughout the novel Maximov creates vivid portraits of people who have allowed their "official duties" and political zeal to nullify their humanity. On one occasion Vlad meets a journalist from the West, a smug advocate of socialist ideas and "progress," who dismisses the Russians' religious faith as naïve. Vlad is unimpressed with this soulless foreigner; Vlad has witnessed the socialist experiment at first hand and knows it to be only a political abstraction in which the value of human life becomes unreal. An especially poignant image is his recollection of the prison riot at Butyrki, where he overheard the disturbing plea of "Let me shoot too, Daddy!" coming from the eight-year-old son of the prison warden.

A political structure so prone to inequity inevitably breeds corruption in its individual citizens, and the struggle to retain personal integrity emerges as another challenge to the characters. For Vlad, this comes to mean preserving his artistic integrity, as well, though it may be a handicap to worldly survival. He must walk an even narrower ledge than most: On the one side, he risks having fear and political intimidation silence his literary vision, and on the other, he must avoid the numbing complacency and self-congratulatory inertia of the Russian artistic establishment. It is, in fact, the need for constant movement, both physical and spiritual, that distinguishes Vlad from those around him. He is driven by an almost congenital sense of the ephemeral nature of existence, the realization that life is fleeting and that moments once lived can never be regained. The narrator reflects that "Time refuses to give back what is dearest to us from the past, in order to accustom us to the silence of our ultimate aloneness." Vlad's travels and subsequent return home are his attempt to recoup these losses. He searches for an underlying coherence, yet his fragmented experience yields nothing but a sense of estrangement and personal exile. As the story closes, he finally comes to understand that the thread he has been seeking is himself.

Several critics have complained about the novel's lack of organization, finding the meandering narrative tedious and irksome, and at a first reading the book does seem to be assembled in a rather haphazard fashion. Yet, whether it was the author's intention or not, the style and structure succeed to the extent that they mimic Vlad's, and presumably Maximov's, experience of life: People enter and exit unannounced, perhaps never to be seen again, and the perspective necessary to understand this stream of faces and events cannot be gained fully until the novel's end. In the final chapter, the distinction between the author and his protagonist becomes blurred, and a single voice reflects: "I weep and sob. My soul mourns. Ghosts, ghosts, ghosts! They have been crowding around me, firmly and loudly announcing their right to a word of reminiscence or a brief episode. . . . Nothing is forgotten, nothing! We are like the leaves of a tree: Even when we fall, we retain within us its image and likeness."

Maximov's final message seems to be this: Discreate the Stalinist purges and the hardships of poverty and war if possible, but human life in even the best of societies will always remain fundamentally tragic, infused with a longing that can never be requited. Every individual accumulates moments of experience that shape him or her, and those moments become part of a past to which one can never return, yet which one can never entirely leave behind.

## Critical Context

*Farewell from Nowhere* was Maximov's fourth novel, and the first major work he wrote after leaving his native Russia. His first novel, *Zhiv chelovek* (1962; *A Man Survives*, 1963), earned for him international recognition and established him among the literary elite of the Soviet Union. His domestic standing was lost, however, when he violated the publishing ban on his third novel, *Sem dnei tvoreniia* (1973; *The Seven Days of Creation*, 1974), a blatant denunciation of Soviet Communism. Maximov was expelled from the Writers Union and banished from the U.S.S.R. He settled in Paris, and there wrote *Farewell from Nowhere*, his attempt "to paint all of Russia."

Though not accorded equal stature with Fyodor Dostoevski or Leo Tolstoy, Maximov is credited with continuing the tradition of the great nineteenth century Russian novelists by his epic sense of the human struggle for physical and spiritual liberation. The ideas and images in *Farewell from Nowhere* have prompted associations with another expatriate novelist and a contemporary of Maximov, Aleksandr Solzhenitsyn, who also was exiled for criticizing the Soviet system. Their struggle for uncensored expression finally began to yield rewards that, ironically, have benefited writers other than themselves. For example, early in 1987 it was announced that a novel by Anatoli Rybakov would be published in serial form in a Soviet journal. Critical, as *Farewell from Nowhere* is, of Soviet life during the Stalinist era, the book had twice before been denied domestic publication.

## Sources for Further Study

*Library Journal*. Review. CIV (August, 1979), p. 1590.
*Listener*. Review. C (November 30, 1978), p. 734.
*New Statesman*. Review. XCVI (November 17, 1978), p. 665.
*Observer*. Review. November 12, 1978, p. 35.
*Publishers Weekly*. Review. CCXV (April 30, 1979), p. 173.

*William LaHay*

# THE FAREWELL PARTY

*Author:* Milan Kundera (1929-    )
*Type of plot:* Farce
*Time of plot:* c. the 1960's
*Locale:* Communist Czechoslovakia: Prague and a health spa in a small town
*First published: La Valse aux adieux,* 1976 (English translation, 1976)

> *Principal characters:*
> KLIMA, a popular jazz trumpeter
> KAMILA, his beautiful but jealous wife
> RUZENA, a pregnant nurse at a health spa
> FRANTA, her jealous boyfriend
> DR. SKRETA, the physician who runs the spa
> JAKUB, his friend, a former political prisoner
> OLGA, Jakub's ward, a patient at the spa
> BARTLEFF, a rich American patient at the spa

## The Novel

*The Farewell Party* is divided into five sections corresponding to the five consecutive days during which the action takes place. "First Day" begins with a phone call from Ruzena, a nurse at a health spa, to Klima, a popular jazz trumpeter in Prague, telling him that she is pregnant and that he is the father. (They spent an intimate two hours together some months before, when his band gave a concert at the spa.) The members of Klima's all-male band offer various sympathetic theories on how to deal with the situation. For example, the young guitarist volunteers to run her over with his car:

"Why dillydally? She's a bitch!"
"No. You're an awfully decent fellow. Thanks. But it won't work," said Klima.

Finally Klima decides to curry favor with Ruzena by pretending that he loves her, after which he can persuade her to have an abortion. Meanwhile, bringing flowers, he lies to his suspicious wife, Kamila, about having to attend a conference at the spa the next day—her birthday.

"Second Day" begins with Klima arriving at the spa and consulting his friend Bartleff, a rich American. Bartleff advises him to try to understand Ruzena and be kind, but he agrees to support Klima's abortion plan by enlisting the aid of Dr. Skreta, the physician who runs the spa. The chummy Skreta cooperates, but for a price: Klima and Ruzena must appear before the local abortion commission to seek official approval, and Klima must agree to perform in concert the night before with Skreta and the pharmacist, amateur drummer and pianist, respectively. Now only Ruzena's agreement is lacking.

Klima wines and dines Ruzena, but she says that she will never have an abortion. Then Klima takes her for a drive in his expensive car and dangles before her the prospect of divorce (his), remarriage (to her), and a long honeymoon in Italy. Ruzena changes her mind about the abortion, and everything seems set. A slight complication, however, appears on the scene: an angry motorcyclist (actually Franta, Ruzena's jealous boyfriend) who confronts them and seems strangely familiar with Ruzena. Ruzena says the young motorcyclist is only a "maniac" who has been following her, so they ignore him.

"Third Day" provides an interlude in the main action, as other forces gather at the spa. The former political prisoner Jakub, finally given permission to leave the country, stops along the way to say good-bye to his friend Skreta and his ward Olga. He also wants to return the pale-blue suicide pill that Skreta gave him fifteen years before. Most of this section concerns political/philosophical/religious discussions among Jakub, Skreta, Olga, and Bartleff and the discovery of Skreta's schemes: He wants Bartleff to adopt him and thus give him the legal right to an American passport, and for several years he has been secretly inseminating married women in the region and at the spa (which is primarily a fertility clinic) with vials of his own sperm in order to bring about Czechoslovakian brotherhood. Jakub also has a run-in with Ruzena, Olga's obnoxious apartment neighbor, over a bulldog that he saves from a group of vigilante dogcatchers (including Ruzena's father) who remind him of his former political persecutors.

In "Fourth Day," Klima returns to the spa, ostensibly to attend the evening concert but also to check on Ruzena's resolve. Klima's return to the spa is a good idea, because Ruzena, influenced by her skeptical women friends, has changed her mind again—no abortion. As she makes her announcement to Klima in a restaurant, Jakub observes them from a nearby table, as does Franta, from a park across the street. The watching eyes, especially Franta's, make Ruzena so nervous that she has to take a pale-blue pill, apparently a tranquilizer. When she and Klima depart, Ruzena accidentally leaves her container of pills on the table, and Jakub, examining them, drops his suicide pill inside the container for comparison. At this point Ruzena returns and huffily demands her pills, and Jakub somewhat compulsively lets her take them. Soon feeling guilty, Jakub goes in search of Ruzena to retrieve his pill. Meanwhile, the jealous Franta is trailing Klima. Franta, however, is not the only one: Kamila shows up as a surprise, and after the concert Klima has to sleep with her (which is literally all he can manage) instead of with Ruzena as he planned. Comforted by Bartleff, Ruzena spends a blissful night with him; innocent Olga seduces Jakub; and puzzled Franta paces the street all night long.

In "Fifth Day," however, Franta's vigil is rewarded. Now in love with Bartleff, Ruzena again agrees to the abortion and appears with Klima before the abortion commission, which Skreta manipulates to a favorable decision. Yet while Klima stays behind to give the requisite blood, Franta realizes what is happening and confronts Ruzena in the women's ward, where he screams out his paternity and protests the planned abortion. Her nerves shattered by the scene, Ruzena takes one of her pills and dies instantly. Franta is frantic, blaming himself, but her death is ruled a suicide. Now Klima and Kamila (whose insight into her weak husband has destroyed her love) can return home. Jakub, who leaves without knowing of Ruzena's death, crosses the border believing that the suicide pill was a placebo, but newly enlightened about himself.

### The Characters

Some reviewers of *The Farewell Party*, seeing the novel as just another conventional farce, complained about the shallowness of the characters. Critic Saul Maloff, writing in *The New York Times Book Review*, was more perceptive: "*The Farewell Party* is the kind of 'political novel' a cunning, resourceful, gifted writer writes when it is no longer possible to write political novels." In other words, the conditions of political oppression under which Milan Kundera wrote *The Farewell Party*, at a time when he was out of favor with the Czech Communist regime, must be considered. If they are, then Maloff's interpretation seems to be not only consistent with the nature of Kundera's other novels but also enlightening, offering the best understanding of the characters in *The Farewell Party*.

The farcical characters do not merely provide conventional entertainment; their shallowness also represents a judgment on the political system that produced them. Rejecting the traditional moorings of Christian humanism, the Communists anchor their morality in the ideals of economic justice, brotherhood, and loyalty to the state. The difficulty of realizing these ideals without the traditional moorings, without the deeper sense of personal responsibility and integrity which is espoused by Christian humanism, is apparent in characters such as Klima, Ruzena, and Skreta. With their selfish, self-centered natures, they are no better than petty capitalists. Indeed, Klima enjoys the economic and social benefits of celebrity, Ruzena is attracted to them, and Skreta is a wheeler-dealer entrepreneur within the Communist state. The characters' preoccupation with sex is a measure of their limited freedom, their restricted horizons. Skreta's hilarious notion of brotherhood— reminiscent of various Communist experiments in social engineering—is populating the country with nearsighted, big-nosed kids. The characters use their offices, their influence, and one another scandalously. Few, except for Franta, are even bothered by Ruzena's death. All in all, they are walking parodies who represent the farcical side of Communism.

There are hints in *The Farewell Party* of a sinister side of Communism, which arises from the same shallow morality. Skreta's breeding program vaguely recalls similar Nazi efforts; the characters' easy acceptance of Ruzena's death is reminiscent of the Stalinist persecutions and judicial killings. The main reminder of the political persecutions is the character Jakub, who, on his way out of the country, no longer needs the suicide pill. Ruzena's taking of his pill symbolically binds the two sides of the Communist character and suggests the hidden moral confusion. Ruzena, who might win a contest for Miss Communist Czechoslovakia, is implicated in her own death, but so is almost every other character, particularly Jakub. He is appalled that he could give Ruzena the deadly pill, even if she does remind him of his former persecutors: The persecuted can turn persecutor, just as the persecutor (like Olga's father, who sent Jakub to prison and a few months later was himself executed) can become the persecuted.

Another possible interpretation, however, is represented by Bartleff. He forgives the woman whom he loved but who turned him over to the Gestapo during World War II, and he offers to be legally charged for Ruzena's death. Klima seeks him for advice, Ruzena for solace, and Skreta for adoption. Bartleff is the moral center of the novel—a new role in world literature for rich Americans, but an obvious clue to the novel's political stance. Nor does Kundera leave any doubt whence comes the moral authority: Bartleff talks about saints, paints pictures of saints (with pale-blue halos—a symbolic color), and at one point is even said to glow with a certain mysterious blue aura himself.

## Themes and Meanings

In *The Farewell Party*, Kundera shrewdly adapts the conventions of farce to the purposes of political criticism. The novel offers the typical entertainment of farce—sexual intrigue, suspense, silly characters, and amusing scenes, all combined in a tightly constructed plot that resembles the five acts of a French well-made play. Yet at the same time the novel, like other works by Kundera, has a reflective quality—in the author's style, in the analysis of character, and in the set discussions—that suggests more than mere entertainment. The suggestion points to another sense in which the novel is reflective thematically: The personal behavior of the characters is a reflection of the regime that made them. As in all Kundera's fiction, there is a continuum between the personal and the political.

Aside from character, Kundera makes his point through symbolism, some of which has already been noted. The contrast between pale-blue pills and pale-blue halos plays on a dichotomy between Communism and Christianity, ingestion and emanation, outer dependence and inner strength, Communist character and Christian character, Skreta and Bartleff. Bartleff calls Skreta "one of Jesus's holy disciples, for he knows how to perform miracles," but Skreta's miracles seem decidedly Communist—his uniform spawn of near-sighted, big-nosed children—whereas Bartleff is the genuine article. Just as

Ruzena embodies Jakub's persecutors, so Kamila embodies the beauty in life that he has so far missed, though he might find it where he is going.

## Critical Context

Viewed in the context of Kundera's career, *The Farewell Party* could be termed his personal farewell to his native country. After the Russian invasion of Czechoslovakia in 1968, Kundera was stripped of his university teaching position and his books were banned. He and his wife were allowed to leave Czechoslovakia for France in 1975. Apparently *The Farewell Party* was substantially completed when he emigrated, though there might have been time for revision before the novel was translated into French and published in 1976. Jakub's leave-taking in the novel might reflect Kundera's experience.

In any event, *The Farewell Party* introduced the theme of exile that has been so prominent in Kundera's later novels, *Kniha smíchu a zapomnění* (1978; *The Book of Laughter and Forgetting*, 1980) and *Nesnesitelná lehkost bytí* (1984; *The Unbearable Lightness of Being*, 1984), both masterpieces. *The Farewell Party* also introduced the metaphor of "lightness" to describe lack of moral responsibility. In *The Farewell Party* the theme of lightness is developed through farce and applies to personal behavior. In his later work Kundera has been able to write about the theme more openly and apply it also to a political setting; still, at the same time, much of the comic tone and sexual intrigue of *The Farewell Party* manages to carry over to the later works, despite their heavy themes.

## Sources for Further Study

Donahue, Bruce. "Laughter and Ironic Humor in the Fiction of Milan Kundera," in *Critique: Studies in Modern Fiction*. XXV (Winter, 1984), pp. 67-76.

Harkins, William E., and Paul I. Trensky, eds. *Czech Literature Since 1956: A Symposium*, 1980.

Maloff, Saul. Review in *The New York Times Book Review*. LXXXI (September 5, 1976), p. 4.

"Milan Kundera," in *Contemporary Literary Criticism*. XXXII, 1985. Edited by Jean Stine.

Pochoda, Elizabeth. Introduction to *The Farewell Party*, 1977.

*Harold Branam*